EARLY ENGLISH
TRACTS ON COMMERCE

A

SELECT COLLECTION

OF

EARLY ENGLISH

TRACTS ON COMMERCE,

FROM THE ORIGINALS OF

MUN, ROBERTS, NORTH, AND OTHERS.

WITH A PREFACE AND INDEX.

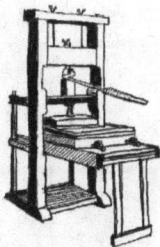

CL Reprints

CL Press | Fraser Institute

CL Press

Published by CL PRESS

A Project of the Fraser Institute

1770 Burrard Street, 4th Floor

Vancouver, BC V6J 3G7 Canada

www.clpress.net

A Select Collection of Early English

Tracts on Commerce

By J.R. McCulloch

A Select Collection of Early English Tracts on Commerce
was originally published in 1856 by Lord Overstone.

First printed: February 2024

Cover image: Cover illustration titled "Gutenberg's Press" by Dave Grey, licensed under a Creative Commons Attribution-NoDerivs 2.0 Generic license.

ISBN: 978-1-957698-12-0

Cover design by John Stephens

Foreword by CL Press, 2024

The present volume was edited by a man with a calling to expound and promote the teachings of political economy. John Ramsay McCulloch (1789–1864) understood the truths and conclusions of political economy to run along classical-liberal lines, in the tradition of Adam Smith. For more than 40 years McCulloch promoted use of the word *liberal* in its original political sense, which is to say its Smithian sense.

Part of McCulloch's calling was to recover the early developments of liberal political economy. He avidly collected books, especially on economic topics. His collection of 8,000 books was perhaps the best collection of the kind of his time.

McCulloch was again a proselytizer, laboring to republish the old literature he found "scarce and valuable." The present volume reprints one of six volumes compiled by McCulloch, volumes consisting of writings from the 17th, 18th, and early 19th centuries. McCulloch wanted people to know of such works, some going back more than 200 years before his own time, works that helped to develop political economy. Financial assistance from Lord Overstone helped McCulloch to edit and publish the six volumes:

1. ***Early English Tracts on Commerce*** (1856) –& CL Press 2024
2. *Scarce and Valuable Tracts on Money* (1856)
3. *Scarce and Valuable Tracts on Paper Currency and Banking* (1857)
4. *Scarce and Valuable Tracts on the National Debt and the Sinking Fund* (1857)
5. ***Scarce and Valuable Tracts on Commerce*** (1859) –& CL Press 2024
6. ***Scarce and Valuable Economical Tracts*** (1859) –& CL Press 2024

The bolded titles are now reprinted by CL Press.

All six of the volumes were republished in 1995 by the publisher Pickering & Chatto, titled *Classical Writings on Economics*, Volumes 1–6. The first volume contains a new general introduction by Denis Patrick O'Brien, who had earlier published *J. R. McCulloch: A Study in*

Classical Economics (1970). O'Brien also edited McCulloch's collected works and Overstone's correspondence.

O'Brien's 1995 general introduction helps with the authorship of the items. We now list the contents of three volumes newly reprinted by CL Press. In the following listing we modernize spellings and abridge the titles for the sake of conciseness:

Early English Tracts on Commerce (1856)

Contents:

1. A DISCOURSE OF TRADE (1621) by Thomas Mun
2. A DISCOURSE OF FOREIGN TRADE (1641) by Lewes Roberts
3. ENGLAND'S TREASURE BY FOREIGN TRADE (1664) by Thomas Mun
4. ENGLAND'S INTEREST AND IMPROVEMENT (1673) by Samuel Fortrey
5. ENGLAND'S GREATEST HAPPINESS; OR, A DIALOGUE BETWEEN CONTENT AND COMPLAINT (1677), authorship unknown
6. BRITANNIA LANGUENS, OR A DISCOURSE OF TRADE (1680) by authorship unknown, possibly William Petty
7. DISCOURSE UPON TRADE (1691) by Dudley North (the first part perhaps written by Roger North)
8. CONSIDERATIONS ON THE EAST-INDIA TRADE (1701), by (probably) Henry Martyn

Scarce and Valuable Tracts on Commerce (1859)

Contents:

1. OBSERVATIONS TOUCHING TRADE AND COMMERCE WITH OTHER NATIONS (circa 1610) perhaps by Walter Raleigh, perhaps by John Keymore
2. NAVIGATION AND COMMERCE, THEIR ORIGINAL AND PROGRESS (1674) by John Evelyn
3. EXTRACTS FROM A PLAN OF THE ENGLISH COMMERCE (1730) by Daniel Defoe

4. AN ESSAY ON THE CAUSES OF THE DECLINE OF THE FOREIGN TRADE (1744) perhaps by **Matthew Decker,** perhaps by a **Mr. Richardson**
5. BRIEF ESSAY ON THE ADVANTAGES AND DISADVANTAGES TO FRANCE AND GREAT BRITAIN WITH REGARD TO TRADE (1750) by **Josiah Tucker**
   —Appended: A LETTER ON THE STATE OF FRANCE IN 1765 by **Tobias Smollett**
6. PROPOSALS FOR REDRESSING AND AMENDING THE TRADE OF THE REPUBLIC (1751) by **Prince William of Orange**
7. A VINDICATION OF THE COMMERCE AND THE ARTS (1758) by **William Temple**
8. NEW AND OLD PRINCIPLES OF TRADE COMPARED (1788) perhaps by **William Vaughan**

Scarce and Valuable Economical Tracts (1859)

Contents:

1. AN APOLOGY FOR THE BUILDER (1685) by (probably) **Nicholas Barbon**
2. GIVING ALMS NO CHARITY, AND EMPLOYING THE POOR A GRIEVANCE TO THE NATION (1704) by **Daniel Defoe**
3. A VIEW OF GREENLAND TRADE AND WHALE-FISHERY (1722) by **Henry Elking**
4. AN APOLOGY FOR THE BUSINESS OF PAWN-BROKING (1744), *authorship unknown but perhaps* **Thomas Wise**
5. EXTRACTS ON POPULATION, COMMERCE, ETC. (1751–74) by **Benjamin Franklin**
6. REFLECTIONS ON THE FORMATION AND DISTRIBUTION OF WEALTH (French 1767; English trans. 1793) by **Anne Robert Jacques Turgot**
7. EXTRACT FROM AN INQUIRY INTO THE CORN LAWS (1777) by **James Anderson**
8. A TREATISE ON THE MARITIME LAWS OF RHODES (1776) by **Alexander C. Schomberg**

9. A DISSERTATION ON THE POOR LAWS (1776) by **Joseph Townsend**
10. THOUGHTS AND DETAILS ON SCARCITY (written 1795, pub. 1800) by **Edmund Burke**
11. AN INQUIRY INTO THE PROHIBITION OF THE USE OF GRAIN IN THE DISTILLERIES (1808) by **Archibald Bell**

In her entry on McCulloch in the *Oxford Dictionary of National Biography*, Phyllis Deane wrote: "It is now apparent that for most of the half-century preceding his death [in 1864] this hard-working, largely self-educated Scot did more than any other economist of this day to introduce the new science of political economy to an interested public." The volumes now reprinted by CL Press show the enduring value of McCulloch's service to those interested in the history of economic thought and the historical arc of liberalism.

This Volume has been printed by the Political Economy Club of London for private distribution amongst its members and their immediate friends The Tracts contained in it are taken from the originals supplied by J. R. McCulloch, Esq., who has also been good enough to contribute the Preface.

ONE HUNDRED COPIES PRINTED

With Lord Overstone's compliments

CONTENTS.

PREFACE.

VARIOUS motives have led to this publication. The Tracts of which it consists are all of great, and some of them of extraordinary rarity. And they are interesting, partly from their containing some of the earliest indications of those liberal commercial principles now so generally diffused—partly from their embodying statements and reasonings that were supposed to demonstrate the truth of theories which, however erroneous, were long universally assented to; and, further, from some of them having been much referred to by subsequent writers. They afford an epitome of the commercial knowledge of the 17th century, both in its theory and practice. And it seemed desirable, by collecting and reprinting treatises of such importance in a separate volume, to provide against the imminent risk of their being lost, and render them accessible to future inquirers.

They are as follows, viz.

I. A Discovrse of Trade, from England vnto the East-Indies; answering to diuerse Obiections which are vsually made against the same. By T. M. 1621.

II.

II. The Treasure of Traffike, or a Discourse of Forraigne Trade; wherein is showed the benefit and commoditie arising to a Common-Wealth or Kingdome,
by the skilfull Merchant, and by a well ordered
Commerce and regular Traffike. By Lewes Roberts,
Merchant and Captaine of the City of London.
1641.

III. England's Treasure by Forraign Trade; or, the
Ballance of our Forraign Trade is the Rule of our
Treasure. Written by Thomas Mun, of London,
Merchant. 1664.

IV. England's Interest and Improvement. Consisting
in the Increase of the Store, and Trade of this
Kingdom. By Samuel Fortrey, Esq. 1673.

V. England's Great Happiness; or, a Dialogue between
Content and *Complaint*, wherein is demonstrated
that a great part of our Complaints are causeless.
By a real and hearty Lover of his King and
Countrey. 1677.

VI. *Britannia Languens*, or A Discourse of Trade:
shewing the Grounds and Reasons of the Increase
and Decay of Land-Rents, National Wealth and
Strength; with Application to the late and present
State and Condition of England, France, and the
United Provinces. 1680.

VII. Discourses upon Trade; principally directed to
the Cases of the Interest, Coynage, Clipping, and
Increase of Money. 1691.

VIII. Considerations on the East-India Trade; wherein
all the Objections to that Trade are fully answered.
With a Comparison of the East-India and Fishing
Trades. 1701. The

The first and third of these Tracts were written by Mr. Thomas Mun, of whom we know nothing, except that he was an eminent merchant of London, and a Director of the East India Company. Though published in 1664, the second and principal Tract had been written several years previously. Mr. Mun's son, in the Dedication to Lord Southampton, which he prefixed to it, says: " my father was in his time famous among merchants," a mode of expression which he would hardly have used had not a considerable period elapsed since his father's death. And Misselden in his " Circle of Commerce," published in 1623, (p. 36,) refers to Mun's Tract on the East India Trade,* and speaks of its author as an accomplished and experienced merchant. Perhaps therefore, we may not be far wrong in supposing, that the " Treasure by Forraign Trade" was written as early as 1635 or 1640. Mr. Hallam is inclined to think it may have been a little earlier.† The doctrines in Mun's tracts are substantially the same; and they are also the same with those in a petition presented by the East India Company to Parliament in 1628, which was written by Mun.

Previously to the formation of this Company, in 1600, it had been the policy of England, as of other nations, to prohibit the exportation of the precious metals, which were then reckoned the only real wealth that a country could possess. But bullion being one of the most advantageous articles of export to the East, this prohibition

---

* The first Edition of this Tract is said to have appeared in 1609, but we have only seen the Second Edition of 1621.

† Literature of Europe, IV. 385.

prohibition was relaxed, under certain conditions, in favour of the East India Company. And whatever may now be thought of it, this, when taken, was a considerable step in advance; and in no long time it was much and strenuously objected to, as being subversive of all sound principle and highly injurious to the public interests. On this occasion Mun came forward in defence of the Company. He did not, however, take his stand on the broad ground that the exportation of bullion to the East was advantageous because it was more valuable there than here. He had recourse to a more subtle theory, and tried to reconcile the interests of his clients with the opinions then generally entertained. In this view he contended that the exportation of bullion by the Company was advantageous, because they employed it to purchase commodities in India, most part of which was afterwards sent to the Continent, whence a greater amount of bullion was imported in their stead than had originally been expended upon them in India. And hence the famous doctrine of *The Balance of Trade,* that is, of an excess of exports over imports; the excess being, it was taken for granted, necessarily paid in gold and silver. No sophistry was ever more completely successful. Its influence was not confined to England, but extended to most other countries. The rule that in dealing with strangers, " wee must ever sell more to them yearly than wee consume of theirs in value"* was looked upon as infallible. Its merits were proclaimed alike by philosophers and merchants, while

statesmen

---

* Post, p. 125.

statesmen exerted themselves to give it a practical effect. Agriculture, commerce, and manufactures, ceased to be objects of public solicitude, The "balance of trade" was regarded as the only source of national wealth, and the only measure of its increase; and all the complex machinery of premiums and bounties on the one side, and of restrictions and prohibitions on the other, was set in motion to render it favourable. It soon, however, became obvious, that customs regulations, how vigilantly soever they might be enforced, were not sufficient to make the golden current flow in the desired channels. Recourse was, consequently, had to still more stringent measures. Treaties and alliances were entered into and set aside, fleets were sent to sea, armies were embodied, and sanguinary conflicts waged in every quarter of the globe, in the vain attempt to realize an imaginary advantage, to seize a mere *ignis fatuus!* And such and so powerful was the delusion, that long after its fallaciousness had been fully demonstrated by North, and Hume, and Smith, and others, it continued to maintain an unimpaired ascendancy. Even in our own times Parliament was annually congratulated on the excess of the exports over the imports. The gilded image of clay and mud stood for more than a century, an object of slavish adoration, after its foundations had been rent in all directions.

The treatises, in which the theory which had such results, was first brought forward, and in which it is most skilfully defended, must always be objects of liberal curiosity and attention. Few delusions have
been

been so widely spread as that to which they gave rise, and of few have the consequences been so disastrous.

The second Tract in this Volume, published in 1641, is by Mr. Lewes Roberts, "merchant and captaine of the city of London." He had previously published, in 1638, in one volume folio, a sort of encyclopædia of commercial knowledge, called the "Merchant's Mappe of Commerce." And it appears from some statements introductory to that work, that after having been in the employment of the Levant Company at Constantinople, he became, subsequently to his return to England, a member of that Company, and of the East India Company. He had evidently been very well informed, and master of all the mercantile knowledge of his time. It is highly to his credit that he should be found at this early period, in favour of the free exportation of gold and silver; of low customs; and of coins of the standard weight and fineness. Roberts' Tract contains the earliest notice of Manchester as a seat of the cotton manufacture.

The fourth of the following tracts, first published in 1663, and re-printed in 1673, was written by Samuel Fortrey, Esq., a gentleman of the King's bedchamber. It contains a forcible argument in favour of enclosures; and the author is favourable to the policy of allowing foreigners to settle in the kingdom, to hold lands, and to enjoy the other privileges of Englishmen, under such restrictions as Parliament may think fit to enact. But this tract is chiefly remarkable for its having power-
fully

fully assisted in raising and perpetuating that prejudice against the trade with France, which resulted not long after in its almost total prohibition. Fortrey gives the substance of a statement which he alleges (but without quoting any authority for the fact) had been presented to Louis XIV, in which the value of the commodities annually exported from France to England is estimated at above 2,600,000*l.*, and that of the commodities exported from England to France at about 1,000,000*l.*; " By which it appears," says he, " that our trade with France is at least 1,600,000*l.* a year clear lost to this kingdom" (p. 234.) And this vague and, indeed, worthless statement, appears to have been generally acquiesced in at the time and for long after. Fortrey's Tract has been referred to over and over again, especially during the discussions on the commercial treaty with France in 1713, in vindication of that *felo-de-se* policy by which we laboured to suppress what had been, and might, but for our interference, have continued to be, an extensive and advantageous branch of trade.

The fifth tract in this volume, a Dialogue by an unknown anonymous author, was published in 1677. The speakers are Content and Complaint, the last of whom dwells on what were then reckoned principal grievances, *viz.* the exportation of money occasioned by the supposed adverse balance in the trade with France, extravagance in living, the influx of foreigners, the inclosure of commons, the too great multiplication of traders, &c. But these and other alleged grievances are satisfactorily disposed of by Content, who shows that

that instead of deserving that name, they are either innocuous or advantageous. The author is at once a decided and an intelligent opponent of restraints on trade, on private expenditure, and on immigration and emigration. Were the tract to be re-written at the present moment, there would be nothing in it to amend, except, perhaps, the style; and in that there is little to object to.

The next, or sixth of the annexed tracts, a considerable treatise, intituled " *Britannia Languens*," appeared in 1680. We have no certain knowledge of the author. The late Mr. George Chalmers ascribes it to Mr. William Petyt, who published some political writings; but this is doubtful.

This treatise exhibits a curious medley of truth and error, intelligence and prejudice. The aim of the author is to show that agriculture, manufactures, and trade, were at the time in a very depressed, or, as he terms it, "consumptive condition." And that this condition was partly a consequence of the exportation of treasure, arising out of the importation of luxuries from France and elsewhere; and partly of the operation of the navigation laws, the monopolies of the East India Company and other trading associations, corporation privileges, &c.

It is certain, however, that the depressed condition of industry for which the author endeavoured to account, was wholly imaginary; that instead of falling off, all sorts of industrial occupations, wealth, and population, were very materially increased between the Restoration and the Revolution; and that the

amount

amount of treasure in the country was considerably greater than at any former period. But notwithstanding this fundamental error, the work contains sundry statements not to be found elsewhere, of much interest in regard to various branches of our domestic resources, and of those of the United Provinces and other foreign states. And though the author erred in estimating the character and influence of some of the institutions and circumstances upon which he animadverts, his observations are, notwithstanding, for the most part, to a greater or less extent, well founded.

The seventh of the following tracts, and the most remarkable in many respects of any that appeared in the course of the century, was written by the Hon. Sir Dudley North, brother to the Lord Keeper Guildford. Having been bred a Turkey merchant, Sir Dudley resided for a considerable period in the Ottoman dominions. After his return home, he was made successively a Commissioner of the Customs, then of the Treasury, and again of the Customs. He was also Sheriff of London during the reign of James II.; and having been afterwards called upon to account for some rather questionable proceedings in that capacity, it must be admitted, that he defended himself in a way more creditable to his shrewdness than to his honesty or straightforwardness. But such conduct was then too common to incur much censure; and whatever might be his defects as a politician, they neither obscured nor perverted his views in regard to questions where party interests and prejudices were not directly affected. His acuteness and experience as a man of business

business, made him peculiarly alive to the many inconveniences and disorders that were occasioned by
the state of the currency, which then consisted principally of silver coins, that were so much clipped and
degraded, that a guinea was ordinarily rated at from
27s. to 28s. or upwards. Having reflected maturely
on the subject, he determined to bring the principles
of the coinage and the state of the coin, with a view
to their amendment, before the House of Commons,
of which he was a member. But losing his seat in that
assembly, he embodied his opinions on the subject,
the importance of which it would not be easy to
exaggerate, in the original, comprehensive, and
admirably written tract now reprinted, which he
published in 1691. It is, however, supposed, that
for some reason or other he had soon after consented
to its suppression. At all events it speedily became
exceedingly scarce, so that, to use his brother's expression, " it hath been ever since utterly sunk, and
a copy not to be had for money."* It was believed,
indeed, to be entirely lost; but luckily this was not
the case. A copy, which had belonged to the Rev.
Rogers Ruding, author of the work on the coinage,
was purchased at the sale of his library by a gentleman of Edinburgh, who printed a few copies for distribution among his friends; and we have since picked
up three copies of the original impression, from one of
which the subjoined reprint has been made.

North is an uncompromising advocate of commercial freedom. He is not, like the greater number

---

* North's *Lives of the Norths*, 8vo. ed. I,II. 173.

ber of his predecessors, well-informed on one subject, and erroneous on others. An Achilles without
a heel, he has no vulnerable points, no bounties,
no duties, no prohibitions. His system is sound
throughout, consentaneous in its parts, and complete. His reasoning in defence of a moderate
seignorage is quite conclusive. Had it been acted
upon, the new silver coins issued during the great
recoinage of 1696–98, would not have begun, almost
immediately, to disappear; and the currency of last
century would, speaking generally, have been vastly
improved. In commercial matters he shows that nations
have the same interest as individuals. He exposes the
folly of thinking that any trade advantageous to the merchant can be injurious to the public; and he ridicules
the efforts to retain the precious metals in a country by
dint of Customs regulations, pronouncing them to be
no better than attempts to hedge-in the cuckoo! "For"
as he truly observes, "no people ever yet grew rich by
policies; but it is peace, and industry, and freedom,
that bring trade and wealth, and nothing else."

The last tract in this volume, "Considerations on the
East India Trade," was published in 1701; and notwithstanding the deference so justly due to North, it
probably also is the ablest and most profound. A con-
troversy was carried on for several years previously to
its appearance between the home manufacturers and
the importers of East Indian silks and cotton stuffs.
The former did not fail to resort to the arguments
invariably used on such occasions, affirming that the
substitution of Indian for English goods occasioned
the

the ruin of our manufactures, the exportation of
the coin, and the impoverishment of the kingdom.
Such arguments could not be successfully resisted
without showing the hollowness of the assumptions on
which they were founded, and, maintaining in opposition to them, that it is for the public advantage to
buy whatever may be wanted, in the cheapest markets.
And this the author has done in a very masterly manner,
with great force of reasoning and variety of illustration.
He has discussed the most specious objections that have
been made, or that may be made, to his doctrine, and
has shown that none of them are well founded; that
the important practical principle which he has laid
down, does not operate by fits and starts, but con-
tinuously at all times and in all places; and that it can
never be departed from without loss and injury to the
public. " He is, also, the first who has conclusively shown
the advantage of employing machinery, and cheaper
methods of production, in the manufacture of commodities; and who has proved that such employment,
instead of being injurious to the labourers is advantageous to them, as well as to the other classes of the
community. And in doing this, he has set the powerful
influence of the division of labour in a very striking
point of view, and has illustrated it with a skill and
felicity which even Smith has not surpassed, but by
which he most probably profited."*

Mr. Macaulay has passed a very high eulogium on
this tract: " The pamphlet on the East India Trade is
excellent, first-rate. I have seen nothing of that age
                                                 equal

---

* *Literature of Political Economy*, p. 100.

equal to it. Davenant's two tracts on the same subject are contemptible in comparison."

It is to be regretted that we have no information in
regard to the author of a treatise, which has been so
commended. We have sometimes been half inclined
to suppose that it might have proceeded from the pen
of Mr. Henry Martin, who contributed some papers to
the *Spectator*. But we are not disposed to lay much
stress on this conjecture.

That this admirable tract should have had, when
published, little or no influence, is wholly to be ascribed
to the author being very far in advance of his age. It
required a long series of still more powerful lights, and
a far wider experience, to dissipate the prejudices which
swayed his contemporaries and their successors.

It may very likely be supposed that we should have
given a place in this collection to the tracts of the
celebrated Sir Josiah Child, long the leader, or rather
dictator, of the East India Company, and one of the
greatest and most successful merchants of his age.
But the statements in his tract on the Trade to India,
published in 1681, are very similar to those in Mun's
tract on the same subject, which we have laid before
the reader; and though his " New Discourse of
Trade," be a work of much merit, and has frequently
been referred to, yet, as it has been often reprinted,
the last time, perhaps, by Foulis of Glasgow, in
1751, and is of common occurrence, it was destitute
of that rarity which has been a principal recommenda-
tion to a place in this volume.

LONDON, January, 1856.

A
DISCOVRSE
of Trade,

From England *vnto the* East-Indies:

Answering to diuerse Obiections which are
vsually made against the same.

The second Impression corrected and amended.

By T. M.

LONDON.

Printed by *Nicholas Okes* for *Iohn Pyper.*
1621.

Brief Notes directing to the
seueral parts which are handled
in the Answeres made to the foure
Obiections against the East-
India Trade in the Dis-
course following.

The parts of the first Obiection,
Page 7.

1. *I*N *the first part is shewed the necessary vse of* Drugges, Spices, Indico, Raw-silke, *and* Callicoes. *page* 8.

2. *In the second part is declared the great summes of ready monies which are yearely saued to* Christendome *in generall, by fetching the wares of the* East-Indies *directly in shipping from thence.* *page* 10.

3. *In the third part, is proued, that the* Trade *from* England *to the* East-Indies *doth not consume, but rather greatly increase the generall stocke and Treasure of this* Realme. *page* 17.

The parts of the second Obiection
Page 23.

1. *In the first part is set forth the noble vse of Ships; and that the timber, planke, and other Materials of this* Kingdome *for the building of Shipping, are neither become scant nor dearer since the* East-India Trade *beganne.* *page* 24.

2. *In the second part is shewed the great strength of shipping*

A DISCOVRSE OF
Trade from England vnto
the East-Indies:

Answering to diuerse Obiections which
are vsually made against the same.

THe Trade of Merchandize, is not onely that laudable practise whereby the entercourse of Nations is so worthily performed, but also (as I may terme it) the very *Touchstone* of a kingdomes prosperity, when therein some certen rules shall be diligently obserued. For, as in the estates of priuate persons, we may accompt that man to prosper and growe rich, who being possessed of reuenues more or lesse, doth accordingly proportion his expences; whereby he may yearely aduance some maintenance for his posterity. So doth it come to passe in those Kingdomes, which with great care and warinesse doe euer vent out more of their home commodities, than they import and vse of forraine wares; for so vndoubtedly the remainder must returne to them in treasure. But where a contrary course is taken, through wantonnesse and riot, to ouerwaste both forren and domesticke wares, there must the money of necessity be exported, as the meanes to helpe to furnish such excesse, and so by the corruption of mens conditions and manners, many rich countries are made exceeding poore, whilst the

people

people thereof, too much affecting their owne enormities, doe lay the fault in something else.

Wherefore, industry to encrease, and frugalitie to
maintaine, are the true watchmen of a kingdomes
treasury; euen when, the force and feare of Princes
prohibitions cannot possibly retaine the same.

And therefore, as it is most plaine, that proportion
or quantity, must euer bee regarded in the importing of
forren wares; so must there also be a great respect of
quality and vse; that so, the things most necessarie
bee first preferred, such as are foode, rayment, and
munition for warre and trade; which great blessings,
when any countrie doth sufficiently enioy; the next
to bee procured are wares, fitting for health, and arts;
the last, are those, which serue for our pleasures, and
ornament.

Now, forasmuch, as by the prouidence of almighty
God, the Kingdome of *England*, is endowed with such
aboundance of rich commodities, that it hath long
enioied, not onely great plenty of the thing before
named, but also, through a superfluity, hath beene much
inriched with treasure brought in from forraine parts;
which hath giuen life vnto so many worthy trades,
amongst which that vnto the *East-India* by name; the
report whereof, although it is already spread so famous
through the world; yet notwithstanding, heere at home,
the clamorous complaints against the same, are growne
so loude and generall, that (my selfe being one of the
Society) it hath much troubled my priuate meditations,
to conceiue the means or true grounds of this confusion. But at the last I resolued my selfe, that the
greatest number of these exclaimers, are led away in
ignorance; not hauing as yet, discerned the mysteries
of such waighty affaires; some haue beene transported
with enuy, as not participating in the said Society, or
beeing thereby hindred (as they conceiue) in some

other trade; and others, wholly corrupted in their affections; who whilst they willingly runne into these errors, doe also labour diligently to seduce others; that so, this good and glory of the Kingdome, might be subuerted by our selues, which by the policie and strength of Strangers, cannot so easily be abated. Wherefore, it is now a fit time to meet with such iniurious courses, by a true Narration of the passages in the said *East-India* Trade; answering to those seuerall obiections, which are so commonly made against the same; That so these mis-vnderstandings and errours may bee made knowne vnto the whole body of this Kingdome, which at this present time is most worthily represented in those noble assemblies of the high Court of *Parliament*; where I hope the worth of this rich Trade, shall be effectually inquired, and so in the end obtaine the credit of an honorable approbation.

The first Obiection.

It were a happie thing for Christendome (say many men) that the Nauigation to the East-Indies, by way of the Cape of Good hope, had neuer bene found out, For in the fleetes of shippes, which are sent thither yearely out of England, Portingall, *and the* Lowcountries; *The gold, siluer, and Coyne of Christendome, and particularly of this Kingdome, is exhausted, to buy vnnecessarie wares.*

The Answere.

THe matter of this Obiection is very waighty, and therefore, it ought to be answered fully; the which that I may the better performe, I will diuide the same into three parts.

1. In the first, I will consider, the necessary vse of

the

the wares, which are vsually brought out of *East-India* into *Europe*; namely, Drugs, Spices, rawsilk, Indico, & Callicoes.

2. In the second; I will intimate the manner & meanes, by which the said wares haue beene heretofore, and now are brought into *Europe*.

3. In the third and last; I will proue, that the treasure of *England* is not consumed, but rather greatly to bee increased by the performance of the said Trade.

The 1. *part concerneth the vse of Indian wares.* Touching the first; Who is so ignorant, in any famous commonwealth, which will not consent to the moderate vse of wholesome Drugges and comfortable Spices? Which haue beene so much desired in all times, and by so many Nations; not thereby to surfeit, or to please a lickorish taste (as it often happeneth, with many other fruites and wines) but rather as things most necessary to preserue their health, and to cure their diseases; euen as it is most notably set forth by

Sir *Thomas Elyos* his Castle of health. *Rembert Dodoneus* his history of *Plants*. The *French Academy* second part, & others. some learned men, who haue vndertaken, to write vpon this subiect; and therefore, it shall bee altogether needlesse heere to discourse vpon their seuerall operations and vertues, seeing that, he that listeth, may be well instructed therein; if hee will peruse the volumes which are penned by the learned, for the benefit of all those, who shall make vse thereof.

But if peraduenture, it be yet further vrged; that diuers nations liue without the vse of Drugges and Spices: The answer is, That either such people know not their vertue; and therefore, suffer much by the want of wares so healthfull, or else, they are most miserable; being without means to obtain the things, which they so much want: but sithence I intend to be briefe, I will insist no further vpon this point; For the Obiecters might as well deny vs the vse of Sugars, Wines, Oyles, Raysons, Figgs, Prunes, and Currandes; and with farre more reason exclaime against *Tobacco*,

Cloth

Cloth of gold and Siluer, Lawnes, Cambricks, Gold & Siluer lace, Veluets, Sattens, Taffaties, and diuers other manufactures yearely brought into this Realme, for an infinite value; all which as it is most true, that whilest wee consume them, they likewise deuoure our wealth; yet neuerthelesse, the moderate vse of all these wares hath euer suted well with the riches and Maiestie of this Kingdome.

But I will come to the Raw-silks and Indico; this being so excellent for the dying of our woollen-cloathes, thereby so much esteemed in so many places of the world; that for ornament, together with the great reliefe & maintenance of so many hundreds of poore people; who are continually imployed, in the winding, *France* and twisting, and weauing of the same; Insomuch, that by the Low the cherishing of this busines (as his Maiestie, for his late yeares part is graciously pleased to performe, in remitting the do make impost of Silke) it may well be hoped, that in short tities of time, industry will make the art to flourish, with no wrought lesse happinesse to this Kingdome, then it hath done wares they (through many ages) to diuerse States in Italy, and were hereto-lately also to the Kingdome of France, and to the from *Italy*. vnited Prouinces of the Lowcountries.

France and the Low countries of late yeares do make great quan-tities of wrought silke, of which wares they were hereto-fore serued from *Italy*.

Now as touching the trade of Callicoes, of many sorts, into which the English lately made an entrance; although it cannot bee truly sayd, that this commodity is profitable for the state of *Christendome* in generall (in respect they are the manufacture of Infidells, and *France, Italy*, in great part the weare of Christians) yet neuerthelesse, *South Bar-*this commoditie, likewise is of singular vse, for this *bary*, and common wealth in particular; not onely therewith to tries. increase the trade into forraine parts; but also thereby, greatly to abate the excessiue prices of Cambricks, Hol-land, and other sorts of Linnen-cloath; which daily are brought into this Kingdome, for a very great

France, Italy, South Bar-bary, and other Coun-tries.

summe

The 2. part Sheweth the manner & the meanes by which Indian wares haue beene and now are brought into Europe.

summe of money. And this shall suffice concerning the necessary vse of the *Indian* wares; In the next place, I will set forth the manner and meanes of their importing into *Europe*.

It is an errour in those men; who thinke that the trade of the *East-Indies* into *Europe* had first entrance by the discouery of the *Nauigation* by the *Cape* of *Good-hope*. For many yeares before that time, the traffique of those parts, had his ordinary course by shipping from diuerse places in the *Indies*; yearely resorting with their wares to *Mocha* in the *Red Sea*, and *Balsera* in the *Persian-Gulfe*: From both which places, the Merchandize (with great charges) were after transported ouer land by the *Turkes* vpon *Cammels*, 50 dayes iourney, vnto *Aleppo* in *Soria*, and to *Alexandria* in *Egypt*, (which are the *Mart Townes*, from whence diuerse Nations, as well *Turkes*, as *Christians*, doe continually disperse the sayd wares by Sea into the partes of *Europe*:) by which course, the common enemie of *Christendome* (the *Turke*) was Maister of the

Rates vpon all sorts of Spices 22. per cent. Raw-Silkes esteemed about 2. per cent. Indico about 8. per cent.

Trade; which did greatly imploy, and inrich his Subiects, and also fill the Coffers of his owne customes, which hee exacted at very high rates; But by the prouidence of almightie God, the discouerie of that *Nauigation* to the *East-Indies* by the *Cape* of *Good-hope* (now so much frequented by the *English*, *Portingalls*, and *Dutche*; and also attempted, by other *Christian Kingdomes*) hath not onely much · decayed the great commerce, betweene the *Indians* and the *Turkes* in the *Red Sea*; and in the *Persian Gulfe* (to their infinite hurt, and to the great increase of *Christian* trade,) but it hath also brought a further happinesse vnto *Christendome* in generall, and to the *Realme* of *England* in particular, for the venting of more *English* commodities; and for exporting of a lesse quantitie of siluer out of

Europe, vnto the Infidells, by many thousand pounds yearely, then hath beene accustomed in former times; as I shall proue most plainly by that which followes.

And First, it will be necessarie to set downe the quantitie of Spices, *Indico,* and *Persian* Raw-silke (which is yearely consumed in *Europe*) and in them all to consider the cost with the charges to lade the same commodities cleare aboard the Shippes from *Aleppo;* and the like of all the selfe same wares, as they haue beene vsually dispatched from the *Portes* of the *East-Indies;* wherein, will appeare that happinesse, which many do so much oppose; especially our owne Countrie-men, vnder the gilded tearmes of the Commonwealth; whilest being indeed either ignorant, or ill affected, they doe not onely grosly erre themselues, but also cause others to hinder as much as in them lieth, the glorie and well-fare of this Kingdome; but leauing them, I will set downe the sayd wares in their quantitie and prizes as followeth; and first,

Such people as affect not the good of this Kingdome.

At Aleppo.

lbs.	*l.*	*s.*	*d.*	
6000000. of Pepper, cost with charges at *Aleppo* at 2s. the ℔.	600000	00	00	The quantitie of Spice, Indico, and *Persian* Raw-Silke, yearely consumed in *Europe.*
450000. of Cloues at 4s. 9d. the pound	106875	10	00	
150000. of Mace at 4s. 9d. the pound	35626	00	00	
400000. of Nutmegs, at 2s. 4d. the pound	46666	13	04	
350000. of Indico at 4s. 4d. the pound	75833	06	08	
1000000. of *Persia* raw silke at 12s. the pound	600000	00	00	
	1465001	10	00	

Now followeth the same wares both for quantitie & qualitie at their seuerall prizes as they are to be bought and laden cleare of charges.

In the East-Indies.

lbs.	*l.*	*s.*	*d.*
6000000. of Pepper cost with charges in *India* 2s. 0½d. the pound........................	62500	00	00
450000. Cloues at 9d. the pound.	16875	00	00
150000. Maces at 8d. the pound...	5000	00	00
400000. Nutmegs at 4d. the pound........................	6666	13	04
350000. Indico at 14d. the pound	20416	12	04
1000000. *Persia* Raw-silke at 8s. the pound	400000	00	00
	511458	05	08

The exportation of the value of 953543.l.sterling out of Christendome into *Turkey* yearely saued. So that by the substance, and summes of these accompts, it doth plainely appeare, that the buying of the sayd quantitie of Raw-silkes, Indico, and Spices, may be performed in the *Indies*, for neare one third part of the ready moneys, which were accustomed to bee sent into *Turkey* to prouide the same; So that there will bee saued euery yeare the value of 953543.l. 4s. 4d. sterling of readie moneys, that heretofore hath beene exporteth out of *Christendome* into *Turkey*; which is a matter of such note and consequence, that it may seeme incredible, before the circumstance bee dulie considered; and therefore least I should leaue the matter in doubt, it is requisite, that I doe make an explanation of some particulars.

And principallie, it must not bee conceiued, that this great aduantage, which hath beene spoken of, is onely the Merchants gaine; for the Common-wealth of *Christendome*, hath a very great part thereof in the cheapenes of the wares, as shall be (God willing) proued hereafter in his due place.

Secondly, the time of the Merchants forbearance, and interest, is verie long: his aduenture and assurance much dearer; his charges of shipping, victuals, Mariners, and factors their wages, far greater, then by the voyage into *Turkey* for the same wares; so that the former great difference must bee vnderstood in these particulars; whereby we may perceiue to our comfort, that the Materialls of the kingdome, & the imployments of the subiects (in liew of readie moneys) becomes a verie great part of the price which is paid for the said *Indian* wares; which cannot hurt the State (as some erroniously suppose) but greatly helpe it, as I shall better proue in that which followeth.

Instance only, that ten shillings imployed in *Pepper* in the *East-Indies*, will require thirty and fiue shillings for all charges whatsoeuer to deliuer it in *London*.

First therefore, I shew for an vndoubted truth, That the *Persians*, *Moores*, and *Indians*, who trade with the *Turkes*, at *Aleppo*, *Mocha*, and *Alexandria*, for Raw-silkes, Drugs, Spices, Indico, and Callicoes; have alwaies made, and still doe make, their returnes in readie money: for other wares, there are but few which they desire from forraine partes; some Chamblets, Cor-rall, wrought silke, woollen-cloth, with some trifles, they doe yearely vent in all, not for aboue 40. or 50. thousand pounds sterling; which is no valuable summ in respect of that wealth which is carried from *Aleppo* and *Constantinople* into *Persia* for Raw-silkes, when least, 500000. pounds sterling *Per annum*: and from *Mocha* about 600000. pounds sterling (likewise yearely into *India*), for returne of Callicoes, Drugs, Sugar, Rice, Tobacco, and diuerse other things. So here is still a very great Commerce maintained betweene those Infidels; not onely for the Callicoes of many sortes, and other wares (which concerne their owne vse) but also for the Raw-silkes of *Persia*, which are altogether transported into *Christendome*.

The great Summes of money which the *Persians* and the *Indians* carrie yearely out of *Turkey*.

How worthy an enterprise is it therefore in the English *East-India* Companie? by whose endeauours, there is now good hope to turne a great part of this wealthy Trade into *England*, by shipping directlie from the *Persian-Gulfe*, whereby the imployments, traffique, and Customes of the *Turkes*, may be still more and

The *East-India* Companie doe endeauour to

more

bring the
Raw-Silkes
from *Persia*
directly by
Sea.

more impayred; & the general Treasure of *Christen-dome* much less consumed; as is alreadie performed for the businesse of Spices and Indico.

And who shall then doubt our want of Siluer to mainetaine the Trade? if by this way wee doe obtaine the Silke, which with more aduantage & conueniencie, will draw the money to this Mart, then it hath beene heeretofore conueyed vnto those remote dominions of the *Turke*.

And least peraduenture it should bee thought, that the traffique in those parts by the *Christians* for the *Persian Silke*, is performed by change for other wares, or by the money which proceedeth of the sales of many rich commodities, which yearely they sell at *Aleppo*, *Alexandria*, *Constantinople*, and these parts:

The answere is, that neither the *Venetians*, *French*, nor *Dutche*, doe vent so much of their owne Country commodities in those parts, as doe prouide their necessarie wants of the proper wares of *Turkes*: such, as are the fine Raw-silke, made in *Soria*, Chamblets, Grogerans, Cotten-woolles, Cotten-yarne, Gaules, Flax, Hempe, Fleece-woolls, Rice, Hides, Waxe, & diuerse other things; so that still their raw-silkes of *Persia*, must be bought with ready money. Only the *English*

Marcellis sendeth yearely to *Aleppo* & *Alexandria* at least 500000.l. sterling, and little or no wares. *Venice* sends about the value of 100000.l. & a great value in wares. The Low-countries

haue more aduantage then any other Nation in this kinde, for they vent so great a quantitie of broade-cloathes, Tinne, and other *English* commodities, that the proceed thereof, doth not onely prouide a sufficient quantitie of part of the said *Turkish* wares (which fit their vse,) but also a proportion of about 300. great balles of *Persia* Raw-silke yeerely.

And if in any yeere, they chance to buy a greater quantitie of silke, then must & do they furnish the same in ready moneys from the *Portes* of *Marcellis*, *Genouay*, *Ligorne*, *Venice*, or the *Netherlandes*. Neither are these the onely meanes, whereby the *Empire* of the

Turke is so abundantly stored with Gold and Siluer, to
the performance of the *Indian-trade.* For, many are
the *Christian* shippes, which yearely lade with corne for
ready moneys in the *Archipelago*; Great is the commerce from *Poland, Hungarie,* and *Germany,* with Gold
and *Dollers,* for Chamblets, Grogerans, and other
things: But that which is very remarkable, is the great
quantitie of gold & some siluer coyned in *Grand-Cairo,*
which by two seuerall *Carrauans* (in bullion) is yearely
brought thither from the *Abissians* countrie in *Ethiopia,*
for returne of many rich commodities, as Veluets,
Sattens, Cloth of Gold, Taffaties, Woollen cloath:
polished Corrall, and other things.

sends about the value of 50000.l. sterling moneys, and little wares. Messina 25000l. in ready money.

Abissians a people in Ethiopia whose influence hath made them dull, lazy, and without artes; enioying diuers Mines of Gold and one of Siluer, which doe procure their wants of forraine wares.

Thus by the coherence of the *Turkish-Trade* with
the *Christians, Persians,* and *Indians,* I haue shewed
both the manner and the meanes, whereby the *East-
Indian* wares haue beene heretofore, and yet are, in
part, procured into *Christendome.* But least it should
seem incredible, that the *Turke* would let so great a
Masse of Treasure yearely to passe his Dominions, to
the *Indians,* and to the *Persians* his professed enemies:
I will make the matter yet more plaine.

And First, concerning the Raw-silkes, it is alreadie
shewed, that hee hath the money from the *Christians,*
besides the benefit he reapeth in their customes, with
great imployments also for his Subiects. And for the
Callicoes (his whole *Empire* hauing litle or no other
meanes for Linnen) he can not possibly be without
them, although it hath, & doth greatly exhaust his
treasure; neither doth he gaine any manufacture by
the same, as the *Christians* haue alwaies done by the
Raw-silke, to the great reliefe of innumerable poore
people, so much prouided for, by the pollicie of all well
gouerned and flourishing common-wealths: As by this
occasion, and in a businesse of the like kind, I may
instance the States of *Genouay, Florence,* and *Luca;*

Turkey hath litle meanes for Linnen but onely from India.

The proceedings of some States in Italy for the maintenance of Arts.

who for the maintenance of Artes and Trade, doe prouide Raw-silkes out of *Sicilia* for the value of 500000
pounds sterling at least yearlie; and for the payment
thereof they doe vent at *Naples, Palermo, Messina,* and
those parts a certaine quantitie of *Florence*-Rashes and
some other wares, for about 150000. pounds sterling
per annum; So the rest, being 350000.l. sterling, is
supplied all in readie moneys; which treasure they doe
willingly forsake, to procure their Trade; for experience hath taught them that Trade is their imployment, & doth returne them treasure, for by those silkes
(being wrought, transported & sould at *Franckforde*
and other Marts) they haue the better meanes, to
furnish their contracts with the King of *Spaine* in
Flanders; and so from *Spaine* the Siluer must returne
again to *Italy*. But if I should runne out in this and
other particulars (fitting our purpose) it would make
me too tedious, and so carrie mee beyond my ayme,
which is to be briefe.

The ready moneys which are yearely carried from some States of *Italy* into *Sicilia.*

Wherefore, I will proceede to cleare some doubts, in
those men, who perhaps not hauing the knowledge of
occurrents in forraine partes, might thinke, that neither
Venice, nor *Marcellis* haue the meanes or yet the
mindes, to exporte such great Sommes of readie
moneys, yearely out of those Dominions; especially
Marcellis being a part of *France,* where neighbour-
hoode doth daily tell vs, that Gold and Siluer may not
be conueied out of that Kingdome, for any valuable
Somme, more then is permitted for the necessarie vse of
Trauellers; Yet neuerthelesse experience hath likewise
taught vs, that for the effecting of those Trades
(whereof wee now speak, & which they esteeme so
much) there is a free extraction out of the sayd places,
of moneys both gold and siluer; whereof with them
there is no want; for, the said wares do procure it
abundantly.

First,

First, to *Marcellis,* it commeth not onely from *Genouay,* Ligorne, *Cartagenia, Malliga,* & many other *Port* townes of *Spaine* and *Italy,* but also from *Paris, Roane, Sainct-Malloes, Tolouse, Rochell, Deepe,* and other Cities of *France;* who want not meanes to haue great store of Rialls and Dollers from *Spaine* and *Germany.*

(marginal note: How Marcellis and Venice are furnished with ready moneys.)

And in like manner, the *Venetians* dispersing the sayd Raw-silkes, and other wares into the seuerall States of *Italy, Germany,* & *Hungarie,* (who haue but few commodities fitting their barter or exchange: but onely moneys) are therewith aboundantly serued; For the mines of *Hungarie* and *Germany* affoord good quantitie of gold & siluer; And likewise the States of *Italy,* especially *Genouay, Florence,* and *Millane,* haue euer store of *Rialls* out of *Spaine* in satisfaction of many great disbursments, which those Merchantes make for that King in his occasions of *Italy* and *Flanders;* of all which, I might make a large discourse, but I conceaue I haue sayd sufficient, to shew how the trade of the *East-Indies* hath beene, and now is brought into *Christendome* generally: what money is yearely sent out; by whom; & the possibilitie, or meanes which they haue to performe it. I will therefore in the next place, satisfie the *Obiectors;* that it is not the *East-India* Trade, which wasteth the Gold, and Siluer, Coyne, or other treasure of this kingdom in particular.

(marginal note: The Italyan Merchants doe furnish the king of Spaine with money in Italy and Flanders.)

For first, who knoweth not, that gold in the *East-Indies* hath no ratable price with Siluer? Neither hath the Siluer coyne of *England* any equall value with the *Spanish* Rialls according to their seuerall prices here; Besides that, his Maiestie hath not authorized the *East-India* Companie, to send away any part of this kingdomes Coyne, either Gold, or Siluer; but onely a certaine limited summe of forraine Siluer yearely;

(marginal note: The third part doth shew how the East-India Trade doth enrich this Kingdome.)

which as they dare not exceede, so neuer haue thcy as yet accomplished the same.

For it doth plainely appeare in their bookes; that from the originall and first foundation of the Trade, in *Anno* 1601. vntill the moneth of *Iuly, Anno* 1620. they haue shipped away onely 548090.l. sterling in *Spanish Rialls,* and some Dollers; whereas by licence, they might haue exported in that time 720000.l. sterling.

How much money and wares the East-India Company haue sent forth euer sithence the beinning of this Trade.

Also they haue laden away in the same tearme of xix yeares, out of this Kingdome 292286.l. sterling in Broad clothes, Kersies, Lead, Tinne, with some other *English* and forraine commodities ; which is a good Addition, and vent of our wares, into such remote places; where heretofore they haue had no vtterance at all.

The vent of English wares increased in the Indies.

And note, I pray you, how time and industrie hath bettered this Trade, when in the last three yeares, there hath beene sent more wares to the *Indies,* then in the xvi. yeares before; and yet our expectation is not at the highest; for those new borne Trades within the *Red Sea,* and in the *Persian Gulfe,* doe bid vs hope for better things, as lately by letters from *Spahan,* we vnderstand of great quantity of Raw silke prepared by the *English* factors, which (by Gods assistance) wee may expect here about the moneth of *August* next; with encouragement also, to vent our *English* cloth, and Kersies in good quantities; the like of Iron, Tinne, & other things; whereof experience (of those alreadie sould) hath giuen vs sufficient approbation of their validitie.

Our stocke may be much increased by Trade from Port to Port in the Indies.

And now (omitting much matter which might be written touching the discoueries of other Trades from one Kingdome or port to another, in the *Indies* : with the commodities thereof, whereby the imployment of our shippes, together with the stocke of money and

goods

goods which is sent out of *England* in them, may be much increased) I will draw to a conclusion of the point in hand; and shew, That whatsoeuer Summes of forren readie moneys are yearely sent from hence into the *East-Indies*, His Maiestie in the letters *Pattents* granted to that Company, hath notwithstanding with singular Care prouided, that the brethren of the Company, shall yearely bring in as much siluer, as they send forth; which hath beene alwayes truly performed, with an ouerplus, to the increase of this Kingdomes treasure.   Neither is it likelie, that the money which is thus contracted for, by the Companie at certaine prices, and to be deliuered them at times appointed, would bee otherwise brought into *England,* but onely by vertue & for performance of the said contracts; for without this assurance of Vent together with a good price for the sayd moneys, the Merchants would vndoubtedly make their returnes in other wares; the vse and extraordinarie consume whereof, would be found lesse profittable to the Commonwealth, when the matter should be duly considered, as I shall yet further endeauour to demonstrate.

The moneys sent to the Indies is all forraine Coyne.

The East-India Companie are obliged to bring in as much money as they carry out of the Realme.

Tobacco, Raysons, Oyles, and Wines, whereof there is no want, but rather too much Smoake.

And here I will suppose, That the *East-India* Companie may shippe out yearely 100000.l. sterling; yet it is most certain, that the Trade being thus driuen with such sums of ready moneys, it will not decay but rather much increase the treasure of the kingdom; which to proue, I will briefely set downe the substance of the *English* Trade vnto the *East-Indies*, concerning the quantitie of the seuerall sortes of wares, to be yearely bought there and sold here: with the vsual prices giuen for them in both places.   And first, I will beginne with their Coste and charges laden cleare aboard the shippes in the *East-Indies.*

In

In the East-Indies.

		l.	*s.*	*d.*
A proportion of such Trade as is hoped yearely to be brought into this Realme from *East-India*.	2500000 lbs. of Pepper at 2*d*. ob. the pound	26041	13	04
	150000 of Cloues at 9*d*. the pound	5626	00	00
	150000 of Nutmegs at 4*d*. the pound	2500	00	00
	50000 of Maces at 8*d*. the pound	1666	13	04
	200000 of Indico at 14*d*. the pound	11666	13	04
	107140 of China Raw silkes at 7*s*. the pound	37499	00	00
	50000 of Callicoes of seuerall sorts, rated at 6*s*. the peece one with another	15000	00	00
		100000	00	00

All the sayd Merchandize haue beene often experienced, or bought at or about the prices aboue written; & we doe hope for our parts (besides the Trade of Raw-silkes from *Persia* yearely, to lade from the *Indies*, such quantitie of the seuerall sortes of wares as are here set downe, (if it shall please his Maiestie, to protect and defend vs concerning the Articles of agreement made with the *Dutche*, that they may not violate any of them to our hindrance or damage) al which wares in *England* will yeelde (as I doe conceaue) the prices hereafter following, *Viz.*

In England.

	l.	*s.*	*d.*
2500000 lbs. of Pepper at 20*d*. the pound	208333	06	08
150000 of Cloues at 6*s*. the pound	45000	00	00
150000 of Nutmegs at 2*s*. 6*d*. the pound	18750	00	00
50000 of Mace at 6*s*. the pound	15000	00	00
200000 of Indico at 5*s*. the pound	50000	00	00
107140 of China Raw silkes at 20*s*. the pound	107140	00	00
50000 peeces of Callicoes of seuerall sorts, rated at 20*s*. the peece one with another	50000	00	00
	494223	06	08

So that here would be our owne money againe; and more, the somme of 394223.l. 06.s. 08.d. aduanced towards the generall stocke of the Kingdome. For although the *East-India* Company shall disburse the greatest part of the sayd somme aduanced vnto his Maiestie for custome and impost; and also vnto the Factors, Officers, and Mariners, for wages, together with the cost of shipping, Victuals, Munitions, Assurance, and the like; yet all these (the Materialls of shipping onely excepted) are but transmutations, and no consumption of the Kingdomes stocke.

But if any man obiect, and say, that the sayd commodities being brought into *England* (as is before written) they are either consumed in the land, or being transported into forraine partes, they are changed into other wares; So that still wee want our 100000.l. in readie money:

1 The answere is; first, that in the occasion of this dispute, wee must conceaue the said wares to be of no vse for this kingdom, but onely for so much, as doe concerne the Trade thereof.

2 And secondly, in the said Trade, wee must cõsider, that although the said goods bee sent out, and returned home in other wares from forraine partes; yet still they are negotiated to the increase of the sayd stocke, & for the imployment of the subiects.

Lastly, if there bee a resolution to determine and end the businesse: who doubteth, that the whole value may not bee presently returned hither in ready moneys? For in *Italy, Turkey*, and other places, where they are most vendible to profit, there likewise is the money free to bee exported at all times and by whomsoeuer.

And as it is most certain, that some other Merchandizes, sent out of this Kingdome were the meanes to bring in the 100000.l. in readie moneys, which is

Side notes:

How much the kingdomes stocke may increase yearely by trading to the *East-Indies.*

2500. Tonnes of shipping will lade home all the wares afore written from the *East-Indies.*

And the materialls of the said shipping (vnwrought) is worth about 15000.l. sterling.

India wares will bring readie moneys into the Realme.

here

We haue no other meanes to procure Treasure but by Trade and Merchandize.

herc supposed to bc sent and imployed in the *East-Indies* (as aforesaid) so likewise, there is the same power in these *Indian* wares, to procure other sums of readic moneys, to be brought into this kingdome: For let no man doubt, but that money doth attend Merchandize, for money is the price of wares, and wares are the proper vse of money; so that their coherence is vnsepa-

The *French &* the *Venetians* send the value of 600000.l. sterling yearely in ready money into *Turkey.*

rable. And if the *French* & the *Venetians* made any doubt of this, they would not so willingly permit the value of 600000.l. sterling, or more in *Spanish Rialls* and *Dollers*, yearely to bee carried out of their Dominions into *Turkey*: whereof three quarter parts at least are imployed, onely for the buying of *Persia* Raw-silkes, which commoditie doth presently enable them with ready money from diuerse other States to performe the

Trade maketh some States very rich which haue little other meanes.

Trade; whereby their wealth doth much increase, and their people are greatly imployed. So to conclude this point, I will onely adde, that the *East-India* Trade alone (although it bee driuen in no amplier manner then is afore written) is a meanes to bring more treasure into this Realme then all the other trades of this kingdome (as they are now managed) being put together.

If the generall Trade of this Kingdome doth export a greater value in wares then it doth import yearely, then doth our treasure increase.

For if the rule be true, that when the value of our commodities exported doth ouerballance the worth of all those forraine wares which are imported and consumed in this Kingdome, then the remainder of our stocke which is sent forth, must of necessity returne to vs in Treasure. I am confident that vpon a diligent and true inquiry it will bee found, that the ouerballance of all our other trades together will not amount vnto so great a summe of money as the *East-India* trade alone doth ouerballance in this kinde.

The trade to the *East-Indies* may

And to make the matter yet more plaine, whereas it is already said that 100000.l. in money exported may import about the value of 500000. pounds sterling, in wares from the *East-Indies*, wee must vnderstand that part thereof to bee properly called our importation that this Realme doth consume, which is about the value of 120000. pounds sterling yearely. So the remainder being 380000.l. is matter exported into forraine parts in the nature of our Cloath, Lead, Tin, or any other natiue commodities, to the great increase of this Kingdomes stocke, and that also in so much treasure, so farre as the *East-India* Trade can bee rightly vnderstood to subsist in this particular. *be said to export 480000 pounds, and to import 120000.l. yearely. So the ouer-ballance is 360000 pounds sterling.*

For as all humane actions haue their termination and ends, so likewise there must be an end assigned vnto the affaires of the *East-Indies*; which are then truely said to be finished, when this Realme is serued, and the remainder of those wares which are sent from hence beyond the Seas, sold there, and conuerted into money; which likewise from thence may bee brought away freely, and without the danger of Law or prohibition. *Euery action ought especially to be considered in his end.*

The East-Indian wares which are sent beyond the seas, are sold and haue their finall end in money, which might bee brought into this Realme in that kinde, if our other trades did not diuert the same

Forasmuch therefore as it is well knowne to many men, that moneys are thus procured by the sales of *Indian* wares to profit, in the parts of *Turkey*, and at *Ligorne, Genouay*, the Netherlands, *Marcellis*, and other places: yet notwithstanding if all the sayd coyne, or any part thereof should bee diuerted from this Realme by some other new imployments or affaires, it must neuerthelesse be granted, that the said *India* wares hath their finall end in moneys. But I will cease to heape vp any more arguments, to prooue a matter which is already made so plaine; wherefore leauing this Obiection, I will endeauour to giue answer to the next.

The second Obiection.

The timber, Plancke, and other materialls, for making of shipping, is exceedinglie Wasted, and made dearer, by the building of so many great Shippes, as are yearely sent to Trade in the East-Indies; *and yet the State hath no vse of any of them vpon occasion. For either they are not here; or else they come home verie weake, and vnseruiceable.*

The Answere.

THis *East-India* Trade seemeth to bee borne and brought vp au Vnthrift, for it wasteth and consumeth all; Neither doth it good to any.

But the Obiection in some part is very weake: and in the rest it is mistaken.

The 1. part concerneth the folly of the Obiection.

For first, concerning the weaknesse thereof; would men haue vs to keepe our woods and goodly trees to looke vpon? they might as well forbid the working of our woolls, & sending forth our cloth to forraine parts; for both are meanes alike to procure the necessarie wares, which this Kingdome wanteth. Doe they not know that trees doe liue and grow; and being great, they haue a time to dye and rot, if oportunity make no better vse of them; and what more noble or profitable vse then goodly ships for Trade and warre? are they not our barns for wealth and plenty, seruing as walles and Bulwarkes for our peace and happinesse? Do not their yearely buildings maintaine many hundred poore people, and greatly increase the number of those Artesmen which are so needfull for this common wealth?

The prouidence of the East-India company for Timber & Plauke.

And is not all this good performed also (with great prouidence) by bringing in yearely store of Timber, and other prouisions from *Ireland?* Why then, where is the great wast and dearnesse? I am sure, the *East-India* Company findes it not; for whereas they do onely buy their prouisions in *Hampshire, Essex, Kent,*

and *Barkeshire*, in all which places they now may haue
both Timber, Planks, Sheathing boards, Trenalls, and
the like, both for goodnesse and price, as cheape (yea
better cheape) than they haue beene this fifteene yeares;
and likewise in all that course of time their bookes doe
plainely shew that those wares haue neuer varied
much; for if they haue risen any smal matter in one
yeare they haue fallen as much the next. And yet
I pray you obserue (besides the *East-India* Companies
buildings) the many goodly shippes, which are daily
made for other priuate Merchants (such as *England*
neuer had before:) and that which is most remarkable,
is, the continuall late buildings of his Maiestie, thereby
yearely adding more strength and glory of great Ships
to his Royall and matchlesse Nauy; so that heere we
see this supposed wast and want is not considerable.

Yea but, say they, the *East-India* shippes are neuer
here, to serue the Kingdome vpon occasion: Or if they
be at home, they are weake, and vnfit for seruice.

In trade of Merchandize our Ships must goe and
come, they are not made to stay at home; yet neuerthelesse, the *East-India* company are well prepared at
all times, to serue his Maiestie, and his Kingdomes,
with many warlike prouisions, which they alwayes
keepe in store; such as Timber, Planks, Iron-workes,
Masts, Cordage, Anchors, Caske, Ordinance, Powder,
Shot, Victualls ready packed, Wine, Sider, and a world
of other things, fitting the present building, repairing
and dispatch of Shippes to Sea: as may be plentifully
seene in their yardes and storehouses at *Deptforde*, and
more especially in those at *Blackewall*; which are
growne so famous, that they are daily visited & viewed
by strangers, as well Embassadors, as others; to their
great admiration of his Maiesties strength, & glory, in one
onely Company of his Merchants, able at short warning
to set forth a fleet of Ships of great force & power.

The East-India Trade hath not indeared the materialls which serue to make shippes.

The 2. part sheweth the mistaking in the Obiec-tion.

The warlike prouision which the *East-India* Company keepe in store.

His Maiesties strength in the *East-India* Com-panie alone.

For it is well knowne to all men who please truely to be informed, That the *East-India* Company (besides their fleete of Shippes, going and comming, & also abiding in the *Indies*) are continually building, repairing, rigging, victualling, and furnishing to Sea, with all prouision needefull for such a long voyage, some 7. or 8. great shippes yearely; which are to bee seene at an Anchor in the Riuer of *Thames* in a great forwardnes some 5. or 6. moneths together, before they commonly depart for the *Indies*, which is about the moneth of *March*: & they are no sooner got off from the coast of *England*, but shortly after, is the season of our ships to returne from the *Indies*; who come not home so weake as some would haue them; for how often hath experience beene made of our shippes which haue performed two or three seuerall voyages to the *East-Indies*? Yet at their returne, they haue beene indocked, new trimmed and lanched out againe, fitted for the like voyages, in lesse then two moneths. But it will be needles to spend any more time in shewing the errors of this 2. Obiection: therefore I will rather come to the handling of that which followeth,

The shippes which returne from the *East-Indies* home, may be repayred in a very short time.

The third Obiection.

The voyages to the East-Indies do greatly consume our victuals, and our Mariners: leauing many poore widdowes and children vnrelieued; Besides, that many Ships are yearely sent forth to the East-Indies, and few we see as yet returned; Also, this Trade hath greatly decaied the Traffique & shipping, which were wont to bee imployed into the Streights: And yet the said Trade of the East-Indies, is found very vnprofitable to the Aduenturers: Neither doth the Commonwealth finde any benefit by the cheapenesse of Spice and Indico, more then in times past.

The

The Answer.

Why, what a world of mischiefes haue wee heere?

1. *Dearth.*
2. *Mortality.*
3. *Destruction.*
4. *Beggerie.*
5. *And neuer a whit the neere.*

A very Teame of calamities, drawing on to misery; is it not then high time to seeke a remedy? Yes verily, and it will be easily done, because these euils neuer were (as yet at least) procured by the *East-India* Trade, as I shall shew, by answering all the parts in order as they stand: and first of *Dearth.*

It is both naturall and iust, that euery Kingdome, State, or Common-wealth, should feed and cherish vp the Natiue people of all degrees and conditions whatsoeuer, to their preseruation of life and health, with such meanes and moderation, as their plentie shall affoord; and this is not only due to them in the time of their aboad at home, but also vpon all occasions of voyages into other Countries beyond the Seas, wherein they shall be imployed for their owne maintenance, and for the good of the Common-wealth. *The first Part concerneth Dearth.*

Now therefore concerning the prouision of victuals (which in this Kingdome is yearely prepared for the setting forth of those Ships which saile to the *East-Indies*) it is well knowen to many men, that it is alwaies proportioned, for about 18. moneths; whereas commonly the voyages proue a yeare longer: so that this ouer-plus of time, is furnished with victuals of forreine parts. *The manner how the East India Company do victuall their ships.*

And likewise for the Bread and Bisket, which is shipped from hence; hath it not alwaies bene made of French Corne, purposely brought ouer hither, (and that at a deare rate) onely to preserue the plentie of owne graine? vntill now of late daies that the Farmers here begin to cry out and say, that the cheapnesse of Corne doth disinable them to pay their deare Rents: Thus doe the *East-India* Company euery way accommodate their proceedings for the good of the Kingdome.

And further concerning their Drinke, is it not a very great part water? Some Wine and Sider, and but little Beere.

Also the Flesh they eate, is Beefe and Porke, and that onely for three daies in a week; the rest of their victuals is Fish, some Butter, Cheese, Pease, Oatemale, and other things; all which is proportioned into a very sparing dyet to euery man by allawance: so that heere is no excesse nor ryot, or any other meanes to make our victuals scant and deare, as is by some erroniously supposed; but rather by this course of life, our plenty is much aduanced. And so I will giue answer to the next part, which is Mortalitie, and great decay of Mariners.

The Second Part concerneth Mortality. The life of man is so precious, that it ought not lightly to be exposed to dangers; And yet we know, that the whole course of our life, is nothing but a passage vnto Death; wherein one can neither stay nor slacke his pace, but all men run in one manner, and in one celeritie; The shorter liuer runnes his course no faster then the long, both haue a like passage of time; howbeit, the first hath not so farre to runne as the later.

Now, it is this length of life which Nature seekes and States likewise endeuour to preserue in worthy men; but none are accounted so worthy in this nature, saue only they, who labour in their vocations and functions, both for the publike good, and for their priuate benefit.

Thus may wee esteeme our good Mariners, to be of

no small vse vnto this Common-wealth: but take them from their laudable and accustomed imployments, for want of voyages to Sea; we see what desperate courses they do then attempt, by ioyning, euen with *Turkes* and Infidels, to rob and spoile all Christian Nations; so that we may conclude, wee must not onely breed vp Mariners, but also seeke by Trade, to giue them a maintenance.

Well, all this is true, but (say they) the *East-India* Company doth neither breed nor maintaine, but destroy the wonted number of our Mariners.

How can this be, when it is most certaine, that *England* (besides the *East India* fleets) had neuer yet more shipping then at this present? neither do any of them stay at home for want of Mariners, no, not at this time, when many hundred Saylers are employed in extraordinary seruice, for his' Maiestie in a royall fleete of ships, now at Sea: besides those great numbers of our best Marriners, which haue beene and daily are wasted and taken prisoners by the *Turkes*; so where is this want, or what is our misery more then the want of true information in those that are so ill perswaded of our Company?

Is it not certaine, that as the *East India* voyages are long, so likewise in Natures course many should die by length of time, although they staid at home? And to recompence the losse of those that die, doe not the *East India* company with great prouidence, yearly ship out at least 400. Landmen in their fleets, which in one voyage proue good Mariners to serue the Kingdome and Common-wealth, vnto which many of them were a burthen before they obtained this employment? And thus is the Kingdome purged of desperate and vnruly people, who being kept in awe by the good discipline at Sea, doe often change their former course of life, and so aduance their fortunes.

Good Mariners are accounted worthy men in a Commonwealth.

The breeding of 400 Mariners yearely. Besides, that the feare of a few mens death ought not to ouerthrow or hinder the performance of honorable actions for the seruice of the King and common-wealth.

Our Mariners owne disordered life, is that which killeth many of them.

Neither indeed are these voyages so dangerous and mortall, as is reported; for how many of our Ships haue gone & come from the *East Indies*, without the losse of fiue men in a hundreth? Others again haue had worse success in the first beginning, when the seasons, the places, and their contagions were not so well known vnto vs; yet time hath taught vs many things, both for the preseruation of health, and speedier performance of our voyage then heretofore. But the Method of my discourse, bids me write more of this in the next part, which is destruction; and this I must diuide into two parts.

In the first I wil consider the want of diuers ships sent to the *East Indies*, which are wasted there.

And in the second, I will answer the supposed ouerthrow of the *Turkey* trade, together with much of our shipping which were wont to be employed thither.

The third Part concernes the decay of shipping which haue beene sent to the Indies.

First therefore concerning the decay of our ships in the *Indies*, it cannot bee denyed, but there hath been great spoile of them in these three last yeares; not by the dangers of the Seas, or by the strength of enemies; but by vnkind and vnexspected quarrels with our neighbours the *Hollanders*, who haue taken and surprised twelue of our ships at seuerall times, and in sundry places, to our vnspeakeable losse and hinderance; toge-

Our troubles with the Dutch.

ther with the death of many of our worthyest Marriners, who haue beene slaine and died prisoners vnder their hands: and this hath so much the more encreased the rumour of their mortality. Neither list I here to aggrauate the fact, more then thus, briefly to giue answere to the obiection: for our late vniou with the *Dutch*, doth promise a double recompence of gaine in time to come.

And they who make this Trade so poore and vnprofitable, are much mistaken in the reckoning; for the present losses which causeth many aduenturers so much

to

to despaire, is not in the substance of the Trade, but
by the euill accidents which haue befalne the same:
and to make this point more plain, I must yet declare
some other particulars: in which I will endeuour very
briefly to set down the summe of the whole businesse,
which the *English* hath hitherto performed in the *East
Indies.*

First, therefore I doe obserue that since the beginning of this Trade, vntill the Moneth of *Iuly* last *Anno*
1620. there haue beene sent thither 79. ships in seuerall
voyages, whereof 34. are already come home in safetie,
richly laden. 4. haue been worne out by long seruice,
from Port to Port in the *Indies*: two were ouerwhelmed
in the trimming there: sixe haue bin cast away by the
perils of the Seas: twelue haue bene taken and sur-
prized by the *Dutch,* whereof diuers will be wasted,
and little worth before they be restored: and twenty
one good ships do stil remaine in the *Indies.* So this
is a true account of our ships.

The summe
of the affaires
to the East
Indies euer
since the
Trade began.

And next concerning our stocke, it is a certaine
truth, that in all in the said ships there hath beene
sent out in ready money as well out of this Realme, as
from all other places wheresoeuer beyond the Sea
(which hath not beene landed in this Kingdome) the
value of 548090. pounds sterling in forraine coine: and
together with the said money, there hath beene shipped
the value of 292286. pounds sterling in sundry sorts of
English and forraine Commodities; all which moneys
and wares amounting vnto 840376. pounds, haue been
disposed, as hereafter followeth.

Account of
all the money
and goods
which hath
beene sent to
the East
Indies euer
since the
beginning of
the Trade.

First, there hath been lost 31079. pounds sterling,
in the six ships which are cast away: and in the 34.
ships, which are returned in safety, there hath beene
brought home 356288. pounds sterling in diuers sorts
of wares, which haue produced here in *England* towards
the generall stocke there of 1914600.l. sterling; for

356288.l.
sterling hath
beene re-
turned from

the East Indies, which did produce here towards charges 1914600.l. sterling.

the charges arising here, is but a change of effects from one to another, as hath beene said before in this discourse: So there ought to remaine in the *Indies*, to be speedily returned hither, 484088. pounds: neither can we conceiue that our charges and troubles with the *Dutch*, will haue wasted more then the odde 84088. pounds sterling: so that I am confident, that there yet remaineth 400000. pounds sterling of good estate, for both the ioynt stockes. And what a great value of *Indian* goods this sum of money may (by Gods blessing) shortly return in our ships, which are there ready to bring them, the example here doth teach vs to make vp the reckoning. So that notwithstanding our great charges of discoueries, our losses by danger of the Seas, our quarrels and infinite hindrance by the *Dutch*: yet heere the kingdome hath, and shall haue her stock againe, with a very great encrease, although the Merchants gaines concerning the two ioynt stocks, will proue but poore, in respect of the former voyages, which haue not had the like hindrance.

There remains yet in the East Indies to be returned home from thence about 400000.l. sterling.

And thus in a few lines may be seene, much matter truly collected with some paines, out of the diuers volumes of the *East Indian* Bookes.

Concerning the decay of shipping and Trade into Turkey.

Now concerning the decay of Trade and shipping, which were wont to be imployed into *Turkey*. I doubt, that in time it will likewise be affirmed, that the *East India* Company, haue hindred the vent of our white Cloath in the *Netherlands*, which to report were a very strange thing. But (praised be God) to our comfort, we see the great increase of goodly Ships, daily built and imployed, by the *Turkey* Merchants, with vent of more of our English Cloath (by the one third part at the least) then in times before the *East India* Trade began.

Yea, but (say they) we haue lost the trade of Spices, and *Indico*, from *Aleppo* into *England*.

Well, I grant they haue; yet the Kingdome hath

 found

found it with more profit by another way; and they likewise are recompenced with a greater Trade, by the exporting from hence of the selfe-same commodities, into *Italy*, *Turkey*, and other places: neither can it be lesse profitable for this Kingdome, to turne the Trade of Raw-silkes from *Aleppo*, and to bring them from the *Persian* gulfe, with one third part lesse money, then it doth now cost in *Turkey*; Besides, that by this meanes, the money proceeding of our English Cloath, Tin, and other wares in *Turkey* (not finding commodities fitting to returne for England) would vndoubtedly be brought home in Gold, as it hath beene performed heretofore, when by superfluitie of stocke The Turkey sent from hence in Spice, together with our English Merchants can and will wares; the Merchants (being thereby furnished with iustifie this a sufficient quantity of *Turkish* commodities) brought truth. home the remainder of their stock of those yeares in gold, for a great value.

Thus doth it plainely appeare, that these reuolutions of Trades, haue and doe turne to the good of the Common-wealth; neither hath the affaires of the *East Indies* impaired or decaied any other trade, Shipping or Mariners of this Realme; but hath mightily increased them all in it selfe. Wherefore let vs now take a view of this noble addition of the kingdomes strength and glory.

But this I must not do, by setting downe the number of our *English* shipping now in the *Indies*, or lately gone that way; for they haue beene heaped thither, these three last yeares together without returne, saue onely fiue ships in all that time; the rest haue beene kept there to oppose the furie of the *Dutch*: but now we are at vnion, we shall (by Gods assistance) daily expect diuers great ships with returnes.

And for the future time, this Trade I do conceiue, The strength will royally maintaine ten thousand tuns of shipping of the East India ships.

continually:

continually: (That is to say) going, and returning, & abiding there in the *Indies*: which said shipping will employ two thousand and fiue hundred Marriners at least: and the building with the repairing of the said ships, here at home, will set to worke fiue hundred men, Carpenters, Cawkers, Caruers, Ioyners, Smiths, and other labourers, besides many officers, and about 120. Factors, in seuerall places of the *Indies*. And so from these matters of great consequence, I must begin to write of Beggerie.

The fourth Part concernes the pouertie of widdowes, &c.

The pouertie of Widdowes and Fatherlesse is matter of great compassion, and doth alwaies moue Christian hearts to commiseration and charitie; whereby many receiue reliefe & help of those whom God hath blessed with better meanes: but how this pouerty should totally be preuented, it seemeth not onely difficult, but altogether impossible: For, besides the euill accidents and miseries, which euer attend on our humanity, we see how many daily (euen through their owne folly and wilfulnesse) do as it were desperately plunge them-selues into aduersity. And thus the number of those is great, who hauing the charge of Wife and Children, are notwithstanding altogether without meanes and artes to procure their maintenance; whereby some of them wanting grace, do run a desperate course, and haue vntimely ends.

The East India Trade doth employ many poore men, & deboist people, which other trades refuse.

Others againe, being better inspired, seeke for imployment, but find it not, or with great difficulty: for, who doth willingly enter-taine a man poore and miserable, charged with a family, and peraduenture debauched in conditions? Neither do any of our other Merchants voyages to forraine parts accept of those Nouices who neuer haue beene vsed to the Sea: So that when all the other

Wages before hand is not giuen in other Mer-

doores of charitie are shut, the *East India* gates stands wide open to receiue the needy and the poore, giuing them good entertainment, with two moneths wages before

hand,

hand, to make their needfull prouisions for the voyage: chants voyages, neither yet so great wages as the East India company pay.
And in the time of their absence, there is likewise paid vnto their wiues for maintenance, two other moneths wages, vpon account of euery yeares seruice: and also if any chance to die in the voyage, the Wife receiueth all that is found due vnto her husband (if he do not otherwise dispose it by will:) and this often happeneth to be more money then euer they had of their own together in any one time.

And likewise, are not many poore Widdowes, Wiues, and Children, of *Black-wall*, *Lime-house*, *Ratcliffe*, *Shadwell*, aud *Wapping*, often relieued by the *East India* Company, with whole Hogsheads of good Beefe and Porke, Bisket, and doales of ready money? Are not diuers of their Children set on work to pick Okam, and other labours fitting their age and capacitie? What might I not say of repayring of Churches, maintenance of some young Schollers, relieuing of many poore Preachers of the Gospell yearely with good summes of money; and diuers other acts of charitie, which are by them religiously performed, euen in the times now of their worst fortunes? for all which I hope there shall be a reward vnto them and theirs. And so I come to the fifth part of this third Obiection.

When did any of these Widdowes beg for reliefe in our Churches, as others often doe?

The East India Company their charity.

And here I must intimate how much they are deceiued, who thinke that Spices and Indico are no better cheape in *England* now, then in times past, before the *East India* Trade began.

The fifth Part concerneth the cheapnesse of Spice and Indico at this present in respect of former times.

For, it is an vndoubted truth, that in those daies we often paid sixe shillings or more for a pound of Pepper, and seldome or neuer lesse then three shillings and sixe pence the pound; whereas since the Trade hath come directly from the *Indies*, it hath been bought commonly at seuerall prices, betweene sixteene pence and two shillings the pound. But I will make the difference of price appeare more plainly, by setting

downe

downe the quantities of Spices and Indico, which are yearely spent in the Realme of *England*, together with the lowest prices, which they were wont to sell at, when wee brought them from *Turkey* and *Lixborne*; and the like concerning their vsuall prices now, that wee bring them from the *East Indies* directly; And first as from *Turkey*.

Prices of Spice and Indico in former times.		
400000.ˡˡ. of Pepper at 3.ˢ. 6.ᵈ. the ˡˡ.	70000.ˡ. 00.ˢ. 00.ᵈ.	
40000. of Cloues at 8.ˢ. the ˡˡ. ——	16000—00—00.	
20000. of Maces at 9.ˢ. the ˡˡ. ——	9000—00—00.	
160000. of Nutmegs at 4.ˢ. 6.ᵈ. the ˡˡ.	36000—00—00.	
150000. of Indico at 7.ˢ. the pound.	52500—00—00.	
	183500—00—00.	

And the selfe same quantitie and sorts of wares, are commonly sold at the prices here vnder written now in these later times.

Prices of Spice and Indico in these latter times.		
400000.ˡˡ. of Pepper at 20.ᵈ. the ˡˡ.	33333.ˡ. 06.ˢ. 08.ᵈ.	
40000 of Cloues at 6.ˢ. the ˡˡ. ——	12000—00—00.	
20000 of Maces at 6.ˢ. the ˡˡ. ——	6000—00—00.	
160000 of Nutmegs at 3.ˢ. the ˡˡ. —	20000—00—00.	
150000 of Indico at 5.ˢ. the ˡˡ. ——	37000—00—00.	
	108333—06—08.	

So that this Trade in Spice and Indico onely, doth saue the Kingdome yearly 74966.ˡ. 13.ˢ. 04.ᵈ. which is a matter worthy to bee obserued; and so much the rather, because it is a certaine truth, that lesse than a quarter part of this sum of money which is thus saued yearely, shall buy in the *Indies* the full quantitie of all the seuerall sorts of wares before written, which doe serue for a yeares prouision for this Realme of *England*; but still it must be remembered, that the custome, impost, wages, victuals, shipping, and other

Lesse than 18. thousand pounds sterling in the Indies, will buy Spice and Indico to serue this Realme for a yeare, which

charges

charges (which are to be added) will be a greater summe then the money which is paid for these wares in the *Indies*; but as I haue noted before, the said charges do not consume the Kingdomes stocke, although it doth greatly abate the Merchants meanes.

And to conclude this point, I will adde vnto that which hath beene said; that the commodities onely which we now send yearely into the *East Indies*, and *Persia*, are of sufficient value there, to returne vs *Indico*, *Spices*, *Drugs*, and all other sorts of *Indian* wares, (*Raw-silkes* of *Persia* onely excepted) for one yeares consume, or more in this Kingdome; So that now all the money which is sent forth in our Ships, doth procure an ouer-plus of the said wares, to the furtherance of Trade from *India* hither, and after from hence to forraine parts againe, to the great imployment of the Subiects, and inriching of this Realme, both in Stocke and Treasurie; all which is matter very worthy to be diligently obserued; And so I come to giue answer vnto the fourth and last Obiection.

is not halfe so much money as it spendeth beyond the seas to buy Currans onely, or to buy Tobacco.

The wares onely which are sent out of this kingdome into the East Indies are of sufficient value to furnish this Realme with an ouer-plus of all manner of Indian wares (Persian Raw-Silkes onely excepted.)

The fourth Obiection.

It is generally obserued, that his Maiesties Mint hath had but little imployment euer sithence the East India Trade began; Wherefore it is manifest, that the onely remedie for this, and so many euils besides, is to put downe this Trade: For what other remedy can there bee for the good of the Common-wealth?

The Answer.

THis fourth obiection may be diuided into three parts:

1. An euill declared.
2. A remedy propounded.
3. And counsell demanded.

The first Part And first concerning the Euill or want of Siluer,
concerneth
his Maiesties I thinke it hath beene, and is a generall disease of all
Mint. Nations, and so will continue vntill the end of the
world; for poore and rich complaine they neuer haue
25000 pounds enough: but it seemeth the malady is growen mortall
waight at
least of Siluer here with vs, and therefore it cries out for remedie:
yearely Well, I hope it is but imagination maketh vs sicke,
melted downe when all our parts be sound and strong; For who
into Plate,
besides old knoweth not the inestimable treasure of this King-
Plate new dome in Plate, possessed by the people thereof, almost
fashioned, as
by credible of all degrees; in such measure, as neuer hath beene
report. seene in former ages?

There hath And for his Maiesties Mint, it is well knowne, that
beene coyned there hath been coyned in fiue yeares together since
great store
of Gold and the *East India* Company began, 6214. pounds waight of
Siluer in his Gold, and 311384. pounds waight of sterling money;
Maiesties
Mint since all which Gold and Siluer doe amount vnto the summe
the East of 1213850. pounds of sterling Money; How then doth
India Trade
began. this Trade turne the currant and imployment of the
Mint?

But vpon the sight of this truth, perhaps it will be
There hath said, That wee must resort vnto the present times, (the
beene little
or no Siluer Mint being idle now.)
coyned in
some yeares, To which I answer, That likewise the Mint had little
when the or no imployment for coynage of Siluer in former
East India
Company times, when the said Company did not export aboue
sent out fifteene or twenty thousand pounds sterling at the
very small
sums of most *per annum*; no, nor yet in the yeares 1608. and
money. 1612: when in the former they shipped out but
6000.^{l}.-00.^{s}.-00.^{d}. and in the latter, but 1250.^{l}.-00.^{s}.-00.^{d}.
sterling. So that both waies we see, that the Mint
hath had very great imployment fiue years together,
since the *East India Trade* began; and also it hath
beene without imployment diuers years, when the *East
India* Company haue sent away but very small summes
of money; wherefore of necessity there must bee some
38   other

other causes and meanes wherby our Siluer is not exported only, but also it is not imported into the Realme as in former times. For we haue not had the meanes by our owne plentie, nor by the scarcity of our neighbours (for the space of the last foureteene yeares together) to send out hundreds of Ships laden with Corne, as in times past, which was returned home in Siluer; but rather of late yeares (as is much to be feared) a great quantity of our money hath beene carried out of the Kingdome, for that corne which hath beene brought vs from the East Countries, and other places, to supply our wants. Thus times doe change, and our fortunes change with them: neither list I to make this matter plaine, by setting downe those meanes, which heretofore brought vs store of money, euen out of *France* and other places, which now are ceased. But without any further medling in the Mint, I will come to the remedy which some propound, by putting downe the *East India* Company.

Some causes and meanes which were wont to bring Siluer into the Realme, are ceased at this present time.

But heere our comfort is, that the Obiectors are not our Iudges, whose wisedome & integrity labouring for the honour of his Maiestie, and the good of his Kingdome, wil soon perceiue the mischiefes of this supposed remedie. And that the pretended euil which many with malice chase, is that great good, which other Nations seeke by pollicie and strength to keepe, and likewise to obtaine. In which proceedings, it concerneth vs, especially to obserue the diligences and practices of the *Dutch*; who with more gladnesse would vndertake the whole Trade to the *East Indies*, then with any reason we can abandon that part therof, which we now enioy; neither can our restraint from the *Indies* keepe our Siluer from thence, as long as the *Dutch* go thither: for we know, that deuices want not to furnish such designes; and when their Ships returne from *India* shall not our Siluer out againe to help to

The Second Part concerneth the putting downe of the East India Trade.

The East India Trade is greatly desired by other Christian Nations.

pay a double price, or what they please, for all those wares which we shall want for our necessities?

The Dutch might grow strong & rich by our destruction.
Thus should the *Dutch* increase their honour, wealth and strength, whilest we abate, grow poore and weake at Sea for want of Trade; and call you this a Remedy; no, rather tearme it Ruine, Destruction, or what you list; And so I come vnto the conclusion, or last part.

The third Part concerneth the councel which the Obiecters demand.
And here I must confesse my selfe aground, for this matter is much too high for my handling: besides, my excuse is faire, hauing already done my task to cleare the *East India Trade* from imputation; the which, for want of learning, although I haue performed without variety of words or eloquence: yet it is done with all integrity of truth, in euery particular, as I shall be ready to make proofe vpon all occasions which may be offered.

And yet before I make an end, although I cannot satisfie euery mans desire, in such measure as is necessarie: yet I thinke it not amisse to performe the same so farre as I am able by common practise, and my obseruations in the Trade of Merchandize, which is my profession.

And first therefore, all men do know, that the riches or sufficiency of euery Kingdome, State, or Commonwealth, consisteth in the possession of those things, which are needfull for a ciuill life.

This sufficiency is of two sorts: the one is naturall, and proceedeth of the Territorie it selfe: the other is artificiall, and dependeth on the industry of the Inhabitants.

The riches of a kingdome is of two sorts.
The Realme of *England* (praised be God) is happily possessed of them both: as first, hauing great plentie of naturall riches, both in the Sea for Fish, and on the Land for Wooll, Cattle, Corne, Lead, Tin, Iron, and many other things for Food, Rayment, & Munition; insomuch, that vpon strickt tearmes of need,

this land may liue without the help of any other Nation.

But to liue well, to flourish and grow rich, wee must finde meanes by Trade, to vent our superfluities; therewith to furnish and adorne vs with the Treasure and those necessarie wares, which forraine Nations do afford: and here industry must begin to play his part, not onely to increase and guide the Trades abroad; but also to maintaine and multiply the Arts at home: for when either of these faile, or are not effected with such skill as their mysterie shall require, then doth the Common-wealth abate and growes poore; neither is this easily perceiued at first, vntill some euil accidents do stir vp our diligence to search out the true causes, that so they being remoued, the effects may cease. And this is the subiect of our discourse which we now pursue.

This kind of industry maketh some Countries which are poor in themselues, to grow rich and strong by other Nations, who haue greater means, and are lesse industrious.

That which I haue hitherto deliuered, hath beene altogether Negatiue, still defending and prouing by arguments, that the *East India Trade* hath not hurt this Common-wealth; and now changing my stile, I must affirme as fast the true causes of those euils which we seeke to chase away.

These causes then (as I conceiue) are principally foure.

Foure Principall Causes which carry away our Gold and Siluer.

1. The first is the breach of Entercourse by forraine Nations.

2. The second is the abuse of the exchanges betwixt vs and other Countries.

3. The third is neglect of dutie in some Subiects.

4. The fourth is our dammage in Commerce with Strangers.

Now concerning all these, I might make a very large discourse; but my purpose is onely to explane the meaning of euery point in order, as briefely as I can.

And first for the breach of Entercourse; by this I

vnderstand

The first Cause concerneth the Standard. vnderstand those Nations, who haue either debased their Standard, or else ouer-valued the price of their Coynes from that equiualence which formerly they had with the Standard and Moneys of this Realme; And also doe tollerate, not onely their owne Moneys, but *Proceedings against enter-course.* also the Coyne of other Countries (and especially of this Kingdome) to be currant with them at higher rates, then the prizes of the Exchange; by which courses (being directly against the Entercourse) there is a greater cause giuen of exportation of the Moneys of this Realme, then otherwise there would be. For although this is done with great danger to the exporters of the same, (it being an acte against the Law of the Land :) yet notwithstanding Couetousnesse, being euer conuersant in wicked actions, thinketh nothing vnlaw-full, which promiseth a certaine gaine; and how to remedie this euill practice, I finde it not easie. For the debasing of the Coyne, or raising the price thereof in this Realme, would much impouerish the estates of particular men, and yet in the conclusion, would prooue a businesse without end: for who doth not conceiue that which would follow beyond the Seas vpon any such alteration here with vs? so that still the euill will remaine, vntill we find some other remedie.

The second Cause concerneth the Ex-changes of moneys with forraine Countries. And for the exchanges of money, vsed betwixt Nations, although the true vse thereof is a very lawd-able and necessarie practise, for the accommodating of Merchants affaires, and furnishing of Trauellers in their occasions, without the transporting of Coyne from one State to another, with danger and losse, both to the publique and priuate wealth; yet is the abuse thereof verie preiudiciall vnto this Kingdome in parti-cular; whilest in the *Interim* the benefit doth arise vnto other Countries, who diligently obseruing the prizes whereby the moneys be exchanged, may take aduantage, to carry away the Gold and Siluer of this

Realme

Realme at those times, when the rate of our sterling money (in Exchange) is vnder the value of that Standard, vnto which place they are conueyed. For in respect the prizes of the Exchanges doe rise and fall according to the plentie or scarcitie of money, which is to be taken vp or deliuered out, the exchange is hereby become rather a Trade for some great monyed men, then a furtherance and accomodation of reall Trade to Merchants, as it ought to bee in the true vse thereof. *The practise of those strangers here in this Realme, who make a Trade by Exchange of moneys.*

And thus many times money may be made ouer hither by Strangers, to a good gaine, and presently carryed beyond the seas to a second profit, and yet the mischiefe ends not here: for by this meanes the takers vp of money in forraine Countries must necessarily driue a Trade to those places, from whence they draw their moneys; and so doe fill vs vp with forraine commodities, without the vent of our owne wares, but for this great euill there is an easie remedie: And so I come to handle the next cause, which is neglect of Dutie. *Forraine wares brought in with our ready moneys carried out of this Realme.*

Neither is it my intent to write of Duties in their seuerall kinds; but onely of that kind of duty which is heere thought to bee neglected by some men in their seuerall vocations. As it might peraduenture come to passe, in those who haue the working of his Maiesties Coyne, either Gold or Siluer: if diligent care be not had in the size of euery seuerall peece, to answer iustly to his weight: for howsoeuer vpon triall of many peeces altogether, the weight may bee found according to the couenants, and within the remedies ordained in the Indentures: Yet notwithstanding many of those peeces may be sized too light, and other as much too heauy; which giueth the greater aduantage to some people, to carry away that which is ouer-weight, and to leaue vs them which are too light, if they leaue vs any. *The third Cause concerneth neglect of duties.*

Our heauy money is conueyed beyond the seas, and melted downe into plate here in the Realme.

And

And this mischiefe is not single; for thereby also some Goldsmiths, regarding profit more then duty, may be the more readily drawne to melt downe the heauy Coyne into Plate, & other ornaments, both of Gold and Siluer.

But what might we thinke of those men who are placed in authority and office for his Maiesty, if they should not with all dutifull care discharge their trust concerning that excellent Statute, wherein it is ordered, *Anno 17. Edw. 4.* that all the moneys receiued by strangers for their Merchandize, shall bee employed vpon the commodities of this Realme? the due performance whereof would not only preuent the carrying away of much Gold and Siluer, but also be a meanes of greater vent of our owne wares: whereof I purpose to write something more in the next part, which concerneth our commerce with strangers.

The fourth Cause concerneth our commerce with strangers. And now I come to the last point, which I feare is not the least amongst the Causes of our want of money (so farre as any such may be:) and let it not seem strange to any man, that Trades should hurt and impouerish a Common-wealth, since it hath beene alwaies accounted an excellent means to help and enrich the same: for, as this truth cannot be denyed with reason, so it is likewise most certaine, that the *Vnskilfull Merchants ouerthrow our Trades.* vnskilfull managing thereof, hath euer proued a great decay vnto those Nations who haue beene entangled with such errors. And are not the examples too frequent in many of our owne Merchants, who not onely by the perils of the Seas, and such like misfortunes, lose their goods, but also euen through want of knowledge, wisely to direct their affaires, doe ouerthrow their whole estates: neither may we properly call this their losse, but rather the Kingdomes losse in them. Wherefore it were to be wished, that this mysterie of Merchandizing might be left onely to them, who haue had education thereunto; and not to be vndertaken by such, who leauing their proper vocations, doe for want of skill in this, both ouerthrow themselues, and others who are better practised.

Merchants by education are onely fit to trade in forraine parts.

But there is yet a farre greater mischiefe by our Trades beyond the Seas, when peraduenture, there might be imported yearely a greater value in forraine wares, then by any way or meanes we doe export of our owne commodities; which cannot otherwise come to passe, then with a manifest impouerishing of the Commonwealth. For as it is a certaine cause to make vs rich, both in stock & treasure, when we shall carry out a greater value of our owne goods then we bring in of forraine wares; so by consequence, a course contrary to this, must of necessity worke a contrary effect.

How rich Commonwealths may become poore.

Neither is this importation meant otherwise then concerning those wares which are consumed in this Realme: for the commodities which are brought in, and after carried out vnto forraine parts againe, cannot hurt, but doe greatly helpe the Commonwealth, by encrease of his Maiesties Customes and Trades, with other imployments of the subiects: by which particulars I might yet set forth the glory of the *East India* Trade, which hath brought into this Realme in 15. months space, not only so much Spice as hath serued the same for the sayd time; but also, by the superfluitie thereof, there hath beene exported into forraine parts about 215000. pounds sterling. So then let all men iudge, for what a great value wee may hope hereafter to export yearely, when vnto these Spices we may (by Gods assistance) adde the infinite worth of Rawsilkes, Indicos, Callicoes, and some other things: All which are to be issued in the nature of Cloth, Lead, Tinne, or any of our owne Merchandize, to the enriching of this Kingdome, by encrease of the Common stocke. So then, to conclude this poynt, we ought not

Forraine wares brought in for Transito, cannot hurt, but greatly helpe the Commonwealth.

Hopes to encrease Trade, by exportation of Indian wares to forraine parts.

to auoid the importation of forraine wares, but rather willingly to bridle our owne affections, to the moderate consuming of the same: for otherwise, howsoeuer the *East India* Trade in particular is an excellent meanes greatly to encrease the stocke of money which we send thither yearely, by returning home fiue times the value thereof in rich commodities; all which (in short time) may be conuerted into Treasure, as is plainly shewd already in Page 21. Yet notwithstanding, if these *Indian* wares thus brought home, cannot be spared to serue for that purpose of Treasure, but must be sent forth together with our owne natiue commodities, and yet all little enough to prouide our excesse and extra-ordinarie consume of forraine wares: then is it like-wise as certaine, that the generall Trade of this Kingdome doth hinder and diuert the comming in of the said Treasure, by ouer-ballancing the value of our wares exported, with the importation and immoderate consume of forraine commodities.

The parti-cular Trade to the East Indies will bring great store of trea-sure into this Realme, if the generall Trade of this Kingdome doe not hinder and consume it.

Therefore, forasmuch as the number of the people in this Realme are thought to be greatly increased of late time (both in themselues and strangers) whereby neces-sarily the commodities of this Kingdome, and also forraine wares, are the more consumed and wasted (a double meanes to abate the Commonwealth) it therefore concerneth vs all in generall, and euery man in his particular, to stirre vp our minds, and diligence, to helpe the naturall commodities of this Realme by industrie, and encrease of Arts; seeing that the mate-rials cannot bee wanting to make such Stuffes, and other things as are daily brought vnto vs from forraine parts, to the great aduantage of Strangers, and to our no lesse dammage. Neither should we neglect the riches which our Seas affoord, whilest other Nations by their labour doe procure themselues great Treasure from the same. And as the diligent performance of

The Dutch in particular, are said to reape such infinite wealth yearely by

these

these things, would plentifully maintaine the poore, and much increase the common stocke of this King- dome : so likewise for the better furtherance thereof, we ought religiously to auoid our common excesses of fodd and rayment, which is growne to such a height in most degrees of people (aboue their abilitie) that it is now beyond all example of former ages.   Neither is it needfull for me to set downe the particulars of these abuses; for they are too well knowne: and I am con- fident, that the wisedome of our Gouernement doth endeuour to see them as well amended, to the glorie
of God, the honour of the King, and the
good of the Common-wealth.
Amen.

this fishing Trade, that without more certain know- ledge thereof I dare not set down the sum, it seemeth so vncredible.

FINIS.

THE
TREASURE
OF
TRAFFIKE
OR
A DISCOURSE
OF
FORRAIGNE TRADE.

Wherein is shewed the benefit
and commoditie arising to a Common-
Wealth or Kingdome, by the skilfull
Merchant, and by a well ordered
Commerce and regular
Traffike.

Dedicated to the High Court of
PARLAMENT *now assembled.*

BY
LEWES ROBERTS, Merchant, and
Captaine of the City of LONDON.

LONDON,
Printed by E. P. for *Nicholas Bourne,* and are
to be sold at his Shop at the South Entrance of
the Royall Exchange. 1641.

TO THE
RIGHT HONOURABLE
THE
LORDS and COMMONS
IN THE
High Court of PARLAMENT
now assembled.

Pardon me Right Honourable, if amongst your other more serious present affaires, I presume to dedicate to your acceptance and perusall this short discourse of forraigne Traffike: It hath ever beene accounted a branch of *Englands* Royall Stem, and a commoditie, that for many yeares, hath brought a wonderfull Revenue to *Englands* diadem; It now presseth to your presence as an agrieved weight, laden with many fetters, imposed thereon by the covetousnesse of some, and by the Envyers of our prosperous Traffike, yet seeing that like religious Pilots you guide the helme of our Kingdome with your hand, whilst your eyes are fixed on heaven, taking from thence the conduct of your earthly directions, it hopes by that

your

your good and gracious aspect to be now freed from
them all, and florish againe in its first lustre. It is
now about forty yeares since it began to be ingrafted
in our English Climate, and ever since found our soyle
proper for its further grouth, but if it find not your
Honors favourable protection and future cherishing,
a few yeares more may see it withred and reduced to
its first nothing. I dare not undertake in this discourse
to demonstrate the burthens that cloggeth it in this
Kingdome, the severall Societies of incorporated
Merchants of the Citie of London being called before
you, will best particularise the same, onely I have
labour'd to shew, what may best gaine it in those parts
of this Kingdome where it is wanting, and augment
that portion thereof in those places where it is settled
already. Let not then, Right Honorable, so excellent
a Jem, and so hitherto profitable and eminent a
revenew, for want of a little of your helpe, die in your
dayes, nor yet perish in our age, but release it from
those subtle *Gives*, that cunningly have been intruded
upon its liberties, and goes about to kill the root
thereof, decking it once againe as primarily, with some
of those lasting and beautiful immunities that can
and may make it live longer, and spred it selfe much
fairer, that the times to come may deservedly attribute
to your names and memory that splendor & glory it
shall obtain by your benignity, so shall the King, our
gracious Soveraigne, have just cause to commend your
care for your preserving to Himselfe and Kingdome,
this so noble a Royalty, your Honours be justly
applauded for imploying your industrious hands and
heads in pruning, and lopping the disordered branches
of so excellent a graft, and the Merchants of this
Kingdome that have hitherto sowne in Expectation, live in hope to reape a fruitfull crop of their
                                                    forraigne

forraigne adventures, and hartily pray for the good successe of all your other weighty affaires, and amongst the rest, so shall ever ascend the devout Orisons of

Your Humble Servant

L. R.   Merchant of London.

To The READER.

*C*Ourteous Readers, It is needlesse for mee here to tell *you, how good a common wealths man a Regular merchant is, nor yet trouble you in relating the severall benefits accrewing to a Kingdome, by his adventrous paines and industry, this short discourse, though unpolished, if well considered, will I hope sufficiently speake the one, and questionlesse make good the other. My well-wishes to our Countries present Commerce, and the enlargement thereof, the great need in the encouragement to the one, and the insensible ruine and decay of the latter, was herein, and still is my greatest hope and obiect:* I have lately discerned that our industrious Neighbours *were ready at a deare rate to purchase that treasure by* Traffike, *which wee our selves, by means of the enviers of our Countreys forraigne Trade, were ready to yeeld them* gratis, *and as it were unsought, and for nothing; yet if it may be rightly said, as undoubtedly it may be accounted, that* Englands *trade is* Englands *treasure, why should our gracious King and his people lose that so excellent a profit in a moment, which cost his Merchants so many yeares to compasse, and so many hazards and charges to obtaine and settle, a few priviledges, and a little protection, a faire aspect, and a gentle encouragement, from both these honourable assemblies, will quickly settle this Kingdomes Traffike, and not only preserve it in its present splendour, but also easily augment and enlarge*

it

it, which will adde a wonderfull honour to our Soveraigns Name, throughout the World, and an eminent commodity and profit to the subjects of all his Dominions, which every true subiect I thinke doth earnestly wish for, and every honest Merchant doth truly pray far, as doth unfainedly,

Lewes Roberts, Merchant, and

Captaine of the City of

LONDON.

THE

TREASURE

OF

TRAFFIKE.

THat we are not borne for our selves, is a saying no lesse ancient, then true: the heathens as well as the Christians have held it a rule worthy to be practised, and every good man, of what quality and profession soever, that will give evidence to the world of his faire intentions, for the benefit, either of the publike or private, are daily seene to follow and observe it.

No Man is born for himselfe, but for his Countrey.

The religious Divine, that with much labour and long study, having learned himself the wayes of Godlinesse, is daily noted to take care and pains, to instruct others therein: the valiant souldier that weares his sword to defend himselfe, yet is ever ready to draw the same in defence of his Countrey; the skilfull Lawyer, that hath learned by the Lawes to make good his owne interest and right, is ever also ready to right the title of others, and the judicious Merchant, whose labour is to profit himselfe, yet in all his actions doth therewith benefit his King, Countrey, and fellow Subjects.

Politicians that have written of State Government,

1   have

Three ways have observed three principall meanes, whereby a King-
whereby a dome may be inriched, the first whereof is by arms
Kingdome is
inriched. and conquest, but this way must be confessed to be,
both chargeable, bloody, & hazardable. The second
is, by planting of colonies, building of well scituated
Townes, and the like, and this is also accounted
uncertain, chargeable, and tedious. But the third
and last is by traffike, and forraigne trade, which is
held the most certain, easiest, and soonest way; money
and time must bee consumed to effect the two former;
but immunities, priviledges, and liberties to the Merchant, will not only assure, but perfect the latter.

The Arts- In the management of these, there is required an
man is still orderly proceeding, and *Salomons* counsell is the safest,
the best coun-
sellor in his that his advice is still to bee taken, who is best versed
own pro- in the way that is prescrib'd; when our salvation is
fession.
doubted, we apply our selvs to the learned Divine;
when our countrey is invaded, the souldier is the best
director: when lawes are to be instituted, the lawyer
proves the best counsellor: so when a Countrey is
properly seated for traffike, and the soveraigne willing,
by forraigne Commerce to inrich his Kingdome, the
Merchants advice is questionlesse best able to propagate
the same.

Parents la- To inrich a Kingdome is a worke of great excellency,
bour to inrich and fittest the study of the Soveraigne, and where
their pos-
terity. many things may concurre to effect it, that only is
to bee chosen, which is most facile, and least troublesome. Many men plant trees, though they are sure
never to see the fruit thereof, and thus the child
oftimes enjoyes his predecessors labours.

King *Henry* the eight did enjoy the benefit of *Henry*
the seventh, and other his Fathers and Predecessors
prohibition of the exportation of our English wool, and
the setling of cloathing here, and the drawing of
Flemings hither, to make our manufacturies in

2   *England,*

England, and this turned him and his Kingdome to more profit than the suppression of so many religious houses, and the annexion of so many old rents to his Crown. *Edward* the sixth, though in his infancy, yet saw how those haunse-townes flourished, where his English Staples were setled, and had he gon forward with his design, of settling the same in *England,* in apt and fit townes, for traffike, as he once intended, doubtlesse it had beene the most politick and surest way to inrich his Countrey, as ever had beene put in practice since the conquest, and his successors should have seene the fruits therof, in the opulency of their Towns, the riches of their Countrey, and abundance of shipping, as now *Holand* doth witnesse unto us.

Edward the sixth, his Staple of Trade.

The consideration of this, and my wel-wishes to the inlarging and benefitting of my Countrey by traffike, and for the advancement of the Merchants thereof, hath drawne mee in this short Treatise to set downe in a briefe manner, the commodities, that doe arise to a Common-wealth, by skilfull Merchants and by a well ordered and regular trade, and Commerce, therewithall shewing, how this Commerce may bee facilitated, and how disturbed, how advanced, and how ruind, and how by the good government thereof, it may prove both profitable and honourable to a Countrey, and how by the ill management and irregular courses thereof, it may bee both prejudiciall and dishonour-able.

The scope of this discourse for the benefit of *England,* and their Traffike.

Statists have noted, that the Arts and Sciences are very many, that are commodious and beneficiall to a Common-Wealth, and which consequently beget abundance, wealth, and plenty, not only to the Prince in his owne particular, but also to his people and Countrey in the generall, but yet amongst all others they confesse none is more conduceable thereto, then Traffike and commerce especially when the same is

No one way more conducible to inrich a Countrey, then is forraigne traffike.

3   governed

6

governed and managed, both by well ordered rules, and by regulate and skilfull Merchants; and to the end, that the youth of this Kingdome, may be incouraged to undertake this profession, the painefull Merchant cherished in the prosecution thereof, and the Prince induced to give them imunities and protection: the particular commodities and benefits, and commodities that arise by Traffike, shall be here demonstrated, and if by my discourse the same shall be found really such, as by me and others it is conceived and here aleaged; the same may in the future be the more furthered and protected, and being found otherwise, it may as in reason it ought, bee both discountenanced and suppressed.

The riches consist in 3 things. Now the aboundance, plenty, and riches of an estate or nation, may be said, principally to consist in three things.

1. In naturall commodities or wares.

2. In artificial commodities or wares.

3. In the profitable use and distribution, of both by Commerce and Traffike.

Naturall commodities or wares, What. Vnder the title of naturall commodities, may be comprehended, such wares as are used in way of merchandizing, & are such as either the earth doth naturally & originally afford, or such as by the labor of the land is brought forth, and these I account the naturall riches, that bring plenty to a Kingdome or Countrey.

Naturall commodities of 2. sorts. Now the earth in it selfe may be said, to produce two severall sorts of naturall commodities, thence drawne from the very intrailes thereof, such as is gold, silver, copper, lead, and the like. The second are wares growing on the face thereof, such as are fruits, trees, graine, &c. and both these I terme naturall commodities, as produced either by the benefit of the Climate, soile, or temperature of the earth, where the

4　　　　　　　　　　　　　　same

same are taken up, planted, or found growing, and
doe become thus to inrich a Countrey, as a man would
say, of themselves; but yet by the meanes of Commerce
and Traffike, contributing thus naturally to the benefit
and use of the inhabitant, and to the furtherance of
universall Commerce; those things whose plenty (otherwise without Traffike, and transport to other Countries,
where such is wanting) would prove altogether fruit-
lesse, unnecessary, and peradventure prejudiciall unto
the owners and possessors, and this hath beene manifested
in some parts of those rich Kingdomes of *India*, some
years past, by their great quantity of spices, drugs,
and Jemmes, which, not by the Commodity of Traffike,
carried thence away, exported and vented into other
parts, and to remoter Countries: these excellencies
which nature herein afforded them, would be prejudiciall to them, and their ground over-laid with sundry
(though otherwise) excellent trees, and exquisite
Minerals, whose fruit or worth would thus not be
requested nor sought after, neither by their neighbours,
nor yet by forraigne Nations, where the same are
wanting, and which would consequently no way benefit
a Countrey, nor yet by Commerce and commutation,
supply them with those things in lieu thereof, that
they in their necessities stand more in need of.

Againe, the earth, though notwithstanding it yeeldeth
thus naturally the richest and most precious commodities of all others, and is properly the fountaine and
mother of all the riches and abundance of the world,
partly as is said before, bred within its bowels, and
partly nourished upon the surface thereof, yet is it
observable, and found true by daily experience in many
countries, that the true search and inquisition thereof,
in these our dayes, is by many too much neglected and
omitted, which indeed proceedeth from a liberty that
every man hath to doe, with that his owne part thereof,

Side notes:

How they
inrich a
Countrey.

Naturall
Commodities
are prejudi-
ciall to a
Countrey,
without the
helpe of
Traffike.

The bene-
fits of the
Earth neg-
lected by
whom, and
how.

5   which

which he possesseth what he pleaseth, proposing commonly to himselfe, a care to find out that which will bee most profitable to him for the present time, and because the rich and great of this world, and those that possesse the greatest part thereof, are seldome or never seene to reside upon their whole estate, nor yet found to husband their owne good, farther in this point (either by their servants or themselves) then by a present benefit and quickest profit, their farmers and tenants are oftnest observed to occupy the same; who like gleaners, sucke and draw thence the present profit

The Farmers eate the marrow of the earth, to the prejudice of the owners.

and daily benefit thereof, eating up the heart and marrow of the same, with greedy art, and continuall labour, not minding, or indeed not regarding the future interest and good of the possessor: & on the other side, where we find the owners themselves to reside upon their owne, yet tis observable, that some of them through Ignorance, some by negligence, and too many by bad husbandry, content themselves with the yearely rents thereof, or at most with the Revenues, that their predecessors drew therefrom before them; as being loath to take the paines, either by industry, improvement or care, to increase those their demesnes and estates, either by planting, cleansing, or manuring a waste or barren piece of ground, or by drayning a marshy bogge, or the like, and thus to inrich themselves by a faire advancement of their own; which in some forraine Countries, hath of late dayes taken such effect, partly by good orders, but especially by example, that Princes themselves, and States have thought it a worke worthy their owne paines, and study, as the

Sundry Princes have studied the advancement of their estates.

late labours of the State of *Venice* in *Polisona de Rovigio*, of the Duke of *Toscany*, about *Leghorne: Pisa* and *Creso*, of the Duke of *Ferrara* in the Valley of *Comachio*, of the States of *Holand*, in sundry and diverse parts of the Low-Countries, doe manifestly

6   witnesse,

witnesse, which hath wrought such good effect, that they have thereby much benefitted themselves and subjects, and by this meanes, have quickned the diligence of the industrious, and punished the negligence of the sloathfull, yet notwithstanding all the laborious hand, and paines of man, to plant, sowe, or bring things growing in, or upon the earth, to their perfection; the excellent temperature of Soyle or Climate, to bring forth either Jemmes, Spice, drugs, or grains, naturally produced from it, and whatsoever else the bounty and goodnesse of the Earth can naturally, or by labour yeeld or affoord to mankind; yet it must be here concluded, that all this would, neither in it selfe, inrich the inhabitants, nor yet bring abundance to a Kingdome or estate without the benefit of Commerce, and Traffike, which distributeth the same into forraigne parts, and by commutation with forraigne Nations, convert this naturall benefit of the Countrey, to the common benefit and plenty of those that are found to possesse, inhabite, and abide thereupon. *No commodity can inrich a Countrey, without the helpe of Traffike.*

The second thing which I observed, that did inrich a Kingdome, is by artificiall commodities and wares, and these by a generall title, I may call the manufactories of all commodities. *The artificiall wares and commodities of a Countrey, what.*

In which two principall things are considerable, conducing to universall Traffike, and to the benefit of a Kingdome. *2 Considerable points therein.*

First the number of the work-men, or Arts-masters, and this in the first place affords the aboundance of the things wrought: and secondly their sufficiency, ability, and skilfullnesse, and this is it that gives the true credit to the fabrikes and worke it selfe, and to the merchandizes so wrought and perfected. *1 The number of work-men.* *2 Their abilities.*

Now the over great number of workmen in all manufactories, would of it selfe be not onely improfitable *Many unskilfull Arts-men, is hurtfull to Traffike.*

fitable to commerce, but also hurtfull, if they were not also as good, skilfull, and as cunning in their Art and mysterie, therefore to the end, not onely to make them such, but also to keepe them so, and multiply them. Wee see in many Countries, many societies and publike houses, erected for all sorts of manufactors, wherein some the poor and needy are instructed, the skilfull and good are cherished, incouraged, and rewarded, and in other the lasie and sluggish punished and imployed.

The excellent industry of the *Germans*, to set men on work.

The *Germans* in this point, I thinke excell all other nations, who willingly admit of all skilfull Arts-men, into their societies and corporations, though otherwise strangers unto them, and of what nation and mystery so ever, incouraging them by large allowances and salaries, to practise with them, and teach and instruct their fellow townsmen. And if otherwise ignorant, yet are they then admitted to learne and practise what they see, by which course it is observed, that some of their Cities and especially their haunse Townes,

The fruits thereof.

flourish in all wealth, and are abounding in all riches, though otherwise peradventure, deprived of all naturall commodities, and furtherances of trade whatsoever. And to this end, was first granted and erected, the

The originall of the Halls in *London*.

Companies, Brother-hoods, Halls, and societies of these mysteries, in the City of *London*, many of which were at first founded with large immunities, and great priviledges, to be incouragements to the said manufactories, and to set the poore of those societies a worke, and the better to cherish these mysteries and Arts.

Many Princes have been free of Halls in *London*.

Many of our Princes have caused their names to be registred, in their societies and Corporations, for honour and incouragement to their Halls and Brotherhoods: and yet when all this is done, it must be granted, that neither the multitude of good able and skilfull worke-men, nor yet the great quantity of reall

8   and

and substantiall manufactories, made and abounding in a Kingdome, can of it selfe either fully and throughly inrich or bring plenty to a place, without the helpe of Commerce, which is the arme and hand that must distribute, and send abroad both that store & quantity of artificiall commodities so wrought, and must export, and vent it into forraigne parts, as being otherwise a superfluity and overplus, and more indeed then the Country it selfe standeth in need of; and in lieu thereof, importeth and bringeth in by commutation and exchange, those things, and such as the place it selfe standeth in want of, and is thereby seene to be onely and properly inriched, for the worke-men by this meanes become to be incouraged, and the manufactories to be preserved, in their reall and substantiall goodnesse, worth, and value, to the honour of the Kingdome, benefit of the inhabitants, & to the furtherance and inlargement of the generall Commerce and Traffike thereof.

Artificiall commodities inrich not a Kingdome, without the helpe of Traffike.

These two points thus considered and granted, and that neither the naturall commodities of a Countrey, be they ner'e so rich or precious, nor yet the artificiall commodities of a Kingdome, be they never so many or excellent, can of themselves, without the assistance of Traffike, benefit a common-weale, or bring plenty or aboundance thereto; and consequently inrich the same. Come we in the next place to the third point, which is this trade it selfe, which of it selfe and by it selfe, can supply all defects, either of naturall or artificiall commodities, and that without the assistance and helpe of either, can yet produce both, and is alone effectuall to accomplish and perfect the same, though in a barren place, affording nether in the prosecution, preservation, and augmentation thereof; foure generall considerations, are in the next place to be noted and observed.

Traffike is only able to inrich a Country, which of it selfe is barren.

Foure considerations in the prosecution, preservation, and augmentation of trade.

9

The

1 What wares to export, and what not.

The first consideration is grounded upon those wares and commodities, that a well ordered Traffike is to export or not to export to the stranger, or forraigne country and people.

2 What to receive, and what not.

The second consideration is grounded upon these wares and commodities, which this trade must receive from strangers or forraigne Countries, and their Entrie or import into a Kingdome or estate, or not to receive them, and banish the Commerce thereof.

3 What may facilitate, and ease this trade.

The third consideration, is grounded upon the facility and ease of this Commerce in generall, collected by practise of forraigne nations, and accompanied with the meanes of the augmentation thereof.

4 What commodity and benefit, this trade produceth to a Kingdome.

The fourth and last consideration, is grounded upon the commodity and benefit of this Traffiike in generall to a Kingdome or estate, where the same is orderly and regularly practised, and that by skilfull and discreet Merchants, bred up thereunto.

First what wares are to be exported, & what not.

First then it is diversly observed, and that in sundry Countries, what the commodities and wares in themselves are which a well ordered Traffike ought to export and carry, into forraigne Countries and nations with whom they have Commerce.

1 Those whereof a place hath aboundance, and how far.

Where in most countries it is generally observable, that those wares are only to be carried out, by way of merchandize, whereof the place it selfe hath aboundance and plenty, of which after that the place or Country is sufficiently furnished, the exportation thereof may be admitted and allowed, as contrarywise those commodities which the place may want, or stand in need of, are in no sort admitted to be exported, nor in like manner those, whereof forraigne parts may use to the hurt and prejudice of the place it selfe, where we abide and remaine, as Armes, Horses, provisions, ammunition, or things designed to Sea or war, or the like. And amongst the rest in many countries, it is noted that the exporta-

Those which a place may stand in need of, are not exportable.

Nor those that may be used to the hurt of the place.

tion

tion of gold and silver, is also forbidden and prohibited, Nor gold, and though in many places ill observed, and in some silver. countries againe, the same is allowed and tollerated, so that the differing lawes of sundry Princes, in divers Kingdomes upon the exportation of gold and silver, as Gold and silver, by some exportable, will in this place be worth our observation, and the and by some rather that the reasons given thereupon, may be ex- not. amined, and the benefit or prejudice arising thereby observed, where the same is either granted or denied.

First it must be considered and granted, that silver The reason and gold is not growing in every Region, and therefore why some as things in themselves scarce, and by all Princes sought Princes forbid the exporta- after, may be accounted a forraigne commodity, and the tion thereof. rather, for that the same carrieth with it, the preheminence, and predominancy over all other commodities, whatsoever the worldly rich doe possesse, and therefore by reason of the excellency, power, vertue, generall use, and need of it, when once it entereth into some countries and Kingdomes; the Princes thereof forbid the exportion and carrying out of the same, upon sharpe penalties and severe punishments for feare of the want and scarcity which may arise, and come thereby, yet it must likewise bee considered, as a thing granted and The same found true by experience, that in some countries and found of no effect, where free Townes, where the exportation thereof is freely the contrary allowed and admitted, and the carrying out openly per- is allowed. mitted by authority; no such want or scarcity is discerned; but contrariwise, all abundance and plenty thereof is noted, so that this being granted, the exportation thereof may bee allowed without prejudice to the state or Kingdome where we abide: now forasmuch as that this point will hardly find admittance in the opinion of many of our Sage Politicians, I will a little enlarge my selfe thereupon, endeavouring by forraigne example to make good this my assertion.

11   There

An example of both for proofe.

There is two differing countries, the one a great Kingdome, where gold and Silver in the greatest plenty groweth, and the prohibition of exportation therof, strictly observed and most looked into, and the other a petty Dukedome, whose Prince is not owner, of neither silver, or gold Mines at all, yet publikely, and by authority admitteth an exportation of this commodity, shall serve here for demonstration and Example of this point.

The King of *Spaine*, richest in Mines, forbiddeth exportation of gold and silver,

The King of *Spaine* then, being possessor of all the rich mines of silver and gold, in the *West-Indies*, found in themselves of farre greater value, then all the other mines yet discovered throughout the world, hath through all his Dominions, strictly prohibited by sharpe lawes, the exportation of his monies, out of any his Countries, and hath by sundry subtile decrees, and politicall ordinances, endeavoured to debarre all other, both neighbouring, and remote Kingdomes, and People else of partaking of his Spanish Reals, yet for all this it is observed, that the necessities of his great and ambitious undertakings, and the urgency of the Com-

Yet finds small benefit by these restrictions.

merce of that his barren and poore Countrey, enforceth a passage and current dispersing, will he, nill he, thereof into all Countries over the face of the earth, so that in the height of all his store and plenty, and when hee was involved in the greatnesse of his greatest aboundance, his Countrey and Kingdomes, were yet notwithstanding, and still are, noted to be both scant, dry, and needy, of both silver and gold, and the common Commerce and Traffike of his most eminent and richest citties, to bee wholly performed by

And his countries are traded most, with black-monies.

the use of blacke, and of Copper monies, to the great disorder and confusion of his trade, and the generall ruine and undoing of his Merchants and people, and

Turkey with whom *Spain*

though by this means, *Turkey*, with whom hee is, and ever hath beene, in greatest enmity, should consequently be more bare of his coynes, yet wee finde, that have is ever in war, yet hath aboundance of *Spanish* Rialls.

either lived, or do Traffike thither, that almost throughout all the Grand Seigniors Dominions, which are both
ample, large, and spacious; there is no silver coyne of
uote currant, but the Spanish Riols, and the same not
carried thither by the hand of war, or the necessity of
his designes in those parts, but by the hand of Commerce, and concurrence of Traffike, which fills all those
Countries, and that in great abundance therewith.

Now the Duke of *Florence*, which is onely the Lord The Duke of *Florence* hath no mines admits exportation, yet hath abundance of Rials.

of a pettie, but pretty Seigniory, barren in its selfe
of mines, both of Silver and Gold, maketh contrariwise no open restriction, nor publike prohibition of exporting, of either gold or silver; and whereas in *Leghorn*, his only noted maritine towne of trade, a million
of Ducats are freely and yearely openly laden, and
shipped away, yet the Countrey wants it not, nor is
found any way to be scant thereof, nor is it seene,
seldom to arise, or fall in price or value; nor yet is
there noted any brasse or copper monies in use
amongst his Merchants in Traffique and Cōmerce, so
that by this experienced demonstration, *Spaine* that
should have most, is the most barren, for all their pro- Note.
hibitions, and *Toscany*, that should have least, affords
the most plenty, by reason of its liberty of exportation
and freedome in the Commerce thereof. But it may
be here alledged, that the naturall infertility of *Spaine*,
and the naturall plenty of *Tuscanie*, may partly occasion, or else inforce the same; to which I answer and
grant, this may have some concurrence, but no neces-
sity; For when as *Spaine* in its lowest ebbe became *Spaine* in its lowest ebbe, came to be the owner of the *West-India*.

fortunately owner of the rich *West-India*, that Prince
then by this meanes had silver, but yet he wanted the
other materials of Commerce, for the performance of
that countries Traffike, which other places could best
afford him, and which his monies might best, and did

13   then

then procure him; and when the *Portugal,* by his happy discovery, had the *East-India* trade alone, yet he wanted Rials to purchase the commodities of *East-India,* which *Spaine* was then best able to afford him, but both these Kingdomes joyned now in one, and bowing to one and the same Scepter, it is observable that the *West-India* afords, now the monies to drive the *East-India* trade withall, and the *East-India* affords the rich spices, and drugs which must procure the sundrie needfull diversity of *European* commodities, to drive the *West-India* Traffike withall; so that a man would imagine *Spaine* as it now stands, should not at this day want any manner of thing to make it abound, either in monies, or in wares and commodities, and yet we find it to be both bare and poore in their Commerce; and notwithstanding, the so strict prohibition of the exportation of their silver and gold, and the authorizing of so much Copper-monies current amongst them, yet still his Kingdomes to remaine in great need and want thereof.

West-India affords the monies to drive the East-India trade, and the East-India affords the spice, & that drives the West-India trade.

And as for the fertility and plenty of *Tuscany,* though it must needs be in some sort granted, yet its riches and aboundance is to be attributed, rather to the trade of the place, and to the excellent government of the Countrey, in matters of Commerce, then to the naturall Climate thereof, or industry of the inhabitants, for it is noted, that three well advised rules in Traffike, hath brought it to this height that now it is.

Tuskanies fertility, is attributed more to the trade, then to the Country.

Observable in 3 rules of Traffike.

1.   The first is the allowance of free and publike exportation of monies.

2.   The second is the easie duties and customes, paid upon all merchandize to the Prince.

3.   And the third is the goodnesse, and reall value of the Coyne current throughout the Duke dome: but this is from my purpose.

This one example then I hope will suffice, to make

good the point before-going, (whereto many others
might be alleadged) to prove that this tolleration of exportation of monies, makes not in it selfe the scarcity
of silver and gold, nether yet the prohibition thereof
makes the aboundance, but I will proceed no further
in this point, save by way of caution, advise all Merchants to submit themselves, to the Lawes and ordi-
uances of Princes, and conforme themselves to the customes of the Kingdomes and places to which they
Traffike; which almost varies in every Countrey, one
commodity being in one Kingdome prohibited, which
iu another is permitted and allowed; as we find, that
Lead, a native commodity of this land, is lawfully exportable in *England*, but is all counted a *Contrabanda*,
and prohibited exportation in *Spaine*, and in many
other Countries, when once it is imported: and we find
that Woolls are prohibited also in *England*, yet allowed
in *Spaine*, Iron againe allowed in *Spaine*, but prohibited in *France*, and Saile-cloth, Canvas, and the like,
allowed in *France*, yet prohibited in *Spaine*; so is gold
and silver, as aforesaid is mentioned, forbidden in *England, Spaine*, and *France*, yet allowed in *Marsellia,
Leghorne, Barbary, Turkey*, and in many other places.

Divers reasons are given by States-men, for the pro-
bition of some peculiar commodities, as I said before,
but indeed many of them are impossible to be observed
in the execution; for that Countrey that will maintaine
a free Commerce with his neighbour, makes in one
Countrey, one commodity lawfull, which in an other is
not lawfull, unlesse all commerce might be made by a
kind of Example, and bartering of Commodities against
commodities, and that also practised in regard of the
merchandise or wares, which are not very necessary,
and not in regard of those that are for the place of our
aboade, and whereof wee cannot passe without; and
in this case Merchants are forced to have recourse to

Marginal notes:
Merchants must submit themselves to the Lawes of Princes, where they Traffike.

Some wares trausportable in some Countries, and prohibited in others.

Reasons for the prohibition of commodities, unpossible to be kept.

15   their

their forraigne parts, and then they must take a law from them, in either giving them other merchandises, which may be as necessary for them, as theirs are for us, or in paying or contenting them with ready monies for the same, however it happen, this is found the generall *A generall* Rule in this point, that a Kingdome and State doth *rule observed* commonly admit of the exportation and carrying out *Commodities.* of those commodities, and wares, which are native and growing in their Dominions, or of that whereof they have store and plenty, not regarding the lawes of other Countries, but yet some prohibitions in these very places, are made of exporting of some commodities of war-fare, as is seene of Iron Ordnance in *England*, and the like, for the possessing thereof by our neighbours, might at one time or other, annoy and prejudice our selves, or the place and countrey of our aboad: within the compasse of this consideration is also comprehended *Artificiall* those artificiall commodities, and wares, which are not *wares which* to be carried out and exported, and such are they as *portable, and* have not received their intire perfection at home, as is *how far.* ordained by wools in *England*, which is not allowable, till wrought into cloath, and yet not in cloath neither, till the same hath received all necessary and fit perfection, by dressing, dying, and the like, for thus the meanes of workeman-ship is taken away from the Artist, and workman, which in some certaine workes, and fabrikes, exceedes the price of the substance, and matter it selfe, and thereby their lively-hoods deprived them, and a powerfull furtherance and helpe of Commerce is by this occasion cut off, and hindred.

The care of This point is by some Princes so narrowly watched, *some Princes* and so vigilantly looked into, that they are not satis- *people on* fied with those materials, that grow amongst them- *worke.* selves, and in their owne countries, but they covet by all industry to draw others from their neighbours, or forraigne nations, to employ their subjects, and to put

16   their

their people on worke, by this meanes, much enriching themselves, and honouring their Countrey; and adding a great helpe to the publike Traffike thereof; selling and venting them thus once wrought, even to those Nations, who many times have first sold and furnished them with the very first materials of the said Manufactories.

Examples of this practise we find many, and that in sundry Countries and places, as the *Florentine*, who of all others exceeds in silk Fabrikes, yet at first provides much of his raw silke, in *Valentia*, in *Spaine*, in *Naples*, and other the neighbouring Countries, and having wrought and perfited the same in *Toscany*, returnes it to the proud and lasie *Spaniard*, and to other places in *Damasces*, Sattins, Taffeta's, and the like; so bringing it backe wrought, to the self same place whence it first came out raw, to be sold and vented. *Examples of the Florentines care, in this point.*

The *Dutch* likewise, buyes his Woolls in *Spaine*, carries it home to his owne house, there spins it, weaves it, and workes it to perfection, then brings it backe into *Spaine*, in Sarges, Sayes, and such like stuffes: and so there againe sells the same to good profit, and vents it. *And of the Dutch, before their last wars with Spaine.*

The towne of *Manchester* in *Lancashire*, must be also herein remembred, and worthily, for their encouragement commended, who buy the Yarne of the *Irish*, in great quantity, and weaving it returne the same againe in Linen, into *Ireland* to sell; neither doth the industry rest here, for they buy Cotten wooll, in *London*, that comes first from *Cyprus*, and *Smyrna*, and at home worke the same, and perfit it into Fustians, Vermilions, Dymities, and other such Stuffes; and then returne it to *London*, where the same is vented and sold, and not seldome sent into forraigne parts, who have meanes at far easier termes, to provide themselves of the said first materials. *And of Manchester.*

Now though it may be wished, that all other parts of our *How far this is to be cherished.*

17

our Countrey, could be so industrious, as thus to procure materials of Fabrikes, for the inriching of themselves, and inlarging of this Kingdomes Traffike, yet we find it in some places, an impossible thing to be performed: for where the Traffike or exportation of a native commodity, is of greater consequence to the Countrey, and over-valueth the commodity imported, it is safer then, and better to preserve the native, and to neglect the forraigne, then by too much preservation of the forraigne, to neglect and ruine the native.

Besides, the native commodity may be rich, and in its selfe, a necessary commodity, but the forraigne a meaner, and tending peradventure more to excesse, and superfluity, then to need and necessity, as the great quantity of native clothes, that are yearely shipped into *Turkey*, by the Levant or *Turkey* Company, having their full workeman-ship, and perfection in *England*, brings in returne thereof, great quantity of Cotten, and Cotten-yarne, Grograme-yarne, and raw silke into *England*, (which shewes the benefit accrewing to this **Staple and** Kingdome by that Company,) for here the said cloth is **native com-** first shipped out, and exported in its full perfection, **modities of a** **Kingdome,** dyed and drest, and thereby the prime native commo-**are in the** ditie of this Kingdome, is increased, improved, and **first place to** **be cared for.** vented, and the Cotten-yarne and raw silke, that is yearely imported and brought in, is more (as experience tells us) then this Kingdome can spend, vent, or any way utter, either raw, in the same nature as it is brought in, or wrought in this Kingdome into manufactories: here the first as the most usefull, native, and excellent is to be first preferred and cared for, and the other yet so much cherished, that it may as much as possible it can, **And the for-** be wrought here, and perfited into Stuffes, partly to **raigne that** **sets the Sub-** give a consumption to the materiall it selfe, partly to **ject on worke,** set the poore Artist here on worke, but principally to **in the next to** **be cherished.** further the generall Commerce of this Kingdome and

18   Countrey

Countrey, and to helpe a valueable returne, for the English cloth exported: some States have seriously entred into consideration of this point, and have indevoured with all posible care, the furtherance thereof, where it was defective, as King *James* of famous Memorie, inordered as I have been informed, that the white cloth shipped hence to the *Netherlands*, by a Nonobstante should have every tenth cloth thereof, died and dressed here, thus indeavoring by a wholesome order, to bring the whole shipping quantity, in use amongst them, that by this meanes, in time to come, all the said shipping might be drawne, to be dyed and dressed in our own Country, and not to be shipped white, as was then in use, and is still, to the great prejudice of that clothing; but had his Majesty then been pleased, to grant the lader thereof, some extraordinary priviledge, or to be free from custome, for any such cloth so shipped, in its full perfection, it would doubtlesse before this time, have wrought better effects in this point, then hitherto we see the former order hath brought to passe.

King James, his provident care in this point.

Some again to further the same, have eased the native manufactories of their Countries, of all customes, imposts, and such like duties in the vent or exportation, thereby incouraging their Subjects to make them, and their Merchants, to send them abroad, and transport them, and some have againe, charged the forraigne Manufactories, which tended not immediately to need or use, with heavie taxes, thereby deterring the importation, and cherishing the native worke-man to make the same, and to indeavour the obtainement of perfection therein at home.

The indeavours of some other Princes in this point.

Some have also eased all raw materials, that have beene imported, being commodities, tending to set the poore subjects on work, as is Cotten, Hempe, Yarne, Flaxe, Woolls, raw silke, and the like; and all these practised in some places, have met with a happy suc-

19   cessc

7

cesse, which hath both inriched the Subject, set the poore native artists on worke, and proved the maine furtherer of the Commerce of that Kingdome, where the same hath been daily, and industriously put in use and practised.

Second consideration what commodities are to be receaved, and what not.

The first point grounded upon the considerable benefit of a well ordered Traffike, being thus handled, and having concluded what wares and commodities may be exported, and what may not, out of an estate or Kingdome, & what hath beene practised by forraigne nations with good successe; I come now to the second consideration before mentioned, declaring what wares and commodities must be receaved, and what must not be receaved into an estate, by the limitation of a well ordered trade and Commerce.

All commodities tending to riot, are to be prohibited importations.

Some observing States-men have noted that a Prince should stop the entry, and importation by Commerce, unto all commodities, that tends to riot or excesse, as the principall meanes that impoverisheth a Kingdome, though many times it inrich the trader, and Merchant, amongst which precious Stones, rich Jemmes, exquisite perfumes, costly unnecessary Spices, and rich Stuffes, which serve more for pompe and show, than for need and use, are principally noted.

With their difficulties.

But how difficult in an age or Kingdome of peace and plenty, this may be effected, I leave to the said statesmen to determine, yet presuppose that these commodities, such as they are, be admitted their importation, the Prince and soveraigne may notwithstanding be in his owne particular a gainer, though the subject or Countrey therein prove loosers, for if the use, or rather abuse of these commodities in a Kingdome, be so inveterate, as that the same cannot be hindred, by a moderate prohibition, yet they may be charged with such great customes and Imposts, as the

20

merchant

merchant or importer may have no great desire to
bring them in any quantity, fearing he shall not obtain
the price they cost him; and the subject will likewise
have no earnest desire to buy them, in regard of the
dearenesse thereof, and though that sometimes this
consideration will not, nor doth not restraine the rich
and wealthy of a Kingdome, from procuring and purchasing such merchandises, yet the soveraignes treasure will by this meanes be augmented, and by this
way it may supply in place of punishment, for the riot
and excesse in private persons, and on the other side,
the Subject desisting from the excesse, though the
Soveraigne gaine not thereby, yet that Commonwealth
will be both improved and benefitted, by this chiefe
and good husbandry.

Now for such other commodities as may be receaved **Needfull wares ever to be receaved.** and imported, those are most welcome, which are noted
to be the most needfull, & what the Countrey and inha-
bitants thereof wants, and such as tend to need or use,
are still the most desired, Graine, Butter, Cheese, and
all provisions for food, should every where be freely
receaved, and that without duties or customes thereupon, as in *Leghorne*, in *Tuskanie*, in *Spaine*, and in
many other places: The Merchants and bringers in of
such, have ever a reward allowed them, to incourage
them to a readinesse at all times, to bring in the same
againe, at another time and season.

Also all ammunition for the defence of our Countrey, **Needfull for wars.** and for the offence of our enemies, as Horses, Armes,
Powder, Cannons, Muskets, Bullets, Match, and all
provision for Shipping, as Planks, Timber, Masts,
Pitch, Cordage, Iron, Saile-cloth and the like, are ever
to be receaved.

Thirdly all such commodities, as may set the poore **And wares that set the Subject a work, are to be receaved.** or richer sort on worke, by making of sundry sorts of
Fabrikes, either of Linen, and Woollen, silke or the
like,

like, as are Cotten Wooll, and yarne, of which is made
Vermillions, Fustians, Demities, & such others, also
fleece-wooll, of which is made woollen-cloth, Sayes,
Sarges, Perpetuanas, Bayes, and sundry other sorts,
comprehended under the name of new Drapery with
us, also Grograme-yarne of which is made, *Iames,*
Grograms, Durettes, silke-mohers, and many others
late new invented Stuffes, Flaxe, Hempe, and the
Yarne thereof, of which is made all sort of Linens,
fine and course, all Ropes, Tackles, Cables, and such
like used in shipping, all raw-silke, and throwne,
whereof is made all manner of Silke-Laces, Sattins,
Plushes, Taffeta's, Cally-mancos, and many others, all
silver and gold in thred, and Bullion, whereof is made
silver and gold Lace, Cloth of gold and silver, and
many others, which may set on worke, not onely the
poore industrious working Subjects, imploy the monies,
and estates of the rich, but also much further Navigation and Commerce, and generally inrich the Prince
and Kingdome, by the second Traffike of these Manufactories.

Yet with cer-
taine Limi-
tations.

Yet many of these commodities and wares, are to
bee receaved with some certaine restrictions, and
limitations, according to the judgement and discretion of the Soveraigne; For if by incouragements or
Immunities, the Merchant brings in the first materiall, as I may say, Cotten-wooll, the yarne thereof may
then be prohibited, for thereby part of the poore
mans labour is taken away, and so in Hemp, and
Flaxe, and the like, if it be imported in good aboundance, the yarne thereof may be prohibited, for the cause
before mentioned, and so may also such petty manufactories be denyed entrance, as playing Cards, gold
and silver thred, and the like, whilst wee have the
principall materials, whereof the same is or may be
composed, & perfitted at home. And thus much

22   shall

shall serve to have said, concerning what wares may be receaved, and what may not be receaved into a Kingdome, by the rules of a well ordered Traffike, the facilitating and acquisition of this Traffike, in a Countrey or place, comes in the next consideration to be handled. *3 considerations is to facilitate, & ease Traffike.*

The politike estate of *Venetia*, the Iudicious Duke of *Tuskanie*, the cunning *Hollanders*, the industrious hauns townes, and others, that much indeavour and studie this point, have noted, and found out many particular points, which they have put in practise, as the most effectuall, operative, and efficient, conducing to the facilitating, ease, and augmentation of Traffike in generall, which gathered out of their practises, wee may put in use, and apply to our selves, for the increase of a Countries forraigne Traffike, which principally are these. *The practises of sundry Princes, to augment Trade.*

First to further by all meanes, the commodious carriage of goods and merchandize both by Land and by water, either by Boates, Cartage, Horses, or other such conveiances, wherein is considerable as a thing necessary, that the Rivers be navigable or made so if possible, by labour, Art and industrie, then to remove all hindring Mills, Bridges, fishing weares,; Bankes, Sholds, and such like impediments that may any way let or hinder the same. *1 To further the commodious carriage of goods &c.*

Secondly, that no Lord, or adjoyning commanding borderer, impose either custome, tolle, taxe, or duties upon the commodities, and wares so carried in Boates, Lighters or Barges, passing or repassing thereupon, or heavie acknowledgements, passing over Bridges, Causeyes, or the like, that may disturbe the publike Traffike, or be a charge to the generall Commerce of a Countrey. *2 No tolle upon Rivers, bridges &c.*

Thirdly, to keepe the Seas, and streames, free and safe from all Pyrats, theeves, and robbers, as the principall disturbers of the universall Traffike, of Kingdomes *3 To free the Seas from Pyrats.*

domes and nations, and the greatest overthrowers of the navigation, and Commerce of Cities and Countries.

4 To maintaine Boyes, Lights, and Castles, &c. Fourthly, to safeguard the Ports, Harbours, Roads, and Sea-Creekes, from them, to maintaine where is necessarie, fortified places, to defend the pursued, and to offend the pursuer, to maintaine and conserve the keyes, Peeres, molds, and other places of moredge, fastnings, anchoredge, and the like, and to set up and maintaine, Beacons, Watch-Towres, Lights by night, Sea-marks, and Boyes, for the safeguard of Mariners sayling either by night or day.

5 To keep the wayes from theeves, &c. Fiftly, to keepe the Land wayes and passages, free and safe also from Theeves and Robbers, to mend Causeys, high-wayes and decayed Bridges, to build alberges, Innes, lodgings and places of safety whare none is, in fit and commodious places, for the reposing and rest of men and beasts of carryage, where all accommodation, both for men and horses travelling, may be had at easie and reasonable rates and prises, and where all needfull things may bee obtained, for the travailer which he may ordinarily stand in need of.

6 To maintaine the Posts, &c. Sixtly, to maintaine posts, and post-horses, by Land, and post barkes by Sea, also all Letter-carriers, and such like foot-posts, with priviledges, and fit stipends, for their paines and care therein.

7 To put downe Monopolies, &c. Seventhly, not to suffer any Monopolies, Pattents, and grants to private men, which may hinder the liberty, and freedome of Traffike, and if such bee discouvered, and found out, to punish the same rigorously and severely.

8 To invite industrious strangers by priviledges. Eightly, to invite by priviledges, the industrious strangers, and Merchants, to bring and import unto us, the wares and commodities, which wee cannot want, and those whereof the Countrey it selfe stands in need of, and that which may either advantage the publike, or the defence of the Countrey it selfe.

24   Ninthly,

Ninthly, to discharge all great custome, heavie
imposts, and duties upon all goods and merchandize,
or at least wise upon the Subjects goods, and upon all
needfull and usefull commodities, or if the same stand
not with the commodity of the Prince, yet at least
wise so much of these customes &c. as the necessity of the state will beare, and trade may well permit,
without overthrowing of the generall Traffike, and
Commerce of the Countrey, and the dependances thereupon.

Tenthly, to establish such Lawes, and ordinances for
Merchants, and merchandizing affaires, and Sea causes,
as that there be not onely faith and assurance, preserved amongst all negociators, Sea-faring men, and
merchants whatsoever, but also amongst all manner of
buyers, and sellers, and that there be likewise severe
punishments decreed for fraudulent & publike deceavers,
bankerouts, and robbers of the common Traffike, of a
nation or Countrey.

Eleventhly, that in case of differences, debates, controversies, and the like accidents, hapning in Traffike
amongst Merchants, there may be a summary, and
speedy Justice executed, either by a quickned law, or
a Court of Merchants, as it is observed and practised
in many Countries, especially in that which concernes
strangers, who oftentimes are noted to forbeare their
Traffike into a place, no lesse, in regard of the charge
and tediousnesse of suits, then for the tretchery and
falshoods of the inhabitants of the Countrey.

Twelfthly, and forasmuch as a permutation of Commodities cannot bee well made, without a certaine price
set downe upon all merchandises, and that they cannot
negotiate with all sorts of people, simply by Exchange,
but that it is necessarie to make use of the monies and
Coynes of Princes, in their severall distinct Countries,
the value, price, and estimation thereof, must be

9 To dis-charge all great customes.

10 To estab-lish Sea Lawes, for Merchants & navigator.

11 To erect a Court of Mer-chants.

12 The Coynes current to be constant and good &c.

therefore

therefore certaine, constant and firme, otherwise it
would bring a confusion to the generall Commerce of
a Kingdome, and every commoditie must then bee
govcrned in esteeme and value, according as the monie
shall bee current in price.

Neither is this onely sufficient, but the reall goodnesse,
and true value of these Coines must bee easie, to bee
judged, and knowne, not onely by the waight thereof;
but also by the eye, and sound of the same, if it bee
possible, the which may bee the easier done, if there
bee no metalls used in Coine current, but onely silver
and gold, which is sufficient in themselves, to expresse
all summes, and quantitie, how little and small soever,
and if everie peece both of silver and gold, bee Coyned
by a certaine waight, thicknesse, and greatnesse, and
in forme of certaine medalles, as the GRECIANS, LATINS,
HEBREWES, PERSIANS, and EGYPTIANS, in old time did
use, it would prove a difficult thing for a man to be
deceived therewith, and it would bee facile for all
strangers, and Merchants, to bee soone experienced,
and acquainted with them.

13 To give
honour to
merchants,
and why ?
Thirteenth, whereas some ignorant estates and forraigne nations, doe contemne Merchants, and merchandizing, and such as exercise Traffike, holding and
undervaluing, the Art of merchandizing in its selfe, as
base and sordid, which too often is found in many
places quickly to decay the publike commerce of some
Kingdomes, for thereby it commeth to passe that they
which have gotten a little wealth, retire themselves
speedily to embrace some other vocation, to the which
the common people carry more respect and honour,
then to this.

It being a thing, which in all civill and well
governed Kingdomes, ought carefully to bee avoyded,
and removed, for the good and furtherance of the
Traffike thereof; now indeed it must be granted, that
there

there bee certaine trades, which should bee left to the
poore and common people, to inrich themselves by;
but there are others, more noble, which they only can
best execute, that are conversant in forraigne Countries,
which is that of Merchandizing in remote parts, by the
benefit and commodity of the Sea, and that by persons Merchan-
qualified and versed in forraigne regions, which in it dizing is the
selfe is the most knowing, profitable, beneficiall, and able in an
excellent in an estate, as shall bee shewed in this fol- estate.
lowing Treatise, and to these more honour and respect
should be attributed, then is now done, both in *France*,
and in some other Countries, for if in all estates, the wise,
judicious, and prudent Counsellours of a Prince, have
thought it fitting, and requisite to invite the Subjects by
honour, to the most dangerous and hazardable attempts
and actions, which may bee profitable and conduce to
the benefit and profit of the publike; these two of
Navigation by Traffike, and of Commerce by navigation, being of that concurrent qualitie, and united disposition, they should propound and attribute more
honour to those that shall deale therein, and exercise
the same, then now it is noted they doe. And if true
Nobilitie should have taken its foundation, (as the Why such
Iudicious and Learned have observed heretofore) from should be
the courage of men, and from their Valour, there is no honoured.
vocation, wherein there is so many usefull and principall parts of a man required, as in these two, for they
are not onely to adventure and hazard their owne
persons, but also their estates, goods, and what ever
they have, amongst men of all nations, and Customes,
Lawes, and Religions, wheresoever they are inhabited.

And that not onely in common casualties, mishaps,
and dangers, but sometimes to wrastle and stand even
against the foure Elements, combined together, to
threaten their ruine, and destruction, which is the
strongest and most remarkable evidence and proofe,

that possibly can bee alledged or spoken, of the con-stant and firme resolution of a man.

This sole point and consideration, hath beene the occasion, that some States have beene of opinion, and thought that this doore should be opened, to the adventuring Merchant to attaine unto Nobility, so as the Father and the Sonne have continued succesfully for some ages therein; and which is seene in some sort to be practised in some places at this day, and if those Noble-men, (the upholders of a Land or Kingdome) who are commonly the richest and greatest in an estate, should practise and addict themselves to this Commerce, and Sea-Traffike (as some beganne to doe in Queene ELIZABETHS daies) being a thing not pre-judiciall, nor hurtfull to their honour, or to their noble condition, doubtlesse it is, and would bee more hon-ourable unto them, then to bee Vsuerers, and Bankers, as is observed in *Italy*, and many other Countries as they are, or to impoverish themselves, in doing of nothing, or nought worthie of note, but neglect their owne occasions, in spending, lavishing, and wasting, when peradventure they never gather any thing to what they have, or what formerly was left unto them, by their Ancestours.

The benefit of the Trade of Nobles and rich in a kingdome.

Hence would grow many advantages, both to the publike and private, for that they that thus deale in traffike, having thus meanes, courage, and sufficiencie, for this Conduct and Enterprise, the same would bee farre greater, and more eminent in it selfe, then now it is, setting thus more ships to sea, and by being con-sequently better armed, and better furnished; and whereof the state in time of need, might make good use of, for its safety and defence; and withall it would carry the reputation of that Nation, farre further into remote Regions; the which they cannot doe, who being poore, and having little or no stock, but of one

ages

ages gathering, or peradventure taken up at Interest, and borrowed from others, wanting both power, meanes, and courage, either to hazard themselves in great, and eminent Enterprises, or to wade through the same, being once entred thereinto.

And for other particular Interest, this Commerce being wisely managed, and discreetly handled, what hazard soever they should run, there is more to be gotten thereby, then to be lost; And if Gentlemen in generall would thus apply themselves to traffike, as some within these late yeares have beene observed to doe, and that without wasting of their estates by vast Expences, or importuning their Soveraigne by disorderly demands and gifts, they should by all likelihoods benefit themselves more in one yeare, by a well govern'd traffike at sea, then peradventure at Court by ten years waiting and solicitations.

Finally, to conclude this point, Experience hath taught, and teacheth us daily, where those of great purses, and good judgements have exercised traffike, and where such have beene backed and encouraged by a gracious and furthering Soveraigne, and by a Prince that loveth Navigation, and favoureth Traffike; it hath mightily enriched both themselves, and the Princes and Estates, under which they have liv'd; as by the late examples of the *Portugal, Hollander, Spaniard,* and *Venetian* is made knowne, and manifested unto all the world.

Next to erect and settle an office of assurance, with fit and skilful Iudges, which should determine, and give speedy Execution in their Decrees and Acts, betweene Adventurers, to avoide demurs, delayes, and hindrances, that happen by tedious suites in adventures at sea amongst Merchants. 14. To erect an assurance office.

Fifteenth, the only meanes conceived to settle the Commerce and Traffike of a Nation into forraigne Countries by sea, in the which the best purses will not 15. To erect some Companies.

29   bee

bee drawne to hazard themselves in the Enterprise, is to compell the Merchants which trade at sea, to one and the selfe certaine place and countrey, to joyn one with another in a corporation, and Company, and not to make their Traffike by themselves asunder, or apart; for although that adventuring apart, the Gaine would probably be the greater to the Adventurers, when the enterprise succeeds happily; yet it is to be considered, that the losse which may happen, would wholly ruine him that attempts the danger alone; and if in making a joynt Company, or Society, the Gaine should turne to be the lesse; yet it is ever more assured, and the disorders by Traffike by a good government is still removed; and the losse being borne by many, it is consequently the lesse to every one that is interested therein; and thus dividing the Trade of the whole, according to either the places, or coasts where the same is made, forbidding them to attempt one upon anothers priviledges; and prohibiting all other private Subjects (of what quality soever) which shall not be Members or free Brothers of those Societies, to negotiate into those parts upon great penalties, and appointing certaine Governours, or others the greatest adventurers, to order and regulate the said Traffike and Companies; which Rules have found such good successe, both in *Holland, England,* and else-where, that it hath beene one of the maine causes, that hath brought the traffike of *London,* and of *Amsterdam,* to that present height and greatnesse, as it is now observed to be.

16. To lend money to the Merchant out of the common Treasurie.

Next, for the furtherance of the Traffike of some Kingdomes, it hath beene observed, that great summes of monies have beene lent *gratis,* or upon easie rates and security, to skilfull Merchants, out of the soveraigne, or common Treasurie, which hath also found such good successe, as that the customes of that Prince have beene thereby much increased, the kingdome

enriched,

enriched, the poore set on worke, and the native Commodities thereof, vented to all parts of the world thereby.

In the next place, it hath beene noted mainely to further the traffike of a Kingdome, the transportation of bils of debt, from one man to another, in liew of monies, as is used in some Countries; for thereby many Law suits are avoyded amongst Dealers, errors in Merchants accounts cleared, the Princes customes increased, the great stocke of the Kingdome, which continually lyeth in all Negotiators hands in dead Bils and Bonds, employed, Traffike it selfe quickned, and such a benefit enjoyed thereby to the Common-wealth, as cannot expressed. 17. By transportation of Bils.

In the next place it hath beene observed in some places, where the poore for want of abilities cannot trade, and where the great or rich have not will, or dare not adventure their Estates in forraigne Traffike, that the examples onely of the Prince hath throughly effected it, and proved a maine Furtherer of the generall Commerce and Traffike of his Countrey; which doth not only hold in this matter of Trade, but in all other state matters whatsoever; for then it will be impossible for the rich Subjects to forbeare, when they see their Soveraigne bend his mind, and addict himselfe therunto. For the wise have observed, that Princes cannot frame an Age unlike unto themselves; and that it is easier (as one said) for Nature to erre, then that a Prince should form a Common-wealth unlike himselfe: Iust if they be wicked, regular if they be dissolute, chaste if they be immodest, and religious if they bee impious. 18. Example of the Prince, a maine Furtherer of Trade. *Cassiod. li.* 3.

Neither is it thus in these our dayes; History it selfe warrants the point, and makes it good in all former ages. For, under *Romulus* it was found that *Rome* was warlike; but under their Soveraigne *Numa* they

31

they were religious, under the *Fabritii* they were continent, under the *Catoes Regular*, under the *Gracchi* seditious, under the *Luculli* and *Antonines*, intemperate and dissolute; under *Constantine* the Great the Empire is Christian, but under *Iulian* idolatrous: Therefore, for conclusion, if the Prince love the Sea, his Subjects will be all Sea-men; and if he be a Lover of trade and traffike, the rich and powerfull of his Kingdomes, will be all Merchants.

19. By erecting a staple of Trade.

In the next place, it hath beene noted as an effectuall meane, whereby traffike may be obtained and settled where none is, is by erecting a staple of trade, and to indow the same with freedome of traffike, which briefly may be termed to containe some of these before recited particulars, especially those of great priviledges, and small customes; for this will gaine Trade where none is, and being gotten mightily increase the same, when this shall fall out to bee in a Countrey, where God and Industry hath blessed the Land and people with wares, that are either rich or usefull, it will soone beget, maintaine, and inlarge the Trade of the place, so made a staple, as above is said.

Now for as much as this staple is in many countries a thing unknown, and that many men are ignorant of the benefit that the same may produce, I will a little inlarge my selfe thereupon, and in few words shew how it may turne a Kingdome to profit, and by perusing the commodity it affordeth to other nations, conceive it may yeeld the like to that Prince that coveteth the same, or putteth this rule in practise: A staple of Trade is a place then, where large immunities and priviledges, are granted to all Merchants of what nation soever; sometimes extending to native commodities onely, and sometimes to forraigne, and sometimes to both, with free liberty, to export and import all manner of wares, custome free, when, whither, and by whom they please,

A staple of trade what.

paying

paying a small acknowledgement onely in liew of the said custome to the Prince, and wheresoever the same hath thus been seene to be settled in a Kingdome, it hath beene noted much to encourage the inhabitants thereof, and force them in a short time to become either great Merchants, or industrious Furtherers thereof; for the same would yeeld them occasion to be sharers in the traffike of other Countries, whereof before they neither had any profit, nor yet the Prince any customes thereby, the benefit of this staple of Trade may be the better discerned by looking upon the practise of those Countries, where the same is put in use, and especially by our Neighbours the Netherlanders, where the same is practised with wonderfull industry, paines, care, and conducible profit, instanced by these examples.

The benefit of a staple by the experience of other Countries.

First it is well knowne to us, and all the world, that they have there no timber, nor yet Forests of any sort, of their own growth, yet the freedome of Trade begets them such fit materials, that the same builds them yearely above a thousand sayle of ships, partly serving to their owne use, but principally to sell to others; and that the huge pales of wainscot, Claboard and Deale are in their staple Cities.

No timber in *Holland*, and yet they have the staple thereof.

Next, they are found to have no corn growing almost in all their countries; for it is the East Countrey that affords the same in abundance; yet wee know that the greatest Store-houses, and staple Granaries of graine, is by the freedome of their trade in the low Countries; for *Amsterdam* (if report may gaine credit) is continually stored with 8. in 100000. quarters, besides what is by trade daily sold away and vented.

No corne there, and yet they have the staple thereof.

The maine shooles, and massy bulke of Herrings, from whence the industry and traffike raiseth to them so many millions yearely, proceeds merely out of our English seas; but yet the great Fishery (to the shame

No fish there, yet the staple therof is in *Holland*.

33   and

and wonderfull dishonour of *England*) is in the Low-countries; wherewith not onely their owne occasions at home are plentifully supplyed, but all Christendome besides abundantly stored, it being computed, that they send forth yearely into other Countries, above one hundred thousand last, which wee may account to bee two hundred thousand tuns.

No Vineyards nor salt in *Holland*, yet they have the staple thereof.

The large and mighty vast Vineyards, and great quantity and store of salt, is noted to be in *France* and *Spaine*, yet the great Vintages, as I may say, and staples both of Salt and Wine, is found in the Netherlands, whereby they imploy yearely above a thousand sayle of their shipping.

No Woolls there, and yet they have the staple of many Factories.

The Wooll, Cloath, Lead and Tinne, and divers staple English commodities, are properly and naturally of *Englands* production, but yet to the dishonour and prejudice of *England,* the great Manufactories of Dying, Dressing, &c. of them are seene in the Low-countries, whereby they not onely imploy their poore by labour, but their Mariners by shipping, and often times under-sell the English, both in their owne countries, and abroad, with these and other our owne commodities.

Light customes in-crease trade, and heavy ruines it.

Many others in this kind may be produced; for it is to be noted, that wheresoever such a staple of trade is erected, kept and maintained, there all forraigne and native commodities doe abound, for the supply of any other countrey, that may or doth want the same; and where the customes upon Merchants goods is small, it easily draweth all nations to trade with them; and contrariwise where great impositions are laid upon Merchants goods, the traffike of the place, will be seen soone to decay, to the prejudice of that place and kingdom.

Example thereof be-tween *England* and *Holland.*

The difference thereof is made evident in any two townes of severall Princes Dominions, in the one, where customes are easie, and there Merchants doe flock

34   together

together from all parts of the world, and abundance of
forraigne commodities are from all countries imported
thither, that benefit the Merchant, the people, and the
Prince; and in the other, where the customes are
heavie and burthensome to a Merchant, and heavie
upon his wares, and there none comes, nor brings any'
commodities, but what hee knows is liable, and must
pay this custome to his and the countries great prejudice; which by an example or two I shall here
manifest.

Two ships laden at *Burdeux*, of equall burthen, and In a ship of
of three hundred tuns, the one goeth for *England*, 300 tuns
and the other for *Holland*; she that commeth into *Eng-* Burdeux.
land, payeth for custome, Prividge, Butleredge, and
other charges thereon by booke of rates, one thousand Paying in
two hundred pounds and upwards, before she bee dis- *England*
charged, and the other going for *Holland* is discharged *Holland* 60.l.
there for threescore pound sterlin, or there abouts; so
that after they have there nnladen their said ship, and
custome being paid, and the wines sold, the buyer can
transport them againe into some other countrey; and, if
hee should in the second place but gaine this custome
that was paid in *England*, yea or halfe so much, hee
would thinke to have gained very well thereby: but it
is not possible for any English man to pay this great
custome in *England*, and to transport them againe into
another Kingdome, but he must be a great loser by
them; for the *Hollander* can still undersell him, and
yet be a gainer thereby.

The like may bee alleaged of two ships, of two hun- In 200. tuns
dred tuns a peece, comming alike laden, with 200. tuns of Tobacco.
of Tobacco from *Barmuda*, Saint *Christopher*, or any
other English Plantation: now, this 200. tuns paying
custome, &c. in *England*, will amount unto 10000
pounds, whereas in *Holland* the said 200. tuns will bee
cleared for 120. pounds. Now though the said 200.

8

tuns of Tobacco should be here againe shipped out within the yeare, and the impost repaid him, yet the Merchant loseth infinitly by bringing it into the kingdome, which he would account for wonderfull gaine, might hee enjoy the same upon all the whole parcell towards all his adventure, interest and charges.

These small customes will increase the totall custome of a Kingdome.

But some Princes may imagine that this will too much diminish their customes, and draw their Revenewes to a low estate : but I rather hold the same will bee a meanes to increase the same; for though a Prince should for the ease of his people, and the augmentation of the trade of his Countrey, take but a small custome upon all forraigne goods imported, and thus exported, with the reservations mentioned in the second consideration of trade; yet he may have a moderate custome to be paid him, upon all goods vented within the Kingdome, as is now used in *England*; and the multiplicity of trade, which will be procured by this staple, and small custome, whereof there is not otherwise accrewing to the Prince any profit at all, will much increase the same in the totall. Presuppose, that this staple of traffike, furthered with such immunities, and smalness of customes, were in some one, two, or three convenient Towns settled here in *England*, let us consider the good in generall, that by the former assertion would produce to us.

Benefit arising to *England* by a staple of trade.

First the Merchants would be enabled, to export the commodities of *France, Spaine, Italy, Turkey,* and *Barbary,* and of the East and West *India,* into the Kingdomes of *Germany, Poland, Denmarke, Swethland, Pomerland, Sprucia,* and *Lifeland,* and the merchandize of those other countries, which are both many and usefull, will againe be transported from the said staple, to those Southerne and Westerne Countries, and hereby the Merchants would mightily flourish by this inlargement of trade.

Secondly.

Secondly, divers sea-Townes, where this staple should be kept would be very much enriched.

Thirdly, the Mariners and shipping of this Kingdome, would hereby come to be very much enlarged and imployed.

Fourthly, many poore people, and other handy crafts men and labourers, would be hereby set on worke, and imployed.

Fifthly, the honour and reputation of this Kingdome will be much advanced in other countries, and much Bullion would thereby come to be imported.

Sixthly, it will keepe all sorts of graine at a reasonable price, both for the buyer and seller, and the countrey should alwayes bee well provided with corne, if dearth should happen, and thereby also retaine our coyne, which upon such an occasion is usually exported.

Lastly, the customes of *England* would be much increased by intercourse of trade, both by Importation and Exportation of all sorts of forraigne commodities, whereof we have no use our selves, and whereof His Majesty hath at present no custome at all, because there is no such course of trade in use.

Having thus shewed how this staple of trade is to be setled, and what benefit it brings with it to that countrey where the same is erected, and may bring to us were the same here settled; and because in all Kingdomes it is a worke of time and much difficulty, and that our ordinary States-men doe neither seriously consider, nor truly weigh the reall benefits that arise to a Kingdome and people by the hand of traffike; I will here in the last place, for conclusion of this consideration, shew that a maine Furtherer of a countries traffike, and the only way for the preservation thereof, being once acquired, is to settle by authority of the Soveraigne a selected number of able and discreet Merchants, with power and sufficient priviledge, to examine the dis-

orders

orders of traffike, and irregular Traders, and to reduce the same to such orders, and constitutions as may stand with the benefit and good of the Soveraigne, his countrey and subjects; and these merchants to be either sworne and admitted into the Princes counsell, or have a superintendency over the generall Commerce of the kingdom, by themselves entituled as State-merchants, or Merchant States-men; the benefit of whose endeavour, skill, judgement, and discretion thus authorised, I shall by these few rules offer to the consideration of the Iudicious.

By inlarge-
ment of
traffike.

It is by all Statesmen accounted a truth undeniable, that the wealth and welfare of all countries (where the subject exerciseth traffike with forraigne nations) is mainely furthered, and much advanced by the regular orders, and merchantlike rules thereof, and more especially in that of *Englands*, by nature commodiously seated to that end, and of purpose; the procurement of which wealth and welfare by the inlargement of Commerce, and the well ordering and regulating thereof, cannot be so fully effected, nor the hindrances fore-seene, nor the prejudices so soone avoided by a meere States-man, as the same can be by a discreet Merchant, qualified with power from the Prince to that purpose.

2 By impor-
tation and
exportation
of *Bullion*.

Secondly, the importation of *Bullion* to the Princes Mint, or exportation of his coyne out of his countrey, cannot be so well fore-seene and prevented as by the Merchant, who by the course of traffike, knowes the impediments of the one, and the preventions of the other.

3. By under-
valuing of
native wares.

Thirdly, the under-valuing of the home-bred, and native commodities of a Kingdome, and the over-valuing in that Kingdome of forraigne commodities, with the discommodity of both to the common wealth, nor the causes thereof, cannot be so well knowne to a

States-man,

States-man, nor by him be prevented, as the same can to a Merchant, qualified with power thereunto.

Fourthly, the inlargement of trade by any new Inventions, Plantations, or Discoveries of new traffikes, cannot be by any so well furthered, as by a qualified Merchant, who best knowes by reason of his trade, what priviledges are fit to be granted, what customes inwards and outwards to be imposed, and for the incouragement of the Merchants, and Vndertakers in these said courses. **4. By new Plantations.**

Fifthly, it is granted that the greatnesse of customes, and other duties upon Merchants goods, in all places diminisheth the trade of a Kingdome, and the smalnesse of the same inlargeth the trade thereof; now a meere States-man conceives not what commodities are fittest to be eased, and which are to be raised for the common good, and profit of the trade of that Countrey. **5. By rising and falling of customes.**

Sixthly, the generall imployment of all the poore of a kingdom in the workmanship of native, and homebred commodities, and forraigne materials imported (now too little regarded by many States-men in many Kingdomes) may with more ease and speed be put in Execution by a States-merchant then by a meere Statesman, as is seene in the dying and dressing of clothes in *England*, and in the prosecution of the Fishing-trade, lately here set on foot by the care and industry of divers noble personages, and lost for want of experienced men in that profession to manage the same. **6. By imployment of workemen in the Manufactories.**

Seventhly, as a matter worthy of a Princes consideration, the furnishing of decayed haven Townes, with inhabitants, Mariners, and shipping in a kingdome, and the needfull helps and furtherances thereto, with a profitable trade to maintaine both, to their, and the Prince and countries good, is better performed by a Merchant, then by a meere States-man. **7. By furnishing decayed towns.**

39   Eighthly,

8. By providing of corne in dearth.

Eighthly, the continuall furnishing of a Kingdome with corne at cheape rates, yea even in times of Dearth, the want whereof some yeares past the last great Dearth, inriched *Holland* for seven yeares following, and impoverished *England* full as long, by their exportation of two millions of pounds, as is conceived that yeare out of all ports of this Kingdome in gold, wherein a meere States-man knows not the way, neither how to provide for the one, nor yet how to prevent the other; which notwithstanding a Merchant can with ease, and better husbandry accomplish and performe.

9. By setling of a staple of trade.

Ninthly, the setling of a staple, or freedome of trade in a kingdome, in commodious and fit places, with fit and advantageable priviledges, and how the same is to be governed and directed, and wherein to be restrained and limited, is onely within the knowledge of a Merchant, and fittest for his direction, which a meere States-man doth not so well understand, nor can judge of.

10. By weakning the enemies by trade.

Tenthly, *Salomon* saith, that wisdome is better then the weapons of warre, therefore a Merchant can in times of warres with forraigne Princes, better direct how to weaken his enemies, in course of their traffike, and preiudice them in the point of their profit, and crosse their designed intentions, for provision of warfare, more then the best States-man can doe by open hostility.

11. By treatises of peace in trade.

Eleventh, In concluding of a peace, or in the making of leagues, and amity with forraigne Princes, the Merchant can advise of the fitting conditions, to bee insisted upon, and obtained in the point of traffike, for the advancement of his King and Countrey, which a States-man doth not so much regard, nay many times not yet understand.

12. By forraigne intelligence.

Twelfth, A Merchant that hath beene resident, many yeares in forraigne parts, and sometimes hath remained

40   all

all that time in one and the same Countrey, and hath afterwards continuall advice from his Factors there resident, by reason of his daily trading thither, of all the occurrences of the place, with their provisions made there for arming of horse, foot, or shipping, must needs consequently understand thereof, and the affaires of those parts, better then those that never were there, or but cursorily to see fashions, and that peradventure many yeares before that time.

Thirteenth, A Merchant knowes by his observations in course of trade, that there bee some trades in a Kingdome, which cannot subsist, nor bee driven without exportation of the coyne of that kingdome and place, or which cause the diversion of *Bullion* from the Mint of that place, which are not to bee cherished, as those trades are which doe neither; all which a meere States-man cannot so well comprehend, and take notice of.

13. By suppressing of trades depending upon exportation of coyne.

Fourteenth, A Merchant doth know that there be some trades againe, which cannot subsist without this exportation of the coyne of a kingdome, and have a necessary dependance thereon, which yet notwithstanding are to be cherished, sometimes equall, sometimes above other trades, by reason that the same trade begets another advantageable trade, that doth more profit to the kingdome, then the exportation of that coyne doth prejudice the same, which a States-man can neither discerne, nor take notice of.

14. By cherishing some trades that subsist by coyne.

Fifteenth, A Merchant doth know what decrees and ordinances made in a Kingdome, doe further and enlarge the trade thereof, and which againe in themselves doe hurt and prejudice the same: also what decrees and ordinances are enacted in forraigne states or countries, that are injurious and hurtfull to the trade and countrey where he abides, and how to meet with, and prevent the same by counter Decrees, and Regulations;

15. By acts prejudiciall to trade.

41

lations; which a meere States-man doth neither know, nor can of himselfe prevent or have notice of.

16. By remedying the forraigne disorders in trade. Sixteenth, A Merchant doth find by his traffike into forraigne parts, what commodities, and what nations are eased by forraigne Princes within their dominions, to the end that by charging of some, and easing of other some, they covet to benefit some nations more then other, and further the vent of some commodities more then others, redounding to the prejudice and ill consequence of the Kingdome of his aboade and residency; which the Merchant can in a short time both prevent and remedy, to the good of that Kingdome where hee lives; but the States-man cannot in a long time find out, nor yet being found out remedy it, till peradventure the remedy be worse then the disease.

17. By carrying out or in of commodities hurtfull or beneficial to a kingdome. Seventeenth, A Merchant knoweth what commodities can bee drawne out of another countrey, to the benefit of his owne, and what commodities are carried out of his owne countrey, to the prejudice (as Iron-Ordnance are in *England*,) or benefit of another, and can by regular orders in the course of traffike hinder the importation, and exportation of what is hurtfull, or any way dammageable to the Kingdome of his aboade, and further the importation and exportation of such commodities as are prejudiciall to the traffike of the strange and remote Countrey; which the States-man for want of knowledge in merchandising cannot effect or accomplish.

18. By importation of materials for Manufactories. Eighteenth, A Merchant can advance his Countrey by the importation of materials for Manufactories to bee wrought at home, and by this meanes set multitudes of poore on work, to the great benefit of the place of his aboade, and can by reason of his travels into forraigne parts, where hee sees the naturall and profitable commodities of other Nations, transport the same, and sometimes plant them in his owne native

soyle,

soyle, for his Countries good and honour; which the
States-man cannot without great difficulty performe
and effect.

Lastly, the Merchant best knowes what Decrees are
constituted in forraigne Countries, that hinder the Navigation, and diminish the shipping of the countrey of
his aboade, and what orders and injunctions are
imposed at home, that insensibly ruine and destroy
the same, either by meanes of grants, made to private
persons to the prejudice thereof: or by innovations
imposed by Farmers, or other Vnder-officers, that
either destroyeth the same, or tendeth to the discouragement of Sea-men; which meere States-men
cannot so soone discerne, nor yet in fitting times
remedy.

To conclude this point, having thus shewed the
courses that are used in sundry Countries, for the
setling, preserving, and augmentation of Commerce in
generall, and withall considered how farre in his owne
person a Merchant is able to benefit, and advance his
Countrey and place of his aboade, and how a staple of
trade may bee erected, settled, and priviledged with
fitting liberties, to gaine an ample traffike where none
is, and shewed withall the commodities that arise to
the Countrey, where the same is so settled and maintained.

I will now, for conclusion of this third consideration,
run through and briefly survey the marvellous care, cost
and paines, that severall Princes have willingly beene
at and undergone, to compasse the same.

By what hath beene saide then in this consideration,
and upon this point, it may be gathered, that the
obtaining and acquisition of a traffike at the first is
very difficult, being as a precious Iewell which must
be sought after, courted and purchased with many
priviledges, liberties & immunities, and sometimes with

19. Forraigne decrees that prejudice navigation and shipping.

The endeavours of sundry Princes to gaine traffike.

43   the

the very example of the Prince himselfe, because that the honour, benefit, and commodity that doth still attend it (as I shall declare in the close of this discourse) extends it selfe both to the Soveraigne, his Nobles, Kingdome, and subjects in generall: and to the end that it may appeare, that all Iudicious Princes, and Politick States-men have thus judged thereof, and found the effects of the same answerable to this my assertion; I will here briefly declare, and shew the industrious paines, and painefull endeavours of sundry the wisest Princes of *Europe*, to acquire, purchase, and obtaine this so excellent a Iewell.

The practise of the Duke of *Florence* to get the trade of *Leghorne*. The Dukes of *Toscany*, being ever accounted expert Exchangers, finding that their Dukedome, by reason of the want of a Sea-port, for the receit of shipping, was very unfit to entertaine a trade by Navigation, purchased the town and Territory of *Leghorne*, of the Common-wealth of *Genoa*, at the rate (as some report) of one hundred and twenty thousand Dollers (it being then a poore Fisher-towne, capable only to receive small Barkes, and that of no considerable burthen) and did, for the inlarging of his traffike by sea, adde a faire and pretty new-built Towne to the old, fortifying the same with Wals, Ditches, Castles, a Bannia for his slaves, and a Lasseretta, or a Pest-house, to receive both the goods and persons of such as should arrive there from contagious and infected parts; then he gave a dwelling to all for seven yeares *gratis*, that would come to inhabit there, then hee erected a watch-Tower with a strong mould to preserve the ships that anchor there from the violence of all weathers; he gives his Merchants many priviledges, cuts a ditch for twenty miles, to convey and cary up all commodities to *Pisa*, and so to *Florence* the Metropolis of his Dukedome; to conclude, by making it a free scale, and that all manner of goods, wares, and monies may bee freely

shipped

shipped inwards, and outwards, without any charge or
custome; and that when commodities doe arrive, which
the purses of his subjects will not, or cannot purchase,
he hath himselfe bought up the same, and that sometimes to his losse and prejudice, he hath I say by these
and other the like meanes within this 25. or 30. yeares,
made this the greatest port of traffike in all the
Mediterranean seas, to his owne great honour, and to
the exceeding profit, and commodity of himselfe, and
all his subjects in generall.

The Hollanders, who have neede of all the politike *Of the Hol-*
helps that can be, to support the charges of their war *landers to*
against a potent enemy, who is continually ready at *support their*
their doores to give them the alarme, yet so well doe *trade.*
study this point of traffike, and make so much of
Commerce in their countrey, where indeed they hold
but a hand-full (as it were) of land to abide in; though,
I say, they have annuall Armies afoot, which doth cost
them infinite, vaste, and great sums to maintaine and
nourish, and that their very bread, meate, and beere
which is eaten by them, doth first pay the States an
excise thereon; yet in all their extremities, dangers
and debts, they have erected many staples of trade in
their countries, and also raised an East-India and
West-India Company of Merchants, with large priviledges, which they have prosecuted with happy &
good success, wheron, notwithstanding their great
disbursements, they impose little or no customes at
all, their interests are easie, their Companies countenanced, and protected by the Estates, and their
Fleets are ready in our Channell, to safe-guard and
defend both the Merchants, Mariners, and Fisher-men
from the depredation, and violence of either enemies or
Robbers.

I am not able to recount how, and with what care *Of the*
and industry the Venetians maintaine their traffike, *Venetians.*

and the liberties of their subjects; in point of Commerce they ease them of customes, give large priviledges to their Mariners, injoyne their ancient gentlemen, and Clarissimi to use the sea, make daily sundry advantagable decrees and orders for the suppressing of forraigne traffike, and advancing of their owne, keepe a selected Court of the best experienced Merchants, to superintend other Commerce, and have a stocke ever in readinesse by the name of Cottimo to expend both in *Turkey* and other places, for the defence of their Merchants and their Estates, from all wrong and injuries.

Of the East Kings of *Portugall.*   Yet none of these comes neere the care and industrious prudence, practised by *Iohn* and *Emanuell*, Kings of *Portugall*, in erecting, prosecuting, and setling the trade of the *East India*, with such provident decrees and immunities for the ordering of their returnes, Lectures for the instruction of their Pilots, and Sea-men, building of Forts and Holds to make good and preserve their traffike, to their exceeding honour and profit in getting those small Ilands of *India*; but of most notable consequence, *Mosambike, Ormus, Dieu, Goa* and *Mallacca*, fit Receptacles of trade and strength, and which have to this day preserved to them the Commerce of all others, the parts of *India. Isabella*, that famous Queene of *Castile*, having by her Christian Piety spent her owne estate in prosecution of the wars against the Moors of *Granada, Murtia*, &c. when yet she and her husband *Ferdinando's* Crownes and Revenues were drawne dry, and farre ingaged in chasing those Barbarians out of their Kingdomes, then when *Henry* the seventh, accounted amongst the wisest of our English Kings, had unhappily refused *Columbus*, the Genoes his offer, for the discovery of the Westerne Continent, now termed *America*, then I say being laden with her greatest debts and engagements, her

Coffers empty, her Church plate spent, and all drawne
to the lowest ebbe by loanes and interests, then did
shee for incouragement to all her subjects, and for to
comply with the resolution of the brave Italian, pawne
her owne wearing Iewels, to set him out in three
Carvels; where how he thrived, and how that Kingdome, Prince and People have beene bettered thereby
ever since, the whole Christian world may witnesse at
this day, as England hath had just cause to repent of
ever after.

But *Henry* the seventh having now seene his errour, *Of Hen.*
and apparently discerned what hee had lost by his *the 7. of*
parcimony, endeavoured to make amends to his King- *England.*
dome, and people, calling hither *Sebastian Cabot*, also
a skilfull Pilot, *Genoes* giving him both encouragement,
honours, and employment; but the issue of his
endeavours did not answer that King's expectation,
though after his life the same was prosecuted in King
Henry the eighth's dayes with various successe.

And though *Margaret* Countesse of *Flanders* did, in
envy to him, set up *Perkin Werbeque* to disturbe the
peace of *England*, and that that mocke Prince came
at length to bee a Scullion in his Kitchin; yet that
wise Prince found another more noble revenge to himselfe, and more profitable to his people, by setling here
the Manufactories of Clothing, and the strict prohibition of the Exportation of English woolls, which
cost him in two yeares (as I have beene informed)
neare one hundred thousand pounds, a mighty masse
of monies, the Prince and times considered: but
England soone found the benefit thereof; for in *Anno*
1515. the English having removed their staple from *Anno* 1515.
Bridges to *Antwerpe*, where the aforesaid Kings of
Portugall had then settled their Contractors, for the
vent of their new gained East-Indian spices, it was
noted by those Registers of Commerce kept in that

place, and left to posterity by *Guicciardin*, that hath written their Chronicle, that the English Company of Merchant-adventurers did bring thither clothing to the summe of   , which was in value 9. of 15. parts of all the other commodities and wares brought thither of all other the nations whatsoever.

Of *Edward* the 6.

What a brave designe *Edward* the sixt his Grandchild had, for the setling of sundry staples for that and other commodities in *England*, and how that by reascn of the then poverty of his Merchants, hee intended, upon security, to lend them out of his Treasury great summes for the effecting thereof; I have briefly touched before, and for conclusion of this

Of Queene *Elizabeth*.

point, looke a little into Queene *Elizabeths* dayes, who though she was ever accompanied with state affaires of mighty consequence, sometimes at home, and sometimes abroad, yet was she ever so careful to set forward traffike, and encourage Navigators, that both Earls, Lords, Knights, Gentlemen, and of every degree, willingly thrust themselves in search of new traffikes and adventures, and to her dayes are wee beholding for the trades of *Barbary* and *Italy*, and other places, and for the discoveries of *Turkey*, *Egypt*, *India*, *Russia*, *Muscovia*, and *Greenland*, and the trades setled by the English therein; which hath since found such fortunate successe, to the benefit of our now happy Soveraigne, and his Crownes, that the customes were in her time, some yeares before her death, farmed but at fourteen thousand pounds, which *Smith*, commonly called

Customes increased in 50. yeares in *England*, from 14 to 500.thousand pounds a yeare.

Customer *Smith*, in one yeare petitioned for reliefe, as having beene a loser thereby, and now in lesse than fifty yeares is come to five hundred thousand pounds yearely, if report gaine credit to the Kings purse; and how much more the Farmers have made thereof, His Majesties custome bookes can best manifest. If then

Princes

Princes of all ages, and the wisest of all Princes, have made it part of their study, and have in many occurrences prejudiced themselves, and their estates, to win this so excellent a benefit, how carefull need all Princes to be when the same is brought to perfection, to preserve and cherish it, and not to suffer the liberties of their Merchants to be incroached upon, the freedome of their traffike, to be fettered by heavy imposts, customes, and Innovations, which are like Cankers that doe insensibly eate out and ruine a trade before the Prince, or the wisest of his Counsellors, can see how to prevent or remedy it.

Princes that have gained traffike must be carefull to preserve it.

The want of this care, and provident foresight hath lost many kings the traffike of their Kingdomes, which were the best Iewels of their Crownes, and the richest flower in their Diadems: The want of good orders in the government of the trade of *Antwerpe*, and the imposing of heavy customes upon the Merchants there trading, hath within this fifty yeares brought that Towne to the lownesse wherein now wee see it. *Lyons* in *France* hath suffered wonderfully by the same inconveniences; and *Marsilia* within the dayes of my knowledge had a wonderfull great traffike for many places of *Turkey, Barbary, Spaine*, and other kingdomes, and was then able to shew many ships imployed in merchandise, carrying thirty and forty peeces of Ordnance, and now which is not above 24. in 25. yeares past, the best of their vessels have not above ten peeces, and of those but very few neither.

Townes that have lost their traffike by want of care and good order.

Antwerpe.

Lyons.

Marsilia.

Here I could also particularize the fetters, Incroachments, and Intrusions that have within these late yeares been laid upon the *East-India* traders of *England*, and their liberties, and what they have suffered both abroad and at home, by the ill wishers of their prosperity; but what will it availe them, or benefit our countrey, to travell into the disturbations,

English East-India trade.

49   crosses,

crosses, and afflictions, which they have, to their
prejudice, felt, and to their losse suffered? It sufficeth
me here to say, that the want of due and timely protection, and incouragement from the Estate, hath
reduced them to that bad point, and low passe, wherein
we now observe them to bee; and that for the future
erecting of such a brave society, a great deale of time,
and money must be expended, and many larger immunities then formerly must be granted, ere the same
can be reduced to that pristine flourishing estate we
lately have beheld it to be in.

Turkey, and Moscovia Company in England. I could also here, by way of addition, say somewhat
of those disturbances, that the *Turkey, Moscovia*, and
other Companies of *London* have groaned under; but
I trust the goodnesse of our Soveraigne, and the
wisdome of his Counsellors, will rectifie the same, or
remunerate them by fitting encouragements some other
wayes; lest thereby the same be reduced to the present
condition of the *East-India* Company, to His Majesties
great losse and dishonour, and to the wonderfull prejudice of his people and kingdomes.

Now, having thus handled the 3. first considerations
of trade, and observed that neither naturall nor
artificiall commodities of a kingdom can inrich a
countrey without the helpe and hand of traffike; and
then shewed what commodities by a well ordered
traffike, a Kingdom must suffer entrance, and what
prohibit, and what againe to send out, and also what
to forbid, and withall shewed the particular meanes
and wayes that Princes are observed to use to gaine,
settle, preserve, and augment the same with the
laborious and studious courses that have beene taken
by sundry late Princes to obtaine and purchase this
so beneficiall a commodity: I come now to the last
The reasons that doe point and consideration before mentioned, wherein the
rest is for the most part comprehended, being the

reasons

reasons and causes that move all estates, Kings and move Princes to covet trade in their King-domes.
Empires to covet the same, which I may say doth
extend it selfe into foure heads and principall parts.

The first is, that traffike with forraigne nations is 1 Honour-able.
notable in respect of the honour and reputation
thereof.

Secondly, excellent in point of riches, both to the 2 Rich.
King, his Countrey, and Subjects.

Thirdly, eminent in regard of strength offensive and 3 Strong.
defensive, that it brings with it to the Countrey and
Princes where it is orderly managed, and regularly
practised by skilfull Merchants.

First then, a well governed traffike, practised in a Traffike is honourable to the people and country.
Kingdome, by judicious and expert Merchants, to
forraigne and remote countries, will easily bee granted,
and confessed to bee both honourable, and of singular
reputation, both to the Soveraigne in his particular,
and to the nation in generall. I need not seeke farre
for examples, nor search much for arguments to make
this good and manifest, but only looke upon this our
kingdome wherein wee live. How had ever the name
of the English beene knowne in *India, Persia, Moscovia,* Experienced in the English.
or in *Turkey,* and in many places else-where, had not
the traffike of our Nation discovered and spread abroad
the fame of their Soveraigne Potency, and the renowne
of that peoples valour and worth? Many parts of the
world had, peradventure even to this day, lived in
ignorance thereof, and never dreamt of the inhabitants
of so small an Iland, had not the traffike of the
Merchants by Navigation made it famous over all
those remote Regions.

Nay, the *Portugals,* and *Hollanders,* an obscure people, And in the Portugall and Hollander.
in comparison of the English, and enjoying but a
handfull of those subjects, that are comprehended
under the Scepter of great *Britaine,* have by this onely
meanes given witnesse and good testimony, to many

powerfull remote nations, of their countries worth and honour.

What brought the *Portugall* nation to be famoused in *Affrica* and *Asia*, or the *Spanish* name to bee notable in *America*, but her traffike and Commerce.

The commerce, and not the conquests of the English have made them famous in *India*.

It is not our conquests, but our Commerce; it is not our swords, but our sayls, that first spred the English name in *Barbary*, and thence came into *Turkey, Armenia, Moscovia, Arabia, Persia, India, China*, and indeed over and about the world; it is the traffike of their Merchants, and the boundlesse desires of that nation to eternize the English honour and name, that hath enduced them to saile, and seek into all the corners of the earth. What part is there unsearched, what place undiscovered, or what place lyes unattempted by their endeavours, and couragious undertakings? most of which hath beene accompanied with such fortunate

League contracted by the English Merchants withforraigne Princes.

successe, that they have contracted Leagues and Amity with the Mogull, Persian, Turke, Moscovite, and other mighty forraigne Princes in their Soveraignes name, and to his honour; which even in our Fathers dayes was not knowne to us, either to have any such condition, or being the Merchants of *England*. And to speak truth of *London*, maintaining now at their charge an Agent in *Moscovia*, an Ambassadour and three Consuls in *Turkey*, and certaine Presidents and Agents also in *India, Persia*, and many other places thereof, which

At their own charge 100000.l. yearely.

by computation cannot cost them lesse then one hundred thousand pounds yearely (which though it may be alledged is for their own profit, & the benefit of their traffike into these parts) yet for as much as that it is not chargeable to their Soveraigne, nor prejudiciall, but profitable to his Kingdomes, it must be granted that the same brings honour to his name, and a great benefit both to him and his subjects; and it is more then can be paralleld in all other Christian or heathen Countries now in the world.

The Danes and Swedish nations are potent, and the French are yet more powerfull iu Europe; yet if you travell into *India, Persia,* and many of those Easterne Kingdomes of the world, they know of no such people, Kings or Countries, but hold all Europe to be inhabited by the Portugals, English and Dutch; nay the French are hardly knowne in *Moscovia* and *Russia,* save by name, but not by their worth or actions; and the Emperour of *Germany,* the greatest of our Christian Princes, for all his eminence and power in Christendome, is not in *India,* knowne, no nor yet in *Persia,* save for some leagues, which the Sophy would sometimes have contracted with him, to the prejudice of *Turkey* and the Ottoman Empire.

The Danes, Sweeds and Germans not knowne in India, &c.

So that by what hath beene said, the Commerce of Merchants, though many times it be accompanied with losse and prejudice to themselves, and estates, and that they are enforced to expose their fortunes to the mercy of mercilesse stormes and tempests, & be subject to the Lawes of Heathenish Princes, and groan under the heavy customes of many Soveraignes and Infidels; yet is it still attended upon with a great deale of honour to their owne Prince, and reputation to his subjects: Therefore I will conclude here this point, that a well ordered traffike managed by skilfull Merchants, hath beene, and ever will be, honourable to that Kingdome and Soveraigne, where the same is duely practised, and carefully protected, and preserved.

The second point is in regard of Riches, and the benefit that traffike bringeth with it, where the same is preserved with fitting priviledges, and practised with regular order and method; and this Riches extendeth itselfe two wayes.

2. *Traffike is excellect in point of Riches, two wayes.*

In the first place to the Soveraigne, his Nobles and Gentry,

1 *To the King and his Nobles.*

Gentry, in the particular of their owne estates and Interests.

Secondly to his subjects, the inhabitants in generall; As to the Sea-men, Husbandmen, Artificers, Labourers, and others.

First for the Prince, or Soveraigne, it particularly inricheth him by his customes and imposts, imposed inwards, and outwards upon all commodities and wares, either imported or exported, in or out of his Kingdomes and. Dominions, by the Merchant, and also by venting, and dispersing of such wares, and merchandises, as hee appropriateth to himselfe, either by purchase, prerogative, or by right of his Crowne; as we find it to doe by the Gabell of Bay-salt, to the King of *France*, by the property of silke to the King of *Persia*, by the Mines of Copper to the grand Signior,
and by the preemption of Tyn to His Majestie of *England*, and next it proveth beneficiall to the Nobility and Gentry, by the improvement of their lands, by the improvement of their lands, by the sale and working of their clothes, by the use of their Timber, by the vent of their Cattle, Graine, and other provisions, and in many regards, which experience daily maketh evident, both in this, and all other Kingdomes where the same is practised.
Secondly, it inricheth the inhabitants of a countrey in the generall, by setting Arts-men on worke, by imploying the poore, by furthering and incouraging of all professions whatsoever; for every Arts-man, Workeman and Artificer, is conducible one way or other to traffike, and every hand is set on worke, where a well governed Commerce is observed to be driven, and exercised by judicious and skilfull Merchants, and to the whole countrey in generall it is found beneficiall by venting the native commodities of that land, as experience tels us, in *Persia* by the vent of their raw

silkes,

silkes, in *France* by the vent of their Wines, Oyles, Lynens, Graine, &c. in *Zante* by the vent of their Corrence, in *Spaine* by the vent of their Wines, Fruits, Sugars, &c. and in *England* by the vent of their Tinne, Cloath, Lead, &c. as the like may be said of many other countries.

Thirdly and lastly, it produceth strength and safety to the Kingdome and people, where the same is duly and orderly practised.

3 Traffike produceth strength two wayes.

Now this strength and safety may be considered two wayes; either defensive or offensive; if my former assertions be granted, That a well ordered trade doth enrich a Prince, his nobles, gentiles and Subjects, as of necessity it must, it will be easie for mee to make good this point also; for that which produceth Riches, doth consequently also beget strength and safety, so farre forth as treasure is accounted the principal nerve and sinnew of war, either offensive, or defensive; but to come to some particulars.

That which begets wealth, also doth beget strength.

It furnisheth the Prince, and his subjects, having maritime ports, with plenty of shipping, and store of Mariners, to manage and sayle the same, in all occasions of the state and countrey by sea; and it furnisheth the same with all fitting Ammunition of and for warre, as Powder, Armes, and other the like necessaries; and by land it maketh the countrey a Magazine, not only for war-like provisions, brought in for the use of the Prince, and the Kingdome it selfe, but also for all other neighbouring countries that stand in need thereof.

How traffike doth beget strength.

I may here fitly bring in *Holland* to make good this point to all the world, who, though exercised in continuall warfare, and daily pressed, and sometimes oppressed by a potent Enemy; yet their industrious traffike into forraigne parts, is handled and practised with so much benefit, countenanced from the State and good Iudgement, that the same doth not onely supply their

An excellent plot of the Hollanders to inrich themselves

owne

owne occasions, with what warlike provisions they want, but withall have thereof in such abundance, that from their owne states they furnish freely all other neighbouring countries whatsoever therewith; for the Artsmen that are by them employed daily, in building of ships, casting of Artillery, making of Muskets, shot, powder, swords, pikes, corslets, cordage, Canvas, and the like Habiliments of warre, doe not only supply their owne turnes, and necessities, and that both cheape and plentifull; but herein proceed so farre, contrary to the politike Rules of many countries, that they sell, and vent their over-plus; yea even to the Spaniards their very enemies conceiving it, no ill trick of thrift, nor yet small point of State-stratagem, to draw thus the monies and wealth of their greatest adversaries to be a reward to their owne labour and industry, and so sell as it may be said (for monies to their foes) the very sword, which peradventure may afterwards be imployed in the cutting of their owne throats, but being instruments considerable, and which must necessarily be had in warre, and which will be by their enemies had elsewhere for monies, if not of them, they chuse rather thus to sell them, and so by permitting an unusuall policy of state, endeavour for their monies to give them with their owne consents, and that voluntarily, and of their owne accord, what they cannot with their best of policie otherwise prevent, and what their enemies will bee furnished withall, in despight of their utmost endeavours else-where.

I need not insist further upon this point, having declared the honour, benefit, and strength, both offensive and defensive, which doth arise to a Commonwealth or Countrey by a well ordered traffike, managed by Regular and Iudicious Merchants, I could here adde to what I have said before in the behalfe of the Merchant, and shew that as hee can in many things

advance

advance his countrey before a meere States-man, so also declare the Nobility of his art, and the excellency of his profession, no one vocation in the world requiring a more generall knowledge, and inspection into all other professions then this doth; and withall make it appeare, that hee is the best of Common-wealths men, both towards his Prince, and fellow-subjects; and that for the most part all other professions live, and have their subsistence from others, hee only giving by traffike a lively-hood to others, and no way dependent, but upon himselfe, and his owne labour and endeavours; as it will easily appeare to any judicious man that shall examine his profession, and compare the same with others.

But I will conclude this discourse, and take it by what hath beene said for granted, as for a truth undeniable, That the excellency of a well ordered traffike, is such and so singular, and the effects thereof so notably beneficiall to a kingdome, and in its selfe so admirable, and the discreet and skilful Merchants endeavours so laudable, and his art so eminently honorable, that it requireth and duly challengeth

A Royall Protection, and Reall Encouragement from all Kings and Princes, a faire respect from all Nobles, a love from all persons, and well wishes from all those their Countreymen, that tender the Profit, Advancement and Honour, both of the King and Countrey, &c.

ENGLAND's

TREASURE

BY

Forraign Trade.

OR,

The Ballance of our Forraign Trade

IS

The Rule of our Treasure.

Written by THOMAS MUN, *of*
Lond. *Merchant,*

And now published for the Common good by his
Son JOHN MUN *of* Bearsted *in the County of*
Kent, *Esquire.*

LONDON,
Printed by *J. G.* for *Thomas Clark,* and are to be sold at his
Shop at the South entrance of the *Royal*
Exchange. 1664.

To the Right Honourable

THOMAS

EARL OF

SOUTH-HAMPTON,

Lord High Treasurer of England,
Lord Warden of the New Forrest,
Knight of the most Noble Order of the Garter,
and one of His Majesty's most Honourable
Privy Council.

MY LORD,

I Present this ensuing Treatise to your Lordship as its proper Patron, to whom, by vertue of your great Trust (the greatest, doubtless, in this Kingdome) the management of his Majesty's Treasure, and improvement of his Revenue, are most peculiarly committed.

The title of it (*Englands Treasure by Forraign Trade*) alone bespeaks your notice, the Argument (being of publick a nature) may invite your perusall, but the Tract itself will, I hope, deserve your Lordships Protection. It was left me in the nature of a Legacy by my Father, for whose sake I cannot but value it as one of my best Moveables, and as such I dedicate it to your Lordship.

He was in his time famous amongst Merchants, and well known to most men of business, for his general
Experience

Experience of Affairs, and notable Insight into Trade; neither was he less observed for his Integrity to his Prince, and Zeal to the Common-wealth: the serious Discourses of such men are commonly not unprofitable.

To your Lordships judgement I submit this Treatise, and my presumption herein to your Pardon.

My Lord,

Your most faithful and
obedient Servant,

JOHN MUN.

THE ARGUMENTS.

CHAP. I.

CHAP.

CHAP. XI.

CHAP. XII.

CHAP. XIII.

CHAP. XIV.

CHAP. XV.

CHAP. XVI.

CHAP. XVII.

CHAP. XVIII.

CHAP. XIX.

CHAP. XX.

CHAP. XXI.

ENGLAND'S TREASURE
BY
FORRAIGN TRADE.
OR,
The Ballance of our Forraign Trade is the Rule of our Treasure.

MY Son, *In a former Discourse I have endeavoured after my manner briefly to teach thee two things: The first is* Piety, *how to fear God aright, according to his Works and Word: The second is* Policy, *how to love and serve thy Country, by instructing thee in the duties and proceedings of sundry Vocations, which either order, or else* act *the affairs of the Common-wealth; In which as some things doe especially tend to* Preserve, *and others are more apt to* Enlarge *the same: So am I to speak of* Money, *which doth indifferently serve to both those happy ends. Wherein I will observe this order, First, to show the general means whereby a Kingdom may be enriched; and then proceed to those particular courses by which Princes are accustomed to be supplied with* Treasure. *But first of all I will say something of the* Merchant, *because he must be a Principal Agent in this great business.*

CHAP. I.

The Qualities which are required in a perfect Merchant of Forraign Trade.

THe love and service of our Country consisteth not so much in the knowledge of those duties which are to be performed by others, as in the skilful practice

1   of

As it is very commendable to know what is to be done by others in their places: So it were a great shame to be ignorant in the duties of our own Vocations.

of that which is done by our selves; and therefore (my Son) it is now fit that I say something of the Merchant, which I hope in due time shall be thy Vocation: Yet herein are my thoughts free from all Ambition, although I rank thee in a place of so high estimation; for the Merchant is worthily called *The Steward of the Kingdoms Stock*, by way of Commerce with other Nations; a work of no less *Reputation* than *Trust*, which ought to be performed with great skill and conscience, that so the private gain may ever accompany the publique good. And because the nobleness of this Profession may the better stir up thy desires and endeavours to obtain those abilities which may effect it worthily, I will briefly set down the excellent qualities which are required in a perfect Merchant.

1. He ought to be a good Penman, a good Arithmetician, and a good Accomptant, by that noble order of *Debtor* and *Creditor*, which is used oncly amongst Merchants; also to be expert in the order and form of *Charter-parties, Bills of Lading, Invoyces, Contracts, Bills of Exchange,* and *Policies of Ensurance.*

2. He ought to know the Measures, Weights, and Monies of all forraign Countries, especially where we have Trade, & the Monies not onely by their several denominations, but also by their intrinsique values in weight & fineness, compared with the Standard of this Kingdom, without which he cannot well direct his affaires.

3. He ought to know the Customs, Tolls, Taxes, Impositions, Conducts and other charges upon all manner of Merchandize exported or imported to and from the said Forraign Countries.

4. He ought to know in what several commodities each Country abounds, and what be the wares which they want, and how and from whence they are furnished with the same.

2

5. He

5. He ought to understand, and to be a diligent observer of the rates of Exchanges by Bills, from one State to another, whereby he may the better direct his affairs, and remit over and receive home his Monies to the most advantage possible.

6. He ought to know what goods are prohibited to be exported or imported in the said forraign Countreys, lest otherwise he should incur great danger and loss in the ordering of his affairs.

7. He ought to know upon what rates and conditions to fraight his Ships, and ensure his adventures from one Countrey to another, and to be well acquainted with the laws, orders and customes of the Ensurance office both here and beyond the Seas, in the many aceidents which may happen upon the damage or loss of Ships or goods, or both these.

8. He ought to have knowlege in the goodness and in the prices of all the several materials which are required for the building and repairing of Ships, and the divers workmanships of the same, as also for the Masts, Tackling, Cordage, Ordnance, Victuals, Munition, and Provisions of many kinds; together with the ordinary wages of *Commanders, Officers,* and *Mariners,* all which concern the Merchant as he is an Owner of Ships.

9. He ought (by the divers occasions which happen sometime in the buying and selling of one commodity and sometimes in another) to have indifferent if not perfect knowledge in all manner of Merchandize or wares, which is to be as it were a man of all occupations and trades.

10. He ought by his voyaging on the Seas to become skilful in the Art of Navigation.

11. He ought, as he is a Traveller, and sometimes abiding in forraign Countreys, to attain to the speaking of divers Languages, and to be a diligent observer of

3   the

the ordinary Revenues and expences of forraign Princes, together with their strength both by Sea and Land, their laws, customes, policies, manners, religions, arts, and the like; to be able to give account thereof in all occasions for the good of his Countrey.

12. Lastly, although there be no necessity that such a Merchant should be a great Scholar; yet is it (at least) required, that in his youth he learn the Latine tongue, which will the better enable him in all the rest of his endeavours.

Thus have I briefly showed thee a pattern for thy diligence, the Merchant in his qualities; which in truth are such and so many, that I find no other profession which leadeth into more worldly knowledge. And it cannot be denied but that their sufficiency doth appear likewise in the excellent government of State at *Venice, Luca, Genoua, Florence,* the Low Countreys, and divers other places of Christendom. And in those States also where they are least esteemed, yet is their skill and knowledge often used by those who sit in the highest places of Authority: It is therefore an act beyond rashness in some, who do dis-enable their Counsel and judgment (even in books printed) making them uncapable of those ways and means, which do either enrich or empoverish a Common-wealth, when in truth this is only effected by the mystery of their trade, as I shall plainly show in that which followeth. It is true indeed that many Merchants here in *England* finding less encouragement given to their profession than in other Countreys, and seeing themselves not so well esteemed as their *Noble Vocation* requireth, and according to the great consequence of the same, do not therefore labour to attain unto the excellence of their profession, neither is it practised by the *Nobility* of this Kingdom, as it is in other States from the Father to the Son throughout their generations, to the

4   great

great encrease of their wealth, and maintenance of
their names and families: Whereas the memory of our
richest Merchants is suddenly extinguished; the Son
being left rich, scorneth the profession of his Father,
conceiving more honor to be a Gentleman (although
but in name), to consume his estate in dark ignorance
and excess, than to follow the steps of his Father as
an Industrious Merchant to maintain and advance his
Fortunes. But now leaving the Merchants praise we
will come to his practice, or at least to so much
thereof as concerns the bringing of Treasure into the
Kingdom.

There is more honor and profit in an Industrious life, than in a great inheritance which wasteth for want of vertue.

CHAP. II.
The means to enrich this Kingdom, and to encrease our Treasure.

Although a Kingdom may be enriched by gifts
received, or by purchase taken from some other
Nations, yet these are things uncertain and of small
consideration when they happen. The ordinary means
therefore to increase our wealth and treasure is by *Forraign Trade*, wherein wee must ever observe this rule; to
sell more to strangers yearly than wee consume of
theirs in value. For suppose that when this Kingdom
is plentifully served with the Cloth, Lead, Tinn, Iron,
Fish and other native commodities, we doe yearly
export the overplus to forraign Countreys to the value
of twenty two hundred thousand pounds; by which
means we are enabled beyond the Seas to buy and
bring in forraign wares for our use and Consumptions,
to the value of twenty hundred thousand pounds: By
this order duly kept in our trading, we may rest
assured that the Kingdom shall be enriched yearly two
hundred thousand pounds, which must be brought to
us in so much Treasure; because that part of our

Forraign Trade is the rule of our Treasure.

stock

stock which is not returned to us in wares must necessarily be brought home in treasure.

For in this case it cometh to pass in the stock of a Kingdom, as in the estate of a private man; who is supposed to have one thousand pounds yearly revenue and two thousand pounds of ready money in his Chest: If such a man through excess shall spend one thousand five hundred pounds *per annum*, all his ready mony will be gone in four years; and in the like time his said money will be doubled if he take a Frugal course to spend but five hundred pounds *per annum*, which rule never faileth likewise in the Commonwealth, but in some cases (of no great moment) which I will here-after declare, when I shall shew by whom and in what manner this ballance of the Kingdoms account ought to be drawn up yearly, or so often as it shall please the State to discover how much we gain or lose by trade with forraign Nations. But first I will say some-thing concerning those ways and means which will encrease our exportations and diminish our importa-tions of wares; which being done, I will then set down some other arguments both affirmative and negative to strengthen that which is here declared, and thereby to show that all the other means which are commonly supposed to enrich the Kingdom with Treasure are altogether insufficient and meer fallacies.

CHAP.

Chap. III.

*The particular ways and means to encrease the exporta-
tion of our commodities, and to decrease our Consumption of forraign wares.*

THe revenue or stock of a Kingdom by which it is
provided of forraign wares is either *Natural* or
Artificial. The Natural wealth is so much only as can
be spared from our own use and necessities to be
exported unto strangers. The Artificial consists in our
manufactures and industrious trading with forraign
commodities, concerning which I will set down such
particulars as may serve for the cause we have in
hand.

1. First, although this Realm be already exceeding
rich by nature, yet might it be much encreased by
laying the waste grounds (which are infinite) into such
employments as should no way hinder the present
revenues of other manured lands, but hereby to supply
our selves and prevent the importations of Hemp,
Flax, Cordage, Tobacco, and divers other things which
now we fetch from strangers to our great impoverishing.

2. We may likewise diminish our importations, if we
would soberly refrain from excessive consumption of
forraign wares in our diet and rayment, with such often
change of fashions as is used, so much the more to
encrease the waste and charge; which vices at this
present are more notorious amongst us than in former
ages. Yet might they easily be amended by enforcing
the observation of such good laws as are strictly practised in other Countries against the said excesses ;
where likewise by commanding their own manufactures
to be used, they prevent the coming in of others,

7 without

without prohibition, or offence to strangers in their mutual commerce.

3. In our exportations we must not only regard our own superfluities, but also we must consider our neighbours necessities, that so upon the wares which they cannot want, nor yet be furnished thereof elsewhere, we may (besides the vent of the Materials) gain so much of the manufacture as we can, and also endeavour to sell them dear, so far forth as the high price cause not a less vent in the quantity. But the superfluity of our commodities which strangers use, and may also have the same from other Nations, or may abate their vent by the use of some such like wares from other places, and with little inconvenience; we must in this case strive to sell as cheap as possible we can, rather than to lose the utterance of such wares. For we have found of late years by good experience, that being able to sell our Cloth cheap in Turkey, we have greatly encreased the vent thereof, and the *Venetians* have lost as much in the utterance of theirs in those Countreys, because it is dearer. And on the other side a few years past, when by the excessive price of Wools our Cloth was exceeding dear, we lost at the least half our clothing for forraign parts, which since is no otherwise (well neer) recovered again than by the great fall of *The State in* price for Wools and Cloth. We find that twenty five *some occasions* in the hundred less in the price of these and some *may gain* *most, when* other Wares, to the loss of private mens revenues, may *private men* raise above fifty upon the hundred in the quantity *by their re-* *venues get* vented to the benefit of the publique. For when Cloth *least.* is dear, other Nations doe presently practice clothing, and we know they want neither art nor materials to this performance. But when by cheapness we drive them from this employment, and so in time obtain our dear price again, then do they also use their former remedy. So that by these alterations we learn, that

8   it

it is in vain to expect a greater revenue of our wares than their condition will afford, but rather it concerns us to apply our endeavours to the times with care and diligence to help our selves the best we may, by making our cloth and other manufactures without deceit, which will encrease their estimation and use.

4. The value of our exportations likewise may be much advanced when we perform it our selves in our own Ships, for then we get only not the price of our wares as they are worth here, but also the Merchants gains, the charges of ensurance, and fraight to carry them beyond the seas. As for example, if the *Italian* Merchants should come hither in their own shipping to fetch our Corn, our red Herrings or the like, in this case the Kingdom should have ordinarily but 25*s*. for a quarter of Wheat, and 20*s*. for a barrel of red herrings, whereas if we carry these wares our selves into *Italy* upon the said rates, it is likely that wee shall obtain fifty shillings for the first, and forty shillings for the last, which is a great difference in the utterance or vent of the Kingdoms stock. And although it is true that the commerce ought to be free to strangers to bring in and carry out at their pleasure, yet nevertheless in many places the exportation of victuals and munition are either prohibited, or at least limited to be done onely by the people and Shipping of those places where they abound.

5. The frugal expending likewise of our own natural wealth might advance much yearly to be exported unto strangers; and if in our rayment we will be prodigal, yet let this be done with our own materials and manufactures, as Cloth, Lace, Imbroderies, Cut-works and the like, where the excess of the rich may be the employment of the poor, whose labours notwithstanding of this kind, would be more profitable for the Commonwealth, if they were done to the use of strangers.

9   6. The

6. The Fishing in his Majesties seas of *England*, *Scotland*, and *Ireland* is our natural wealth, and would cost nothing but labour, which the *Dutch* bestow willingly, and thereby draw yearly a very great profit to themselves by serving many places of Christendom with our Fish, for which they return and supply their wants both of forraign Wares and Mony, besides the multitude of Mariners and Shipping, which hereby are maintain'd, whereof a long discourse might be made to show the particular manage of this important business. Our fishing plantation likewise in *New-England*, *Virginia, Groenland,* the *Summer Islands* and the *New-found-land*, are of the like nature, affording much wealth and employments to maintain a great number of poor, and to encrease our decaying trade.

How some States have been made Rich. 7. A Staple or Magazin for forraign Corn, Indigo, Spices, Raw-silks, Cotton wool or any other commodity whatsoever, to be imported will encrease Shipping, Trade, Treasure, and the Kings customes, by exporting them again where need shall require, which course of Trading, hath been the chief means to raise *Venice*, *Genoa*, the *low-Countreys*, with some others; and for such a purpose *England* stands most commodiously, wanting nothing to this performance but our own diligence and endeavour.

8. Also wee ought to esteem and cherish those trades which we have in remote or far Countreys, for besides the encrease of Shipping and Mariners thereby, the wares also sent thither and receiv'd from thence are far more profitable unto the kingdom than by our trades neer at hand; As for example; suppose Pepper to be worth here two Shillings the pound constantly, if then it be brought from the *Dutch* at *Amsterdam*, the Merchant may give there twenty pence the pound, and gain well by the bargain; but if he fetch this Pepper from the *East-indies*, he must not give above

10   three

three pence the pound at the most, which is a mighty *The traffick to* advantage, not only in that part which serveth for our *the East* own use, but also for that great quantity which (from *most profit-* hence) we transport yearly unto divers other Nations *able trade in* to be sold at a higher price: whereby it is plain, that *both for King* we make a far greater stock by gain upon these *Indian* and *King-* Commodities, than those Nations doe where they *dom.* grow, and to whom they properly appertain, being the *We get more* natural wealth of their Countries. But for the better *wares than* understanding of this particular, we must ever dis- *the Indians* tinguish between the gain of the Kingdom, and the *themselves.* profit of the Merchant; for although the Kingdom *A distinction* payeth no more for this Pepper than is before sup- *Kingdoms* posed, nor for any other commodity bought in forraign *gain and the* parts more than the stranger receiveth from us for *profit.* the same, yet the Merchant payeth not only that price, but also the fraight, ensurance, customes and other charges which are exceeding great in these long voyages; but yet all these in the Kingdoms accompt are but commutations among our selves, and no Privation of the Kingdoms stock, which being duly considered, together with the support also of our other trades in our best Shipping to *Italy, France, Turkey,* the *East Countreys* and other places, by transporting and venting the wares which we bring yearly from the *East Indies;* It may well stir up our utmost endeavours to maintain and enlarge this great and noble business, so much importing the Publique wealth, Strength, and Happiness. Neither is there less honour and judgment by growing rich (in this manner) upon the stock of other Nations, than by an industrious encrease of our own means, especially when this later is advanced by the benefit of the former, as we have found in the *East Indies* by sale of much of our Tin, Cloth, Lead and other Commodities, the vent whereof doth daily

11   encrease

encrease in those Countreys which formerly had no use of our wares.

9. It would be very beneficial to export money as well as wares, being done in trade only, it would encrease our Treasure; but of this I write more largely in the next Chapter to prove it plainly.

10. It were policie and profit for the State to suffer manufactures made of forraign Materials to be exported custome-free, as Velvets and all other wrought Silks, Fustians, thrown Silks and the like, it would employ very many poor people, and much encrease the value of our stock yearly issued into other Countreys, and it would (for this purpose) cause the more forraign Materials to be brought in, to the improvement of His Majesties Customes. I will here remember a notable increase in our manufacture of winding and twisting only of forraign raw Silk, which within 35. years to my knowledge did not employ more than 300. people in the City and suburbs of London, where at this present time it doth set on work above fourteen thousand souls, as upon diligent enquiry hath been credibly reported unto His Majesties Commissioners for Trade. And it is certain, that if the said forraign Commodities might be exported from hence, free of custome, this manufacture would yet encrease very much, and decrease as fast in *Italy* and in the *Netherlands*. But if any man allege the *Dutch* proverb, *Live and let others live;* I answer, that the Dutchmen notwithstanding their own Proverb, doe not onely in these Kingdoms, encroach upon our livings, but also in other forraign parts of our trade (where they have power) they do hinder and destroy us in our lawful course of living, hereby taking the bread out of our mouth, which we shall never prevent by plucking the pot from their nose, as of late years too many of us do practise

to the great hurt and dishonour of this famous Nation;
We ought rather to imitate former times in taking
sober and worthy courses more pleasing to God and
suitable to our ancient reputation.

11. It is needful also not to charge the native commodities with too great customes, lest by indearing
them to the strangers use, it hinder their vent. And
especially forraign wares brought in to be transported
again should be favoured, for otherwise that manner
of trading (so much importing the good of the Commonwealth) cannot prosper nor subsist. But the Consumption of such forraign wares in the Realm may
be the more charged, which will turn to the profit of
the kingdom in the *Ballance of the Trade,* and thereby
also enable the King to lay up the more Treasure out
of his yearly incomes, as of this particular I intend to
write more fully in his proper place, where I shall
shew how much money a Prince may conveniently lay
up without the hurt of his subjects.

12. Lastly, in all things we must endeavour to make
the most we can of our own, whether it be *Natural* or
Artificial; And forasmuch as the people which live by
the Arts are far more in number than they who are
masters of the fruits, we ought the more carefully to
maintain those endeavours of the multitude, in whom
doth consist the greatest strength and riches both of
King and Kingdom: for where the people are many,
and the arts good, there the traffique must be great,
and the Countrey rich. The *Italians* employ a greater
number of people, and get more money by their industry and manufactures of the raw Silks of the
Kingdom of *Cicilia,* than the King of *Spain* and his
Subjects have by the revenue of this rich commodity.
But what need we fetch the example so far, when we
know that our own natural wares doe not yield us so
much profit as our industry? For Iron oar in the

Mines

Mines is of no great worth, when it is compared with
the employment and advantage it yields being digged,
tried, transported, bought, sold, cast into Ordnance,
Muskets, and many other instruments of war for
offence and defence, wrought into Anchors, bolts,
spikes, nayles and the like, for the use of Ships,
Houses, Carts, Coaches, Ploughs, and other instruments for Tillage. Compare our Fleece-wools with
our Cloth, which requires shearing, washing, carding,
spinning, Weaving, fulling, dying, dressing and other
trimmings, and we shall find these Arts more profitable
than the natural wealth, whereof I might instance
other examples, but I will not be more tedious, for
if I would amplify upon this and the other particulars
before written, I might find matter sufficient to make
a large volume, but my desire in all is only to prove
what I propound with brevity and plainness.

Chap. IV.

The Exportation of our Moneys in Trade of Merchan-
dize is a means to encrease our Treasure.

THis Position is so contrary to the common opinion,
that it will require many and strong arguments to
prove it before it can be accepted of the Multitude,
who bitterly exclaim when they see any monies carried
out of the Realm; affirming thereupon that wee have
absolutely lost so much Treasure, and that this is an
act directly against the long continued laws made and
confirmed by the wisdom of this Kingdom in the High
Court of Parliament, and that many places, nay *Spain*
it self which is the Fountain of Mony, forbids the
exportation thereof, some cases only excepted. To all
which I might answer, that *Venice*, *Florence*, *Genoa*,

the *Low Countreys* and divers other places permit it, their people applaud it, and find great benefit by it; but all this makes a noise and proves nothing, we must therefore come to those reasons which concern the business in question.

First, I will take that for granted which no man of judgment will deny, that we have no other means to get Treasure but by forraign trade, for Mines wee have none which do afford it, and how this mony is gotten in the managing of our said Trade I have already shewed, that it is done by making our commodities which are exported yearly to over ballance in value the forraign wares which we consume; so that it resteth only to shew how our moneys may be added to our commodities, and being jointly exported may so much the more encrease our Treasure.

Wee have already supposed our yearly consumptions of forraign wares to be for the value of twenty hundred thousand pounds, and our exportations to exceed that two hundred thousand pounds, which sum wee have thereupon affirmed is brought to us in treasure to ballance the accompt. But now if we add three hundred thousand pounds more in ready mony unto our former exportations in wares, what profit can we have (will some men say) although by this means we should bring in so much ready mony more than wee did before, seeing that wee have carried out the like value.

To this the answer is, that when wee have prepared our exportations of wares, and sent out as much of every thing as wee can spare or vent abroad: It is not *Money begets* therefore said that then we should add our money *trade and* thereunto to fetch in the more mony immediately, but *trade encreaseth mony.* rather first to enlarge our trade by enabling us to bring in more forraign wares, which being sent out again will in due time much encrease our Treasure.

15   For

For although in this manner wee do yearly multiply our importations to the maintenance of more Shipping and Mariners, improvement of His Majesties Customs and other benefits: yet our consumption of those forraign wares is no more than it was before; so that all the said encrease of commodities brought in by the means of our ready mony sent out as is afore written, doth in the end become an exportation unto us of a far greater value than our said moneys were, which is proved by three several examples following.

1. For I suppose that 100000.*l.* being sent in our Shipping to the East Countreys, will buy there one hundred thousand quarters of wheat cleer aboard the Ships, which being after brought into *England* and housed, to export the same at the best time for vent thereof in *Spain* or *Italy*, it cannot yield less in those parts than two hundred thousand pounds to make the Merchant but a saver, yet by this reckning wee see the Kingdom hath doubled that Treasure.

Remote trades are most gainful to the Commonwealth.

2. Again this profit will be far greater when wee trade thus in remote Countreys, as for example, if wee send one hundred thousand pounds into the *East-Indies* to buy Pepper there, and bring it hither, and from hence send it for *Italy* or *Turkey*, it must yield seven hundred thousand pounds at least in those places, in regard of the excessive charge which the Merchant disburseth in those long voyages in Shipping, Wages, Victuals, Insurance, Interest, Customes, Imposts, and the like, all which notwithstanding the King and the Kingdom gets.

3. But where the voyages are short & the wares rich, which therefore will not employ much Shipping, the profit will be far less. As when another hundred thousand pounds shall be employed in *Turkey* in raw Silks, and brought hither to be after transported from hence into *France*, the *Low Countreys*, or *Germany*,

16   the

the Merchant shall have good gain, although he sell it
there but for one hundred and fifty thousand pounds:
and thus take the voyages altogether in their *Medium*,
the moneys exported will be returned unto us more
than Trebled. But if any man will yet object, that
these returns come to us in wares, and not really in
mony as they were issued out,

The answer is (keeping our first ground) that if our
consumption of forraign wares be no more yearly than
is already supposed, and that our exportations be so
mightily encreased by this manner of Trading with
ready money, as is before declared: It is not then
possible but that all the over ballance or difference
should return either in mony or in such wares as we
must export again, which, as is already plainly shewed
will be still a greater means to encrease our Treasure.

For it is in the stock of the Kingdom as in the
estates of private men, who having store of wares, doe
not therefore say that they will not venture out or
trade with their mony (for this were ridiculous) but
do also turn that into wares, whereby they multiply
their Mony, and so by a continual and orderly change *The Proverb*
of one into the other grow rich, and when they please *saith,* He that
turn all their estates into Treasure; for they that have hath ware
Wares cannot want mony. hath mony
by the year.

Neither is it said that Mony is the Life of Trade, as
if it could not subsist without the same; for we know
that there was great trading by way of commutation
or barter when there was little mony stirring in the
world. The *Italians* and some other Nations have
such remedies against this want, that it can neither
decay nor hinder their trade, for they transfer bills of
debt, and have Banks both publick and private, wherein
they do assign their credits from one to another daily
for very great sums with ease and satisfaction by
writings only, whilst in the mean time the Mass of

Treasure which gave foundation to these credits is employed in Forraign Trade as a Merchandize, and by the said means they have little other use of money in those countreys more than for their ordinary expences. It is not therefore the keeping of our mony in the Kingdom, but the necessity and use of our wares in forraign Countries, and our want of their commodities that causeth the vent and consumption on all sides, which makes a quick and ample Trade. If wee were once poor, and now having gained some store of mony by trade with resolution to keep it still in the Realm; shall this cause other Nations to spend more of our commodities than formerly they have done, whereby we might say that our trade is Quickned and Enlarged? no verily, it will produce no such good effect: but rather according to the alteration of times by their true causes wee may expect the contrary; for all men do consent that plenty of mony in a Kingdom doth make the native commodities dearer, which as it is to the profit of some private men in their revenues, so is it directly against the benefit of the Publique in the quantity of the trade; for as plenty of mony makes wares dearer, so dear wares decline their use and consumption, as hath been already plainly shewed in the last Chapter upon that particular of our cloth; And although this is a very hard lesson for some great landed men to learn, yet I am sure it is a true lesson for all the land to observe, lest when wee have gained some store of mony by trade, wee lose it again by not trading with our mony. I knew a Prince in *Italy* (of famous memory) *Ferdinando the first*, great Duke of *Tuscanie*, who being very rich in Treasure, endeavoured therewith to enlarge his trade by issuing out to his Merchants great sums of money for very small profit; I my self had forty thousand crowns of him *gratis* for a whole year, although he knew that

18   I

I would presently send it away in *Specie* for the parts of *Turkey* to be employed in wares for his Countries, he being well assured that in this course of trade it would return again (according to the old saying) with a Duck in the mouth. This noble and industrious Prince by his care and diligence to countenance and favour Merchants in their affairs, did so encrease the practice thereof, that there is scarce a Nobleman or Gentleman in all his dominions that doth not Merchandize either by himself or in partnership with others, whereby within these thirty years the trade to his port of *Leghorn* is so much encreased, that of a poor little town (as I my self knew it) it is now become a fair and strong City, being one of the most famous places for trade in all Christendom. And yet it is worthy our observation, that the multitude of Ships and wares which come thither from *England*, the *Low Countreys*, and other places, have little or no means to make their returns from thence but only in ready mony, which they may and do carry away freely at all times, to the incredible advantage of the said great Duke of *Tuscanie* and his subjects, who are much enriched by the continual great concourse of Merchants from all the States of the neighbour Princes, bringing them plenty of mony daily to supply their wants of the said wares. And thus we see that the current of Merchandize which carries away their Treasure, becomes a flowing stream to fill them again in a greater measure with mony.

There is yet an objection or two as weak as all the rest: that is, if wee trade with our Mony wee shall issue out the less wares; as if a man should say, those Countreys which heretofore had occasion to consume our Cloth, Lead, Tin, Iron, Fish, and the like, shall now make use of our monies in the place of those necessaries, which were most absurd to affirm, or that the

19

the Merchant had not rather carry out wares by which there is ever some gains expected, than to export mony which is still but the same without any encrease.

But on the contrary there are many Countreys which may yield us very profitable trade for our mony, which otherwise afford us no trade at all, because they have no use of our wares, as namely the *East Indies* for one in the first beginning thereof, although since by industry in our commerce with those Nations we have brought them into the use of much of our Lead, Cloth, Tin, and other things, which is a good addition to the former vent of our commodities.

Again, some men have alleged that those Countries which permit mony to be carried out, do it because they have few or no wares to trade withall: but wee have great store of commodities, and therefore their action ought not to be our example.

To this the answer is briefly, that if we have such a quantity of wares as doth fully provide us of all things needful from beyond the seas: why should we then doubt that our monys sent out in trade, must not necessarily come back again in treasure; together with the great gains which it may procure in such manner as is before set down? And on the other side, if those Nations which send out their monies do it because they have but few wares of their own, how come they then to have so much Treasure as we ever see in those places which suffer it freely to be exported at all times and by whomsoever? I answer, *Even by trading with their Moneys;* for by what other means can they get it, having no Mines of Gold or Silver?

Thus may we plainly see, that when this weighty business is duly considered in his end, as all our humane actions ought well to be weighed, it is found much contrary to that which most men esteem thereof, because they search no further than the beginning of the work,

20   which

which mis-informs their judgments, and leads them *Our humane* into error: For if we only behold the actions of the *actions ought* husbandman in the seed-time when he casteth away *especially to be considered* much good corn into the ground, we will rather accompt *in their ends.* him a mad man than a husbandman: but when we consider his labours in the harvest which is the end of his endeavours, we find the worth and plentiful encrease of his actions.

CHAP. V.

Forraign Trade is the only means to improve the price of our Lands.

IT is a common saying, that plenty or scarcity of mony makes all things dear or good or cheap; and this mony is either gotten or lost in forraign trade by the over or under ballancing of the same, as I have already shewed. It resteth now that I distinguish the seeming plenties of mony from that which is only substantial and able to perform the work: For there are divers ways and means whereby to procure plenty of mony into a Kingdom, which do not enrich but rather empoverish the same by the several inconveniences which ever accompany such alterations.

As first, if we melt down our plate into Coyn (which suits not with the Majesty of so great a Kingdom, except in cases of great extremity) it would cause Plenty of mony for a time, yet should we be nothing the richer, but rather this treasure being thus altered is made the more apt to be carried out of the Kingdom, if we exceed our means by excess in forraign wares, or maintain a war by Sea or Land, where we do not feed and cloath the Souldier and supply the armies with our own native provisions, by which disorders our treasure will soon be exhausted.

Again,

Again, if we think to bring in store of money by
suffering forraign Coins to pass current at higher
rates than their intrinsick value compared with our
Standard, or by debasing or by enhancing our own
moneys, all these have their several inconveniencies
and difficulties, (which hereafter I will declare), but
admitting that by this means plenty of money might
be brought into the Realm, yet should we be nothing
the richer, neither can such treasure so gotten long
remain with us. For if the stranger or the English
Merchants bring in this money, it must be done upon
a valuable consideration, either for wares carried out
already, or after to be exported, which helps us nothing
except the evil occasions of excess or war aforenamed
be removed which do exhaust our treasure: for otherwise, what one man bringeth for gain, another man
shall be forced to carry out for necessity; because there
shall ever be a necessity to ballance our Accounts with
strangers, although it should be done with loss upon
the rate of the money, and Confiscation also if it be
intercepted by the Law.

*How we must
get Treasure
to make it
our own.* The conclusion of this business is briefly thus. That
as the treasure which is brought into the Realm by
the ballance of our forraign trade is that money which
onely doth abide with us, and by which we are enriched: so by this plenty of money thus gotten (and
no otherwise) do our Lands improve. For when the
Merchant hath a good dispatch beyond the Seas for
his Cloth and other wares, he doth presently return to
buy up the greater quantity, which raiseth the price of
our Woolls and other commodities, and consequently
doth improve the Landlords Rents as the Leases expire
daily: And also by this means money being gained,
and brought more abundantly into the Kingdom, it
doth enable many men to buy Lands, which will make
them the dearer. But if our forraign trade come to a

stop or declination by neglect at home or injuries
abroad, whereby the Merchants are impoverished, and
thereby the wares of the Realm less issued, then do
all the said benefits cease, and our Lands fall of price
daily.

CHAP. VI.

*The Spanish Treasure cannot be kept from other King-
doms by any prohibition made in Spain.*

ALL the Mines of Gold and Silver which are as
yet discovered in the sundry places of the world,
are not of so great value as those of the *West-Indies*
which are in the possession of the King of *Spain :* who
thereby is enabled not onely to keep in subjection
many goodly States and Provinces in *Italy* and elsewhere (which otherwise would soon fall from his obei-
sance) but also by a continual war taking his advantages doth still enlarge his Dominions, ambitiously
aiming at a Monarchy by the power of his Moneys,
which are the very sinews of his strength, that lies
so far dispersed into so many Countreys, yet hereby
united, and his wants supplied both for war and peace
in a plentiful manner from all the parts of Christendom, which are therefore partakers of his treasure by
a Necessity of Commerce; wherein the Spanish policy
hath ever endeavoured to prevent all other Nations
the most it could: For finding *Spain* to be too poor
and barren to supply it self and the *West-Indies* with *The policie*
those varieties of forraign wares whereof they stand in *and benefit of*
need, they knew well that when their Native Com- *Spain by the*
modities come short to this purpose, their Moneys *East Indies.*
must serve to make up the reckoning; whereupon they
found an incredible advantage to adde the traffick of

23   the

the *East-Indies* to the treasure of the *West*: for the last of these being employed in the first, they stored themselves infinitely with rich wares to barter with all the parts of Christendom for their Commodities, and so furnishing their own necessities, prevented others for carrying away their moneys: which in point of state they hold less dangerous to impart to the remote Indians, than to their neighbour Princes, lest it should too much enable them to resist (if not offend) their enemies. And this Spanish policy against others is the more remarkable, being done likewise so much to their own advantage; for every Ryal of Eight which they sent to the *East-Indies* brought home so much wares as saved them the disbursing of five Ryals of Eight here in *Europe* (at the least) to their neighbours, especially in those times when that trade was only in their hands: but now this great profit is failed, and the mischief removed by the English, Dutch, and others which partake in those *East-India* trades as ample as the Spanish Subjects.

It is further to be considered, that besides the disability of the *Spaniards* by their native commodities to provide forraign wares for their necessities, (whereby they are forced to supply the want with mony) they have likewise that canker of war, which doth infinitely exhaust their treasure, and disperse it into Christendom even to their enemies, part by reprisal, but especially through a necessary maintenance of those armies which are composed of strangers, and lie so far remote, that they cannot feed, clothe, or otherwise provide them out of their own native means and provisions, but must

The effects of different wars concerning Treasure. receive this relief from other Nations: which kind of war is far different to that which a Prince maketh upon his own confines, or in his Navies by Sea, where the Souldier receiving mony for his wages, must every day deliver it out again for his necessities, whereby

the

the treasure remains still in the Kingdom, although it be exhausted from the King: But we see that the *Spaniard* (trusting in the power of his Treasure) undertakes wars in *Germany*, and in other remote places, which would soon begger the richest Kingdom in Christendom of all their mony; the want whereof would presently disorder and bring the armies to confusion, as it falleth out sometimes with *Spain* it self, who have the Fountain of mony, when either it is stopt in the passage by the force of their enemies, or drawn out faster than it flows by their own occasions; whereby also we often see that Gold and silver is so scant in *Spain,* that they are forced to use base copper money, to the great confusion of their Trade, and not without the undoing also of many of their own people.

But now that we have seen the occasions by which the Spanish treasure is dispersed into so many places of the world, let us likewise discover how and in what proportion each Countrey doth enjoy these Moneys, for we find that *Turkey* and divers other Nations have great plenty thereof, although they drive no trade with *Spain,* which seems to contradict the former reason, where we say that this treasure is obtained by a Necessity of Commerce. But to clear this point, we must know that all Nations (who have no Mines of their own) are enriched with Gold and Silver by one and the same means, which is already shewed to be the ballance of their forraign Trade: And this is not strictly tyed to be done in those Countries where the fountain of treasure is, but rather with such order and observations as are prescribed. For suppose *England* by trade with *Spain* may gain and bring home five hundred thousand Ryals of 8. yearly, if we lose as much by our trade in *Turkey,* and therefore carry the mony thither, it is not then the *English* but the *Turks* which have got this treasure, although they have no trade with *Spain* from

whence

whence it was first brought. Again, if *England* having thus lost with *Turkey*, do notwithstanding gain twice as much by *France, Italy,* and other members of her general trade, then will there remain five hundred thousand Ryals of eight cleer gains by the ballance of this trade: and this comparison holds between all other Nations, both for the manner of getting, and the proportion that is yearly gotten.

But if yet a question should be made, whether all Nations get treasure and *Spain* only lose it? I answer no; for some Countreys by war or by excess do lose that which they had gotten, as well as *Spain* by war and want of wares doth lose that which was its own.

Chap. VII.

The diversity of gain by Forraign Trade.

IN the course of forraign trade there are three sorts of gain, the first is that of the Commonwealth, which may be done when the Merchant (who is the principal Agent therein) shall lose. The second is the gain of the Merchant, which he doth sometimes justly and worthily effect, although the Commonwealth be a loser. The third is the gain of the King, whereof he is ever certain, even when the Commonwealth and the Merchant shall be both losers.

Concerning the first of these, we have already sufficiently shewed the ways and means whereby a Commonwealth may be enriched in the course of trade, whereof it is needless here to make any repetition, only I do in this place affirm, th at such happiness may be in the Commonwealth, when the Merchant in his particular shall have no occasion to rejoyce. As for example, suppose the *East-India* Company send out

one

one hundred thousand pounds into the *East-Indies*, and receive home for the same the full value of three hundred thousand pounds; Hereby it is evident that this part of the Commonwealth is trebled, and yet I may boldly say that which I can well prove, that the said Company of Merchants shall lose at least fifty thousand pounds by such an adventure if the returns be made in *Spice, Indico, Callicoes, Benjamin, refined Saltpeter,* and such other bulkey wares in their several proportions according to their vent and use in these parts of *Europe.* For the fraight of Shipping, the ensurance of the adventure, the charges of Factors abroad and Officers at home, the forbearance of the Stock, His Majesties Customs and Imposts, with other petty charges incident, cannot be less then two hundred and fifty thousand pounds, which being added to the principal produceth the said loss. And thus we see, that not only the Kingdom but also the King by his Customs and Imposts may get notoriously, even when the Merchant notwithstanding shall lose grievously; which giveth us good occasion here to consider, how much more the Realm is enriched by this noble Trade, when all things pass so happily that the Merchant is a gainer also with the King and Kingdom.

In the next place I affirm, that a Merchant by his laudable endeavours may both carry out and bring in wares to his advantage by selling them and buying them to good profit, which is the end of his labours; when nevertheless the Commonwealth shall decline and grow poor by a disorder in the people, when through Pride and other Excesses they do consume more forraign wares in value then the wealth of the Kingdom can satisfie and pay by the exportation of our own commodities, which is the very quality of an unthrift who spends beyond his means.

Lastly, the King is ever sure to get by trade, when

both

both the Commonwealth and Merchant shall lose severally as afore-written, or joyntly, as it may and doth
sometimes happen, when at one and the same time our
Commodities are over-ballanced by forraign wares consumed, and that the Merchants success prove no better
than is before declared.

But here we must not take the King's gain in this
large sense, for so we might say that His Majesty
should get, although half the trade of the Kingdom
were lost; we will rather suppose that whereas the
whole trade of the Realm for Exportations and Importations is now found for to be about the yearly value
of four millions and a half of pounds; it may be yet
increased two hundred thousand pounds *per annum*
more by the importation and consumption of forraign
wares. By this means we know that the King shall
be a gainer near twenty thousand pounds, but the
Commonwealth shall lose the whole two hundred thousand pounds thus spent in excess. And the Merchant
may be a loser also when the trade shall in this manner
be increased to the profit of the King; who notwithstanding shall be sure in the end to have the greatest
loss, if he prevent not such unthrifty courses as do
impoverish his Subjects.

Chap. VIII.

*The enhansing or debasing our Moneys cannot enrich
the Kingdom with treasure, nor hinder the exportation
thereof.*

THere are three ways by which the Moneys of a
Kingdom are commonly altered. The first is
when the Coins in their several Denominations are
made currant at more or less pounds, shillings or pence
than

than formerly. The second is when the said Coins are altered in their weight, and yet continue currant at the former rates. The third is when the Standard is either debased or enriched in the fineness of the Gold and Silver, yet the Moneys continue in their former values.

In all occasions of want or plenty of Money in the Kingdom we do ever find divers men, who using their wits for a remedy to supply the first and preserve the last, they fall presently upon altering the moneys; for, say they, the raising of the Coins in value will cause it to be brought into the Realm from divers places in hope of the gain: and the debasing of the monies in the fineness or weight will keep it here for fear of the loss. But these men pleasing themselves with the beginning onely of this weighty business, consider not the progress and end thereof, whereunto we ought especially to direct our thoughts and endeavours.

For we must know, that money is not only the true measure of all our other means in the Kingdom, but also of our forraign commerce with strangers, which therefore ought to be kept just and constant to avoid those confusions which ever accompany such alterations. For first at home, if the common measure be changed, our Lands, Leases, wares, both forraign and domestique must alter in proportion: and although this is not done without much trouble and damage also to some men, yet in short time this must necessarily come to pass; for that is not the denomination of our pounds, shillings and pence, which is respected, but the intrinsique value of our Coins; unto which we have little reason to add any further estimation or worth, if it lay in our power to do it, for this would be a special service to *Spain*, and an act against ourselves to indear the commodity of another Prince. Neither can these courses which so much hurt the Subjects,

Money is the measure of our other means.

A notable service for Spain.

29   any

any way help the King as some men have imagined: for although the debasing or lightning of all our mony should bring a present benefit (for once only) to the Mint, yet all this and more would soon be lost again in the future great In-comes of His Majesty, when by this means they must be paid yearly with mony of less intrinsique value than formerly; Nor can it be said that the whole loss of the Kingdom would be the profit of the King, they differ infinitely; for all mens estates (be it leases, lands, debts, wares or mony) must suffer in their proportions, whereas His Majesty should have the gain only upon so much ready mony as might be new Coined, which in comparison, would prove a very small matter : for although they who have other estates in mony are said to be a great number, and to be worth five or ten thousand *l. per* man, more or less, which amounts to many millions in all, yet are they not possessed thereof all together or at once, for it were vanity and against their profit to keep continually in their hands above forty or fifty pounds in a family to defray necessary charges, the rest must ever run from man to man in traffique for their benefit, whereby we may conceive that a little mony (being made the measure of all our other means) doth rule and distribute great matters daily to all men in their just proportions: And we must know likewise that much of our old mony is worn light, and therefore would yield little or no profit at the Mint, and the gain upon the heavy, would cause our vigilant neighbours to carry over a great part thereof, and return it presently in pieces of the new stamp; nor do we doubt that some of our own Countrymen would turn Coiners and venter a hanging for this profit, so that His Majesty in the end should get little by such alterations.

Yea but say some men, If His Majesty raise the mony, great store of treasure would also be brought

All the ready mony in this Kingdom is esteemed at little more than one million of pounds.

into

into the Mint from forraign parts, for we have seen by experience that the late raising of our Gold ten in the hundred, did bring in great store thereof, more than we were accustomed to have in the Kingdom, the which as I cannot deny, so do I likewise affirm, that this Gold carried away all or the most part of our Silver, (which was not over-worn or too light) as we may easily perceive by the present use of our Moneys in their respective qualities: and the reason of this change is, because our Silver was not raised in proportion with our Gold, which still giveth advantage to the Merchant to bring in the Kingdoms yearly gain by trade in Gold rather in Silver.

Secondly, if we be inconstant in our Coins, and thereby violate the Laws of forraign Commerce, other Princes are vigilant in these cases to alter presently in proportion with us, and then where is our hope? or if they do not alter, what can we hope for? For if the stranger-merchant bring in his wares, and find that our moneys are raised, shall not he likewise keep his Commodities untill he may sell them dearear? and shall not the price of the Merchants exchange with forraign Countries rise in proportion with our Moneys? All which being undoubtedly true, why may not our Moneys be carried out of the Kingdom as well and to as much profit after the raising thereof, as before the alteration?

But peradventure some men will yet say, that if our Moneys be raised and other Countries raise not, it will cause more Bullion and forraign Coines to be brought in than heretofore. If this be done, it must be performed either by the Merchant who hath exported wares, or by the Merchant who intends to buy off our Commodities: and it is manifest that neither of these can have more advantage or benefit by this Art now, than they might have had before the alteration of the

Money.

Money. For if their said Bullion and forraign Coins
be more worth than formerly in our pounds, shillings
and pence, yet what shall they get by that when these
moneys are baser or lighter, and that therefore they
are risen in proportion? So we may plainly see that
these Innovations are no good means to bring treasure
into the Kingdom, nor yet to keep it here when we
have it.

Chap. IX.

*A Toleration for Forraign Coins to pass currant here
at higher rates then their value with our Standard,
will not encrease our Treasure.*

THe discreet Merchant for the better directing of
his trade and his exchanges by bills to and from
the several places of the world where he is accustomed
to deal, doth carefully learn the Parity or equal value

Merchants do of the monies according to their weight and fineness
or ought to compared with our Standard, whereby he is able to
know the know perfectly the just profit or loss of his affairs.
weight and And I make no doubt but that we trade to divers
fineness of places where we vent off our native commodities yearly,
forraign to a great value, and yet find few or no wares there
Coins. fitting our use, whereby we are enforced to make our
returns in ready mony, which by us is either carried
into some other Countries to be converted into wares
which we want, or else it is brought into the Realm
in Specie; which being tolerated to pass current here
in payment at higher rates then they are worth to be
Coined into sterling mony; that seemeth very probable
that the greater quantity will be brought in : but when
all the circumstances are duly considered, this course
likewise will be found as weak as the rest to encrease
our Treasure.

First,

First, the toleration it self doth break the laws of entercourse, and would soon move other Princes to perform the same acts or worse against us, and so frustrate our hopes.

Secondly, if mony be the true measure of all our other means, and forraign Coins tollerated to pass current amongst us, at higher rates than they are worth (being compared with our Standard) it followeth that the common wealth shall not be justly distributed, when it passeth by a false measure.

Thirdly, if the advantage between ours and forraign Coins be but small, it will bring in little or no Treasure, because the Merchant will rather bring in wares upon which there is usually a competent gaine. And on the other side if we permit a great advantage to the forraign Coins, then that gain will carry away all our starling mony, and so I leave this business in a *Dilemma*, and fruitless, as all other courses will ever prove which seek for the gain or loss of our treasure out of the ballance of our general forraign trade, as I will endeavour yet further to demonstrate.

CHAP. X.

The observation of the Statute of Imployments to be made by strangers, cannot encrease, nor yet preserve our Treasure.

TO keep our mony in the Kingdom is a work of no less skill and difficulty than to augment our Treasure: for the causes of their preservation and production are the same in nature. The statute for employment of strangers wares into our commodities seemeth at the first to be a good and a lawful way leading to those ends: but upon th' examination of

33   the

the particulars, we shall find that it cannot produce such good effects.

*The use of
Forraign
Trade is
alike to all
Nations.*
For as the use of forraign trade is alike unto all Nations, so may we easily perceive what will be done therein by strangers, when we do but observe our own proceedings in this waighty business, by which we do not only seek with the vent of our own commodities to supply our wants of forraign wares, but also to enrich our selves with treasure: all which is done by a different manner of trading according to our own occasions and the nature of the places whereunto we do trade; as namely in some Countrys we sell our commodities and bring away their wares, or part in mony; in other Countreys we sell our goods and take their mony, because they have little or no wares that fits our turns, again in some places we have need of their commodities, but they have little use of ours; so they take our mony which we get in other Countreys: And thus by a course of traffick (which changeth according to the accurrents of time) the particular members do accommodate each other, and all accomplish the whole body of the trade, which will ever languish if the harmony of her health be distempered by the discases *How forraign* of excess at home, violence abroad, charges and restric-
*Trade is
destroyed.*
tions at home or abroad: but in this place I have occasion to speak only of restriction, which I will perform briefly.

There are three ways by which a Merchant may make the returns of his wares from beyond the Seas, that is to say in mony, in commodities, or by Exchange. But the Statute of employment doth not only restrain mony (in which there is a seeming providence and Justice) but also the use of the Exchange by bills, which doth violate the Law of Commerce, and is indeed an Act without example in any place of the world where we have trade, and therefore to be considered,

34   that

that whatsoever (in this kind) we shall impose upon
strangers here, will presently be made a Law for us in
their Countreys, especially where we have our greatest.
trade with our vigilant neighbours, who omit no care
nor occasion to support their traffique in equal privileges with other Nations. And thus in the first place
we should be deprived of that freedom and means
which now we have to bring Treasure into the Kingdom, and therewith likewise we should lose the vent of
much wares which we carry to divers places, whereby
our trade and our Treasure would decay together.

Secondly, if by the said Statute we thrust the
exportation of our wares (more than ordinary) upon
the stranger, we must then take it from the *English*,
which were injurious to our Merchants, Mariners and
Shipping, besides the hurt to the Commonwealth in
venting the Kingdoms stock to the stranger at far
lower rates here than we must do if we sold it to them
in their own Countreys, as is proved in the third
Chapter.

Thirdly, whereas we have already sufficiently shewed,
that if our commodities be over ballanced in value by
forraign wares, our mony must be carried out. How
is it possible to prevent this by tying the Strangers
hands, and leaving the English loose? shall not the
same reasons and advantage cause that to be done by
them now, that was done by the other before? or if
we will make a statute (without example) to prevent
both alike, shall we not then overthrow all at once?
the King in his customes and the Kingdom in her
profits; for such a restriction must of necessity destroy
much trade, because the diversity of occasions and
places which make an ample trade require that some
men should both export and import wares; some export
only, others import, some deliver out their monies by
exchange, others take it up; some carry out mony,

35

others

others bring it in, and this in a greater or lesser quantity according to the good husbandry or excess in the Kingdom, over which only if we keep a strict law, it will rule all the rest, and without this all other Statutes are no rules either to keep or procure us Treasure.

Lastly, to leave no Objection unanswered, if it should be said that a Statute comprehending the English as well as the stranger must needs keep our money in the Kingdom.   What shall we get by this, if it hinder the coming in of money by the decay of that ample Trade which we enjoyed in the freedom thereof? is not the Remedy far worse than the Disease? shall we not live more like Irishmen than Englishmen, when the Kings revenues, our Merchants, Mariners, Shipping, Arts, Lands, Riches, and all decay together with our Trade?

Yea but, say some men, we have better hopes than so; for th' intent of the Statute is, that as all the forraign wares which are brought in shall be imployed in our commodities, thereby to keep our money in the Kingdom: So we doubt not but to send out a sufficient quantity of our own wares over and above to bring in the value thereof in ready money.

Although this is absolutely denied by the reasons afore written, yet now we will grant it, because we desire to end the dispute: For if this be true, that other Nations will vent more of our commodittes than we consume of theirs in value, then I affirm that the overplus must necessarily return unto us in treasure without the use of the Statute, which is therefore not onely fruitless but hurtful, as some other like restrictions are found to be when they are fully discovered.

36   Chap.

Chap. XI.

It will not increase our treasure to enjoyn the Merchant that exporteth Fish, Corn or Munition, to return all or part of the value in Money.

Victuals and Munition for war are so pretious in a Commonwealth, that either it seemeth necessary to restrain the exportation altogether, or (if the plenty permits it) to require the return thereof in so much treasure: which appeareth to be reasonable and without difficulty, because *Spain* and other Countries do willingly part with their money for such wares, although in other occasions of trade they straightly prohibit the exportation thereof: all which I grant to be true, yet notwithstanding we must consider that all the ways and means which (in course of trade) force treasure into the Kingdom, do not therefore make it ours: for this can be done onely by a lawful gain, and this gain is no way to be accomplished but by the overballance of our trade, and this overballance is made less by restrictions: therefore such restrictions do hinder the increase of our treasure. The Argument is plain, and needs no other reasons to strengthen it, except any man be so vain to think that restrictions would not cause the less wares to be exported. But if this likewise should be granted, yet to enjoyn the Merchant to bring in money for Victuals and Munition carried out, will not cause us to have one peny the more in the Kingdom at the years end; for whatsoever is forced in one way must out again another way: because onely so much will remain and abide with us as is gained and incorporated into the estate of the Kingdom by the overballance of the trade.

Some restrictions hinder Trade.

This may be made plain by an example taken from

37 an

an Englishman, who had occasion to buy and consume
the wares of divers strangers for the value of six
hundred pounds, and having wares of his own for the
value of one thousand pounds, he sold them to the
said strangers, and presently forced all the mony from
them into his own power; yet upon cleering of the
reckoning between them there remained onely four
hundred pounds to the said Englishman for overballance of the wares bought and sold; so the rest
which he had received was returned back from whence
he forced it. And this shall suffice to shew that
whatsoever courses we take to force money into the
Kingdom, yet so much onely will remain with us as
we shall gain by the ballance of our trade.

Chap. XII.

*The undervaluing of our Money which is delivered or
received by Bills of Exchange here or beyond the
Seas, cannot decrease our treasure.*

THe Merchants Exchange by Bills is a means and
practice whereby they that have money in one
Countrey may deliver the same to receive it again in
another Countrey at certain times and rates agreed
upon, whereby the lender and the borrower are accom-
modated without transporting of treasure from State
to State.

These Exchanges thus made between man and man,
are not contracted at the equal value of the moneys,
according to their respective weights and fineness:
First, because he that delivereth his money doth respect
the venture of the debt, and the time of forbearance;
but that which causeth an under or overvaluing of
moneys by Exchange, is the plenty or scarcity thereof

in

in those places where the Exchanges are made. For example, when here is plenty of money to be delivered for *Amsterdam*, then shall our money be undervalued in Exchange, because they who take up the money, seeing it so plentifully thrust upon them, do thereby make advantage to themselves in taking the same at an undervalue.

And contrariwise, when here is scarcity of money to be delivered for *Amsterdam*, the deliverer will make the same advantage by overvaluing our money which he delivereth. And thus we see that as plenty or scarcity of mony in a Common-wealth doth make all things dear or good cheap: so in the course of exchange it hath ever a contrary working; wherefore in the next place it is fit to set down the true causes of this effect.

Plenty of Mony makes the Exchange cheap, and all other things dear.

As plenty or scarcity of mony do make the price of the exchange high or low, so the over or under ballance of our trade doth effectually cause the plenty or scarcity of mony: And here we must understand, that the ballance of our trade is either General or Particular. The General is, when all our yearly traffique is jointly valued, as I have formerly shewed; the particular is when our trade to *Italy, France, Turkey, Spain,* and other Countreys are severally considered: and by this latter course we shall perfectly find out the places where our mony is under or overvalued in Exchange: For although our general exportations of wares may be yearly more in value than that which is imported, whereby the difference is made good to us in so much treasure; nevertheless the particular trades do work diversly: For peradventure the *Low Countreys* may bring us more in value than we sell them, which if it be so, then do the *Low Countrey* Merchants not only carry away our treasure to ballance the accompt between us, but also by this means mony being plen-

What kinds of plenty or scarcity of money make the Exchange high or low.

tiful

tiful here to be delivered by exchange, it is therefore undervalued by the takers, as I have before declared; And contrariwise if we carry more wares to *Spain*, and other places than we consume of theirs, then do we bring away their treasure, and likewise in the Merchants exchange we overvalue our own money.

Yet still there are some who will seem to make this plain by Demonstration, that the undervaluing of our money by Exchange doth carry it out of the Kingdom: for, say they, we see daily great store of our English Coins carried over, which pass current in the Low-Countries, and there is great advantage to carry them thither, to save the loss which the Low-Countrymen have in the Exchange; for if one hundred pounds sterling delivered here, is so much undervalued, that ninty pounds of the same sterling money carried over *in specie* shall be sufficient to make repayment and full satisfaction of the said hundred pounds at *Amsterdam*: Is it not then (say they) the undervaluing of our Mony which causeth it to be carried out of the Realm?

To this objection I will make a full and plain Answer, shewing that it is not the undervaluing of our money in exchange, but the overballancing of our trade that carrieth away our treasure. For suppose that our whole trade with the Low-Countries for wares brought into this Realm be performed onely by the Dutch for the value of five hundred thousand pounds yearly; and that all our commodities transported into the said Low-Countries be performed onely by the English for four hundred thousand pounds yearly: Is it not then manifest, that the Dutch can exchange only four hundred thousand pounds with the English upon the *Par pro Pari* or equal value of the respective Standards? So the other hundred thousand pounds which is the over ballance of the trade, they must of necessity carry that away in mony. And the self same loss of treasure must happen if there were no exchange at all permitted: for the *Dutch* carrying away our money for their wares, and we bringing in their forraign Coins for their commodities, there will be still one hundred thousand pounds loss.

Now let us add another example grounded upon the aforesaid proportion of trade between us and the *Low Countreys.* The *Dutch* (as aforewritten) may exchange with the *English* for four hundred thousand pounds and no more upon the equal value of the monies, because the *English* have no further means to satisfie. But now suppose that in respect of the plenty of money, which in this case will be here in the hands of the *Dutch* to deliver by exchange, our mony (according to that which hath been already said) be undervalued ten *per cent.* then is it manifest that the *Dutch* must deliver four hundred and forty thousand pounds to have the Englishmans four hundred thousand pounds in the *Low Countreys:* so that there will then remain but 60000. pounds for the *Dutch* to carry out of the Realm to ballance the accompt between them and us. Whereby we may plainly perceive that the undervaluing of our money in exchange, will not carry it out of the Kingdom, as some men have supposed, but rather is a means to make a less quantity thereof to be exported, than would be done at the *Par pro pari.*

The undervaluing of our mony in Exchange is the Strangers loss and our gain.

Further let us suppose that the English Merchant carrieth out as much wares in value as the Dutch Merchant bringeth in, whereby the means is equal between them to make their returns by exchange without carrying away of any mony to the prejudice of either State. And yet notwithstanding the Dutch Merchant for his occasions or advantage will forsake this course of exchange, and will venture to send part of his returns in ready mony.

To this the answer is, that hereupon it must follow

41   of

of necessity, that the Dutch shall want just so much means in exchange with the English, who therefore shall be forced to bring in the like sum of mony from beyond the Seas, as the *Dutch* carried out of this Realm; so that we may plainly perceive that the monies which are carried from us within the ballance of our trade are not considerable, for they do return to us again: and we lose those monies only which are made of the over-ballance of our general trade, that is to say, That which we spend more in value in forraign wares, than we utter of our own commodities. And the contrary of this is the only means by which we get our treasure. In vain thereforefore hath *Gerard Malynes* laboured so long, and in so many printed books to make the world beleeve that the undervaluing of our money in exchange doth exhaust our treasure, which is a mere fallacy of the cause, attributing that to a Secondary means, whose effects are wrought by another Principal Efficient, and would also come to pass although the said Secondary means were not at all. As vainly also hath he propounded a remedy by keeping the price of Exchange by Bills at the *par pro pari* by publick Authority, which were a new-found Office without example in any part of the world, being not only fruitless but also hurtful, as hath been sufficiently proved in this Chapter, and therefore I will proceed to the next.

Marginal notes:
1 *The Canker of* Englands *Common-wealth.*
2 *Free trade.*
3 Lex Mercatoria.
4 *The Centre of trade.*

CHAP. XIII.

The Merchant who is a mere Exchanger of money by Bills cannot increase or decrease our treasure.

THere are certain Merchants which deal onely upon all advantages in th' Exchange, and neither

export

export nor import wares into the Kingdom, which hath caused some men to affirm, that the money which such mere Exchangers bring in or carry out of the Realm is not comprehended in the ballance of our forraign trade; for (say they) sometimes when our sterling mony hath been undervalued and delivered here for *Amsterdam* at 10. *per cent.* less than the equal value of the respective Standards, the said mere Exchanger may take here one thousand pounds sterling, & and carry over onely nine hundred thereof *in specie*, which will be sufficient to pay his Bill of Exchange. And so upon a greater or a lesser summe the like gain is made in three months time.

But here we must know, that although this mere Exchanger deal not in wares, yet notwithstanding the money which he carrieth away in manner afore-written must necessarily proceed of such wares as are brought into the Kingdom by Merchants. So that still it falleth into the ballance of our forraign trade, and worketh the same effect, as if the Merchant himself had carried away that money, which he must do if our wares be overballanced, as ever they are when our money is undervalued, which is expressed more at large in the 12. Chapter.

And on the contrary, when the mere Exchanger (by the said advantages) shall bring money into the Kingdom, he doth no more than necessarily must be done by the Merchant himself when our commodities overballance forraign wares. But in these occasions some Merchants had rather lose by delivering their money at an under-value in Exchange, than undertake to hazard all by the Law; which notwithstanding these mere Exchangers will perform for them in hope of gain.

CHAP.

CHAP. XIV.

*The admirable feats supposed to be done by Bankers
and the Merchants Exchange.*

ALthough I have already written something concerning the Merchants Exchange, and therein of
the undervaluation of our money, and of the mere
Exchanger, with their true causes and effects; Nevertheless it will not be impertinent to pursue this business yet a little further, and thereby not only to
strengthen our former Arguments, but also to avoid
some cunning delusions which might deceive the unskilful Reader of those books entituled, *Lex Mercatoria,
pag.* 409. and *The maintenance of free trade, pag.* 16.
wherein the Author *Gerard Malynes* setteth down the
admirable feats (as he termeth them) which are to be
done by Bankers and Exchangers, with the use and
power of the Exchange: but how these wonders may
be effected he altogether omitteth, leaving the Reader
in a strange opinion of these dark mysteries, which
I cannot think he did for want of knowledge, for I
find him skilful in many things which he hath both
written and collected concerning th' affairs of Merchants, and in particular he discourses well of divers
uses, forms and passages of the Exchange, in all which
as he hath taken great pains for the good of others, so
do his Works of this kind deserve much praise: but
where he hath disguised his own knowledge with
Sophistry to further some private ends by hurting the
public good; there ought he to be discovered and
prevented, unto which performance (in this discourse
of treasure) I find my self obliged, and therefore I
intend to effect it by shewing the true causes and
means whereby these wonders are done, which *Malines*

　　　　　　　　　　　attributeth

attributeth to the sole power of the Exchange. But first for order I think it fit to set down the particular feats as they stand in his said books.

The admirable feats to be done by Exchange.

1. To lay their mony with gain in any place of the world where any exchange lyeth.

2. To gain and wax rich, and never meddle with any Princes commodities.

3. To buy any Princes commodity, and never bring penny nor pennyworth into the Realm, but doe that with the Subjects mony.

4. To grow rich and live without adventure at Sea or travaile.

5. To do great feats having credit, and yet to be nought worth.

6. To understand whether in conjecture their mony employed on Exchange, or buying of wares, will be more profit.

7. To know certainly what the Merchants gain upon their wares they sell and buy.

8. To live and encrease upon every Princes subjects that continually take up mony by Exchange, and whether they gain or no.

9. To wind out every Princes treasure out of his Realm whose Subjects bring in more wares than they carry out of the Realm.

10. To make the Staple of money run thither where the rich Prince will have it to be brought, and pay for it.

11. To unfurnish the poor Prince of his provision of mony, that keeps his wares upon interest mony, if the enemy will seek it.

12. To furnish their need of mony that tarry the selling of their wares in any Contract untill they make them come to their price.

45 13. To

13. To take up mony to engross any commodity either new come or whereof they have some store, to bring the whole trade of that commodity into their own hands to sell both at their pleasure.

14. To hide their carrying away of any Princes mony.

15. To fetch away any Princes fine money with his own or any other Princes base money.

16. To take up Princes base mony and to turn into his fine mony, and to pay the deliverer with his own, and gain too.

17. To take upon credit into their hands for a time all the Merchants mony that will be delivered, and pay them with their own, and gain too.

☞ 18. To make the Realm gain of all other Realms whose Subjects live most by their own commodities, and sell yearly the overpluss into the world, and both occupie that encrease yearly, and also their old store of treasure upon exchange.

19. To undoe Realms and Princes that look not to their Commonwealth, when the Merchants wealth is such, that the great houses conspire together so to rule the Exchange, that when they will be deliverers, they will receive in another place above the Standard of the Mint of the Princes mony delivered: and when they will be takers, they will pay the same in another place under the Standard of the Mint of the Princes money taken up.

20. To get ready mony to buy any commodity that is offered cheap.

21. To compass ready mony to get any offered bargain out of another mans hands, and so by out-bidding others oftentimes to raise the wares.

22. To get a part and sometimes all his gains that employeth mony taken up by Exchange in wares, and so make others travail for their gain.

23. To

23. To keep Princes for having any Customs, Subsidies or Taxes upon their mony, as they employ it not.

24. To value justly any Wares they carry into any Countrey by setting them at that value, as the mony that bought them was then at by Exchange in the Countrey whither they be carried.

If I had a desire to amplifie in the explanation of these wonders, they would afford me matter enough to make a large volume, but my intent is to do it as briefly as possibly I may without obscurity. And before I begin, I cannot chuse but laugh to think how a worthy Lawyer might be dejected in his laudable studies, when he should see more cunning in *Lex Mercatoria* by a little part of the Merchants profession, then in all the Law-cases of his learned Authors: for this Exchange goes beyond *Conjuring*; I think verily that neither Doctor *Faustus* nor *Banks* his Horse could ever do such admirable feats, although it is sure they had a Devil to help them; but wee Merchants deal not with such Spirits, we delight not to be thought the workers of lying wonders, and therefore I endeavour here to shew the plainness of our dealing (in these supposed feats) to be agreeable to the laudable course of Trade.

And first, *To lay our Money with gaine to any place of the World where Exchange lieth.* How can this be done (will some men say) for *Amsterdam*, when the losse by Exchange is sometimes eight or ten *per cent.* more or lesse for one moneths usance? The answer is, That here I must consider, first, that the principal efficient cause of this loss, is a greater value in Wares brought from *Amsterdam* then we carry thither, which make more Deliverers then Takers here by Exchange, whereby the Money is undervalued to the benefit of the

The principal efficient cause of loss by Exchange.

taker:

taker: hereupon the Deliverer, rather then he will lose by his Money, doth consider those Countreys, unto which we carry more Wares in value than we receive from them; as namely, *Spain, Italy,* and others; to which places he is sure (for the reasons aforesaid) that he shall ever deliver his money with profit. But now you will say, that the money is further from *Amsterdam* than before; How shall it be got together? yes, well enough; and the farther about will prove the nearest way home, if it come at last with good profit; the first part whereof being made (as we have supposed) in *Spain,* from thence I consider where to make my second gain, and finding that the *Florentines* send out a greater value in cloth of Gold and Silver, wrought Silks, and Rashes to *Spain,* than they receive in Fleece Woolls, West-India Hides, Sugar and Cochineal, I know I cannot miss of my purpose by delivering my money for *Florence;* where (still upon the same ground) I direct my course from thence to *Venice,* and there finde that my next benefit must be at *Frankfort* or *Antwerp,* untill at last I come to *Amsterdam* by a shorter or longer course, according to such occasions of advantage as the times and places shall afford me. And thus we see still, that the profit and loss upon the Exchange is guided and ruled by the over or under ballance of the several Trades which are Predominant and Active, making the price of Exchange high or low, which is therefore Passive, the contrary whereof is so often repeated by the said *Malines.*

To the second, fourth, fourteenth, and twenty-third, I say, that all these are the proper works of the meer Exchanger; and that his actions cannot work to the good or hurt of the Commonwealth, I have already sufficiently shewed in the last Chap. and therefore here I may spare that labour.

To the third. It is true, I can deliver one thousand

pounds

pounds here by exchauge to receive the value in *Spaine*, where with this Spanish money I can buy and bring away so much Spanish wares. But all this doth not prove, but that in the end the English money or commodities must pay for the said wares: for if I deliver my thousand pounds here to an English-man, he must pay me in *Spain*, either by goods already sent or to be sent thither; or if I deliver it here to a Spaniard, he takes it of me, with intent to employ it in our wares; so that every way we must pay the Stranger for what we have from him: Is there any feats in all this worthy our admiration?

To the fifth, thirteenth, twentieth, and twenty first, I must answer these Wonders by heaps, where I finde them to be all one matter in divers formes, and such froth also, that every Idiot knowes them, and can say, that he who hath credit can contract, buy, sell, and take up much money by Exchange, which he may do as well also at Interest: yet in these courses they are not alwayes gainers, for sometimes they live by the losse, as well as they who have less credit.

To the sixth and seventh. Here is more poor stuff; for when I know the current price of my Wares, both here and beyond the Seas, I may easily conjecture whether the profit of the Exchange or the gain which I expect upon my Wares will be greater. And again, as every Merchant knows well what he gains upon the Wares he buyeth and selleth, so may any other man do the like that can tell how the said Merchant hath proceeded: But what is all this to make us admire the Exchange?

To the eighth and twelfth. As Bankers and Exchangers do furnish men with money for their occasions, so do they likewise who let out their money at interest with the same hopes and like advantage,

which

which many times notwithstanding fails them, as well
as the Borrowers often labour onely for the Lenders
profit.

To the ninth and eighteenth.   Here my Author hath
some secret meaning, or being conscious of his own
errours, doth mark these two Wonders with a ☞ in
the Margin.   For why should this great work of enriching or impoverishing of Kingdomes be attributed
to the Exchange, which is done onely by those means
that doe over or under-ballance our Forraign Trade,
as I have already so often shewed, and as the very
words of *Malynes* himself in these two places may
intimate to a judicious Reader?

To the fifteenth and sixteenth, I confess that the
Exchange may be used in turning base money into
Gold or Silver, as when a stranger may coin and bring
over a great quantity of Farthings, which in short time
he may disperse or convert into good money, and then
deliver the same here by exchange to receive the value
in his own Countrey; or he may do this feat by
carrying away the said good mony *in specie* without
using the exchange at all, if he dare venture the
penalty of the Law.   The Spaniards know well who
are the common Coiners of Christendome, that dare
venture to bring them store of Copper money of the
Spanish stamp, and carry away the value in good Ryals
of Eight, wherein notwithstanding all their cunning
devices, they are sometimes taken tardie.

To the 17.   The Bankers are always ready to receive
such sums of mony as are put into their hands by
men of all degrees, who have no skill or good means
themselves to manage the same upon the exchange to
profit.   It is likewise true that the Bankers do repay
all men with their own, and yet reserve good gain to
themselves, which they do as well deserve for their

                                                   ordinary

ordinary provision or allowance as those Factors do
which buy or sell for Merchants by Commission: And
is not this likewise both just and very common?

To the 11. I must confess that here is a wonder Lex Merca-
indeed, that a poor Prince should keep either his wars toria, *pag.*
or wares (I take both together as the Author sets them *Maintenance*
down both ways differing in his said two books) upon *of free trade*
interest mony; for what needs the Enemy of such *p. 17.*
a poor Prince deale with the Bankers to disapoint him
or defeat him of his mony in time of want, when the
interest it self will do this fast enough, and so I leave
this poor stuff.

To the 19. I have lived long in *Italy*, where the
greatest Banks and Bankers of Christendom do trade,
yet could I never see nor hear, that they did, or were
able to rule the price of Exchange by confederacie,
but still the plenty or scarcity of mony in the course
of trade did always overrule them and made the
Exchanges to run at high or low rates.

To the 22. The Exchange by bills between Mer- *Exchange*
chant and Merchant in the course of trade cannot *hinders not*
hinder Princes of their Customs and Imposts: for the *their cus-*
mony which one man delivereth, because he will not, *toms.*
or hath not occasion to employ it in wares, another
man taketh, because he either will or hath already
laid it out in Merchandize. But it is true, that when
the wealth of a Kingdom consisteth much in ready
mony, and that there is also good means and con-
veniencie in such a Kingdom to trade with the same
into forraign parts, either by Sea or Land, or by both
these ways; if then this trade be neglected, the King
shall be defeated of those profits: and if the exchange
be the cause thereof, then must we learn in what
manner this is done; for we may exchange either
amongst our selves, or with strangers; if amongst our
selves, the Commonwealth cannot be enriched thereby;

51   for

for the gain of one subject is the loss of another. And if we exchange with strangers, then our profit is the gain of the Commonwealth. Yet by none of these ways can the King receive any benefit in his customes. Let us therefore seek out the places where such exchanging is used, and set down the reasons why this practice is permitted; in search whereof we shall only find one place of note in all Christendome, which is *Genoua*, whereof I intend to say something as briefly as I can.

The present estate of the commonwealth of Genoua.

The State of *Genoua* is small, and not very fertile, having little natural wealth or materials to employ the people, nor yet victuals sufficient to feed them; but nevertheless by their industry in former times by forraign trade into *Ægypt, Soria, Constantinople,* and all those Levant parts for Spices, Drugs, raw Silks and many other rich wares, with which they served the most places of *Europe,* they grew to an incredible wealth, which gave life unto the strength of their Cities, the pomp of their buildings, and other singular beauties. But after the foundation and encrease of that famous City of *Venice,* the said trades turned that way. And since likewise the greatest part thereof doth come into *England, Spain,* and the *Low Countreys* by navigation directly from the *East Indies,* which alterations in the traffique, hath forced them of *Genoua* to change their course of trading with wares, into exchanging of their mony; which for gain they spread not only into divers Countreys where the trade is performed with Merchandize, but more especially they do therewith serve the want of the *Spaniards* in *Flanders* and other places for their wars, whereby the private Merchants are much enriched, but the publique treasure by this course is not encreased, and the reasons why the Commonwealth of *Genoua* doth suffer this inconvenience, are these.

52   First

First and principally, they are forced to leave those trades which they cannot keep from other Nations, who have better means by situation, wares, Shipping, Munition and the like, to perform these affairs with more advantage than they are able to doe.

Secondly, they proceed like a wise State, who still retain as much trade as they can, although they are not able to procure the twentieth part of that which they had. For having few or no materials of their own to employ their people, yet they supply this want by the Fleece-wools of *Spain,* and raw Silks of *Sicilia,* working them into Velvets, Damasks, Sattens, Woollen-drapery, and other manufactures.

Thirdly, whereas they find no means in their own Countrey to employ and trade their great wealth to profit, they content themselves to do it in *Spain* and other places, either in Merchandize, or by exchanging their monies for gain to those Merchants who trade therewith in wares. And thus wheresoever they live abroad for a time circuiting the world for gain; yet in the end the Center of this profit is in their own Native Countrey.

Lastly, the government of *Genoua* being *Aristocracie,* they are assured that although the publique get little, yet if their private Merchants gain much from strangers, they shall doe well enough, because the *richest* and *securest Treasure of a Free State, are the riches of the Nobility* (who in *Genoua* are Merchants) which falleth not out so in a Monarchy, where between the comings in of a Prince, and the means of Private Men, there is this distinction of *meum & tuum,* but in the occasions and dangers of a Republick or Commonwealth, where Liberty and Government might be changed into Servitude, there the *Proper substance of private men is the publique Treasure,* ready to be spent with their lives in defence of their own Soveraignty.

58

To the 24. If a Merchant should buy wares here with intentions to send them for *Venice*, and then value them as the Exchange comes from thence to *London*, he may find himself far wide of his reckoning: for before his goods arrive at *Venice*, both the price of his Wares and the rate of the Exchange may alter very much. But if the meaning of the Author be, that this valuation may be made after the goods arrive, and are sold at *Venice*, and the money remitted hither by Exchange, or else the money which bought the said wares here may be valued as the Exchange passed at that time from hence to *Venice;* Is not all this very common and easie business, unworthy to be put into the number of *Admirable feats?*

To the tenth. Although a rich Prince hath great power, yet is there not power in every rich Prince to make the staple of Money run where he pleaseth: for the Staple of any thing is not where it may be had, but where the thing doth most of all abound. Where-upon we commonly say, that the Spaniard, in regard of his great treasure in the *West Indies*, hath the Fountain or Staple of money, which he moveth and causeth to run into *Italy, Germany*, the *Low Countreys*, or other places where his occasions doe require it, either for Peace or War. Neither is this effected by any singular Power of the Exchange, but by divers wayes and means fitting those places where the money is to be employed. For if the use thereof be upon the confines of *France* to maintain a War there, then may it be safely sent *in specie* on Carriages by Land; if in *Italy*, on Gallies by Sea; if in the *Low Countreys*, on Shipping by Sea also, but yet with more danger, in regard of his potent enemies in that passage. Where-fore in this occasion, although the Exchange is not absolutely necessary, yet is it very useful. And because the Spaniards want of Commodities from *Germany* and

the

the *Low Countreys* is greater in value than the Spanish Wares which are carried into those parts, therefore the King of *Spain* cannot be furnished there from his own subjects with money by exchange, but is and hath been a long time enforc'd to carry a great part of his treasure in Gallies for *Italy*, where the Italians, and amongst them the Merchants of *Genoua* especially, do take the same, and repay the value thereof in *Flanders*, whereunto they are enabled by their great trade with many rich commodities which they send continually out of *Italy* into those Countreys and the places thereabouts, from whence the Italians return no great value in wares, but deliver their money for the service of *Spain*, and receive the value by Exchange in *Italy* out of the Spanish Treasure, which is brought thither in Gallies, as is afore-written.

How the Italians are enabled to furnish Spain with money in Flanders.

So that by this we plainly see, that it is not the *power of Exchange* that doth enforce treasure where the rich Prince will have it, but it is the money proceeding of wares in Forraigne trade that doth enforce the exchange, and rules the price thereof high or low, according to the plenty or scarcity of the said money; which in this discourse, upon all occasions, I think I have repeated neer as often as *Malynes* in his Books doth make the Exchange to be an essential part of trade, to be *active, predominant, over-ruling the price of Wares and Moneys, life, spirit, and the worker of admirable feats.* All which we have now briefly expounded; and let no man admire why he himself did not take this pains, for then he should not onely have taken away the great opinion which he laboured to maintain of the Exchange, but also by a true discovery of the right operation thereof, he should utterly have overthrown his *par pro pari;* which project (if it had prevailed) would have been a good business for the Dutch, and to the great hurt of

this

this Common-wealth, as hath been sufficiently proved in the 12. chapter.

Now therefore let the learned Lawyer fall cheerfully to his books again, for the Merchant cannot put him down, if he have no more skill than is in his Exchange. Are these such *admirable feats,* when they may be so easily known and done in the course of trade? Well then, if by this discovery we have eased the Lawyers minde, and taken off the edge of his admiration, let him now play his part, and take out a *Writ of Errour* against the *Par pro Pari;* for this project hath mis-informed many, and put us to trouble to expound these Riddles.

Nay, but stay awhile, can all this pass for current, to slight a business thus, which (the Author saith) hath been so seriously observed by that famous Council, and those worthy Merchants of Queen *Elizabeth* of blessed memory, and also condemned by those French Kings, *Lewis* the 9th. *Philip the fair,* and *Philip de Valois,* with confiscation of the Bankers goods? I must con-fess that all this requires an answer, which in part is already done by the Author himself. For he saith, that the wisdome of our State found out the evil, but they missed of the remedy; and yet what remedy this should be no man can tell; for there was none applyed, but all practise and use in Exchange stand still to this day in such manner and form as they did at the time when these Feats were discovered, for the State knew well that there needed no remedy where there was no disease.

Well then, how shall we be able to answer the proceedings of the French Kings who did absolutely condemn the Bankers, and confiscated their goods? Yes, well enough, for the Bankers might perhaps be condemned for something done in their exchanges against the Law, and yet their profession may still be

lawful

lawful, as it is in *Italy* and *France* it self to this day. Nay we will grant likewise that the Banks were banished, when the Bankers were punished; yet all this proves nothing against Exchangers, for Kings and States enact many Statutes, and suddenly repeale them, they do and undo; Princes may err, or else *Malynes* is grossly mistaken, where he setteth down 35. several Statutes and other ordinances enacted by this State in 350. years time to remedy the decay of Trade, and yet all are found defective; only his reformation of the Exchange, or *Par pro pari*, is effectual, if we would believe him; but we know better, and so we leave him.

Maintenance of free trade, p. 76, 77, 78, and 79.

I might here take occasion to say something against another project of the same brood that lately attended upon the success of this *Par pro pari*, as I have been credibly informed, which is, the changing and re-changing here within the Realm, of all the Plate, Bullion and Monies, Forraign or Sterling, to pass only by an office called, *The Kings Royal Exchanger, or his Deputies*, paying them a *Peny* upon the value of every *Noble*: which might raise much to their private good, and destroy more to the publique hurt. For it would decay the Kings Coinage, deprive the Kingdom of much Treasure, abridge the Subjects of their just liberty, and utterly overthrow the worthy trade of the *Goldsmiths*, all which being plain and easie to the weakest understandings, I will therefore omit to amplify upon these particulars.

57   CHAP.

Chap. XV.

Of some Excesses and evils in the Commonwealth, which notwithstanding decay not our Trade nor Treasure.

IT is not my intent to excuse or extenuate any the least excess or evil in the Commonwealth, but rather highly to approve and commend that which by others hath been spoken and written against such abuses. Yet in this discourse of Treasure, as I have already set down affirmatively, which are the true causes that may either augment or decrease the same: so is it not impertinent to continue my negative declarations of those enormities and actions which cannot work these effects as some men have supposed. For in redress of this important business, if we mistake the nature of the Malady, we shall ever apply such cures as will at least delay, if not confound the Remedy.

Let us then begin with Usury, which if it might be turned into Charity, and that they who are Rich would lend to the poor freely; it were a work pleasing to Almighty God, and profitable to the Commonwealth. But taking it in the degree it now stands; How can we well say, That as *Usury encreaseth so Trade decreaseth?* For although it is true that some men give over trading, and buy Lands, or put out their Money to use when they are grown rich, or old, or for some other the like occasions; yet for all this it doth not follow, that the quantity of the trade must lessen; for this course in the rich giveth opportunity presently to the *younger & poorer* Merchants to rise in the world, and to enlarge their dealings; to the performance whereof, if they want means of their own, they may, and do, take it up at interest: so that our money lies not dead, it is still traded. How many Merchants,

58   and

and Shop-keepers have begun with little or nothing of their own, and yet are grown very rich by trading with other mens money? do we not know, that when trading is quick and good, many men, by means of their experience, and having credit to take up money at interest, do trade for much more than they are worth of their own stock? by which diligence of the industrious, the affairs of the Common-wealth are increased, the moneys of Widows, Orphans, Lawyers, Gentlemen and others, are employed in the course of Forraign Trade, which themselves have no skill to perform. We find at this present, that notwithstanding the Poverty we are fallen into by the Excesses and Losses of late times, yet that many men have much money in their chests, and know not how to dispose thereof, because the Merchant will not take the same at interest (although at low rates) in regard there is a stop of trade in *Spain* and in *France*, whereby he cannot employ his own meanes, much lesse other mens moneys. So that for these, and some other reasons which might be alledged, we might conclude, contrary to those who affirm, that Trade decreaseth as Usury encreaseth, for they *rise and fall together*.

In the next place, we hear our Lawyers much condemned; the vexation and charges by multiplicity of Sutes do exceed all the other Kingdomes of *Christendome*, but whether this proceed from the Lawyers Covetousness, or the Peoples Perverseness, it is a great question. And let this be as it may, I will inquire no farther therein than our present discourse doth require, concerning the decay of our Trade, and impoverishing of the Kingdom: Sure I am, that Sutes in Law make many a man poor and penniless, but how it should make us trade for less by one single penny, I cannot well conceive. For although amongst the great number of them who are vexed and undone by controversies,

versies, there be ever some Merchants; yet we know,
that one mans necessity becomes another mans opportunity. I never knew as yet, a decay in our Trade
and Treasure for want of Merchants, or Means to
employ us, but rather by excessive Consumption of
Forraign Wares at home, or by a declination in the
vent of our Commodities abroad, caused either by the
ruinous effects of Wars, or some alterations in the
times of Peace, whereof I have spoken more fully in
the third Chapter. But, to conclude with the Lawyers,
I say, that their noble Profession is necessary for all,
and their Cases, Quillets, Delayes and Charges, are
mischievous to many; these things indeed are Cankers
in the Estates of particular men, but not of the
Common-wealth, as some suppose, for one mans loss
becomes another mans gain, it is still in the Kingdome,
I wish it might as surely remain in the right places.

Lastly, all kind of Bounty and Pomp is not to be
avoided, for if we should become so frugal, that we
would use few or no Forraign wares, how shall we then
vent our own commodities? what will become of our
Ships, Mariners, Munitions, our poor Artificers, and
many others? doe we hope that other Countreys will
afford us money for All our wares, without buying or
bartering for Some of theirs? this would prove a vain
expectation; it is more safe and sure to run a middle
course by spending moderately, which will purchase
treasure plentifully.

Again, the pomp of Buildings, Apparel, and the like,
in the Nobility, Gentry, and other able persons, cannot
impoverish the Kingdome; if it be done with curious
and costly works upon our Materials, and by our own
people, it will maintain the poor with the purse of the
rich, which is the best distribution of the Common-
wealth. But if any man say, that when the people
want work, then the Fishing-trade would be a better

60   employment,

employment, and far more profitable; I subscribe willingly. For in that great business there is means enough to employ both rich and poor, whereof there hath been much said and written; It resteth only that something might be as well effected for the honour and wealth, both of the King and his Kingdoms.

Chap. XVI.

How the Revenues and Incomes of Princes may justly be raised.

NOw that we have set down the true course by which a Kingdom may be enriched with treasure; In the next place we will endeavour to shew the ways and means by which a King may justly share therein without the hurt or oppression of his Subjects. The Revenues of Princes as they differ much in quantity, according to the greatness, riches and trade of their respective dominions; so likewise is there great diversity used in procuring the same, according to the constitution of the Countreys, the government, laws and customs of the people, which no Prince can alter but with much difficulty and danger. Some Kings have their Crown Lands, the first fruits upon Ecclesiastical Livings, Customs, Tolls and Imposts upon all trade to and from forraign Countries; Lones, Donations and Subsidies upon all necessary occasions. Other Princes and States leaving the three last, do add unto the rest, a custom upon all new wares transported from one City, to be used in any other City or place of their own dominions, customs upon every alienation or sale of live Cattel, Lands, Houses, and the portions or marriage mony of women, licence mony upon all Victualling houses and Innkeepers, head mony, Custom

upon

upon all the Corn, Wine, Oyl, Salt and the like, which grow and are consumed in their own dominions, &c. All which seem to be a rabble of oppressions, serving to enrich those Princes which exact them, and to make the people poor and miserable which endure them; especially in those Countreys where these burdens are laid at heavy rates, at 4, 5, 6, and 7. *per cent.* But when all the circumstances and distinction of places are duly considered, they will be found not only necessary and therefore lawful to be used in some States, but also in divers respects very profitable to the Commonwealth.

First there are some States, as namely *Venice, Florence, Genoua,* the united Provinces of the *Low Countreys,* and others, which are singular for beauty, and excellent both for natural and artificial strength, having likewise rich Subjects: yet being of no very great extent, nor enjoying such wealth by ordinary revenues as might support them against the suddain and powerful invasions of those mighty Princes which do inviron them; they are therefore enforced to strengthen themselves not only with confederates and Leagues (which may often fail them in their greatest need) but also by massing up store of treasure and Munition by those extraordinary courses before written, which cannot deceive them, but will ever be ready to make a good defence, and to offend or divert their enemies.

Neither are these heavy Contributions so hurtfull to the happinesse of the people, as they are commonly esteemed: for as the food and rayment of the poor is made dear by Excise, so doth the price of their labour rise in proportion; whereby the burden (if any be) is still upon the rich, who are either idle, or at least work not in this kind, yet have they the use and are the great consumers of the poors labour; Neither do the

rich

rich neglect in their several places and callings to advance their endeavours according to those times which do exhaust their means and revenues; wherein if they should peradventure fail, and therefore be forced to abate their sinful excess and idle retainers; what is all this but happiness in a Commonwealth, when vertue, plenty and arts shall thus be advanced all together? Nor can it be truly said that a Kingdom is impoverished where the loss of the people is the gain of the King, from whom also such yearly incomes have their annual issue to the benefit of his subjects; except only that part of the treasure which is laid up for the publique good; wherein likewise they who suffer have their safety, and therefore such contributions are both just and profitable.

Yet here we must confess, that as the best things may be corrupted, so these taxes may be abused and the Commonwealth notoriously wronged when they are vainly wasted and consumed by a Prince, either upon his own excessive pleasures, or upon unworthy persons, such as deserve neither rewards nor countenance from the Majesty of a Prince: but these dangerous disorders are seldom seen, especially in such States as are aforenamed, because the disposing of the publique treasure is in the power and under the discretion of many; Neither is it unknown to all other Principalities and Governments that the end of such Excesses is ever ruinous, for they cause great want and poverty, which often drives them from all order to exorbitance, and therefore it is common policy amongst Princes to prevent such mischiefs with great care and providence, by doing nothing that may cause the Nobility to despair of their safety, nor leaving any thing undone which may gain the good will of the Commonalty to keep all in due obedience.

But now before we end this point in hand, we must

remember

remember likewise that all bodies are not of one and
the same constitution, for that which is Physick to one
Some States man, is little better than poyson to another; The
cannot sub- States aforewritten, and divers others like to them
sist, but by cannot subsist but by the help of those extraordinary
the means of contributions, whereof we have spoken, because they
heavy taxes. are not able otherwise in short time to raise sufficient
treasure to defend themselves against a potent enemy,
who hath power to invade them on the suddain, as is
already declared.   But a mighty Prince whose dominions are great and united, his Subjects many and
Loyal, his Countries rich both by nature and traffique,
his Victuals and warlike provisions plentiful and ready,
his situation easy to offend others, and difficult to be
invaded, his harbors good, his Navy strong, his alliance
powerfull, and his ordinary revenues sufficient, royally
to support the *Majesty of his State*, besides a reasonable
sum which may be advanc'd to lay up yearly in trea-
Princes, who sure for future occasions : shall not all these blessings
have no just (being well ordered) enable a Prince against the sud-
cause to lay dain invasion of any mighty enemy, without imposing
extraordinary
and heavy those extraordinary and heavy taxes? shall not the
taxes upon wealthy and loyal subjects of such a great and just
their Subjects. Prince maintain his Honour and their own Liberties
with life and goods, alwayes supplying the Treasure of
their Soveraign, untill by a well ordered War he may
inforce a happy Peace? Yes verily, it cannot otherwise be expected.   And thus shall a mighty Prince be
more powerful in preserving the wealth and love of his
Subjects, than by treasuring up their riches with unnecessary taxes, which cannot but alter and provoke
them.

Yea, but say some men, we may easily contradict
all this by example taken from some of the greatest
Monarchs of Christendome, who, besides those Incomes
which here are termed ordinary, they adde likewise all,

or the most of the other heavy Contributions. All which
we grant, and more; for they use also to sell their
Offices & Places of Justice, which is an act both base
& wicked, because it robbeth worthy men of their
Merits, & betrayeth the cause of the innocent, whereby
God is displeased, the people oppressed, and Vertue
banished from such unhappy Kingdomes: Shall we
then say, that these things are lawfull and necessary
because they are used? God forbid, we know better,
and we are well assured that these exactions are not
taken for a necessary defence of their own right, but
through pride and covetousness to add Kingdome to
Kingdome, and so to usurp the right of others: which *The sinister*
actions of Impiety are ever shadowed with some fair *ends which*
pretence of Sanctity, as being done for the Catholic *some great*
Princes have
Cause, the propagation of the Church, the suppression *in laying*
of Hereticks, and such like delusions, serving onely to *heavy taxes*
upon their
further their own ambition, whereof in this place it *subjects.*
shall be needless to make any larger discourse.

CHAP. XVII.

Whether it be necessary for great Princes to lay up
store of Treasure.

BEfore we set down the quantity of Treasure which
Princes may conveniently lay up yearly without
hurting the Common-wealth, it will be fit to examine
whether the act it self of Treasuring be necessary: for
in common conference we ever find some men who do
so much dote or hope upon the Liberality of Princes,
that they term it baseness, and conceive it needless for
them to lay up store of Treasure; accounting the
honour and safety of great Princes to consist more in
their Bounty, than in their Money, which they labour

to

to confirm by the examples of *Cæsar, Alexander*, and others, who hating covetousness, atchieved many acts and victories by lavish gifts and liberal expences. Unto which they add also the *little fruit* which came by that *great summ of money* which King *David* laid up and left to his son *Solomon*, who notwithstanding this, and all his other rich Presents and wealthy Traffique in a quiet reign, consumed all with pomp and vain delights, excepting only that which was spent in building of the Temple. Whereupon (say they) if so much treasure gathered by so just a King, effect so little, what shall we hope for by the endeavours of this kind in other Princes? *Sardanapalus* left ten millions of pounds to them that slew him. *Darius* left twenty millions of pounds to *Alexander* that took him; *Nero* being left rich, and extorting much from his best Subjects, gave away above twelve millions of pounds to his base flatterers and such unworthy persons, which caused *Galba* after him to revoke those gifts. A Prince who hath store of mony hates peace, despiseth the friendship of his Neighbours and Allies, enters not only into unnecessary, but also into dangerous Wars, to the ruin and over-throw (sometimes) of his own estate: All which, with divers other weak arguments of this kind (which for brevity I omit), make nothing against the lawful gathering and massing up of Treasure by wise and provident Princes, if they be rightly understood.

For first, concerning those worthies who have obtained to the highest top of *honour* and *dignity*, by their great gifts and expences, who knows not that this hath been done rather upon the spoils of their Enemies than out of their own Cofers, which is indeed a Bounty that causeth neither loss nor peril? Whereas on the contrary, those Princes which do not providently lay up Treasure, or do imoderately consume the

same

same when they have it, will sodainly come to want *Excess and bounty brings beggery, which makes most men devise in their heads how to extort and get mony into their hands.* and misery; for there is nothing doth so soon decay as Excessive Bounty, in using whereof they want the means to use it. And this was King *Solomons* case, notwithstanding his infinite Treasure, which made him over-burthen his Subjects in such a manner, that (for this cause) many of them rebelled against his Son *Rehoboam,* who thereby lost a great part of his dominions, being so grosly mis-led by his young Counsellors. Therefore a Prince that will not oppress his people, and yet be able to maintain his Estate, and defend his Right, that will not run himself into Poverty, Contempt, Hate, and Danger, must lay up treasure, and be thrifty, for further proof whereof I might yet roduce some other examples, which here I do omit as needless.

Only I will add this as a necessary rule to be observed, that when more treasure must be raised than can be received by the ordinary taxes, it ought ever to be done with equality to avoid the hate of the people, who are never pleased except their contributions be granted by general consent: For which purpose the invention of Parliaments is an excellent policie of Government, to keep a sweet concord between a King and his Subjects, by restraining the Insolency of the Nobility, and redressing the Injuries of the Commons, without engaging a Prince to adhere to either party, but indifferently to favour both. There could nothing be devised with more judgment for the common quiet of a Kingdom, or with greater care for the safety of a King, who hereby hath also good means to dispatch those things by others, which will move envy, and to execute that himself which will merit thanks.

CHAP. XVIII.

How much Treasure a Prince may conveniently lay up yearly.

THus far we have shewed the ordinary and extra-ordinary incomes of Princes, the conveniency thereof, and to whom only it doth necessarily and justly belong, to take the extraordinary contributions of their Subjects. It resteth now to examine what proportion of treasure each particular Prince may con-veniently lay up yearly. This business doth seem at the first to be very plain and easy, for if a Prince have two millions yearly revenue, and spend but one, why should he not lay up the other? Indeed I must confess that this course is ordinary in the means and gettings of private men, but in the affairs of Princes it is far different, there are other circumstances to be *Forraign* considered; for although the revenue of a King should *Trade must* be very great, yet if the gain of the Kingdom be but *give propor-* small, this latter must ever give rule and proportion *tion to a* *Princes trea-* to that Treasure, which may conveniently be laid up *sure which is* yearly, for if he should mass up more mony than is *laid up* gained by the overballance of his forraign trade, he *yearly.* shall not *Fleece*, but *Flea* his Subjects, and so with their ruin overthrow himself for want of future sheer-ings. To make this plain, suppose a Kingdom to be so rich by nature and art, that it may supply it self of forraign wares by trade, and yet advance yearly 200000*l.* in ready mony : Next supppose all the King's revenues to be 900000*l.* and his expences but 400000*l.* whereby he may lay up 800000*l.* more in his Coffers yearly than the whole Kingdom gains from strangers by forraign trade; who sees not then that all the mony in such a State, would suddenly be drawn into the

Princes

Princes treasure, whereby the life of lands and arts must fail and fall to the ruin both of the publick and private wealth? So that a King who desires to lay up much mony must endeavour by all good means to maintain and encrease his forraign trade, because it is the sole way not only to lead him to his own ends, but also to enrich his Subjects to his farther benefit: for a Prince is esteemed no less powerful by having many rich and well affected Subjects, than by possessing much treasure in his Coffers. *A Prince whose Subjects have but little forraign Trade cannot lay up much mony.*

But here we must meet with an objection, which peradventure may be made concerning such States (whereof I have formerly spoken) which are of no great extent, and yet bordering upon mighty Princes, are therefore constrained to lay extraordinary taxes upon their subjects, whereby they procure to themselves very great incomes yearly, and are richly provided against any Forraign Invasions; yet have they no such great trade with Strangers, as that the overbalance or gain of the same may suffice to lay up the one half of that which they advance yearly, besides their own expences.

To this the answer is, that stil the gain of their Forraign Trade must be the rule of laying up their treasure, the which, although it should not be much yearly, yet in the time of a long continued peace, and being well managed to advantage, it will become a great summe of money, able to make a long defence, which may end or divert the war. Neither are all the advances of Princes strictly tied to be massed up in treasure, for they have other no less necesssary and profitable wayes to make them rich and powerfull, by issuing out continually a great part of the mony of their yearly Incomes to their subjects from whom it was first taken; as namely, by employing them to make Ships of War, with all the provisions thereunto

belonging,

belonging, to build and repair Forts, to buy and store up Corn in the Granaries of each Province for a years use (at least) aforehand, to serve in occasion of Dearth, which cannot be neglected by a State but with great danger; to erect Banks with their money for the encrease of their subjects trade, to maintain in their pay, Collonels, Captains, Souldiers, Commanders, Mariners, and others, both by Sea and Land, with good disci-

Munition for war ought to be kept in divers places of the State, to prevent the loss of all by trechery in one place.
pline, to fill their Store-houses (in sundry strong places) and to abound in Gunpowder, Brimstone, Saltpeter, Shot, Ordnance, Musquets, Swords, Pikes, Armours, Horses, and in many other such like Provisions fitting War; all which will make them to be feared abroad, and loved at home, especially if care be taken that all (as neer as possible) be made out of the Matter and Manufacture of their own subjects, which bear the burden of the yearly Contributions; for a Prince (in this case) is like the stomach in the body, which if it cease to digest and distribute to the other members, it doth no sooner corrupt them, but it destroyes it self.

Thus we have seen that a small State may lay up a great wealth in necessary provisions, which are Princes Jewels, no less precious than their Treasure, for in time of need they are ready, and cannot otherwise be had (in some places) on the suddain, whereby a State may be lost, whilest Munition is in providing: so that we may account that Prince as poor who can have no wares to buy at his need, as he that hath no money to buy wares; for although *Treasure is said to be the sinews of the War*, yet this is so because it doth provide, unite & move the power of men, victuals, and munition where and when the cause doth require; but if these things be wanting in due time, what shall we then do with our mony? the consideration of this, doth cause divers well-governed States to be exceeding

provident

provident and well furnished of such provisions, especially those Granaries and Storehouses with that famous
Arsenal of the *Venetians,* are to be admired for the
magnificence of the buildings, the quantity of the
Munitions and Stores both for Sea and Land, the
multitude of the workmen, the diversity and excellency
of the Arts, with the order of the government. They
are rare and worthy things for Princes to behold and
imitate; for Majesty without providence of competent
force, and ability of necessary provisions is unassured.

Chap. XIX.

Of some different effects, which proceed from Naturall and Artificiall Wealth.

IN the latter end of the third Chapter of this Book,
I have already written something concerning Natural and Artificial Wealth, and therein shewed how
much Art doth add to Nature; but it is yet needful to
handle these particulars apart, that so we may the
better discern their severall operations in a Common-
wealth. For the effecting whereof, I might draw some
comparisons from *Turkey* and *Italy,* or from some other
remote Countreys, but I will not range so far, having
matter sufficient here in *Great Britain* and the *united
Provinces* of the *Low Countreys,* to make this business
plain: wherefore in the first place, we will begin with
England briefly, and onely in general terms, to shew
the natural riches of this famous Nation, with some
principal effects which they produce in the disposition
of the people, and strength of the Kingdome.

If we duly consider *Englands* Largeness, Beauty,
Fertility, Strength, both by Sea and Land, in multitude of warlike People, Horses, Ships, Ammunition,

71   advantagious

advantagious situation for Defence and Trade, number of Sea-ports and Harbours, which are of difficult access to Enemies, and of easie out-let to the Inhabitants wealth by excellent Fleece-wools, Iron, Lead, Tynn, Saffron, Corn, Victuals, Hides, Wax, and other natural Endowments; we shall find this Kingdome capable to sit as master of a Monarchy. For what greater glory and advantage can any powerful Nation have, than to be thus richly and naturally possessed of all things needful for Food, Rayment, War, and Peace, not onely for its own plentiful use, but also to supply the wants of other Nations, in such a measure, that much money may be thereby gotten yearly, to make the happiness compleat. For experience telleth us, that notwithstanding that excessive Consumption of this Kingdome alone, to say nothing of *Scotland*, there is exported *communibus annis* of our own native commodities for the value of twenty two hundred thousand pounds *Sterling*, or somewhat more; so that if we were not too much affected to Pride, monstrous Fashions, and Riot, above all other Nations, one million and an half of pounds might plentifully supply our unnecessary wants (as I may term them) of Silks, Sugars, Spices, Fruits, and all others; so that seven hundred thousand pounds might be yearly treasur'd up in money to make the Kingdome exceeding rich and powerful in short time. But this great plenty which we enjoy, makes us a people not only *vicious* and *excessive*, wastful of the means we have, but also improvident & careless of much other wealth that shamefully we lose, which is, the Fishing in his Majesty's Seas of *England, Scotland,* and *Ireland*, being of no less consequence than all our other riches which we export and vent to Strangers, whilest in the mean time (through lewd idleness) great multitudes of our people cheat, roar, rob, hang, beg, cant, pine, and perish, which by this means and main-

The fruits of idleness, which are Englands common reproches among Strangers.

tenance

tenance might be much encreased, to the further
wealth and strength of these Kingdomes, especially by
Sea, for our own safety, and terrour of our enemies.
The endeavours of the industrious Dutch do give sufficient testimony of this truth, to *our great shame, and
no less perill,* if it have not a timely prevention: for,
whilest we leave our wonted honourable exercises and
studies, following our pleasures, and of late years
besotting ourselves with pipe and pot, in a beastly
manner, sucking smoak, and drinking healths, until
death stares many in the face; the said Dutch have
well-neer left this swinish vice, and taken up our
wonted valour, which we have often so well performed
both by Sea and Land, and particularly in their *The Nether-*
defence, although they are not now so thankful as to *landers in-*
acknowledge the same. The summ of all this is, that *gratitude.*
the general leprosie of our Piping, Potting, Feasting,
Fashions, and mis-spending of our time in Idleness and
Pleasure (contrary to the Law of God, and the use of
other Nations) hath made us effeminate in our bodies,
weak in our knowledg, poor in our Treasure, declined
in our Valour, unfortunate in our Enterprises, and
contemned by our Enemies. I write the more of these
excesses, because they do so greatly wast our wealth,
which is the main subject of this whole Books discourse: and indeed our wealth might be a rare discourse for all *Christendome* to admire and fear, if we
would but add *Art* to *Nature*, our *labour* to our *natural
means*, the neglect whereof hath given a notable advantage to other *nations*, & especially to the *Hollanders*,
whereof I will briefly say something in the next place.

But first, I will deliver my opinion concerning our
Clothing, which although it is the greatest Wealth and
best Employment of the Poor of this Kingdome, yet
neverthelesse we may peradventure employ our selves
with better Safety, Plenty, and Profit in using more

Tillage

Tillage and Fishing, than to trust so wholly to the making of Cloth; for in times of War, or by other occasions, if some forraign Princes should prohibit the use thereof in their dominions, it might suddenly cause much poverty and dangerous uproars, especially by our poor people, when they should be deprived of their ordinary maintenance, which cannot so easily fail them when their labours should be divided into the said diversity of employment, whereby also many thousands would be the better enabled to do the Kingdom good service in occasion of war, especially by Sea; And so leaving *England*, wee will pass over into the *United Provinces* of the *Netherlands*.

As plenty and power doe make a nation vicious and improvident, so penury and want doe make a people wise and industrious: concerning the last of these I might instance divers Commonwealths of Christendom, who having little or nothing in their own Territories, do notwithstanding purchase great wealth and strength by their industrious commerce with strangers, amongst

The Hollanders *improvement and industry.*

which the united Provinces of the *Low Countreys* are now of greatest note and fame: For since they have cast off the yoke of *Spanish* slavery, how wonderfully are they improved in all humane policy? What great means have they obtained to defend their liberty against the power of so great an Enemy? and is not all this performed by their continual industry in the trade of Merchandize? are not their Provinces the *Magazines* and *Storehouses of wares* for most places of Christendom, whereby their Wealth, Shipping, Mariners, Arts, People, and thereby the publique Revenues

Those Princes which do willingly support the Dutch, *would as resolutely resist the* Spaniard.

and Excizes are grown to a wonderful height? If we compare the times of their subjection, to their present estate, they seem not the same people; for who knows not that the condition of those Provinces was mean and turbulent under the *Spaniards* government, which

brought

brought rather a greater charge than a further strength
to their ambition; neither would it prove over difficult
for the neighbour Princes in short time to reduce those
Countreys to their former estate again, if their own
safety did require the same, as certainly it would if the
Spaniard were sole Lord of those *Netherlands;* but our
discourse tends not to shew the means of those muta-
tions, otherwise than to find out the chief foundation
of the *Hollanders* wealth and greatness; for it seems a
wonder to the world, that such a small Countrey, not
fully so big as two of our best Shires, having little
natural Wealth, Victuals, Timber, or other necessary
amunitions, either for war or peace, should notwithstanding possess them all in such extraordinary plenty,
that besides their own wants (which are very great)
they can and do likewise serve and sell to other Princes,
Ships, Ordnance, Cordage, Corn, Powder, Shot, and
what not, which by their industrious trading they
gather from all the quarters of the world: In which *Much Policy,*
courses they are not less injurious to supplant others *but little*
(especially the English) than they are careful to *Honesty.*
strengthen themselves. And to effect this and more
than hath been said (which is their war with *Spain*)
they have little foundation besides the Fishing, *which
is permitted them in His Majesties Seas,* being indeed
the means of an incredible wealth and strength, both
by Sea and Land, as *Robert Hitchcock, Tobias Gentleman,* and others have pulished at large in print to
them that list to read. And the *States General* themselves in their proclamation have ingeniously set out
the worth thereof in these words following, *The great* Part of the
Fishing and catching of Herrings is the chiefest trade States Pro-
and principal Gold Mine of the United Provinces, clamation,
whereby many thousands of Housholds, Families, Handi- Hague, 19.
crafts, Trades and Occupations are set on work, well July 1624.
maintained and prosper, especially the sailing and navi-
gation,

gation, as well within as without these Countreys is kept in great estimation; *Moreover many returns of mony, with the encrease of the means, Convoys, Customs and revenues of these Countreys are augmented thereby and prosper,* with other words following, as is at large expressed in the said Proclamations, set forth by the States General for the preservation of the said trade of Fishing; without which it is apparent that they cannot long subsist in Soveraignty; for if this foundation perish, the whole building of their wealth and strength both by Sea and Land must fall; for the multitude of their Shipping would suddainly decay, their revenues and customs would become small, their Countreys would be depopulated for want of maintenance, whereby the Excize must fail, and all their other trades to the *East Indies* or elsewhere must faint. So that the glory and power of these *Netherlanders* consisteth in this *fishing of Herrings, Ling and Cod in His Majesties Seas.* It resteth therefore to know what right or title they have thereunto, and how they are able to possess and keep the same against all other Nations.

The answers to these two questions are not difficult: for first, it is not the *Netherlandish* Author of *Mare Liberum,* that can entitle them to Fish in His Majesties Seas. For besides the Justice of the cause, and examples of other Countreys, which might be alleged, I will only say, that such titles would be sooner decided by swords, than with words; I do beleeve indeed that it is free for the Fish to come thither at their pleasure, but for the *Dutch* to catch and carry them away from thence without His Majesties licence, I harbour no such thought. *There may be good policy to connive still, and so long to permit them this fishing as they are in perfect league with* England, *and in war with* Spain. But if the *Spaniards* were Masters of the *United*
Provinces

Provinces as heretofore, it would neerly concern these Kingdoms to claim their own right, and carefully to make as good use thereof for increase of their wealth and strength, to oppose that potent enemy, as now the *Netherlanders* do, and are thereby well enabled for the same purpose: by which particular alone they are ever bound to acknowledge their strong alliance with *England,* above all other Nations, for there is none that hath the like good means to lend them such a powerful maintenance. Nor were it possible for the Spaniard (if he had those Countreys again) to make a new Foundation with the power of his money, to encrease his strength, either by Sea or Land, to offend these Kingdoms, more than he is now able to perform with the conveniency of those Provinces which he hath already in his possession; for it is not the Place, but the Employment, not the barren Netherlands, but the rich Fishing, which gives Foundation, Trade, and Subsistence to those multitude of Ships, Arts and People, whereby also the Excises and other publick Revenues are continued, and without which Employment all the said great Dependences must necessarily disbandon and fail in very short time. For although I confess, that store of money may bring them materials (which they altogether want) and Artsmen to build them Shipping, yet where are the wares to fraight and maintain them? if money then shall be the onely means to send them out in Trade, what a poor number of Ships will this employ? or if the uncertain occasions of War must support them, will not this require another Indies, and all too little to maintain the tenth part of so many Ships and Men as the Hollanders do now set on work by the Fishing and other Trades thereon depending? But if it be yet said, that the Spaniard being Lord of all those Netherlands, his expence of the present War there will cease, and so

Money and fishing compared.

this

this power may be turned upon us. The answer is,
that when Princes send great Forces abroad to invade
others, they must likewise encrease their charge and
strength at home, to defend themselves; and also we
must consider, that if the Spaniard will attempt any
thing upon these Kingdomes, he must consume a great
part of his Tresaure in Shipping, whereby the means
of his invading power of Money and Men to land will
be much less than now it is in the *Low Countreys*:
Nor should we regard them, but be ever ready to
beard them, when our Wealth and Strength by Sea
and Land might be so much encreased by the possession and practise of our Fishing, of which particular
I will yet say something more where occasion shall be
offered in that which followeth. And here in this
place I will onely add, that if the *Spaniard* were sole
Lord of all the Netherlands, he must then necessarily
drive a great trade by Sea, to supply the common
wants of those Countreys, whereby in occasion of war,
we should have means daily to take much wealth from
him; whereas now the *Spaniard* using little or no
trade in these Seas, but imploying his Ships of warre
to the uttermost of his power, he only takes, and we
lose great matters continually.

Now concerning the second question, *Whether the
Hollanders be able to possess and keep this fishing
against all other Nations.* It is very probable, that
although they claim now no other right than their
own freedome in this Fishing, seeming to leave the
like to all others; yet if the practice of any Nation
should seek either to Fish with them or to supplant
them, they would be both ready and able to maintain
this Golden Mine, against the strongest opposition
except *England*, whose harbours and In-lands with
other daily reliefs are very needful, if not absolutely
necessary for this employment, and whose Power also

by

by Sea, is able (in short time) to give this business disturbance, and utter ruin, if the occasion should be so
urgent as is afore supposed: Neither is it enough for
any man to contradict all this by saying the *Hollanders*
are very strong by Sea, when both Sea and Land
encounter them with a greater power: we must observe
from whence their strength doth grow, and if the root
may once be spoiled, the branches soon will wither;
and therefore it were an error to esteem, or value them
according to the present power and wealth, which they
have obtained by trade or purchase; for although this
were far greater then indeed it is, yet would it soon be
consumed in a chargeable war against a potent enemy,
when the current of those Accidents may be stopt
and turned by preventing the substance it self (which
is the Fishing in His Majesties Seas) that gives Foundation, and is the very Fountain of their strength and
happiness: The *United Provinces* (we know) are like
a fair bird suited with goodly borrowed plumes; but
if every Fowl should take his feather, this bird would
rest neer naked: Nor have we ever seen these Netherlanders as yet in their greatest occasions to set forth
neer so many ships of war at once as the English have
often done without any hinderance of their ordinary
traffique; It is true indeed, they have an infinite
number of weak Ships to fish with, and fetch Corn,
Salt, &c. for their own victualling and trading, the like
to fetch Timber, Plank, Boords, Pitch, Hemp, Tar,
Flax, Masts, Cordage, and other Ammunitions to make
those multitudes of Ships, which unto them are as our
Ploughs to us, the which except they stir, the people *The Nether-*
starve; their Shipping therefore cannot be spared from *landers*
their traffique (as ours may if occasion require) no not *Ploughs.*
for a very short time, without utter ruin, because it is
the daily maintenance of their great multitudes which
gain their living but from hand to mouths upon which

also depends the great excises, and other publique revenues, which support the State it self: Neither indeed are those Vessels strong or fit for war; and in their proper use of Fishing and trade they would become the riches, or the purchase of a potent Enemy by Sea, as they partly find by one poor town of *Dunkirk*, notwithstanding their great charge of Men of war, strong Convoys, and other commendable diligence, which continually they use to prevent this mischief: but if the occasion of a more powerful enemy by Sea should force them to double or treble those charges, we may well doubt the means of their continuance, especially when (by us) their fishing might nevertheless be prevented, which should procure the maintenance.

Men who speak by affection or tradition, not from reason. These and other circumstances make me often wonder, when I hear the *Dutch* vain-gloriously to brag, and many *English* simply to believe, that the *United Provinces* are our Forts, Bulwarks, Walls, out-works, and I know not what, without which we cannot long subsist

The Hollanders *main supportance is* Englands *good Alliance.* against the *Spanish* forces; when in truth, *we are the main fountain of their happiness, both for war and peace; for trade and treasure, for Munition and Men, spending our blood in their defence; whilst their people are preserved to conquer in the Indies, and to reap the fruits of a rich traffique out of our own bosoms;* which being assumed to ourselves (as we have right and power to do) would mightily encrease the breed of our people by this good means of their maintenance, and well enable us against the strongest enemy, and force likewise great multitudes of those *Netherlanders* themselves to seek their living here with us for want of better maintenance: whereby our many decayed Sea-towns and Castles would soon be re-edified and populated in more ample manner than formerly they were in their best estate. And thus these forces being united, would be ever more ready, sure, and vigorous

than

than a greater strength that lies divided, which is always subject to delays, diversion, and other jealousies, of all which we ought not to be ignorant, but perfectly to know, and use our own strength when we have occasion, and especially we must ever be watchful to preserve this strength, lest the subtilty of the *Dutch* (under some fair shews and with their mony) prevail, as peradventure they lately practised in *Scotland*, to have had a Patent for the possessing, inhabiting, and fortifying of that excellent Island of *Lewis* in the *Orcades*; whose scituation, harbours, fishing, fertility, largeness and other advantages, would have made them able (in short time) to offend these Kingdoms by suddain invasions, and to have defended the aforesaid Fishing against his Majesties greatest power, and also to send out and return home their Shipping prosperously that way, to and from the *East* and *West Indies*, *Spain*, the *Straights*, and other places, without passing through his Majesties narrow Seas, where in all occasions this Kingdome now hath so great advantage to take their Ships, and prevent their best Trades, which would soon bring them to ruine, whereby (as they well know) we have a greater tie and power over them than any other Nation. And howsoever the said Island of *Lewis* might have been obtained in the name of private men, and under the fair pretence of bringing Comerce into those remote parts of *Scotland*; yet in the end, when the work had been brought to any good perfection, the possession and power would no doubt have come to the Lords, the States Géneral, even as we know they have lately gotten divers places of great Strength and Wealth in the *East Indies*, in the names and with the purse of their Merchants, whereby also their actions herein have been obscur'd and made *less notorious* unto the world, untill they had obtain'd their *ends*, which are of such consequence, that it doth much

concern

concern this Nation in particular, carefully to observe their proceedings, for they notoriously follow the steps of that valiant and politick Captain, *Philip of Macedon,* whose Maxim was, *That where force could not prevail, he always used bribes, and money to corrupt those who might advance his fortune;* by which policy he gave foundation to a Monarchy; & what know we but that the Dutch may aim at some such Soveraignty, when they shall find their Indian attempts and other subtil plots succeed so prosperously? Do we not see their Lands are now become too little to contain this swelling people, whereby their Ships and Seas are made the Habitations of great multitudes? and yet, to give them further breed, are they not spared from their own wars to enrich the State and themselves by Trade and Arts? whilest by this policy many thousands of strangers are also drawn thither for performance of their martial employments, whereby the great revenue of their Excises is so much the more encreased, and all things so subtilly contrived, that although the *forraign souldier* be well paid, yet all must be there again expended; and thus the Wealth remains still in their own Countreys; nor are the strangers enriched which do them this great service.

I have heard some Italians wisely and worthily discourse of the natural Strength and Wealth of *England,* which they make to be matchless, if we should (but in part) apply ourselves to such policies and endeavours as are very commonly used in some other Countreys of *Europe;* and much they have admired, that our thoughts and jealousies attend only upon the Spanish and French greatness, never once suspecting, but constantly embracing the Netherlanders as our best Friends and Allies; when in truth (as they well observe) there are no people in Christendome who do more undermine, hurt, and eclipse us daily in our

Where force fails, yet money prevails; thus hopes the Hollanders.

Navigation and Trades, both abroad and at home; and this not only in the rich Fishing in his Majesty's Seas (whereof we have already written) but also in our Inland trades between City and City, in the Manufactures of Silk, Woolls, and the like, made here in this Kingdom, wherein they never give employment or education in their Arts to the English, but ever (according to the custome of the Jewes, where they abide in *Turkey*, and divers places of Christendome) they live wholly to themselves in their own Tribes. So that we may truly say of the Dutch, that although they are amongst us, yet they certainly are not of us, no not they who are born and bred here in our own Countrey, for stil they will be Dutch, not having so much as one drop of English bloud in their hearts.

More might be written of these Netherlanders pride and ambitious endeavours, whereby they hope in time to grow mighty, if they be not prevented, and much more may be said of their cruel and unjust violence used (especially to their best friends the English) in matters of bloud, trade, and other profits, where they have had advantage and power to perform it: but these things are already published in print to the view and admiration of the world; wherefore I will conclude, and the summ of all is this, that the United Provinces, which now are so great a trouble, if not a terrour to the Spaniard, were heretofore little better than a charge to them in their possession, and would be so again in the like occasion, the reasons whereof I might yet further enlarge; but they are not pertinent to this discourse, more than is already declared, to show the different effects between *Natural and Artificial Wealth:* The first of which, as it is most noble and advantagious, being alwayes ready and certain, so doth it make the people careless, proud, and given to all excesses; whereas the second enforceth Vigilancy, Lite-

rature,

rature, Arts and Policy. My wishes therefore are, that as *England* doth plentifully enjoy the one, and is fully capable of the other, that our endeavours might as worthily conjoyn them both together, to the reformation of our vicious idleness, and greater glory of these famous Kingdomes.

Chap. XX.

The order and means whereby we may draw up the ballance of our Forraign Trade.

NOw, that we have sufficiently proved the Ballance of our Forraign Trade to be the true rule of our Treasure; It resteth that we shew by whom and in what manner the said ballance may be drawn up at all times, when it shall please the State to discover how we prosper or decline in this great and weighty business, wherein the Officers of his Majesties Customes are the onely Agents to be employed, because they have the accounts of all the wares which are issued out or brought into the Kingdome; and although (it is true) they cannot exactly set down the cost and charges of other mens goods bought here or beyond the seas; yet nevertheless, if they ground themselves upon the book of Rates, they shall be able to make such an estimate as may well satisfie this enquiry; for it is not expected that such an account can possibly be drawn up to a just ballance, it will suffice onely that the difference be not over great.

How we must value our Exportations and Importations. First therefore, concerning our Exportations, when we have valued their first cost, we must add twenty-five *per cent.* thereunto for the charges here, for fraight of Ships, ensurance of the *Adventurer*, and the *Merchants* Gains; and for our Fishing Trades, which pay no Custome to his Majesty, the value of such Exportations may be easily esteem'd by good observations which have been made, and may continually be made, according to the increase or decrease of those affairs, the present estate of this commodity being valued at one hundred and forty thousand pounds issued yearly. Also we must add to our Exportations all the moneys which are carried out in Trade by license from his Majesty.

Secondly, for our Importations of Forraign Wares, the Custome-books serve only to direct us concerning the quantity, for we must not value them as they are rated here, but as they cost us with all charges laden into our Ships beyond the Seas, in the respective places where they are bought: for the Merchants gain, the charges of Insurance, Fraight of Ships, Customes, Imposts, and other Duties here, which doe greatly indear them unto our use and consumption, are notwithstanding but Commutations amongst our selves, for the Stranger hath no part thereof: wherefore our said Importations ought to be valued at twenty five *per cent.* less than they are rated to be worth here. And although this may seem to be too great allowance upon many rich Commodities, which come but from the *Low Countreys* and other places neer hand, yet will it be found reasonable, when we consider it in gross Commodities, and upon Wares laden in remote Countreys, as our Pepper, which cost us, with charges, but four pence the pound in the *East Indies,* and it is here rated at twenty pence the pound: so that when all is brought into a *medium,* the valuation ought to be made as afore-written. And therefore, the order which hath been used to multiply the full rates upon wares inwards by twenty, would produce a very great errour in the Ballance, for in this manner the ten thousand bags of Pepper, which this year we have brought hither from

85   the

The Trade to the East Indies is not onely great in it self, but it doth also make our other trades much greater than they were.

the *East Indies*, should be valued at very near two hundred and fifty thousand pounds, whereas all this Pepper in the Kingdomes accompt, cost not above fifty thousand pounds, because the Indians have had no more of us, although we paid them extraordinary dear prices for the same. All the other charges (as I have said before) is but a change of effects amongst our selves, and from the Subject to the King, which cannot impoverish the Common-wealth. But it is true, that whereas nine thousand bags of the said Pepper are already shipped out for divers forraign parts; These and all other Wares, forraign or domestick, which are thus transported Outwards, ought to be cast up by the rates of his Majesties Custome-money, multiplied by twenty, or rather by twenty-five (as I conceive) which will come neerer the reckoning, when we consider all our Trades to bring them into a *medium*.

Thirdly, we must remember, that all Wares exported or imported by Strangers (in their shipping) be esteemed by themselves, for what they carry out, the Kingdom hath only the first cost and the custom: And what they bring in, we must rate it as it is worth here, the Custom, Impost, and pety charges only deducted.

Lastly, there must be good notice taken of all the great losses which we receive at Sea in our Shipping either outward or homeward bound: for the value of the one is to be deducted from our Exportations, and the value of the other is to be added to our Importations: for to lose and to consume doth produce one and the same reckoning. Likewise if it happen that His Majesty doth make over any great sums of mony by Exchange to maintain a forraign war, where we do not feed and clothe the Souldiers, and Provide the armies, we must deduct all this charge out of our

86   Exportations

Exportations or add it to our Importations; for this expence doth either carry out or hinder the coming in of so much Treasure. And here we must remember the great collections of mony which are supposed to be made throughout the Realm yearly from our Recusants by Priests and Jesuits, who secretly convey the same unto their Colleges, Cloysters and Nunneries beyond the Seas, from whence it never returns to us again in any kind; therefore if this mischief cannot be pre- *Two Contra-* vented, yet it must be esteemed and set down as a *ries which are both* cleer loss to the Kingdome, except (to ballance this) we *pernicious.* will imagine that as great a value may perhaps come in from forraign Princes to their Pensioners here for Favours of Intelligence, which some States account good Policy, to purchase with great Liberality; the receipt whereof notwithstanding is plain Treachery.

There are yet some other petty things which seem to have reference to this Ballance, of which the said Officers of His Majesties Customs can take no notice, to bring them into the accompt. As namely, the expences of travailers, the gifts to Ambassadors and Strangers, the fraud of some rich goods not entred into the Custom-house, the gain which is made here by Strangers by change and re-change, Interest of mony, ensurance upon English mens goods and their lives: which can be little when the charges of their living here is deducted; besides that the very like advantages are as amply ministred unto the English in forraign Countreys, which doth counterpoize all these things, and therefore they are not considerable in the drawing up of the said Ballance.

Chap. XXI.

The conclusion upon all that hath been said, concerning the Exportation or Importation of Treasure.

THe sum of all that hath been spoken, concerning the enriching of the Kingdom, and th' encrease of our treasure by commerce with strangers, is briefly thus. That it is a certain rule in our forraign trade, in those places where our commodities exported are overballanced in value by forraign wares brought into this Realm, there our mony is undervalued in exchange; and where the contrary of this is performed, there our mony is overvalued. But let the Merchants exchange be at a high rate, or at a low rate, or at the *Par pro pari*, or put down altogether; Let Forraign Princes enhance their Coins, or debase their Standards, and let His Majesty do the like, or keep them constant as they now stand; Let forraign Coins pass current here in all payments at higher rates than they are worth at the Mint; Let the Statute for employments by Strangers stand in force or be repealed; Let the meer Exchanger do his worst; Let Princes oppress, Lawyers extort, Usurers bite, Prodigals wast, and lastly let Merchants carry out what mony they shall have occasion to use in traffique. Yet all these actions can work no other effects in the course of trade than is declared in this discourse. For so much Treasure only will be brought in or carried out of a Commonwealth, as the Forragn Trade doth over or under ballance in value. And this must come to pass by a Necessity beyond all resistance. So that all other courses (which tend not to this end) howsoever they may seem to force mony into a Kingdom for a time, yet are they (in the end) not only fruitless but also

hurtful:

hurtful: they are like to violent flouds which bear down their banks, and suddenly remain dry again for want of waters.

Behold then the true form and worth of forraign Trade, which is, *The great Revenue of the King, The honour of the Kingdom, the Noble profession of the Merchant, The School of our Arts, The supply of our wants, The employment of our poor, The improvement of our Lands, The Nurcery of our Mariners, The Walls of the Kingdoms, The means of our Treasure, The Sinnews of our wars, The terror of our enemies.* For all which great and weighty reasons, do so many well governed States highly countenance the profession, and carefully cherish the action, not only with Policy to encrease it, but also with power to protect it from all forraign injuries: because they know it is a Principal in Reason of State to maintain and defend that which doth Support them and their estates.

FINIS.

Englands

INTEREST

AND

IMPROVEMENT.

Consisting in the Increase of the Store, and Trade of this Kingdom.

By *Samuel Fortrey*, Esquire.

LONDON,

Printed for *Nathanael Brook*, at the Sign of *Angel* in *Cornhil*, 1673.

To

The most High and mighty

MONARCH.

CHARLES the II.

May it Please your most Ex-

cellent Majesty,

HAving some years since (with so great boldness) presumed to present this unworthy Treatise to your most Sacred *MAJESTY*; the which having received, not onely your *Majesties* pardon, but Favour and Countenance; I am incouraged to renew it again with the satisfaction to have had thoughts, sutable to your *Majesties* inclinations, as appears by your *Majesties* gratious approbation of many particulars contained in it; By which great success I am imboldned

imboldned, once again humbly to crave your *Majesties* favorable Pardon and protection, having no greater ambition than, The onely being,

your Majesties most Loyal and
faithful Subject and
Servant,

SAMVEL FORTREY.

To the Reader.

I Have been often ashamed at my own confidence; in giving to any so much trouble, or loss of time, as the reading this undeserving paper. But it having been first Published in the year 1663. when my zeale to the Publick, more than my ability prevailed with me, to venture the hazzard of such an Undertaking; And since finding my Endeavour more acceptable, than I had reason to expect, and no more Copies remaining whereby to gratifie such friends as seemed very desirous of them: I have again renewed them without any alteration; That it may appear, how many things have hapned since, according to my wish; and how my mean thoughts have found concurrence, in the worthiest Councils. And if my endeavours herein have been any wayes successefull, or beneficiall to any, I have attained the end I aimed at.

Sam. Fortrey.

ENGLANDS
INTEREST
AND
IMPROVEMENT.

*E*NGLANDS Interest and Improvement consists chiefly in the increase of store and trade.

Store comprehendeth all such commodities, as either *Of store and* the soil, or people of this nation are capable to produce, *trade in* which are either usefull at home, or valuable abroad. *general.*

Trade is the means, by which a nation may procure what they want from abroad, and vent to the best advantage, what ever may be spared of their own increase at home.

Of store there are properly two sorts, natural and artificial.

Our natural store may also be divided into three parts.

First, the annual increase of the soil, which consists chiefly in corn of all sorts, and all the best sorts of cattel.

Secondly, the product of our Mines, of lead, tin, iron, coal, allum, and the like.

Thirdly, the great plenty of fish our seas naturally afford, of which we might reap unknown advantages, were our fishing trade rightly improved.

Our Artificial store consists in the manufacture and Industry of the people, of which the chiefest in this nation are the manufactures of woollen clothes, and all

7   other

other sorts of woollen stuffs, linen cloth, silk, stuffs, ribbandings, stockings, laces, and the like.

In trade there may be likewise said to be two kinds.

The one, trade at home, one with another: the other, our trade, or traffick abroad with strangers.

And in each of these particulars, by the bounty of nature and divine providence, this nation doth not onely equal any neighbour countrey, but far excels all in the most profitable advantages.

Of the trade of France.

France we know to be a nation, rich, populous and plentifull; and this onely by the increase of its own store, raised both by the fruit of the soil, and industry of the people; consisting in corn, wine, and many sorts of fruits, and great manufactures of all sorts of silks, linen clothes, laces, and many other rich commodities, which do not onely store them at home, with what they need, but by the overplus provides for all things else, they necessarily want from abroad; with plenty of money to boot.

Of the trade of Holland.

Holland hath not much of its own store, especially not answerable to supply the wants of that nation; and yet by their industrious diligence in trade, they are not onely furnished with whatsoever the world affords and they want, but by the profit of their trade they excel in plenty and riches, all their neighbour nations.

Riches & People necessary to increase the greatness and power of a nation.

Two things therefore appear to be chiefly necessary, to make a nation great, and powerfull; which is to be rich, and populous; and this nation enjoying together all those advantages with part whereof onely, others grow great and flourishing; and withall, a Prince, who above all things delights and glories in his peoples happiness: this nation can expect no less then to become the most great, and flourishing of all others.

The prejudice private interests often are to publick advantages.

But private advantages are often impediments of publick profit; for in what any single person shall be a loser, there, endeavours will be made to hinder the

8   publick

publick gain, from whence proceeds the ill succes that commonly attends the endeavours for publick good; for commonly it is but coldly prosecuted, because the benefit may possibly be something remote from them that promote it; but the mischief known and certain to them that oppose it: and Interest more than reason commonly sways most mens affections.

Whereby it may appear, how necessary it is that the publick profits should be in a single power to direct, whose Interest is onely the benefit of the whole.

The greatest thing therefore that any Prince can aim at, is to make his dominions rich and populous, and by what means it may be effected in this nation, beyond all neighbour countreys, I shall endeavour to demonstrate: People and plenty are commonly the begetters the one of the other, if rightly ordered.

And first, to increase the people of this nation, per- *How to* mission would be given to all people of foreign coun- *increase the* treys, under such restrictions as the state shall think *people of this* fit, freely to inhabit and reside within this kingdom, *nation.* with liberty to buy or sell lands or goods, to import or export any commodities, with the like priviledge and freedom that *English* men have.

This would quickly increase the number of our people, and multiply our riches: for those people that would come from other countries to inhabit here, would also bring their riches with them, which if they laid out in the purchasing of estates, or improvement of our trade, or were onely their persons rightly employed, it might very much increase, both the riches and power of this nation.

But it may be demanded why we should expect that *Why* people should leave their own native contreys to come *foreigners* and inhabit here, when they enjoy already as many *desire to inha-* priviledges as here are offered them. *bit here.*

These reasons may be given,

9   First,

16

The first reason.

First, that this countrey in it self is as pleasant, or more pleasant, healthfull, fruitful and temperate then any other.

The second reason.

Secondly, that our laws, government, and disposition of the people, I may say, are not onely as good, but much better then any other, for the ease, quiet, peace and security of a people.

The third reason.

Thirdly, if our trade and manufactures were but improved to that advantage, as they are capable of, there would be no countrey in the world, where industrious people might improve their estates, and grow more rich, then in this; and the hope of gain commonly bears so great a sway amongst men, that it is alone sufficient to prevail with most.

The fourth reason.

Fourthly, this being the most eminent and intire countrey of all others, that profess the Protestant Religion (which profession is very numerous in most of the other countreys of *Europe*, but many of them under constraint and danger, and the free liberty of mens consciences with security to their persons, being above all things most desirable) it cannot be doubted, or denied (were those impediments removed, that now may hinder) but we might be sufficiently stored with wealthy and industrious people, from all parts of *Europe*.

Reasons shewing the advantages the Prince of this nation hath by preferring the Protestant Religion only.

And were there not so many divine reasons to prefer the Protestant Religion before all others, as being doubtless above all the most free from vain and superstitious beliefs and ceremonies, being the onely model of true piety and vertue, without those allays of pretended pious evils, that some abound with; contriving by murder, treason and mischief, to advance their opinions: I say, if there were not these reasons for it, but that the Protestant Religion wanted this unvaluable worth, to prefer it before others, and suppose it onely equal with the rest; yet in humane prudence it

10   is

is most eligible, and to be preferred by the Prince of this nation before all others.

First, because thereby, he remains the onely Supreme, *The first* under God, in these dominions; and controllable by *reason.* none: whereby his power in government is much confirmed, and the peace of his people secured; when if it were otherwise (as in some it is) that mens consciences were at the dispose of others; who use their power onely to the advancement of their own wealth, pride & greatness; it cannot be avoided, but that the Princes Interest and theirs may often differ; which can never happen but to the Princes great hazard, and peoples ruine; of which truth, there have been already too many sad examples in this kingdom; so as I conceive, there needs little more to be said to perswade a Prince, to prefer his own peace, security and freedom, above the perswasions of any, that onely seek their own private Interest and advantage.

Secondly, for the Prince of this nation, to profess *The second* the reformed Protestant Religion, is a matter of greatest *reason.* policy & prudence, for the advance of his own power and greatness: For as it is said before, considering how desireable the countrey is in it self, and the only chief in *Europe* of this profession; and the hazardous and dangerous condition of those in other countries, & the power that the perswasions of mens consciences have to prevail with them, he may always be assured of this, that where any of this profession in other countreys, shall happen to be persecuted or injured by a stronger party of a contrary belief, their refuge will certainly be to him, either to be received as his Subjects in his own countrey, or else to offer their service to help him to become Lord of their own; or otherwise, if quarrels or differences should happen to arise between this Prince and the Prince of any other neighbour country, if they should make war upon him, he

11   would

would be assured of friends abroad to help to divert
them, or if he should find it fitting to attach others, he
cannot want confederates and assistants in the prosecution of his design, especially if there be any thing of
pretence of Religion in the case: which is seldom
wanting, where it is any ways serviceable to advance
a design.

But by the way it is to be observed, that as this may
be of certain advantage to this Prince against others,
so would it be of like mischief to himself or worse,
should he suffer the Interest of any other Prince to
have the like advantage against him; and in this kind
there is but one profession which is so considerable,
either amongst our selves at home, or in countreys
abroad, that is worthy the taking notice of, and it is so
Catholick as I shall not need to name it.

The danger for the prince of this nation to tolerate any other Religion. And though Christians ought not to persecute one
another, and that onely for small differences in opinion,
when what is right or wrong for the most part remains
a doubt and uncertain; whil'st the evils are onely certain
that such disputes produce.

And as it may be truly said, Morality may be short
of true Religion, yet it is most certain, that no Religion
can be pure that wants true morality; I shall onely
therefore make this short observation, That that Religion which shall endeavour to advance it self by all
immoral and wicked ways and means, must needs be
in that particular much defective. And though this
be commonly practised by most, yet certainly the
danger is greater from that whose profest principle it
is, than from such others, who (though often guilty)
yet wholly disown it. And what Prince, or state is
likely to escape mischief, or be secure; when opportunity is offered to those, who by ties of conscience are
obliged to ruine it; and have Interest and subtilty
enough to contrive the same? all which being rightly

12   weighed

weighed and considered, it is evident, how perilous, and desperate a thing it might prove, if it were onely on account of policy, and self-preservation, for a Prince to admit or countenance such things, which have not the least shew or appearance of good, or advantage, but in all likelihood, of most certain hazard and ruine, both to Himself and State.

But granting what is said to be true, yet what can be objected against the countenancing, or at least toleration of all such other sorts of Christian professions, who pretend they have not the will, nor probably can have the power, to contrive or act any thing considerable to the damage, or disquiet of the Prince or State.

It may be answered, that the toleration of all such in it self doth not appear altogether so dangerous to the Prince, or State: But if the nature of man be rightly considered, together with the common zeal in matters of Religion, you shall finde that commonly things of the smallest consequence make the greatest differences: and, as the same faith and belief, doth very much increase love and affection, so contrariwise difference in opinions, do only beget & engender contempt, & animosities towards one another; by which means the Prince shall at no time be either quiet, or secure. For should the Prince suffer all indifferently, and not elect some one which should always be countenanced, and maintained as the chief, and most universal profession of his kingdom: the confusions would be so great, and the Princes Interest so small amongst them, for want of any dependency on him; that a kingdom so devided against it self, could not stand.

And on the other side, should the Prince first settle a government in the Church, as it is at this day, and then give toleration to all others; the mischievous consequence would not be much less: for first, all such

as

as would withdraw, would not without grudging pay
their dues to Parsons, from whom they receive no
recompence, nay rather, whom they contemn and hate.

Secondly, upon all invasions from abroad, or rebel-
lions at home, the Prince shall be sure to have all such
for his enemies, as shall be so tolerated.

First, because of their certain hatred to the present
Church-government: by which they conceive, that they
receive many injuries, and oppressions.

Secondly, in hope every one to advance their own
party, could they remove the power in being; each
imagining their own opinion as the most worthy, would
first take place.

And lastly, where such advantages are offered, to
strengthen any discontented party, no Prince can hope,
or expect to be long quiet or secure.

These mischiefs and inconveniences, having of long
time been so obvious, it hath been thought by some,
that a strict uniformity in Church-government, is the
onely means to prevent all the aforesaid inconveniences.

*What is
chiefly re-
garded in
settling a
strict uni-
formity.*

I conceive it cannot well be denied, but then care
would be taken, that what is so imposed, be onely such
things as are barely necessary and such as may agree
best with the quiet and preservation of the State. And
in this also good regard would be. had, to the most
sober way of the same profession in other countreys;
which would much advance the design aforesaid, and
in all likelihood would preserve the Princes power more
entire, and his people in greater fidelity, love and
peace.

But to return to the cause that first moved this
discourse, as a means to multiply people, and enrich
the kingdom, it may be objected;

*Objections
against the
ways and
means to mul-
tiply people.*

First, that it doth not appear that people are wanting,
but rather that we have already too many, if we consider the number of poor people that are found in

14   every

every place; and it might be prudence, first, to employ these, before we endeavour to multiply more.

Secondly, that to give the like liberty and priviledge to foreiners, that *English-men* have, might be a means to undo the natives; for foreiners by their Correspondents abroad, and industry at home, will gain all the trade to themselves, and also by purchasing of estates, will make our land much the dearer.

It is answered first; It is true considering our *The Objections* present condition, how trade is decayed, and the little *answered.* encouragement people have to industry, we have already more people then are well employed; but I conceive, it is so much the greater damage to the Prince, to have his people both few and poor; but if the manufactures and other profitable employments of this nation, were rightly improved and encouraged, there is no doubt but the people, and riches of the kingdom might be greatly increased and multiplied, both to the profit, and honour of the Prince.

Secondly, that any *Englishman*, of the like ingenuity as a stranger, will have the like advantage of trade, as any stranger can have, as to the exportation or importation of any commodities, for they may have their correspondents abroad as well as the other: yet, suppose they could not, it would be no damage to the kingdom, but an advantage, if the Subjects by this means be more plentifully and cheaply provided with all forein commodities, & may gain a better price, and vent for their own, and the number and Interests that can pretend to suffer hereby, are so few, & inconsiderable that it bears no proportion with the advantage.

And further, by this liberty to foreiners, we should quickly attain to the perfection of those manufactures, which now we so highly value and purchase so dear from abroad: for many of the best Artists of other countreys, no doubt in short time would be transported

15   hither

hither, perhaps no less to the benefit of this nation, then the like encouragement hath been in former times, by the improvement of our art of clothing; and by which practice the *Hollander* at this day reaps unknown advantages.   And as for raising the price and value of our lands, or of any thing else that is our own; it is of so great an advantage, that it might be wished, nothing were cheap amongst us but onely money.

Of our natu-ral store.

But to proceed in order, and first of our natural store, and annual increase of the soil, the annual prcfit and increase of the soil of this kingdom, consists chiefly in corn of all sorts, flax, hemp, hops, wooll, and many more such like; and also the best sorts of cattel, as bullocks, horse and sheep; and the greater our in-crease is of any of these commodities, the richer may we be; for, money, and all forein commodities that come hither, are onely bought by the exchange of our own commodities; wherefore by how much our own store doth exceed those necessaries we want from abroad, by so much will the plenty of money be increased amongst us.

Those things to be chiefly increased that are raised at least charge, and are of greatest value abroad.

Our care should therefore be to increase chiefly those things which are of least charge at home, and greatest value abroad; and cattel may be of far greater advan-tage to us, then corn can be, if we might make the best profit of them; for that the profit we can make of any corn by exportation, is much hindred by the plenty that neighbour countreys afford of that commodity, as good or better than we have any.   Wherefore, could we employ our lands to any thing of more worth, we could not want plenty of corn, though we had none of our own; for what we should increase in the room of it, of greater value by exportation, would not onely bring us home as much corn as that land would have yeelded, but plenty of money to boot.

16   Of

Of cattel, the most considerable are horse, sheep, and bullocks, in all which we do not onely excel in goodness all other countreys, whereby we can vent the profits of them at far greater rates, but we may also by our singular advantage, in the increase of those cattel, have the sole trade, being able so far to exceed our own wants, as to furnish all our neighbours, who must be forced to good rates, no other countrey affording the like for goodness, or scarce sufficient for their own use.

And might we freely have the liberty to export them, or so much of them as may be fitting, we should need no laws to hinder the exportation of corn; for we should find thereby a profit, so far exceeding that which might be raised out of every acre, that we might better afford to give a far greater price to buy it, than we can now sell it for. For the profit of one acre of pasture, in the flesh, hide and tallow of an Ox; or in the flesh, wooll and tallow of a sheep; or in the carcase of a horse, is of so much greater value abroad, than the like yield of the earth would be in corn; that the exportations of this nation might be at least double to what it is, if rightly disposed. Wherefore it is to be wished, that the Supreme power would so far tender the publick good, in which it is so much concerned, as to remove all impediments, and promote all endeavours, which tend to so great and publick an advantage.

The greatest impediments in this Improvement are chiefly these, *The impediments of this improvement.*

First, men cannot make the best of their own lands.

Secondly, when they have, they cannot sell the increase of it to the best advantage. And these may be thus amended.

First, by a liberty for every man to enjoy his lands in severalty and inclosure; one of the greatest Improvements this nation is capable of; for want whereof, we *How to remove them, and first by inclosure. The damage*

17 find

that happens for want of inclosure. find by daily experience, that the profit of a great part of the land and stock in this kingdom, as now imployed, is wholly lost. And this appears, in that the land of the common fields, almost in all places of this nation, with all the advantages that belong unto them, will not let for above one third part so much as the same land would do inclosed, and always several. And on the great Commons, a house with commoning wil not let for one quarter so much, as it would do were its proportion several unto it. And all this by reason of the many several Interests: whence it is, that men cannot agree to employ it to its properest use, and best advantage: whereby much land is tilled with great labour, and small profit; and much land fed to the starving of the cattel, and the impoverishing the inhabitants; to the increase of nothing but beggery in this nation; all which inconveniences, would by inclosure be prevented.

Objections against inclosures. But it may be objected, that many other inconveniences would happen by inclosure; and chiefly, it would cause great depopulations and scarcity of corn, as hath been conceived by former Parliaments; which appears by their opposing, rather than advancing of it: upon this opinion, that inclosure would convert the land to pasture; one hundred acres of which, will scarce maintain a shepherd and his dog, which now maintains many families, employed in tillage; and by experience it is found, that many towns, which when their lands were in tillage had many families, now they are inclosed, have not so many inhabitants in them.

To this I answer,

The Objections answered. First, that inclosures would not have been opposed, had it not appeared, that most landlords endeavoured it; which is a greater argument of Improvement: for, did not the landlord suppose it would improve his land to a higher value, he would never have been perswaded

18   to

to do it; and the reason why it would have been of greater advantage to the landlord, is, because the tenant could make more profit of it, or else we should not finde them so greedy after pasture, at so high a rate, when they may have arable enough for half the value; and this proves inclosure is profitable, since the same land is thereby raised to a far greater value.

Secondly, as for Corn, it would be nothing the scarcer by inclosure, but the rather more plentifull, though a great deal less land were tilled : for then every ingenious husband would onely plow that land that he found most fitting for it, and that no longer than he found it able to bring him profit: so as he would out of one acre, raise more corn than in the common field can be raised of two, whereby one acre would be saved for other uses, besides the charges of mens and cattels labours; whereas in the common fields, where the tenant doth not plow, the profit of the land is lost; whereby he is forced to a continual plowing, though to the ruine and damage both of the land, and of himself: so as that land, labour, and charge is lost, which otherwise might be imployed, to the profit and advantage of the kingdom.

Thirdly, as to depopulations by inclosures, granting it increaseth plenty, as cannot well be denied, How increase and plenty can depopulate, cannot well be conceived: nor surely do any imagine that the people which lived in those towns they call depopulated, were all destroyed, because they lived no longer there; when indeed they were onely removed to other places, where they might better benefit themselves, and profit the publick.

Certainly they might as well think the nation undone, should they observe how *London* is depopulated in a long vacation, when men are only retired into the countrey, about their private and necessary employ-

19   ments

ments; and the like might they think of the countrey
in the Term time, yet a man is not thereby added, or
diminished to the nation.

Fourthly, as many or more families may be maintained and employed, in the manufacture of the wooll
that may arise out of one hundred acres of pasture,
than can be employed in a far greater quantity of
arable; who perhaps do not always finde it most convenient for them to live, just on the place where the
wooll groweth; by which means cities and great towns
are peopled, nothing to the prejudice of the kingdom.

Wherefore then if by inclosure the land it self is
raised to a greater value, and a less quantity capable
of a greater increase, and if really it causeth no depopulations, but at most a removal of people thence;
where without benefit to the publick, or profit to themselves, they labored and toiled, to a more convenient
habitation, where they might with less pains greatly
advantage both: And if the manufactures and other
profitable employments of this nation are increased, by
adding thereto such numbers of people, who formerly
served onely to waste, not to increase the store of the
nation, it cannot be denied, but the encouragement of
inclosure, where every mans just right may be preserved, would infinitely conduce to the increase and
plenty of this nation, and is a thing very worthy the
countenance and care of a Parliament.

Of our Mines.   In the next place, the product of our Mines of lead,
tin, iron, coals, allum, and the like, may also be
accounted amongst the annual increase of the soil, and
the product of these are onely obtained by the labour
and industry of the people, and are very serviceable at
home and profitable abroad; and therefore the increase
of them doth very well deserve all just encouragement.

Of our   Lastly, the great plenty of fish our seas naturally
fishing-trade. afford may be accounted amongst our other annual

increases,

increases, and the profit of these onely depend on peoples labour, and that in such a kinde as it doth not onely increase the plenty and wealth of the kingdom, but also may be very serviceable to preserve and increase the honour and safety of our nation, by increasing our shipping; especially if some course were taken to prevent others from robbing us of so great a treasure, and therefore very worthy of the publick care to maintain and incourage; but the concernment of this is already so well known to every one to be so great, as it is not needfull to discourse it further.

In the next place, our manufactures are to be considered, on which chiefly depends both the wealth and prosperity of this kingdom: for by the increase and encouragement thereof, the Subjects are employed in honest and industrious callings, maintained and preserved from want, and those mischiefs which commonly attend idleness: the people furnished at home with all things both of necessity and pleasure; and by the overplus procure from abroad, what ever for use or delight is wanting. *Of our manufactures.*

The chief manufactures amongst us at this day, are onely woollen clothes, woollen stuff, of all sorts, stockings, ribbandings, and perhaps some few silk stuffs, and some other small things, scarce worth naming; and these already named so decayed and adulterated, that they are almost out of esteem both at home and abroad.

And this, because forein commodities are grown into so great esteem amongst us, as we wholly undervalue and neglect the use of our own, whereby that great expence of treasure, that is yearly wasted in clothing, furnitures, and the like; redounds chiefly to the profit of strangers, and to the ruine of his Majesties Subjects. *Our manufacturers very much decayed. The reasons.*

And this will more plainly appear, if we examine the vast sums of money the *French* yearly delude us of;

either

either by such commodities as we may as well have of our own, or else by such others, as we might as well in great part be without: whereby no doubt our treasure will be soon exhausted, and the people ruined, as this particular may make appear, which not long since was delivered in to the King of *France*, upon a design he had to have forbidden the trade between *France* and *England*; supposing the value of *English* commodities sent into *France*, did surmount the value of those that were transported hither.

A catalogue of French commodities yearly transported into England. 1. There is transported out of *France* into *England*, great quantities of velvets plain and wrought, sattins plain and wrought, cloth of gold and silver, Armoysins and other merchandises of silk, which are made at *Lions*, and are valued to be yearly worth one hundred and fifty thousand pounds.

2. In silk, stuffs, taffeties, poudesoys, armoysins, clothes of gold and silver, tabbies, plain and wrought, silk-ribbands and other such like silk stuffs as are made at *Tours*, valued to be worth above three hundred thousand pounds by year.

3. In silk ribbands, gallowns, laces, and buttons of silk, which are made at *Paris, Rouen, Chaimont, S. Estienes* in *Forrests*, for about one hundred and fifty thousand pounds by year.

4. A great quantity of serges, which are made at *Chalons, Chartres, Estamines* and *Rhemes*, and great quantities of serges made at *Amiens, Crevecoeur, Blicourt*, and other towns in *Picardy*, for above one hundred and fifty thousand pounds a year.

5. In bever, demicastor and felt hats, made in the city and suburbs of *Paris*; besides many others made at *Rouen, Lions*, and other places, for about one hundred and twenty thousand pounds a year.

6. In feathers, belts, girdle, hatbands, fans, hoods, masks, gilt and wrought looking-glasses, cabinets,

watches,

watches, pictures, cases, medals, tablets, bracelets, and other such like mercery ware, for above one hundred and fifty thousand pounds a year.

7. In pins, needles, box-combs, tortois-shell combs, and such like, for about twenty thousand pounds a year

8. In perfumed and trimmed gloves, that are made at *Paris, Rouen, Vendosme, Clermont,* and other places, for about ten thousand pounds a year.

9. In papers of all sorts, which are made at *Auvergne, Poictou, Limosin, Champayne* and *Normandy,* for above one hundred thousand pounds a year.

10. In all sorts of iron-mongers wares that are made in *Forrests, Auvergne,* and other places, for about fourty thousand pounds a year.

11. In linen cloth that is made in *Britainy* and *Normandy,* as well course as fine, there is transported into *England,* for above four hundred thousand pounds a year.

12. In household-stuff, consisting of beds, matresses, coverlids, hangings, fringes of silk and other furniture, for above one hundred thousand pounds a year.

13. In wines from *Gascoigne, Nantois* and other places on the river of *Loyer,* and also from *Bourdeaux, Rochel, Nante, Rouen* and other places, are transported into *England* for above six hundred thousand pounds a year.

14. In aqua vitæ, sider, vineger, verjuice, and such like, for about one hundred thousand pounds a year.

15. In saffron, castle-sope, honey, almonds, olives, capers, prunes, and such like, for about one hundred and fifty thousand pounds a year.

16. Besides five or six hundred vessels of salt, loaden at *Maron, Rochel, Bouage,* the isle of *Oleron,* and isle of *Rhee,* transported into *England,* and *Holland,* of a very great value. So as by this calculation, it doth

appear

appear, that the yearly value of such commodities as are transported from *France* to *England*, amount to above six & twenty hundred thousand pounds.

And the commodities exported out of *England* into *France*, consisting chiefly of woollen clothes, serges, knit stockings, lead, pewter, allum, coals, and all else, do not amount to above ten hundred thousand pounds a year. By which it appears that our trade with *France* is at least sixteen hundred thousand pounds a year, clear lost to this kingdom:

Whereby the King of *France*, finding it would prove to his loss, to forbid the trade with *England*, soon laid aside the design; however raised the customs of some of our *English* commodities, by which means the vent of those commodities is very much lessened and hindred.

Hereby it may appear how insensibly our treasure will be exhausted, and the nation begger'd, whil'st we carelessly neglect our own Interest, and strangers abroad are diligent to make their advantages by us.

Means to redress this mischief. But most of these evils would be easily prevented, if only his Majesty would be pleased to commend to his people, by his own example, the esteem and value he hath of his own commodities, in which the greatest Courtier may be as honourably clad, as in the best dress, *Paris*, or a *French* Taylour can put him in; besides it seems to be more honourable for a King of *England*, rather to become a pattern to his own people, than to conform to the humours and fancies of other nations, especially when it is so much to his prejudice.

This alone, without further trouble, would be at least ten hundred thousand pounds a year to the advantage of his people; for the Courtiers always endeavour to imitate the Prince, being desirous to obtain his favour, which they can no way better do, than by approving his actions in being of like humour:

and the Court being the copy that the Gentry strive to write after, and the rest of the people commonly follow; it appears of what great consequence and advantage the good example of a Prince, is to the benefit of his people.

And whereas it sometimes hath been thought prudence in a Prince, to forbid and discountenance the excess of apparel in his Subjects; whereby many of the nobility themselves have ruined their families, and most of the Gentry have been impoverished; whereby the great expence and waste of treasure in that vanity doth appear: yet I conceive, in a convenient manner it rather ought to be maintained, and encouraged, onely observing these rules. *Expence in apparel to be countenanced under some restrictions.*

First, that the vanity of the expence do not depend on such commodities, as have too much of the substance of gold, silver, or silk; whereby the publick treasure is wasted and lost.

Secondly, that we impoverish not ourselves to enrich strangers, by that unnatural vanity, in preferring foreign commodities though worse, before our own, that are better.

Thirdly, that the excess of this expense consist chiefly in the art, manufacture and workmanship of the commodity made in our own countrey; whereby ingenuity would be encouraged, the people employed, and our treasure kept at home, so as the Prince would be nothing damnified by the excess: for the ruine of one would raise as much another of his Subjects; and money would thereby be more moving, which would be a great encouragement, and satisfaction to the people.

To name the particulars of such commodities as would hereby be increased, would be endless and needless, when in a word it is, whatever at present we purchase from abroad, which we might as well raise of

our

our own at home. But some perhaps may say, that this would destroy our trade abroad, for many of our commodities are vented, by the exchange of them for other commodities we bring home in return.

I answer, it is no prejudice to lose that trade which is a loss to keep; and if our importations of forein commodities be of far greater value than our own exportations, our treasure must needs be wasted to even the balance; and so our own people remain idle & poor, for the vent of one thousand pounds worth of commodities abroad, is of little advantage to the people, if thereby they are hindred of the vent of two thousand at home.

The Interest of the Prince, to increase the manufactures and trade of his people. Concerning our trade abroad, & what is freely to be exported. Wherefore these particulars considered, it is evident of what great concernment it is to a Prince, to encourage and increase the trade, and manufacture of his own people. And so much concerning trade at home.

In the next place concerning our trade abroad with strangers: and this would also be encouraged, and increased by all means possible, and when any commodity is raised to the greatest height it is capable of, it should be free for exportation, under so reasonable customs, that the Merchant may afford his commodity abroad, as cheap as others, or else he would not be able to vent it.

What freely to be imported. Secondly, all forein commodities that are usefull, to improve our own manufactures and trade abroad, and cannot be raised here, should be brought unto us under easie customs, the better to enable us at an easie exchange, to vent our commodities abroad.

What to be hindred and prevented. Thirdly, all forein commodities whatsoever, that are only useful to be spent within the nation, & that have already all their perfection, as fruits, sugars, wines, linen cloth, laces, silks, & what else can receive no addition here, and are not to be again transported; such commodities should pay extraordinary customs,

but

but should not be forbidden to be brought in: For by
this means, these commodities will be so dear to the
people, that it will much wean them from so lavish an
use of them, as might otherwise be, and for such things
as we are capable to raise, it will much increase it of
our own; whereby the State will raise a good revenue,
and the countrey save their wealth, that would be
wastfully spent abroad, and so increase our own manufactures at home.

Fourthly, the increase of our land in any kinde
(except sheep alive and mares) that have already all
the perfection that we can add unto them, should be
free for exportation, under reasonable customs; and of *The exporta-*
all things this nation is capable to raise, there is not *tion of horses*
of greatest
any one of so great profit, as the exportation of horses, *advantage.*
which of all commodities is of least charge to be raised
at home, and of greatest value abroad. But to this
may be many objections.

First, that it will make horses dear. *Objections.*

Secondly, that the exportation of stone-horses may
be prejudicial, by furnishing others with our breed.

Besides, it may enable our enemies who may invade
us, and we shall also weaken our selves by sending
away our best horses; with other such like objections.

But to these it is answered,

First, as for the dearness of any thing we sell to *The Objections*
strangers, the more money we get for it by how much *answered.*
the dearer it is; and the only way to be rich, is to
have plenty of that commodity to vent, that is of the
greatest value abroad; for what the price of any thing
is amongst our selves, whether dear or cheap, it matters
not; for as we pay, so we receive, and the countrey is
nothing damnified by it; but the art is when we deal
with strangers, to sell dear and to buy cheap; and this
will increase our wealth.

Secondly, to vent stone-horses, would be of far better

profit

profit then to vent geldings; for that a stone-horse will give far more money, with the same charge to us, besides the loss of many horses in gelding; and as for any prejudice to our breed, I conceive it no danger, if mares be not transported; for one horse will cover twenty mares as well as twenty horse may do: wherefore the increase of the horses do nothing increase the breed; and in *France* where we should best vent our horses, they have always horses enough, and of very great value and goodness, sufficient for stallions; but they have neither mares nor conveniency to breed; for the contrey generally is all champion, corn-fields, and vineyards, and also so unsafe to venture any cattel of such worth without stone walls to guard them, that scarce all the summer, either horse or cow is left abroad in the night, without a guard; besides, if they could breed, the breed of it self would prove degenerate, and soon be lost, the countrey being naturally improper for it.

As for enabling our enemies to invade us, I conceive there is but little danger in that. At present we have amity with all those countries that desire our horses, and if at any time it should be found fitting, to forbid the transportation of them, the prejudice that might happen by those already transported, would soon be past; for of five hundred horses that should be transported, I verily beleeve in less than five years, there would scarce be five remaining.

Yet further, it doth not concern us to fear any such power in our neighbours, we having no frontiers subject to sudden incursions; but our defence consists chiefly in another strength which is our ships at sea, which should they be insufficient to guard us, I doubt the enemies want of our horses would be but small security.

And as to the weakening of our selves, by sending away our best horses, whereby we may want for our

own

own use, this I conceive is a groundless fear, and
wholly mistaken; for the good profit we should make
by a free vent of this commodity, would encourage
every ingenious husband, to be well provided with what
is so profitable; and every man would endeavour, not
onely to increase his breed but also to be curious in
the goodness of them; so as it will rather be a double
advantage to us; for as by the profit of those we send
abroad, we shall greatly increase our wealth, and far
more by this means than by any other this countrey is
capable of, out of its own store; so we shall also have
more choice, and plenty of this so serviceable and
profitable a creature, both for use and pleasure.

By the improvement of our trade as aforesaid, both *Concerning*
at home and abroad, whereby our exportations of com- *the return of*
money by
modities would exceed our importations, a very great *exchange.*
& signal advantage would acrue not commonly taken
notice of, and it is the profit we should then make of
our returning money, by bills of exchange, in which *The prejudice*
at this present we suffer an unvaluable loss: for as it *at present.*
is said before, our importations exceeding our exportations, our coin & treasure must needs be wasted to
even the balance and consequently more money drawn
by exchange out of the countrey than is returned back
again; whereby we are forced to give far more than
the intrinsick value of the thing, to receive our monies
beyond the sea, to supply our occasions, the number
being greater of those that desire to receive moneys
abroad, then of those that want it at home; for it is in
this as in all other commodities, Where the commodity
is scarce, and the vent great, the purchase is alwaies
dear; and the forein Merchant finding our necessity, *Our coin and*
makes his advantage upon us incredibly to our loss; *bullion trans-*
so that by this means it also happens, that our coin *ported, and*
the reason.
and bullion is transported; it being found more profitable then returns by exchange, for the reasons afore-
29   said:

Our gold transported and the reason.

said: and our gold being of less value at home then it is abroad it hath been all conveyed away within these few years: and laws to prevent it shall always prove fruitlesss, when it is advantageous to do it; there being means sufficient to be found to effect it, by such as shall find it profitable.

Laws to prevent it fruitless.

Wherefore to make laws to hinder the exportation of coin or bullion, I conceive altogether useless.

First, because it doth nothing prevent it where it is intended; and Secondly, in many cases it is most advantageous to do it. For in some countreys, some commodities are no way to be purchased at cheaper rates, than by money *in specie*: and if by the right ordering and disposing of our trade, our exportations did exceed our importations, in value; our coin and bullion would be daily increased; there being no other means to even the balance of trade.

Concerning our money and coin.

And here it may not be altogether improper, to speak something concerning our money and coin, which is also a commodity as well as the rest; in which these particulars are chiefly to be respected.

How chiefly to be considered in relation to other nations.

First, to consider and examine if the gold to silver, in *England*, be of the like proportionable value; as the gold to silver, in *France, Spain, Holland*, and other forein countreys.

Secondly, to consider the allay of gold, and silver, in *England*, to that of other countreys.

Thirdly, to consider if the coin be of equal value with the currant price of bullion, the charge of coining onely deducted.

Lastly, how to order our coin, so as may be most honourable and profitable to the nation.

To the first, it doth appear that the gold in *England* doth not bear so good a value to silver as it doth in *France*, and other forein countreys; whereby all our gold is exported, and not our silver.

　　　　　　　　Secondly,

Secondly, the allay both of gold and silver in *England*, is finer than in other parts; which is rather a prejudice, then an advantage, it giving no more in forein countreys, than onely according to the weight by their standard, without consideration to the purenesss.

Thirdly, our coin is not equal to the true value of the silver, the coinage onely deducted; for by the imperfection of our mint, the pieces of the same value are made so various, that some shillings will weigh fourteen pence, and some not above eight pence; which afterwards, being new weighed over, and culled by the goldsmiths, through whose hands most of our bullion passeth, the heavy ones are picked out, and onely the leight ones, and those of under value, pass for currant; which is a most eminent abuse and wrong to the publick.

Wherefore lastly, in prevention to these inconveniences, First, our gold would be raised in proportion to silver, at least equal with what it bears in *France*, and other countreys; and if it be desired to increase, chiefly, that *species*, a small addition to the value will soon do it.

Secondly, the allay would be made the same, with that in other countreys of *Europe*, with whom we chiefly traffick. *The imperfection of our mint and abuses at home.*

Thirdly, the abuses happening by the imperfection of our mint, as light and false money in abundance; any ill-favoured and imperfect false stamp being hardly to be distinguished from the true, might easily be prevented, by a more exact and curious stamp, as may easily be made by the way of milling; whereby not only the coin will be more beautifull, but also more equal in weight, and much more difficult to be clipped and counterfeited: especially if care be taken, to make the pieces large and thin; which will not onely shew more great and noble, but will many ways be more easie to be distinguished from false, as by the sound, stiffness, weight and colour: it being both so difficult, and *How to order our mint, so as to prevent most of these abuses and inconveniences.*

chargeable

chargeable, to counterfeit money so formed, as few will hazard to undertake it.

Concerning our shipping and naviga- tion. Next, in order to our trade abroad, and safety at home, our shipping and navigation is to be considered; the increase and preservation whereof, is of great concernment to the Interest, safety, and well-being of this nation; for which the late act for trade, by the late pretended Parliament, did wisely provide, by ordering that no foreiner should bring any commodity hither, but what was the growth of their own countrey; Whereby the *Hamburger* and *Flemming*, that run hackney all the world over, were a little stayed from coming hither crowding so thick, with all forein commodities as they were wont to do; whereby little, or no employment could be found for our own vessels; every thing being so plentifully brought hither by them; and at cheaper rates, than we our selves could fetch them.

Objections against it. But some perhaps may object, that, Sure it was an advantage to us, to be so cheaply and plentifully stored with forein commodities, when we cannot be so cheaply furnished by own shipping; for that we are at far greater charge, both in goodness of shipping, number of our men, and chargeable maintaining of them more than others.

The Objections answered. I answer, It is true, that the same commodity brought hither in any of our own vessels, cannot be afforded so cheap as what might be brought by others; by reason indeed, that our shipping is much more chargeable, and better manned than any other: but this being rightly considered, it is rather an advantage than a prejudice to the publick; for, if commodities be thereby any thing the dearer, here at home, yet, we buy them as cheap abroad as any other; and all that others would have gained of us by the carriage, will now be earned by our own people; and whatever it costs the dearer to the purchaser here, is no prejudice to the publick, when our own nation receives the profit of it; especially it

being

being by the increase of that, in which consists the greatest honour and safety of the kingdom. Some might therefore think, that it might be of no less advantage, to forbid other nations to fetch any of our commodities, but to keep to our selves the benefit of the portage of them by our own shipping.

I answer, should we do this, we can expect no less, but that other nations would do the like towards us, whereby we should be very much prejudiced.

First, in that we should then lose the advantage which now we have, in bringing forein commodities home; and besides, we should perhaps, want the vent of our own commodities, which certainly will always sell best, wher most chapmen are found to buy them; so as by how much the cheaper they can transport them, so much the more they will be contented to give us here; moreover, the greatest part our Manufactures, are of so great value, and so light of carriage, that a small advantage in the price, or a little better vent, will soon compensate the loss of the portage of them; but indeed, if the *Hamburger* and *Flemming*, were prevented in the carriage of some of our more sluggish commodities, as sea-coal, lead, iron, allum, fish; or the like, where the charge of the carriage many times is greater, than the whole value of the commodity it self, this might possibly increase something our Navigation, and yet hinder nothing the vent of those commodities, which others cannot at all be without; and we shall not much need to fear their requiting us in the same kinde; for neither the *Hollander*, nor *Hamburger*, have any such commodities of their own, as we need care to fetch; who are the onely nation, that employ themselves in this kinde of trade.

It may not also be improper, to reflect a little upon the benefit this nation doth, or may receive by forein Plantations. *Of forein plantations.*

I conceive

What chiefly to be considered in the increasing and preserving them. I conceive, no forein Plantation should be undertaken, or prosecuted, but in such countreys that may increase the wealth and trade of this nation, either in furnishing us, with what we are otherwise forced to purchase from strangers, or else by increasing such commodities, as are vendible abroad; which may both increase our shipping, and profitably employ our people; but otherwise, it is always carefully to be avoided, especially where the charg is greater than the profit, for we want not already a countrey sufficient to double our people, were they rightly employed; and a Prince is more powerful that hath his strength and force united, then he that is weakly scattered in many places. But, To descend to particulars, *viz.* what commodities are most desireable and of greatest advantage, and what countreys and climates are most proper to increase them, would be too tedious to treat of here.

Concerning Merchants associating themselves in companies. There yet remains something to be said concerning Merchants, associating themselves in companies; the benefit or prejudice whereof hath been often controverted, but something difficult to determine.

Objections against it. The objections answered. It is true, It is opposed by many, conceiving the free liberty of trade would be much more advantageous in the general, because these companies, keeping the trade to themselves onely, will have what commodities are to be vented abroad at their own price, and at an under-value; none having occasion to buy them but themselves: wherby the workmen are many times discouraged, and sometimes undone. And on the contrary, what commodities are brought home in exchange, they sell at what unreasonable rates they please, the whole commodity remaining in their hands; whereby the people in general, are very much damnified, and the companies onely enriched; whereas, if the trade were free, our own commodities having more chapmen, would sell at better rates, and what is brought home

34　　　　　　　　　in

in return, would be distributed at much cheaper prices amongst the people.

This is for the most part a truth, yet, rightly considering the thing, it rather seems an advantage in the whole, then the least prejudice; for indeed, as they make their profit at home, so they make no less advantage abroad; for the whole commodity being in their hands, they will make the most that can be made of it; none having the like commodities to undersell them: and the like advantage they have again in what they buy; whereby in truth, our own commodities are sold the dearer to strangers, and forein commodities bought much the cheaper; when both would happen contrary in a free trade; where each will undersel the other, to vent most; and also purchase at any rates, to prevent the rest: besides, many times the trade is wholly lost, particulars being often too weak to maintain and undergo it, and there is nothing less of a commodity vented by a Company, than by single persons: for they will always furnish, as much as the trade requires; the more they vent, the more being their profit. Whereby it may appear, that Companies both vent our own commodities to the best advantages and buy cheapest what we want from strangers; and the prejudice that may happen by them to the workmen, or home-chapmen, is fully recompensed by the clear profit they return to the publick; of which they are members, as well as others. But if their particular profits be thought too great, it may be something moderated by a free liberty, that every one that please, may be admitted of the Company, on fit and reasonable terms.

In the last place, concerning the use of money; which being the life and sinews of trade, it hath been the opinion of some that, The greater use were allowed for money, the more would be the profit of the publick; for that strangers, finding a greater benefit to be made

What Interest most proper to be allowed for the use of money.

35 of

of their money here, then other where, would send it hither; whereby money would be much more plentifull amongst us.

Indeed, I should be of their opinion, if as soon as by this means, great sums of money were transported hither, all their money should be confiscate to the publick; but if otherwise, sure it cannot be denied, but the greater the use the more the profit to the usurer, and loss to the debtor; so as in a few years, we should finde our selves so little enriched thereby, that when the principal should be again recalled, we should find but little money left; all our own being wasted in use: wherefore indeed the true benefit to the publick is, to set the use of money as low, or rather lower than in our neighbour-countreys it is; for then they would make no profit out of us, by that means; but rather we on them.   And it is the clear profit that we get out of our own that will make this Nation rich; and not the great sums we are indebted to others.

Many particulars more might seasonably be discoursed of, and this already touched, possibly by some other might be more exactly and amply treated on; but these being the, most material things that I could call to memory, and most conducing (in my opinion) to the emprovement and prosperity of the Nation, and consequently to my present design; I shall satisfie my self with this Essay; hoping the subject being so worthy, some other and more skilful and knowing Pen, may be provoked to enlarge it further.

F I N I S.

The Contents.

First

Concerning

The Contents. 249

FINIS.

ENGLAND'S
Great Happiness;

OR, A

DIALOGUE

BETWEEN

CONTENT *and* COMPLAINT

WHEREIN

Is demonſtrated that a great part of our
Complaints are causeless.

And we have more Wealth now, than
ever we had at any time before the Restauration of his sacred Majestie.

By a real and hearty Lover of his King
and Countrey.

---

*Say not thou, What is the cause that the former daies were
better than these? for thou dost not enquire wisely concerning this.* Eccl. 7. 10.

LONDON,
Printed by *J. M.* for *Edward Croft*, and
are to be sold at the *Printing-Press*
in *Cornhill*. 1677.

THE
CONTENTS
OF THIS
DIALOGUE.

Multitude

254 The Contents.

The Author to his Book.

MY little Book, when you do look
 Into the World that's curious;
You must take care, you don't ill fare
 From those men that are furious.

Against all things that reason brings
 To contradict their humours;
And scarce are pleas'd, unless they're eas'd
 By spreading forth false rumours.

But if that they ought 'gainst thee say,
 And make it truth appear;
Then I'l submit and think it fit,
 That you the blame should bear.

But if they will be murm'ring still,
 Partic'larizing men, that idly spend,
Or fates do lend a hand to Ruine: then
 'Twill be but meet Poor Robin see't,
And answer them with glee, because such fools
 Are the fit tools T'employ such men as he.

ENGLAND'S
Great Happiness;
OR, A
DIALOGUE
BETWEEN

Content and *Complaint*.

Content. **H**Ow do you do, Mr. *Complaint?*
  Complaint. Your Servant Sir, I'm glad to see you well: What News?

Cont. Why, all the talk is of the *Blazing Star*, and Whale that's come to *Colchester*.

Compl. God grant they forbode no ill News, I'm afraid on't. The French King they say is at *Callice*.

Cont. Well, what then, I hope he knows the way back to *Paris*.

Compl. Nay he need not come hither, here are enough already to eat us up, I profess there's no trade, I don't know what we shall do, there is not a penny stirring, and men break like mad, if these times hold we shall be all undone.

Cont. You Complainants are a sort of the worst condition'd people in the World, I won't say 'tis impossible for God to please you, but I'm sure his Blessings of Peace and Plenty won't.

Compl.

Compl. Plenty say you! yes, here's plenty enough of broken Merchants and Citizens.

Cont. True, one of them of a sort is too much, but yet I dare say there is more wealth in *England* at this time, than ever was at any before his Majesties Happy Restauration.

Compl. What then makes the Complaint?

Cont. Because such as you are hardly ever well when you are doing otherwise.

Compl. You talk strangely.

Cont. Well, I think 'tis so easie to make out, that while we are drinking a glass of Wine, I may convince, or put you to a non-plus.

Compl. Say'st thou so? Well I'le try, but instead of Wine let's drink a dish of Coffee; for I profess whatsoe're you think, I find them hard times.

Cont. Well, a match, but I suppose you go thither because 'tis the Complaining School, and you may be entertain'd with false jealousies an hour for a penny. Come Boy give me a dish of Tee, for I'm for something that heats and wets, and by its sweet taste give some reason to be contented.

Compl. For all this give me some Coffee.

Cont. Well, now let's hear your Complaints, and we'l consider them one by one.

Compl. There are a great many at present, I'le only mention five, *viz.*

1. Carrying the Money out of the Nation.
2. People's over high living.
3. The too many Foreigners.
4. The Enclosure of Commons.
5. The multitude of people that run into trade, and sell so cheap that one can't live by another.

Cont. Are these your great Complaints? I can hardly forbear laughing, for these rightly considered are some of our main temporal advantages. A great

8   encrease

encrease whereof would make us so rich as to be the envy of the whole world.

Compl. I should be glad if 'twere so, I pray let's hear what you can say for the exportation of money. There's law against it, and a great many wise men complain of the *East India Company* for that reason.

Cont. I must not gainsay Law; there was once a law to stint the making of Malt; but some of our Gentlemen are now of other minds, witness the Act for exportation of Beer, Ale, and Mum. The complaints against the *East India* Company, if they were for the Nation's happiness, would they were encouraged, and let it go as our Parliament shall in their wisdom think fit, but some wise men think it best as 'tis, however 'tis our great advantage to export Money: For the aforesaid Company brings in a great many more goods than we consume, the over-plus whereof is exported: By which part I suppose none will dispute a profit. Wherefore whatsoever they bring in more, must be all exported, (we being already over stockt) which undoubtedly will enrich us according to its proportion. But this they cannot do without money. For I suppose them men that very well understand their own interest (by which I am apt to judge all) and do think that if they could sell that cloth in *India* for two and twenty Shillings, which costs them here twenty, and sell enough, they would never carry out one penny: for they pay no freight out, and two and and twenty Shillings if it be really two and twenty Shillings, will buy more goods than twenty shillings will do. But if the *Indians* will not buy our goods, they must have our money, or we must knock off that Trade which the *Dutch* will heartily thank you for, and give you a golden god to boot.

Comp. Ah but we consume abundance of their Commodities here.

Cont. Best of all, for the more *Callico* we use, the

Our great advantage to exportmoney.

It is more less profitable for

9

us to consume
Callico, than
other foreign
linnen.

less other linnen, and that saves abundance of wealth by being to us (at first hand especially) much cheaper; and also pulling down the price of forreign linnen, I have heard some say almost half. But about this *India* trade you may see more at large by ingenious Mr. *Mun;* and a Letter call'd The *East-India* trade a most profitable trade to the Kingdom, printed 1677.

Norway
trade a profit-
able trade.

Comp. This is something, but what think you of the *Norway*-trade that takes away so many of our Crown pieces?

Cont. I think well of that too, for that kind of timber we cannot be without, and I suppose our land can be better imploy'd than in great groves of such like. It also employs a great shipping, and makes us build Houses, Ships, and Cases for Merchandise, at cheap rates, and if we might have a thousand Saw-Mills, for ought I know they might do us as much kindness as Engine Looms, and for all the talk of the short sighted Rabble, employ twice the people too.

Compl. You speak plain, but what think you of the *French* trade? which draws away our money by wholesale. Mr. *Fortrey* whom I have heard you speak well of, gives an account that they get sixteen hundred thousand pounds a year from us.

The *French*
Trade a pro-
fitable Trade.

Cont. 'Tis a great sum, but perhaps were it put to vote in a wise Council, whether for that reason the trade should be left off, 'twould go in the negative. For Paper, Wine, Linnen, Castle-Sope, Brandy, Olives, Capers, Prunes, Kid-skins, Taffaties, and such like we cannot be without; and for the rest which you are pleas'd to stile *Apes* and *Peacocks* (although wise *Solomon* rankt them with Gold and Ivory) they set us all a-gog, and have encreas'd among us many considerable trades: witness, the vast multitudes of Broad and Narrow silk Weavers, Makers of Points, and white and black Laces, Hats, Fanns, Looking-Glasses, and

10   other

other glasses as I'm told the best in the world, Paper,
Fringes, and gilded Leather, which in a short time is
like to be made as cheap here, as in *Holland* or any other
place. Wine of several fruits, Sider, Saffron, Honey,
Spirits, and such like: and some cause improvements
by farther Manufacture, others we export with great
profit, and have a great variety to satisfie all sorts of
Markets, causing their Neighbours that sell the like, as
Salt, Wine, Linnen, &c. to sell as much cheaper with
abundance other advantages. I must confess I had
rather they'd use our goods than money, but if not, I
would not lose the getting of ten pound, because I can't
get a hundred; and I don't question but when the *French*
gets more foreign trade, they'l give more liberty to the
bringing in foreign goods. And I think you'l be
ashamed to deny the Canary's a little when *Spain* yields
you so vast quantities. I'l suppose *John a Nokes* to be a
Butcher, Dick a Styles an *Exchange man,* your self a
Lawyer, will you buy no Meat or Ribbands, or your
wife a fine *Indian* Gown or Fann, because they will not
truck with you for Indentures, which they have no need
of? I suppose no, but if you get money enough of
others, you care not though you give it away *in specie*
for these things: I think 'tis the same case.

Compl. 'Tis well if it be as you say, but what think
you of your next proposal? Our High Living.

Cont. He that spends more than he is able to pay
for, is either fool or knave, or in great necessity; but
I suppose not this to be the Nations case; for if it
were we must owe more to other Nations than they to
us, though we gave them all we have to boot, which
if you think, most of the Merchants that have foreign
Factories in the *East* or *West Indies, Africk, Streights,
Spain, Portugal, Baltick, East Countrys, Hanse-Towns,
Scotland, Ireland,* with *France* and *Holland* too, will
condemn you. But our height puts us all upon an

[margin note: Variety of Wares for all markets a great advantageous.]

[margin note: A general High Living a great improvement to arts.]

11   industry,

industry, makes every one strive to excel his fellow, and
by their ignorance of one anothers quantities, make
more than our markets will presently take off; which
puts them to a new industry to find a foreign Vent,
and then they must make more for that market; but
still having some over-plus they stretch their wits farther,
and are never satisfied till they ingross the trade of the
Universe. And something is return'd in lieu of our
exportations, which makes a further employment and
emprovement.

If it won't do this, why do you complain of *France*
getting our money for their trifles? if it will, why
should we not encrease it as high as ever it is possible?
If we make six considerable Laces and export but one,
I suppose for it we may bring in more money than the
first cost of them all; which is far better than to
import one and let our people sit idle for want of
imployment.

The *Venetian, Spaniard, Portugeeze, Dutch,* and
English have drove the great trade of the world, and
fetcht the gold and silver: but when they had done,
they eagerly carried it to *France* to buy their guegawes,
and thereby made them always considerable: and I had
rather get a thousand pound by lace and fringes, than
nine hundred by the best broad-cloth that ever I
yet saw.

The former great traders.

That honest way that finds most employment and
gets most money, is sure the best for any Nation, and
this fine manufacture joyn'd to our shipping will perhaps make us the most potent the Sun shines on.

Take away all our supernecessary trades, and we
shall have no more than Tankard-Bearers, and Plow-
men; and our City of *London* will in short time be like
an *Irish* Hut, or perhaps *Carthage* mentioned in *Virgil
Travestie.*

If you have reason, here's enough to satisfie: but if

12   not,

not, should I bring ten thousand undeniable arguments you'd still complain.

Compl. I meet but with very few of your mind: but I pray let's hear your thoughts of the next proposal? which is, That 'tis our happiness to have abundance of Foreigners, for I'm sure the general cry is that they eat the bread out of our mouths, they sell their goods when we can't, they work cheaper than we, live in holes, pay neither scot nor lot; and if we should have many more of them, sure we should have nothing to do.

Cont. You are never well full or fasting; you cry up the *Dutch* to be a brave people, rich, and full of Cities, that they swarm with people as Bee-hives with Bees; if a plague come, they are fill'd up presently and such like; yet they do all this by inviting all the World to come and live among them. You complain of *Spain* because their Inquisition is so high, they'l let no body live among them, and that's a main cause of their weakness and poverty. You find fault because some of our people go to *Ireland* and the Plantations, and say we want people at home to fill our Cities and Countrie towns, and yet you'l allow none to come and fill up their rooms. Will not a multitude of people strengthen us as well as the want of them weaken *Spain?* sure it will. Would you not be glad if the Duke of *Lorrain* should destroy as many Villages in *France* as are destroy'd in *Alsatia,* and thereby destroy 100000 people? I dare say the most part of you would. I pray then would it not do as well if an hundred thousand *French* would run away leaving their houses to drop, and fight against the *French* King, or at least work for money to pay taxes to them that will? I think you won't gainsay it. In Sr. *Walter Raleigh's* observations concerning the causes of the magnificency and opulency of Cities, 'twas the best policy that old *Rome*

Invitation of Foreigners a great advantage.

The advantages of Multitudes.

13   had

had, and by it they were brought to their height. *Tamerlan* the great was of the same mind, and *Constantinople* owes its greatness to the same contrivance. Would not Foreigners living here consume our corn, cattle, cloth, coals, and all kind of things we use? and would not that cause our lands to be better till'd, and our trades increas'd? would they not bring several new trades with them, or help to encrease those we have? witness the Flemmings in the time of *Edward* the third, the Colonies of *Colchester, Canterbury,* and *Norwich,* the Silk-trade in *Spittle-Fields,* the Tapistrey-makers in *Hatton Garden, Clerkenwel,* and elsewhere, Mr *Todin* the rare Pewterer in St. *Martins Lane,* the Husbandmen in the *Fenns,* and divers others, and doth not every Trades-man among them employ two or three *English* to attend them either in making tools, winding silk, or such like, besides buying all their materials here? Do you think the first rough materials of a piece of silk of six pound a yard costs twenty Shillings? is not the other five pound better earnt and spent here, than to give the whole six pound to *France* for't? No man in *England* loves it better than I, and I love no Nation more than another, but for their vertues, or as they relate to the welfare of *England:* but some of our great complainers will spend a groat when they are not worth two pence, and work but two or three days in the week, therefore others out-do them.

Strangers pay neither scot nor lot, tis true, but 'tis because they are disturb'd, and are hardly suffer'd (or at least encourag'd) to take houses, but otherwise they'd quickly be like us, and the next generation would not be known from English.

You seldom hear of any disturbance they make in the State, for they are not all of one mind, and cannot agree if they would, they come for safety, quietness, and livelyhoods, for which and other good reasons, if the Parliament think fit, I could wish there would twenty thousand come in next year. A hearty Wish.

Compl. At this rate all the World would be invited hither.

Cont. Amen, say I; for then our King would be universal Monarch, and I'd never fear a prejudice either to Church or State if all were to be hang'd that should teach them causeless complaining principles.

Compl. Enough of this, but if you are for Enclosures the poor will complain of you, and curse you to the pit of Hell; and a great many of the rich will give you but little thanks.

Cont. All this signifies nothing; one good reason pre- Enclosure and vails more with me than all their cries and curses, if they were ten fold: and I'm sure that God is a God of reason. As for the Gentry I respect them highly, but a great many are more rul'd by a vulgar error, and false maxims, than the dictates of their own reason. But if I thought it would not be much for the advantage both of Gentry and Commonalty I would not say a word more on't. But I pray consider that inclos'd ground will sometimes yield treble to what common Its advantage will, but if sow'd with Clover, Sant-foin or such like, sometimes six, eight, or tenfold, when Corn bears a good price, and 'tis for the Land's advantage 'tis plow'd too, and after the Crop is off sow'd with Turnips or such like, and this with the help of good tillage and dung (which our good Husbandmen know now pretty well how to procure) done every year, when the other must lye wast one in three.

A great deal will be turn'd into Orchards and Gar- Horticulture a great advantage. dens, four or five acres of which sometimes maintains a family better, and employs more labourers than fifty acres of other shall do. Hops, Saffron, Liquorish, Onions, Potatoes, Madder, Artichocks, Aniseeds, and

15 Coleseeds

Coleseeds will thrive but ill in Common Fields, and I suppose none will denie an Acre of these to yield more money than so much Wheat: Whither goes it then? why, surely into the owners purse or labourers pockets.

For the cry that the poor will be starv'd, it is not worth a rush, for few of them make the benefit for lack of stock, and perhaps they spend as much time in looking after their titts, runts, and tupps, as would gain them by an indifferent Handy craft, twice the profit.

And how that parish that traded but for ten thousand pounds a year, and now for twenty thousand, should be more likely to famish, and twice or thrice the employment for the poor starve them, I confess is to me a paradox. Ever since old *Tusser's* time, it has been observed that where there's most common, there's least good building and most poor.

Enclosure must needs encrease more great and small cattle, and an encrease of Hydes, Tallow, and Wool, with finer manufactures of them than formerly, can never either depopulate or impoverish.

Compl. I must confess that most men yield it to be most profitable. But is it lawful to take away that we have enjoy'd time out of mind? and we must not do evil that good may come on't.

Whether it be lawful to enclose.

Cont. I must confess this is your main argument, and I being neither Divine nor Lawyer perhaps may not give to it so good an answer as ten thousand wiser men can do. But 'tis well that I have prov'd it profitable: But I suppose this Island before it was inhabited to be all Common; which was something altered by the first Occupants, and encreas'd according to the good husbandry, populacy, and needs of the people, and why this prescription should not prevail as much as yours, I know not. It doth in *America*, and I believe all the world over. In *China* I hear there is not an Acre of Common Land.

I must

I must confess I know no Statute that gives full power to enclose all the Common-Fields, in the Kingdom; but in my weak judgment there are several that do much encourage it. Especially when it is for the advantage of the whole; witness the two first Acts for enclosing the Fenns, and the 4 *Jac.* II. for part of *Herefordshire,* caus'd by the good husbandry of some of the inhabitants. And I think the 3 *Edw.* 6. & 3. will go a great way. And the inducement and ground of the Act call'd Trade encouraged 15 *Car.* 2. 7. runs thus *verbatim.*

Forasmuch as the encouraging of Tillage ought to be in an especial manner regarded and endeavoured, and the surest and effectuallest means of promoting and advancing any trade, occupation or mystery, being by rendring it profitable to the users thereof, and great quantities of Land within this Kingdom for the present lying in a manner waste, and yielding little, which might thereby be improv'd to considerable profit and advantage (if sufficient encouragement were given for the laying out of cost and labour on the same) and thereby much more Corn produced, greater numbers of People, Horses, and Cattle employed, and other Land also rendered more valuable. The reasons for the Act call'd Trade encouraged.

How far the inducements and grounds of Acts of Parliament run, I know not, but they shew their designs; and how this can be done better than by Enclosure, my ignorance won't reach to; but I have prov'd it most advantageous to the owner, and I think wealth and a treble labour, will quickly encrease People, Horses, and other Cattle, the plenty whereof, of necessity must quickly make other Land more valuable.

17   If

19

If leave were given, all the barren land in *England*
I suppose would soon be improv'd.

I believe you'l be asham'd to urge the 25. of *Hen.* 8.
and 13. because the cheapness of our Corn, Cattle,
Wool, Pigs, Geese, Hens, Chickens, and Eggs, are in a
great part the ground of your complaint.

I chiefly aim at that we call Common Field-Land,
where men claim a propriety, and can say, Thus many
acres are mine; but for the other that lye always open,
if the Lord of the Manor gets all in his own hand, or
the Parishioners can agree, I wish 'twere all so serv'd,
and I think there's few with good reason can be
against it.

As for the King's Forests and Chaces, if they were
imparkt, and kept to himself, I believe timber would
thrive ne'r the worse, or the neighbouring corn, nor
perhaps would there be a less breed of good Horses;
But arguments are endless. Boy give me t'other dish
of Tee.

Compl. I pray do nothing rashly, but drink first.
Well suppose I grant that you have law and reason
enough on your side: what will you do against the beg-
garly multitude, that will pull down your Fences, turn
Cattel in, and spoil your Corn, or what other improvements you shall make in your new Enclosure?
if you sue them you know the old Proverb, *Sue a
Beggar,* &c. and they have nothing to lose, their
punishment will ne'r make you satisfaction, and except
you have a large purse, and courage too you may
chance be tired.

Cont. 'Tis true, this is a great impediment to the
good work, but a great many have conquer'd it, and I
believe had the former ages went the same way to
work, which an ingenious Justice, and another of my
good friends (whom you well know) have done, we

A way to in-
close in spite
of the Rabble.

18   should

should long e'r this have had more Milk and
Honey. For instead of narrow Ditches and high banks,
which might quickly be thrown down and fill'd with
ease, they have made their Ditches, seven, eight, or
ten foot wide, six foot deep, and carried away all that
should make a hurtful bank, planted quick, and with
Damms, stop water to fill up as high as they can or
think necessary. By this means the Rabble want materials to refill, unless they'l bring it with them, or
dig one ditch to fill another. But as what relates to
Ryots, Trespasses, and other law tricks, the Countrey-
Men I believe are wise enough.

Compl. This is a way indeed, surely this will do or
nothing, but let them inclose or do in the fields what
they will, what can you say for the multitude of
Trades-men?

Cont. Say for them! I have said enough in what I
said just now of Foreigners: but however something
more.

Multitude of
traders a
great advan-
tage.

That man that gets most money over and above his
expences, surely will be richest: so likewise will that
trade: but suppose there were formerly twenty Linnen-
Drapers, (or any other Traders) and they clear'd each
five hundred pounds a year, it will amount to ten thousand pounds; but now there are forty Drapers, and by
under-selling each other they clear each but four
hundred pounds a year, this will make sixteen thousand
pounds. I suppose this Company do plainly thrive:
But should eighty get but three hundred pounds each,
it would amount to four and twenty thousand pounds
besides the employment of four times the Ships and
Labourers, with the the like encrease of his Majesties
Customs, and this is the case of most of our old trades,
only besides the quantity of men, the particulars have
most of them so much increas'd their quantities, that

19   with

with less profit they every year spend more, and give
their Children better portions.

Moreover there are a multitude of new Trades; and
that variety of Arts should undo a Nation, I believe
was never known in this world or in *Utopia.*

When you keep Bees, you are loth to suffer Drones
among them. Good Bees are the seventeen Provinces,
and you cry them up to the skies, and say that two or
three years peace will make amends for all the Calamities they have endured this War: but the like Industry in *England,* added to a prodigious Plenty, will
quite spoil us.

The advanta-
ges of many
Traders.

Do not some of our Trades-men spend one or two
hundred pounds a year, whose parents never saw forty
Shillings together of their own in their lives? Doth
it not make the Capons and Custards go off at a good
rate? Doth it not mightily encrease his Majesties
revenue, by Customs, Excise, and Chimney-Money?
Doth it not make a tax light, by having many Shoulders
to bear the burden? And were it not for this, his
Majestie must like *Spain* and *Denmark,* when he hath
occasion to hire ships, from perhaps his ill-humour'd
Neighbours. But God be thanked things are in a
better case, and if I should live forty years longer, I
hope to see *London* as big again, and all the Towns in
England strive to imitate it

Compl. Well, I'l trouble you no more at present,
and confess that what you say seems to have a great
deal of truth in't; but I don't know, people do complain.

A disswasive
from mur-
muring.

Cont. And ever will; but I prithee leave off this
humour of murmuring, either disprove what I have
said, or for shame blush to complain. Remember that
you are a rational creature, don't make your own and
others lives uncomfortable by refusing to enjoy those

Blessings

Blessings Providence hath heap'd upon you: St. *Paul*
with far less liv'd a happier life. What Comfort can
his Majestie have, when for all his good Government,
Care, and Protection, you reward him with a mess
of Complaints? Don't Judaize and complain more
when you are fed with Manna and Quails, than when
you fed on Leeks and Garlick. Murmur not like *Corah*
and his Crew when your King is *a Moses*. You know
that of 600000. that came from *Ægypt*, there went but
two into the *Land of Canaan*. Most of the rest perished
for this crime. When *Moses* beg'd any great Matter
of God, he commemorated his former loving kindnesses,
and O God of *Abraham, Isaac*, and *Jacob* was of great
concern in a Jews petition. 'Tis the remembrance of
the *French* King's Victories makes him go on with
courage: And would we but consider the great things The word *im-*
we have done, it would perhaps make us believe nothing *possible* a
to be impossible either in Arms or Arts. Let's bless rager of Arts.
God for all his mercies, and particularly for our good
King, whose greatest Care hath been to keep us in
peace, and procure us plenty, which I think will prove
better arguments to gain any needful thing, than the
irksom and causeless camplaints of a thousand generations. The sum of all is this; If we have great Magazines for War, and multitudes of brave Ships; If we Signs of
have a Mint employ'd with more Gold and Silver than Wealth.
in a considerable time they can well coin; If it be an
affront to cause one to drink in any worse mettle than
Silver, if great part of our utensils be of the same: if
our Trade be stretcht as far as any trade is known; if
we have six times the Traders and most of their Shops
and Ware-houses better furnisht than in the last Age;
if we have abundance of more good debts abroad than
credit from thence; if many of our poor Cotagers
children be turn'd Merchants and substantial Traders;

if

if our good Lands be made much better, and our bad have a six-fold improvement; if our houses be built like Palaces, over what they were in the last Age, and abound with plenty of costly furniture; and rich Jewels be very common; and our Servants excel in finery the Great ones of some Neighbour-Nations; if we have most part of the trade of the World, and our Cities are perhaps the greatest Magazines thereof; if after a destructive plague and consuming fire, we appear much more glorious; if we have an universal Peace, and our King in such renown that he is courted by all his Neighbours, and these only the marks of poverty, then I have been under a great mistake: But if it doth otherwise appear, as certainly it doth to all rational men. Then I may still go on with my maxime and say,

We have more wealth now, than ever we had at any time before the Restauration of his Sacred Majestie.

A Comparison.

The Jews were never well setled till the time of *Saul*, and then Wealth flow'd in like water spilt upon the ground: you might see it coming, and it being a stranger they stood gazing and cry'd ahah! witness,

2 Sam. 1. 24. *David's* lamentation over *Saul, He clothed them in Scarlet, and put ornaments of Gold upon their apparel.* But in *David's* own time it grew to a pretty handsom brook; but in *Solomon's* time to a profound River.

Our now complaints.

But then the custom of their Wealth took away the sense of it, they cry'd that times were hard, there was nothing to be got, they were the old ones that got estates, he that would get one then, must have tug'd hard for't; and that such like talk they had, is witness *Solomon's* reproof, *Say not thou, the former times were better than these, for thou dost not enquire wisely concerning this.*

Just thus it hath been with *England*, Queen *Elizabeth's* time was like *Saul's*, when by taking a few

22   *Spanish*

Spanish Ships, and almost beginning a Navigation, made us cry ahah! In the time of King *James* and *Charles,* for want of Silver the Gold made a pretty handsom glistering, but now Gold doth much abound, and Silver is hard-any thing esteemed of. It flows in so often like a deep river, there is hardly any notice taken of it.

Compl. I must confess I can't answer you, but surely that which every body saith, must needs be true.

Cont. Well if you are so wilful as not to be convinc'd, I'm sorry, but however this advantage to my self I'll reap, I'l give God thanks for his great Bless- **A good reso-** ings, and enjoy them while you sit murmuring and **lution.** repining for what you don't want, and like *Midas* starve in a monstrous plenty.

However consider what follows.

Neither murmur ye as some of them also murmured, 1 Cor. 10. 10. *and were destroyed of the destroyer.*

Wo unto them, for they have perished in the gainsay- Jude 11. *ing of* Core.

These are spots in your Feasts of Charity. 12.

And are murmurers and complainers, walking after 16. *their own lusts.*

Your murmurings are not against us, but against the Exod. 16. 18. *Lord.*

Do all things without murmurings. Phil. 2. 14.

And the people spake against God, and against Moses, Numb. 21. 5. *wherefore have you brought us up out of Ægypt, to die in the Wilderness? For there is no Bread, neither is there any water, and our soul loatheth this light bread.*

And the Lord sent Fiery Serpents among the people, 6. *and they bit the people, and much people of Israel dyed.*

Many when a thing was lent them reckoned it to be Ecclus. 29. 4. *found, and put them to trouble that helped them.*

Till he hath received he will kiss a mans hand, and for 5.

his

his Neighbours money he will speak submisly: but when
he should repay, he will prolong the time and return

Rev. 22. 11.   *words of grief, and COMPLAIN OF THE TIMES.*

He that is filthy let him be filthy still.

Come Boy take money.

However dear Friend, farewel.

F I N I S.

Britannia Languens,

OR

A DISCOURSE

OF

TRADE:

SHEWING

The Grounds and Reasons of the
Increase and Decay of Land-Rents, National
Wealth and Strength.

WITH

Application to the late and present
State and Condition of *England, France,* and
the *United Provinces.*

Dum singuli pugnant universi Vincuntur, Tacitus
in Vit. Agricolæ, speaking of the *Britains.*

London, Printed for *Tho. Dring,* at the *Harrow* at *Chancery-Lane* end in *Fleet-Street,* and *Sam. Crouch* in *Popes-head-Alley* near the *Royal Exchange* in *Corn-hill.* 1680.

The Preface.

Courteous Reader,

MY *Original Design was to examine by what means our* English Land-Rents, lately fallen, *might be universally* advanced; *which I have principally pursued; but have found such a* Concatenation and Sympathy *between the interest of* Land and Trade, *and between these, and that of the* Government; *That I have been carried into all the Considerations you will meet with; a Task I little expected when I first began, and which I could never have supported with any Alacrity, but upon hope, that when it shall undeniably appear to every one,* that these Interests are the same, *there may follow that general* Amity and mutual Assistance *to each other, which render a Nation* happy and secure.

Though my Intention be thus, Just and Innocent, yet I cannot but doubt what Approbation this Discourse may meet with from many of those who have a main suffrage *in crying up a* new Book; *since it is upon a Subject much out of mode; so much, that the very naming it is a matter of* Ridicule *amongst many of our* sprightly men: *It is really of such a nature, that it hath not lead me to seek for* Smiles, Dinners, *or other more* solid Gratifications, *by flattering any predominant humours,* Vices *or* Passions, *or to make an Interest by espousing or canvasing any* doubtful Points in Religion: *As little can I hope from the* Criticks, (*I mean our great Masters in Expression:*) Trade *being a matter of business, and the business of the ordinary people, at least, equally with the*
rest;

The Preface.

rest; I have not endeavoured to dress it up with Curiosity
of Phrase, *by conforming myself to the* Laconick *or* Cice-
ronian way, *studying for* Metaphors, *spruce words, or the*
renowned Antithesis; *nor do I find these flowers will very
aptly mingle with the Notions of* Trade; *which are so unfortunate, as to have little or* no Cognation with Love and
Honour, *or those other common Themes of Wit which deno-
minate a man a* neat *Author by the Elegancies they inspire
him with: But this is not all, I am afraid you will think
Trade is the very* Antipodes *to all good breeding, when I
shall further tell you, that (had I been sufficiently qualified)
it hath not permitted me to gratifie the* Learned *with any of
the niceties or finismes of our most fashionable Studies; nay
it hath obliged me to hazard the very enmity of others, by
impeaching many private and oppressive Interests, whose* Silver-
Smiths *may be highly provoked; and when I thought to qua-
lifie any Resentments of that nature, by waving all* Reflections *on particular persons, I am now told, that perhaps my
Caution this way may disgust others; whence I cannot but be
sensible that these Papers want much of those endearments which
render many of our Prints so acceptable; And being under these
Apprehensions, I could not but have some Compassionate
thoughts of my* Book-Seller; *who must look very melancholly,
when some of his customers shall ask for the* Ancient Forreign Histories *and* Poets, *the new* Philosophical Comple-
ments, *and* Books of Astrology, *the Treatise of the* Art of
Memory, *or* Swimming; *or such like Rarities;* Others *for
the Monstrous* Leviathan, Behemoth, *and* Garagantua:
Others for the new French Romance, *the* Spick and Span
new Play, *and* the new Satyrs; *Others for the new* Books of
Cookery, *(for we are arrived to a mighty judgment in eating:)
Others for the Books of the* World in the Moon, Terra Incog-
nita, Lues Venerea, *and* Westminster Drollery, &c. *But
upon the sight of the Title Page of this, (because it is of*
Trade) *shall condemn it as fit only to be read by* Milleners
and Exchangemen.

*But recollecting, that we have yet a far greater number of
others, under all Characters and Professions, who bear a*

due

The Preface.

due affection both to our Government and People, *I have adventured upon making this Discourse publick; as not despairing of their Vindication, being assured* they *will never think he hath deserved* ill, *who hath done no more than* endeavour *to advance and secure the common Interests of both; in which I should be always happy to be instrumental, but especially* then, *when the Nation is under present difficulties and eminent dangers; For then certainly it more imports every man to seek the* Common Safety, *than any the most tempting Additions to his own* private Fortune. *Should the* Mariners *in a Ship stand* trifling and sporting, *or* contending for Offices, *or other gain, on the* Decks, *whilst a gaping* Leak *in the* Keel *lets in the Ocean, we should think them little better than* phrenetical; *surely in such an Exigence every man on board ought to give his utmost assistance; he that hath no* share *in the* Cargoe *hath yet a* life *to lose, no man would then slink back to escape the dirt, or for fear he should be lookt on as a* busie-body. *How far the present Condition of our Trade will bear such a* Simile, *I shall submit to your Consideration upon* what follows; *wherein I have, not knowingly, mis-represented any thing, but with my utmost application endeavoured to discover and speak the* truth *of as much as I have thought fit for me to meddle with.*

Yet I am not so very a Jockey, *nor so arrant a* Tradesman in writing, *as to desire your implicite belief that all I am about to utter is without Imperfection. I am assured you will least expect it upon a* Subject *which hath the reputation of being so* Comprehensive *as this, and seems to require the ascertaining of so great a variety of* Facts, *that no man upon his* single experience *can pretend to know them; The consideration whereof might have deterred me from engaging in it, and may you from the perusal, were it not that some of these* Facts, *which make the* Constitutions of Trade, *and therefore the* Causes *of the rest, are notorious and capable of little Controversie, whence the rest being the effects may be easily calculated; a course used and allowed in all* Arts *and* Sciences, *and I conceive with more certainty on this* Subject *than on any other; from whence greater and more notable*
                                                                    Discoveries

The Preface.

Discoveries have been made, than by the most vigilant Disqui-
sitions into all the Revolutions of Facts: Columbus *found*
out the Indies *in his Study; so did* Archimedes *the most*
stupendous Conclusions in the Mathematicks. *It must be*
confessed many of those other Facts *relating to* Commerce,
which are the effects, *are of greater obscurity, most of them*
being Forreign, and are so numerous, that they branch into
almost as many parts as there are humane Actions; yet of
these, some are more obvious, *and more* important *than others,*
whereof, as occasions offer, I have endeavoured to give you
some accompt where I can speak with any good assurance;
wherein, if you meet with any defect, you may please to attri-
bute it to this, *That I am neither* Omniscient *nor* infallible; *I*
have also the old excuse at hand, viz. Importunity of Friends,
that common Midwife of Books, besides the frequent Interruptions *I have really received by my own ordinary Affairs,*
which ('tis probable) has caused many abrupt breaks *and* mis-
expressions, *which I have not had time to review and rectifie;*
hoping that I have however spoken Intelligibly; *and profes-*
sing, that I have as well considered and digested the deliberative *and* reasoning *part as my Intellectuals will give leave:*
and if I do not fail in that shall be contented, since it must
be admitted that I have written as becomes a man, who hath no
better or more discerning faculty than that of his reason: *I*
have no ambition to be accompted an Irrefragable, *or* Printed
Author; *being sensible the most* Angelical *Writers have had*
their failings, and that whosoever Publishes his thoughts in
Print, breaks that (oftentimes profitable) *reserve which* cunning men *affect, and exposes his quiet to the* Malice *and* Im-
pertinences *of* vulgar *Reflections; which nothing but a sincere*
love to my Country, *and the Consideration of its present*
Circumstances could oblige me to dispense with.

   I shall be well satisfied if I have served the Public a little,
or made a step *towards it, which, at least, I hope I have done,*
if in a matter of high Consequence I have but stirred *ques-*
tions necessary to be cleared by abler heads; Experience hath
been shown what admirable performances have ensued, when a
weak Essay hath kindled a Common Emulation, *for then*
certainly

The Preface.

certainly must the brightness *of* Truth *appear (discharged from that* rust *and* foulness *which* time or corruption *hath brought upon it) when the Intellectuals of men are carried into a* rational ferment; *this I take to be the* true use, *and* most *virtuous* design *of writing, and is all I desire; let those men wear* Bays *and* Lawrel, *and be* hum'd, *and* clapt, *who are fonder of such Trophies than*

Your humble Servant,

Philanglus.

THE

THE
Introduction.

IT hath been the Common Design and Business of Individual Men in England, as elsewhere, to obtain sufficient Revenues in Money to the end they may secure themselves from Necessities and Shifting, and live plentifully; And yet it may be undeniably and uncomfortably observed, That whilst every one hath eagerly pursued his private Interest, a kind of Common Consumption hath crawled upon us; Since our Land-Rents are generally much fallen, and our Home-Commodities sunk from their late Price and Value; our Poor are vastly increased, and the rest of our People generally more and more feel the Want of Money; This Disease having grown upon us in times of Peace, when no Forreigners have Exhausted us by War-like Depredations, may very justly amuse us; and the more, when at the same time, we observe that some of our Neighbour-Nations, lately our Equals, or much our inferiors, are become so prodigiously Rich and Powerful on a sudden, (I mean the French and Dutch:) Certainly these mighty Productions must have some great and vigorous Causes, which have been very furiously working of later years, and such as have not fallen under Common Observation: The Nations and Races of People are the same, and the

1   Countries

Countries of England, France, *and* Holland, *stand where they did, they are not removed an Inch; nor do the* English *seem to have lost their Understandings; they are as* cunning *in their private Contracts as ever, and appear nothing inferior to the* French *and* Dutch *in most parts of* Literature; *I question not but that they know all the* Ancient Languages *and* Histories *as well, that our* Academicks *are as subtile in all the* Criticisms *of* Aristotle; *that they have travelled as far into the most abstruse parts of his* Logick, Physicks, *and* Metaphysicks; *and yet have we still grown poorer and poorer; So have we excelled in divers* necessary parts of Learning; *We have had as Able, Eloquent, and Eminent* Lawyers *and* Clergy-men *as ever, and as Notable* Physitians, *and the Nation seems to have grown more* Learned, *and therefore* Wiser *than before, by the late vast increase of these Ranks of men.*

The present Disadvantages we are under, are therefore commonly attributed to Accidents *of divers kinds, as mens present particular* Fancies *dictate, in which the greatest part are contented to rest satisfied without farther enquiry, whilst they have some Prospects of* Gain *in the* Imployments *they are severally educated to; Some ascribe the* fall of Rents *to an over-great increase of Corn, by the* ploughing up of Parks; *Others to the modern* Parsimony in Housekeeping, *the lessening of Gentlemens* Retinues, *and leaving off the old laudable Custom of plentiful* Suppers, *which they suppose occasions a less Consumption of Victuals: others attribute this, and the want of Money in the Country, to the great resort of People to* London, *and quarrel at the* New Buildings, *as the Hives and Receptacles which draw them thither; others to the* banking up of Treasures *in the Coffers of some unknown* Grandees, Church-men, Lawyers, *or* Citizens, *of which they are highly confident, for else, they say, what is become of the money? then for the late*

2   *Progress*

Progress and Trophies of the French, *many look upon them as the meer effects of the* Despotick *or* Arbitrary Power *of that* Monarchy *or of the personal* cunning *of some men now living in* France; *I remember I heard one Gentleman say, that the* French Genius *was up, where-with he gave himself and others good satisfaction:* Others *will have it, that the late Enemies of the* French *wanted* Valor *and* Conduct, *but that if the* French *had the* English *to contend with, their Glory would soon be laid in the Dust: For the* Dutch, *there are those who will argue their* Riches *and* Populacy *to proceed from the* peculiar Industry *of that Nation, and that such an Eternal Toil is not supportable by any other; Others, to their small Expense in* Diet *and* Habit, *others to particular Circumstances in the time and manner of their* Defection *from* Spain; *to their* Register *of* Titles *and* Contracts, *and their* cheap *and easie decision of* Law-Suits.

Of all other things we seem to be most secure *in the matter of* Trade; *we have many who taking themselves to be* born *or intitled to so much a year in* Land, *do consider* Trade *as no otherwise necessary in a Nation, than to* support *younger* Brothers, *and are ready to thrust all* Publique Taxes *upon* Trade, *that they may ease the Land; Others who pretend to enquire into it, hear the Customs are much risen of late years, and then rest satisfied that we have a mightier* Trade *than ever: We have also some* Merchants *and* Shopkeepers *who get Estates, and buy Land on a suddain, which is lookt upon as an Argument of a good* Trade; *We find their mighty and numerous* Shops *and* Warehouses, *full of goods, and do not hear them complain of* Trade, *Or that Land is brought to* 14 *or* 16 *years purchase, or that they buy at a much* abated yearly value.

Some, indeed, justly apprehending a Disease *in our* Trade, *by the decay of our* Home Manufactures, *and*

3   *an*

an excess of Forreign Importations, *have judiciously expressed themselves in it; these Notions whilst in* Embrio, *have been* ralleured *by our Modern* Drolls, *in their new Manufacture of* Plays.

There are others, who with more Design *and* Gravity, *tell us, That the Notions and Improvements of* Trade, *are of a* dangerous tendency, *because they threaten part of the present* Jurisdiction *of our* Spiritual Courts, *and the gain of many* Offices, *by some requisite Toleration of* Conscience, *and other mittigations relating to* Trade, *and upon this Occasion the same Objectors proceed to argue the Improvements of Trade to be of as bad Consequence to the* State, *by filling the Nation with Trading-Religious Dissenters, or by a necessary moderating of the present* Custom-Rates: *They also insinuate, that we ought not to look for such a perfection of Trade under a* Monarchical Government, *but to dispose of our selves otherwise as we can; We have others that say, Trade is a* misterious thing, *and not intelligible in any part of it, without a long Apprentiship, and therefore wholly refer themselves to the* Merchants *and* private Traders; *Others that 'tis* Mechanical, *and not Gentleman-like.*

But if it fall out that these are all mistaken Opinions, if Trade *alone hath produced the afore-mentioned Effects in* England, France, *and* Holland, *If the rise and fall of* Rents *absolutely depend upon it; If* Liberty *and* Property *be made valuable by Trade only, and are not valuable or safe without it; If a* Nation *may be made* strong *or* weak *by the meer different Operations of* Trade; *If the* Taxing *or burthening of* Trade *must reduce all Land-Revenues, if the* easing *of* Trade *either in the particular Custom-Rates, or otherwise, will make the whole Revenue of the* Customs *greater, or else much enhance all other publick as well as private Revenues; If a mighty Trade be consistent with a* Monarchical Government? *(where*

there

there is Property and Liberty :) *If it be a false and officious* Scandal *to this form of Government, to affirm the contrary, if* England *of all other Nations, be naturally most capable of the Advantages of* Trade, *but yet the* Trade *of* England *of late years hath been* Consumptive; *If the late Policies of our Neighbour-Nations have rendered our* old established *Methods of* Trade *insufficient, if we have divers late* innovated Obstructions *in our* Trade, *if this hath caused an* over-ballance of Forreign Importations, *If our National Industry hath been* imployed *to enrich* Forreigners, *if our own Treasures have been* exhausted *by our own Trade, and will soon be swept away in the present course of it, Nay, even notwithstanding our* late Prohibition of French Goods, *if the Objections against the enlarging and bettering of our Trade arise from* private Interests, *in contradiction to the Publique, or from* Passion *or* Humour, *and if this be intelligible to every man of sense, that will take the pains to enquire into it. Then certainly it must follow,*

That it does much import all English Gentlemen, Owners of Land, *and others, who take themselves to be sharers in the* National Interest, *to examine the past and present State of our* Trade, *and to seek for a* legal Regulation *of it; And that all* private Interests *destructive to our Trade ought to be relaxed, and given up for the future.*

Private Interest *is that many-headed* Monster, *I am chiefly to encounter with, in which if any particular person shall take himself to be concerned, I shall desire him to consider, whether his own Condition would not be more truly* honourable *and* safe *under more open Methods of* Trade? *I shall pray him to look into the nature of* meer private Interest, *which if he do, he must confess it the same Principle that leads men into* Cheats, Thefts, *and all those other base mercyless and execrable* Villanies,

5   *which*

which render the Actors Criminous, and odious by the Sufferings and Injuries they bring upon others.

Then if any man's particular way of Gain be so prejudicial to Trade, as to occasion the continual Beggery *of* Thousands *of his Countrymen, is not this more then equally mischievous to so many* thousand *Thefts? But what if this Beggery must unavoidably cause many thousand* actual *Thefts, nay* Murders *and* Enormities *of all kinds, and as it grows more Universal, must bring the Nation into an* impotent *and indefenseable* weakness? *Have we any amongst us that will be yet* tenacious *of such ways of Gain? Will they tell us that they are not punishable by any* Laws in force? *'tis pity they are not.   So there was a time when in* Old Rome, *there was no direct Law against* Parricide: *But that they may no longer shelter themselves under this* Umbrage, *it were highly necessary that* Laws *were made to control them, and to remove all Obstructions in our* Trade.

That Trade *is of this National* Importance *and* Influence, *and that the Trade of* England *in particular, hath been and continues under these* Disadvantages, *will, I think, sufficiently appear to any indifferent Reader, by the following Discourse; Of which having given the Reader a tast, by way of* Introduction, *I shall proceed to what I have undertaken, and shall begin with some* Preliminaries, *of which part are* self-evident, *and for those that are not (being not able to say all at once) refer the Reader to the following* Sections.

SECTION I.

*Trade National or Private, Home or Forreign Treasures
Imported by Trade, thence Land-Rents, Populacy
increased, the Revenues of all Ranks of men depend
upon Trade, People and Treasure make National
Strength, particular Advantages in Treasure, the difference between Ancient and Modern Wars, Navigation supported by Trade, this necessary for the Security of an Island, and therein the farther scope of
the whole.*

T Rade is either *National or Private :* The *National
Trade* doth influence the Wealth and Strength
of a *whole Nation,* and therefore is not the only Concern of *Merchants.*

   Private Trade hath regard to the particular Wealth
of the Trader, and doth so far differ in the scope and
design of it from the *National,* that a private Trade
may be very beneficial to the private Trader, but of
hurtful, nay of very ruinous Consequence to the whole
National; as will appear.

   I shall speak of National Trade, which is properly
divided into *Home* Trade, and *Forreign* Trade.

   The Home Trade in every Nation hath dependance
on the Forreign Trade: if a Nation hath no Gold or
Silver-Mines within its own Territory, there is no
practicable way of bringing *Treasure* into it (in times
of Peace) but by Forreign Trade: And if such a Nation be not enriched by Imported Treasure, its Home

7

Trade

Trade can only be managed by *Exchange of Goods for Goods*.

But if Treasure be Imported, then may its Home Trade be managed by buying and selling for *money*.

And from hence may the *Lands* in such a Nation come to yield a *money Rent*, which is the produce or profits of Land sold for *money*.

In which Case the *price of Home Commodities*, and consequently the yearly *Rent of Lands* in a Nation which hath *populacy* and *property*, will hold proportion with the quantity of the National Treasure; and will rise or fall as the Treasure does increase or diminish.

For where there is an increase of *Treasure* in a Nation which hath *property*, this will ordinarily diffuse amongst the people by the necessity and succession of *Contracts*; and then the people having universally more money than before, the *Seller* will not be so *necessitous* for money as before, and will have a greater *choice of Chapmen*, who will be more able and ready to buy.

These numbers of Chapmen will inevitably raise the Market one upon the other, as is demonstrable by common and undeniable Experience and Fact; And therefore I shall lay it as a ground in Commerce, That the *plenty of Chapmen*, who have *plenty of money*, will cause a higher and quicker Market for any desireable Commodity, especially if the *Seller* be not so *necessitous* for money as to be forced to *snap* at the first offer.

And that on the other side, where there be fewer Chapmen, who have less money, and the Sellers themselves are more necessitous, they must and will sell lower; This must inevitably happen in a Nation where there is little money.

For instance, If there were but 500*l*. Sterling in *England*, an Ox could hardly be worth a peny, nor could the Revenue of all *England* be 500*l. per annum*, or not above;

It

It follows then, that a Forreign Trade (by increasing the National Treasure) will advance *home Markets,* and the value of *Lands* in *England.*

I shall admit that if a Nation can be *Victorious in War,* and can plunder the Conquered, some Treasures may happen to be Imported this way; But certainly those who consider it, will rather desire to be enriched by Trade than by War, since in the Course of Trade, far mightier Treasures may be gotten with *Peace, Innocence, Security, and Happiness to the People,* who cannot be Victorious in War without Bloodsheds, Rapines, Violences, and Perpetrations of all kinds; they also must be subject to perpetual difficulties and hazards in the hardships and event of War, which will disturb or subvert the Home Trade, nor can the Treasure of a People so imployed circulate in the Markets to any advantagious degree; or should we have any such *Bravoes* or *Knights Errant* as would rather purchase Wealth by Fighting than by Industry, yet are these imaginary Conquests absolutely impracticable at this day without the assistance of Forreign Trade; as will be shewn.

But first upon the former grounds I shall add, that a Forreign Trade (if managed to the best advantage) will yet further advance the values of Lands, by necessitating a vast *increase of people,* since it must maintain great multitudes of people in the very business of Trade, which could not otherwise be supported, (as will also further appear): All which having the Rewards of their Labours in their hands, will still enlarge the choice of Chapmen to the Sellers, and there being so many more persons to be fed and cloathed, there must be a far greater home Consumption of all the products of Land.

And hence must arise a kind of Competition amongst the people who shall farm or purchase Land, when the

9   Revenue

Revenue of Land is certain, and grows higher daily, as the Treasure and People increase, which must cause Land to rise as well in the years' purchase, as in the years' value; nay, the very Earth must receive an inevitable *Improvement* by their Industrious numbers, whilst every one will be able and willing to possess and manure a greater or lesser part, according to his occasions; there is hardly any Land in *England* but may be improved to double the value, and very much to treble and more.

This necessary Improvement of Rent and Land is verified in the Forreign instance of *Holland*, and in such of our *English* Lands as lie near great and populous *Corporations*; And on the other side, we see that in *Spain* and *Turkey*, and also in such parts of *England* and *Ireland*, where there is little Trade, and fewer people, there lie great quantities of Land which yield little or no profit; and hence I conclude, That the Revenue and Value of Land will simpathize with the National Trade.

There are indeed certain Ranks of Men of honourable and necessary Imployments and Professions in every Nation, whose Revenues do not so immediately arise from Trade; such are *Officers* greater and less, *Lawyers*, *Physicians*, and such like.

But though these are not placed in the direct Channel of Trade, yet 'tis very plain they derive their Revenues from it; being supported in their Grandure and Gains at the cost of the Land-Holders and Traders; who will be more capable and willing to give them greater Gratuities and Fees, when their own pockets are fuller; and as the People, Trade, and Contracts do increase, there will be more Law-Suits and Diseases, and ordinarily more Fees and Gratuities, so will there be more Houses built, more Apparel made, and more Imployment of all sorts for *Masons*, *Carpenters*,

Taylors,

Taylors, and men of all other middle and inferior Callings.

And from hence it also follows, That a Forreign Trade managed to the best advantage, will make a *Nation vastly stronger than naturally it was,* because money and people do ordinarily make National strength.

Money is necessary for the purchasing of many Provisions for War by Land or Sea, as Arms, Victuals, Ammunition, materials for Shipping, and many others, which being gotten, yet neither Souldiers nor Seamen will now adventure themselves at the mouths of Cannon and Musket without pay, whereof the further Consequence is that the Prince and Nation which hath the greatest Treasure, will finally have the Victory, and probably with little or no fighting.

For being enabled by their Treasure to keep themselves in *a posture of War,* they will oblige their Enemies to the like Expence, till their Enemies Treasures are exhausted, and then their *Armies* and also their *Councils* will dissipate.

This shews the difference between the *ancient* and *present* Course of *War,* for anciently the event of War was tried by frequent Battles, and generally succeeded as one Nation was Superior to the other in personal Strength and Roughness; But since the Wealth of the *Indies* came to be discovered and dispersed more and more, Wars are managed *by much Treasure and little Fighting,* and therefore with little hazard to the richer Nation.

And hence also doth it appear that in the present condition of the World, it is in a manner impossible for a Nation to gain Riches by Conquest and Plunder, unless it hath first store of Treasure at Home, which cannot otherwise be gotten than by Forreign Trade.

Also *money* will command the *Service and Lives* of any *poorer and rougher Nation,* It will purchase the

11   *Assistance,*

Assistance of Forreign *Princes,* It will *indear* their great *Ministers,* open their *Cabinets,* engage true and close Correspondencies, and *poison* their *Councils:* It will pass unseen through Rampiers, Fortifications, and Guards, into Cities and Forts, and will surprize them without the tedious hazards of Seiges; It will purchase Governors and Generals, and like Lightning will consume the *Heart* of a poorer Nation, whilst its *Countenance and Outside* shall remain fresh.

So are *people* necessary to Guard the Treasures, and defend the Nation, who will be more or less true and serviceable to the National Interest, as they have a greater or lesser *share in it;* he that hath somewhat of his own, and lives Comfortably, will stoutly defend the Nation against Invaders; But if a People be poor and miserable, their Condition being uneasie, it will be indifferent to them who is Conqueror; nay they will hope for a better Condition by turning the Tables; so is it of dangerous Consequence that the People should become *vitious,* because it generally weakens their Bodies, Courages, or Faiths: In all which the excellency of a great and well regulated Forreign Trade may be discerned, since it will render the People Rich, and ordinarily Virtuous; as will also appear.

But Forreign Trade may bring a particular advantage to an *Island* by a great *Navigation,* without which its impossible for any Island long to defend it self against a Forreign Enemy potent in Shipping, for the *Invaders* circling an Island with their Ships, may sail from Place to Place, and Rob, Spoil, and Kill, before the Natives can, by long Land-Marches, apply their Courage and Land-Forces to resist them; which must necessarily distract and weary out the most valiant People on the Earth: this hath been evident by many Demonstrations in *England,* which hath been often Conquered by Forreigners for want of a sufficient *Naval Force,* parti-

12   cularly

cularly by the *Romans*, nay by the *Saxons, Danes,* and *Normans*; but hath more often repulsed Forreigners, whilst we have been most *powerful at Sea*; and therefore the constant Policies of this Kingdom have long aspired too, and enjoyed a *Soveraignty of the Sea,* and kept a narrow and jealous watch on Neighbour-Nations, lest they should aggrandize their Naval Strengths.

SECT. II.

The several kinds of Forreign Trade, of trading with Home or Forreign Navigation, some general Application.

IT will be then proper to consider how a Forreign Trade may be driven to most Advantage for the increase of *National Treasure, People, and Navigation.*

A Forreign Trade may be driven by a Nation with *Forreign Navigation,* or with *Home Navigation.*

A Forreign Trade driven with *Forreign Navigation,* is when a Nation sells its Commodities at Home to such Forreigners as come thither to Buy and Export them.

This sort of Forreign-Trade may enrich a Nation with Treasure more or less, as the Commodities so sold are of greater or lesser quantity and value.

But it is very plain, that if the Natives had *Exported* the same Commodities to the same Forreigners in *Shipping of their own,* the same Commodities would have yielded a greater Rate in the Forreign Ports, because the Natives must have been also paid for the *Carriage*; which by so much would have increased the National Gain; wherefore it is more advantagious for a Nation to Export its own Commodities by Navigation of its own.

13   But

But it will not follow, that 'tis therefore necessary or fit to confine all Exportations to Home Navigation by Penal Laws, especially in *England,* as will be shewn.

Nor does it follow that a Nation which doth Export its own Commodities, shall be always richer than another that sells at home ; for the Commodities of one Nation sold at home may yield ten times more money at home than the Commodities exported by the other shall yield abroad, and therefore must make it ten times richer.

This may be verified in the Trade of *France ;* whose Commodities sold at home to the *Dutch, English,* and others, for many years past, have brought vast quantities of money into *France,* perhaps more than all the Neighbour Nations have gotten by their exported Commodities, by which means, and no other, *France* is become the Terrour of the World, as I shall more particularly and fully shew.

A beneficial Forreign Trade, with home Navigation, may be said to be of two sorts.

The one consists in the meer *Exportation* of home Commodities into Forreign Nations where they may be vended, of which I have spoken before.

The other, in Trading and Huxtering *from Port to Port.*

The benefit of Trading or Huxtering from Port to Port consists in buying Commodities cheaper in one Forreign Port, and selling them dearer in some others ; in which case the Nation Trading ordinarily gets more or less, in proportion, as the Merchants buy for less and sell for more, and as the Stock and Navigation imployed in this sort of Trade is more or less.

The *Dutch* being to buy much of their Victuals, Cloaths, and other necessaries from abroad, and having little Commodities of their own to Export, put themselves upon this Trading *from Port to Port ;* which Trade

14   they

they have improved to that degree, that they are become, as it were, the Common Carriers of the World,
imploying near 30000 Trading-Vessels, (including those
which belong to their Fishery.) In this way of Trade
have this Industrious People yearly bought up vast
quantities of *French* Manufactures and Commodities,
and uttered them again for present profit in other parts
of the World, not foreseeing those dangers they have
been bringing upon themselves and all *Europe*.

The *English* have never attained to near so Universal
Manufacture as the *French*, or so general a huxtering
Trade as the *Dutch;* But yet until this last Age had a
greater proportion of each then the *Dutch* or *French;*
their Trade hath chiefly consisted in the Exportation of
their own Commodities, and Manufactures made of
their own home Materials ; of which that of our *Wooll*
being the Principal, was long thought and really still
is, or might be, the greatest and richest in the World;
This, with our exported *Tin, Lead, Iron, Allome, Fish,*
and other valuable things, brought in a sufficient quantity of Forreign Commodities to serve our National
Occasions, Pomp and Ornament, and left an Annual
Increase of Imported Treasure, which in length of time
had much enriched the Nation, though our neat Annual
Gain by Forreign Trade did never bring in much above
250000*l.* or 300000 *per annum* increase of Treasure, one
year with another (taking any number of 20 years
together) as may be reasonably collected by what will
follow ; nor was that a Contemptible Gain (as the Trade
of this part of the World formerly stood) since it had
rendred this Kingdom as Rich and Happy at home, and
as formidable abroad, as any in *Europe*.

SECT.

SECT. III.

Of Forreign Trade consisting in Exportation, of the advantages of home Manufactures, and Manufactures, incidently other home Trades, and Imployments are considered; and which of them enrich a Nation; of the Fishing-Trade, and the annual exporting of Corn.

THe National Gain, by Forreign Trade, consisting either in vending home Commodities to Forreigners, or in Trading from Port to Port; It may be fit to be considered how these branches of Trade may be improved to the utmost.

Home Commodities vendible and exportable to Forreigners, are either such as are Capable of little or no *Manufacture*, as Coals, &c.

Or else such as may be manufactured, which may be called the *Principles or Materials* of Manufacture; such are Wooll, Silk, Flax, Hemp, Tin, Iron, Skins, Corn, and others.

Most materials of Manufacture are of small value whilst raw and unwrought, at least in Comparison of the Manufacture, since by Manufacture they may be made of five, ten, or twenty times their first value, according to the *Workmanship;* which is proved by the Woollen, Silk and Linnen Manufactures, and almost infinite others; wherefore if a Nation hath naturally any Materials of Manufacture, it is far more advantagious to Export them in Manufacture, rather than the raw Materials, because the Manufacture is so much more valuable, and will make a return of five, ten, or twenty times more *Treasure* to the Nation than the raw Materials.

Besides, it is most dangerous to Export the Materials

of

of Manufacture, since it may transfer the Manufacture
it self into some Neighbour Nation, and with it the incident Riches and Populacy : by which means a Neighbour-Nation may become five, ten, or twenty times
richer and stronger than that Nation which doth Export
its Materials, and those innocent Materials may in a
short time return in the shape of *armed Men and Ships*,
to the Terror and Confusion of an unwise and lazy
People.

But if Forreigners will vend their *raw* Materials of
Manufacture, it is necessary, or highly convenient for a
Nation to Import them, and put them into Manufacture
at home; after which, this Manufacture may be either
exported and sold for much more than the Materials
cost, or being used at home, will prevent the necessity
of *Importing* the like from abroad, by which the Nation
will *save* to the value of the Manufacture: Thus do the
French and *Dutch* manufacture Forreign Silk, *Spanish*
and *English* Wooll, and many other Forreign Materials,
which they Export and sell again with prodigious
advantage.

The *sorts* of Manufacture are so various, and almost
infinite, that there is no People so great or numerous
but may be universally imployed by it; There are many
which relate to *Eating and Drinking*, many more to
Apparel of all sorts, Furniture of *Houses*, *Equipage*,
Navigation, *War*, *Literature* and *Science*, unnecessary,
but acceptable *Toyes*, to gratifie the humors and follies
of Men, Women, and Children, under all which generals,
there are so many *species* of Manufactures, that the
very naming of them would make a Volume; some are
of *simple* Materials, some of *mixt*.

The Labours of the People bestowed this way, must
necessarily glomerate the Riches of the World, and
must render any Nation a prodigy of Wealth; for
whilst

21

whilst vast numbers of Manufacturers are thus continually improving the value of some Commodity or other, they work for the *Nation* where they live as well as for themselves; If 100000 Manufacturers get 6*l. per annum* a piece, the Nation must gain or save 600000*l. per annum* by their Labours, (supposing the Materials to be meliorated only to the value of their *Wages;)* If the number of the Manufacturers be greater, or if the same number gain more a piece, then is the National gain still greater and greater in proportion: All which is too evident in the present instance of *France,* and the contrary of that of *Spain,* which although supplied with the Wealth of the *Indies,* is, for want of home Manufactures, the poorest and weakest of all Nations, and the most *dispeopled.*

For by Manufactures, a Nation may support many hundred thousands of Families, besides the meer Tillers of Lands and Keepers of Cattel, which increase of *people* shall live well, without being a clog and vexation to the Landholders, and shall be highly beneficial to the rest of the Natives in times of Peace, as otherwise they will not be; and as the people increase, so may the kinds and quantities of Manufacture; the very *Women and Children* may ordinarily get good Livelihoods in Manufacture.

Hence must follow a sweet Harmony in a Nation which hath property, when every one's Hand and Head is employed, and when there comes a reciprocation of advantage to the Landholders, and all others, as necessarily there must; And as Manufacture seems a kind of *debt* to the *laborious* part of the people, who by nature are intitled to live; so it is the highest of all *Charities*; as it is most substantial and universal; What signifies the distribution of a little *broken meat* amongst a few Wretches, in Comparison of the support of hundreds

dreds of thousands of Families? And lastly, it is attended with the promised Rewards of Charity, *viz. Plenty, Glory, and Prosperity to a whole Nation.*

This, and what hath been said in the last Section, may administer occasion to consider what sorts of Trades, Imployments, and Professions do *add to the Riches of a Nation, and what not.*

It is evident that all sorts of home Manufactures must advance or save the National Wealth, the like may be said of those who are imployed in the *Fishing-Trade,* so may the Trade and Profession of a *Merchant* add to the National Riches.

There are another sort of home-Traders, who live meerly by *buying cheaper and selling dearer at home,* such are *Retailers* of all sorts in the City and Country, whom we call *Shopkeepers;* of which a convenient number are necessary in every Nation to keep open *Marts and Markets* for the vending of Commodities; These may advance their private Stocks and Estates by buying cheaper and selling dearer, but cannot (meerly by this way of Trade) add a peny to the National Riches, so that it may truly be said of one poor Manufacturer, that he adds more in a year to the Wealth of the Nation than all such Retailers and Shop-keepers in *England.*

And if these Shop-keepers deal over-much in *Consumptive Forreign Wares,* they may assist in the *beggary* of the Nation; so may the Trade of a Merchant *export and exhaust* the National Riches, if he trade over-much in meer *Consumptive Importations.*

And therefore though the *gain* of the persons imployed be one main end and design of all Trades and Imployments, and in that respect they are all alike; Yet they differ in this; That in some of them the persons imployed do immediately or ultimately gain money from *Forreigners;* But in the other, they gain from the *people,* and from *one another.*

19   Of

Of the last sort, are all Imployments relating to the Law and Physick, so are *Offices* of all kinds (which I do not say to insinuate any of these Imployments to be *useless* in a Nation, or to diminish from that due respect which ought to be given to Men of Place.) There is no question but they are highly necessary for the Regulation of the Body-Politick, and the Body-Natural; so are the *Clergy* for the Information of Mens Consciences; and therefore in every Nation convenient numbers of the people ought to be set apart for these purposes; But as far as they are *Imployments,* and intended for *private gain,* 'tis plain they add no Treasure to the Nation, but only enable the persons so imployed to share and heap up the Treasures already Imported; The like may be said of all other ways of living by meer *Literature and the Pen,* and some inferior In-land Imployments mentioned before; It must therefore be of dangerous Consequence if the Trade of a Nation run into over-much *Shop-keeping,* or if too many of the people withdrawing themselves from Manufactures, and the beneficial parts of Trade, should throng themselves into the *Clergy, Law, Physick, Literature,* and such other Professions as bring no *increase* of National Riches; And the rather, because these Imployments and Professions are *narrow,* and can support but a *few* Families in a Nation with convenience; so that it may endanger *Depopulation,* and by their numbers will prejudice one another; Whereas Manufacture and a great Forreign Trade, will admit of and oblige an increase of people even to infinity: And the more the Manufacturers increase, they will the more enrich one another, and the rest of the people; It may then be proper to inquire how the *Manufactures* of a Nation may be *increased and improved.*

This may be done either by enlarging former Manufactures, or by introducing new ones.

20   New

New Manufactures must be first taught, and then encouraged, and if made of Forreign Materials, the Materials must be Imported, after which, as the people find the sweet of their Labours, it is not to be questioned but that they will throng into the Imployment; they that want Bread, Cloathes, and other necessary Comforts, will be glad to obtain them honestly; Thus our King *Edward* the Third (a Wise and Victorious Prince) invited over the *Flemmings* to teach his Subjects the Woollen Manufacture; And thus have the *French* Policies invited over the most Exquisite Manufacturers into *France* from all parts of the World; these with their Schollars were first imployed at the Charge of the Government; but the Manufactures soon afterwards diffused into the gross Body of the people.

Without these primary Encouragements and Superintendence of the Government, it will be hard to nourish up any new Manufacture, or to enlarge any old ones, at least, suddenly, to any great degree.

Amongst the Exportations, the *Fishing-Trade* ought not to be forgotton, since according to modern Calculations, the meer Fishing-Trade for *Herring and Cod* on the Coasts of *England* and *Scotland* imploys above 8000 *Dutch* Ships or Vessels, 200000 of their Sea-men, and Fishers; And the Herrings and Cod sold by the *Dutch* in Forreign Countries, do bring an Annual profit of about 5000000*l. per annum* Sterling to that Nation: besides which, 'tis accounted that there are at least 250000 people more imployed and maintained at Home about this particular Navigation, making of Fishing-Nets, and the curing, ordering, and preparing of the Fish, &c. besides the *Island, Newfound-Land,* and *Greenland,* fishings of very great advantage.

See Mr. *Smith* of Improvements, *pa.* 268, 269, 270, computes the whole profit of this Fishery to be ten millions sterling: *per annum,* in a manner, all gained by otherNations.

But the ordinary Exportation of *Corn* out of the

Annual

Annual increase, hath been accounted most dangerous, and of all others the most unprofitable, because of the possibility of a dearth; which besides the hardships of it, will give opportunity to Forreigners of drawing away vast Treasures in a trice.

But if a Nation doth *store* up Corn in cheap years, the people will be secure against a Dearth, and yet when Corn is excessive dear in Neighbour-Nations, may then take their time to furnish them, and by that means will make much greater Advantages than by ordinary Exportation; And for this reason have the modern Policies of some wise Nations in Trade, contrived and erected *publick Storehouses or Conservatories for Corn.*

I shall conclude with the words of Sir *Walter Rawleigh,* in his excellent Observations upon Trade, presented to King *James.* "*Amsterdam* is never without "700000 quarters of Corn, a dearth in *England, France,* "*Italy,* or *Portugal,* is truly observed to enrich *Holland* "for seven years after; For example, the last Dearth "six years past, the *Hamburghers, Embdeners,* and *Hol-* "*landers,* out of their *Storehouses* furnished this King- "dom, and from *Southampton, Excester,* and *Bristol* "only, in a year and half, carried away near 200000*l.* "Then what great quantities of Corn did they Trans- "port from round about the Kingdom? from every "*Port-Town,* from the City of *London,* and other "Cities? it cannot be esteemed less than two Millions: "to the great decay and impoverishment of the Peo- "ple, discredit to the Merchants, dishonour of the "Land, &c."

Suppose then a Dearth or Scarcity of Corn happen once in twenty or thirty years, the Annual Labours of the People in the produce of the exported Corn are lost; 'tis also a *bulky* Commodity, and makes but a small yearly return, and the Forreign price and vent of it is

very

22

very casual, and incertain, for which Reasons, of latter years, the ordinary exporting of Corn is used only by some poor Nations, who have little other Trade: 'tis said the *French* King hath Ordered publick Stores and Conservatories of Corn.

SECT. IV.

Of Forreign Trade from Port to Port, the Nature and Advantage of it, differs from meer Carriage, and meer Importation; the necessity of a Home Storehouse: The ordinary Exporting of Money or Bullion, of dangerous consequence; how to be avoided: The Fishing-Trade, and Trade from Port to Port, are the Nursery and Support of Sea-men, and Sea-towns; The Condition of Ours; The National Advantages of England for all sorts of Trade, yet hath the least share.

SInce the Trade from *Port to Port* will cause a great *Navigation*, and also bring in very much *Treasure*, and therefore if it be added to the Trade of *Exportation*, must render a Nation the Miracle of Riches and Power; I shall next consider what this Trade from Port to Port really consists in, and by what methods it may be driven most advantagiously to a Nation.

A Trade from *Port to Port* may be most properly so called, when a Merchant of one Nation buying Goods in another, the Property becomes his, and he carries them to a third Forreign Market on his own account;

thus

thus the *Dutch* buy up, Export and sell the *French* Manufactures and Commodities; But if a *Dutch*-man carry *French* Goods to be sold in a Forreign Market, on a *French-man's account*, taking a certain Rate for the Hire of his Ship; this is not properly a Trade from Port to Port, but is *meer Carriage;* which sort of Imployment (though it may seem least reputable) may increase the National Treasure, as the Navigation used in it is more or less, and may imploy many Sea-men.

A Trade from Port to Port doth also differ from *meer Importation,* which is, when the Merchant does Import Consumptive Commodities, which are spent at Home, in which case, if the importations are *excessive,* it may truly be called *The Disease of Trade,* since it must cause an Exportation of the National Stock of Treasure, and thereby may soon ruine a Nation, as will be shewn; But so cannot a Trade from Port to Port, truly so called, because the Goods bought being sold or bartered off, at other Forreign Ports, must be ultimately converted into more and more money, and thereby increase the home Treasure.

This Trading from Port to Port, does not wholly consist in the Carriage of a Commodity from one Port directly to another; nor can be so driven to any great, or ordinary Advantage; for the Merchants thus Imployed, must either Trade *little,* or else must *glut* the Ports they go to with an over-great quantity of Goods of the same kind; and therefore for the full improvement of a Trade from Port to Port, it is generally necessary, That the Merchants should first unlade at Home, which will inevitably render a Nation so Trading a compleat and mighty *Storehouse* of all Forreign Manufactures and Commodities; and then from this infinite Miscellany of Goods (as the Merchants observe their time for a Market and the Ports they go to) they may freight their Ships with such *sortible Commodities and*

Cargoes

Cargoes as are proper and vendible to advantage; Thus
are the *Dutch* Provinces become the mighty *Storehouse* See Sir *Wil-*
of the World; the Plenties of the World do grow and in- *liam Temple's*
crease in other Countries, but there are the Stores, and *Dutch Cap. of*
thence do their Merchants furnish themselves for all *Trade,* pag.
sorts of Voyages; "Thus they Transport the Merchan- 210, 232.
"dizes of *France, Spain, Portugal, Italy, Turky,* the *East*
"and *West Indies* to the East and North-East Countries
"of *Pomerland, Sprusland, Muscovy, Poland, Denmark,*
"*Norway, Liefland, Swedeland, Germany*; and the
"Merchandizes of the last mentioned Kingdoms they
"transport into the Southern and Western Nations,"
as Sir *Walter Raileigh* long since noted, nor is a Trade
from Port to Port practicable, or can be improved to
any considerable or valuable degree, unless the Nation
be made an universal Storehouse.

In the Trade from Port to Port there must be some
kinds of *Original Exportation*, because the Merchant
cannot purchase Forreign Goods in a Forreign Port
for nothing.

And one would think it should hardly be a question,
whether in this way of Trade it be most profitable to a
Nation *to Export Manufacture, or other home Commodities, or Money, or Bullion.*

But of late years many of our Merchants very much Stat. restrain-
contend for a Liberty to Export Money or Bullion ing the Ex-
                                                     portation of
as advantagious to the Trade of the Nation, and have Money and
gotten an Act of Parliament to Legitimate the ex- Bullion are 9
porting of Bullion, contrary to many other former 2 *H.* 4. 5*th* 5
Statutes, and now Bullion and Money also are become *R.* 2. 2 *H.* 6.
our usual exportable Commodities.   6*th* 4 *H.* 7. 23.
                                                     19 *H.* 7. 5.
But I shall oppose the ordinary Exporting of Money The Expor-
                                                     tation of Bul-
or Bullion in Trade, especially as the Constitution of lion Licensed
our Trade now is, for the Reasons following: by a short
                                                     Clause of 15
First, I shall admit that the exporting of Treasure *Car.* 2, *Cap.* 7.
in the Trade from Port to Port may increase Treasure, intituled
                                                     Trade
25   provided *Incouraged.*

provided that the Merchant makes wise Bargains, and his Ships return safe, neither of which is altogether certain; But supposing the Merchant be both so wise and fortunate, yet 'tis very plain that in this way of Trade the Merchant cannot bring more new Treasure to the *Nation* than the Merchant by his judicious and prosperous dealing and Voyage can *Add* to the Original Sum he *carried out.*

But had the *Merchant* taken off and exported to the same value in home *Manufacture or Commodity,* 'tis as plain that the very vending or bartering of that Manufacture or Commodity, would have been a farther Gain to the *Nation,* to the full value of the Manufacture or Commodity exported; since the Manufacture or home Commodity sold would finally resolve into Treasure, nay, though the *Merchant* gain but little or nothing in this case, yet the *Nation* must be a Gainer to the value of the Manufacture or other Commodity exported.

As suppose a *Dutch* or *English* Ship go with exported Treasure to *France,* where the Merchant buys *French* Wine for 1000*l.* which afterwards he carries into the *Sound,* and there sells it for 1300*l.* the Merchant hath brought but 300*l.* new Treasure or Credit to the *Nation;* But had the Merchant Exported Herrings or home Manufacture, and by Sale or Barter of his Fish or Manufacture had purchased the same quantity of Wines, which afterwards he sold for 1300*l.* the *Nation* must presently have a new Addition of Treasure or Credit for the whole 1300*l.* In which last Case the *Nation* gets a new 1000*l.* by the labours of the Fishers or Manufacturers, besides the 300*l.* got by the Merchant; if the Merchant had got nothing, yet the *Nation* had gained 1000*l.*

Secondly, In this last Case great numbers of Manufacturers, Fishers, &c. are kept and well maintained at Home, whereas the ordinary Exportation of Money

must

must make them idle and useless; whereof the further
Consequence is, that the ordinary Exportation of Money
must inevitably *depopulate* a Nation, if it be of any
great extent of Territory; so must the Exportation of
Bullion be attended with the same mischiefs for the
same reasons : The Exportation of Bullion does also
open a way for the Exporting of Coined Treasure,
without any hazards of Seizure, by *melting* down the
most valuable Coin into Bullion.

But I expect to be told that *Hamburgh* and *Holland*,
&c. do allow of and use the Exportation of Treasure.

To which I answer, That there is no parallel between
such Countries as these and *England*; For these are
little Territories, much consisting of Merchants, their
Agents, Factors, and dependents, who live by meer
Merchandize, that the rest of the people being but few
(in Comparison of what are necessary to people so great
and fertile a Nation as *England*) may be supported with
much fewer and lesser Manufactures and home Employments; and therefore that the Exporting of Treasure
must be less dangerous, and perhaps may be the more
necessary there, because by the fewness of people, and
consequential restraint of Manufactures, their Merchants
may be confined in the bulk and variety of home Commodities to Export.

If it be said that no Nation can be so stored with
home Commodities, as to answer all Forreign Ports
and Markets, and therefore that it may be sometimes
necessary to Export Treasure in every trading Nation;
This perhaps may be true in some degree; But this is
another question; and in the mean time it remains that
it is most profitable to a Nation to Export home Commodities (where it may be done) rather than Money or
Bullion, and therefore that the Merchants ought to be
restrained from it as much as it is possible.

Then as to the other question, how far it may be

27   *necessary*

necessary in a Nation to Export Money in Trade, It
must depend upon the greater or lesser Improvement
of the National Trade.

For as a Nation hath a more universal Manufacture
and Fishery, more Drinks, Fruits, Curiosities, and Delicacies of its own, its Merchants will be more and more
enabled to Fraight themselves outwards with home
Commodities; These mighty Stores of home Commodities can only be had in great fertile and populous
Nations.

But suppose a Nation be not, or cannot be so fully
stored with home Commodities as to Answer all Forreign
Markets, yet its Merchants first Exporting home Commodities to Ports where they are Vendible, may by a
Barter, Sale, or Exchange of these, and an eternal
Succession of Voyages and Contracts, make the Nation
where they live a *Storehouse* to Perfection; and will
then have the choice of all Merchandizes on the Earth
to Export; and therefore may ordinarily and beneficially
Trade to any Forreign Port without exporting Treasure;
And if they may, they will, because else they will loose
the benefit of the Market for the goods they may re-
Export; Thus even the *Dutch* originally Exporting
Herring, Cod, Earthen Wares, Woollen Cloth, Linnen,
and of late Silks, and other home Commodities, and
having by the Barter or Sale of these compleated their
home Storehouse, can ordinarily buy at Foreign Markets,
without Exporting Treasure; By this means are the
Dutch enabled to Trade as they do to *Swedeland, Liefe-
land,* and *Norway,* where by selling or bartering of their
own and Forreign Commodities, they provide themselves with the materials of Pitch, Tar, Hemp and Flax,
necessary for Navigation, and with Timber, and other
Commodities, for their use at Home, and Trade abroad,
whilst the same Commodities cost the *English* some
100000*l. per annum,* since the decay of our Cloth-Trade

into

into those Ports; which kind of Trade is doubtless advantagious to some Merchants (else they would not continue it;) But does help to drain the Nation of its Treasure.

I do not say the *Dutch* never Export Treasure, but that by reason of their Forreign Storehouse, they are under no such ordinary necessity to do it; and in fact Export little or none to many other Countries, where the *English* Trade with much: whereof I shall have occasion to say more.

I shall conclude, that where the Home and Forreign Trade of a great and populous Nation is duly Regulated, and sufficiently Improved, there will be little necessity to *Export Treasure.*

To which I shall add, That the Exporting of Treasure in a Nation, having ill methods of Trade, must be yet more dangerous, because it facilitates *meer Importation,* and in *England* is chiefly serviceable to it, as will appear.

If a Trade from Port to Port be Improved to any great degree, it must necessarily very much increase the National Treasure, and numbers of people, especially *Sea-men.*

If 20000 Trading Vessels add 300*l. per annum* a piece to the National Stock yearly, the yearly National Gain must amount to 6000000*l. per annum,* and so in any greater or lesser proportion, as the Navigation or Gain is greater or less; of which we have a plain Example in the *Dutch,* who in about Ninety or 100 years time have arrived to a wonderful Wealth and Strength by it, though they have been always forced to buy much of their Victuals and Materials of Clothing, all their Materials of Shipping, and many other chargeable Necessaries from Forreigners, which must be a prodigious Annual Expence.

A Fishing-Trade is one great and certain *Nursery of Sea-men,* and brings Wealth and Comfort to *Sea-Towns;*

But

But a Flourishing Trade from Port to Port will make better and more Sea-men, inrich Sea-towns more, and will Imploy very considerable numbers of people at Land, in Building, Manufacturing, Repairing, and other ordering of the Shipping, Tackle, and Goods Imported and Exported, besides the Merchants and their more immediate Dependants; Thus do we see the Towns upon our opposite Shores abound in Riches and People, whilst our own Sea-towns languish more and more.

And from hence it may appear, that for the utmost advance of this Trade, it is necessary there should be very much Shipping in a Nation, multitudes of Sea-men, great Stocks continually imployed in Merchandize, great numbers of Merchants, and lastly safe Ports and Harbours.

I shall end this with some retrospect to the last Section, by observing, that no Nation in the World is naturally so adapted for a mighty Trade of all sorts as *England.*

First, Because it hath more excellent *Native Commodities* than any one Nation in the World, as Copper, Lead, Iron, Tin, Allome, Copperas, Saffron, Fell, the mighty Commodity of Wooll, Corn, convertible into Beer, and Transportable, besides near 100 others, which are capable of near 1000 sorts of Manufactures, as *Sir Walter Rawleigh* observes.

That it is one of the most *Fertile* of Kingdoms, and therefore out of its own Stores might support almost infinite numbers of people both for Manufactures at home, and Trade abroad, especially as the Island might be improved.

That it hath more and safer *Ports* and Harbours than almost all the Nations in *Europe* put together.

That it is *better scituated* for the Northern, Eastern, Southern and Western Trades than any other Nation.

That the *Herring and Cod,* with which the *Dutch*

drive

drive so mighty a Trade, are caught in our *English* Seas, upon our own Coasts and Shores, and may be managed with more ease and advantage by the *English*, than by any other Nation.

And to conclude, That our *People* are strong and able for Work at Home, generous and adventurous abroad, and such as all the rest of the World *have* most coveted to commerce with, and naturally as ingenious, industrious, and willing to labour as any part of Mankind, so long as they can have a reasonable fruit of their Labours, which hath been evidenced by many former undeniable Experiences.

Notwithstanding all which Advantages, *England* hath had very few considerable Manufactures, some of which are lost, and the rest decaying; nor have we any considerable remaining Trade from Port to Port, or Fishing-Trade, of which there are doubtless some Reasons and Causes very fit to be understood and regulated, since the *Wealth, Strength, Happiness and Safety of England* immediately depend upon it; I shall therefore in the three next ensuing Sections give an Account of such particular *Obstructions in our Trade,* as have fallen under my notice.

SECT. V.

That our Home and Forreign Market is Incumbered, and
prejudiced by extraordinary and unequal Charges, and
Cloggs in our Merchandize above what are in our
Neighbour-Nations, viz. In the building and furniture
of our Ships, Victuals, Sea-mens Wages, Customs,
Interest-Money, &c. with the Consequences in our
Manufactures and Forreign Trade; more particularly
of the decay of our Woollen Manufacture: our Ex-
portations now confined to our Importations and Im-
ported Treasure, how to be enlarged, our casual
dependence on the Trade of Spain.

SUpposing this or any other Nation had all the
aforesaid Grounds of Trade, *viz.* All sorts of Home
and Forreign Materials of Manufacture, sufficient numbers of People, and those instructed in Manufacture,
supposing them never so industrious, that there were
no want of Ships, Sea-men, or Stocks of Money, Ports
or Plenties at home, yet there is another thing necessary, which is a *good and quick Vent and Market* for
Commodities; without which all Manufactures will
decay and expire, all other Exportations must fail, and
the Trade from Port to Port can be no longer practicable or valuable.

For if the Manufacturer cannot sell his Manufacture,
he hath laboured to his great loss; so if a Merchant
buy Goods at one Forreign Port which he cannot sell
at another Forreign Port, he hath at least lost his
Voyage, and the Charge of it; so if the Market be not
absolutely closed up, yet if it be prejudiced and spoiled
to any great degree, the Merchant or Manufacturer
will either discontinue presently, or will Trade less and
less, and will fling up speedily if the Market doth not

mend;

mend; for if men of Trade cannot sell for reasonable profit, but will be forced to live much worse and poorer than other men of the like degree and estate in the same Nation, they will not continue long in so unprofitable a Toil.

The *Home* and *Forreign Market* bear such a Simpathy one with the other, that Obstructions in the Market at home, may arise from Obstructions in the Forreign Market, as well as immediately from Causes at home.

For if the Forreign Market for Exportable Commodities fail in any degree, there must be a less and worse Vent and Market at home for these Commodities; if the Forreign Market come to take off a *lesser quantity* yearly than before, or at a *lesser price*, the Natives must sell a lesser quantity, and at a lesser price, to their Exporters and Merchants, who will not buy more than they can Vend again, nor so dear that they cannot vend them with sufficient profit.

Now the course of our *English* Forreign Merchandize hath begotten an Obstruction in the Forreign Market, because our Merchants are liable to *greater Charges* in their way of Trade than the Merchants of our Neighbour Nations.

For all necessary Charge of the Merchant in his course of Trade is super-added to the Original Cost of his Commodity, so that the Merchant, upon sale of the Commodity Exported, is under an Obligation to pay himself his Charge, and yet to sell so, that he may make himself a reasonable gainer besides.

Then if a Forreign Merchant bring the same Manufacture or Commodity to the same Forreign Port with less charge, he will be able to under-sell the *English* Merchant as much as his charge is less, and yet shall get reasonable profit.

And if the Merchants of other Nations be able to sell for less, they will, nay perhaps must, (supposing

33   that

22

that they drive an open Trade, and upon their distinct Stock) for then being incapable of *combining* to Impose prizes, and desiring a quick Market (which is the life of Trade,) they will be worked down by the Forreign Buyers to take as moderate profit for their Goods as they can afford them at.

The Consequence of this is, that the *English* Merchant must either forbear Exporting, or else must sink his prizes on the *English* Manufacturers, whereby the *English* Manufactures must be stifled or discouraged.

'Tis true, That if a Nation hath some rich and necessary Material and Manufacture within it self, exclusive to other Nations, it hath the *Monopoly* of this Manufacture to the rest of the World, and therefore cannot be under-sold, but may vend it so as to pay all extraordinary Charges with sufficient gain to the Manufacturer and Merchant; which was heretofore the Case of *England* in the *Woollen Manufacture.*

But if a Manufacture or Commodity be common to *England* and *Holland,* or *England* and *France,* and the *Hollanders* or *French* can bring this Manufacture or Commodity cheaper to a third Forreign Port than the *English,* the *Hollanders* or *French* under-selling the *English,* will beat the *English* out of the Manufacture; It is accompted that the odds of two *per cent.* nay of one *per cent.* will produce this advantage.

An inequality of Charge on Merchandize must also influence the Trade from Port to Port; For if the *English* and *Dutch* Merchant coming to the same Port with the same Forreign Commodity, the *Dutch* can ordinarily under-sell the *English;* it must also be of the same Consequence in this ·rt of Trade.

This happens to be the Case between the *English* and *Dutch,* the *Dutch* being upon their defection from *Spain,* driven into great Exigencies, and therefore becoming studious and emulous how to advance their

Trade

Trade, have contrived all imaginable ways how to *Trade cheap,* whose Example other Neighbouring-States and Kingdoms have followed in a great degree, and the *French* amongst the rest, whilst the *English* do not only proceed in their former more chargeable methods of Trade, but have clogged their Navigation and Merchants more and more, whereof I shall give some Instances, and shall leave the Computation of the odds to the Reader.

First, The *Dutch* have found and long used such a way of *building* their ordinary Trading *Ships* and *Vessels,* that they will sail with eight or ten men, when an *English* built Ship of about the same Burthen shall not sail without near thirty men, so that the *English* Merchant must ordinarily be at more Charge for *Wages* and *Victuals* by two Thirds than the *Dutch.*

Secondly, The *English Customs* for Forreign Goods Imported and Re-exported (though half the Customs paid are returned upon Re-exportation) are near twenty times greater than the *Dutch* Customs, and for some home Commodities Exported, if not for all, are greater than the *Dutch* or *French* Customs, which does work a further Charge on the *English* Merchants. For,

Thirdly, By this means our *English* Merchants are ordinarily forced to keep near a fourth part of their Stocks dead at home to answer Customs, so that a *Dutch* Merchant may drive the same Trade with a much less Stock.

Fourthly, The late *Act of Navigation,* and the Act of 14 *Car.* 2. *Cap.* 11. confining the *English* Trade to Shipping built with *English Timber* (which is now exceeding scarce and dear.) The *Dutch, French, Danes, Hamburghers, &c.* can have Ship-Timber in *Germany, France* and *Denmark,* for less than half the price of ours. So by means of the same Acts of Navigation,

35   have

have the *Dutch* and *French* their Cordage, Masts, Sails, Tackle, Pitch and Tar, (being all necessary and chargeable Ingredients of Navigation) very much cheaper than the *English*, so that the *Hollanders*, or *French*, or *Danes*, nay, almost any other of our Neighbours, can build and apparel a Ship, or fit up and repair, at a less charge by half than the *English* can do; the reason of this is more at large Discoursed by Mr. *Roger Cooke* in his late Ingenious Treatises *Of Trade*.

18 Car. 2. Cap.
2. & 20 Car.
2. Cap.

And Fifthly, By means of the late *Irish Acts* against Importation of Cattel the *Dutch* and *French* can and do *Victual* their Ships cheaper with *Irish* Victuals than the *English* can do in *England*, whereas before, *England* could Victual cheaper than any Nation in *Europe*.

Note, no Interest is allowed in *France*.

Sixthly, The *English* pay 6 *per Cent. Interest for Money*, and the *Dutch* but 3 *per Cent.* or less, which is to our *English* Merchants of a strange ill Consequence, if we consider our extraordinary Charges in Victuals Wages, Shipping, and the money kept dead to answer Customs, besides the Interest of the Stock actually imployed in Merchandize and Wares; for the Interest, with Interest upon Interest running up continually, does still increase the Charge and Clogg upon our Merchants, but especially must disable us to make *England* a Storehouse of Forreign Goods, since although they should be bought and Imported as cheap as in *Holland*, they must yet become dearer for Re-exportation by the odds in the Interest; if the Annual Interest *per Cent.* were the same, yet the odds in the Stock imployed would produce a vast odds in the Interest.

Seventhly, The Act of Navigation obliging us to sail with ¼ of our *English Sea-men* (of which we have but a few in Comparison of the *Dutch*, who have at least ten times more than we) hath given occasion to our Sea-

36

men

men to raise their Wages: To all which may be added our present Charge of Passes, supposing that any Forreign Nation can Trade without *Passes,* or procure them for less money: the like may be said of our late Charge of *Ballastage, &c.*

Nay the *Dutch* are so curious, that for more cheapness and convenience, they build Ships of *divers makes, sorts of Timber, and manner of Tackling,* for almost every Trade: whereas the *English* build or use but one sort, and that the most chargeable.

Suppose then, that the *English* and *Dutch* should both Manufacture Silk, Linnen, Woollen, &c. and that an *English* and *Dutch* Merchant buying up these *Manufactures* at the same Rate at Home, should Export them to a third Port where they are Vendible, 'tis plain that the *Dutch* Merchant being at less charge by at least two thirds for Wages and Victuals, at less charge for Customs or Port-Duties, at a less charge by half in building and fitting up his Ship, and being so much eased in the Interest of money, and other the said particulars, may under-sell the *English* Merchant a great many times 2 *per Cent.*

But much more will he be able to under-sell the *English* Merchant in the Trade from *Port to Port,* because of the excessive height of our Customs for Goods Imported and Re-exported, or if an *English* Merchant go directly from one Port to another, he will still lie under the other inequalities of Charge.

Nor are the *English* for the same Reason capable of any Imployment in *meer Carriage* for any Forreigners, unless, perhaps, during the Convulsions of a War amongst other Nations.

And for the same Reasons the *English* can never drive any considerable *Fishing-Trade,* though we pay no Custom for Fish.

This cheapness of the *Dutch,* and other Forreign

Sir *Walter Rawleigh,* in his time, observes, That if an *English* and *Holland* Ship of 200 Tun a piece be at *Dantzick,* the *Hollander* should serve the Merchant cheaper by 100*l.* than the *English,* being sailed with nine or ten Mariners, but ours with thirty, yet our

Navigation

English Carpenters keep their old way of building to this day, and know no other.

Navigation and Trading, doth not only give advantage and preference to their own Manufactures, but to the Manufactures of all other Nations where there is an open, free and reasonable Market; as suppose the *Dutch* buy *French*, *German*, or *Italian* Manufactures as cheap as the *English* Merchant can buy the like Manufactures in *England*, he may be able to under-sell the *English* Merchant and Manufacture in a third Port, with gain to himself.

And hence it is that the *Dutch*, and other Forreign *cheap* Navigation, hath given rise and growth to the *French*, *Dutch*, *German*, *Italian*, and other Forreign Manufactures; which, with the difficulties on our Trade at home, hath worked us out of near all our Manufactures, except what remains to us of our Cloathing-Trade.

So the cheapness of the *Dutch*, and other Forreign Navigation and Trading, hath in a manner beaten us out of all the Trade from Port to Port, and Fishing-Trade; the *English* retaining little from Port to Port, but the *East-India Trade*, for Callicoes, Pepper, &c. a Trade which continues upon a particular reason, distinct from all the rest, as I shall also shew in the next Section.

And upon the former Reasons, and others mentioned in this and the two next Sections, we must expect that the *Dutch* and *French* may in a short time destroy our remaining *Woollen Manufacture;* the *Dutch* taking advantage of our mis-management of our Cloth-Trade, of which I shall give a further account, found ways of getting our fine Wooll, which mixing with fine *Spanish*, and by that mixture making a cheaper and more serviceable fine Cloth than with all *Spanish*, have been long high our Competitors in the Trade of fine Cloth, and have near actually beaten us out in the *Northern Eastland and German Trades*, and share with

us

us in the *Turky-Trade,* both *Dutch* and *French* getting
what quantities they please of our long and middling-
Wooll out of *England* and *Ireland* (which they now
have cheaper than the *English* Clothiers from *Ireland*)
do mix it with *French, Polonia,* or other Forreign
Woolls, (which are two thirds cheaper than ours) and
therewith make vast quantities of coarse Cloths, Druggets and Stuffs, which being acceptable and Merchandizable, they Export to *Spain, Portugal, Germany,* and
most other Parts.

Their *Competition* in the Cloathing-Trade, joined
with some *Polonian, Silesian, German,* and other later
Manufactures of coarse Woolls, have already sunk our
Forreign *Market* and Vent; this hath sunk the *price*
of our raw Wooll, as necessarily it must, and as their
Manufactures increase, and ours does expire, the *French*
and *Dutch* must have our Wooll for what they please;
and if they cannot have it at their own Rate at one of
our Ports, they will go to another, and our necessitous
People having their Wooll in their hands, will sell
almost at any Rate; which is so far the Case in *Ireland*
already, that is there openly Exported at 6 or 7*s.* the
Tod; and then if we compute what a Tod of Wooll
may stand the *French* or *Dutch* in, considering their
cheap mixtures of *French, Polonish,* and other course
Woolls, we may very suddenly expect to have our
English Woolls at about 4*s.* the Tod; for if the *English*
Clothier gives more for his *Materials* than the *French*
or *Dutch,* he cannot live: It is now in most parts of
England at about 12*s.* or 13*s.* the Tod, in some places
at 10*s.* where of late years it was 30 and 40*s.* the Tod.

The *French* and *Dutch* have long maligned this
English Manufacture, and have now made a mighty
progress towards its extirpation, and therein of the
great support of our *English* Nation; (doubtless the
Wooll-Sacks were placed in our House of Parliament

to

to give us a precaution of it :) The *Dutch* of late have been somewhat checked in the *Turky-Trade* by the War; but the *French* are more vigilant and vigorous in the increase and vent of their Woollen Manufacture than ever; and the *Dutch are now at Peace again.*

I know some alledge, that these Nations may support their present Woollen Manufacture without our Wooll, which our own *English Clothiers*, on their own experience, deny; They say that a mixture of fine *English,* and fine *Spanish,* makes a Cloth so much cheaper and more serviceable than of all fine *Spanish,* That it must needs beat out any Forreign Manufacture made of all fine *Spanish,* (which is always near twice as dear as our finest *English* Wooll) and therefore have the *English* and *Dutch* near subverted the *Venetian* Cloth-Trade in *Turkey;* On the other side, They say that the *German, Polonia, Silesian,* and *French,* are so coarse of themselves, that although they may be wrought into an ill sort of Composition, perhaps fit for Sailors, or such like; yet it is not *Merchandizable;* but in mixture with *English* or *Irish;* good dressing and dying will make very vendible and serviceable Stuffs, Druggets, and coarse Cloths.

Nor is there any shadow of reason to believe otherwise, considering how Ravenous the *French* and *Dutch* have been after our Wooll, since they set up their Woollen Manufactures; why have they and their Agents been lurking on our Coasts and in our Creeks to filch it away for so many years? why have they given *treble* as much for it as for *Polonia* or *French?* shall we think the *Dutch* and *French* such Fools and mad-men as to make so *laborious* and *dear* a Purchase of an unnecessary Commodity? We are told of some fine *Sclavonian* Woolls which the *Dutch* make use of, but withall that they are not comparable to ours; nor of any considerable *bulk;* and are assured by those who

40   should

should best understand it, that no Nation but *England* hath a sufficient store of Wooll to drive a Forreign Trade of any Consequence.

There is no question, but that if we did manufacture all our Wooll, we might again near Monopolize the Merchandize and Forreign Trade of Woollen-Cloathing, though perhaps some Forreign Manufactures of coarse Woolls might be kept up for the use of the ordinary poorer people at Home; at least it must be admitted, that if we did manufacture all our *English* and *Irish Wooll*, it would find vent in the World, since it is now all manufactured in *England, France* and *Holland,* and doth find vent in the aforesaid *mixtures*; by which the bulk of the Manufacture must be much increased.

Then if the question be how we shall arrive to the sole Manufacture of our own *English* and *Irish* Wooll, it must appear upon what hath been said, that the only safe Expedient must be by *easing* our Navigation and Trade equally with Forreigners, in which Case having so much advantage in the Materials, we could not fail of an answerable success in the Manufacture; long Experience hath demonstrated that the *meer prohibiting* of the Exportation of Wooll is but a Cobweb, the *Dutch* and *French* being constantly supplied with what quanties they please to have, and ever will be, as long as their advantages in Trade will enable them to give more for our Woolls than our *English* and *Irish* Natives: for so long the Interests of our People will teach them ways to Elude or Baffle the Prohibition; For this reason our late Act of 12 *Car.* 2. *Cap.* 22. which makes it Felony to Export Wooll, hath nothing remedied the mischief. Upon what hath been said, I may further add, That those who think to better our Trade in general by the forceable subversion of the *Dutch* Trade and Navigation, are as much mistaken; since the *Hamburgers,* and other Trading States, the *French,* and

41   other

other Kingdoms, who have eased their Merchandize and Navigation, would then take the place of the *Dutch*, and would share the Trade, and exclude the *English*, unless our Trade were equally eased.

I shall conclude this Section with this farther Observation, That for the opening of a sufficient Forreign Vent and Market for our Home Commodities, whether Manufactures, Fish, or others; it is not only necessary to remove all unequal cloggs on meer Exportations, but also those on Imported Goods; because that whilst the *English* Merchant, by the Charges on Imported Goods, is ordinarily disabled to Trade from Port to Port, the value of our *English* Exportations must be in a manner *confined* to the value of the *Goods Imported*, and consumed at Home, and the Treasure we Import *in specie* yearly.

Whereas were the cloggs on our Imported Goods taken off, we might yearly vend of our own Home Commodities to the value of all the Forreign Goods we should then Import and Re-export, to serve the Occasions of all other Nations, (for these we might purchase by Barter or Sale of our own) whereby our Exported Home Commodities would then amount to much more, probably to more than ten times the value they now do yearly; All which in the course of Trade from Port to Port would resolve into more and more Treasure and Riches of all sorts.

And therefore, let the Treasure now Imported *in specie* be more or less, 'tis evident, that were our Merchants enabled to Trade from Port to Port, as the *Dutch* and others can and do, as our Manufactures, and other Home Commodities, Exported yearly, would be vastly more in quantity and value, so would the Treasure Imported yearly.

Secondly, The Exportation of *English* home Commodity is yet farther confined, when instead of home

Commodity

Commodity to answer the Imported Goods and Treasure, we Export so much Treasure as we do; In which Case if the Treasure Exported be more than is Imported yearly, this Kingdom must insensibly be beggered by meer Trade.

This may be feared to be our Case, because there are very few Forreign Nations (I think none worth the naming but *Spain*) where our Merchants can ordinarily sell our Commodity for ready money, or with so much advantage, that they can afford to return with the price received, but will be obliged to better their Adventures by laying out the money again on Consumptive Forreign Goods, or else apply it to satisfie Forreign Debts by Bills of Exchange; This many of our *Spanish* Traders do, so that our Merchants Import much less Treasure than they receive; and it may not be improper to be added here, that whilst the virtue of our whole Trade (as now managed) does still depend so much on that with *Spain*, our Support is very *single* and *casual*, and the Consequence must be fatal, should the *Spaniard* be rendred either *unable* or *unwilling* to Trade longer with us; our Case is already thus far worse than it was, that *Spain* is grown poor and weak, and the *Dutch* and *French* share and grow upon us in this Trade.

SECT.

SECT. VI.

Other Cloggs on our Trade, viz. The late Acts of Navi-
gation, which, with the other difficulties, have begot
Monopolies; made our Navigation yet dearer, so
Forreign Materials of Manufacture cause meer Im-
portations, hinder our Forreign vent of Victuals,
obliges a sudden Consumption of our remaining Ship-
Timber, particular dangers and consequences thereof;
Our Navigation cannot be increased whilst we are
restrained in Trade: The Exhausting of our Treasure
must subvert our Navigation: The advantages of For-
reigners, of Trading by Companies, and the different
Nature of ours, more particularly of our African *and*
East-India *Companies and Trade: divers ill Conse-*
quences of Joint-Stocks; therein more of Monopolies.
Long Land Carriages to London; *the Market there*
delayed. Odds in Interest-Money must prejudice our
Manufactures: private Interest observed. Our affec-
tation of Forreign Commodities: the prejudice of
obstructing the vent of Manufactures. Our Manu-
facturers liable to be imposed upon by our Merchants,
and by Ingrossers, a disadvantage by the Restitution
of half Customs on the Re-exportation.

IT being natural, That the continuance of one inconvenience should beget many others, it hath so fallen
out in *England.*

Our Natives discerning the odds of Charge between
our own and Forreign Navigation, and being therefore
tempted to Trade in Forreign Ships, or to deal with
Forreign Importers, (which threatned the subversion of
our *English* Navigation, and the *Importing Trade* of
44

our

our *English* Merchants) instead of Regulating our Navigation, the late Act of Navigation was made, whereby, and by other Acts, our *English* Exporta- tions are expressly or virtually confined to our own *English* built Shipping, so is the Importation of For- reign Goods, or else to the Forreign Natives of whose growths or productions they are; which restraint hath *begotten,* or (jointly with the other cloggs on our Forreign Merchandize) hath *heightned,* these farther Inconveniences.

12 Car. 2. ca. 18. 13 Car. 2 c. 14. 14 Car. 2. ca. 11. 15 Car. 2. c. 7.

First, It hath given a *Monopoly to our own Merchants* upon our Manufacturers and People, for our own ex- portable Manufactures and Commodities.

Secondly, It hath given a *Monopoly to our own Merchants* upon all the people of *England,* for Goods Imported.

Thirdly, The said Act of Navigation obliging the *English* to buy Imported Goods only at those Ports, or of those Natives, of whose growths and productions they are, hath given *Monopolies to all Forreigners* on the *English* for Goods of their respective growths and productions; the *Danes* (for instance) taking ad- vantage of it, very much raised their Prizes and Cus- toms upon us, for Pitch, Tar, and Timber, forcing us to pay near double what we did, and to pay them in money, where we used to barter with them for Com- modity; the like may be said of the *French,* those of the *Canary*-Islands, and others, particularly the *Leif- landers,* for raw Hemp and Flax; at the best we are but at mercy.

See Mr. *Coke's* Third Trea- tise *of Trade.*

Fourthly, this Act hath made our Navigation yet *more chargeable* than before, because the aforesaid For- reign Materials of Pitch, Tar, raw Hemp and Flax are thereby made very much the dearer; It doth also render *English* Ship-Timber still dearer and dearer, which must more and more disable and discourage us in the

building

building of Ships for Trade, and gives a great and dangerous advantage to our Neighbours in the building of *Ships of War* so much cheaper than we.

Fifthly, This dearness of Shipping must the more prejudice the vent of our Manufactures made of our *own Materials*, and disable us in the Trade from Port to Port, for the Reasons in the last Section.

Sixthly, The same *dearness of Shipping, with the other unequal charges on our Forreign Merchandize*, must render all *Forreign materials of Manufacture* imported much dearer in *England* than in other Neighbour-Nations, (such are Hemp, Flax, Silk, and many others of great consequence) and then our Manufacturers buying the Materials dearer, are obliged to sell their Manufactures dearer, which must hinder their vent at home as well as their Exportation abroad, and consequently the rise and growth of all our Manufactures made of Forreign Materials, and accordingly we see our Manufactures of Linnen, Cables, Sails, Sea-Nets, and Silk of all sorts, are some of them in a manner lost, the rest much decayed ; which I the rather mention, that this, and what I say elsewhere, may take off some ignorant and unreasonable Reproaches against the *English* Manufacturers, for not selling some Manufactures so cheap as in other Nations, since they are necessitated to it by these and some other difficulties upon them, which I shall take notice of in this and the next Section, as I shall have occasion.

Seventhly, This restraint to our dear *English* Navigation, *and Charges on our Merchandize*, does by Consequence tend to introduce the *Disease of Trade*, consisting in *meer Importation;* for as our Manufactures expire, there is a farther occasion of Importing Forreign Manufactures, especially if on this, and other Accounts, they may be sold cheaper here than our own: And hence it is, that we have a prodigious increase of

Imported

Imported Linnens, Silks, &c. and that we are of late forced to buy much more of our Cables, Cordage, Sails, and divers other Manufactures from the *Dutch, French, Germans, &c.* than formerly we did; in all which our Merchants must be greater gainers *for a time,* because our occasions for Forreign Goods being greater, they Import and sell the more at home; and from more and greater Sales must get the more money of *our Natives,* and the rather, because of their *Monopoly* on the rest of the people for Imported Goods, which does enable them to sell so at home, as to reimburse themselves all their Charges, with extraordinary profit.

Eighthly, The said Restraint excluding great numbers of Forreign Ships from our Ports must hinder the vending of great proportions of our Beef, Pork, Corn, Beer, Clothing, and other Necessaries.

Ninthly, The dearness of the *English* Timber, arising from the scarcity of it, the said Act doth oblige us to a kind of impossibility, there being not Timber enough in *England* to support any considerable Navigation, at least for any continuance of time; which small remnant of Timber we are forced to spend so fast in the building or repairing of ordinary Vessels, that we shall soon see the end of it, and then in any great Exigence we must seek out for Forreign Timber to build Ships of War, for which the Timber now remaining might be reserved.

Tenthly, Whereas the increase and support of Navigation depends on the ordinary Imployment of Ships and Sea-men in Trade, of which far the greatest numbers are to be maintained in the Fishing-Trade, and Trade from Port to Port, the *English* being, by the Acts of Navigation, and *other difficulties,* disabled from those Trades, can never increase their Navigation, and upon a small increase of Shipping must be *over-clogg'd.*

Eleventhly,

Eleventhly, The Act of Navigation giving *Forreigners*

See Mr. *Coke's* Treatises *Of Trade,* this largely and most rationally discoursed.

election either to sell their Goods to the *English* at home, or to Import them into *England,* is so far from incouraging our Navigation, that it hath put it into the choice of Forreigners whether theirs or our Shipping shall be imployed, which, with the dearness of ours, hath already increased the Navigation of our Neighbours, but hath reduced ours.

And lastly, As the dearness of our Navigation and course of Merchandize established by this Act does run us into an *Excess of Importations,* our Treasures must be exhausted, and then the remnant of our Shipping must be becalmed, and our Sea-men will leave us, as they already do, which I shall more particularly observe in the following Sections.

In the mean time it must be apparent, that if we had disposed our selves to a cheaper way of building and sailing our Trading-Ships (being as practicable here as in *Holland*) and had eased our Merchandize and Trade to an equal degree, these, and all other the aforesaid Mischiefs, had been prevented, and we might have supported a more swelling and beneficial Navigation than that of the *United Provinces;* who are so far from making use of any Expedient of this Nature, that they allow *Free Commerce* to all Forreigners, and their Ships; nor can the like Expedient be found in any Nation on the Earth, who have or aspire to a great Navigation or Trade; 'Tis confessed the like Act was made by the *Rump,* but 'twas on the occasion of their *Dutch War,* and intended (as 'tis said) to exclude the *Dutch* from the benefit of our Trade and Ports; however it were, we are not to learn the *Rump* might be mistaken in their Calculations.

If the people of a Nation have free Liberty to sell at home to all Merchants, they must necessarily have

48   the

the utmost choice of Chapmen for Manufactures and home Commodities, and by consequence the *best and utmost Market and Vent* as far as the Stocks, Treasures, Industry, Navigations and Occasions of the *World* will bear, and it is known that the most *thrifty* Merchants, and *near Livers,* and those that Trade most *universally,* and with the *greatest Stocks,* and *cheapest,* are ordinarily able to buy dearest, and sell cheapest; and if our Natives were un-confined, they would have Liberty to deal with any Forreigners on the Earth thus qualified; But our Natives being restrained to our own Merchants, and their own National Stock in Merchandize; let the particular Stocks of our Merchants be never so *small,* let them Trade never so *dear,* or so *little,* let them live never so *high and costly,* yet our Natives Manufactures and others must *pay for all,* by selling cheaper to our Merchants, and buying of them dearer; for the Merchants are in a capacity to buy so and sell so at home, as to satisfie themselves, and maintain the Equipage they live in, with much overplus.

But our *Clothiers,* and some others, have complained, that they are yet farther confined in their *choice* of Chapmen, since of the *English* Merchants they are confined to the *Trading Companies* and their stocks; which does first give me occasion to consider the *Constitutions* of our *English* Forreign Trading-Companies, and of what *consequence* they are in Trade.

This I shall do (as I think it will appear) without any partiality, protesting that I bear no malice or personal ill will against any Company, or Member of any Company, in *England,* but on the contrary, have an high esteem for as many of these and other Merchants as I am acquainted with, having found them very worthy men, and such as much desire the general Good, and therefore hope they will close with the Common Interest in what relates to themselves.

Particular

332 Of Cloggs upon our Trade, viz. Companies, &c.

Particular men have too long flattered themselves with a corrupt opinion, that they may gain by the common loss, and that it will *hold out their times*, which I do not say with any particular Reflection on these, or any other Traders; being the ordinary *maxim* or *prudential* of our *cunning men* of all kinds.

Of the first and more ancient sort are our *Regulated Companies*, or such as are so called, such are the *Turky*, *Hamburgh*, *Muscovy*, and *Eastland* Companies, whose Incorporations have been always accompted *Legal*, being *intended* for the better Regulation of some particular Forreign Trades, and for the raising and support of Common Charges, and for those purposes are enabled to *act by Committees*.

The Members of these Companies trading on their *distinct stocks*, seem to leave the same choice of Chapmen to our Manufacturers, wherefore I cannot observe but that such Companies might consist with a Flourishing Trade, if according to their appellations they be *really Regulated*, (that is) provided all *English*-men (according to their Right) be left at liberty *to become Members*, and Trade, upon Terms that are not *oppressive*. Secondly, That these Companies be not permitted to make such *By-Laws* for their private ends, as may prove advantagious to the Members of the Company, but prejudicial to the Nation; a thing very practicable, as suppose they should prolong their times of buying our home Commodities, or confine the Market to some such particular *places* at home as may be convenient for themselves, but injurious to our Manufacturers, or other Natives, or should Trade to few Ports where they can have extraordinary Rates and Terms, when they might Trade to more, and consequently vend more Commodity; or should endeavour to set the Dice on Forreigners, by Arbitrary prizes, or otherwise, whereby Forreigners may be disaffected with our Commerce;

50   experience

experience hath shown that private interest hath carryed some of them into such or the like irregularities,
it would be too long to instance in particulars, I shall
only say, that those of the last sort made Forreigners
the more Impatient till they had set up their woollen
Manufactures.

Our *East-India* and *Affrican Companies* are of another
kind, and of a latter creation, having gotten *Pattents* of
the Sole Trade of great part of the World *exclusive* to the
rest of his Majesties Subjects, which they manage upon
Joynt-stocks; of which I shall shew the generall ordinary consequences, and then examine how far they are
applicable to the particular Cases of these Companies.

The present *East-India* Pattent, granted 13 *July* 1660. That to the *African* Company since.

First, in the *nature* of such Companies they must be
as injurious as may be to all home-Manufactures made
of our own materialls, and the vent of our other exports, because by trading on a *Joynt-stock* they make
but *one buyer*, and therefore have a *Monopoly* for all
exportable goods proper *only* for the Forreign Nations
within their pattents, and must contract the choice of
Chapmen *for all other goods* proper for these and other
Countrys; now the confining of the Market and choice
of Chapmen in any degree is dangerous and prejudiciall to Trade, and in a larger sence may be called a
Monopoly, but it is far more mischievous when the
Election is totally lost, for then those who have the
Monopoly *may*, and therefore *will*, buy at their own
prizes.

Secondly, for the same reason they must be yet more
injurious to home-Manufactures made of forreign materialls; for first, they will sell the materialls as *dear*,
and then buy the Manufacture as *cheap as they please;*
which must subvert any Manufacture in a trice, especially if made of forreign materials bought cheaper by
forreign Manufacturers; suppose then the *East-India*
Company by their Commodity of Money, should so far

51   divert

divert the market as to beat out the *Turky Company* in
the trade of *Raw-Silks,* at what rates would our *Silk-weavers* buy raw-silks? or will it be said a Company on
a Joynt-stock, will so much value the National interest
as to sell as low as the Commodity is sold for in other
Nations? or if it will be said, who will believe it? was
ever any such thing done either by the English, Dutch,
or *East-India Companies?* did they ever yet endeavour
to beat out one another in trade by low selling? No,
this is never the effect of choice; were a third *East-India* Company in *France* on a Joynt-stock, they would
hold up the prizes; the advantage got to a Nation by
underselling is the effect of necessity, or high convenience; when the Sellers being infinite, some of them
are ready, and all long for dispatch and a new adventure, whereby they work down one another to as low a
prize as the Commodity can be afforded at; of all which
we have an undenyable example in the present *Affrican
Company,* who were no sooner Constituted, but they
raised the price of imported *red-wood,* which before
was sold at 26. and 28*l. per* Tun, to 80*l. per* Tun, which
must make our exported dyed Cloaths of all sorts so
much the dearer; and being an intolerable rate, put
our Dyers upon finding out the use of *Saunders,* which
they still continue; and as a farther confirmation of
this, and what I said before, I shall add, that after the
Erection of this Company, all goods proper for that
Trade only sunk at least 15*l. per Cent.* nor would the
10*th* part of the same goods be vended to the said
Company as there was before, to our Merchants driving
an *open Trade.*

Thirdly, For the same reason such a Company must
be as injurious to the Trade from *port to port;* For
having also a Monopoly in selling, they may and will
impose Arbitrary prizes on the buyers, and then the
Merchants or Re-exporters who buy goods so dear,

must

must be undersold by any other Nation which drives a *free and open Trade* to the same place from whence they are Imported ; this is self-evident, and therefore I should not instance in Fact, but that I have it on good Authority; that even in the *East-India* Trade, which is *Alledged* to be out of the common Rules of Trade, whilst the Trade was open, *viz.* In the years 54, 55, and 56, our Merchants sold the *Indian* Commodities so low, that they furnished more parts of *Europe* then since we have done, nay, *Holland* and *Amsterdam* it self; and that this very much sunk the Actions of the *Dutch East-India Company :* a thing which stands with reason ; and which therefore recommends an *open Trade* to India, *if it may be so driven with long continuance,* whereof I shall farther consider.

Fourthly, These Companies having also *Monopolies on these Forreign Natives* with whom they Trade, may set Arbitrary prizes upon them, for our home-Manufactures exported ; and will get more, by selling a little very dear, then by selling much more at moderate profit : and though the Joynt-stock imployed *be not sufficient* to manage the Trade any thing near the full advantage, yet those interested in it will have reason to be satisfyed with the returns they make, since in proportion to the Stock, they may be very great ; and for the same reason, may be well contented to Trade to a *few Ports* where they can have *great rates.*

5*ly,* The industry, courage and ingenuity of all the rest of the Natives (by which as much as by stock all Trade is improved) are shut out, which must not only be a prejudice to the Trade in general, but is a hardship put on the rest, *who by their birth-rights are equally intituled to all Trade;* upon all which accompts, the *Legality* of sole importing, sole buying, and sole vending, hath been formerly brought in question, and

denyed

Stat. 21.
Jacob. 3. 12.
Hen. 7. cap.
6th. 3. Jac.
cap. 6th.

denyed in our greatest Judicatures; and should it be generally admitted, by the same reason, the rest of our Forreign Trade might be inclosed to two or three more Companys, and then we should have but three or four Chapmen or Shops for all Exported and Imported Commodities; nay the whole might be granted or reserved to *one Company,* or *one man:* in any of which Cases what would become of *property?* Such is the Case of *the general body* of our *Merchants* already, that having in a manner lost the *Eastland* and *Northern* Trades, they are shut out of the *Affrican, Indian,* and *Persian, Chinese,* and other mighty Trades within those *Patents :* since this out of the *French* trade, and therefore are thronged into the *Streights,* and other narrow remnants, and yet is this the usual preferment of most of the younger Sons of the *Gentry of England.*

Sixthly, Though our other Merchants on their single accompts export much treasure, yet cannot it so easily be done, or not in so great Quality, as by such a Company; whose Joint stock having a great credit, can take up as much ready money as they want; whereas those who will not trust a single trader with a 100*l.* in *mony* will trust him with 500*l.* worth of Commodity, as common experience shews: and 'tis affirmed, that during our trade in 54. and 55. we exported more Commodities, *viz.* cloth, and other things, then since we have done.

To this is Objected, that the *East-India* trade so far differs from others, that it cannot be supported, *or not with so much advantage and security, (which I admit to be all one)* without a Joynt stock, which if true, there is no doubt but it ought to be so managed. This then is one great Question, in the mean time I hear nothing of this so much as alledged for the *Affrican* Company : the reasons given, depend upon pretended *Facts* in *India,* viz. the necessity of great common charges in

　　　　　　　　　　gratifying

gratifying and corresponding with the *Indian Princes*, and keeping *Forts and Forces* for the defence of our Factories there, which they say could never be supported but out of a Joynt stock in Trade.

To which others answer, 1*st.* that it may be true, great common charges are necessary, *& much greater then our Company are at,* but that *common charges* may be rais'd by a *regulated company* on *Goods* imploy'd in Trade, or on other parts of the Traders Estates, if the Company are Impower'd to make Levies, which is no more then every Parish are enabled to do for Church-Poor and other things: and that 'tis the same thing for a man to be assubjected to Levies out of that part of his distinct stock which is not in trade, as 'tis to make good any publick charge or loss out of his Joynt-stock.

Or Secondly, they say, that if this Trade be taken into the protection of the *Government,* it will have the Joint stock of the *Kingdom* to secure it, the same by which we are all secured: they offer what we were able to do in our open Trade in 1654. 55. and 56. But as a demonstration, urge the example of the *Portuguese,* who in an open Trade (I do not mean in an *Anarchy* nor without *conduct* and *order)* made near or full as great a progress in this Trade as the *Dutch,* whilest their Government gave sufficient assistance, which they say, also answers what hath been objected from the *supposed disorder of our Trade in those parts, should it lye open, and the capacity the Natives would be then in, of setting the dice upon the English:* and as a further answer to this they say, the same thing may be objected against all other open Trade in the World.

But then those for our Company, object the example of the *Dutch,* who being a Nation so wise in Trade, successfully manage the *East-India* Trade by a Company on a Joint stock; which being matter of fact, is beyond all the Argument in the World.

To

To which is answered, that this Example proves that a Company in a Joint stock may make a great progress in it, but does not disprove the like, or a greater progress under a regulated or open Trade.

2ly. That on the first constitution of this Company, and ever since, the *Dutch*, had most of the Trade, from Port to Port, and carriage throughout the rest of the World; and therefore might with less disadvantage to the rest of the Dutch Merchants inclose this to a Company.

3ly. That that Company was occasioned by the distinct Bands or voluntary Associations of Merchants in the several Provinces, who first undertook this Trade, which being soon after the Union, and the Provinces having Originally seperate rights, the said Associations had not so good a correspondence as was necessary, which could never fall out under a regulated Company of one Nation.

See the present state of the low Countrys, Printed in 69. Written by *M. A.* Fellow of the Royal Society p. 154, 5, 6, 7, 8, 9.

4ly. That the constitution of this Company being intended for a present Reconciliation of these interests, was Originally but for 21. Years, and was afterwards continued, because the Company growing so rich and powerfull both abroad and at home, the Members were generally *chosen States*, and therefore above any attacque at home from the rest.

See *Mandelsloe's* Travels, p. 285.

5ly. That as the *Dutch* Company is constituted, and have managed this Trade, it hath redownded to almost, if not fully to as *general* an advantage, as if managed by an open or regulated Trade: in which they say our Company is much defective; & that supposing a Joint stock necessary, or highly convenient, yet if we might manage ours to more National advantage, it were but fit it should be done.

To prove this might be done, those for a more open Trade urge, that our now *East-India patent* contains near or fully *one third part of the World*, and there-

fore

fore must have many hundreds, if not thousands of parts, that whereas their *priviledge* begins at the *Cape of good Hope*, it is from thence above 4000 Miles, upon the Coast of *Affrick* to the *Red Sea*, in all which they do not Trade to one Port, and very little, if any thing, in the *Red Sea;* which they say might be done to considerable advantage, and much more to *Persia,* then we now do ; That in *India*, our Company do not Trade to above 20. or 30. Ports, nor vend our Woollen Manufactures at above 3. or 4. Ports, and there *very dear,* who sell again much dearer, and to *Ingrossers,* which hinders the vent: that in *China,* or *Japan,* they have no Trade at all, ' where (to use the words of the Author of the Book ' in defence of the Company,) in all likelyhood more ' considerable quantities of our Woollen Manufactures ' might be vended, and from thence, in return thereof, ' *Gold, Silver, and Copper,* might be brought to supply ' at least, in a great measure, the Trade in other parts ' of *India*, without carrying so much out of *Europe* : ' But these Trades (he says) are not so easily gained ' as some fancy, great hazards of considerable stocks ' must be run, *&c.*'

Note the *African* Companys Patent contains from the *Streights* Mouth to the *Cape of good Hope.*

Printed in (77.) pag. 21.

Whereas, they say were a greater share of the industry and vigour of the Nation now pent up, and greater stocks now worse imployed, or idle, let into this Trade, we might hope for a great Trade to the Ports now of no use to the Company, for that in fact the *Dutch* Company Trade to all Ports in *India, China, Japan, &c.* and drive a mighty Trade to *Persia* with the Commodities of those Countreys, *viz.* Spice of all sorts, *&c.*

2dly. They say by this our want of a sufficient Commerce in *India* there is a very *small Navigation* imployed in this mighty Trade, of what might be, being not above 20. or 30. Ships *to and from India* in a direct course, and *in India* so inconsiderable that it is

57   not

not worth the noting : That for this reason, and because
we there vend so little Commodity, our Company does
Trade with vast quantities of exported *Treasure,* insomuch that upon search of the Custome books of the
Port of *London* only, it appeared by the Entrys, that
the Gold and Silver exported for *India* by the said Company from the 2d. of *March* 1673, to the 11th. of
March 1674, amounted to 500. sixty odd thousand
pounds Sterling ; besides what might be entred in the
out-ports, and without entry privately exported, which
those that understand this Trade will not think a little :
the Author of the aforesaid Pamphlet confesses, that
from the end of the Year 1674, to the beginning of the
Year 1675, was exported to *India* about 400000*l.* more,
in which perhaps we have reason to be suspitious of his
modesty : (It were a Nationall work to search the entrys for this and the other Years succeeding) that 'tis
the exporting of this Money that endears our Company
to the *Indian Princes,* and buys their protection, who
otherwise might destroy them if they would, our Company, having not above 2 or 300 people in their fort
St. *George,* including Factors and Agents of all sorts, and
at *Bombey* fewer.

Whereas, that on the other side the *Portuguese* whilst
they had the Trade of the *Indys,* though under no
Company, supported a *vast Navigation* there to serve
the occasions of those mighty Empires and their own ;
that since the *Dutch* have supplanted the *Portuguese ;*
they have yet a greater, having there thousands of Ships
Trading from Port to Port in the *Indies, Persia,* &c.
Besides 50, or 60, (if need be) more *Men of War,* and
keep great *Armies* in pay : That they have gotten many
spacious *Countrys, Islands,* and *Populous Citys* of their
own, whereof *Batavia* is near as big and rich as *Amsterdam ;* besides divers *Tributary Kingdoms,* whom they
have forced into a profitable complyance, and were it

not for fear of the English power at home, could dayly ruin us at their pleasure; that by the greatness of their Trade in these parts, they gain so considerably, that they can fraight home their great Fleets with the most valuable Commodities in the *Indies;* being the result of their industry in those parts, not of their exported Money.

3ly. That the *Subscribers* to our *East-India* Stock were originally but few, and the Stock but small, that divers of the shares being now bought in and consolidated into particular hands, there are not above 60. or 80. persons or thereabouts considerably concerned in the Joynt stock; that although the Stock be not near sufficient to manage even the present Trade, and therefore could admit of more *Depositums* of Money, which would let in a greater number of our people, the Company to prevent the necessity of it, do take up 4 or 500000*l.* at Interest at 5 *per Cent.* which by their dear Sales at home yields them 20 or 30 *per Cent.* or more; that as the Trade redounds to the benefit of few at home, so to as few in *India,* the Companies, Factories and imployments being few, and most lye divided amongst men of mean condition, who will depend solely on the Company, being originally *Hospitall Boys* or such like, and all others restrained to *Traffick, Frequent* or *haunt* the *Indies,* or places within their Pattent, by a Clause therein, under penaltys of *Imprisonment, Seizures* and *Confiscations,* frequently and severely exerted by the Company, *how legally* I leave to be examined: That upon this accompt, even those few Seamen or others whom they permit to deal for themselves, can make little profit, being charged with great *Mulcts,* made payable to the Company at their discretion for all the Commodities they export or import.

Whereas the original *Stock* of the *Dutch* company was 600000*l.* and this in the year 1602. and the *Number* See *Mandelsloes Travils* 285. State of the Low

59

Countrys 159. 160. In 1608. the *Dutch East-India* Stock was made up near 3 Millions Sterling, besides great dividends. Present State of the United Provinces pa 163 our *East-India* Stock actually paid 1660 was but 368000*l.* the Trade so ill, that in 1665. our effects were sold at 70 *per Cent.* and farther Subscriptions refused : but the act of 15 *Car.* 2 Licencing the Exporting of *Bullion* and forreign Coyne, and the Company betaking themselves to this Commodity, hath occasioned the support of this Trade to the present degree.

ber of the Sharers in the *Dutch* Company of all sorts, and of those considerably concerned, are vastly more, than in our English Company, proved by their Ordinary Councils or Chambers of Curators of this their Company in each Province; besides their Superiour Assemblies, amounting to great Numbers, all which are but *Deputies* of far greater Numbers; that besides their *Navigation Trade, Judicature,* and *War* in the *Indies,* let in Multitudes of others, into very profitable imployments, so that in effect they make up another *potent Government,* for the aid of their Nation in all exigencies.

I have been the more copious on this particular Subject, first, because of the apprehensions or pretences of some, that our stupendious advantage in this Trade gives us a kinde of National security, so that no sooner can others mention any defect in our Trade, but they are presently told of our Trade to the *Indies,* the wealth of the *Indies,* and our Navigation to and in the *Indies.*

And yet I shall admit, though with little reputation to the rest, that our *East-India* Trade, such as it is, seems the most flourishing branch of the whole, and therefore that the Gentlemen concerned in this Company have evidenced their conduct in the *present way of Trade.*

2ly. I shall not much contest but that the Indian Commodities consumed at home, and re-exported, may (as the rest of our Trade is now managed) *prevent* the exportation of near as much money to our Neighbouring Nations, *viz.* by the use of Callicoes instead of other Linnens, by a Barter of these and the rest of our *Indian* Commodities in *France* and other parts *for other Consumptive goods;* in which there is an advantage, because the less money we part with to our Neighbours, they will be in the less capacity to hurt us, but this does not prove the *Indian* goods re-exported bring in the Treasure exported to *India,* since the whole, or a great share of it may be, and is by the circulation of forreign contracts, *finally resolved* into other consumptive Importations; of so dangerous a consequence it is to export money.

But suppose the *Indian* goods, re-exported, bring us in more Treasure, yet is it evident from such Facts as I have mentioned before as are admitted by the Company, and such as are indisputable, that this part of our Trade (which before 1654. was managed by the like Company) was never improved to any great or considerable degree, in comparison of the progress made by all other Nations which have undertaken it: whereof there must be causes and reasons highly necessary to be examined and regulated; I shall add, that for those other Facts relating to the present debate which seem of less notoriety, they are such, as to my knowledge were affirmed by many credible witnesses, and by them intended to be proved before a Committee of the *House of Commons,* upon the occasion of a Petition there formerly exhibited by the *Clothyers,* but having attended several days, were never heard, because the Parliament was engaged in other things, and afterwards Prorogued; but I doubt not they are all ready to attest the same and more before that Judicature; which I say, that it may not be thought that I have lightly or officiously reported any of the aforesaid allegations to the same Judicature, I shall leave it to be determined by what expedients to enlarge this Trade, being in a matter of this Importance contented to have opened some questions and Facts relating to it: I am so free from any malice to the Company, or any man so much as concerned in it or envying their gains, that for a more easy Composure of things, I hartily wish there may be found some more beneficiall Nationall and comprehensive way of Managing this Trade by a Joynt stock, that thereby the present Interests of the *Gent.* of this

Company

Company may be secured, nay and improved; if this
cannot be done, then submit it to farther consideration
how just and reasonable it is that these Gent. should
have compensation for what they shall really lose by
the Dissolution of the Company.

I shall conclude this with remarking, First, that the
Dutch East India Company Trading on a Joynt-stock,
and therefore with as much disadvantage to their re-
exporting Merchants as the English, hath been a
means to preserve us this Limb of Trade from Port to
Port in *Callicoes, Pepper,* &c. and propably the rather
because our Trading in Money hath so far debosh'd
the *Indian* Market, that the *Dutch* are not over-ready
to deal for these Commodities, and therefore principally apply themselves to their richer *Spice Trade,*
whereof they have the Monopoly.

This restraint of our Market to our own Merchants
and Companies, hath yet brought a farther mischief
upon our Manufactures, because our Companies being
seated in *London,* our Natives are forced to bring their
Manufactures thither by *Land Carriages,* some of which
are so long that they are as chargeable as a Voyage to
Spain or *Turky,* Quantity for Quantity; all which is
superadded to the originall charge of the Manufacture;
our Clothiers have also complained, that when they
have brought their Cloaths to *London,* they have been
frequently and long *delayed* before they have been able
to vend them; which whether it hath proceeded from
any correspondence or Intelligence between the Companies, their Committees or Agents, their want of
Stocks or universall Trade, or from the dearness of our
course of Merchandize, and the consequentiall obstructions in the forreign Market, or from all together, I
shall not positively undertake to say: But certain it is
that in this case our Clothiers for want of a quick
Market lose the Interest of so much of their Stocks as

lyes

lyes dead, which also is super-added to the first cost of their Manufacture; but yet being made necessitous by delay, and confined to the *London* Market, are forced to sell cheap: and then are the poor Manufacturers most miserable, when on the one hand the charges they are at oblige them to sell dear, but yet are confined in their just demands.

It may be remembered here that the odds in *Interest of Money* between *England* and *Holland,* and *England* and *France,* (where none is allowed to be taken under the highest penaltys) must as much prejudice our Manufactures as our forreign Trade, by the unequall charge it brings on our Manufacturers, which charge is still increased as they are longer delayed.

The freedom of the Market being of so great importance; it must also follow, that the like Cloggs and incumbrances put upon the Trades of Ware-house keeping and Shop-keeping, must have ill effects on the National Trade, because these Trades make up the publick Marts and Markets, as hath been said.

From the Contents of this and the last Section it may be observed, that is not only necessary to ease the *course of Merchandise,* but to remove all other Cloggs and restraints on the *home Market* ; for though our Merchants should be able to Trade as cheap as forreigners, yet if it should lye in their disposition to impose on the rest of the people, (whether Manufacturers, Shop-keepers or others) the Merchants might gain much more then now they do, but our Manufacturers and other Natives might be still sufferers in some degree; 'tis too apparent that our English Clothiers have made so ill Markets at *London,* that they have lived poorly and got little or nothing, whilst the Merchants have lived splendidly and laid up money, the like may be said of others.

And here it may be farther observed how predominant

nant private interest hath been amongst us, and how finely it hath spun the thread; our *Land-holders* have thought to ease themselves by thrusting great part of the publick Charges upon Trade, the Merchants in Exchange have gotten *Monopolies on the Land-holders,* and people for all goods exported and imported; and of these some Companies trading on Joint Stocks have got *Monopolies exclusive to the rest*; but at the same time we have given all forreign Nations *Monopolies on the English,* in all which we have been eagerly seeking to get advantages on one another, but have laid our selves open to Forreigners; who (whilst we scramble for the present wealth in the Nation) take it out of our fingers at their pleasure.

To which may be added as a farther obstruction to the growth of our Manufactures, that our people have gotten a vain and imoderate *affectation and use of forreign Manufactures and Comodities;* which must necessarily sink the Market at home for our own of the same kind; for the same quantity of home Commodity wanting of its former vent, must stagnate and lye on the owners hands, who either will not be able to sell it at any rate, or must sell it much the cheaper.

This *deadness and cheapness* of any Manufacture, on this or any other occasion, will have a very ill Consequence; for it must presently sink the Manufacturers *wages* and discourage the Master of the Work; and then in case the Market doth not mend in some reasonable time, they will withdraw both their labour and Stock.

Nay this, or little better, must be the ordinary fate of all our Manufactures, by the meer want of a Forreign vent; for as any of our Manufactures which supply our National use, draws in more and more of our people till the Manufacture becomes too bulkey to receive a full vent at home, it must then equally stagnate on the hands of all that are concerned in it; at least render

64   them

them necessitous, and endanger the Manufacture: the increase of imported raw-silk from *Turky* in barter for our Cloath, occasioned the increase of our Silk Manufacture; what is now like to become of it may be seen.

Before I go to the next Section, I shall yet observe these farther inconveniences from the aforesaid constitutions and course of our Forreign Merchandize.

First, That our Manufacturers being confined to buy of our own Merchants and Companies, are not only subject to buy Forreign materials of Manufacture at such prizes as they can and will please to afford them, but must be contented to buy *worse materials* than other nations make use of, in case our Merchants for their own gain, or by negligence of their Factors, import worse.

2dly, That Forreign materials of manufacture being thus straitly Imported into *England*, gives our Traders frequent opportunity to *ingrosse Imported Commodities*, (both materialls of Manufacture and others,) and thereby to impose 3 times the currant price in other Nations upon our Manufacturers or other buyers, which must not only disable our Manufactures, but hinder re-exportation; this ingrossing Trade is the daily design of a sort of *Cunning men* amongst us; which with *stealing Customes*, and importing and vending *Prohibited goods*, are the ordinary methods of getting *an Estate on a suddain*.

3dly, The seeming ease we have by a *restitution of half Customes upon re-exportation*, is so far from being really such, that it not only leaves the great disproportion and charge mentioned in the last Section, but in Cases where our imported materials of Manufacture are re-exported, bring a further unequall charge on our English Manufacturers; because that when re-exported and sold, the Forreign buyers are eased of about half the duties paid, especially if sold so near as *Holland* or

65   *France;*

France; of what consequence then must this be in the Silk-Manufacture? (Supposing *Holland* or *France* could no be otherwise provided of Raw Silk) and so in others, but more particularly in our Imported *Dying Stuffs, and Raw Sugars from the West Indyes,* which are materialls peculiar to the English; but by this disadvantage in re-exportation are now mostly Manufactured by Forreigners; of which I shall have occasion to say more, upon Consideration of our present Plantation-Trade, in the mean time, upon what hath been already said, and what I shall adde in the next Section, let any man Judge how causelessely our poor people are taxed with dear Selling their Manufactures, with Sloath and other inconsiderate Reproaches by such as *live at ease.*

SECT. VII.

Forreigners eased in Trade; Other clogs and difficulties upon ours; Want of populacy, incidently of extream prizes of victuals, and how the duration of Land-Rents may be secured, our people restrained from Manufactures; the Abuse of the Act of 43 Eliz. 2. Act of 5 Eliz. cap. 4. Meer prohibitions of no value. Freedomes and pre-emtions of Corporations, with the consequences: Free-Schools and Scholar-like Imployments: Forreign Protestants hindered from transporting hither; want of Toleration of Protestants Dissenters; the objections briefly considered: Elections in Corporations. Monopolyes of New Manufactures: delay and charge in some Law-Suits. Tyths of Hemp, Flax, and Fish, more of Customes, and incidently of Taxes.

FRom the foregoing Sections, it appears how dangerous it is to clog Trade. It is like putting a pound weight at the end of a pole, which is heavier then

66

then 20 times so much placed at the hand, for so a small impost or difficulty on Trade shall work down all *Land revenues* more then the sums actually paid : Nay Land-Rents will rise under greater Taxes, where home and Forreign Trade is left open and free, as experience hath shown in *Holland* and elsewhere.

2dly. That the charges and Clogs on Trade are to be estimated tolerable or inconvenient *by Comparison,* as they are more or less than the charges on Trade in other Nations, and therefore, That it is of high importance to watch the pollicies of other Nations in Trade; if other Nations Trade with as much disadvantage to their Natives as the English, they never can out-strip us; But if they ease and facilitate their Trade at home and abroad, So must we, else they will beat us out.

What then are we to expect whilest our neighbouring Forreigners continue to have the aforesaid advantages upon us in course of Forreign Merchandize, when also the home-vent of their Manufactures is not confined to the Merchants of one Nation, nor Companyes of one Town, when their Manufacturers are not obliged to the charge of long Land-carriages, nor opprest with delays, but can sell when and where they please, and to all Merchants Aliens, as well as to their own, and therefore have an unlimitted and most profitable market.

The *odds in Populacy* must also produce the like odds in Manufacture; plenty of people must also cause *cheapnesse of wages :* which will cause the cheapnesse of the Manufacture; in a scarcity of people wages must be dearer, which must cause the dearnesse of the Manufacture; But this populacy I speak of, must not be understood of those people which the *Extent of Territory* makes necessary for the meer tilling of the ground, keeping of Cattle, &c. for in this sence there is no doubt but the grand Seigniors or Spanish Domi-

nions

nions are more populous then *Holland;* The populacy I intend and which only can be serviceable to Manufacture, are those exuberant numbers which cannot find Imployment in husbandry, nor otherwise but in Trade; in which sence *France* and the *United Provinces* are most populous; their Trade and people have grown up together, having nourished one another; the like may be said of some parts of *Germany* and *Italy.*

But on the other side *England* never was so populous as it might have been, and undenyably must now be far lesse populous then ever, having so lately peopled our vast *American Plantations* and *Ireland;* the decay of our Manufactures hath much depopulated our Inland Corporations of the Villages Adjacent; the decay of our Fishing Trade our Sea-Towns; I know this want of people is hardly credible with many who see no farther then their own ease and gain; they will tell us, we have so many people already that we know not what to do with them; which is true, and so they have in *Spain*, where their Villages are in a manner forsaken, and many of their great Cities and Towns lie half empty; most of their ordinary people having no employment at home, are gone to *America*, those that remain chiefly consisting in Gentlemen, Lawyers, Officers and Shopkeepers, with their necessary men of husbandry and servants: I must not omit Priests and beggars, since to the honour and comfort of *Spain* they make about a fourth or fifth part of the whole; there little or no support for other ranks of men: how near this we are in *England* let any man judge, or how soon we shall come to it through the decay of our Manufactures; What an uproar have we already in an English Parish if a poor young couple happen to marry, or a man with Children chance to get into a house? how they are tossed from Justice to Justice, and from pillar to post, by vertue of the several Acts for settlement of poor?

See Sir *William Temples* Book of the *United provinces,* Ch. 6.

The peopling of *Ireland* here intended was to supply the losse by the Irish Massacre being computed at about 150000 persons besides what the growing plentys of *Ireland* have invited over dayly.

Stat 39 *Eliz.* 4th 7. *Jacob.* 4. 14 *Car.* 2. 12

poor? And what joy there is when these clogs are removed? which acts and prosecutions regularly and daily force many out of the Nation, and in effect *banish them by Act of Parliament;* 'Tis like, that besides the Inquisition, the proud *Spaniards* had some such expedients as these to be rid of this kinde of lumber; they would be now glad of those laborious drudges to encounter the populous *French*.

Being upon this Subject I cannot omit to observe, the bad consequences of some others of our late Laws, made to raise *the prizes of Victualls*, which doubtless were projected for the raising *Land Rents*, viz. the *Acts for Transportation of Corn*, and the Acts against *the Importing* Irish *and* Scotch *Cattle*, which had they the full effects intended, must much assist both in depopulating the Nation, and Subverting our remaining Manufactures; For if the Manufacturer buys his Victualls at excessive rates, at what rates must he sell his Manufacture, or how shall he live? especially in a time when his Manufactures fall upon his hands daily? but this will mainly dissatisfy some, who will have no Manufacture or Trade, if the price of the Victualls must not be excessive, for then say they, how can the vallue of Lands be raised? to which I answer, First, that the products of Lands do not wholly consist in Victualls, and that much Land is to be applied to many other as profitable, and (perhaps more profitable ways) than for meer Victualls, *especially in a Nation abounding in Trade and People;* for this I shall refer to our Copious Books of Husbandry, which then may do us much good, but little or none before.

Secondly, That though Victualls be not at a very excessive price, yet if there be *a quick and great market* at a midling price, it will raise and hold up the vallue of Lands, as experience hath proved of late years.

But Thirdly, it is impossible the vallue of Lands

69 can

can be much raised by the meer raising of the price of
Victualls, especially in a Nation but thin of people;
nor would such a Revenue endure or be tollerable; perhaps the Spanish Dons did once raise the prizes of
Victualls, or suppose they should do it now, what
weighty effect would it have, unless to drive all the rest
of the Spaniards into *America;* But that which will
most *certainly and durably* raise the Revenue of Land
must be the *encrease of Treasure and Trading people;*
suppose the people of *England* were trebled, 'tis plain
that the Land must yield treble the produce in meer
Victualls, else the people must starve; but these people
will not starve, especially *trading people,* nor will they
live needily or scarcely, if they can help it, and will
therefore set themselves and others to the improving of
all corners of Land in the Nation, till our Lands produce more then treble the Victualls they now do, a
thing very practicable, and then supposing Victualls as
cheap and cheaper then now, Land will ordinarily be
treble its present vallue, especially if we consider how
much may be then applyed to raise Hemp, Flax,
and other necessary and profitable things, with the
By the Maps increase of Wool, Hides, Tallow, &c. And as the
of *England* people increase, so will the vallue of the Land: there is
it is found
to contain no doubt but *England* upon the utmost improvement
29568000 might maintain 6 times its present number of people,
Acres besides
that which is nay 10 times, with an indifferent use of that mighty
allowed for plenty of Fish our own Sea affords us; there is as little
High-ways,
all the United doubt but upon a great increase of people and money,
Provinces are Victualls will be rather too dear, and that Laws may
hardly so big
as *Yorkshire.* be then requisite to restrain the price.

Such was the ancient populacy of *England,* that we
had formerly Statutes made in restraint of the exportation of Corn, our Flesh also found vent, though our
people kept Lents, Ember-weeks, and Fasting days;
wherein they fed on Fish and white meats, and yet we

read

read of Famines in those days; whereas now we finde it necessary to export all the Corn we can, we eat very little Fish, and have made Acts against the importation of Forreign Cattle (which by the way gave a *Monopoly* to a few English and Welch breeding Counties on all the rest of the Nation,) and yet we thought our markets over-clogged.

But *England* is not only prejudiced by the paucity of people, but we have another rank of Statutes which hinder very many of those we have from applying themselves to Manufacture: one is the Stat. of *43th Eliz. cap.* 2. which according to the intention of it seems necessary now when we have such a vast increase of poor; but such is the Arbitrary latitude given by the Act to Over-seers and Justices, that many of our Laborious people well able to work, by clamour or favour get Parish maintenances, choosing rather to live lazily by this means, assisted with some pilfering.

Then we have the Stat. of *5th Eliz. cap.* 4. which (though it gratifies the blinde avarice of some of our Corporation men) is more prejudicial, by restraining our people to work in Manufacture, unless they have served an *Apprentiship full seaven years,* which is so long a term of drudgery and slavery before they can reap any fruit of their labors, that Parents are deterred from putting their Children Apprentices to Manufacture; nor will many of our Youths or young men be brought to it especially the most apt and docile, and those of ripeness of years, of which many would be more perfect in 3 or 4 years then others in 10, and therefore they betake themselves to other more easy and ready Imployments, or else live Idle.

The same Act does very strangely provide that no man shall take an *Apprentice* for Woollen Manufacture in any Town Corporate, unlesse such *Apprentice* be his Son, or the Father or Mother of such *Apprentice* have

71 · the

the clear yearly vallue of 40*s*. Inheritance, nor in any
Market-Town or Village unless he be his Son, or his
Father or Mother have the clear yearly value of 3*l*.
Inheritance, which clause apparently shuts out at least
5 parts of the people in 6, from the Woollen Manufacture; and by consequence tends to the *depopulation*
of our Inland Towns, the increase of Rogues, Vagabonds and poor; These difficulties on Trade begot
the Act of the 43. *Eliz*. and many others of the like
nature, and thereby much work for our Justices.

Which by the way may give occasion to observe how
vain it is to make Acts against Rogues, Vagabonds, or
Poor, nay against thefts or Murthers, how little the
Houses of Correction, Whipping-posts, Pillories, or
Gallows can prevail, whilst our other Constitutions
drive our People into necessities, nor any *prohibitory
or penal Law*, ever have the intended effect, unless the
Grounds and Causes of the mischiefs be removed; of
which I shall say more when I come to speak of our
late Prohibition of *French* Goods. Amongst the restraints on our *English* Trade, the inclosure of Trade
to the *Freemen of Corporations and Guilds*, may be
deservedly mentioned as one.

This Priviledge is claimed by most, or all of our
ancient Corporations, and might be well intended at
first by the Donors, but as now used is very prejudicial;
for the Power of admitting Free-men being generally
lodged in a Councel or Committee of *a few Free-men*,
any Forreigner (and such they call all those who are
not Sons or Apprentices of seven years standing to a
Free-man in the same Town) must *buy* his Freedom
before he can exercise any open Trade there; for which
these Free-men are left at liberty to demand as great
and arbitrary Price as they please, or if they will, may
wholly refuse; whence it commonly follows, that most
Beginners in Manufacture, and other Trades, being

Forreigners, and having but small Stocks, can never obtain Freedom, and without it are burthened and plagued with by-Laws, Penalties, Distresses, and Seizures; nay, if a Man be exquisite in his Trade, he shall hardly get a Freedom for Money, in a Corporation where there are more free of the same Trade, for then he is lookt on as *a dangerous person,* and likely to *eat the bread out of their mouths,* (as they phrase it) in which they will gratifie, and influence one another, being the common cause, and can easily do it: The fewer Free-men there are in a Trade, they think the rest may get the more; and thus are most of our ancient Corporations and Guilds become *oppressive Oligarchies,* excluding or discouraging the *English* Subjects from Trading in our greatest and best situated Towns, where the *Markets* are; and which are therefore the most proper and ready *Seats* for Manufacture, and other Commerce: For this, and the Act of the 5*th* of *Eliz.* our Corporation-men have only this to say, That care ought to be taken, that none but persons *skilful* should exercise any Trade, which is true; but the Law of necessity, common sense, and experience, provides sufficiently for this, since an unskilful Artificer or Trader will not find imployment, and therefore must receive due punishment by his own *Ignorance:* 'Tis confessed, Manufactures may be made *deceitfully,* which may disgrace and prejudice our vent abroad; but this fraud is an Act of Skill, which cannot be discovered or prevented, without the daily scrutinies of Judicious Persons; for which our other former Statutes have already made *some provision,* but *defective;* it were to be wished, there was a constant Judicature of Men knowing in Trade in every County to supervise the sufficiency of Manufactures: In the mean time this Argument for the support of the Act of the 5*th* of *Eliz.* and Freedoms must appear very fallacious, since

73   both

both the Act and the Freedoms serve only to exclude the *English* Subjects, and of those many of the most skilful, from Trade, and by inclosing Manufactures to a few, hinder their growth, and make them far dearer.

A farther inconvenience of these Freedoms is, That *the pre-emption of our Manufactures, and Imported Goods,* in most of our inferiour Corporations and Cities, as well as in *London,* is in a manner inclosed to the *Number* and *Stocks* of the Free-men, and is very much subject to their pleasures, by reason of their union and correspondence in Counsels: So that he who would escape the long Land-Carriages to *London,* and *London* Companies, must fall into the hands of these other Free-men; these Free-men have generally so brave a time of it, that they can live in ease and plenty, (every Shop resembling an Office) whilst the laborious part of our Traders are ready to perish; which Priviledges could not have survived the Statute of 21 *Jac.* against Monopolies, but that they are *saved by a special Proviso in that Statute*; *so civil were the Burgesses of Corporations at that time.*

Our Trade being thus clogged, and the very Avenues to Manufactures so much narrowed and choaked up, it doth not a little help to the subverting of our Manufactures, and other Trade, that the Passages to other Preferments are made so open and easie, at present I mean all those that depend *upon Literature,* in which our Youth are led from step to step by all manner of Incouragements; First, by the multitude of our late endowed *Free Schools,* where every ordinary Man's Son is taught *Latin, Greek,* and *Hebrew,* for a small matter; and then is above Manufacture: Then we have two mighty endowed Universities, where there will, at least, be hope of preferment, let the throng be never so thick; and thence they have farther and more comfortable prospects; and in the mean time live easie, at

little

little or no charge, as Servitors, or on small Stipends, till they become Scholars of Houses, &c. others of these Free-School-Boys grow Pen-men of all sorts; and all these are a sort of *Gentlemen-like* ways of living, which intitle them to be called *Masters*, which gives a main temptation both to parents and Children; who on the other hand, see the *contemptible* and *miserable* condition of our poor Clothworkers, and other ordinary Artificers, who at the best are called *Mechanick Fellows*; and what is yet farther mischievous is, that our Youth thus educated, never reading any thing of Manufacture, Exportation, or Importation, in *Homer* or *Virgil*, or their Colledge Notes, and being from thence carried to other Studies, which have no cognation with Trade, can ordinarily have no sensation of the advantages of it; like a Bowl which hath a rub at hand, the farther they go, the more they are divided from it; whence it hath unfortunately ensued, that our *Men of Learning* are either generally silent in this matter, or else, being inclin'd to think it the sole concern of the *dirty* and *servile* part of the People, speak of it with contempt, and some with reflection; by whom most others being influenced, we are still pretending to be more accurate in Logick and Philosophy, (which howsoever otherwise useful, do not add two-pence a year to the Riches of the Nation) we continue to squeeze all the sapless Papers and Fragments of *Antiquity*; we grow mighty well acquainted with the old *Heathen Gods*, *Towns*, and *People*; we prize our selves in fruitless Curiosities; we turn our Lice and Fleas into Bulls and Pigs by our *Magnifying-glasses*; we are searching for the World in the Moon with our *Telescopes*; we send to weigh the Air on the top of *Teneriffe*; we invent *Pacing Saddles*, and Gimcracks of all sorts; all which are voted Ingenuities, whilst the Notions of Trade are turned into Ridicule, or much out of fashion.

In

In all which we are very short of the Policies of our Neighbours, the *French, Dutch,* and other trading and wise Nations; who on the one hand have no Laws or Constitutions to restrain or exclude their People from Manufacture, nor to Ferret them away; and on the other, do consider *Trade* as an *Honorary* and almost *Sacred* thing, and do highly esteem and cherish their Manufacturers, as well as their other necessary Traders.

Now should these restraints and discouragements on our own People and Trade be removed, it would doubtless much advantage our Trade in some time; but would not bring us so sudden an increase of People, Manufactures, Ships, and Riches, as is highly requisite for the carrying on of a mighty Trade, or perhaps for our National security; nor can these so suddenly be had, but from other parts of the World, where they are moving; Men, Ships, or Riches, do not grow on the Trees, nor yet drop out of the Clouds.

Besides the Common Law these Statutes, 1 *R.* 3. 9. 21 *H.* 8. 16. 22 *H.* 8. 13. 32 *H.* 8. 16. 25 *H.* 8. 9. 14 *H.* 8. 3. 4 *H.* 7. 23. and many others of former date, to which are added 12 *Car.* 2. 16. 14 *Car.* 2. 11. and 15 *Car.* 2. 7.

But we have such another rank of Laws against *Forreigners,* that we are not to hope Forreigners will come hither; I mean those which disable Forreigners from trading in *England;* therefore we must first have a Law of general *Naturalization* of *Protesiunt*-Forreigners, though to the displeasure of many of our own self-interested ignorant Traders, nor will that do, without a Repeal of the Act of the *5th Eliz. Cap.* 4. and a compleat Regulation of our Trade; for neither Manufacturers or Merchants will remove from their own Countries hither to sit idle; nor will all this bring us over any great Numbers, without some *Toleration* of their *Consciences,* no not of Forreign *Protestants,* who differ much from us in several Points which *they think* material; all which is demonstrated in Fact by the success of *His Majesties Proclamation* at the beginning of our last *Dutch* War; by which Forreigners, then under the utmost terrors, were invited to the Liberties

76   and

and Plenties of *England;* but we see few or none of
them came or stay'd with us on this incouragement:
In this the *Dutch* have a further advantage upon us, See Sir *Wil-*
since they allow free Ports, free Trade, and all other *liam Temples*
National Freedoms to Forreigners; whereby their Peo- *Dutch, Chap.*
ple of all sorts, their Navigation and Stocks in Trade, the 6*th.*
have increased continually.

So are the most considerable *French* Ports *Free,*
(unless for Goods *prohibited,* as in *Holland* some are;) no
sooner was *Dunkirke* in the Hands of the *French King,*
but he made it a Free Port; so hath he invited all Forreign Artificers into *France,* by granting them as great,
or greater Freedoms than his own Subjects enjoy.

There are yet others of our Laws, which must prejudice our Trade of all sorts, and give a farther advantage to the *Dutch* and *French,* I mean those which
inflict Penalties on *Protestant Dissenters;* not only
because they may hinder the transplanting of Forreign Protestant Artificers or Merchants, but because they disable many of those we have in *England*
already, from carrying on any manner of Trades; and
if so, then in effect they are not People, since they
cannot answer the ends of People, but are rather the
Trunks and Signs of Men in a Nation, their Industries
and ingenuities being lock'd up; Suppose two or 300000
of our own People disabled, it may be presumed more
than a Million *per Annum* loss to the Nation; what
then may be our loss by the shutting out a far greater
number? perhaps ten times the number of Forreign
Protestants, and those of the richest, the most mercantile, and the best Manufacturers of *Europe.*

That this is the Case of dissenting Protestants in *England,* must be very plain to those who shall consider the
Statute of 20*l.* a month, and those Volumes of other
Statutes made before and since the King came in
against *Non-Conformists;* most of which were intended

against

against Papists, and occasioned by former Popish Treasons, but reach all Protestant Dissenters, who, besides the bare Penalties, are liable to the daily charge and trouble of *Informations, Actions,* and *Indictments* in our Courts of *Law,* and as many or more *Libels and Presentments* in our *Spiritual Courts;* our *Constables, Church-wardens,* and *Grand-Juries* are upon their Oaths constantly bound to accuse them; if they omit, 'tis at *every other Mans pleasure* to inform, and some or other will not fail of it; thus are Dissenters brought into the hands of the *Officers* of both Courts, whose duty it is to prosecute; these may delay for a time, whilst they are *paid for their favours,* or until *notice* be taken of it, but no longer, and then must follow a Seizure of Dissenters *Persons* or *Estates,* or both; Besides all which, particular *Justices of the Peace* are by several late Statutes authorized and obliged to *Convent, Convict, and make Levies;* which sufferings being accompanied with a continual *Anxiety of mind,* our *Protestant* Dissenters cannot possibly apply themselves or their Stocks to Manufacture or other Trade.

See Sir *William Temple, Chap.* of Religion.

Whilst on the other hand, both the *Dutch* and *French,* and most other of our neighbouring Nations, any thing famous for Trade, allow Liberty of Conscience to *Protestant* Dissenters, at least to such a degree, *as to enable them to trade:* Which is all that the Interest of Trade requires; 'tis true, that now of late we have heard the *French King* hath given some greater discountenance to Protestants than heretofore, (whether to gratifie the *Romish* Clergy, who may be otherwise very useful to his present designs, and whom he daily and visibly endears by all signal demonstrations of favour, (if we may believe our Gazets) or for what other reason, I shall not undertake to say) however not so, as *to disable* the *French* Protestants from Trade.

What farther hardships he may put upon *French*

Protestants, or other his Trading Subjects, in case they shall have no other *Asylum* or *Shelter* to repair to, time may shew.

This being the case in the matter of Toleration between us and these our subtile and potent Neighbours, the Question is, what is to be done? A long *Surfeit* of experience hath demonstrated, that the Penal Laws, though accumulated and imbittered to as great a degree as hath been desired, are not a sufficient expedient to reduce Protestant Dissenters. To propose any thing which shall subvert our present Church of *England*, is that which I shall not do; conceiving it for the honour and safety of the Nation to support a *flourishing* National Church, and that the present *Protestant Church of* England hath in all respects the best Title to it.

On the other side, to rest under our present Disadvantages by the want of a convenient Toleration of Dissenting Protestants, must disable us from making that sudden, and full improvement of our Trade, as otherwise we might, and as perhaps may be found necessary for our support against those Forreigners who already do, and daily will more exceed us in *Treasures and People,* if they shall let in, and we continue to shut out, so mighty a share of each.

Here then there seems a difficulty, which deserves and requires our utmost prudentials to clear, by a *Toleration of Protestant Dissenters,* consistent with the preservation of our present *Church of England* in all its Rights; I am perswaded none of the *Generous Dignitaries,* or Members of our Church, would oppose such a Toleration; some there have been, who could never think themselves happy, unless others were miserable, and have loved Cruelty for Cruelty's sake; the most infamous for this was *Phalaris,* who was at last brought to roar in his own *Brazen Bull;* nor is this a time for Men to gratifie their humours or passions this way, if

it

it may prove perilous towards the whole; rather let our
Hearts melt with a tender and charitable Commiseration to these our Fellow-Country-men, who by their
Birth-right are intitled to *Magna Charta* equally with
our selves, but are incapacitated to enjoy the advantages
of it, meerly for *Conscience*, when by no other overt
Act they have forfeited their Hereditary Claims, when
their sufferings undeniably demonstrate they are no
Hypocrites, and therefore that they suffer for what they
cannot help; let us observe, that *God* never planted or
propagated his Truth by *Temporal Power*, that he was in
the *small Voice*, not in the *Thunder*, or the *Whirl-wind*:
Let us consider the *original meekness* of Christians,
whose *Anathema's* against Dissenters were only accompanied with *Admonishments*, and meer *Excommunica-
tions*, without any *Writ* to take the *Body*, or make
Levies on Mens *Estates*; Let us remember that we
have flung off the Yoke of *Papal Tyranny, founded* on
a pretended infallible conclusive *Church Authority*,
superinduced upon Christians by a Conspiracy of *Romish
Priests*, as subservient to their Ambition, Pride, Ease,
and Luxury; that if persecution were *then* wholly un-
warrantable, it is *now* far more *incoherent*. When our
present Church professes it self *fallible*, both our
Church, and all Protestant Religion it self, are derived
from no other Principle than the Fallibility of all
Churches, at least in their Decrees; when our first
most famous Protestant Doctors carried on the Reformation in opposition to their National Churches and
Laws, such were *Luther, Calvin, Beza*, and many others
abroad, and our *Martyrs* at home, whose Glorious
Mr. *Fox.* Sufferings are celebrated by one of our own former and
most Learned and Pious Divines, as the chief *Gemms*
which truly beautifie our *present Church*: Let it never
be said, that the *Interests* or *Temperaments* of our present Church are *inconsistent* with our National *Wealth*,

80 *Happiness,*

Happiness, and *Security,* or *obstruct our progress* towards them; this would give too great an advantage to her publick and private Enemies: Let us industriously amass all the just Considerations we can to facilitate *these great ends,* by some Toleration of *Protestant* Dissenters, being it is so important, I say of *Protestant* Dissenters, because these having no forreign dependance on the *Pope,* have reason to be endeared and knit up to the National Interest by the common protection and security of their Estates and Families, equally with the rest: As for the *Popish Party,* I am confident that after so many late accurate Treatises, and Authentick Narratives, of the dangerous Principles, and horrid treasonable Practises, of the Priests, and others of the same Party, none will think it necessary, or possible, that I should add one syllable to prove that Party unfit for a Toleration.

Such being the high Motives to make us wish for a Toleration of *Protestant* Dissenters, I shall, with all deference to Authority, and without any of those passionate reflections which usually incumber this debate, briefly endeavour to examine the dangers objected, which are,

First, an apprehension of a necessary great *increase of Dissenters,* and this (as *some* will have it) to such a degree, as to swallow up the present Church; a very strange *supposition* for those who have *Scripture* and *Antiquity* on their side: On the contrary, it may be justly hoped, that the *Church of* England may then reconcile all those whom *Penalties* cannot reduce; and the rather, because when the *Penalties* are gone, all Parties must resort to *reasoning* and *sanctity,* which are the proper and only means of making Impressions on Mens *Understandings* and *Consciences; Penalties* may bring in *Atheists* and *Hypocrites,* but can never work a real change in any Mans *opinion,* unless when the

81

25

the sufferings of Dissenters proselyte others, (being a
kind of Argument of the truth of what is so asserted,
at least amongst the vulgar or middle sort;) our present
Protestant *Church of* England must therefore have an
advantage this way; and yet on the other side, will retain
that of being vindicated by the Government, in as much
as all publick *Divine Service* in the Parish Churches will
remain in the form now used in our *present Church*, and
all *Church preferments* inclosed to the Clergy of the
same Church; which Priviledges, being consistent with
a Toleration, may continue secured to our Church by our
present Penal Laws in force for that purpose, with an
addition of such others as may be thought necessary;
whence it will follow; first, that it will be more for the
ease and *convenience*, nay and Interest of the Laicks to
conform, rather than to seek farther for Dissenting Con-
venticles, whose Ministers they must help to maintain;
which *Convenience*, with the *Countenance* of *Authority*
given to the National Church, is a great matter, since
it will bring in all those, who being good Christians in
the main, are yet little affected with the Points in difference, which are the *generality*, as may be seen by
their equal resort to the Parish Churches before and
since His Majesties Restoration. But secondly, it will
then be yet more the interest and advantage of all
Clergy-men to conform, by the great and *Honourable
preferments* they may this way hope for, which they
cannot otherwise obtain.

Dr. Heylin observes, that after the Toleration of Protestants in France, the other Party in Religion having the countenance of the State, and the Prescription and Posses-sion of so many years to confirm the same, is in as prosperous a condition, both for Power and Patrimony, as any that acknowledgeth the Authority of the Popes of Rome. Geogr. 176.

The other grand Objection against a Toleration of
Protestants, is the danger of the Temporal Government; which seems yet stranger than the other, if we
consult our *Reasons*, which must tell us, that Men at
ease will be better satisfied than when in *pain;* that
Men who are kept innocently and profitably *busie*, who
by their Industry can live well, support their Families,
and gain Estates, will be less apt to study, or do mis-

chief to the Publick than those, who being disabled
from all such Imployments, are daily goaded with
penal Laws, a condition which perhaps may be thought
more grievous in *England* than the like hardships in
Turky and *Muscovy*, where all suffer alike, when in
England our Protestant Dissenters hear much of *Magna
Charta*, and see others enjoy the full fruit of it, but are
precluded themselves, and this for meer difference in
Religious belief. But why should I labour to evince
that which *Experience* hath demonstrated; we have the
great Instance of *France*, and the like in the Kingdom
of *Poland*, in *Holland, Switzerland, Hamburg*, and other
parts of *Germany;* All which Nations have been at
peace, at least about Religion, ever since the Tolerations
given, as some of them could never be before, particularly *France :* which must appear to proceed from
the *pacifique virtue* of Toleration, not from the *coercive*
power of *Standing Forces*, or *despotick Monarchy*, as
some would have it, because *that* of *Poland* is *regulated*,
and the rest are *Republicks*. 'Tis notorious that before
the *French* Toleration many of that National Church
had or pretended to have as fearful Apprehensions of
the effects of it; but we see what Councils did prevail
even amongst the *Popish Party*, and what hath followed? We find *France* the most powerful of Nations,
and the *French* King so confident of his *Protestants*,
that he long intrusted his mighty Armies, in the hands
of *Monsieur Turenne*, a *Protestant* till near his death :
On the other side we have the Example of *Spain*, whose
execrable and inexorable Cruelties towards dissenters
hath mainly Assisted in the present poverty and weakness of that Nation : We may then conclude that Persecution is a stale piece of policy, which perhaps might
have born a debate in *Harry the 8th's time*, but is now
tryed to our hands : And let any man judg whether
the *French* or *Spanish Church* be now most flourishing,

or most likely to continue; the *French Church* and
Church-men will certainly get ground with the *French
Victories*, for which they are as much beholding to the
French *Protestants* as to the rest. Let us not therefore be wholly insensible that the Church of *England*
may fall under the worst circumstances of danger,
otherwise than from *Protestant* Dissenters; as suppose
England should ever be reduced to such a condition as
to be no longer able to bear up against foreign Powers,
what then would become of our *present Church?* what
sort of men would then push into our *Bishopricks,
Deaneries*, and other Church-Preferments? a Fatality
which we ought therefore to provide against by a Union
of Protestant interests and affections and increase of
Traders, as far as safely we may; in which Foreigners
are grown so nicely vigilant, that not long ago we
might observe the policies of the great *French King* and
the great *Duke of Tuscany* curiously Angling for the
Jews; for when the *French King* had made *Marseilles* a
free Port (which was about 12 years since) the *Jews*
planted at *Leghorn*, induced by an offer of protection
at *Marseilles*, and the sweeter situation of that place,
resolved to transplant, which the Great *Duke* dis-
covering, applyed his utmost endeavours to prevent it;
which he did by making an Edict, That if any Christian
bought a Jews house, it should be forfeit. In *England*
a Jew cannot buy a house. I am no Advocate for Dissenters or Jews, but for the *Common Interest* of *England*, by which that of the Church of *England* must
stand or fall. And being now speaking of somewhat
that concerns Religion, there occur to my memory two
plain Texts of Scripture, one is, *that of two evils we are
to choose the least*, and another that a *Kingdom divided
cannot stand*. I shall desire the Reader to couple these
considerations with what I shall say in the following
Sections concerning the present posture of this and our

84   Neighbour

Neighbour Nations, and then he will not accuse me of
having made an unnecessary digression.

Whilst we are calculating the best expedient to bring
in *forreign* Protestant Artificers, and *forreign* Manufacturers, it is fit that notice should be taken of that
Clause in the Act of 21 of King *James chap.* 3. which
leaves the Inventers of new Manufactures at liberty to
obtain *Patents* for *Monopolies* for one and twenty years,
which Statute being in *construction* extended to all
Manufactures already used by Foreigners that are not
used here, hinders the introducing, or growth and perfection of any new forreign Manufactures, and makes
it the business of our more observant Travellers to
hauk after Monopolies.

There is no question but several other obstructions
to the Trade of *England* might be observed, particularly that the carrying on of *Elections* in Corporations of latter years with so much drinking, is very
prejudicial to our Manufactures; for men (upon this or
any other occasion) being once *debauched,* hardly ever
retrieve themselves, and are therefore lost to Manufacture and the Nation.

Our Fishers have complained that in several parts
they are forced to pay *Tyth* for the *Fish* they catch on
their own Coasts, in which the *Dutch,* and other Fishermen have the advantage to the value of the Fish, and
must therefore disable our Trade of Fishery in those
parts.

It hath also been noted that the payment of *Tyth*
out of our *Hemp* and *Flax,* does as much disable the
increase of Hemp and Flax in *England,* the rest being
made so much the dearer to the owner, that it is not
vendible, as otherwise it would be; and thereby prevent our great forreign Importation of Hemp and Flax.
These being things of so great Importance to the
Nation, may deserve a full Examination and remedy,

85   whatsoever

whatsoever the particular interests of some Incumbents of Churches may suggest to the contrary.

Lastly, we have a farther complaint from the Traders of all sorts, of the tedious and chargeable proceedings in some Courts of Justice, occasioned by *Writs of Error*, and *Suits in Chancery*, in which last Court many are hung up for seven years and more, and are forced to expend much more than the money they justly sue for; *Our little Courts*, especially about *London*, are as destructive to poor Seamen, Manufacturers and other laborious people, where in a Suit for a disputable Groat, or meer malice, they are easily led in, or forced to spend three or four pound; if but thirty or forty shillings 'tis enough to ruine such poor wretches and their Families, which hath caused many thousands to perish in Goal, or fly from their Habitations and Countrey, since the erection of several new inferior Jurisdictions.

Here again we may look back and observe the mischievous effects of private and mistaken interests, pride and humor; which I shall not recapitulate, but should here conclude this Section; but that having mentioned the *greatness* of our *Customs* amongst the incumbrances on our Trade, I am willing to clear my self from insinuating or wishing any Diminution of His Majesties Revenue; nor would the moderation of the Customs work any such effect, (at least in the Judgments of wise men who have considered it) were the other obstructions on our Trade regulated; of this Sir *Walter Raleigh* took notice of very early in his Observations upon Trade, presented to *King James*, in these words.

' Of this their smallness of Custom, (meaning in ' *Holland, Hamburgh*, &c.) inwards and outwards, we ' have daily experience; for if two *English* Ships, or ' two of any other Nation, be at *Burdeaux*, both laden ' with Wine of 300 Tun apiece, the one bound for *Hol-*
land,

' *land,* or any other of the Petit States, the other for
' *England ;* the Merchant shall pay above 900*l.* here,
' and other duties, when the other in *Holland,* or any
' other Petit State shall be cleared for 50*l. and so in all*
' *other Wares and Merchandizes accordingly* ; which
' draws all Nations to traffick with them ; and although
' it seems but small duties which they receive, yet the
' multitudes of all kind of Commodities and Coin that
' is brought there, and carryed out by themselves and
' others, is so great, that they receive more Customs
' and Duties to the State by the greatness of their Com-
' merce in one year, than *England* doth in two years ;
' for the 100*th* part of the Commodities are not spent
' in *Holland,* but vented into other Countries ; which
' make all the Country-Merchants to buy and sell, and
' increase Ships and Mariners to transport them.

' My travels and meaning is not, neither hath been,
' to diminish your Majesties Revenues, but exceedingly
' to increase them, *&c.*

' All Nations may buy and sell freely in *France,* and
' there is free Custome outwards twice a year; at which
' times our Merchants do there make their sales of
' *English* Commodities, and do buy and lade their Bulk
' with *French* Commodities to serve for the whole year ;
' and in *Rochel* in *France,* and in *Brittain,* free Custom
' all the year long; except some small Toll, which
' makes free Traffick, and makes them flourish.'

To this he adds an Instance in *Genoua,* formerly the
Store-house of *Italy :* But after they had set a Custom
of 16 *per Cent.* all Nations left trading with them ; but
that on the other side, the *Duke of* Florence, by setting
a *small Custom* at *Leghorn,* had brought all the Trade
thither : Thus did this great Man of his time express
himself.

But admitting, that by the moderation of our Customs Rates, our present publick Revenue in Customs

should

should be somewhat sunk; yet how easily might this Revenue be made good by a Land-Tax, or by some *Excise* upon Extravagancies, and Forreign consumptive Commodities spent at home, without the least prejudice to Trade? Thus do the *Dutch* raise far more than the Revenue of our Customs; and if by this means the private Revenue of our Land must universally rise, and the people better be enabled to pay any other Taxes, why should the Land-holders, or any on pretence of Service to His Majesty, oppose it? Suppose His Majesty had a Custome of *5s.* in the Pound on all the *English* Treasure exported, would any Man for the sake of the Custom, and out of zeal to His Majesties Interest, promote the Exportation of all the *English* Treasure? How much this is the Case of the present *English* Customs, doth, and more largely will appear.

Certainly it was very unfortunate for *England,* That when Sir *Walter Raleigh* wrote these and other his excellent Observations on Trade, our Councels were under an earnest pursuit of the *Plantation-Trade,* on which great Customs were projected; for so it hath hapned, that whilst our Neighbour Nations have been vigilant to ease and facilitate their ways of Trade, the Trade of *England* hath continued under the former disadvantage, and is incumbred with new charges and difficulties of later years; all which in Conjunction have worked us out in all the Particulars mentioned before, and in divers others; and in recompence of these losses, our *Plantation-Trade* hath robbed and prevented us of some Millions of our Poople; amongst which very many being, or might have been Manufacturers, the Nation hath also lost many more Millions of Pounds in the loss of their Manufactures.

SECT.

SECT. VIII.

That a Nation may grow poor by Forreign Trade, viz. by an excess of meer Importations, illustrated by some Observations : this facilitated by exporting Money or Bullion; the fatal Consequences and Symptoms of a Consumptive Trade, decay of Manufactures, other ways of living over-stocked, fall of Rents, general Poverty, an increase of Criminals of all sorts, Depopulation; some Application to the present Case of England, *and amongst others the occasion of the new Buildings about* London ; *of Incontinency, Cunning,* &c.

AS a *Nation* may grow *Rich and Populous*, and consequently *strong* by Forreign Trade; so may a Nation grow *poor* and *dispeopled*, and consequently *weak* by Forreign Trade; nor is there any possible or practicable way for the Treasure of a Nation in peace, to be exhausted and exported into another Nation to any considerable and sensible degree, but by Forreign Trade.

This must necessarily happen by the excess of *meer Importation*, viz. when the Commodities imported from abroad, and spent at home, do cost more than the National gain by Trade amounts to; as suppose such yearly Importations into *England* should cost two Millions, and the National gain by Exportations or otherwise should amount but to 1500000*l.* the *Nation* of *England* must yearly lose 500000*l.* of its Treasure by Trade, because so much must yearly be exported by the *English* Merchants to satisfie the over-ballance.

That the *English* Trade might fall into such a Consumption, is easily and highly credible.

For

For suppose the utmost neat gain of our former *English* Trade amounted to but 300000*l. per An'* one year with another; then if the Exportations and beneficial Merchandize of *England* should become worse by 400000*l. per An'* one year with another than before, the *Nation* of *England* must lose 100000*l. per An'* of its National Treasure, though our yearly Importations be no more in value than before; whence it appears, that by this means the *same Importations* may become *excessive.*

So though our Exportations, and the beneficial part of our Merchandize, continue as valuable as before, yet if our yearly Consumptive Importations grow to be more in value by 400000*l. per An'* than before, the Nation must also in this case lose 100000*l. per An'* by Trade.

But what if both the beneficial part of the Trade grow worse, and also the Importations increase? Certainly this must cut deepest on the National Stock, and must soonest grind it out; for then if the beneficial part grow worse by 400000*l.* and the Importing part be increased 400000*l. per An'* value, the Nation must then lose 500000*l. per Annum*; or suppose but to half those values in each, the Nation must lose 100000*l. per Annum.*

To accommodate these Hypotheses to *England*; first, we may conclude, that the beneficial part of our Trade hath grown much less and worse yearly, by reason of the unequal cloggs and difficulties on our Home and Forreign Trade.

And that on the other side our Importations must as necessarily be increased, both by the decay of our own former Manufactures at home, and by our modern gawd'ry and affectation of foreign Goods; and as our Trade from Port to Port hath become more impracticable to any advantage, the Exporters of our remain-

ing

ing Manufactures and other home-Commodities, must
either come back empty, or else must freight themselves
homewards with such consumptive foreign Commodities,
as for Gawdry, Novelty, Cheapness, or Lyquorishness,
will dazle, tempt and bewitch our People to buy them;
in which course of Trade our Merchants may gain considerable proportions of our remaining Treasures as long
as there is any in the Nation.

Nay, rather than sit idle, they will, and do freight
themselves outwards with meer Ballast and *Bills of*
Exchange (by which the Importation of foreign Bullion
or money is prevented:) or if Bills of Exchange cannot reasonably be had (as they usually cannot to those
Countries where we are overballanced in Trade) then
they export Mony and Bullion, and buy and import
Consumptive Goods which are spent at home; which
kind of Trade deserves rather to be called *Foreign*
Pedling, than Merchandise.

See Mr. *Mun* of Foreign Trade, Chap. 12. p. 83, to 92. and that the over bal- lance of Trade in any par- ticular Coun- try, causes the Exchange to be high, so that the ex- porting of money shall save the Mer- chant 10*l. per Cent.* or more, as the ex- change is.

It may be remembred here, how much the beneficial
part of our Trade may be prejudiced by the loss of
100000 of our Manufactures, and what odds the same
loss may produce in our Importations, since if they get
but 6*l. per Ann.* a peice, it must sink the former gain
by Trade no less than 600000*l. per Ann.*

And on the other side, that if a *Million* of Families
or Persons in a Nation, do one with the other consume
to the value of 20*s. a piece* more, yearly in foreign
Manufactures, Drinks, &c. than before, this must increase our Importations to the value of a Million *per*
Ann. which I observe here to shew how imperceptibly
an over-ballance of Importation may creep upon a
Nation; and that the Reader may with the less difficulty conjecture at the late and present ballance of
Trade in *England*.

It must also much assist this Importing Trade, if the
Merchants shall export Mony, or Bullion; especially in

such

such a Nation as *England,* where a Trade from Port to Port is not ordinarily practicable to any advantage: for in that Case the Goods Imported being spent at home, the Treasure Exported must be lost to the Nation; and as long as the English Merchant can have Bullion or Mony to Export, and can have a vent for his Importations at home, his private gain will never oblige him to complain of the want of. Exportable home-Manufactures, or the Clogs upon Trade, especially in *England,* where our Merchants have such a *Monopoly* of those Importations on the rest of the People.

This Consumptive Importing Trade must be of very fatal Consequence in its Nature; for first, whilest the National Stock is greater, it will exhaust the Treasure almost *insensibly ;* but as the Treasure grows less and less, it will work more *palpably and grievously,* because it will consume more and more of that little which remains.

And as the National Treasure comes to be more and more diminished, the People must generally have less and less, which must cause the price of all home-Commodities, and consequently *Land-Rents* to fall continually, the home Manufactures must be choaked and stifled by Importations, so that both the Farmers and Manufacturers must fling up; the values of their Stocks must be contracted, and will be eaten out by Rent, Wages and other standing charges before they are aware; men cannot provide against misfortunes which have unseen Causes: and as home-trade grows worse and worse, Industry it self must be tired and foiled, to the great amazement, as well as affliction of the People.

For at the same time *Liberty and Property* may remain inviolated, many *Merchants* shall grow rich and shall be well satisfied as long as there is *Vanity* and *Money* at home; so shall their *Retailers* and *Salesmen* of foreign Wares, such are Mercers, Lacemen, Linnen-

Drapers

Drapers, Exchange-men, Grocers, Vintners and most others; there may seem to be the same Navigation for a time, the *Customs* must also necessarily much increase as the Importations increase (especially in *England* where the Customs on Importations are so high) and by that means may cause a reputation and *sound* of Trade amongst many, when indeed such a swelling of the Customs does only denounce their growing poverty and ruine.

It may be these ranks of men, who stand not in the direct Channel of Trade, may seem to flourish for a time, as *Officers, Lawyers, Physitians,* and others : nay perhaps some *Officers* may have greater opportunities of gain during the first Convulsions of a growing Poverty ; since the necessities of men obliging them to be more Criminous, it may for a while occasion greater and more frequent gratuities, and a more absolute sub-servience ; so may many Lawyers get more than ever whilst mens Estates are rending to pieces, *(as doubtless did some Bricklayers get Estates by the burning of the City).* So perhaps sickly men whilst they can, may strain hard to secure the *Faith* and *Care* of their *Phy-sitians* with as good Fees as before, so some *Clergy-men.* *Scriveners* and *Pen-men* of all sorts, Usurers and such others may seem to stem the torrent better than the *Landholders* and *Manufacturers,* whose Revenues im-mediately depend on the home-market, and who make up the gross body and strength of a Nation; many of these former rankes of men (being at ease themselves) may seem insensible of the Common Afflictions, but must be gradually involved with the rest.

And the sooner, because as men fling up their Farms and Manufactures, and others are discouraged, mul-titudes of those that want Imployments, observing what other sorts of men continue to live at some ease, will naturally and inevitably throng themselves into the

93   like

like, *viz.* *importing Merchandise, Retayling, Shop-keeping, the Law, Clergy, and Priesthood of all sorts, Offices, Scrivening, Solliciting, and Physick :* by which these Imployments must be so over-clogged, that they will be hardly able to live by one another ; vast numbers of others must betake themselves to *Inn-keeping, Ale-keeping, Victualing, &c.* and those who have little or no stocks or literature, and therefore cannot crowd themselves into some of these ways of Livelihood must lye on the Parish, or being higher or worse minded must fall to *Cheating, Canting, Shifting, Perjury, Forgery, Whoredom, Sherking, Chipping, Coyning, Buffooning, Tumbling, Pimping, Pilfering, Robbery, &c.* for their ordinary maintenances; the more honest or industrious will transport themselves into *foreign parts,* as soon as they have opportunity, rather than live miserable at home, especially if they have an *Ireland and Plantations* to go to ; nor is it possible (as I conceive) for any Laws or Penalties effectually to restrain the swelling numbers of any of the former professions, but by opening the beneficial and Comprehensive Imployments of Manufactures, Farming, &c.; nor can the daily increase of Ale-houses, or of Frauds, Perjuries and Criminals of all sorts be otherwise corrected ; *no Statutes,* nay, or *Preaching,* though never so *learned* or *florid,* can prevail with necessitous men.

But the increase of these former more Gentleman-like, Scholar-like, Retailing and Shopkeeping-Imployments, must yet bring a farther inconvenience, *viz.* a more general *affectation of Finery and Gawdery,* than before; for these being sedentary and easie professions, will not only admit of, but occasion greater curiosity in Apparel, Modes, and dresses than the active and laborious ways of living by Farming or Manufactures. And as this Gawdery grows more in use it will spread amongst the rest, and the People emulating one another, will be gawdy as long as they can, though never *so poor*; which must support and increase Foreign Importations, whilst every one is contending who shall have the *finest Foreign Livery*, so will People thus at leisure most naturally fall into the habits of *drinking* and other ill Courses.

Too many of these symptoms of a Consumptive Trade may be generally observed in *England*; of late years any man who had but an indifferent Stock might have set himself to *Tillage, Grazing, Daiery, Cloathing, Fulling, &c.* in almost any part of *England*, and might not only have maintained his Family plentifully, but as his Stock and Ingenuity were more or less, might have left an Estate behind him; it was not extraordinary for a man thus employed to get an Estate of 3, or 4000*l.* some 10, some 20, some 30000*l.* whereas now, and of these later years these home-imployments have been the usual Shipwracks of mens Stocks and Estates in most parts of *England*, or so dull and cold that men can hardly endure to live so meanly.

Our *late Wealthy Yeomanry* are impoverished, or much reduced in their stocks, a man shall hardly find three in a County able to rent 3, or 400*l. per Ann.* they are forced to *sink their Rents* on the Gentry continually, or else to fling up their Farms; much Land is fallen a fifth part, some a fourth part, some a third part, some to half of the late Rent, (unless in some few Countys in whose benefit the *Irish* Acts were made, and there Rents are not risen and are now like to fall low enough:) by which continual contracting of Rents the very earth seems to shrink and consume under us, and whilst many of our *late opulent and mighty Gentry* since the general decay of their Revenues have been striving to support the antient honour and dignity of their Families, they are become immerged and fettered in inextricable debts and securities; great numbers of our *Clothiers* and other

95 Manufacturers

Manufacturers are undone, or have given up; the rest remain under a languishing hope of better Markets: and multitudes of those people, whose Labours brought Mony, Trade and Comfort to our Corporations, are now become chargeable burthens: it being computed that our *Poor* are increased to near ten times their late number within this last twenty years, and that their maintenance doth cost the Nation 400000*l. per Ann.* constant Tax.

On the other side, the increase of those sorts of men, whose Imployments either may prejudice, or else can add no increase of Treasure to the Nation, is very visible: by which increase the inconveniencies must be still the greater; for where the foreign Trade of a Nation is so much driven in importations, the increase of *Merchants* will oblige an increase of Importation; so an increase of *Retailers* dealing in foreign Goods, will open a greater vent for Importations; suppose such a Retailer sells for 10*l. per Cent.* profit, the *Nation* must lose about nine pence for every peny he gets, what then shall the Nation lose by the Trade of a Merchant or Retailer, who by *vending Foreign Wares* shall get an Estate of 10, or 20000*l.* over and besides a profuse maintenance? Or what will it signifie to the Wealth or Glory of a Nation, or City, to have many such 10000*l. men* as these? Have we any reason to rejoyce in such a flourishing Trade? These Retailers and Shop-keepers, gleaning the Mony, from the People, hand it up to the *Importers*, who export this *Commodity in Trade* as occasion does require; and as our Manufactures have decayed, so have *Shop-keepers* of all sorts increased; our Cities and Corporations are stuffed with them more and more; there being at least ten times more in the Nation than were 20, or 30 years since.

Thus also have we multitudes of more *Lawyers, Attorneys, Solicitors, Scriviners, and Pen-men of all sorts,*

96   than

than of late years we had ; which occasions more Querks, Tricks, and Cheats in the Law.   We have vastly more *Scholars and Clergymen*, which a late Author observing, thought it necessary to export *Tunns of Divines* instead of Manufacture: This does cause an universal compe-tition for Benefices; of which the needy Laity taking advantage, make Simonaical presentations, and thence must follow perjury in Institutions, and thence seared Consciences; but of all other Imployments we have the greatest questing after *Offices;* Men will almost give any thing, say any thing, or do any thing for an Office; so that some *Offices* which were thought hardly worth the medling with of late years, will now yield near ten years purchase for one life, which competition hath also in a manner virtually repealed the Statute against buying and selling of Offices, and obliges those who buy trusts to sell trusts.   We have also far more Physitians, men of Medicine and Quacks, especially *Pox-Doctors* than ever, so have we (with our poverty) far more *Finery and Gawdery*, more *Daintyness, Delicacy* and *Luxury*.

So have we a vast increase of *Inn-keepers and Ale-keepers* both in City and Country, by which the com-mon-people are debauched, made impious, poor and effeminate: all which mischiefs do in union cause the vast increase of *new Buildings* in and about *London;* for most of the Offices are in *London,* or there to be gotten, there is also the ready access to Church-pre-ferment, and the best and most easie Imployments for Lawyers, Solicitors, Scriviners, Physitians, and such others, and the rather, because the publick Taxes and Importing-trade drawing the mony up to *London,* it will there be stirring as long as we have any in the Nation; whilst the Country is left poorer and barer every day; and therefore besides these higher ranks of men, the ordinary People who used heretofore to begin

Author of the grounds and reasons of the contempt of the English Clergy. paq. 141.

97   upon

upon Farming or Manufacture, hearing of *mony* in *London*, do post from the starving Country, and apply themselves to the selling of Ale, Brandy, Tobacco, Coffee, Brokery of all sorts, letting of Lodgings in or about *London*, and such like Imployments, which too commonly end in Bawdery and the Gallows, by which there is room made for new Comers and Tenants; I have heard it said, that *Madrid* is grown much bigger and more Populous of late years.

From these and other sorts of People, both in City and Country, we have more and more *Criminals* of all the sorts and species mentioned before; our Gaols are fuller and fuller, great numbers of which are yearly executed or transported; vast numbers of others have betaken themselves to voluntary exile from this their Native Country, in hopes of a better condition, rather than to endure certain poverty or persecution for Conscience at home; besides those gone into *Ireland*, and the *Plantations*, there are many thousands of Protestants gone from us into the *Low Countries*, into *France*, into *Germany*, and into *Poland*, where being Woollen Manufacturers, they have taught, and set up this Manufacsure, and thereby helped to work our ruine. These being of the most strong and able part of our People, leave their Wives and Children, and other impotent and lazy People at home.

And thus shall a Nation be inevitably *dispeopled*, as well as impoverished by a consumptive Trade; Nay, it shall hinder the ordinary increase of People by procreation, especially in a Nation where *venereal sins* are become general, habitual and shameless; for the People being poor, or vicious, or both, dare not, or care not to engage in the charge or virtuous Obligations of *Marriage*, (unless here and there where a man gets a Catch with a Wife which shall be equal to an Office,) but will rather use unlawful *promiscuous Copulation*, which breeds no Children, but infinite *Claps and Poxes* to the common weakning of Posterity, and present scandal of a Nation: (thus have our Women also lost their choice of Chapmen for Husbands :) how many of our most beautiful Women (which might have made good and vertuous Wives, and brought forth numbers of as beautiful Children,) are for want of convenient Matches tempted, or forced for a little mony, to sell their souls to the Devil, and their delicate bodies to lust and rottenness, nay to the Gallows, when proving with Child, the remains of their natural modesty, will not in their extremities permit them to call Witnesses of their shame, whilst the *Gallants* which beget them go free, and glory in their great performance.

All which mischiefs of a consumptive Trade are yet more fatal, because the growing vice and poverty which attends it, will generally bring a languor and difficulty on mens understandings ; as men sink in their Estates, their Spirits and Thoughts will be lower and narrower, and their Minds clouded with anxieties and cares, this (with the common disability of making advantages upon Forreigners in the course of Trade) leads them into a kind of unhappy *Cunning*, consisting in the over-reaching of one another at home; and he will be accounted wise, who by any means can shift himself out of the common wants, nor will he think his own happiness small, (*especially if his beginnings were low*) when (like one standing on the Sands) he can behold the Shipwreck of others.

SECT. IX.

*That a Consumptive Trade must render a Nation still
weaker and weaker: How far the meer establishment
of Absolute Power, or meer Liberty and Property, may
alter the Case.*

FRom what hath been said in the first Section and
since, it must also follow, that a *Consumptive Trade*
must render a *Nation* still weaker and weaker.

First, because it must still exhaust more and more
of the National Riches, and sink the value of Mens
Estates.

If the value of private Stocks or Revenues are contracted, Men will be less and less able to pay publick
Taxes; it is impossible for those that have no Money to
pay Money, or for those that have less to pay as much
as those that have more; and less Taxes must then also
be more grievous than greater were before; if a Man
having 100*l. per An'* or 100*l.* Stock, sink 40*l. per Cent.*
of his Revenue or Stock, it is equal to any direct Tax
of 40*l. per Cent.* and then if a Tax or publick Charge
of 5 or 10*l.* be super-added, it is equal to a former Tax
of 45 or 50*l. per Cent.*

It must also disable a Nation to continue the *Charge
of a War,* because the quantity of Money diffused
amongst the People will sooner be drawn out of the
Home-Markets; and then they can no longer raise
Taxes, and when the Taxes fail, what hope or dependance can there be in the courage of Officers, Soldiers,
or Sea-men? or how shall the continual Supplies of
Warlike Provisions of all sorts be purchased at home
or abroad?

There are yet other Concomitants of a growing
Poverty, which must render any Nation much the

100 weaker

weaker, *viz. discontents, uneasiness,* and *heart-burnings,* which when begun, are easily fermented into *Convulsions,* by which a Nation may be disabled to exert even its remaining strength.

2. *Perfidy* and *Treachery* amongst all sorts; needy Men are readily tempted to make a Merchandize of their own Souls and other Mens Lives and Estates, and those who will betray one another for Money at home, will be equally wrought upon by forreign Money, and then may be brought to barter of both Princes and Countries; for being once corrupted, they must, *like Women,* for ever remain slavishly true to the Intrigue, lest the *Gallant* should tell, of which Histories give us many sad Examples.

But in a Nation where the value of Land, or Home-Commodities, are risen 40 *per Cent.* he that had 100*l.* Revenue or Stock, paying 40*l.* Tax, retains what he had; and if the National Treasure be much greater, it will support the charge of a War much longer, and can hardly ever be totally exhausted, where there is a considerable Annual Increase of Treasure by Forreign Trade: This exuberance of a National Treasure will also generally support and secure the Spirit and Fidelity of all sorts of Men.

It must therefore be of most dangerous consequence to a Nation impoverished by Trade, if any other neighbour-Nation hath at the same time grown much richer in Treasure, since in the case of a War it will produce the like inequality of Power; nay if any such richer Nation shall think fit to keep great Armies and Navies in pay, (though in times of Peace) so must the poorer Nation, or else be devoured at pleasure; and thus may a Nation, drained by the over-ballance of Trade, be beggered, and consequently overcome without fighting, as hath been intimated before.

So if a Nation grow generally more vitious, soft,

effeminate

effeminate, debauched, dispeopled, and undisciplined than before, it must be much weaker than before, wherein the danger must be much greater if any neighbour Nation grow far more warlike, more populous and better disciplined than before.

In which case the better situated, more useful, strong, plentiful, and blessed the Country so impoverished naturally is, and the more it doth abound in beautiful Buildings, Women, or other delicacies, it will the more forcibly provoke the Appetite of a stronger Nation to its Conquest, the mighty *Hunters* of the World are for the most desirable prey; so if a Nation thus weakned hath formerly been famous and redoubted for Arms and War; those who affect glory by Conquest, must have the greater Ambition to vassalize its People.

From what hath been said it must appear; first, That a Nation must be estimated *weak or strong by comparison,* with the strength or weakness of Neighbour Nations; if a Neighbour Nation grow ten times as strong as before, the Nation which only retains its usual and former strength is *weak;* but the Case must be yet worse, if whilst the one hath grown *ten times stronger, the other hath grown much weaker.*

2. That in the present state of the World a Nation cannot grow poor by a consumptive Trade with any Security.

In such a Case the *meer absoluteness of a Monarchy* would not prevent the approaching fatality, (which I add because *Hobbs* and others call it a strong Government) absolute Power may suddenly force away that Treasure which the People have, but cannot *create* any, nor can it carry on a War, or even *support it self* without continual *vast expences;* and then when the Treasure is drawn off into the hands of Officers and Soldiers, (who pay no Taxes) it will be found, that the People (who have it not) can no more make Brick without

Straw

Straw in this Age, than heretofore; and will be naturally desirous to change their Masters upon hope to be
treated with less rigor.

Nor on the other side will the meer preservation of a
legal Liberty and Property secure a Nation thus impoverished, without a concurrent improvement of Trade,
for the Reasons before given; the Blessings which
usually attend these Freedoms wholly, or very much
depend upon the Riches the People are possessed of.

It must be confessed these Freedoms make a necessary step towards the improvement of Trade; where an
absolute Power is exerted, the conditions of Men are
little better than that of Brutes, being continually lyable
to Imprisonments, Death, and Confiscations, at the
Pleasure of others; nay perhaps are worse, by the fears
and terrors Men must be always under, even whilst they
do not actually suffer; which will take away the edge
and life of Industry, and will ruine or drive away the
Merchants, and those who have Stocks in Manufacture,
who neither will, nor can labour all their lives for Wealth
under daily expectations of losing what they painfully
get, which in this last Age hath obliged the *French*
Monarchy to permit divers Immunities to their Manufacturers, and of late to their Fishers and other Maritime Traders, which have now gotten the reputation of
established Laws; at least they are such as are satisfactory *to the French Natives*, who cannot have, nor are
acquainted with better terms, and who are of themselves
so numerous, that they stand in no need of Supplies of
People from abroad; and therefore of no greater invita-
tions of this nature to bring in Forreigners, and the
rather, because their Trade is otherwise so much eased
and incouraged (of which I shall have occasion to say
more;) so have the *great Dukes of Tuscany* in this
last Age been curiously vigilant to provide for the
Freedom of Traders, both Domestick and Forreign:

The

The *Dutch, Venetians, Hamburghers,* and other Trading States do yet farther secure the Liberties and Properties of their Natives, and others, under their several Jurisdictions, by fundamental and unalterable Constitutions.

Which being admitted, it doth not follow that a Nation which hath meer Liberty and Property, without other requisite incouragements, shall drive any great Trade; we have an Example in *Genoa,* at this day, a *Republick,* where, because they set a Custom of 16 *per Cent.* on Goods Imported, they lost their Trade of Forreign Merchandize to *Leghorne,* made a free Port by the *Duke of Tuscany;* what then may we hope for from the meer Liberty and Property of the *English,* when in *England* the Customs are generally higher, and our other difficulties on Trade are yet more grievous than the Customs? by the Accompt we have from our first Discoverers and Planters in *America,* most of these poor Nations had a Home-Liberty and Property.

SECT. X.

Further presumptions of our late National Overballance in Trade; an Account from the Mint in November 75. *and thence our former Ballance of Trade estimated.*

AS a further Evidence that our National Trade hath been *Consumptive,* and that I may silence the prevarications of some whose private Interest or Passions (which are but the fermentations of their Interests) teach them to affirm the contrary, I shall take notice of the following Accompt taken and Printed in *November* 1675. for the clearing a Debate then before a Committee of Parliament, intituled as followeth.

An Account of all the Gold and Silver Coined in his Majesties Mint within the Tower of London, *from the first of* October 1599. *being the forty first year of the Reign of* Queen Eliz. *to* November 1675. *being* 76 *years, divided into four parts; shewing how the Coin of this Kingdom did increase in the three first parts, proportionable to the increase of Trade and Navigation, and how much it hath decreased in the fourth part.*

Gold and Silver Coined.	*Totals by Tale.*			*Yearly Medium.*		
From the first of *Octob.* 1599. to the last of *March* 1619. was Coined four Millions seven Hundred seventy nine Thousand three Hundred and fourteen Pounds thirteen Shillings and four Pence; which was *per An'* two Hundred forty five Thousand ninety two Pounds Eleven Shillings & six Pence.	*l.*	*s.*	*d.*	*l.*	*s.*	*d.*
	4779314	18	4	245092	11	06
From the last of *March* 1619. to the last of *March* 1638. was Coined six Millions nine Hundred thousand forty two Pounds eleven Shillings and one Peny; which was *per An'* three Hundred sixty three thousand one hundred & sixty Pounds two Shillings one Peny farthing . .	6900042	11	1	363160	02	1¼

From the last of *March* 1638. to *May* 1657. was

Coined

Gold and Silver Coined. Totals by Tale. Yearly Medium.

Coined seven Millions seven Hundred thirty three Thousand five Hundred twenty one Pounds thirteen Shillings fourpence farthing; which was *per An'* four Hundred and seven thousand and twenty seven Pounds nine Shillings one Peny $\frac{1}{2}$ penny.

	l.	*s.*	*d.*	*l.*	*s.*	*d.*
	7733521	13	4¼	407027	9	1½

From *May* 1657. to *Nov.* 75. being 18 years and a half, was Coined three Millions two hundred thirty eight thousand nine hundred ninety seven Pounds sixteen Shillings and three farthings; about one Million of which was Harp and Cross Money, and broad Gold, *&c.* re-coined; which deducted, there remains but 2 Millions two hundred thirty eight thousand nine hundred ninety seven Pounds 16*s.* three farthings; which was *per An'* but one hundred twenty one thousand 26*l.* eighteen Shillings and four Pence.

	2238997	16	¾	121026	18	04

The total of all Gold & Silver Coined in these

106   76 years

Gold and Silver Coined. *Totals by Tale.*

76 years from the first of *Octob.* 1599. to *Novemb.* 1675. was Coined twenty one Millions eight hundred fifty one thousand eight hundred seventy six Pounds fourteen Shillings seven Pence half-peny. . .

	l.	*s.*	*d.*
	21851876	14	7½

The Coin yearly increased in the 2*d* part, from the last of *March* 1619. to the last of *March* 1638. more than in the first part, one hundred and eighteen thousand sixty seven Pounds ten Shillings seven pence farthing; the Total thereof is two Millions two hundred forty three thousand two hundred eighty three Pounds one Shilling two pence. . . . . .

Yearly Increase.   *Total Increase.*

l.	*s.*	*d.*	*l.*	*s.*	*d.*
118067	10	4	2243283	01	02

The Coin yearly increased in the 3*d* part, from the last of *March* 1638. to *May* 1657. one hundred sixty one thousand nine hundred thirty four Pounds 17*s.* 7½*d.*, the Total thereof is three Millions seventy six thousand seven hun-

dred

Gold and Silver Coined. Yearly Increase.   Total Increase.

	l.	*s.*	*d.*	*l.*	*s.*	*d.*
dred sixty two Pounds fourteen Shillings ten pence half-peny. . .	161934	17	7½	3076762	14	10½

The Coin hath yearly decreased in the fourth part, from *May* 1657.to this present *November* 1675. being the last eighteen years and half, two hundred eighty six thousand Pounds ten Shillings nine pence halfpeny; the total whereof is five Millions two hundred ninety one thousand and nine Pounds nineteen Shillings four pence farthing. . . .

	l.	*s.*	*d.*	*l.*	*s.*	*d.*
	286000	10	9½	5291009	19	4¼

This prodigious decrease of Coin in the last eighteen years, does undeniably evidence a vast decay in our Trade: but since, even in these latter years, there hath been somewhat above 120000*l. per An'* Coined, as appears by the Account, it doth seem to administer an Objection, that still there hath been some National gain by Trade, though much less than before.

But this does not follow, for if more Money hath been exported yearly during these last eighteen years than hath been Coined, the National Treasure must be diminished: Now if we have been over-ballanced, more Money must be exported; so that it will resolve into the former Question.

It is a vain thing to say, that the exportation of Money in *Specie* stands still *prohibited*; so is the exporting of Treasure prohibited in *Spain* under the

the

highest Penalties; and yet because *Spain* is over-ballanced by consumptive Importations, Forreigners continually carry it away; so that were it not for their Mines, there would not have been the value of a Peny left in *Spain* many years since; nor can their *Mines* so answer this mighty *drain* by a consumptive Trade, but that the Treasures of *Spain* are drawn lower than in any Nation in *Europe*.

And therefore though the ordinary trading with exported Money is condemnable, as that which tends to the subversion of Manufacture and People, and facilitates meer Importation; yet I cannot recommend prohibitory Laws as a means to stop the exportation of Money, unless at the same time the Methods of Trade be regulated.

'Tis now become more practicable by the Liberty given for the Exportation of Bullion; for upon any great emergency, for Bullion, (as for instance) upon the going out of *an East-India Fleet*, Standard-Silver hath risen from 5*s*. the Ounce to 5*s*. 4*d*. the Ounce; which being about 10 *per Cent*. must not only hinder the Coining of Bullion, but must cause our weighty Coin to be melted into Bullion, and so exported as it hath been noted before.

And upon the like occasions 'tis observable, that Guinnies rise to 22*s*. apiece, & broad Gold to 24*s*. apiece, which does evince, that those who use that Trade do not confine themselves to Bullion.

So 'tis notorious to those who understand our *Northern* and *Eastern* Trades, and our Trade to *France*, the *Canaries, Turkey*, &c. that we yearly export great quantities of Treasure to those and other Countries, and that we do not stick at *Coined Money*, being closely put up in Packs of Goods or Barrels, or however may be made lawful and laudable Merchandize by melting; whence it is come to be so commonly asserted a Com-

109   modity;

modity; and then if we look back and observe how little hath been Coined in the 18 years since (57) being but 121026*l. per An'*, it must be highly credible, that we have exported much more Money yearly than we have Coined.

But to make the over-ballance yet more evident, it will be necessary to find out, if possible, what was the yearly Treasure the Nation gained by Forreign Trade, at any time in this last Age; and in the next place, how much our Exportations and beneficial part of our Trade have since failed, and our Importations increased in quantity and value.

The increase of Home-Treasure must either be in Coined Money, or in Plate, made up for Home-uses; for all Bullion imported must either be converted into one of these at home, or else be re-exported, and then 'tis not superadded to the National Home-Treasure.

Now if we look back to the Accompt from the Mint, we may conclude, that during those 76 years, our Trade did never add more to our Coin yearly than 407027*l.* 9*s.* 1¼*d.* for any number of 20 years together; this being the utmost Medium comprized in the Accompt.

Plate Coined by the King at Oxon, and Parliament at London. And this being in the 18 years before (57,) was not all the meer product of the Trade of these very years, for 'tis well known that during those years we had good quantities of our own Plate Coined into Money, 'tis not possible for me to ascertain how much; but if it were a Million, it ought to be deducted out of the Medium of those years.

So during those 18 years, our Trade might yet add less to our Coined Money, *viz.* in case our Forreign Trade did then export any of our Coined Money, the like may be said of any other of the said 18 years or Mediums in the Accompt; and then must all the Money so exported be also deducted out of the Annual Gain of those years.

I believe none will expect that I should adjust the yearly quantity of Money exported by stealth in our Forreign Trade before (57,) I shall leave it to the consideration of the indifferent Reader upon what I shall add; but 'tis evident, that our Merchants did formerly use to export Money, by the prohibitory Statutes made on that occasion.

It may be also further evident, that the yearly quantity of Money so exported before 57 was considerable; for before the 76 years mentioned in the Accompt, we must have had some stock of Money in the Nation, which supposing to be but six Millions, then adding what more was Coined during the said 76 years, we must have had near 30 Millions of Coin in the Nation before 57, had none been exported; whereas no intelligent Man will say we had then half that Sum; which if doubted I shall have occasion to enforce further; and if this be admitted, the Consequence must be, that our Forreign Trade and occasions did even before 57 carry off near half as much Money as was yearly Coined; and then our National yearly Gain in Coined Treasure would not be near to the aforesaid full Mediums Coined, nor to above half the Mediums, (taking any number of years together.)

Nor can we reckon or allow of above 50000*l. per Annum* for increase of *Home-Plate*, during any of the said 18 years, considering that much Plate is always brought back to the Mint, or turned into Bullion, as other new Plate is made; and that at this allowance for Plate, in any twenty years time there would be a Million increase of Home-Plate in the Nation.

Upon the whole the Reader may observe what our utmost National Gain in increase of Treasure possibly might be, and upon the aforesaid grounds may deduct from any of the Mediums as he shall think reasonable, wherein I shall not pretend to confine him, though in

my

my private Judgment I cannot estimate our utmost National increase of Treasure by Trade during any of the said 76 years to be above 250000*l. per Annum,* or thereabouts, for any twenty years together.

Considering which, if the indifferent Reader shall reflect on what hath been said in the 5*th,* 6*th,* 7*th* and 8*th* Sections, if he there find that our Trade hath been under such difficulties, as must necessarily work us out of all the parts of it, whilst our Neighbours are enabled to snatch it from us: If he there find undeniable Instances of it in some Particulars, he may for the same Reasons conclude the like in all others; and by Consequence that our National Trade long before this, became less beneficial than it was by 250000*l. per Annum*; it hath been always found most safe to be governed by the Causes and Reasons of things, but the concurrent impoverishment of our People, and other the Symptoms, Plague-sores, and Spots of a consumptive Trade do further evidence it.

It is confessed it would be of great use, if the odds in our past and present National Forreign Trade might be certainly stated; a difficult, if not impossible task: Since it requires an antient, as well as modern experience in Forreign Trade, and not of any one Trader only, but of so many as have traded into all Parts; of those that are curious, intelligent, and impartial, and have minded the *publick Interest* as well as their *own;* perhaps if a sufficient number of such as these did assemble, they might, upon debate, and with reference to their Books, bring the Compute very near the truth; but nothing of this hath been done of late; and whosoever shall promiscously consult our Traders apart, will find them various: Then for our Custom-Books old or new, though they might be useful for some things, yet they cannot ascertain us in the odds of the Forreign values of any Exported or Imported Goods, nor of the

quantity

quantity of Imported prohibited or smuggled Goods, nor (as I conceive) of our former or present Fishing-Trade, (Fish paying no Custom) nor of the gain of Carriage, nor of the Trade from Port to Port; without which the certain odds in the Ballance cannot be calculated; and therefore for my own part I rest chiefly on what hath been said; believing myself secure whilst I keep my self to the *rational part,* which cannot be refuted but by Reason: Whereas I am apprehensive that should I descend to examine our Ballance of Trade by the particular *effects* of the foregoing *Causes,* these being matters of *Fact,* and very many, and most of them Forreign, and of less Notoriety, may be liable to Exceptions or Cavils of particular Men, as their different Sentiments or Interests may dictate; it being as easie to deny as affirm, and as hard for many Readers to determine the truth in these matters; whereby the sincerity of the Relator may be drawn into question; and at such times, when he shall have no opportunity to defend himself: and I am not insensible, that amongst so many Facts as the nature of this Subject hath forced me to mention, (whereof I must speak much upon the credit I give to others) 'tis impossible there may be some slips, even by the transcribing of Papers: Upon these Considerations, I had thoughts of laying aside part of the three next Sections as needless, and neglected somewhat of that Curiosity I intended, but being perused and approved by some Friends amongst the rest of these Papers, they have perswaded me to publish them as they are, upon apprehension that they will enforce what I have already said, though left so general, and will give the Reader a further useful light into the past and present nature and condition of our Trade and Nation: and since they do not bind up the Reader to precise Quantities and Values, can admit of little altercation; in which I have been

the

the more ready to comply, upon hopes that I may awaken and spur on the *virtuous emulation* of others to a more compleat disquisition into the several branches of our Trade, and that the Reader will think me the more excusable in this and the rest I have undertaken, when he shall observe the present Subject so *Copious*, and so little laboured by other Writers, that I have no common Places or beaten Tracks to follow, as in other Studies.

This I assure the Reader, that amongst the following instances, or elsewhere, there are no wilfull or affected errors, and that I have not affirmed any thing which I do not know, but upon such Authority as I have reason to believe *highly* credible, and am confident that whatsoever mistakes in Fact the Curious may find out in what I have already said, or shall say, there are none such as do in the least impeach the *force* or *reason* of this Discourse, and then must be admitted immaterial.

To which I shall add, that by the following Essay, I do not pretend to that difficult work of adjusting the present Ballance of our Trade, but to evince, that the former Ballance of our Trade (as it may be computed from the aforesaid Accompt, from the Mint or otherwise) is grown consumptive in *some degree ;* which I think will appear to the indifferent Readers satisfaction, upon consideration of some late decays and defalcations in our Trade, wherein I shall confine my self to such as have happened long after the beginning of the 76 years mentioned in the Accompt, from the Mint, many of them within 20 years last.

SECT. XI.

*Particular decays in our Exportations, and the beneficial
parts of our Trade; Instances in the decay of our
Foreign-Trade for Woollen Clothing, in the several
Countries and Ports we Traded to, in the sinking of
the foreign price of this Manufacture, so of exported
Wooll in our foreign victualling Trades for Flesh,
Butter, Cheese, &c. in our* Irish *Trade, and* Scotch *Trade
for almost all sorts of Commodities:* Irish *Wooll increased: The Expiration of the* Irish *Acts will not now
revest that Trade, but prejudice us more, and in what :
decays in our several former and late Fishing-Trades, in
our Foreign-Trade for Stockings and Hats in our exports to the* Canaries, *in the Foreign-Price of our exported Tyn and Lead, and the Price and quantity of
exported Pewter, in our Trade from Port to Port, our
former and late prejudices in our Plantation-Trade,
incidently of our Navigation and other things.*

I Shall begin with our Exportations, and as I shall pass
from one particular to another, in this and the next
Section, shall desire the indifferent Reader to put such
an estimation on our losses in Trade, as he shall think
reasonable; and shall first instance in our Woollen
Manufactures, as being our principal Commodity, and
certainly of the most general and necessary use, (and
therefore in its nature the best) in the World.

Before *Edward the thirds* time the *Flemings* Manufactured our Wooll, and had the Merchandize of it,
which gave the original Foundation to the former Wealth
and Popularity of the *Netherlands.*

Edw. 3. observing the great advantages the *Flemings*
made of our Wooll, brought over some Flemish Manufacturers, who by degrees taught the Manufacture of

Cloaths of all sorts, *Worsted* and divers others, particularly mentioned in our *Statutes* of former times: and as the *English* more applied themselves to it, and increased ours (as soon as they did) so did that of the *Flemings* decay.

For first, the *English* had the materials cheaper than the *Flemings*, not only by the odds in the carriage out of *England*, but because the raw Woolls afterwards exported were charged with great *Customs* and *Duties* to the King, as appears by the Acts and Writings of those times.

Secondly, Because the Manufacture was continually incouraged, and taken care of by Laws for that purpose, as also appears by our *Statute-Book*.

Thirdly, At that time we had none of the present Clogs on our Manufactures, which have either become so by the better Methods of Trade first contrived by the *Dutch* States, or have been grafted upon us by private or mistaken interests long since *Edw. 3ds* time. I do not find that there was any absolute *Prohibition* of exporting Wooll till the Statute of the 12th of His now Majesty, chap. 32. yet the example of our cunning Neighbours now tell us, that *Prohibitions*, accompanied with a due Improvement of Trade at home, are not to be condemned.

The *Flemish* Cloath-trade was long since so far reduced, that we had the sole Merchandize of it, yet it cannot be denied but the *Flemings* kept up a Manufacture of a sort of *Stuffs* and *Sayes*, (but of no great bulk) the make whereof the *English* had not been taught, till the *Duke* of *Alva* about 100 years since by his Tyranny and Persecution for Conscience, drove away their Manufacturers, whom *Queen Elixabeth* like her wise Predecessor *Edward the third* entertained, seating them in *Norwich*, *Colchester*, and *Canterbury*, whereby these Manufactures became incorporated into

116   the

the *English*, to the great advantage of those parts, and of the Nation in general: they also taught us the art of making *Tapestry*.

Before this the *English* exported great quantities of our Manufacture into *Flanders*, but doubtless more afterwards, for which we kept a rich Staple at *Antwerp*, the *Dutch* long after they became States were ignorant of this Manufacture, whom we therefore wholly supplied, exporting vast quantities of our Cloaths thither, most Whites, which were there dyed and dressed, and from these parts transmitted into the *Southern* and *South-east* Countries of *Germany*, and many other Nations: we had also the sole trade up the *Elbe*, and thereby to the *North* parts of *Germany*, *Jutland* and *Holsteyne*.

We had the sole Trade into *Denmark*, *Norway*, *Swedeland* and *Liefland*, and to the great Territory of *Poland* (through *Dantzick*) by our *Eastland Company*, formerly very flourishing, and called the *Royal Company*.

We had also the sole Trade to the vast Empire of *Muscovy*.

All which Trades are sunk to a small matter, the *Dutch* having set up mighty Woollen Manufactures of all sorts, and the *Flemings* renewed or enlarged theirs, our exports to *those* parts are very much reduced.

Our *Hamburgh Company*, by whom the *North* parts of *Germany*, *Jutland* and *Holsteyne* were supplied, do not vend near half what they did, the *Dutch* and other Manufactures having prevailed upon us in those parts, both for the Finest and Coarsest Cloaths: what we now export to *Hamburgh* are a sort of Cloaths of between 3, and 7*s.* a Yard, and of those not near the former quantity.

Then for our *Eastland Trade* it is sunk more, I have heard several Estimates, all near concurring with what I find in Mr. *Coke's* third Treatise of Trade, dedicated Pag. 33, 34.

to *Prince Rupert, viz.* That this Company only heretofore usually exported above 20000 Broad Cloaths, 60000
Kerseys, and 40000 Doubles yearly; but of late years
not above 4000 Broad Cloths, 5000 Kerseys, and 2000
Doubles. To give this worthy Gentleman his due, he
hath written more materially on the present subject
than any man in this Age, in which he hath not only

Pag. 112.
demonstrated his deep Judgment, but his great sedulity
and sincerity in the discovery of the truth, professing
himself ready to make out whatsoever he hath reported,
before any Judicature. There is too much reason and
fact to warrant the great decay of this *Eastland Trade*,
when the *Dutch* Manufacture is arrived to such a degree,
besides which the *Silesian* and *Polonian* Manufactures
of Coarse Woolls are mightily increased, so that at
Dantzick, our late great staple, we now sell so little
that 'tis not worth the naming; we now trade *thither*
with Treasure, whence we used to Import much; the
like may be said of other Ports this Company formerly
traded to.

Then for *Swedeland*, the Natives have lately set up a
Manufacture there of their Coarse Woolls, as well as
Denmark, Liefland and *Norway*, are very much supplied
by the *Dutch*, imposing greater Prices and Customs
upon us for what they vend, and insisting to have
Treasure of us, where before they bartered for Commodity.

To which I may add, That our late great *Muscovy*
Trade is in a manner lost; the same Mr. *Coke* takes
notice that the *Dutch* send 1500 Sail of Ships into the
Sound in a year, and 40 to *Muscovy*, we do not send
above seven into the *Sound* in a year, of which two are
laden with woollen Manufactures, the other five with
Ballast, (and are therefore to buy their foreign lading)
and to *Muscovy* we hardly send two in three years;
during the late War we have sent somewhat more.

We had also the sole trading for woollen Cloathing into *France,* of which we vended there to the value of 600000*l.* yearly ; but the French having for these later years set up this Manufacture at home, do now supply themselves ; and as their own hath increased, so have they laid greater Impositions upon ours, till in (67) the *French* King set an intolerable Tax of about 50 *per Cent.* on all our Cloathing imported into *France,* by which our Cloathing-trade to *France* became in a manner impracticable, nor have the *French* any occasion to open this Trade to us again. 000000

This value of our exported Cloathing to *France* is avouched by our Antient Traders thither and so asserted in the Printed Book in (77) in defence of our *East India* Company.

We had also the sole Cloathing-Trade into *Turkey, Spain* and its Dominion ; and it must be confessed, that we have supported our *Turkey-Trade* better than any other, much occasioned by our importation of raw Silk from those parts, for which we used to barter : but of late years the *Dutch* are great Competitors with us in the *Turkey-Trade,* (though the *English* may have had the advantage whilst the *Dutch* have been engaged in the late War ;) the *French* have been long nibling at this Trade, and both the *French* and *Dutch* largely share with us in the *Spanish-Trade.* . 000000

But what is yet more grievous, we import much *Fine Cloath* from the *Dutch* yearly, and till of late great quantities of *Stuffs* and *Druggets* from the *French,* which *French* Importation (only) amounted to the value of 150000*l. per Annum,* as Mr. *Fortrey* in his Book of Trade reports ; how much of these, or other *French* Goods may be imported for the future, may be guessed from what I shall say in the last Section concerning the *late Prohibition of French Goods* ; in the

mean

mean time it may be observed, how far our late *Monopoly* of the Woollen Manufacture is *vanished*.

We had also the sole Trade for Woollen Manufactures to the Kingdom of *Portugal*, which Trade hath been decaying several years, because of the Competition of the *French* and *Dutch*, but of late hath been worse than ever; by reason that the Government of *Portugal* since the year 1660 hath prohibited the wearing of *English* Cloath; having set up this Manufacture of their own Woolls; we still drive a Trade thither for *Stuffs*, in which the *French* and *Dutch*, as before, are great sharers, and of late the *Portuguese* have been attempting at these Manufactures, having gotten over some of our *English* Manufacturers. . . .   000000

We had also the sole Trade into *Italy*, in which the *French* and *Dutch* are also sharers, besides the *Venetians*, who Manufacture and vend much Cloath in those parts.

Stat. 18, & 20 *Car.* 2.   So till of later years the *English* had the sole Trade to *Ireland* for Woollen Cloathing of all sorts, but since the late *Irish* Acts, the *Irish* have set up a considerable Woollen Manufacture of their own, for Frize and Stuffs, and now make good Cloath; or if they want, are in a great measure furnished from the *Dutch* or *French*, with whom they now Commerce; these *Irish* Manufacturers increase very much.   000000

Besides which, by the late competition of Foreigners in the Trade of Woollen Manufacture, our *Cloaths* have gradually and generally *sunk* in the foreign Market from their former *price and value* being (according to

120   the

the best estimate I can meet with) sold for near a third less than they were sold for within 30, or 40 years last past, taking the sales made in one Country with another; some say at less than a third; if at less by a fourth or fifth than before, this odds alone seems sufficient to turn the Ballance of our Trade; since our whole Woollen Manufacture lately exported hath been generally agreed to yield near two Millions *per ann.* Whatever it were, our gain in this our principal Commodity must be sunk in proportion, to which must be added what we fail of the former *quantity.* 000000

All which by a necessary sympathy is verified in the present condition of our *English* Towns and Clothiers; of which we may take one obvious instance in the Town of *Reading*; where the late number of Clothiers being about 160, are reduced to about 12, and the Poor so increased that they cost the Town about 1000*l.* *per Annum;* perhaps in some Towns where Provisions are cheaper, the Clothiers may bear up somewhat better; but he that will examine into any other of our Cloathing Towns, will find the Trade decayed in some greater or lesser degree, and will hear the Complaints of these Clothiers, who continue in the Manufacture.

I may add, that our *exported Wooll* is sunk to about a third of its late price. 000000

And whereas before the said *Irish Acts,* Foreign *Ships* did use to *victual* themselves out of the plenties of *England,* the *Irish* being since forced to fat their own Cattle at home, and by the cheapness of their Lands being enabled to sell cheaper than the *English,* Foreigners do now victual their Ships out of the new stores of *Ireland,* and cheaper than we can in *England;* by which we are beat out

121

of

of the Trade of *Foreign Victualing :* nay, what
is yet harder upon us, the very *English Ships*
do now ordinarily victual from *Ireland :* this
Trade of *Victualling* is also much prejudiced
by our late *Act of Navigation,* which does
exclude much Foreign Shipping from our
Ports ; and of what yearly loss this must be
to the *English* Nation, and more particularly
to the *English* Landholders, I submit to
Judgement.   000000

Also the *English,* before the said *Irish Acts,*
Exported vast quantities of *Butter* to *France,*
Spain, Portugal, Flanders, Italy, and into
Ireland itself, and *Cheese* also; but the *Irish*
by the Stop of Importation of lean Cattle,
being put to make another Rent of their Land,
have set themselves to the making of Butter
and Cheese, and do not only supply themselves, but by the cheapness of their Lands do
under-sell us to these Foreigners, and have
therefore in a manner beaten us out of this
Trade; and how much this must affect the
Dairies and *Rents* of *England,* and what the
yearly loss to *England* may amount to, I also
submit to Judgment.   000000

So before the said *Irish Acts, England* did
furnish *Ireland* with *Hats, Stockings, Dying*
Stuffs, Hides, Fruit, Sugars, Tobaccoes, Silks
of all sorts, Gold, Silver, and Silk Lace, and
Ribbons of all sorts. And before the Act of
15 *Car.* 2. *cap.* 7. Intituled, *Trade Incouraged*
(by which the Importation of *Scotch* Cattle
was stopt) *England* did furnish *Scotland* with
wrought Wire of all sorts, Haberdashers Ware,
as Hats, Ribbons, Gloves, Buttons, Bandstrings
of all sorts, Upholsterers Ware, as Hangings,

Stools,

Stools, Chairs, &c. *all sorts of Cutlers Ware,
as Knives, Scissers, Sickles, Scithes, all sorts
of Slop-sellers Ware, as Stockings, Caps, course
Shifts, and Frocks :* By all which, the *English*
Manufacturers and Nation made considerable
Gain.

But the Commerce between *England* and
Ireland, and *England* and *Scotland,* being stopt
by reason of the said Acts, the *Irish* and *Scotch*
do otherwise supply themselves with these
Manufactures, partly by the like Manufactures
set up at home, partly by such other Foreigners with whom they now Trade : And the *Scots*
upon occasion of the said Act of 15 *Car.* 2.
imposed a Tax of 90 *per Cent.* on all *English*
Commodities Imported into *Scotland.* 000000

It is a hard matter to put a just Estimate on these
yearly Losses; for the present I shall leave it to be
computed by our *Melancholick English* Tradesmen.

By means of the same *Irish Acts,* we have
also lost the Exportation of *English Hops and
Beer* from the Eastern, Southern, and Western
Parts of *England* into *Ireland.* 000000

And whereas before the said *Irish* Acts, *England* was the *Storehouse* of *Ireland,* and did
furnish the *Irish* with *Foreign imported Wares*
of all sorts, and our *Irish* Trade did maintain
above 100 *Sail of our Ships sailing between,*
besides what were employed outwards with
Commodities of the growths of *Ireland;* since
the said Acts, the *Irish* are supplied by the
Dutch, or other Foreign Stores and Navigation,
and are much *increased in Shipping of their*
own. 000000

And as if the mischief of these Acts would
never have an end, it may be further observed,

they

they were the occasion of *Increase of Sheep*,
and thereby of a vast *increase of Wool* in
Ireland, by which the *French* and *Dutch*
Woollen Manufactures are now more plenti-
fully supported, and rather cheaper than the
English.   000000

And now the *Irish*, for the former Reasons,
also furnish our *Foreign Plantations*, with very
much of their Butter, Cheese, Clothes, and
other necessaries of the growth and product
of *Ireland :* Considering which, and that those
of *New England* of late furnish the rest with
Flower, Bisket, Salt, Flesh, Fish, &c. (all which
were formerly Exported from hence) we may
expect our *Plantation-Trade* for *Sugar, Tobacco,* &c. must ere long be wholly driven
with *Exported Money, or with foreign Goods
bought with Exported Money,* since by this
means, by the insufficiency of our own home-
Manufactures, and the *growing Luxury* of our
Planters, we are forced to send vast quantities
thither already, particularly, *foreign Linnens
of all sorts, Paper, Silks, and Wines of all
sorts, Brandies,* and other things mentioned
in the next Section, besides great quantities
of Wines sent from the *Madera's,* paid by Bills
of Exchange drawn on our Merchants in *Lis-
bon.* The consequence of the Whole is, that
the loss of the *Irish Trade,* and the consequences thereof, have much assisted in the
Impoverishment of the *English,* (who bear
almost all the Charge of the Government) and
will eat upon us more and more daily; and
on the other side the *Irish,* who lately dealt
so cruelly by us, and are a Conquered People,
are made far richer on a suddain, and that the

Irish Lands do much rise in Rent, whilest the
English sink. 000000

Having given this Accompt of our direct and Consequential Losses by *the Irish Acts,* I expect to be
Answered by some, That howsoever these Acts may
have prejudiced us for the time past, they are *now
expired,* and that by Consequence we shall now be let
into all the advantages we had before the Acts made.
This I shall examine before I go further, and with that
Impartiality as I think becomes an *Englishman,* without
being byassed by the Situation of my Lands: which if
any man does, this Consequence must appear mistaken.

For first, The Manufacturers set up in *Ireland,* will
still Continue to the same prejudice of ours; and 'tis
highly probable (if not certain) that they will Improve,
by the cheapness of their Provision and Wages.

Secondly, Having now long used to fatt their Cattle
(with which they do not only continually Victual all
sorts of Ships, but Forreign Towns, Armies and Nations, particularly the *French,* and those of the United
Provinces, besides the Return they make by the Vent
of their Hides and Tallowes) it is not to be Imagined
that they will be so mad as to give up this far more
profitable Trade.

Thirdly, They will breed, manufacture, and Export
as much Wooll, Butter, Cheese, &c. as before.

Fourthly, These Exportations obliging them to Commerce with the *French* and *Dutch,* as before, it must be
expected that they will generally still buy such Commodities as they want of the *Dutch* and *French;* and
much the rather, because the *Dutch* and *French,* for
Reasons before mentioned, can and will afford them
much cheaper than the *English.*

What Advantages shall we then have by the expiring
of the *Irish Acts?* 'tis confessed, that their Territory

    being

being large, most Fruitful, and now plentifully stored
with Cattle, they may carry on their other Trades, and
yet furnish us with abundant Stores of Cattle for our
Money; which they already do, sending many of their
Cattle near or altogether *fatt :* supposing them *lean,*
yet will not this Nation get 3d. a year by it, but will be
a yearly loser.

For the meer Importing of *Irish* Cattle, did never
advantage this Nation otherwise, than as it secured the
Irish in that base way of Trade, and from turning their
National Industry into a Competition with the *English*
in other Trades; during which time, what Money they
received for their Cattle, they generally laid out in
London, or elsewhere in *England,* for the Commodities
I mentioned before, and others, by which *Ireland* was
stored; But now I do not see how it can be avoided,
but that they will carry out all or the greatest part of
the Money they receive, in *Specie,* which may probably
be little less than 100000*l. per Annum,* I conceive much more than double that Sum, Considering what Victuals and other Commodities
we freight from thence in our Voyages Yearly;   000000
so that the Importing of these Cattle will not
only greatly sink the *Welch* and *Northern*
Rents, but all *other Rents* in a little time;
which must demonstrate the further necessity of Easing
and regulating our Trade equal to the *Dutch* or *French,*
who will otherwise thrust us out of this Trade and all
other, and will give a greater Vent to the *Irish* Commodities daily.   In the mean time we may observe,
that we ought not to be governed by such narrow
Principles as the Situation of our *English Lands,* but
by the National Interest.   Lastly, I shall add, That
should we suppose a Compleat restitution of our losses
in and by the *Irish Trade,* Yet Considering our other
defalcations

defalcations in Trade, and our present Poverty, it would not restore the Ballance of our Trade, or not to any such degree, as to secure the Nation.

Our *Fishing Trade* hath decayed continually of later years; we formerly supplied *France, Spain, Muscovy, Portugal,* and *Italy,* with great quantities of White Herring, Ling, and Cod-fish, which Trade is now lost to the *Dutch, French,* &c. We have only the Trade of *Red Herrings,* which we retain; because, before the *Dutch* can bring their Herrings upon their own coasts, they grow too stale to be cured for Red Herrings: and what a miserable thing is it for our poor starving Natives to see the *Dutch,* and other Foreigners draw such Inestimable Treasures out of our own Seas, and at our Doors? This Fishing Trade (bringing in *no Custom*) was insensibly lost in the pursuit of our *Plantation-Trade,* on which great *Customs* are Imposed. 000000

Mr. *Smith* cited before, reasonably computes other Nations gain, 100000000*l. per annum* by this Fishing Trade only, whereof th e *Dutch* above 50000000*l.* Mr. *Mun* in 63. saith, It was found that all our Exported Fish, of all sorts,amounted to but 140000*l. per annum,* Pag. 184.

So is our *Iseland Fishing* very much decayed, where we have not a fourth part of the Trade we had twenty or thirty years since; the like may be said of our *Newfound-Land Fishing;* and our *Groenland Fishing,* where we had the sole Trade, is quite *lost:* the *Dutch* had far beaten us out of these Trades, but the *French* of later years have struck into a good share of the Whole, beating out the *English* more and more; And by the loss of our Fishing Trade, our National Gain must not only be vastly sunk, but our Sea Coasts are generally impoverished to a lamentable and almost incredible degree, and our Nation is deprived of this great and necessary *Nursery of Seamen.* 000000

Our Foreign Trade for Woven *Silk-Stock-*

ings,

ings, and *Knit Woollen Stockings*, is much decayed, by reason that these Manufactures are
set up in divers foreign Countries, which
(though perhaps they are not, nor for Woollen
Stockings can ever be so good as ours) yet
they greatly hinder our Foreign Vent; and
our late great Trade and Exportation of English *Hats* to *Spain*, is in a manner lost, being
now mostly supplied by the *French*.   .   .   .   000000

Our Exportations to the *Canary Islands* are
vastly sunk in quantity and value, from what
they formerly and lately were; of which I shall
speak more particularly in the next Section .   .   000000

Amongst many other Excellent Materials,
we have in *England* great store of *Tyn and
Lead*, capable of rich and mighty Manufactures in mixture, and otherwise, as appears by
our Imported *Tynned Plates* from *Germany*,
which are computed to cost *England* near
100000*l. per Annum ;* and then what does that
Manufacture bring into *Germany* from other
Countreys?   This Art the *English* were never
taught, but have had a Manufacture of *Pewter*,
made of our Tyn and Lead, of which we made
and exported far greater quantities to *Spain*,
than of late Years we have done, since the
Dutch and others came to share with us in
that Trade, so did we export more of it into
France and *Holland*, in which Countreys 'tis
now prohibited.   We now Manufacture very
little of our Tyn and Lead, but export these
materials to be Manufactured in other Nations,
to whom we are little better than the Miners;
and though some Forreigners have lately
taught us to make better Pewter than before,
yet the bulk and exportation of it is much less.

Our

Our exported *Tyn* is sunk more than *half* its
former forreign *Price*, and our exported *Pewter*
above *a third*, as is also our exported *Lead.* . 000000

Perhaps more instances might be given of decayes in
our Exportations of late Years, though it may be considered that we never had many Exportable Manufactures of very great bulk and value, nor in truth any but
that of our Wooll; so that if we so much fail of our
former gain in this Commodity, it must strike deep on
our former Ballance; But much more if we also fail in
so many other Exportations and Beneficial Trades.

And after these losses in our Exporting Trade, a
further Estimate ought to be made of the decay in our
Trade from *Port to Port;* for though the *English* never
were, nor since the *Dutch* began to trade could be,
considerably Masters of this kind of Trade; Yet may it
be presumed, that whilst we kept the *Monopoly of Cloth*,
our Merchants by the Barter and Vent of this Commodity had then more advantagious Opportunities of
Buying and Selling Forreign Goods in Forreign Ports;
and the rather, because it not only gave the *English*
an extraordinary Reputation, but a real preference in
those Parts they then principally Traded to; besides,
the former *Privileges* the *English* long enjoyed in *Muscovy*, enabled them to so much of this kind of Trade as
related to that Empire, which advantage we have lost by
the resumption of those Priviledges, whereof I shall say
more.

But perhaps I may be told, That all our before mentioned Defalcations in the beneficial parts of our Trade,
have been made good by the Accession of the *Plantation-
Trade* in the Reign of King *James*, (being within the
Compass of the 76 Years mentioned in the Accompt
from the Mint) and by the Increase of it since; and I
the rather expect this Objection, because this Trade
remaining inclosed to the Subjects of the Crown of

England, who for Want of other Trade are *thrust* into it, it makes a great *noise* amongst us; I shall therefore speak more particularly to it, than yet I have, that I may leave no Holes for Starters.

It may be Alledged, and must be Confessed, That this Trade hath imployed a good number of Ships, and hath brought in great Customs; but nothing of this is to the present question, being only, Whether it hath advantaged the Nation in its Annual gain of Treasure; which I conceive this Trade hath not, if ballanced with the losses the Nation hath received by it.

All the Gain *England* can or ever could receive by this Trade, must be in the Return and Result of those Commodities we import from the *Plantations*, (*viz.* Sugars, Tobaccoes, Dying Stuffs, &c.) in Exchange for so much of our Butter, Cheese, Beer, Woollen Cloaths, Hats, Shoes, Iron-work, and other home-Commodities as we Export thither.

Now that the Labours of the same People in Fishing or Manufactures *at home* did, and would have produced a greater Profit to the Nation than these *Plantation-Commodities*, I think no man, considering what hath been said before, can so much as make a question. In fact our Fishing for White Herring and Cod was deserted for this Trade, and the Continual transplanting of multitudes of our Manufactures and other people, hath inevitably more and more *sunk* and *disabled* us in all Manufactures and home-Employments.

Then for the supposed advantage we have in the Vent of our home-Commodities to the Plantations, 'tis plain they are but our own People; and it must be undeniable, that had the same People stayed in *England*, they would have taken off a far greater Quantity; for whereas we now furnish them with some small part of their Victuals, we should then have supplyed them with All, *viz.* with Bread, Flesh, Fish, Roots, &c. which now we do not; and they would have taken off far more of our Butter, Cheese, Cloathing, Drink, and other home Commodities, when they had them at hand, and had been put to no other shifts.

But our infelicity is yet greater; for our Plantation-Trade (though at the best far less valuable to the Nation than the same People and their Labours at home) is yet grown much worse than it was 20 or 30 Years since, and must grow worse and worse Continually.

This must notoriously appear by what hath been said See before. in this Section, when by means of the late *Irish* Acts, and for other Reasons there mentioned, we are forced to Export unto, and furnish these our Plantations with so much less quantities of our own, and so much greater quantities of Forreign Goods than formerly and lately we did.

Besides which, by a further Improvidence we have lost other advantages in this Trade: Our Re-exporters being to receive back half the Customs (which in this Trade are very mighty) it hath followed, that the *Dutch* coming to be furnished with our *Sugars and Dying Stuffs* much cheaper than the *English*, (as being charged not with half the Customs) have been by that means able to set up and beat us out of the Forreign Trade of *baked Sugars*, of which they bake and vend above 20 times the quantity the *English* do; so do they now use far the greatest part of our *Dying Stuffs*, gaining near as much, if not more, by these Manufactures than the raw materials yield the *English*.

Then, if this Trade did originally subvert or weaken several better Trades, and besides is now less valuable than it was, instead of an Improvement, it ought to be reckoned amongst the defalcations in our present Trade. . . . 000000

And though it be not so direct to the present ques-

131   tion

tion, I shall adde, That we have little reason to boast
of our *Navigation* in this Trade, when it was the occasion of the loss of a more certain and beneficial Nursery
of Seamen and Shipping in our Fishery, when at the
same time the Strength and Business of the Nation
have been so much contracted by the loss of our People,
when our Planters of *New England* having gotten a
Considerable Navigation of their own, do Trade from
Port to Port in *America*, and have in a manner beaten
us out of that kind of Imployment in those Parts; and
when the *Irish Shipping*, together with the growing
Plenties of *Ireland and New England*, threaten the like
in the Trade of *Exportation and Importation.* To all
which may be added, what we ought to expect in case
the *Dutch* may retain and Cultivate *Surinam* as far as
'tis capable, since it will produce as good *Sugars and
Tobaccoes* as any part of *America*, and as much as will
serve the greatest part of the World, if not all.

Nay, these *Plantations* may be Considered as the
true Grounds and Causes of all our present Mischiefs;
for, had our Fishers been put on no other Employment,
had those Millions of People which we have lost or been
prevented of by the *Plantations* continued in *England*,
the Government would long since have been under a
necessity of Easing and regulating our Trade; the
common Wants and Cryes of our People would infallibly
have obliged it; but much of the Industry of the
Nation being turned this way, and the *Plantations*
affording room and hopes for Men of *necessitous and
uneasie Conditions*, and our Lawes mentioned in the
Seventh Section, posting them away, they have deserted
the Nation Continually, and left us intricated and
fettered in private Interests and destructive Constitutions of Trade. And thus, whilest we have been projecting the *Increase of Customs*, we have fed our selves
with the *Shadows* of Trade, and suffered other Nations

132   to

to run away with the *Substance.* I am assured, that
the *English* at *Jamaica* are now near, if not fully treble
what they were when Sir *Thomas Muddiford* was
Governour there, and then they were at least 20000 ;
whence some Conjecture may be made at the rest.

SECT. XII.

Instances in late Increases and Excesses of our Forreign
Importations, and therein of the Decay of some other
of our own Manufactures which supplyed our Home
Uses, viz. *in Linnens of all sorts, more dear fine*
Linnens used; incidently of the late and present
Huswifery of English *Women: In Ticking, in Im-*
ported Woollen Manufactures from Holland, France,
and Ireland; *In Cordage, Cables, Sayls and Sea-*
Nets; in Iron, in Brandy, in Wines of all sorts,
these risen in price; the particular odds in our for-
mer and present Canary-Trade; in Coffee, in Earthen
Ware, Pitch, Tarre, Hemp, Flax, and Forreign Timber
bought dearer, and far more Timber Imported: In
Imported Silks of all sorts; in Laces, and many
other things, and thereupon our late French *Over-*
ballance Considered. To which Added, our late losses
by the French Capers, *and Money Exported to* France
by our Travellers, &c. The National Overballance
inferred, this cleared by a Deduction of our Trade,
with Relation to the Dutch *and* French, *and therein*
of their gradual Increase, and our Decay in Trade;
Whence the Growth of the French *and* Dutch *Reve-*
nues and Strengths observed; a farther Calculation
of our late and present Overballance; incidently of
some further Advantages in Trade Forreigners have
upon us.

IN order to take a right Measure of the *Overballance,*
it is observed in the Eighth Section, That if the

beneficial

beneficial part of our Trade become worse, and the Consumptive Importations increase, it will sooner induce an Overballance, and will cut deepest on the National Stock of Treasure.

Now it will much evidence the Increase of our Importations, if any of our own Manufactures which are of necessary Use at home, are lost, or impaired in any Considerable degree of later Years, because, the People must be then supplyed by the like Forreign Goods, to a greater degree than before.

I shall first instance in *Linnen,* lately a Considerable Manufacture in *Cheshire, Lancashire,* and the Parts adjacent; it was also the Huswifery of our *English Ladies, Gentlewomen* and other *Women;* which general Employment of our *Women,* (although most designed for the private Uses of Families) did keep very many Thousands of Linnen Looms at work in *England,* and did supply the greatest part of our National occasion for Houshold and Coarse Linnens of all sorts.

But all this Manufacture of *Linnen* in *Cheshire, Lancashire,* and elsewhere, is now in a manner expired; and the Huswifely Women of *England* now employ themselves in making an ill sort of Lace, which serves no National or Natural Necessity; most of the rest spend their times much worse, or are *idle,* bringing a Scandal on themselves and their Families; so that there is hadly a working Linnen Loom left in a County: which Idleness and Unprofitable living of our *Women,* gives the *Dutch* a farther great Advantage upon us, whose *Women* are mainly serviceable in Trade.

And hence hath followed a great Increase of Forreign *Imported Linnens* from *Holland* and *Germany, Dantzick,* &c. much of which since the Decay of our Cloth-Trade into those Parts, we buy for Money, Bullion, or by Bills

134   of

of Exchange, besides a prodigious Increase of *Imported Linnens* from *France*, which of later Years hath been estimated to cost the Nation at least 500000*l. per Annum,* which must now be supplyed from other Forreign Parts, and dearer, if our new Prohibition be observed. It hath also occasioned a far greater Home-Consumption of *Indian Callicoes,* &c. bought with Money; and the rather, because the *English* of all sorts use more Linnen than ever, in their Apparel, Beds, Curtains, Hangings, &c. 000000

This Importation of Linnen is also become far more chargeable, by the more general Use of Dear *Fine Hollands,* and other *fine Forreign* Linnens of great Value; which till of later Years were only worn by some People of Quality, and by them very sparingly 000000 Thus also is our Manufacture of *Ticking* in *Devonshire* and *Somersetshire* much impaired, and much more Forreign Ticking Imported: Such is our Importation of Linnen, that at this day an *English* Linnen-Draper who deals for 80000*l. per Annum* in Linnen, doth hardly sell 200*l. per Annum English* of all sorts . . 000000

Suppose all the People in *England* one with another bestow 5*l.* a piece more in Forreign Linnen Yearly, than they used to do; what a Vast Summe must this amount to? And this being of so Universal Use, how soon may the Increase of this Importation alone turn the *Ballance* of the *English* Trade? There is hardly any Nation in *Europe* but hath a Manufacture of Linnen, at least for Home-Uses, except *England;* from *Scotland* we have much, and in *Ireland* it is a growing Manufacture much encouraged.

To this may be added the New Importation of *Woollen Manufactures,* viz. *Cloths, Stuffs,*

and

and *Druggets* from *Holland* and *France*, of a
great yearly value, mentioned in the Eleventh
Section, but proper to be remembered here   000000

And it ought not to be forgotten, that no
sooner had the *Irish* learned to make *Frize*,
but presently *Irish Frize* became a great fashion in *England*   000000

Our Manufactures of *Cordage for Ships,
Cables, and Sea-Nets*, are also much decayed
from what they were, much occasioned by the
late dearness of Imported Hemp and Flax, as
hath been intimated before, and we are therefore forced to import much more of these
Commodities from the *Dutch* and *French; the
Act of Navigation not Prohibiting the Manufacture;* which is worthy to be observed . .   000000

There hath been a great Increase of imported *Iron* from *Swedeland, Flanders,* and
Spain; by this means many Iron-Works are
laid down already in *Kent, Sussex,* and *Surrey,*
and elsewhere; and the rest must suddainly
follow (if the Importation continue,) which
will bring at least 50000 Families in *England*
on the Parish-Charge, and must sink the
price of all the Woods now employed for Iron-
Works to little or nothing. Imported Wire
hath already beat out our home Manufacture
of Wire   000000

Our *English* Distillations of *Strong Waters*
of all sorts, did formerly serve the National
Uses, but of late years, our people at home,
and Mariners abroad, have been supplied with
Imported *Brandy* from *France* and *Germany,*
which being hardly known in *England* within
less than 20 years, hath of late cost the Nation above 100000*l. per Annum*   000000

So hath the Importation of all sorts of *Foreign Wines*, vastly increased of later years, especially out of *France*. We have also bought *French* Wines *dearer* than formerly, and have bought them with our *Money, Bullion,* or by *Bills of Exchange;* but formerly with *our Exported Commodity* 000000

Besides which, we have vast quantities of Imported *Spanish Wines,* which till of later years, we also Purchased with our *exported Commodities,* at the rate of 10*l. per* Pipe, but now at about 20*l. per* Pipe, and mostly with *Money, Bullion,* or *Bills of Exchange;* so that 'tis Computed that of later years it hath cost *England* near 200000*l. per Annum,* in Imported *Spanish Wine,* over and above the value of our Commodities Exported to the *Canaries* 000000

The Canary Wines are computed at about 13000 Pipes yearly, which at 20*l. per* Pipe, amounts to 260000*l. per Annum;* and that our Commodities Exported thither do amount to about 65000*l. per Annum*

So, even *before the stop of French Wines,* we had very much more *Portugal* and *Rhenish Wines* Imported and consumed at home than ever; besides *Italian, Greek,* and *Smyrna* Wines; if the Importation of *French Wines* continue prohibited, we must expect as much more of these and *Spanish Wines* as will answer our present General Debauchery: many of these Wines were hardly *known* in *England* of late years, and the rest far more sparingly drunk; but our Imported Wines do now in the Whole cost the Nation the greater part of a Million *per Annum* 000000

Thus do we *swallow and piss* out inestimable Treasures, and contemn our own excellent and more wholsom Drinks, which might be improved to a much greater Perfection, both for our Use at home, and Trade abroad; and whilst every one is an Ambitious

137   Pretender

Pretender to a Critical Palate in Wine, and is ready to impeach the Guilty Drawers for *Mixtures, Molossus,* and *Arsenick,* we are contented to let our Brewers abuse our own Liquors as they please.

And as if the *English* could affect every thing because it is Foreign, we have also a new chargeable Importation of *Coffee,* which of all others seems to be most useless, since it serves neither for Nourishment nor Debauchery   000000

We have also had a vast Increase of imported *earthen Ware* from *Holland,* most of it made of *our own Earth and Lead*   000000

To these ought to be added such other *Importations,* as are now bought much *dearer* than *formerly,* spoken of before, but fit to be remembered here: Such are *Pitch, Tar, Hemp, Flax,* and *Timber* from *Norway* and *Liefland,* being also mostly bought *with Money,* since the decay of our Cloth-Trade into those Parts; and of these the yearly *quantity* of *imported Timber* of all sorts is vastly *increased* of later years, by reason of the Decay of our *English* Timber; so that we are overballanced in our Trade for these Commodities several 100000*l. per Annum*   000000

Nay our so much boasted *Turkey Trade* is so far infected by the general Disease, that we now yearly Export almost as much *Treasure* to *Turkey,* as the value of our Cloth Exported thither amounts to. Of late years we Exported little or no Treasure thither; Nay, I have heard that formerly we imported Treasure thence. In Exchange for the Treasure and Cloth now Exported, the principal Commodity we Import is *raw Silk,* this serves our own Silk Manufactures most consumed at home, except Silk-Stockings, for which our chief remaining Foreign Markets are *Cales* and *Hamburgh*. This Cloth-Trade depending on the vent of Imported Silk at home, is already considerably checked by the continual Increase of *Imported raw Silk* from the *East Indies*, where our *Indian Company* buy it with *Exported Treasure*; this year they have Imported more than ever. This last Sale they exposed to be sold no less than 563 Bales of Raw Silk 000000

The *English* formerly wore or used little Silk in City or Countrey, only Persons of Quality pretended to it; but as our National Gaudery hath increased, it grew more and more into Mode; and is now become the Common Wear, nay the ordinary Material for Bedding, Hanging of Rooms, Carpets, Lining of Coaches, and other things : and our *Women*, who generally govern in this Case, must have *Foreign Silks ;* for these have got the Name, and in truth are most curious, and perhaps better wrought, as being most encouraged. Of the same humour are their Gallants, and such as they can influence; and most others. Our ordinary People, especially the Female, will be in Silk more or less, if they can; though never so plain, stained or tattered : Whence hath followed a vastly *greater Importation, and home-Consumption of the dear Silk-Manufactures* from *Venice, Florence, Genoa, France,* and *Persia,* and of late from *Holland;* where they have improved their Silk Manufacture to a considerable bulk and perfection. This our Affec-

tation

tation and Use of foreign Silks having apparently much increased, within about Twenty or Thirty years past, must produce a great Odds in the Ballance, and besides hath much contracted the *home-vent* of our *Woollen-Stuffs and Cloths*, and *Beggered our own Silk-Weavers*. And it may be here taken notice of, as one of the mischievous Consequences of our present *Importing Trade*, That our Merchants to preserve their *only* home-Market, must bring in such curious and serviceable Foreign Manufactures as will beat out our own. This Importing Trade agrees well with our Shop-keepers, who can get more by Foreign Commodities, (of which, few or none know the Prices but themselves, and the Merchants)   000000

We have also of late a very chargeable *Importation of Laces* from *Venice* and *Genoa*, but most of later years from *France*, all which are commonly called *Points de Venice*, amounting to a vast Sum yearly   000000

Of All others our late *Overballance* in the *French Trade*, hath been most Prodigious; and such have been the Arts to attain it, that it would require a particular Treatise by it self: But it will be necessary to what I have undertaken, to give some brief Accompt of it, and in what it did consist; and the rather, that something of the Variety of the *French* Exportable Manufactures and other Goods may Appear. I shall In *Anno* (63) begin with what Mr. *Fortrey* reports in his Book twice and (73). Printed, and Dedicated to his *now Majesty*, and therefore I presume of good Authority.

He tells us, That upon a Jealousie the *French King* had conceived of the Ballance of the *English* Trade, there was an Estimate thereof given in to the *French*

King;

King; whereby it appeared, that there was yearly Exported of *French* Goods by the *English*, to the value of 2500000*l. viz.*

1. In Velvets plain and wrought, Sattins plain and wrought, Cloth of Gold and Silver, Armosynes and other Merchandizes of Silk which are made at *Lions*, of a great value.

2. In Silk-Stuffs, Taffeties, Poudesoys, Armosyns, Clothes of Gold and Silver, Tabbies plain and wrought, Silk Ribbands and other such like Silk-Stuffs as are made at *Tours*.

3. In Silk Ribbands, Galloons, Laces, and Buttons of Silk, which are made at *Paris, Rouen, Chaimant, S. Eslieres* in *Forests*.

4. A great quantity of Serges, which are made at *Chalons, Chartres, Estammes*, and *Rhemes;* and great quantities of Serges made at *Amiens, Crevecoeur, Blicourt*, and other Towns in *Picardy*.

5. In Bever, Demicaster, and Felt-Hats, made in the City and Suburbs of *Paris*, besides many others made at *Rouen, Lyons*, and other places.

6. In Feathers, Belts, Girdles, Hatbands, Fans, Hoods, Masks, gilt and wrought Looking-Glasses, Cabinets, Watches, Pictures, Cases, Medals, Tablets, Bracelets, and other such like Ware..

7. In Pins, Needles, Box-Combs, Tortoiseshell-Combs, and such like.

8. In Perfumed and Trimmed Gloves, that are made at *Paris, Rouen, Clendosme, Clermont*, and other places.

9. In Papers of all sorts which are made at *Auvergne, Poictou, Limosin, Champaigne*, and *Normandy*.

10. In all sorts of Ironmongers Wares that are made in *Forrests, Auvergne*, and other places.

11. In Linnen Cloth that is made in *Brittany*, and *Normandy*, as well Course as Fine.

141   12. In

12. In Houshold-stuff, consisting of Beds, Mattresses, Coverlids, Hangings, Fringes of Silk, and other Furniture.

13. In Wines from *Gascoigne, Mantois,* and other places on the River of *Loyer,* and also from *Burdeaux, Rochel, Nante, Rouen,* and other places.

14. In Aqua-vitæ, Cyder, Vinegar, Verjuise, and such like.

15. In Saffron, Castle-Soap, Honey, Almonds, Olives, Capers, Prunes, and such like.

16. Besides 5 or 600 Vessels of Salt loaden at *Maron, Rochel, Bovage,* and the Isle of *Oleron,* and Isle of *Rhee.*

But that the Commodities *Imported* out of *England* into *France,* consisting chiefly of Woollen Cloathes, Serges, Knit Stockings, Lead, Pewter, Allom, Coals, and all else did not amount to above a Million yearly, which left the over-ballance 1600000*l.*

'Tis true, that since this there was an Estimate of the *French* Overballance taken in *England* by some *English* Merchants, from the Entries of the Port of *London,* by which it was computed, that the *French* Overballance amounted to about a Million; This was presented by our Merchants to our Lords Commissioners upon a Treaty of Commerce with *France* in (74.) (which came to no conclusion) and afterwards to the *Parliament;* which seems to impeach the Estimate of the *French* Overballance reported by Mr. *Fortrey,* as to the *Quantum.*

This I need not contend, since if the *French* Over-ballance had been no more than a Million, it was enough to impoverish us, considering our Importations from other Forreign Nations; But that I may not totally desert Mr. *Fortrey,* I shall take notice, that this *English* Computation was taken from the Entries of the Port of *London* only, from whence there may

not

not be any so Just a calculation for all the rest of our
Ports; and that the Entries do not comprehend any
of those *French* Commodities which were prohibited
by our former Laws, and are therefore Imported without Entry, which are accompted to amount to some
Hundreds of thousand pounds yearly, perhaps near to
another Million. But on the other side, that the
French Entries must be certain as to the Exportations
from *France;* that Mr. *Fortrey* would not be willing to
falsify with *His Majestie* of *England,* nor the *French*
Ministers with the *French King,* in a matter so important.

Nor is it to be thought that our Importations from
France decreased in quantity or value since Mr. *Fortrey*
wrote, to the time of the Prohibition, but rather increased; whereof our Merchants then gave an instance
in *Wines and Brandies,* from the Entries of the Port
of *London,* as followeth :

'From *Mich.* 1663 to *Mich.* 1664. There was Im-
' ported into the Port of *London* 6828 Tuns of French
' Wine, and then the quantity of Brandy was so small
' and inconsiderable, that it deserves not to be noted.

'From *Mich.* (67) to *Mich.* (69) There was imported
' into the Port of *London* in the said two years, 17000
' Tuns of French Wine, and of Brandy about 3000
' Tun.

'From *Mich.* (72) to *Mich.* (74) Was Imported into
' the Port of *London* 22500 Tuns of French Wine.

'From *Mich.* (71) to *Mich.* (73) Was Imported to
' *London,* 7315 Tuns of Brandy.

'From *Mich.* (73) to *Mich.* (74) Was Imported to
' *London,* as near as can be computed, 5000 Tuns of
' Brandy, and every Tun of Brandy consuming about
' 5 Tuns of Wine, makes the quantity of 25000 Tuns
' of Wine.

This I the rather take notice of here, because from

hence

hence it doth also appear, that the Additional Impositions on French Wines and Brandies by our Parliament in (67) did not make the Importation of them less tolerable or practicable than before, and therefore were only Impositions on the English Subject.

Nay, the *French* have been able to *raise* the Prices of *their Wines* and *Brandies* upon us, even since (67) as the same Merchants represented.   For,

' In (67) Langoon Wine in *France* was not above ' 43 Crowns *per* Tun, clear aboard.

In *Anno* (68) the price was . .	47 Crowns.
In *Anno* (69)	54 Crowns.
In *Anno* (70)	52 Crowns.
In *Anno* (71)	55 Crowns.
In *Anno* (72)	50 Crowns.
In *Anno* (73)	56 Crowns.
In *Anno* (74)	70 Crowns.

' And all sorts of Clarrets are risen double the price, since the year (67).

So said the Merchants in the year (74) and whosoever will take the pains to look into the Custom-Books, will find a mighty Increase of Imported French Wine and Brandy since (74) to the time of the Prohibition; and that, for several years last past, our Importation of French Linnen, Silks, and other Commodities, have also continually grown upon us, whereof we have an infallible Evidence in the continual Rising of our Customs.

I have heard that the quantity of French Wines Imported in 1676 made about 36000 Tuns of Wine, and that about the years (50) (51) and (52) the quantity yearly Imported was about 3000 Tuns of Wine.

But on the other side, the *French Policies* have been as industrious to suppress our *English Trade*, upon which they have gradually imposed more and more Taxes, and at last so great, that it amounts to a Pro-

hibition

hibition; as may be instanced in our Woollen Manufacture.

' In the year 1632, the Duty on an English Broad
' Cloth Imported into *France*, was 6 *Livres.*

' In *Anno* (44) it was raised to 9 *Livres.*

' In *Anno* (54) to 30 *Livres.*

' In *Anno* (64) to 40 *Livres*, and yet did the English
' continue to Export considerable quantities of our
' Woollen Cloathes into *France.*

' But in *Anno* (67) being after Mr. *Fortrey* wrote, it Mr. *Fortrey*
' was raised to 80 *Livres*, which is about 50 *per* first Printed
' *Cent.* his Book in (63).

' A piece of Serge in *Anno* (32) *per* 1 *Livre.*

' In *Anno* (54) 5 *Livres.*

' In (64) 6 *Livres.*

' In (67) 12 *Livres*, which also amounting to about
50 *per Cent.* was equal or worse than an express Prohibition; so that all our Exportations of our home-
Commodities to *France* in the year 1669, amounted
but to 171021*l.* 6*s.* as it was Calculated from our own
Entries (if my Copy be true.)

It will not be a Digression to shew how Industrious
the *French* Polices have been to suppress our Trade to
other Nations.

It is now about five years since that our Merchants,   Mr. *Mun*
observing the *Dutch* & other Neighbour Nations to of Forreign
be in War, but ours in Peace; they had now golden Trade *pag.*
hopes of driving a mightier Forreign Trade than ever; 149. Notes,
' That all the
for which purpose they thought it convenient to buy ' great Losses
' we receive
many *Dutch-built* Ships, and somwhat the rather ' at Sea in
because they had lost many Ships in the late War: ' our Ship-
' ping, either
But the Act of Navigation standing in their way, they ' outward or
obtained His Majesties License for it. ' homeward
' bound,
But thereupon, there presently came out a *French* ' ought to be
Edict for the seizing of all *Ships bought in any Enemie's* ' considered
' in the Bal-
Country, which did discourage many of our Merchants ' lance; for
145   from ' the value of

from buying any Ships, yet many were bought and escaped safe to our Ports; these and many *English* Ships our Merchants forthwith freighted and sent out, in prospect of a swelling Trade, and vast Returns of Treasure.

But immediately there came out swarms of *French Capers*, who seized on those Dutch-built ships, though they had all necessary Passes; and from thence, finding the sweetness of it, they fell to taking of our *English-built Ships*, on pretence they carried Enemies Goods, whereof they themselves would be the Judges, and did actually seize all sorts of *English*-built Ships, laden meerly on the account of *English* Merchants, they took meer *English Coasters*; nay, they *retook* many of our Ships which had been actually *discharged* in *France*; they plunder'd our Ships, and grievously beat and wounded our generous Seamen (who never before dream't of any thing but the Sovereignty of the Sea) and killed many.

Then were our Ships carried into the *French* Ports, and our Merchants put to prove the property of their own Ships and Goods before *French Judges*, in the new erected *French* Admiralties, by a long and tedious proceeding; by which, and also in the *French* Court, and by the *Treachery of their own Agents*, they were put to vast Expences.

There were about 400 Sail of our Merchants Ships seized in this manner, many of which the *French* thought fit absolutely to condemn; and such as were released were kept, some three Months, some six Months, some twelve Months, and some longer, and then were Discharged with great Damage, by Plunder and Expence in *France*, besides the first Violences; and after all, lost the intended Fruit of their Voyages, of which, doubtless the *French* were very sensible: And what is yet worse, the *French King* making the

utmost

utmost advantages of every thing, got Thousands of
our Seamen by extraordinary Pay, to engage in his
Service, to which he doth still indear them by Money,
and all imaginable encouragements.

All which being done in times of Peace, could only
be intended to impoverish and disable our Merchants
Trade and Nation, notwithstanding their pretence of
carrying Enemies Goods: this is evident as well from
the *said Edict*, and from the Nature of the whole
Transaction, as by another *Edict* set forth by the
French King about the same time, giving Liberty of
Trade to any Nation (without exception) that would
take *French* Passes; for it being foreseen that the
English would not take any, because of the *English*
Claim to the *Sovereignty of the Seas*, it left other
Nations then at enmity with *France*, at Liberty to
take Passes, and by Consequence to Trade; who
accordingly did, and traded without controul, particu-
larly the *Dutch:* So did the *Swedish* Ships at the same
time openly Trade *to and from Holland*, and other
Countries then at *enmity with France;* without any
Disturbance from the *French* Capers.

This might administer further Considerations; I
shall only at present accommodate it to the Matter in
question, being the *Overballance of Trade;* which must
needs have been the higher upon us, as our Merchants
received more Injuries and Losses of this Nature.

To this I shall add, that it is an incredible Sum of
Money which our English *Gentlemen and Travellers*
of all sorts spend yearly in *France*, to learn unprofitable Apish affected *French* Fashions, and Modes in
their Carriage, Talk, Cloaths, Eating and Drinking.
It is below any of these *English Mounsieurs* to enquire
into the *Trade* of *France;* This Expence is not near
ballanced by the Expence of the *French* Travelling
Gentry, or others in *England;* the *French* that come
hither,

Here may be added the vast Sums and Riches which already are, and Annually will be Transported by Papists to France, and other Parts; but principally to France.

hither, being ordinarily such as come to *get Estates* by
vending *French* Manufactures, Wines and other Commodities, Dancing, Cookery, &c. and when they are
grown Rich, do generally Transport themselves, and
their Estates into *France*, and so Spirit away our
Wealth.

Many of these Losses by the *French*, being
not comprised in the former instances, require a further ample Valuation 000000

I believe other instances may be given of
the late Increase of our Importations, our
National Luxury and folly being such, that our
Merchants find a home-Vent for almost all
sorts of Forreign Goods and trifles in the Universe: These I leave to be added by the observation of others 000000

In the mean time, considering what the utmost gain
of our Trade might be, during the 76 years mentioned
in the Accompt from the Mint, it must be evident
from what I have already said, that we have been *Over-
ballanced* many 100000*l. per Annum*, of later years.
The Particulars I have mentioned in this, and the last
Section, being such as have happened, or worked more
signally and vigorously upon us during the years mentioned in the said Accompt; which (that I may prevent
Alterations) I shall endeavour to clear, by a brief
Deduction of our Trade during the same 76 years,
which I cannot do without some Relation to the *French*
and *Dutch* Trades; of whose *Rise* and *Growth*, and
their Consequential Increase of *Strength* and *Power*, I
shall therefore also give some Accompt.

I shall begin with that of the *English*:

Before the *Dutch* were cemented into States, the
English had far greater Advantages in Trade than any
Neighbour Nation, by *the greater Plenty of our more
excellent Oak-Timber, Victuals, Numbers of Seamen,*

home-

*home-Materials of Manufacture, our great Woollen-Manu-
factures, our Fishery, and other our valuable Commodities
mentioned before :* Besides the *German, Flemish,* and
French Trades. That of the *Sound,* and *Streights,* our
Adventurous Merchants and Mariners in *Edw.* the
Sixth's time Discovered the North-East Passage by
Sea to *Muscovy,* which Trade was before driven by the
Merchants of the *Hans-Towns* a-cross the *Baltick :*
Such was our good success, that by the great Commerce our Merchants brought, and by the Embassies
and Applications of our succeeding Princes, especially
Queen *Elizabeth,* the *Czar* granted them a *Free Trade*
at his Port *Archangel,* (that is) without paying any
Impost ; which he would not grant to others : whereby
the *English* became possessed of the whole Trade of a
great Advantage; besides which, our Woollen-Manu-
factures were not a little improved in Bulk and Value,
by means of those *Flemmings* or *Walloons* driven out
by the Duke of *Alva,* and entertained by Queen *Elizabeth ;* spoken of before.

In this Condition was our Trade when the *Dutch*
United Provinces came to a Settlement, being about
90 Years since ; the *Dutch* hereupon found themselves
obliged to study all Imaginable wayes of Gain by Trade;
For the People driven into these Provinces by the
Spanish Tyranny and Persecution for Religion, were
very *Numerous,* the Country very *narrow,* and yielding
little of the *Necessaries of life,* and the Long and Continual Charge of their War with *Spain* very great;
from which *Necessity* followed much *Contrivance* and
Industry, and thence those *Arts and easie Methods of
Trade* which have wrought so great Changes in most
Parts of *Europe,* if not throughout the world.

First there followed these Alterations in the *Trade* of
Europe ; the *Dutch* fell into a mighty Trade or Employment of *carrying and dealing from Port to Port,* far

beyond

beyond what was ever used in these Parts before; which Trade they engrossed, beating out the *Antwerpians, English,* and all others, Except in what related to *Muscovy,* (secured to the *English* by our Privileges there) and what related to *Spain* during the Wars with that Crown; the *Portuguese,* having before found out the way by Sea to the *East-Indies,* and having by that cheaper passage beat the *Venetians* out of that Trade, and planted mighty Factories and Forces in the *Indies;* the *Dutch* before, the Year 1600, being informed of the Riches of that Commerce by one *Cornelius Houtman* a Fugitive from the *Portuguese,* engaged in a Trade thither, and in the Year 1602, by the Authoity of their Union, established their *East-India* Company; who upon their original Fund, being 600000*l. Sterling,* made so great a progress in that Trade, that besides several Considerable Dividends before made, upon a Compute in the Year 1608, their Stock was increased to near Three *Millions Sterling:* and in this great Carriere very speedily supplanted the *Portuguese* in this Trade: their success was little less in the Fishing Trade for *White Herrings, Ling and Codfish* on the Coasts of *England* and *Scotland,* which they extended beyond what we ever did, incroaching daily on the *English,* being enabled thereto by their more easie Methods of Trade; and the *English* the more disabled by our Application to the Plantation-Trade in the time of King *James,* whereof the Wise Sir *Walter Raleigh,* by the *occasion* of his Travels, taking notice, about 60 years since gave a Caution of it to King *James,* shewing the Reasons, and proving that the *Dutch* then got 1372000*l. per Annum* Sterling by this Trade, by the Accompts he took at several Ports, (and yet he mentions not their Trade in the *Streights,* and but one Port in *France,* viz. *Roan:*) notwithstanding which the *Dutch* still getting advantages upon us, had near beaten us

out

out before the end of King *James* his Reign; and soon after became Compleat Masters of it.

Thus was this our *Fishing-Trade*, of great and certain Profit, and of high Importance for the Support of our Navigation aad Coasts, supplanted; in the place of this, we had our *Plantation-Trade*, of which having spoken so much before, I shall say no more, than that it brought *in great Customes :* Yet, not forgetting, that *King James* succeeding Queen *Elizabeth*, (who to reduce the late portentous greatness of the *Austrian* Family, had supported the *Dutch*) made a Peace *with Spain*, which gave the *English* a particular Advantage in the Trade of *Spain* for a time, *viz.* till the *Dutch* made a Peace with that Crown; and since that hath continued a very beneficial Market for many of our Commodities, being there vended for ready-money: Our Trade to *Muscovy* remaining secured to us by our Privilege there, and our Clothing Trade by our Wooll, and the ignorance of other Nations in that Manufacture. We had a remaining Fishery at *Groenland, Iseland,* and *Newfoundland;* we continued some other Exports of lesser Note mentioned before; but the Woollen-Manufacture being our chief Jewel, we kept the Monopoly of it during the Reign of *King James,* and for the greatest part of the Reign of *King Charles* the First, and generally raised the prices; by all which, and for that our *Imports* were less than of late they have been, the Ballance of our Trade, during the Reigns of these Princes, was kept up to the degree, we may Compute it by the Accompt from the Mint, which though somewhat, was but a *narrow scantling,* considering how prodigiously the *French* and *Dutch* Trades were improved and grew up *by us* continually; yet have we since lost, or much Impaired all these principal Advantages in Trade, as I have already shewn.

Before I shew how these Limbs of our Trade became

151   so

so much disabled, it will be necessary to observe *what Influence* the *Dutch Trade* had upon the *French.*

All the *Exportable Commodities* of any Note the *French* formerly, and till this last Age pretended to, were *Corn, Wine,* and *Salt :* whereof that of Corn was as Considerable as any; the other two being but sparingly Exported, at least in Comparison of what have been Vended of late Years: besides these, they had *Skins, Tallow,* and *Woad,* and some Fruits of little Consequence; which whole Trade could bring in no great matter.

But the *Dutch* being ravenous after Trade, and like Bees thrusting themselves into every Creek or Corner for Commodities to sell again, and barter away for Profit, presently gave a far mightier Vent to the *French Wines,* with which they not only plentifully supplyed most other Nations, but drank good store themselves, being their principal Home-*Consumption;* of *Salt* they took off yet greater quantities, not only for present Merchandize, but to use in their prodigious Fishery. As the Vent of these grew greater, more were provided in *France;* hence also did their *Infant*-Manufactures of Linnen, Silk, Paper, Brandy, and those Numbers of others enumerated by Mr. *Fortrey,* and doubtless many more, grow up to *Gyants;* the hungry *French* tasting the sweet of the Gain, did not fail to supply this busie People, though doubtless not without the Conduct of an extraordinary Wisdom; Since 'tis apparent, that the *Dutch* manner of Trading made the same Overtures See before in to other Neighbour Nations; the wise Sir *Walter* Section the *Raleigh* observed how free and easie they had made 7th Pag. their Commerce by lowering their Customes and Duties; they let in the *French* Protestants by a Toleration, and carefully Superintended the Increase of their Manufactures. Thus as the *French* Shop came to have more things of *Delicacy and Variety,* it drew

in

in more Customers, and the *English* amongst the rest;
and as a great part of Trade is driven in *Fantastical
Dresses*, and Toys of many sorts, the *French* took care
to provide an Abundance, with which they *gulled* the
rest of the World: Hence were their *Princes* at first
called *Fashion-mongers*; but they did not rest there,
they soon became *Portentous Tradesmen* in the most
solid and valuable Commodities in the World, and
thence *Lord Mayors* of the Continent; doubtless the
present *French King* thinks it his high Concern, and
values himself upon it, of which we have an Evidence
in his nice and early looking into his great *Shop-Books*
or Entries, to find out the *Ballance* of his Trade with
England, and by making his Shop *easie* in the Approach
viz. by his increasing his *free Ports,* (for in truth, it
would be a very strange Project of Gain, for a Tradesman to set a Toll on every man that comes in at his
Door) the same appears by an hundred other instances.

Thus have the *Dutch* in a *blind* pursuit of their particular Interests, built up a *Prodigie of Power,* which
(having of late propagated a great Navigation of its
own, as I shall more particularly shew) is now so swelling, and of so *Serpentine* a Nature, that it is ready to
devour those who first gave it life.

The yearly value of the late and present *Exports* from
France, may be computed by what the *English* only
took off, which supposing to be more moderate than
Mr. *Fortrey* Reports, (which yet I do not admit) *viz.*
but *two Millions Sterling,* what a vast yearly Sum must
it amount to? Since there is great reason to think,
and I speak upon the best Authority I can meet with,
that the *Dutch* have taken off *seven or eight times* more
yearly than the *English;* For besides the mighty quantities of *Salt, Wine, and Brandy,* which they themselves
Consume, they Export vastly more of these, and *All
other French Commodities,* to other Nations; the *French*

Trade being indeed the *principal foundation* of most of
the ordinary *Dutch* Trade *from Port to Port.*

Besides the *Dutch,* the *Hamburghers, Lubeckers,
Swedes, Danes,* and most or all other Mercantile Nations in this Part of the World, do yearly Freight
themselves at the *French* Ports, (which must be one
reason, and perhaps *as yet* the principal, why the
French Language is become so *Universal:*) whilest the
French take very little Consumptive Commodity from
these, nor yet from the *Dutch* or *English,* but *East-India*
Spice, Callicoes, &c. a Trade which the *French* King
hath also manifestly designed to engage in, by an Asso-
ciation and Contribution of Stock in *France,* and his
Attempts to get footing in divers places of the *East-
Indies;* some time will shew what his Success may be,
or whether *at a Lump,* he hopes to unite the *Dutch*
Trade and Strengths in those Parts to himself, by an
Union of the *Dutch* Provinces and their Navigation to
his present Empire; and whether then our *English* Factories there will be able to preserve themselves against
daily Violations, and utter Extirpation. In the mean
time upon what hath been said, let the Reader compute,
how many Millions Sterling must already yearly enter
into *France,* by the Annual Vent of so Prodigious a
Store of Commodities; it must be much the better part
of *Twenty Millions.* I find it affirmed by a small Piece
lately Printed, Intituled, *An Accompt of the* French
Usurpations upon England; which seems written by a
man of good Judgment, That from the Northern Countries only, the *French Wines* now bring in 25 Millions
of *Florens;* their *Salt,* 10 Millions of *Florens; Brandy,*
5 Millions; their Silks, Stuffs, Toyes, and Fripperies,
40 Millions of *Florens* more. What then do the *French*
receive from all the other Regions of the World, for
these, and other things?

All which hath been visible in the *gradual Increase*
of

of the *French Power*, from the time the *Dutch* Provinces began to Trade. It must be admitted that both before and since the *French* Monarchy became Absolute (this being a great and populous Nation) was able to bring Considerable Armies into the Field ; but they could get little or no ground by Arms on any of their Neighbours, or soon lost what they got : The People were abject and recreant, and more the Ridicule, than the terror of their Neighbours ; the *English* and *Spanish* Treasures and Strengths were notoriously too big for them ; the *English* Conquered them several times ; the *Spaniards* more lately beat them out of *Navarre*, *Naples*, and *Millan*, and by their Faction in *France*, drove *Henry* the 3d. out of *Paris*, and most of his other best Cities, and afterwards not above 80 years since supported the *Holy League* with Arms and Money against *Henry* the 4th, under the Conduct of the *Duke* of *Mayence*; both which Princes fell by the hands of *Priests*; for the *Spaniards* were then the *strongest side.* This Superiority of the *Spanish* Power made all the Kings of *France* from *Charles the 8th*, to *Lewis the* 13th *inclusive*, glad to seek a Support from the *English;* and the more to endear themselves, got to be *Knights* of the *Garter* (except *Francis the 2d.* a King of one year, and no more) these were, *Lewis the 12th*, *Francis the 1st*, *Henry the 2d*, *Charles the 9th*, and the said *Henry the 3d*, and the *4th;* if we go higher to *Lewis the 11th*, who next preceded *Charles the 8th*, we may Compute his Treasure and Grandure by a Reckoning found in the Chamber of Accompts at *Paris*, *of 2s. for new Sleeves to his old Doublet, and three Half-pence for liquor to grease his Boots;* 'Tis like he was the poorer, because he and the rest paid a kind of *Tribute* of 50000 Crowns *per Annum* to the King of *England* for 100 years together; before this, they were almost continually wasted by the *English*, till our *Dissentions at home* called our Forces away,

Heylin's Geogr. 236.

leaving

leaving *Charles the 7th*, Predecessor of this *Lewis the 11th*, to take Possession of what he pleased, except *Calais*.

But soon after the *French* Ports were frequented by the *Dutch* Navigation, we find the State of *France* begin to alter; the said *Henry* the *4th*, having reduced the Holy League, grew a *Mighty Prince*, added *la Bresse*, *Bearne*, and *Basse Navarre* to the Crown, and enjoyed a 10 years Peace, though at last Murthered. *Lewis* the 13*th.* was yet more powerful; besides the *Reduction of the Huguenots*, and of above 300 *Walled Towns* then in their hands, he added or revested to that Crown, the Dukedoms of *Barre*, and *Lorrain*, and other acquests in *Germany*, *Italy*, the *Belgick Provinces*, and other parts of the *Spanish* Dominions; in which, and in *Italy*, he was able at once to maintain *five Royal Armies in the Field*; keeping no less than 120000 Men in Pay and Action for many years together, besides his Garrisons; and yet is the Power of *France* since vastly increased, whereof every man is or has reason to be sensible. I shall refer the particular Consideration of it till the last Section.

He began his Reign in the year 1589, and Reigned till 1610. Next Lewis 13th, who died 1642, and since, the present Lewis the 14th.

In the mean time, I shall only add what I find in Dr. *Heylin's* Book of *Geography*, p. 238, (who being to give an Accompt of the Revenue of that Countrey) tells us, 'That *Lewis* the 11*th* gathered one Million and an ' half of Crowns, *Francis* the 1*st.* brought them to three ' Millions; his Successor *Henry* the 2*d.* to six; *Charles* ' the 9*th.* to seven; *Henry* the 3*d.* to ten; *Henry* the ' 4*th.* from two to five Millions, Sterling.' This he attributes meerly to the more *Despotical Power*, and greater Tyranny of the later Princes; and might be so in some measure : For in the time of *Charles* the 7*th.* whilst in War with the *English*, there was an Act by the Three *French* Estates, that the King might raise Money in case of Necessity; which Power, 'tis likely,

was

was not at first used so immoderately as it was after : However we cannot think *Henry* the 4*th* could *leap* from two Millions to five Millions Sterling, without a great Importation of Treasure, which does not grow on the Peoples backs like Wooll ; the advance of the *French* Trade, and Treasure being the true Reason, we may believe the Revenue of *Lewis* the 13*th.* was raised to more than double this, *viz.* Ten Millions Sterling ; and that since it is doubled again, *viz.* Twenty Millions, (as good Judges of it as I can meet with say, 'tis now above Twenty Millions Sterling) For the Treasures of the World being drawn into *France,* as into a *Gulf,* must answerably advance that King's Revenue, and diminish the Treasures of other Nations ; which 'tis probable is partly the Cause that the Price of most Commodities in *Europe* are sunk ; since according to the former Maxims, if there be less Money in the hands of other Trading Nations than before, they must and will buy for less.

Having thus far pursued the Growth of the *French Trade,* and *Power;* I shall now return to the *English,* as they were invested with the several Trades before mentioned in the time of our two last Kings, *viz.* King *James,* and King *Charles* the First, and shall endeavour to shew, First, how we come to lose the Monopoly of the *Woollen Manufacture;* which was the Effect of many Concurring Causes; the *Dutch* were generally vigilant after all Trade, and particularly this, so much they shared with us long before, that they Dyed, Dressed, and Vended vast quantities of our white Cloaths Exported thither, by which they made an incredible Gain. Sir *Walter Raleigh* about 60 years since, in his Observations on Trade presented to King *James,* proves, *England* in 55 years, had lost 55 Millions of pounds by the *Dutch* Dyeing and Dressing our white Cloaths ; But withal, the *Dutch* by their vast Navigation and Universal Trading, gave them a greater *vent* than we

otherwise

otherwise could do, unless by an equal Regulation of
our Trade, the *English* had been made as Capable;
without any thing of that, this course was taken; one
Sir *William Kokayne,* and other Merchants, hoping to
make an advantage to *themselves,* got a *Patent* for the
Dyeing and Dressing of our Cloaths, with Power to
hinder the Exportation of our white Cloaths; wherein
we have our two usual Expedients in Trade, *viz.* a
Restraint to a Company, and a *Prohibition;* by which
our Vent was lessened, and the *Dutch* the more provoked
to attempt this Manufacture at home; to which they
had great encouragement by their *Situation* for the
Trade of *Germany;* and the rather because our *Hamburgh Company,* who by their Patent have the sole
Trade on that Coast, for about six or seven hundred
Miles, kept but two Staples, *viz.* at *Hamburgh* and *Dort,*
remote from each other, and from many of those Countries which they supplied: So as many of those who
come to our Markets, must pass and repass, through
several Principalities, with much Danger and Payments
of Tolls and Taxes; and besides, we raised our Prices,
and set such terms on the Buyers, that others as well
as the *Dutch,* were much *disaffected;* whereupon an
Opportunity was offered: For about the year 1636.
Two hundred Families of our Manufacturers being
about to forsake *Norfolk* and *Suffolk,* and Transport
themselves to our Plantations, *by reason of the then
Persecution of Dissenters,* the *Dutch* invited them into
Holland, where the *Dutch* did not only entertain them,
but in *Leyden, Alkmaer,* and other places, planted them
Rent-free, and Excise-free, seven years. After these
went more and more *Colonies,* which settled at *Rotter-
dam, Middleburgh,* and *Flushing,* where a fourth part of
the Inhabitants are *English,* or of *English* Extraction:
Besides vast numbers of *English* dispersed elsewhere in
those Provinces.

The *Dutch* having gotten the Manufacturers, had half done their work; they wanted nothing but *Wool*, which if they might have on any tolerable Terms, their Advantages in the way of Trade, must enable them to out-doe us, this they Imported from *Spain, England,* and *Ireland,* and elsewhere, falling amain upon the Woollen Manufactures of all sorts; so that about the year 1640, they pretended to something of a Cloth Trade in *Germany,* and soon afterwards took occasion to supply our *Eastland and Northern* Markets more and more; especially with *fine Cloth;* getting ground upon us continually, they bought our Woolls dearer at first, but have gradually sunk the Prices; our Vigilant Neighbours, *the French,* started with them, or soon followed their Example, as did the *Flemings,* the *Silesians, Polanders,* and some others mentioned before; by all which, these and other Parts of the World were as much supplied with Coarse *Cloths, Druggets, and Stuffs;* but the *Dutch* would not rest here; Trade was their business, and they observed, the virtue of ours (such as we had) depended wholly on *Accidents,* and particularly that of *Muscovy* on our *Privilege;* which therefore they found ways to evacuate, by bestowing Money amongst the Grandees of that Court, and furnishing them with an Objection against our Merchants, as being *Londoners,* and therefore (as they insinuated) must be concerned as Actors in the *horrid* Murther of His late *Sacred Majesty,* which it was in vain for our Merchants to dispute, when the Judges were Fee'd on the other side; this powerful Metal (whereof the *Dutch* are never sparing on such occasions, and therein have a farther advantage upon us) had so radicated their Interests with the *Boyars,* that notwithstanding all Applications in an Honourable Embassy to the *Great Czar* from his *now Sacred Majesty,* by the *Earl of Carlisle,* our Privilege could never be regained.

Soon

Soon after this, there followed two things convenient to be taken notice of for the prevention of misapprehensions on either side; one was, that between the year (50) and (60) we had an Accidental Opportunity of increasing our Treasure with the loss of our People, *viz.* by the Stocking *Ireland* with Inhabitants and Cattle, after the Reduction of the *Irish* Rebels, and by furnishing it with all sorts of Goods and Necessaries, then much consumed or spoiled by the Wars and Disorders there; which on a sudden, brought us almost all the Treasures of *Ireland;* which supposing but a Million and an half, or but a Million, was considerable.

Another, which prevented us of as much Money as we thus got, if not of more, and doubtless exhausted us of some; In the year 1654. the late Usurper *Oliver Cromwell* (whose guilty fears made him Jealous of the *English,* and seek a support from *France*) did in Conjunction with *France* make a fatal War upon *Spain;* which, besides the seisure of our *Spanish* effects, and our vast Losses at Sea in that War, interrupted our Trade *with Spain,* and gave the *Dutch* better footing, but *opened* our *French Trade;* at once weakening the Ballance of our Trade, and the *Ballance of all* Europe.

Thus it was before the year 1660. But in regard our Imports were then of far less quantity and value than they were after, 'tis presumeable that our Trade might be yet beneficial, especially considering our then *Irish* Trade; but our Importations increasing, we find what Mr. *Mun,* a *Principal English Merchant* thought of it, by what he saith in his Book of Trade, Printed in (63.) But, as appears by the Preface, was Written some time before; the words are these, " The whole Trade of "the Realm for Exportations and Importations is now "found to be about the yearly value of four Millions "and a half of Pounds; It may be yet increased "200000*l.* more by the Importations and Consumption

Pag. 61.
As for Mr. *Mun's* proposal to Export Money in Trade, I have spoken to it before;

160   " of

"of Foreign Wares, by this means we know the King
"shall be a Gainer near 20000*l.* (*viz.* by the Customs;)
"but the Common-wealth would lose the whole 200000*l.*
"and the King shall be sure in the end to have the
"greatest loss, if he do not prevent such unthrifty
"courses as do impoverish his People." By which words,
I take it as very plain, that before he wrote, our Exportations and Importations were computed to stand
even; which is the more enforced by the latter words,
viz "That the Commonwealth would lose the whole
"200000*l.* the People be impoverished, and the King
"the greatest loser at last.

and besides, he recom-mends the Reduction of the Customs, and easing of Trade, which (if fully done) it might be then con-venient.

Then if we compute our Losses since (60),
nay, or (63), *viz.* By the means of the Acts of
Navigation, which (though first begun by the
Rump, to the prejudice of Trade in their time)
have been since made Laws, and continued to
our greater and daily growing prejudice. . .   000000

    By all our direct and Consequential Losses
from the *Irish* Acts mentioned before . . .   000000

    By the Loss or decay of our *Scotch* Trade .   000000

    By the Stop of our Exported Cloathing into
France   000000

    By the setting up of more Woollen Manu-
factures in *Portugal, Swedeland,* and the *Pala-
tinate,* (to which last Countrey went some
Thousands of our Manufacturers within less
than Twenty years) and by the Increase of
these, and of the *Silesian, Polonian, Dutch,
French,* and *Flemmish* Woollen Manufactures
ever since, by which our Vent must be answerably Contracted.   000000

    By the continual sinking of the Forreign
Price of our Cloathing.   000000

    By the decay of our *Iseland, Groenland,* and
Newfound-Land Fishing-Trades.   000000

To these and all the rest, add what losses have accrew'd by inclosing our African Trade to a Company and Joynt-Stock, and by the Act of 15 Car. 2. 7. Licensing the East India Company, and all others to Export Treasure and such other late losses, as being men-tioned in the 4th, 5th, 6th, 7th, or 8th Sections, have been omitted in this and the last By Section.

By the sinking of the Foreign Price of our
other Exports mentioned before. . . . .　000000

And lastly, in a Lump by a continual vast
Increase of our Importations of all Sorts and
Species mentioned in this Section, with an
Exportation of Treasure answerable to the
Whole. . . . .　000000

Our Overballance appears to me to be so much of
late years, that it might be wondred how any of our
late Treasures could yet remain amongst us, did we not
also Consider that our Trade by degrees, in length of
time, had before the year (60) brought a great Treasure
into *England*, and that these our latest Prejudices and
Losses have not been working upon us many years.
But if the Overballance continue, it must soon sweep
away what remains; which Mr. *Fortrey* Prophetically
foretold in these words :

"Hereby it may appear how insensibly our Treasures
"must be exhausted, and our Nation Beggared, whilst
"we carelessly neglect our own Interests, and Strangers
"abroad are diligent to make their advantages upon us.

Sir *William Temple*, in his excellent Treatise of the
Dutch, does presage the like.

Pag. 231, 232, 234.　Having laid it as a Ground, That "Whatever the
"Exportation wants in value, to Ballance, the Importa-
"tion must of necessity be made up with ready Money ;
"he tells us, That by this we find out the Foundation
"of the Riches of *Holland*, as of their Trade, by Cir-
"cumstances already rehearsed ; for never any Countrey
"Traded so much, and consumed so little ; they buy
"infinitely, but 'tis to sell again, either upon Improve-
"ment of the Commodity (*viz.* by Manufacture) or at
"a better Market : (*viz.* in the Trade from Port to Port.)

"By all this Accompt of their Trade and Riches, it
"will appear that some of our Maxims are not so
"certain, as they are Currant in our Common Politicks :

"As

" As first, That the example and *encouragement of*
" *Excess and luxury,* if employed in the Consumption
" of Native Commodities, is of advantage to Trade; the
" Custom or humour of Luxury, and Expence cannot
" stop at certain bounds; what begins in Native, will
" proceed in Forreign Commodities; and though the
" *example rise among idle Persons, yet the Imitation will*
" *run into all degrees,* even of those, by *whose Industry*
" *the Nation subsists :* and besides, the more of our own
" we spend, the less we shall have to send abroad; *and*
" *so it will come to pass that while we drive a vast Trade,*
" *yet by buying much more than we sell, we shall come to*
" *be poor.*

" Whereas, when we drive a very smal Traffick abroad,
" yet by selling so much more than we bought, we were
" very Rich in proportion to our Neighbours. This
appeared in *Edward* the Third's time, when he maintained so mighty Wars in *France,* and carried our Victorious Arms into the heart of *Spain,* Whereas in the
28*th* year of that King's Reign, the Value and Custom of all our Exported Commodities, amounted to
294184*l.* 17*s.* 2*d.* and that of our Imported, but
38970*l.* 03*s.* 06*d.* ; so as there must have entred that
year into the Kingdom, in Coin or Bullion, or else have
grown a Debt to the Nation, 255214*l.* 13*s.* 08*d.* and
yet we then carried out our Woolls unwrought, and
brought in a great part of our Cloaths from *Flanders.*

Whence Two things may be remarked : First, That
'tis much in vain to increase the value of our Exports,
if at the same time we increase our Imports to a yet
greater value, being now (perhaps) an 100 times more
than *their then* value.

Secondly, That although *Edward* the Third revived
the Order of the *Round Table,* he did not perform his
great Atchievements by the meer virtue of Knight
Errantry ; there is no doubt but our succeeding Princes

were

were enabled to make their Conquests in *France*, by the advantages of our former Trade, then far more considerable than the *French*.

I shall only add, that this Consumption by our Importations, will not be prevented, but rather augmented by our *late Prohibition of* French *Goods;* as I shall demonstrate in the last Section.

SECT. XIII.

That a Considerable part of our late Treasure is exhausted: Application to our Publick and Private Revenues: Objections Answered, viz. *The Plenty of Money to be let on Securities, Stores of Money in* London, *Stocks in Merchandize, the Over-weightiness of our Coin,* &c.

After what hath been said, it may seem little requisite to enquire whether Mr. *Fortrey* Prophesied a-right, when he foretold the Exhausting of our Treasure.

If the Diffusive Body of the People be much Poorer than before, they have much less Treasure than before; For Poverty is but the privation of Treasure. Now if the Question be whether the Nation be Poorer, it must be undeniable from all those Badges of Poverty I have mentioned before, if any of those particular Men who find themselves *at ease*, are yet unwilling to believe it, they may be further convinced from the universal Cries of the People, (at least from the Land-holders, remaining Manufacturers, and their Dependants who make up the gross and stanch Body of the Nation) they remember when it was otherwise, when there was a far greater plenty of Money in all our inferiour Cities, Corporations, and Villages; when our Farmers had their Rents before

164   hand,

hand, and had Stocks for every Farm; when they and our Manufacturers got Estates, and when vast Taxes could be readily raised; and therefore are the most proper Judges of the odds, who feel the present Scarcity, and want of Money; they cannot conspire in a Falsity of this Nature, but in so general and near a Concern, The Voice of the People hath been taken to be like the *Speech of God.* Those that find their Stocks wasted, or much Contracted, their late Revenues sunk, their home-Commodities of much less value, their labours in Manufactures turn to less Profit, or to none at all, the poor and their Maintenances vastly increased, the Nation involved in Debts, Money very hard to be gotten or raised in the way of home-Trade, with other Common hardships, cannot be argued out of their Senses; *Crede quod habes & habes,* is no Logick in matters of Interest, but amongst Fools and Madmen; or let Men be never so good at perswading or believing, yet when their Estates and Stocks are thus sunk, they cannot answer the Publick Emergencies by Payment of as great Taxes as before.

I should not say more to prove our National Treasure is much diminished, (taking it to be indisputable; and being sensible, that the over-labouring a Truth, may bring it in question) but having something to offer, by which (as it seems to me) some nearer Conjecture may be made of the Quantity of Money thus exhausted, I shall present it to the Reader, desiring his Excuse, if he think it unnecessary.

So great was the Quantity of our late *Harp and Cross Money,* before the year (60) that according to the best Estimate I can make or meet with, it made about 10 or 15 *per Cent.* of our Common Money in tale in the *Countrey,* and more in *London,* which I do not take to be the meer Effect of our extraordinary Exports in

165 Trade,

Trade, for the years then last preceding, but partly of the Plate then lately Coined, and our Stocking *Ireland ;* but more than either, from our far less yearly Imports of all kinds several years before 1660.

I must refer it to the Memory, or other Information of the Reader, whether he can comply with me in the aforesaid late quantity of *our Harp and Cross Money ;* whatsoever it were, this Money being taken in to be recoined in the year (60) must, when recoined, produce the like Quantity of His *Majestie's Coin ;* besides which, according to the said Accompt in *November* (75) there had then been 2238997*l.* more Coined since His Majestie's Restoration, and since the said Accompt, there hath been yet *more* Coyned; which supposing to be but 600000*l.* had the Money so Recoyned, and since Coyned with His now Majestie's Impression, continued in the Nation, the new Money under His Majestie's Impression, must have been much above Three Millions, I conceive near Four Millions; and then supposing we had Twelve Millions in the Nation, it would have been above 30 *per Cent.* of our currant Money in Tale, more, were our whole Treasure less than Twelve Millions.

Whereas we see at this day, that the new Money of His now Majestie's Impression, does not amount to above 5 *per Cent.* of the currant Money in *the Countrey,* taking one Payment with another, (especially in such Counties as lye any thing remote from *London*) I think not so much.

'Tis true, that in *London,* where the Mint and Merchants are, there is some greater quantity of new money; and perhaps somewhat more of late than usually; because that by occasion of the *late Forreign Wars,* we have had somewhat a better Vent for our *English* Cloths, and a greater Exportation of our *Annual produce* of Corn: But yet in *London* it does not

make

make near 30 *per Cent.* taking one Payment with another; nor I conceive, more than equal the quantity of our late Harp and Cross Money.

Now if the Money *in His now Majesties Impression,* be *less* in quantity than the *Harp and Cross Money,* it must follow, that notwithstanding all the Money since Coyned, we have less Money in the Nation than we had in (59;) if our present new Coyn but equal the Harp and Cross Money, it follows, that we have now no more Money than in (59). And in either Case, that as much of our new Coyn as amounts to the said whole 2238997*l.* and all the other Money Coyned since *November* (75) is also Exported: For though we may still have some Coyn of each of the succeeding years since (59;) yet if all of it put together amounts to no more than the quantity of the Harp and Cross Money we had in (59,) our Stock of Treasure cannot be more than it was in (59:) if less, then our present Stock is less.

And if Millions of our *new Money,* Coyned since (59) be gone, as, I take it, 'tis evident they are; we may reasonably Collect that as much or more of *our old Coyn,* is also Exported (by the old Coyn, I mean such as was Coyned in the Reigns of King *James* and King *Charles* the First, and before) of which we had lately a mighty Store, almost all of it valuable and unclipped, especially *the Gold,* whereof we had an abundance commonly passing in home-Trade and Payments, there is no reason why these Coyns, being as valuable or more, should not be as good a Commodity in Trade as the new.

And accordingly we may to our Comforts observe, that this late mighty Store *of old Gold,* is in a manner totally vanished, those few pieces which remain, being almost taken as Medals, never to be parted with.

If it be said that part of our old Gold is Coyned into

Guinnies,

Guinnies, this will not alter the Case, since our whole new Coyn is no more in proportion to the old, than before is noted.

So of our old Silver Coyn, there is very little remaining, but what is much Clipped, or worn; and therefore not valuable for Exportation. We have those yet alive who can remember what a flowing Treasure we had in all Parts of *England*, before we had any Harp and Cross Money, and are now sensible of the general scarcity and Want of it.

This does let in a further Presumption, that our new Coyn is diminished to a much greater degree, than it appears to be: For, suppose we have now but a moiety of all the old Coyn we had in the year (59), 'Tis plain, that a moiety of the Harp and Cross Money (had it remained) would now hold the same proportion to the old, as the whole did in (59), and so will a moiety of our new Coyned Money: and thus will it be in any lesser proportions.

If the new Coyn come to be *less in proportion* to the old, than it was before, it is an infallible evidence of the *Diminution* of our Treasure, because the old Coyn *could not increase*; But if the new Coyn come to be *more in proportion* to the old Coyn than before, this is no manner of Demonstration of the increase of Treasure, since the decrease of the old Coyn may produce this Odds.

Thus after the Consumption of our old Gold, we have more than twenty Guinneys to one Broad Piece; but I think no body will press it as an Argument of more Gold in the Nation than we lately had; so having lost so great a part of our valuable old Silver Coyn, 'tis no Wonder if our new Silver Coyn seems so much as it doth, especially about *London*; perhaps it hath been a kind of Providence that we have had so much Clipt and worn Money; since otherwise we might have had as little old Silver, as we have old Gold; and might have been re-

duced

duced to our present Store of new Silver Coyn, as we are to our Guinneys, which might have afforded a weighty Argument of the increase of our Treasure.

Upon these Grounds, and upon the common Wants, Necessities, and Decays mentioned before, it may reasonably be concluded, That besides the loss of most of those Millions Coyned since His Majestie's Restauration, we have lost many more Millions of the old Coyn in Silver and Gold; I shall leave the quantity to be computed by the indifferent Reader: Those who set out the said Accompt from the Mint, taking notice of the great consumption of our Treasure by reason of its being Exported, did by the same Paper, then estimate it to be reduced to about four or five Millions, and by the Nature of that Accompt, they seem no unfit Persons to make some competent Judgment of this Matter.

Whatsoever our Coyned Treasure was when this Accompt was made, 'twas plainly much less then, than it would have been, had none been Exported; and though it must be admitted, that our late Exportation of our Annual Corn, and what other advantages we had during the late War, may have somewhat helped us, yet we have reason to think it farther diminished now, especially considering our losses at Sea by the *Dutch,* and others, before we dis-engaged from the late War, and since by the *French* and *Algiers* Pirates, and the mony lately and daily exported by *Papists* departed hence; to which may be added what we must now further export by the expiration of the *Irish* Acts, and the *dear buying* of these goods we imported from *France,* already added to the former Overballance of our Importations.

Then let the Reader judg what we are to hope for in our *private and publick Revenues,* I shall only endeavour to put him into a method of conjecturing, leaving the compute to his greater ingenuity and leisure. Suppose

we

we have now 5, 6, or 7 Millions of Treasure in the Nation; let him consider how much of this must constantly lye in the *hands of Traders* to attend the payment of Customs, and the buying up of our vast importations; how much always is, and must be *actually collected* in *Taxes,* and either lies in the *Exchequer,* or in the hands of Officers; and how much does, and always will lye dead in *Banks* and other private hands; and then, how much will at the same time (*I say at the same time*) be employed in the home-Markets to buy of the annual *Produce of Lands;* perhaps it will not be half of the Whole: Then recollecting that we have 29568000 Acres of Land in *England,* what *Rent* can they yield, one with the other. Admitting this whole Treasure at the same time stirring in the home-Markets, our whole Land-Revenues could not be much; all the help we have is, that we have many *great wasts,* which yielding little or nothing, a greater quantity of this floating money is applicable to the rest; and yet to our sorrow we have found that our rents are mightily sunk, which having not abated so much or speedily as was requisite, our Yeomanry are generally impoverish't.

Then for our *publick Revenue,* 'tis as plain, it must be confined to the stock of Treasure be it greater or less. We have many who seem to resent the narrowness of his Majestie's Revenue and Supplies, and are ready to expostulate why they should not be equal to the *French King's;* let them consider what may possibly be paid out of our Land Revenues thus contracted, and constantly charged with the maintenance of our numerous poor; and besides, that the *English* having by the constitutions of the Government an undoubted *liberty* and *property,* are accustomed to live well, and their Representatives, being a part of themselves, in whose disposition it lies to give supplies or

not,

not, will have regard to their own and the peoples abilities; should they give extravagantly it would be like *Diego's* Will, and must induce many of those sad consequences mentioned before; what then if we should be involved in any long Foreign War, or obliged to any great extraordinary publick Charge in time of Peace, whilst we remain under a consumptive Trade? which I intimate once more to show the necessity of improving our Trade.

I shall now answer some common Objections.

The most usual is, That there is now *as much money to be let on good Securities in* England, *as there are Securities,* or rather more; from whence some infer that there is as much, or more money than ever in *England.*

To this I answer, That on the contrary, it only proves the scarcity of Securities, and therein the poverty of the Nation; for *personal Security* for money being in a manner *lost;* all the floating money to be let out at interest is thrust upon Land-Securities; which (were they all good) would take off much less money than was let out at interest when both Land and Personal Securities stood: But, as the National Poverty hath subverted Personal Security, so hath it crept into the Land; for mens estates are already so entangled with Debts, that there is not one Land-Security in twenty that is good, as dear experience hath now taught us. Then, the Securities being grown so scarce and narrow, 'tis no wonder that there is now as much money to be let out as there are Securities, and more. Thus if a man had 1000*l.* in the Isle of *Shetland,* he would there hardly find any Security for it; which at this rate of arguing would prove the Isle of *Shetland* richer than the Isle of *Great Britain.*

And upon this occasion I shall add, That there is no possible way for restoring the Securities and Credits of

England,

England, but by restoring its Riches; no *Register* can
do it, at least comparable to the other; we may Register our common Poverty, but nothing will make an
ill man value his credit, or able to satisfie for a Cheat,
but his own private wealth; nothing can make a man
who is honestly inclined to do a foul thing, but Poverty
and Necessity.

Another Objection, partly answered before, is, That
there is still as much money in and about London, *as
ever;* from whence they would argue as much money
in the Nation as before.

I cannot admit this fact; if I did, the consequence
is lame and frivolous; however, because there hath
been such a pother made about the money in *London,* I
shall give some further account of it.

I agree that there are considerable quantities of
money always lodging in and about *London,* in some
particular hands: But the reason is, because the King's
Revenue is paid in, and issued out, in and about *London.* There is also the *Mint,* and there do our *principal
Merchants* live, who Trade with so much exported
money or bullion, and keep money dead for the Customs. This is also the great Port for Forreign Importations; and the Country Retailers, who buy them
there and vend them to the people, must send up their
money to *London:* Upon which and the like occasions,
'tis thought near half the money in *England* is in
London: The more is the pity; it were much better for
the Nation that there were more *home-Manufacture,*
with Forreign *Stores* of re-exportable Goods, and a less
proportion of our money; and the rather because it
stagnates for a time in the hands of Merchants, Ban-
quers, and Scriveners; and facilities the culling, melting, and exportation. This being the great *Sluce* of
our Treasure will necessarily draw it from all parts, as
long as we have any in the Nation.

These

These Stores of money in *London* must rather evidence the poverty of the people, who being over ballanced by the money drawn out for Importations and Taxes, and therefore incapable of answering those payments by Bills or Returns to *London;* very much of our Taxes have been sent up in *Carts and Waggons,* and our Country Retailers continually send up money in specie *by the Carriers;* which must drein away that which remains, in a little time: Nor do those Stores of money much spread, or benefit the general body of Traders, even in *London;* who were never so poor or broke so fast (tho never so fine) as now. It is impossible that the occasions, vanities, or the remaining stock of the Kingdom can ever support such a prodigious Increase of Retailers and Shop-keepers as are in and about *London,* being near 100000 in number, when in *Amsterdam* there are not 5000.

Nor is it to be objected, That I have not computed *our present Stores of Merchandize* or Forreign Effects as part of the National wealth.

First, because the present question is about the actual *fruit and produce* of a National Trade in new Treasure; and not about the quantity of our Stores of Merchandize or Forreign Effects.

'Tis true, That if a Nation whose Trade is truly regulated, hath a great *Store-house* of *Forreign Goods, as in* Holland, *or great Forreign effects,* 'tis very possible and likely that these may produce new Treasure; and if they do, then is the National gain in Treasure to be computed, and not before.

For on the other side 'tis possible (even in a Nation that hath a due ballance of Trade) that such Stores and Effects may produce no Treasure; for the Forreign Stores being re-exported may be lost by the perils of the Sea, or Seisures of Princes or Pirates: we may remember the late seisures of the *English,* by the

French

French Capers; the like casualties do attend Forreign Effects, for which we may also remember when our Effects were seized in *Spain*.

But Secondly, Supposing none of those Casualties, yet (as a National Trade may be managed) these stores and Effects shall produce no new Treasure to the Nation; as when these Forreign Goods and Stores are, and must be spent at home; and the Forreign Effects are continually by Bills of Exchange, applied to pay for those Forreign Goods; so if the Merchants are sometimes forced to Import and Coyn some Forreign Bullion yearly, but yet Export it, or the like quantity of Money or Bullion, the Nation gets nothing; and if more Treasure be Exported than is yearly Imported, the Nation loses: in which Case the stock so imployed in Trade doth prejudice the wealth of the Nation; since in the Whole it makes up a monstrous Engin for the Bulgeing out of its Treasure; and that this hath been the Case of our *English* Trade, is plain enough.

Nor can the *Forreign Stock* in such a Consumptive Trade be of any great value, since as some Effects are gotten by our Merchants in one Forreign Countrey, so are debts contracted in another, as long as our Merchants can have credit; and then perhaps our Forreign debts may be near the value of our Forreign Effects, and probably more; or however, cannot be thought equal to our former stock in Trade, when we were not over ballanced.

There are yet other objectors, who admitting much of our Treasure Exported, will excuse our Trade, and assign the cause of it in the *over weightiness of our Coyn*, and the *undervaluing* it in our *Forreign Bills of Exchange, &c.*

These are old inconsiderate fancies, sufficiently refuted before, yet I should be more particular in it, had not Mr. *Mun* in his Book of Trade taken the pains to clear this and the like objections by evident reason and instances, in six several Chapters, beginning at *pa.* 62. proving withal, that nothing but the Overballance of Trade can exhaust the National Treasure; to which therefore I refer the Reader.

SECT. XIV.

People and Treasure the true Pillars of the National strength: The Odds in the different Vse and imploy-ment of people. The absoluteness of the French *Monarchy no cause of the present* French *Grandure: The late Application of the* French *Councils to the Increase of Trade, People, and Treasure; and the occasion thereof. The greater excellency of the Form of our* English *Government. The farther necessity of Improving our Trade from the Modern Treasures and Powers of the* French; *of their Naval force, the* Algiers *Pyracy; how the* French *design to engross all Maritime Commerce; our dangers from* France; *of the present condition of the* Dutch: *That our late Prohibition of* French *Goods will not disable that Monarchy, nor better our Trade; meer Prohibitions of no value: Our great advantages in Trade above* France *and* Holland: *That a speedy Regulation of our Trade, &c. would secure us against all Forreign Powers, and Dangers at home: Of Excises, and other Taxes. The certain Increase of his Majesties Reve-nue; hence, what occasion for a Parliament, &c.*

FRom what hath been said, it is evident that *National power* is not Chimerical, but is founded on *People and Treasures;* and that, according to the different condition of these its true Pillars, it imme-

diately

diately grows more vigorous or languid; that sufficient stores of Treasure cannot otherwise be gotten, than by the industry of the people; and, That till they have it, they cannot pay.

People are therefore in truth the chiefest, most fundamental, and pretious commodity, out of which may be derived all sorts of Manufactures, Navigation, Riches, Conquests, and solid Dominion: This *capital material*, being of it self *raw* and indigested, is committed into the hands of the Supreme Authority; in whose prudence and disposition it is, to improve, manage, and fashion it to more or less advantage; if any individual Manufacturer should permit his *raw materials* to be Exported into Forreign Countreys, or should himself make great store of knots and felters in his Yarn, he would soon have a very slender, or difficult business of it: so great an odds there is in the different disposition of the ordinary industry of the people, that on the one hand, they may be thrust on in the pursuit of private interest, destructive to the publick, and be obliged like *Cannibals* to live by devouring one another, (by which they must continually and inevitably wound and weaken the publick:) when on the other, their ordinary labours, more aptly and industriously methodized, shall as unavoidably aggrandize that Government which protects them; and this without the Midwifery of those Arts, Shifts, and Projections, which otherwise may be found necessary for its more present Support.

More particularly it appears, That the present *French power*, which is now the admiration and terror of the World, hath no other foundation; and therefore is not derived from the meer *despotick Form* of that Government, as some would insinuate, but from a prudent *Relaxation* of the Rigor of it towards the persons and Stocks of the Trading part of that people; this Form of Government being in its nature the most incom-

patible

patible with Trade, of all others; nor probably had Trade ever received any encouragement in *France*, but upon a *necessity*; this Monarchy being become absolute, was yet low, poor, and despicable; beset round about with *Spanish* Forces, Territories, and Allies, and poisoned with *Spanish* Pensions within, and therefore ready to become a *Spanish* Province: It was then that this Monarchy found *absoluteness* without sufficient Treasure was but a trifle: That Arbitrary power might force store of *Blood and Tears* from the people, but not of *Money*, unless they had it: It was then that the opening and growth of the *Dutch* Trade presented an expedient of drawing in greater quantities of the diffused Treasures of the World into *France* by a Machine of home-Manufactures, than the *Spaniards* could directly from their Mines; which therefore was embraced by the *dying hands* of this Monarchy, and supported and improved ever since by a Succession of understanding men: which apparently was not done by any peculiar virtue in this *Form* of Government, but by a necessary Abating of its inherent rapaciousness, which otherwise would have swallowed up every *Sols* of the stocks imployed in Manufactures and other Trade, and thereby would have driven away the people; as may be seen in the *strong* Governments of *Turkey*, *Muscovy*, *Spain*, and others.

The *French* Councils discerning where the true strength of Empire lay, were not so bewitch't with the *lusciousness* of their Arbitrary power as to seek any such extreme execution of it; their policies have long gone another way, as may be infallibly collected from the effects, and by other lights: so long ago as *Henry* the Third's time of *France*, *Bernard de Gerrard* Lord of *Haillan*, a great Politician in his time, presented an excellent piece to that King, intituled, *The Estate and Success of the Affairs of* France, thereby representing

177 *by*

31

by what courses that Kingdom had been, or might be
aggrandized or weakened; amongst others, he highly
recommends the *Support of the Populacy,* beginning

Pag. 195. thus. " The people are by Justice to be preserved in
" *liberty,* as well to *Trade* as to *Labour,* and to do every
" thing belonging to their degree; by these the King-
" dom are *maintained,* and *enriched* in general, and
" particular; if they bear the charge of Tailles, so are
" they to be cherished, defended, and sustained by the
" Nobles, as formerly they were, and now ought to
" be, from the violences and oppressions of their
" Neighbours, and by the King and Justice from the
" *insolence* of the Nobles." For so it was, that the
Nobles or Gentry, being discharged of the Tailles, had
given up the Constitution of Estates; for which, *they*
had been indulged with a kind of *despotick power,*
within their own particular *Fiefs;* from whose barbarities proceeded the greatest sufferings of the people;
whereof this Author is not nice or sparing to give
several instances too long to recite. I have troubled
you with this citation, because this piece was by the
Author Re-dedicated to *Henry* the Fourth, whom the
Author tells in his Epistle, *That his Predecessor* Henry
the 3d. used to read it with an Appetite, and yet the
Author goes so far as to applaud the Antient Constitution of the Estates or *Parliaments* in *France,*
Pag. 207. affirming them to have been the *mutual Succour, Medi-*
cine, and Remedy both of the King and People in all
their Calamities. If we come to the Reign of *Lewis*
the 13th. under the Administration of Cardinal *Riche-*
lieus, we may Judg how vigilant the *French* Councils
were in his time, for the Increase of People and Trade,
by two great Instances mentioned before : First in the
Toleration of Protestants, after a Victorious Reduction
of all their strengths by force of Arms : this mighty
Prince and his wise Ministers overcame all *resentments*

to

to advance and cement the glory of his Empire; so
that 'tis observed by Dr. *Heylin*, "That the Protest- *Geo gr. 176*
" ants never had the exercise of their Religion with so
" much freedom, as they had after the reducing of
" their Forts and Garrisons to this King's obedience.
Secondly, by *moderating of Customs* and Port-duties *Bernard de*
on Merchandizes, which in the Reigns of his Prede- *Gerrard* of
cessors had been raised and accumulated by about *Finances.*
Twenty several *Edicts;* but in *his* time were in a manner taken off, as appears by what Sir *Walter Raleigh* See before
Represented to King *James* about sixty years since, *Sect. 7th.*
cited before; but if we would at once discover how far
the *French Politicks* have inclined this way, we may
observe them as they are Digested and Refined in the
prodigious Book, so entitled, written, as appears,
several years since, (the Authority of which piece,
though already famous, I shall give a farther account *French* Poli-
of) where in the Chapter of Finances, it being first ticks pag.
observed, " That a State is no further *Powerful* than 108, 109.
" proportionably to the Richness of its publick Treasury,
" and the greatness of the yearly Income that main-
" tains it :" it is laid as a farther unalterable Maxime,
" That the *Fundamental* Wealth of a State consists in
" the *multitude of Subjects;* for its Men that *Till the*
" *Ground, produce Manufactures, that manage Trade,*
" *that go to War, that people Colonies, and in a word,*
" *that bring in Money.* To make way in *France* for
the multiplying of Men, divers courses are there dictated *to oblige both Men and Women to Marry, viz.*
By Freedoms and Exemptions in Case they do, and
have many Children, (now established by an *Edict*)
and by Penalties in case they do not; whence it may
be observed, what Estimate the *French* Politicks put
upon *Marriage.*

In the Chapter of the 3*d* Estate thus, " There can- Pag. 67.
" not be too great a number of *Husbandmen* in *France,*

" by

Pag. 68

" by reason of the Fertility of the Countrey; and our
" Corn being Transported into Forreign Countries, we
" ought *to make great Stores of it,* and *have as much as*
" *may be in a readiness,* (which I am told is also so
" ordered by an *Edict.*) *Handicraftsmen and Artificers*
" are no less useful; for besides that Manufactures do
" keep men at work, and *engage them,* they are the
" Cause that the Silk, the Wool, the Skins, the Flax,
" the Timber, and the other Commodities that grow in
" *France* are made Use of, and that Countrey People
" have the means to Barter these things, and put them
" off; especially being wrought into Wares, not made
" in Forreign Parts, we shall grow further Principal
" Manufacturers, as we already are of *Hats for* Spain,
" *and Stuffs for all* Europe; *a Matter of exceeding great*
" *Consequence.* All this quickens Trade, and makes
" *Money* pass to and fro, *which promoteth the Publick,*
" *and therewith at once every one's private advantage:*
" There must be *Merchants* also, for without their
" Industry, the Artificers Shops would be Stores never
" emptied, the Granaries would remain full of Corn,
" and the Cellars of Wines, &c. In the Chapter of
General Orders, Usury is thought fit to be Prohibited
(which is accordingly suppressed by an *Edict :*) I shall
leave it to Enquiry, whether most of the rest of these
Politicks relating to matters at home, are not established by other *Edicts;* if the Reader would further
observe, how curious the *French* Politicks are to provide for the Increase and true Use of Populacy, I shall
refer him to the Thirteenth Chapter of this admirable
Tract, directing the *Education of Children,* and when
'tis fit to *Marry* them; and to the Chapter of *Commerce,* or rather to the whole piece. By all I have
said, it appears, that although the *French* Kings have
assumed an Arbitrary Power, the *French* Politicks have
not *rested* upon this as a *Security,* but for the Aggrand-

izing of that Monarchy, have found it necessary to *relax and retire* from the severity of this Power, and to resort to *popular Principles :* a Matter which may deserve the Consideration of our *New Polititians* the *Hobbists,* who place all the virtue of the *French* Government in its *absoluteness :* In the mean time I shall add, that notwithstanding what I have said, I do not pretend that the Condition of the *French* People, though made tolerable to the *French,* is comparable to the happiness of those whose greater Freedoms and Enjoyments are secured by Fundamental Laws and Constitutions : But this I shall observe, That whereas formerly, when this People were wretchedly poor, almost every small new Imposition begot an *Insurrection* in *France,* as the said *De Gerrard* takes notice, the *French* now pay twenty times greater Taxes, with much more Satisfaction, because they are enabled so to do; and besides can live far more plentifully than before, many of the Traders splendidly, and gain considerable Estates; To all which may be added another particular, in which the late *French* Politicks deviate from the usual *Jealous Maxims* of *Arbitrary Government ;* which is a general care to instruct the *Plebeians* of all sorts, in the *Discipline of Arms.*

The late swelling Power of *Spain* after the Suppression of the *Spanish Cortes* or Estates derived from the *accidental* Discovery of the *Indian* Mines, and the present Power of *France* after the Suppression of the *French* Estates, from as *accidental* an Improvement of their *Trade,* have been the occasion that some, out of mistake, or design, have much applauded *that Form* of Government, when it must be Confessed that the same *Indian* Treasure and Trade, would have rendred the same Nations, under the continuance of the Estates, or *England* under its *present Government,* much stronger

181   and

and *more secure*, and this, by the advantages in *this Form* of Government.

Despotick, or *Arbitrary Monarchy*, was for many Ages as great a Stranger in this Part of the World, as *Republican Government*; As the *European* Nations by degrees cast off the *Roman Yoke*, they had before their eyes the Example of their former *Mistress*, the *Common-wealth* of *Rome*, which became Vassalized to her own *Servants*, by the unlimited Power committed to Dictators and Generals; these assuming the Empire *by force*, and *without title*, were uncontrollable by Law, and therefore did not only gratifie *their own* Lusts and just Fears of being supplanted, by all manner of Cruelties, but their *Masters the Soldiers* also, by the Spoils of the Provinces; nay, and of *Italy*, and *Rome* itself; and yet were they very frequently killed, deposed and changed by the same force which set them up: To avoid the Mischiefs on each side, as the Members of this Empire resumed their National Rights, they universally cemented into a third Form of Government, much the same with *ours;* which, if we truly consider it, appears purposely, and wisely Calculated to prevent the Inconveniences of the other two, and yet to take in all that is *excellent in either;* For first, we have a fixt Royal Legal Sovereignty, which filling the seat of Majesty, frustrates the Ambitious hopes of others from stepping into it; Then we have the Constitution of *Parliaments*, by whose Intervention, Liberty and Property are preserved: Thus Revolutions and Oppressions *at home* are prevented. Then for the strength of this Government *outwards* upon Forreign Nations, it must *in the Nature of it*, equal, if not exceed any other, especially absolute Monarchy; not only because its greater *freedoms* capacitate the People to Trade with more advantage, as I shall yet more particularly shew,

182   but

but because the same *freedoms* beget a kind of Generosity and Bravery even in the *common sort,* when Absoluteness of Government debases their Spirits, and reconciles them to the Ignominy of being *beaten,* at least till they acquire a kind of *insolence* by long Service in War, which can hardly be called *Courage.* All Experience hath warranted this odds between Freemen and Slaves; but there is yet a farther odds, when the Quarrel is *National,* especially if espoused both by the King and Parliament; for then the *individual* Animosities of the *Whole* being engaged, the People do not meerly fight for Pay, but out of *Principle,* and in defence of those greater Enjoyments they have at home, when the Vassals of Absolute Monarchy are driven on by the fear of their *Despotical Power,* which they would be glad to see subverted, and themselves delivered.

In an *Absolute* Monarchy, the Fate of the Whole depends upon the *Prudence* of the Monarch; be his Empire never so flourishing, he may by one *temerarious Edict,* or other Act, bring all into Confusion: How great must the Danger then be, when the wisest of Mortal men are often transported by Passions, and otherwise liable to Mistakes? The voluntary Councils of such a Monarch must gratifie his Power by Applauding or Complying with his Resolutions and Sentiments: But what if there come a *weak* Prince? against which there is no Security? Or suppose the King be left an *Infant?* then all goes to wrack: those Armies which were the *support* of the last Predecessor, wanting Business and Conduct, fall into *Mutinies;* all are working their Ambitious ends, many contending for the *Tuition* and Publick Administration; those that have it not, supplanting those that have, whereby the Government is endangered: all which was visible during the whole Infancy of the present *French King,* though

he

he had a *Mother,* and so faithful and wise a Minister
as *Mazarine:* The high Animosities of the *French
Princes* and *Nobles,* carried them into continual Distractions and Civil Wars; so that had the *English,* or any
other neighbour Nation, then been in a Condition to
have supported the Male-contents, they might have Subverted the *French Empire: which mischiefs* are totally, or
in a high measure avoided by the Constitution of *Parliaments;* without whose consent, Laws cannot be altered,
or Publick Innovations made; and who by their course
of *Impeachments* are a continual Check and Awe upon
men of indirect and Ambitious designs: So that
(according to the excellent Motto of our own Sacred
Prince) it may be truly said of *such a Monarchy,* and
its *Parliaments,* that they are to each other *Decus &
Tutamen;* what would have become of the *French*
Monarchy when their King *John* was Prisoner in *England,* had it not been for their Estates, or *Parliaments?*
we have reason to believe, That were that *Crown and
Nation* brought into great Exigencies and Distresses *by
any Forreign Power,* they would be convened again,
the Constitution being not *there* absolutely *dissolved,*
as the said *De Gerrard* observes; nothing can be fatal
to such a Government, but a disunion between the
Prince and Parliament, and therefore a great part of
the transcendent Policy of this our Form of Government consists in the high *Obligations* and *means* of a
Union: the Prince being invested with the mighty
Prerogatives of making War and Peace, Calling, Pro-
rogueing and Dissolving *Parliaments,* and as many
others as fill Volumes, hath such a Controll on the
Parliament, that it is generally to be presumed, they
will ever gratifie him in whatsoever is any way consistent with that *Trust* they are under; on the other
side, the *Parliament,* being the great and High Council,
and their Consent requisite to all new Taxes, whenso-

184   ever

ever the Prince on any emergency desires their Advice,
or a Supply of Money, the People must necessarily
have time to represent their true grievances to him,
whose Princely favour and occasions, will then equally
call upon him to redress what is really amiss; *in which
Commutation* he must have a far greater advantage
than any *bare Tax* he receives; since as it appears, the
true strength of all Monarchies and Governments
depend upon well-being Abilities, and Increase of the
Populacy; which no other Prince hath Comparably so
certain a means to understand and Improve, as he that
hath a Parliament: To all which may be added, that
mutual Affection which must naturally follow these
Endearments, and which must render the Prince and
Nation much the stronger, never to be hoped for in
any other kind of Monarchy: There are yet farther
Obligations to this *Union* between the Prince and
People from a just sense of those fatalities which must
follow a *disunion;* we need not resort farther than to
the Fable where we have an Accompt of a quarrel
between the several Limbs of the Body Natural, whereof
the Consequence was, that every part grew presently
Languid and Impotent, and ready to yield it self a
Feast to the *Ravens.*

If then there be the utmost Advantages on the one
side, and Mischiefs on the other, this is all humane
Prudence can provide; God himself hath done no
more in those Divine Institutions which he hath projected for the Support, Felicity, and Security of Mankind: against which, it hath never yet been accounted
any Objection that they have ben violated; nor is it
any against the form of our Government, that it hath
fallen into some Convulsions; as long as Men are Men,
there will be pravity and irregular Appetites amongst
them, which in some Ages and Circumstances may be
able to give greater Disturbances than in others; if in

any

any Society of Men, unreasonable and destructive Propositions are insisted upon, or reasonable and necessary ones refused, disunions are inevitable : This I say in general, 'tis no part of my design to Rub up old Sores, nor will it, I presume, be expected I should embroil the present Subject by vindicating Sides or Parties ; let the Consequences of former disunions be remembred.

But why should I dwell longer upon Arguments to evince the admirable Frame of our Government, when it is so unanswerably demonstrated by its former Splendid continuance for near 600 years? by the glory of our Princes, who, in Conjunction with their Parliaments, ever were, and thought themselves the greatest and happiest in *Europe :* by their stupendous Atchievements in War, and by the former ready Adherence, and large Contributions of our Parliaments, in what tended to the Advantage or Honour of *England ;* we had no other form of Government in our *Edward* the Third, or *Henry* the Fifth's time, who Successively found Supplies of English *Treasure* and *Courage* enough to Conquer *France ;* our Queen *Elizabeth* since, baffled the *Despotick,* and then tremendous Monarchy of *Spain,* which continuing absolute, is (notwithstanding its vast extent of Territory) one of the weakest in *Europe :* had our *Henry* the Seventh entertained the Overtures of *Columbus,* or our Councils in the Reign of King *James,* or since the wise Observations of Sir *Walter Raleigh,* or followed the example of *France,* and other Neighbouring Nations, in easing and improving our Trade, there is no doubt but the *English* Treasures and Power had far surmounted both the *Spanish* and *French* at this day ; It is notorious that the Subjects of the late *Dukes* of *Burgundy,* under the Constitutions of Estates, or *Parliaments,* for many succeeding Ages, drove a mighty Trade, which gave those Dukes a long Superiority over the *Absolute French* King's, till the

Dukedom

Dukedom became annexed to *Spain,* and the *Spaniards* See Sir *William Temple* of the *Dutch,* cap. 1. by their Persecution for Conscience, and Tyrannous Attempts after Arbitrary Government lost both the Trade and Traders, and Seven of the Provinces, whom they forced into a Republick.

Treasures are those *Vehicles* which carry out men of *daring Spirits,* mighty *Thoughts and Abilities* into the Conquests of Forreign Countries: there is no Nation but hath a *breed* of People naturally more fit for these great Performances than any other, who growing Generals or other Commanders at Land or Sea; or Intendants in the greatest Negotiations, might, this way, prove highly Serviceable to the Publick, and find business for *Pen-men* to write their *Memoirs,* as in *France* they do: whereas, by the want of a sufficient home-Treasure, the more Couragious sort must either be *Hackneys* to Forreigners, or degenerate into *Hectors* or *Thieves* at home, and are killed in Brawles, or are hanged for Murthers or Robberies. The more *Deliberative* generously regarding the common Exigencies, more than their own, may lie under the frowns of Fortune, and great Men, and be thought burthensom and dangerous: there are many other Disadvantages which follow a National Poverty, as hath been noted before, which ought not to be ascribed to this or that mere Form of Government, or temper of the People.

That a speedy and Compleat Regulation of our *English* Trade may yet further appear highly necessary, I shall briefly observe what have been the more Modern Effects of this mighty Trade in *France.*

This may too plainly be seen by the great performances of the *French* in these last Wars, in which, the *French* King hath been able to maintain above 250000 Men in Arms, whom he hath duly paid; and yet such have been his Treasures, That he hath not been obliged to put the event of the War to the *push* of a Battel; but

187   wearies

wearies out his Enemies with Expence from year to
year, and being able to lay up mighty Stores, can keep
the Fields in the *Winter*, when his Adversaries, though
as valiant People as any on the Earth, are fain to lye at
home : Thus watching his Advantages, he hath Taken
and Burnt many strong Towns, laid many Provinces
wast, breathing out Death and Devastations as he goes.
This he hath done in the face of the world, in a War
with near 20 Princes and States, whose lamentable
Sufferings, with the Cries of their People, have long
pierced our ears ; whilst the *French* King grows more
Vigorous and Powerful, and his Armies grow better
Disciplined continually, and hath at last reduced the
Dutch and *Spaniards* to the Terms of a dishonourable
Peace, by exposing their Allies to the *French* Power ;
which hath obliged the rest to a Complyance on his
own Terms ; and now he gives the Law to them All,
keeping mighty Armies on foot to Invade whom he
pleases : But that which is yet more Prodigious is, that
even during this War, he hath been able to carry on
the Building of his present *great Fleet*, consisting of
about 200 Ships of War, plentifully Armed with Brass
Guns, and accurately built for Service ; he hath also
furnished himself with abundant Naval Provisions of
all sorts, at an immense Charge, every Ship having its
distinct Stores and Storehouse, and therefore may be
made ready on a suddain : At the same time, he
hath imployed multitudes of Men in cutting of Canals
through Rocks and Mountains, in making, cleansing,
and securing Havens upon the Coasts opposite, or near
to *England* (whither by degrees, in these two or three
years past, he hath drawn down the greatest part of
his Navy) and at the same time hath answered mighty
Annual Pensions to the *Swedes*, and *Swisses*, (whose
lives he buys with his Money :) besides all the other
vast private Pensions, Gratuities and Aids he bestows

in the Courts and Countreys of other Princes, (by which, perhaps he hath made as great Advantages as by his Arms:) and yet 'tis probable, that in all this he hath not exceeded the bounds of his ordinary Revenue.

That which most threatens the Trade of *England,* is his *Naval Force,* which none of his Predecessors ever had, and were checked if they pretended to it; Queen *Elizabeth* forbad *Henry the 4th.* of *France* (on a suddain called the Great) building great Ships, else she would fire them in his Harbours: Since which the *French* have desisted, till about the year 1664. as may appear by that excellent Treatise, intituled, *A free Conference,* Printed in 1667. by the special Appointment of the truly Honourable the Lord *Arlington,* where *Pag.* 49. we find these words, " Not above three " years ago, *France* was hardly able to set out 20 Ships; " (that is to say, Men of War) now they have 60 large " Vessels ready furnished, and well Armed, and do " apply their Industry in every part to Augment the number, &c. I shall forbear repeating some sharp Reflections which next follow.

And that the *French* King might want no *Seamen* of his own, and might at least *share* in the Gain of *Navigation,* he hath for several years past endeavoured by all Imaginable Encouragements to establish a mighty Navigation in *France;* so that for one Trading *French* Ship there was 20 or 30 years since, there are now 40. For this purpose he hath Propagated a Sea-Fishery, to a very great degree, which Improves daily to the prejudice of our remaining *English* Fishery; and besides, hath yearly educated Supernumerary Seamen on Board the *French* Trading Ships, at his own Charge; so that 'tis to be feared he will stand in little need of Forreign *Seamen* for his Ships of War; or if he do, the *Dutch* have Store, which perhaps he may have for his Money, as 'tis probable he may the Fleets of *Swedeland, Por-*

189   *tugal,*

tugal, and *Algiers*; these his Allies of *Algiers*, (as 'tis said, by the assistance of his Money upon a general Redemption of *French* Slaves) are on a sudden gotten from 10 to above 40 Men of War; and as soon as our Applications in *France* had prevailed with the *French* to desist from taking our Ships, these *Algiers* Pyrats fell upon us, and have continually pick't up our Merchantmen, and Vassalized our Seamen and other People ever since; they now do it before our faces, in our Channel, finding Harbour in the *French* opposite ports, which makes a great Addition to our late Losses; and, which is yet worse, hath so terrified our *Seamen* and *Merchants*, that many already think it necessary to trade in *Dutch* and *French Bottoms*, a Consequence which 'tis probable might be foreseen by some of our Neighbours, who wish we had neither Ships nor Seamen.

<small>Note, most of that Fleet which the *Algerines* had (which was but small) was destroyed by the *English* at Cape *Spartell*, and *Bugia*, about eight years since; They have since Built 40 Men of War, from 20 to 50 Guns and upwards, besides Brigantines, Gallies, &c.</small>

At the same time our Gazetts weekly tell us of great Squadrons of *French* Men of War, proudly ranging in all Quarters of the World, in the *Mediterranean*, in the *East* and *West Indies*, and in our own Seas, viewing the Strengths and Weaknesses, and Sounding and Commanding the Harbours of other Nations.

We find it said in the *Free Conference*, " That " *France* is our Hereditary Enemy, and hath so often " tryed what we are able to do against the enlarging of " their Empire, who have graven it deep on their " hearts, the injury of the Title, which to their shame " *England* bears in all Public Treaties, and her Trophies " in reference to that Crown; This very *France* hath " no greater desire than to take the *Dominion* of the " *Sea* from us, &c.

If we look into the before-mentioned *French Politicks*, they assure us of the same; of which piece, because I so often cite it; I shall first give the Reader some *present* Accompt; and *farther*, when I have done

with it : " The *English* Preface tells us, the Author
" was a person bred up under Monsieur *Colbert,* and
" to shew his Abilities, writ this Treatise, and in Manu-
" script presented it to the *French* King, which was
" favourably received; but afterwards Vanity prompting
" him to publish it in Print, the King look't upon him
" as one that had *discovered his Secrets,* and turning his
" favours into frowns, caused him to be Imprisoned in
" the *Bastile,* where he continued a long time, and
" afterwards was Banished, &c. 'tis like to some place
where he should not be able to aver the same, or
disclose more Secrets; what opportunities he might
have of learning Secrets by his Attendance on Monsieur *Colbert,* whether he might over-hear the Debates
and Results of the *French* Councils, or whether Casu-
ally, or by order he had a View of the Papers, and was
but the servile Compiler, or bare Porter of this Scheme
or Manual of Policies, I leave to be examined; a stupendious piece it is, which being written seven or eight
years since, and presaging so great a part of what hath
followed, gives so considerable an Authority to it self,
that its Credit need not depend upon that of the Author
of the *Growth of Popery;* who, as 'tis hinted in the
English Preface, calls it the Measures of the *French*
King's Designs.

These Politicks having first delineated the Compre- Pag. 162, 163.
hensive and steddy Foundations of the *French* Monarchy, as built upon Trade, Treasure, and Populacy at
home, they then proceed to look abroad, and first they
project the Ingrossing of all Commerce at Sea, and
this *at a lump,* by imploying part of this Treasure in
Building a Fleet of Men of War able to Command it,
in which they say, " All things Conspire to give the
" *French* hopes of Success; the work however is such
" as must be *leisurely* carried on, and perfected by little
and little, so *great a Design continually Alarming*
191 *Europe,*

Europe, Asia, Africa, and *America,* Friends and Foes;
" a Precipitation of it would be its Ruine, Six or Ten
" years time might be Allotted for it: The King may
" keep 100 Gallies, and 100 Ships in the Mediterra-
" nean, and 200 Sail upon the *Ocean,* the more Vessels
" he shall have, the more enabled he will be to recover
" the Expence made about them: The Sea will yield
" Maintenance for the Sea, either by Commerce or
" War; There is Timber in *France,* there is Cordage,
" there are Sails, there is Iron and Brass, *&c.*   When
" things have taken their Course, Seamen will be had
" in time, and the profit that will accrew will afford
" Store, and bring them in *from all Parts of the*
" *World.*

Pag. 165.   " The Fleets with the King might keep upon the
" *Ocean,* would make him Master of all the *Powers*
" *and Trade* of the *North;* yea, though the *Hollander*
" and *English* should *Unite* against *France,* they could
" not avoid their Ruine *in the end;* for how could the
" one or the other make good their Commerce (which
" is all they have to trust to) if they were forced to
" keep great Armadoes to continue it?   The Point of
" *Britain* is the *Gate* to enter into, and go out of the
" *Channel:* Fifty Ships of War at *Brest,* would keep
" this *Gate fast shut,* and they would not open it but
" by the King's Command.—*Thus there would need no*
" *War almost to be made for all these things, nor His*
" *Majestie's Forces hazarded: It will be sufficient to*
" *give his Orders to Forreigners; nor will it be difficult*
" *to cut them out work in their own Countries,* and by
" this means stay their Arms at home, and make them
" spend their strengths there; something of this in its
" place hereafter.

" His Majestie's Power being thus strongly setled
" in each Sea, it will be easie to *secure* Commerce in
" *France,* and even *draw* the Merchants thither from

192   " all

" all parts; I say *secure* Commerce; for till this be
" done, it will ever be incertain and dangerous.

It may not be improper to observe, with some
reference to what hath been debated in the preceding
Sections, what further Expedients the *French* Politicks
dictate in this Chapter, for the *securing* of Commerce:
Amongst others we there find this Caution: " It must
" be studiously prevented that Commerce introduce
" not into a *State, Superfluity, Excess,* and *Luxury,* Pag. 169.
" which are often followed with Ambition, Avarice, and
" a *dangerous Corruption of Manners:* It is added, Pag. 171.
" That it hath been a question offered to debate,
" whether Traffick in *France* should be *managed by Sub-*
" *jects or Forreigners,* to make a short decision; 'tis
" evident that Forreigners must be allowed to gain by
" our Merchandizes, if we would have them take them
" off, if we carry them into their Ports, we shall make
" less Sales; yet, That our Merchants may *share in*
" *the profit,* they may enter into Partnership with
" them, or be their Commissioners here, or Freight
" them themselves, provided they sell at somewhat
" *cheaper Rates,* and *so be content with moderate Gain.* See Sir *Wil-*
Which passages I have cited to shew, That 'tis no *liam Temple*
part of their Politicks *to increase Luxuries or Excess;* Pag. cited be-
nor to inclose their home and Forreign Market to fore, *Sect.* 12.
their *own Navigation or Merchants.*

I have been thus long tracing the *French* Politicks,
and our own unfortunate Methods in the matter of
Trade, and this out of a hope to occasion the Restitution and Increase *of ours*; but have gone so far in the
pursuit, that on a sudden I have step't into a Scene
of Horrors, by a necessary and inevitable Apprehension of the Dangers we are in, from the present *French*
Powers; it is impossible for any man to close up the eye
of his Reason, when he sees a Ghastly Troop of Ruins

making

making their regular Approaches against his Prince and his Countrey, and therein threatening many Millions of poor Innocents, and of these some Millions, who hardly *know their right hands from their left*, with Butcheries and Violations of all kinds; in such a Case, Silence would be the greatest and foulest of Barbarities, and no better than an Apostacy from the sacred Duties of *Allegiance* and *Self-Preservation*.

Shall we flatter our selves with an opinion that the *French* have no inclination to turn their mighty Treasures, Land and Sea-Forces upon us? How poor, weak, incertain and dishonourable is such a Security? Are we so tenacious of every little pretence of Right at home, and so busie to get a Penny, and yet shall be content to enjoy our Lives and Estates by no better a Tenure than the discretion of the *French?* whose Councils are dark and inscrutable, and who by their late Invasion of *Flanders*, contrary to former Leagues and Sanctions, and the then Assurances of the *French* Ministers, have at least demonstrated, that they most intend what they least profess; Is *England* become so despicable a Spot, as not to be worth the Acquest? Is it not equal to *Flanders*, or the *Island* of *Sicily?* Is it not evident that the present *French* King aims at the Trade of the World, and particularly of the North? doth he not want Ports? will it not be more grateful to him to engross the Woollen Manufacture by securing the *English Wooll*, than to stand to our Courtesie? Hath not *England* most other valuable *Materials*, by which he might yet mightily enlarge the Trade of *France?* Can he hope to proceed in his Conquests on the Continent, whilest he leaves so dangerous an Enemy *at his Rere?* Doth he not know the *Spirit* of our People? Are our *Talbots*, and *Bedfords* forgotten? Did he not see us raise a considerable Army the other

See *The Buckler of State and Justice,* Printed in (67) by the special Appointment of the Honourable the Lord *Arlington.*

194   day

day to check his Progress? Is he not exasperated by
our late Prohibition of *French* Goods, which touches
him in the most tender Concern of his Trade? Doth he
not think himself affronted in the face of the World?
What can be so grateful to a Prince Ambitious of Glory,
and to the *French* Nation in general, as to render
those *English*, their *Hewers of Wood*, and *Drawers of
Water*, who have so often Triumphed in *France?* Will
they not endeavour to obliterate that *Title England*
bears in her publick Treaties? Will not such an
Acquist ennoble the name of the present *French* King,
above all those of his Ancestors? What a mighty and
useful Purchase will he have in a *Seminary* of *able Men*
and *Horses*, whose value he hath reason to understand,
and which he may then draw out into his Wars at his
pleasure, what spacious Possessions and Commanderies
would *England* and its *Dominions* afford to his *French*
Officers, to whom it may be no little Temptation to
have the deflowring and violating of our most beautiful
Women, being such as the whole Earth cannot Parallel: A thousand other particulars might be accumulated,
of which it is not the least that here would be a vast
accession of Preferments for the numerous *French
Popish Clergy*, and then what would become of ours?
And shall we think the *French* Councils are insensible
of these Advantages? Have they who have been
nicely *winnowing* all the rest of their Neighbouring
Countreys, forgotten ours? if we resort again to the
French Politicks, we shall have no reason to think so;
we see before what they design upon our Commerce,
from thence they proceed to project Conquests at Land;
The *French Romances* speak us nothing but *Love and
Honour*, and in truth make a very *pleasing divertise-
ment*; but their politicks denounce *Subjugation and
Vassallage :* if we follow them from Countrey to Countrey, what they say of *ours* will appear more considerable;

Pag. 153.

derable; thus they begin: " It *were to be wisht*
" *that the King did add to his Kingdom all the Low*
" *Countries* to the *Rhine,*—It would make him *Master*
" *of the Northern Seas,* &c. (what Progress the *French*
King hath made towards *this Conquest,* and why he
found himself obliged to desist for the present, need
not be repeated, no doubt but the French *bear it in*

Pag. 154.

Memory.) " Secondly, it were convenient the King had
" *Strasburgh* to keep all *Germany* in *quiet,* &c. (Our
Gazetts may inform us what Advances he hath made
towards the reducing this great strength, and that he
is now storing all his adjacent Magazines). " In the
" third place *he had need to have the* French Comte to
" lay a restraint upon the *Swisses,* &c. (This he hath
since gotten). " In the fourth place, *Millan* is ne-
" cessary in respect of *Italy,* &c. (Of this we have yet
heard no more than that he hath been *bargaining* for a
passage by *Casall*). " In the fifth place, *Genoa;*—
" Genoa *would make the King Master of the Mediter-*
" *ranean Sea,* &c. (This he hath so far proceeded in,

The *Genoeses*
of late appear
unwilling.

that he hath obliged the *Genoeses* to harbour his Ships,
and to almost what other Conditions he pleases. In

Beginning
Pag. 183.

the fifth Chapter, Dictating how *France* should act with
Forreign Princes after a most exquisite Scrutiny into
the ill adjusted Councils, and Luxuries of the *Spanish*

Pag. 186.

Grandees, 'tis said, " Their Forces are not to be feared,

Pag. 187.

" Sicily *might easily make an Insurrection,* &c. (We

Pag. 188.

have seen what followed). " *Portugal* is a perpetual In-
" strument for *the weakening* Spain, *&c.* (*So it hath*
" *remained.*) " The *Venetians* and People of *Italy* are
" wise; to reduce them to our Intentions, we must
" work by down-right force, *&c.* The *Pope* will ever
" Consider *France, because of the County of* Avignon:
" The *Hollanders* will keep themselves to our Alliance
" as much as possibly they may,—They are rich. *It*
" *were expedient the King did interpose in their Affairs,*
196   " *and*

" *and that some divisions be sown amongst them :* (we
see what hath ensued :) " The *Swisses* are *Mercenaries,* Pag. 189.
" who will always serve the King for his Money : (*so*
" *they have done ever since*). The King of *Denmark* is
" a Prince whose State is but small, &c. *Sweden* will
" never break off from the Interests of *France,* we Pag. 194.
" ought to consider them as instruments which *for our*
" *Money* we may make Use of to divert the *Eng-*
" *lish* or *Holland* Forces, when His Majesty makes any
" *Enterprize* which *pleaseth them not,* &c. (*Success
hath verified this, and may further :*) " *The Friendship* Pag. 195.
" *of the* Turk *is good for* France, to be made Use of on
" occasion against the *Emperor :* (our Gazetts have informed us what Essays there have been; and at last
the *Turk* was brought upon *Muscovy,* whereby the
Swedish Army in *Livonia* was let loose upon the Confederates.)

   Of All others, these Politicks speak most confi-
dently of the Conquest of the *English;* they observe
that " *We have no Friends,*—and are positive, " that a
" War of *France for three or four years,* would ruine
" us: (which 'tis evident must be said out of a sense Pag. 189.
they have of their *odds* in *National Treasure;* for by Pag. 190.
the Import of the words and Context, they cannot be
spoken on supposition the *French should attacque us
unawares,* (which God prevent) : Hereupon it follows,
" so it seems reasonable that we should make no Peace
" with them, *viz.* the *English: but on Conditions of the
" greatest Advantage to us,* unless the King think fit
" to defer the Execution of this *Project* for another
" time : To make *sure and quick work,* 'Tis farther
thought fit that ways should be found to disable our
Government by great Expences, and by Disunions and
Convulsions; from which 'tis manifest, the *French* are
well aware in what the *virtue* of our *Government* consists, and therefore know how to strike at the *root :*

There

There are divers indirect Expedients proposed, which I shall forbear, being somewhat Prolix, and mixt with Contemptuous and Reflective Expressions: It is enough to observe here from whence these *French Politicks* hope for their *English Harvest*, and that this is the *work at home* before intended to be cut out for us.

See before, Pag.

This *great Prince* hath thought fit hitherto to defer a *formal War* upon us, at least, under that Denomination; but whether he hath deferred the *Project* as these Politicks call it, may depend upon a Consideration of what he hath been *visibly* doing ever since; he hath been since building his Fleet, amassing his Naval Stores, Educating and Providing Seamen and Harbours, wasting and disabling those Neigbouring Empires and States, who being jealous of his Power, might otherwise have interposed in his Carriere, getting those great Passes and Strengths into his hands, by which they might have entred his Countrey; he hath been disciplining a victorious and mighty Army, and exhausting us by his Trade, with a great Addition of loss by his Capers; (the *French* are very curious at Cooking their Morsels before they eat them) and at last hath, as it were, *forced* a general Peace, even whilst he was Victorious, by which he is left at entire Liberty: of which Peace, whilst it was under Negotiation, and drawing to a Conclusion, a wise and noble Lord of our time, gave this his sence to both our Houses of Parliament: " The influence such a Peace may have upon " our affairs, is fitter for *Meditation* than discourse, " only this is *evident*, that by the Preparations we have " made for *War*, (*viz.* in the raising of our late Army, " &c.) and by the *Prohibition* we have made of Trade, " we have given no small Provocations to so mighty a " King, who may be at leisure enough to resent them " if he please; and therefore it will Import us so to " strengthen ourselves both at home and abroad, that

The present Lord Chancellour in his Speech to both Houses Parliament, on the 23d of *May*, 1678.

"it

" it may not be found a cheap and easie thing to put
" an Affront upon us. I need not inform any *English*
Reader, what fatal Apprehensions the same Parliament
had of the Consequences of such a Peace; they are in
ordinary Memory; can we think this Fleet of Men of
War is built to be employed in the Fishery, or to lye
and rot in their Harbours? Can this Army profitably,
or safely be supported Idle? Will he suffer them to be
tainted with Luxury? Will he hazard Animosities or
Factions amongst the numerous *French* Nobles (by
whom this Army is Officer'd) the Mutinies of the Soldiers, or Insurrections of his own People? Will he
not rather send these Armed Heards to graze in our
sweet Meadows, and to gather him fresh Laurels out
of our *English* Gardens?

The Gazett for Monday, *Decemb.* 29. gives us this Advertise-ment. *Hamburgh, Dec.* 22. The *French* have hired all the Vessels in this River, and the *Weser*, which used to go to *France*, and return with Wines, on which they mean to Transport great Quanti-ties of *Oats*, *and other Corn.* (which they are therefore *buy-ing up in these Parts*) to *Calais*, *Dunkirk*, *and other Places on that Coast.*

It may reasonably add to our Fear, that we see the
French King hath lately made so strict Alliances with
Spain, and with *Bavaria*, by which he is farther secured
from any Inroads from those Parts; and that we also
find him so vigilant to prevent our Leaguing with the
Dutch, and to come to some closer Conjunction with
them himself; in which his Ministers use the utmost
Arts, mixt with a sort of Menaces; I cannot but resort
again to the *French Politicks*, where in the close of
those Methods by which the *French* King may obtain
an easie and intire Conquest of *England*, we find it
farther dictated thus, " On the other hand, *our League*
" *with the* Hollanders *should be renewed, and they put*
" *into a belief*, that *we should give them all the Trade*
" *still*, because they have the knowledge of it, and are
" proper for it; whereas (*as 'tis to be suggested*) the
" *French* have no Inclination that way, and Nature
" cannot be forced; they *must be told* that now they
" are come to *the happy time* for advancing their Affairs,
" and ruining their Competitors in the Sovereignty of the

Pag. 192.

199   " Northern

" Northern Seas: we see these Politicks go through stitch in the business. And that upon the Whole they were very unfit to be Printed: no man who had so much Wit as to be the real Author, could have so little as to publish them; and the rather, because of Another Secret amongst the rest very improper to be divulged at that time, *viz.* a Projection how to suppress the Exercise of the Protestant Religion in *France,* as soon as it might be done with Security, in respect of what Assistance or Places of retirement, they might have from Neighbouring Protestants, and yet the Methods proposed are not by direct Severities, which may give us occasion to call to mind *that discountenance of Protestants,* we lately hear of in *France ;* of what Extraction this piece is, I leave to be considered; only adding, that it seems incredible a private *French-man* out of the Mint of his own Brain, could foretel so great part of the *French* Actions for the years succeeding ; That the style of it is Majisterial, much in the *Imperative Mood,* a sort of Expression we find in the Emperour *Justinian's* Institutions, but little suitable to the Address of a Subject to a Sovereign ; 'tis also visible how little labour he uses to evince the highest Conclusions and Maxims of State, which are mostly proposed single, as if agreed upon; should it be admitted the sole work of the supposed Author, the Consequence presses us more nearly, when we see private *Frenchmen* arrived to that ripeness of Policy, and in particular, know *our* Circumstances so well ; What then are we to conjecture of the *Capital* French *Councils ?* I am not so vain as to think so great a Prince as the *French* King, is wholly and meerly Governed by this, or any other Scheme of Politicks, he could doubtless take new measures, as subsequent Negotiations or Accidents, then unseen, have offered; but 'tis as little to be doubted, but there was a time when

he

he sate down and considered the grand Materials of that mighty Tower which we already see mounted so high.

What Success the present Overtures of the *French* King will receive in *Holland*, a little time may shew; perhaps things are gone so far, that the *Hollanders* will not easily be flattered into an Opinion they shall be *Sovereigns of the Sea:* But whether they may close with him upon his Assurances of being Protected in a great degree of Freedoms and Trade, may be a question. They know the *French* King is a Considerate Prince, and must be sensible that they are his *Porters,* That their Countrey being naturally a *bogg,* can be no otherwise valuable to him than by supporting a Trade there, and keeping the People together: They may be told, that the *French* King having already so vast a Revenue, will stand in need of less Taxes from them than they already pay, and can live without picking their Bones; and so it may be, as long as he pleases; 'tis certain this People are exhausted by the War, and know the Strength, and will therefore fear the wrath of this mighty Borderer; the *French Politicks* say, that he will be able to ruine them and us in *Conjunction,* by disturbing our *Commerce at Sea:* He is now in a far better Capacity, by the Neighbouring Acquests at Land he hath since gotten: how soon therefore may he *disable,* or *influence* this People, should they become our *Allies;* and how necessary is it upon the Whole to trust to, and *suddenly* Improve our own Strengths? We see but the other day how they were forced to desert, and give up their late Allies, and are advised by *the best of Councellors,* not to lean too much on a *broken Reed,* lest it *pierce our hands:* This of all others, would be the most fatal, and certain Expedient of our Ruine.

For my own part, I am one of those many whose Life and Interests are imbarqued in the Publick, and

who,

who, upon a general *Shipwrack*, have no Prospect to
get off in the *Long-boat*; but must expect to be swallowed
up in the Common inundation, or if I survive, to die
daily by a sence of my own misery, and the Sufferings
of those that are as near and dear to me as my life.
Self-preservation is a Principle to which God, Nature,
and the Fundamental Constitutions of Humane Society
require us to adhere; I do not project my own Security
only, but that of my Countrey, and therefore hope none
amongst us will be offended at it; if any be, let them
examine with their own Consciences, and others judge,
whether *their* designs are not very *different*; I make no
doubt but that all the generous part, even of the great
French Nation, will think I have done but my *Duty*;
and that, should it ever lye in their Power to afflict or
ease me, which God divert, I could not more certainly
intitle my self to their favour, than by having once
asserted the Interests of this my Native Country.

I shall add, that those our other formidable Neighbours the *Dutch*, having now made Peace with the
French, remain the same Government and People, and
under the same Constitutions and Capacities of out-
stripping us in Trade, as before; nay, of offending us,
especially in Conjunction with *France*, whose Commodities they Buy and Barter off as before; their
Necessities are such, that they will utter more than
ever; unless, perhaps, for Politick Reasons restrained
by some Act of their State.

And now having examined the Different Policies and
Constitutions of Trade in *France*, the *United Provinces*,
and *England*, with the different Operations of it, and
the present Posture of things between us; It must
appear, that in order to our future National Security, it
is indispensably and speedily necessary to improve and
regulate our Trade to the utmost.

And here I was about to conclude, but that several

Persons

Persons have objected, that our Trade is sufficiently regulated by our late *Prohibition of* French *Goods;* this, by what I have said already, must appear a mistake: But that I may leave no umbrage for private Interest, I shall more particularly apply my self to clear it.

Perhaps this *Prohibition* hath *somewhat* prejudiced the Trade of *France,* and may for the next year, which yet I shall not admit.

But supposing this, yet it will not *better* the Trade of *England* (though it might tend to the Security of *England* should the prejudice it brings to the *French* Trade, be so great as to disable the *French* Monarchy,) But this it will not do, for which I shall give these Reasons.

First, upon the Question how much it may prejudice the *French* Trade, I shall observe that the Prohibition it self extends only to *Wines, Brandy, Linnen, Salt, Silk, Paper, Vinegar and Manufactures made or mixed with Silk, Thread, Wooll, Hair, Gold, Silver, or Leather;* Now if we look back in Mr. *Fortreys* Accompt, we shall find many other chargeable Commodities imported from *France;* 'tis true many of them were prohibited by former Laws, but then were, and still may be Imported as freely as before the late Prohibition: The Yearly value of these very Imported Commodities thus formerly Prohibited, have been usually computed at above 500000*l. per Annum.*

Secondly, 'Tis already found, and 'twill be more and more discovered every day that great quantities even of the Goods Prohibited by the late Act, are and will be Imported; For I shall again observe here, that *meer Prohibitory Laws* never did, or can answer the ends they were intended for, being made in restraint of the Effects, without removing the Causes, whilst it remains the Interest of Traders to elude the Prohibition: Nay, the Importation of *French* Goods is now become a far

more

more gainful business than ever; for now the mighty Customs are taken off; which is so much clear gain to the Importers.

Therefore there is no doubt but that private Traders (whose business it is to increase their private Stocks) will Import if they can: Then let it be considered who they are who must make the Seisures; These are the *Officers of Ports*, viz. Searchers, Waiters, &c. upon whose integrity and Diligence all the virtue of this or any Prohibition does depend; Now how Indigent, Mercenary, and Negligent many of these are, we are not to learn; nor are we to expect their extraordinary Industry or Fidelity in this Case; because this Prohibitory Act gives them nothing for their pains; so they must spend their Money and Time in Seisures, and Suits, and all for nothing; besides, we have long Tracts of Coasts and Creeks in *England*, where hardly any Officers attend, or if they do, cannot hinder Clandestine Importations; the Insufficiency of meer Prohibitory Laws is verified by the Prohibited Exportation of Money out of *Spain*, *Portugal*, and *England*, Wooll out of *Ireland*, and *England*, and the Exuberant Importation of many sorts of Goods from *France*, and other Parts long *since Prohibited by our former Statutes*; and yet these Laws give sufficient incouragement to Informers.

See 3 *Edw. c.* 4. 1 *Rich.* 3d. 12. 5 *Eliz.* 7.

Then if the Goods *last Prohibited* may be *Imported*, they will certainly find *Vent*. How few in *England*, if any, can positively Swear this or that is *French* Manufacture on the meer *view?* Nor are our People apt to Inform; and will be less, when it shall come to be the Common Interest of Traders to connive; Nay, our learned Wine-Drinkers will tell us, that the very Wines may be vended in mixtures, making Sack of White Wine and Malaga, Sherry of White Wine and Brandy, Rhenish of White Wine, Porto-Port of Clarets; these

they

they say are ordinary Performances: But to prevent this trouble, our Vintners commonly sell *French* Wine as before.

Upon the Whole, I shall leave it to be computed how *near a Million* our *French* overballance may be, even during the Prohibition, not forgetting the Curtesie of our Merchants, who hearing of the Prohibition, Imported a Store of *French* Goods, to the value of about a Million.

Then considering the mighty Trade the *French* still drive with other Nations, the *French* Monarchy must be so far from being disabled by our late Prohibition, that we must expect it will grow more vigorous and formidable; and the rather because of the flowing Treasures already Imported, and Warlike Stores provided in *France*; so Politickly hath the *French* King managed the matter, that (except his Forreign Pensions) his Wars have Exported little Treasure, since it hath circulated back into *France* by the hands of his *French* Purveyors and Sutlers, and thence again passes to his Exchequer.

I shall now Consider, whether the late Prohibition may better *our* Trade, and how much; which is a question wholly distinct from the other, (though the violence of our common resentments against the *French* make it seem almost the same:) For it does not follow that every thing which will prejudice the Trade of one Nation, shall better the Trade of another: But this falls out to be so, or not, as other Nations are by their Constitutions in Trade more or less capable of Trade; for Example, If the *French* Trade should fail, it would not better the *Spanish* Trade, who by their high Customs and other Cloggs on Trade, are made incapable of it; nay it would hinder the *Dutch* Trade, because the *Dutch* Trade consists so much in Carriage, at least till the *Dutch* could be furnished with the same bulk of

vendible

vendible Commodities from some other Nation; so would the ruine of the *Dutch* Trade from Port to Port injure the *French* Trade, till *their* own, or some other Neighbouring Navigation, could supply the Room of the *Dutch*.

Now if we look back to the Grounds and Reasons of the decay of our *English* Trade, we shall find them to be no other than our own ill Constitutions in Trade, which are not a whit remedied by the *French* Prohibition, and therefore will prevent any advantage we might perhaps otherwise receive from it.

Our Home and Forreign Markets remain obstructed as before, we retain the same chargeable Navigation in all the before mentioned particulars ; we are over charged with Customs, and Interest Money; we are under the same disadvantages by our Act of Navigation, by the Monopolies of our Merchants, of our Trading Companies, and Freemen ; nay of Forreigners upon us : Our Manufactures and other Exportations are now as much confined to the value of the Goods imported, as before ; we have no more Manufactures, Merchants, or other People, no more Ships, or Stocks, in Home, or Forreign Trade, than before; no more National Riches than before ; we have still the same Acts of 5 *Eliz.* 4. The same Acts against Protestant Dissenters : The *Irish* and *Scotch* Trades remain diverted, the same encouragements of Scholar-like Educations, and necessity of the Increase of Shop-keeping; we have the same Laws against the Naturalizing of Forreigners; against the introducing of Forreign Manufactures, Stocks, and Riches ; the same debauched Elections, and all the other burthens on our Trade mentioned before, with the Consequential difficulties : There is the same Exportation of Wooll from *Ireland*, and *England*, and there remains the same Delicacy, Luxury, Drunkenness, and Debauchery.

The Consequence is, That the same Causes will have the same Effects; the growth of our Manufactures will be stifled at home, and their Forreign Vent will remain obstructed: The *French* and other Forreigners will supply the Forreign Market with their Manufactures as they did before; if our Prohibition hath any effect, it will cause the *French* to sell cheaper than they did, which will help them to beat us out more than ever. Which of our Manufactures can receive any greater Forreign Vent?

I expect 'twill be said our Woollen Manufacture, (for we have *Hobson's* choice, and shall wear it threadbare with often naming,) this at the best may be a question; Nay, whether our Vent for it will not be less: *France* will receive no more of it, the *Dutch* and *French* still remain our prosperous Competitors in other Parts, all the other Forreign Woollen Manufactures are still supported and increased, by which the Forreign Markets are already over-clogged with it, whereof the same Causes remain: And now will Forreigners (which have been exhausted by the late Warr) be more hungry and vigilant in this and all other Trade than before: Besides, when the Prohibition of *French* Goods shall make Forreigners see we are under a greater necessity for their Commodities, we must also expect they will take advantage of the Monopoly given them by the Act of Navigation, as the *French, Danes,* and others have done, and will insist to have our sweet Commodity called Money, and reject our Woollen Manufactures; this they can have of our Neighbours the *Dutch,* and *French,* and perhaps cheaper, and as good, if not better; we already buy much of our Linnen at *Hamburgh* with Money.

If our poor Clothiers cannot help us out, I know not what will, for I hear of no new improving Manufactures in *England,* but that of *Perriwiggs;* then for our Trade

       from

from Port to Port, we have as melancholick a Prospect that way: The Prohibition will not better us to the value of a Scullars wages: The *Dutch* and other Forreigners for the reasons before given will run away with it as before, so will they shut us out of the Fishing Trade.

In the mean time our Merchants being confined in their Exportations from home, and disabled from the Trade from Port to Port, as much as before, they must resort to their present Commodities of Bullion, and Money, for ordinary Exportation; and must Import Consumptive Forreign Commodities to be spent at home as before, or else lye still.

Our late particular Overballance in the *French* Trade swelled so high, because the *French* Shop had so great variety of valuable Commodities, and somewhat cheaper, and was nigh hand; which was an ease and advantage to our Importers.

Now suppose they are forbid to go to this particular Shop, and will Religiously observe the Prohibition; yet they may and will furnish us with the same things from other Ports; they will bring us more Silks, Laces, and Baubles from *Italy, Flanders, Holland*, &c. More Linnens and Paper from *Holland, Hamburgh*, and *Genoa*, &c. And more Wines from *Italy, Portugal, Germany, Spain*, and *Turky*; from *Germany* more Brandies: There is hardly any of the *French* Commodities, but what may be had else-where; but with this odds, that they will cost dearer in any other Nations than in *France*, which by so much must increase our National charge in Importations; nay, we must expect that in this alteration of the course of our Trade, our *Importers* will find out new trifles and gewgaws for our silly people: How suddenly do we find all the Women and Children of any account in *England*, in *Amber* Necklaces? Which at the rate they are sold at, must cost

England at least 100000*l*. And now we have a new Sawce called *Catch-up*, from *East-India*, sold at a Guiney a Bottle.

But should it be admitted, That our new Prohibitions would any thing correct our ballance of Trade; yet,

First, The Prohibition is to indure but a year and a little more.

Secondly, A general Prohibition of Goods, being looked on as a most injurious thing in all Nations, and a kind of Denuntiation of War, we must not think to perpetuate ours, unless we resolve to be always under a State of Enmity and War, with the *French*. Then, if this be thought highly inconvenient, what mighty Effects of our new Prohibition can we hope for in such a time?

Thirdly, Should this Prohibition somewhat correct the ballance of our Trade, yet if it does not perfectly restore the ballance, we shall be Annual losers by our Forreign Trade, and compleat the beggary of the Nation.

But fourthly, Should we suppose that it would restore the ballance; nay, that it should render the National Trade of *England* somewhat beneficial, yet it must be confessed, That a compleat Regulation of our Trade would render it prodigiously more beneficial, (perhaps more than all the Trade of *Europe* besides) considering how our advantages in Trade would reduce the Trade of our Neighbour Nations, as ours does improve.

Lastly, The meer restoring of the ballance of our Trade, nay, or a Trade which shall be but a little beneficial, must be very insecure to *England*, in the present posture of things, when some of our Neighbour Nations do already so much surmount us in Treasures and strengths acquired by Trade; and by the future course of their Trade must grow so much richer, and stronger daily. From the whole I conclude, That our new Prohibition is not a sufficient or satisfactory Regulation

of

33

of our Trade, but leaves us open to many fatal and threatning Consequences.

The Reasons of the decay of our *English* Trade being understood, the Disease may be the more easily cured, and the Nation thereby secured, of this we need not to despair, provided the Medicines be *speedily* applied; which I shall endeavour to demonstrate; That after so many *soure Herbs*, I may leave a more Agreeable rellish with the Reader, and so conclude; in order to this, I shall first remember some of our Advantages in Trade.

We have a particular high advantage over *France* in the *Nature of our Government*; under which Liberty and Property are, by Law and publick Constitutions, secured, which must be a vast Incouragement to Trade and Traders, as is noted before.

Whereas the *French* Traders are daily liable to Taxes ahd Seisures at pleasure, which is as great a discouragement.

'Tis true, that the late Councils of *France* having been successively studious how to improve the *French* Trade, have exerted this Power very Judiciously towards Traders, yet are the Taxes high, and Arbitrary, and the Sufferings of the greatest part must make the rest uneasie.

And whatsoever freedoms of Liberty and Property the *Dutch* allow, the *English* have the advantage in the *sweetness and healthiness* of their Countrey, and in the extent of it, the *Dutch* Territory being very narrow, naturally loathsom, and most unhealthy, *nor are the* English *liable to suddain Inroads and Depredations*, as the *Dutch* are on the Continent; which odds will invite Forreigners to plant in *England*, rather than in the *United Provinces*.

But what is yet more, the *English Ports* are numerous, deep, safe, and open all the year; the *Dutch* Ports but few, dangerous in the Approach, unsafe within, and

usually

usually frozen three or four Months in the year, the *French* Ports much fewer, and but five or six that will carry Ships of any great Burthen, and those very far asunder.

England hath, or may have, all the most considerable and desireable *materials of Manufacture* of its own growth, except Silk : which is of a Prodigious Advantage, because the charge of Importing is saved, and its Manufactures may rest *undisturbed by a War at Sea:* whereas the *Dutch* have none, and the *French* fewer than we, particularly they want the excellent Material of Wooll, by which Millions of People at home may be most profitably Imployed.

England is the most *fertile of Nations,* and out of its own Stores, as it might be cultivated, might maintain almost infinite *Numbers of People.* The *United Provinces* so scanty of Provision, that they are forced to buy most or all their Meat and Drink of Forreigners, except Fish (by which as many might be supported in *England*) ; *France* (though fruitful) doth not yield near so much Cattle and Flesh-meat; which is most strengthning and grateful to all, especially Laborious men, and is necessary for Victualling of Ships.

Both in *France* and *Holland* are *great Excises* on most, or all, *ordinary* Meats and Drinks, in *England* on part of our *Drink* only, *viz.* That in Alehouses, and Publick Brewings, (I hope there never will be any such as shall burthen Trade.)

Our great *Wasts, and void Lands,* which are our present Grief and Scandal, may on the Regulation of our Trade, prove highly beneficial to us, since they will afford present room for a vast Increase of People, whether Forreign Planters, or others; in the *United Provinces,* or *France,* none such are to be found.

And lastly, *England* is far better *situated for the Fishing Trade,* and other Forreign Trade than either

France,

France, or the *United Provinces,* and its People are
naturally far more *Adventurous* and *Valiant* than theirs,
as Experience hath shewn, which makes no small odds
upon National Contests, between Nations emulous in
Trade, when they fight upon equal Terms of Treasure,
and Warlike Preparations: and there is no question
but our *National Industry* in Trade, would be also more
Vigorous and Successful, were it put into suitable
methods; but otherwise can no more Exert it self than
a generous Courser in a Horse-Mill.

From all which it must be evident, that were our
Trade eased as in Neighbour Nations, *England* would
have the Superiority, since the same Causes must produce greater Effects in *England,* being invigorated with
these our National Advantages, which no other Nation
doth or can enjoy.

The *present Power* of the *French* King would infallibly much *Contribute* to it, which being arrived to such
a swelling and tremendous height, does not only inti-
midate all men of Trade and Wealth in *France,* especially Protestants; but all the adjacent Provinces and
People on the Continent, who either already groan
under the insupportable Oppressions and Insolencies of
the *French,* or are under deep and Continental Apprehensions of being wasted by his numerous Troops,
grown Proud and Wanton with Success, and ready to
make irresistable descents upon any *private Order;* in
which these his Neighbours can never think themselves
secure, because of his late sudden Invasion of *Flanders:*
and would therefore flye to our *English* World, as a
blessed and safe *Asylum, were it put into a posture of
being so.* Then if the suddain Populacy, Treasures,
Trade, and strength of the small *Dutch Provinces,* were
the Effects of the then *Spanish* Tyranny in the Low-
Countreys, what might we not hope for from far greater
Confluences of the richest and most Mercantile and

Industrious

Industrious Protestants, or such as would be so, even
from *Holland* and *France,* as well as from many other
parts of *Europe?* whose Stocks being transported by
Bills of Exchange, and their Manufactures with their
Persons, and this on a suddain, would give the odds of
Strength and Treasure to the *English,* who no longer
need to trust to the fallible Security of *Leagues,* which
are so often obstructed and broken by the humour or
perfidie of particular men, or frustrated by incapacity
and accidents: And therefore this patching and piecing
a Strength together by *Leagues,* is the dependance of
small and weak estates, such as those of *Italy* and *Germany;* where they are always tricking and betraying
one another; yet at this time Leagues (though not to
be wholly rested upon) *may be* of great, and good consequence to *England.*

Had the *French* Monarchy never over awed the rest
of *Europe,* as it now does, it must be evident, that if
our Trade had been regulated and eased equally with
the *Dutch,* all those Merchants and People which have
setled in *Holland,* would have planted here, where
besides the former advantages, the extent of our Territory renders the Burthen of Taxes far easier on particular men than in *Holland,* where they are also at a
much greater *necessary* charge for Garrisons on their
Frontiers; nay the very *Dutch* would have forsaken
those Provinces for *England,* or if any had remained,
they would have been Carriers for the *English,* as they
have been to the *French,* and will rather be so for the
future, if our Shop were sufficiently furnished, because
they will more willingly transfer the wealth of the
World to a Countrey where they themselves may securely share in it, when they please, than to an *Arbitrary Power,* which may in a moment swallow it up,
and oppress those that brought it to any the most
barbarous degree; from all which, these things are

most

most manifest: First, That nothing does or can so
formidably threaten the Trade, and by Consequence
the Monarchy of *France*, as the Modern Freedoms of
the *English*, and some other Neighbouring Countreys.
Secondly, That the *English* Freedoms are at this day
so great an advantage to his most Sacred Majesty of
England, that they are a Weapon left in his hands,
with which, and a Concurrent Regulation of our Trade,
he may with ease and assurance attain a Superiority
over all the Monarchs and Powers of *Europe* put together; he will cut the Grass under their Feet, and *draw*
away their Treasures and People, notwithstanding all
the Policies can be used: no *mere Prohibition* can stop
those whose Interests, quiet, and safety, shall oblige
them to depart: In which, besides a *sufficient* Guard at
Sea, (to use the words of the *French* Politicks) *there
would need almost no War to be made, nor His Majestie's
Forces hazarded.* Thirdly, That for these Reasons it
is most evident, that it doth highly import the *French*
Monarchy, that the Freedoms of the *English*, and all
others in these parts should be subverted and evacuated,
of which, whether the *French* Councils, who have been
so long and so curiously projecting the Grandure of
that Monarchy, are insensible, I leave to be considered.
Fourthly, 'Tis also as evident, that upon such a Regulation of our Trade His Majestie's Revenue being (by
some *Excise* added to the *then* smaller Customs, and
other his present Funds) made *but equal* to what now
it is, would infallibly swell higher and higher yearly, as
Trade, People, and Treasures shall increase; if *these*
shall become *double, treble,* or *six fold* what they now
are, so would his *Revenue:* then what extraordinary
Supplies in Parliament might he not expect, upon a
National Emergence; nay, or for his own proper occasions, when by an increase of People, the Burthen
upon *particular men* will be answerably eased, and by

the increase of Treasure, and the advance of private
Revenues and Stocks, these People should be enabled
to give *largely*, and *often;* and this without any prejudice to their home-Trade, or Land-Rents, and therefore
with such an Alacrity, as is agreeable to that true
Honour and Affection they really bear him.

I need not observe how much it will be in His
Majestie's Power to secure the making up of his present Revenue by new Funds, should he graciously
think fit to compute by a Moderation of the Customs;
but since I have now, and before mentioned *Excises*,
and have observed some men of Parts, almost to *startle*
at the *naming* of a new *Excise*, I shall thus far explain
and vindicate my self, and the proposal: First, I shall
agree that such *Excises* as affect and over-burthen the
beneficial parts of Trade, are of pernicious Consequence.
Secondly, that an Universality of *Excise* is both inconvenient and unnecessary; But that there may be *Excises* Imposed on many Superfluities, and Excesses, in
Meats, Drinks, or Equipages, or upon some imported
Goods *Consumed at home*, which would be no prejudice
to any kind of Trade; being no clog upon our Exports,
or Re-exports; or perhaps, a very small *Excise* on
ordinary Meats, Drinks, and Apparel, might be supportable: I do not propound all, but some of these, in
this Course there will be this odds of advantage on the
part of the King, That the *Users, Wearers, and Consumers*, being this way made chargeable, His Majesty
would be less liable to be defrauded than in the Customs, which are perpetually smuggled, and then the
Imported Goods openly Vended, and used; This, on
the part of the People, That it will bring the like
Obligations of charge on men of *Visible and Invisible
Stocks*, in, or out of Trade, as on the Land-holders;
and therefore I do not see any shadow of reason why
Excises should appear such Bugbears in *England*, espe-

cially

See Sir *W. Temple* of the *Dutch*, Pag.

cially to Land-holders, any more than in *Holland* and in other Trading Nations, where the Publick Revenues are made to swell high by these small and almost insensible Payments. It is Confessed, that it will be highly fit to provide for a fair and easie Collection, and against the Extortions, Insolencies, and Abuses of Officers; for which we need to go no farther than to learn by what Methods they are collected and ascertained in *Holland*, if any shall misbehave themselves, we have a free recourse to the Law, as in *Holland* they have, but in *France* they have not, though perhaps now more than ever. Nor are *Excises*, or somewhat in the Nature of them, so new amongst us, if we regard the Ancient *Tolls* for things bought and sold in home-Markets; which, although they now seem small, were before the Discovery and Diffusion of the *Indian* Treasure Considerable, and originally belonging to the Crown, but since appropriated to private hands by Grants, or long usuages founded on Grants from the Crown, which having also given *Exemptions* to some Towns, we may presume them first intended for the ease of Manufacturers, of which the Government had an especial regard: having said this, if the Reader will reflect on All that I have said, he cannot think I have any design in beggaring the *English* Subjects by an invention of new Taxes; 'twas Sir *Walter Raleigh's* Opinion, that the smaller and more numerous Payments of Custom, would rise far higher than before, which he Confirms with Fact; be they more or less, the National Wisdom is at Liberty to exert it self in further Levies, by Excise, Land-Tax, Poll, or otherwise as there shall be cause.

Having now written what I intended on the present Subject, the Nature of it may sufficiently assure the Reader, that I have not designed any peculiar Ends of my own: On the contrary it hath been a trouble, which

I wish an abler hand had undertaken, and being for the Publick, may expect what usually ensues, when men engage upon the cutting new of Common Rivers, wherein they must have Contests with every one, who hath a *Lands End* abutting upon the Work, who will set a greater value upon six foot of Earth, than upon all the Good the Countrey, and therein themselves, and all their Posterity, might reap by the Accomplishment of the Business; in which they are generally so tenacious, that they ordinarily ruin the *Undertaker*, and thereby make great store of mirth for the *Cunning men* of the adjacent Villages. I am not insensible how many mens Animosities I have hazarded, by incountring their private Interests, or contrary Inclinations; a thing no way grateful to me, being not one of those (if any there be) that, out of any petulancy of humour, love Contention, or Innovations, or that would appear considerable by opposing something that is already thought so; or that delight in stirring Sediments, or raking into fedities; I affect quiet as much as any man, and account it my ordinary duty to give the least offence I can, even to the little ones. Nothing but a Consideration of our present Difficulties, and a hope to be Instrumental to the publick felicity, could have moved me an inch beyond these common Prudentials: to which I have yet conformed as far as I can; I have touched no man's Person, and I presume I need not say I have forborn Reflections, in which I do not think any one obliged to me, being but what I have judged requisite for a Composure of things; it hath been absolutely necessary that I should represent our ill *Constitutions in Trade*, and some of the *most important Consequences*, that from a general apprehension of the Common Interest, there may ensue a National Union in those Methods which may be most for the Publick

Advantage,

Advantage, and this upon the *mighty Basis* of our present form of Government, and under our present most gracious Prince, whose Glories I hope to see expanded by an exuberant increase of National Treasures, People, and Royal Revenues, and to such a degree, as that the days of our Queen *Elizabeth* shall appear but a faint Type, or dawning of the greater Lustre and Happiness of His now Majestie's Reign: This is what I wish for, and have to my utmost endeavoured, and therein the real Advantage of all Ranks of Men in the Nation; If then these Excellent Ends appear obstructed by a sort of antient or Innovated Laws or Usages, who can speak of them, without much Resentment? In which, I hope, I am Excusable. These are the *Spells* by which our innocent People are inevitably lead into Courses destructive to the Publick.

How can our Merchants or Shop-keepers now avoid Trading in Forreign Consumptive Goods? Have they any sufficient Stores of Home-Manufactures? Can our Merchants Trade from Port to Port as the *Dutch* and others do? or must Men that are bred up to these Gentile professions, that are Men of *Family, Industry,* and *Fortune,* fling up, live lazily, or poorly? Who doth not know how many generous and intelligent Men are to be found amongst our *Merchants* and *Shop-keepers* of all sorts? Such as bear a true affection to their Country, and are an honour to the Nation, and such as wish for a Régulation of our Trade, and would be ready and capable to give all farther assistances, were they called to it? This I wish to see, being not so conceited, as to think I have said all that is material on this Subject; but on the contrary apprehend, That there are very few Paragraphs of what I have written, but may admit of farther Informations: In the mean time, from what hath been already said, it must be

apparent

apparent to these and others, That as an open and free
Trade would be far more profitable to the generality of
Merchants, so would it be far more honourable to all;
That the Consequential Increase of People and Wealth,
would better support our great Increase of *Shop-
keepers, Lawyers, Solicitors, Pen-men,* &c. (of which
the present Numbers would then hardly be sufficient).
That the benefices of our *Clergy* must receive an inevitable Improvement by it. And that our great and
famous City of *London* (which is the Seat Royal, where
our National Courts of Justice are, which is contiguous
to our most secure Harbour for Ships, which hath the
sweetest and most Commodious situation of any City
in *Europe,* and is so vastly peopled already) must by
these advantages, for ever, have the greatest resort and
Trade of the Nation, (even under the utmost Improv-
ments of our Trade) which must then be incomparably
more than now: Besides, the vast advantage our *Gentry*
would infallibly reap by the continual Rising of their
Rents, even such of these as desire more business, or
gain, will then have other and farther daily opportunities, by putting Stocks into Manufactures, or Forreign
Trade, and projecting and solliciting the Improvement
of either, or both. In *Florence,* the very *Nobility* and
great *Duke* himself are *Traders;* hence might our
Members of Parliament be continually prepared to
make the most suitable Laws for the facilitating of
Trade.

Lastly, Nothing can so effectually and certainly
secure the peace of the Nation, as the Regulating of
our Trade, since it will set all Mens heads and hands
at work in all manner of Innocent and Profitable
Imployments, and introduce a general satisfaction and
Harmony.

Then, and never 'till then, shall we make up that
invincible

invincible *Phalanx,* which must not only be terrible to all Forreign Nations, but to all Enemies of the Government at Home, when they find it supported by the solid Pillars of Trade and Treasure, and a Consequential swelling Populacy and Navigation; which will deter Men of sence from Treasonable Machinations, and of Fools there needs no fear: Whereas the defect of these Supports must continually administer temptation to all such as by reason of their particular circumstances, can hope for any greater advantage or security, by the general ruin. The Body Politick being in this like the Natural, more subject to new Distempers when it is infirm before, but when stanch in every part easily bears off the Corruption or Acidity of any malignant humours.

The *Trade of the World* hath long *courted England,* but never with *so much importunity,* or with so much *advantage* as now: This *great Lady* affecting Freedom and Security, hath no Inclination to continue under the *Arbitrary Power* of the *French,* nor the *Uncertain fate* of the *Dutch;* with *these* she hath resided only as a *Sojourner,* but is ready to *espouse* our Interest and Nation, and with her self to bestow upon us the Treasures of the World; but if we still continue inexorable and stubborn, things are grown to such a Crisis, That we may have reason to fear this is the last time of her asking, and that she may suddenly turn this Kindness into such a Fury as we shall not be able to withstand.

Shall we then embrace so advantagious Overtures, or shall we still proceed in our present Methods? I have heard it was a hard matter to reclaim the *Irish* from drawing with their *Horses Tails;* shall the *Irish* now beat us out of our Trade? Shall we continue rolling in Forreign Silks and Linnens? or be still

sotting

sotting in Forreign Wines, whilest they pick our pockets?   Shall we be Curious in Trifles, sneaking after our private interests? or like the blind *Sodomites* groping after our filthy Pleasures, whilest the Wrathful Angels of God stand at our elbows?   Shall we like the Reprobated *Jews* be under continual Decimations within, whilest our Enemies are at the Gates?   Shall those of the *High City*, those of the *Low City*, and those in the *Temple* be picking out one anothers Eyes to facilitate the Aggressions of more powerful Forreigners? or shall we be hunting or grasping after false Shadows, and Imaginary Forms and Ideas, and neglect that most valuable substance which we have already in our Mouths, and which would turn into the most solid Nutriment, would we take the pains to chew it?

See *Josephus* of the Siege and Destruction of *Hierusalem.*

Which leads me to say, There is yet a farther Requisite to our happy procedure in the Whole, of greater importance than any other; *viz.* a general Humiliation of our selves towards *God*, accompanied with an abhorrence of our past Intemperances, Corrupt Passions, Pride, Avarice, Lusts, Prophaneness, mutual Oppressions, Perfidies, and other Impieties, with such a Christian Meekness, Charity, Purity, Truth, Holy Zeal and Resolution as may render us Capable of his Mercy and Protection; perhaps one *false step* at this time, may be more Irreparable than ever: 'tis certain we shall never be able to make a *true one* whilest we are under the displeasure of the Almighty.

It is as undeniable, that the Laws which obstruct our Trade, cannot be *Repealed*, or *new ones* requisite for its *Improvement* or *Security* be *made*, otherwise than by *a Parliament* : Whether therefore, upon this and other important Considerations, the *Convening* and *Holding* of a Parliament be not under *God*, *(who does not work*

221   *by*

by Miracle) a necessary means to prevent the Ruine of this Nation, and how Long it may *now* with *any* security be deferred, is that, which I most humbly submit to the Determination of Authority.

F I N I S.

The CONTENTS.:

The Contents.

The Contents.

fatal Consequences and Symptoms of a Consumptive Trade, decay of Manufactures, other ways of living overstocked, fall of Rents, general Poverty, an increase of Criminals of all sorts, Depopulation; some Application to the present Case of England, and amongst others the occasion of the new Buildings about London, of Incontinency, Cunning, &c.

The Contents.

Hemp, Flax, and Forreign Timber bought dearer, and far more Timber Imported: In Imported Silks of all sorts; in Laces, and many other things, and thereupon our late French Overballance Considered. To which are Added, our late losses by the French Capers, and Money Exported to France by our Travellers, &c. The National Overballance inferred, this cleared by a Deduction of our Trade, with Relation to the Dutch and French, and therein of their gradual Increase, and our Decay in Trade; Whence the Growth of the French and Dutch Revenues and Strengths observed; a farther Calculation of our late and present Overballance; incidently of some farther Advantages in Trade Forreigners have upon us.

SECT. XIII.

That a Considerable part of our late Treasure is exhausted: Application to our Publick and Private Revenues: Objections Answered, viz. The Plenty of Money to be let on Securities; Stores of Money in London; Stocks in Merchandize; The Over-weightiness of our Coin, &c.

SECT. XIV.

People and Treasure the true Pillars of the National strength: The Odds in the different Use and imployment of people. The absoluteness of the French Monarchy no cause of the present French Grandure: The late Application of the French Councils to the Increase of Trade, People, and Treasure; and the occasion thereof. The greater excellency of the Form of our English Government. The farther necessity of Improving our Trade from the Modern Treasures and Powers of the French; of their Naval force, the Algiers Pyracy; how the French design to engross all Maritime Commerce; our dangers from France; of the present condition of the Dutch: That our late Prohibition of French Goods will not disable that Monarchy, nor better our Trade; meer Prohibitions of no value: Our great advantages in Trade above France and Holland: That a speedy Regulation of our Trade &c. would secure us against all Forreign Powers, and Dangers at home. Of Excises, and other Taxes. The certain Increase of his Majesties Revenue; hence, what occasion for a Parliament, &c.

Discourses

UPON

T R A D E ;

Principally Directed to the

CASES

OF THE

$\left.\begin{array}{l}\textit{Interest}\\\textit{Coynage}\\\textit{Clipping}\\\textit{Increase}\end{array}\right\}$ *of* MONEY.

LONDON:

Printed for *Thos. Basset*, at the
George in *Fleet-street*. 1691.

The Preface.

THese Papers came directed to me, in order, as I suppose to be made Publick: And having transmitted them to the Press, which is the only means whereby the University of Mankind is to be inform'd, I am absolv'd of that Trust.

The Author is pleas'd to conceal himself; which after perusal of his Papers, I do not ascribe to any Diffidence of his Reasons, the Disgusts of Great Men, nor over-much Modesty, which are the ordinary Inducements for lying hid; but rather to avoid the Fatigue of digesting, and polishing his Sentiments into such accurate Method, and clean Style, as the World commonly expects from Authors: I am confident he seeks only the Publick Good, and little regards Censure for the want of Neatness, and Dress, whereof he seems to make a slight account, and to rely wholly upon the Truth, and Justice of his Matter; yet he may reasonably decline the being noted, for either a careless, or an illiterate Person.

The Publick is an acute, as well as merciless Beast, which neither over-sees a Failing, nor forgives it; but stamps Judgment and Execution immediately, tho' upon a Member of itself; and is no less Ingrateful than common Beggars, who affront their Benefactors, without whose Charity their Understandings would starve.

Wherefore I cannot but excuse our Friend's Retirement, and shall take advantage of his absence so far, as to speak of his Discourses with more freedom, than I verily believe his Presence would bear.

As for the Style, you will find it English, such as Men speaks, which, according to Horace, is the Law and Rule of Language. Nor do I perceive that the Gentleman intended

more

The Preface.

more than his Title holds forth; common Discourses, which possibly were taken by an Amanuensis, *and dispatcht without much Correction.   Surely no Man would refuse the Conversation of an ingenious Friend, because he doth not speak like* Tully; *And if the Conversation be so desirable, why should we quarrel with the same thing in Writing?   Nay, it is very impolitick, by such Exactions of Labour and Pains, to discourage all Ingenious Persons from medling in Print, whereby we lose the benefit of their Judgment, in matters of common concern.*

Words are indeed a Felicity, which some have in great perfection; but many times, like a fair Face, prove Temptations to Vice; for I have known very good Sence neglected, and post-poned to an Elegance of Expression; whereas if Words are wanted, the whole Effort is made by pure strength of Reason, and that only is relied on.

The Lawyers in their Deeds, wave all the Decorums of Language, and regard only incontrovertible Expressions. The Merchants in their Policies and Exchanges, use no one Word but what is necessary to their Point, because the Matter and Substance only is intended, and not the Dress; Why then should Reasoners be incumbred, beyond what is necessary to make their Reason understood?

To speak very short, and yet clear, is a Vertue to be envyed; and if directed to Persons, or Assemblies whose business is great, or made so by many Mens interposing in it, it is absolutely necessary; for your Discourse, if it be tedious, is better spared than the time; but it is not so in dealing with lazy Ignorance of any sort, or an Ear-itching Rabble, who are actually impertinent (as well as impetuous) and not sensible of cheat.   And I may add, That in Writing, unless in the Epistolary way, (which being supposed hasty, ought to be short and figurative) an abundance of Words is more pardonable than obscurity, or want of Sence, because we take our own time, and have leisure to peruse it.

I will grant that amongst opulent and idle Persons, as well as Schollars, whose business lies in Words, the bare polishing of Language, is one of the most commendable Entertainments;
and

The Preface.

and to them we resign it; for to Men of business, it is the most hateful thing, I mean, meer Idleness.

I grant also, that delicacy of Words, now most used in Poetry, is useful for disposing wayward People to learn, or make them endure to read. But the World is not at such low ebb of Curiosity in this Age. Men are forward enough to run their Noses into Books, especially such as deal in Faction and Controversie: And it were well if they were either Wrote or Read with as much Integrity as Industry; we have no need of Sugar-plum devices to wheedle Men into Reading, they are Inquisitive enough; and if the Subject be their own Interest, I am of Opinion, if you can make 'em understand it, you may trust them.

As for the Method used in these Papers, there is so little of it affected, that I am afraid some will say there is none at all. I never thought that true Method consisted in affected Divisions, and Sub-divisions, Firsts, Seconds, Sub-firsts, &c. tho' all that is very useful in Works intended to be consulted as Repertories; but where the Understanding is to be informed, it is meer trash, and the business is often lost in it.

And in such Designs it is enough, if Things lie in the Order of Nature, and the Conclusion is not put before the Premisses, so that the course of the Argument is limpid, and intelligible: A Friend of mine used to say, That if the First Chapter were before the Second, it was all the Method he cared for, meaning only what I have observed, which I suppose you will find here.

This drudgery of Digesting, is another Excise upon Sence, which keeps back a great deal of it from coming forth; and without a singular tallent, and much exercise, it makes composing extreamly difficult. I do not understand why other Men, as well as Mountaigne, may not be indulged to ramble in Essays, provided the Sence fails not.

The Scalligerana, Pirroana, Pensees, and Mr. Selden's Table-talk, are all heaps of incoherent scraps; yet for the wit and spirit esteemed; therefore let that which is most valuable, Reason and Truth, be encouraged to come abroad, without imposing such chargeable Equipages upon it, whereby Writers are made to resemble Brewers Horses, very useful Animals, but arrant Drudges.

Methinks

The Preface.

Methinks when I meet with a great deal of Firsting, and Seconding, I smell one who conceits himself an Author, a Creature as fulsome as any other sort of Impertinents. If there be Reason, and that understood, what could the formal Methodist add? Let me have the Cockle, and who will take the gay shell.

Now after all this it will be injust, not to say somewhat of the Subject-matter of these Discourses, which is Commerce and Trade; and the Author's manner of Treating it.

He seems to be of a Temper different from most, who have medled with this Subject in Publick; for it is manifest, his Knowledge and Experience of Trade is considerable, which could not be attained, unless he were a Trader himself; and yet it is not to be collected from any thing he says, of what Nature his dealing hath been; for he speaks impartially of Trade in general, without warping to the Favour of any particular Interest. It hath been observed formerly, when Merchants have been consulted, and the Questions concerned only Trade in general, they agreed in Opinion; but when opposite Interests were concerned, they differed toto cœlo. As for his Opinion touching Interest of Money, wherein he is clear, that it should be left freely to the Market, and not be restrained by Law, he is lyable to the same suspicion, which attends those of a different Judgment; that is, partiality to his own Interest; the difference is only in the supposed Cause, which in the one, is Wealth, and in the other Want. He hath given his Judgment with his Reasons, which every one is free to canvas; and there is no other means whereby a wise and honest Person can justifie his Opinions in Publick Concerns.

In the next place, I find Trade here Treated at another rate, than usually hath been; I mean Philosophically: for the ordinary and vulgar conceits, being meer Husk and Rubbish, are waived; and he begins at the quick, from Principles indisputably true; and so proceeding with like care, comes to a Judgment of the nicest Disputes and Questions concerning Trade. And this with clearness enough, for he reduceth things to their Extreams, wherein all discriminations are most gross and sensible, and then shews them; and not in the state of ordinary concerns, whereof the terms are scarce distinguishable.

This

The Preface.

This Method of Reasoning hath been introduc'd with the new Philosophy, the old dealt in Abstracts more than Truths; and was employed about forming Hypotheses, to fit abundance of precarious and insensible Principles; such as the direct or oblique course of the Atomes in vacuo, *Matter and Form, Privation, solid Orbs,* fuga vacui, *and many others of like nature; whereby they made sure of nothing; but upon the appearance of* Des Cartes' *excellent dissertation de* Methodo, *so much approved and accepted in our Ages, all those Chymera's soon dissolved and vanisht.*

And hence it is, that Knowledge in great measure is become Mechanical; which word I need not interpret farther, than by noting, it here means, built upon clear and evident Truths. But yet this great Improvement of Reason which the World hath lately obtained, is not diffus'd enough, and resides chiefly with the studious and learned, the common People having but a small share; for they cannot abstract, so as to have a true and just thought of the most ordinary things, but are possest and full of the vulgar Errors of sense: Except in some few things that fall within the compass of their day-labour, and so gives them an Experience; As when a Common-Seaman, with all his Ignorance, proves a better Mechanick, for actual Service, than the Professor himself, with all his Learning.

The case of Trade is the same; for although to buy and sell, be the Employment of every man, more or less; and the Common People, for the most part, depend upon it for their daily subsistence; yet there are very few who consider Trade in general upon true Principles, but are satisfied to understand their own particular Trades, and which way to let themselves into immediate gain. And out of this active Sphere nothing is so fallacious, and full of Error, as mens Notions of Trade. And there is another Reason, why this matter seems less understood, than in truth it is. For whenever Men consult for the Publick Good, as for the advancement of Trade, wherein all are concerned, they usually esteem the immediate Interest of their own to be the common Measure of Good and Evil. And there are many, who to gain a little in their own Trades, care not how much others suffer; and each Man strives, that all others may be forc'd, in their dealings, to act

subserviently

The Preface.

subserviently for his Profit, but under the covert of the Publick.

So Clothiers would have men be forc'd to buy their Manufacture; and I may mention such as sell Wool, they would have men forc'd to buy of them at an high Price, though the Clothier loseth. The Tinners would have their Tin dear, though the Merchant profits little: And in general all those who are lazy, and do not, or are not active enough and cannot, look out, to vent the Product of their Estates, or to Trade with it themselves, would have all Traders forc'd by Laws, to bring home to them sufficient Prizes, whether they gain or lose by it. And all the while, not one of them will endure to be under a force, to Sell, or Let their own Estates at lower rates, than the free Market of things will produce.

Now it is no wonder, that out of these Ingredients a strange Medley of Error should result, whereby seldom any Publick Order, which hath been establisht, and intended, or at least pretended for the good of Trade in general, hath had a suitable Effect; but on the contrary, hath for the most part proved prejudicial, and thereupon, by common consent, been discontinued. But this is too copious Matter for a Preface, and tho' many Instances occur, I leave all, and return to the matter of Vulgar Errors in Trade.

It is not long since there was a great noise with Inquiries into the Balance of Exportation and Importation; and so into the Balance of Trade, as they called it. For it was fancyed that if we brought more Commodities in, than we carried out, we were in the High-way to Ruin. In like manner have we heard much said against the East-India *Trade, against the* French *Trade, with many other like politick conceits in Trade; most of which, Time and better Judgment hath disbanded; but others succeed in their room, according as new Persons find Encouragement to invent, and inspire, for promoting their private Interest, by imposing on those, who desire to be cunning. And now we complain for want of Money in specie, that Bullion is Exported or mis-employed to other uses, than making Money; and ascribe the deadness of Trade, especially of Corn, and Cattel in the Country, to this; and hope by a Regulation of the Bullion-Trade, and stinting the*

Price,

The Preface.

Price, except it be in Money, to make a through Reformation, and give new Life to all things, with much more, ejusdem farina, which I do not particularize, this being enough for a taste.

Now it may appear strange to hear it said,

That the whole World as to Trade, is but as one Nation or People, and therein Nations are as Persons.

That the loss of a Trade with one Nation, is not that only, separately considered, but so much of the Trade of the World rescinded and lost, for all is combined together.

That there can be no Trade unprofitable to the Publick; for if any prove so, men leave it off; and wherever the Traders thrive, the Publick, of which they are a part, thrives also.

That to force Men to deal in any prescrib'd manner, may profit such as happen to serve them; but the Publick gains not, because it is taking from one Subject, to give to another.

That no Laws can set Prices in Trade, the Rates of which, must and will make themselves: But when such Laws do happen to lay any hold, it is so much Impediment to Trade, and therefore prejudicial.

That Money is a Merchandize, whereof there may be a glut, as well as a scarcity, and that even to an Inconvenience.

That a People cannot want Money to serve the ordinary dealing, and more than enough they will not have.

That no Man shall be the richer for the making much Money, nor have any part of it, but as he buys it for an equivalent price.

That the free Coynage is a perpetual Motion found out, whereby to Melt and Coyn without ceasing, and so to feed Goldsmiths and Coyners at the Publick Charge.

That debasing the Coyn is defrauding one another, and to the Publick there is no sort of Advantage from it; for that admits no Character, or Value, but Intrinsick.

That the sinking Money by Allay or Weight is all one.

That Exchange and ready Money, are the same, nothing but Carriage and re-carriage being saved.

That Money Exported in Trade is an increase to the Wealth of the Nation; but spent in War, and Payments abroad, is so much Impoverishment.

In

The Preface.

In short, That all favour to one Trade or Interest against another, is an Abuse, and cuts so much of Profit from the Publick. With many other like Paradoxes, no less strange to most men, than true in themselves; but in my Opinion, clearly flowing from the Principles, and Discourses that follow, which you may freely peruse and censure, for now I have done.

Perhaps my unknown Confident may think me too saucy, for putting my Oar into his Boat, and I will not excuse my self to him, otherwise than by demanding the same Liberty he hath taken; that is, to have a fling at the World; and as yet the Advantage is his, for he hath two, and better, for my one. And so Farewel.

A

A

DISCOURSE

Concerning the

Abatement of INTEREST.

ARguments for Abatement of Interest are many, *viz.*

I. When Interest is less, Trade is incourag'd, and the Merchant can be a Gainer; whereas, when it is great, the Usurer, or Money-owner takes all.

II. The *Dutch*, with whom Interest is low, Trade cheaper, and under-sell us.

III. Land falls in value, as Interest riseth.

With divers others, whereof the Facts may be true, but proceed from another Cause, and conduce nothing to the purpose for which they are alledg'd.

I shall not formally apply my self to answer all the Arguments and Discourses, that commonly are found in Pamphlets, and Conversation upon this Subject; as if I were to Advocate the Cause of Interest: But give my thoughts impartially in the whole matter, with regard to the Profit of the whole Nation, and to no particular Person's project: Wherein I hope to propose that which may resolve any doubt that can be raised, and leave every one to apply it, as they think fit.

1   The

The Question to be considered is, Whether the Government have reason by a Law, to prohibit the taking more than 4*l. per Cent.* Interest for Money lent, or to leave the Borrower and Lender to make their own Bargains.

In the Disquisition of this, many things are to be considered, and particularly such as relate to Trade, of which a true Notion will set right a World of Mistakes, wherefore that now shall be chiefly treated of.

Trade is nothing else but a Commutation of Superfluities; for instance : I give of mine, what I can spare, for somewhat of yours, which I want, and you can spare.

Thus Trade, whilst it is restrained within the limits of a Town, Country, or Nation, signifieth only the Peoples supplying each other with Conveniences, out of what that Town, Country, or Nation affords.

And in this, he who is most diligent, and raiseth most Fruits, or maketh most of Manufactory, will abound most in what others make, or raise; and consequently be free from Want, and enjoy most Conveniences, which is truly to be Rich, altho' there were no such thing as Gold, Silver, or the like amongst them.

Mettals are very necessary for many Uses, and are to be reckon'd among the Fruits and Manufactories of the World. And of these, Gold and Silver being by nature very fine, and more scarce than others, are higher prized; and a little of them is very reasonably esteem'd equal in value with a great quantity of other Mettals, &c. For which reason, and moreover that they are imperishable, as well as convenient for easie stowage and removal, and not from any Laws, they are made a Standard, or common Measure to deal with; and all Mankind concur in it, as every one knows, therefore I need not inlarge further in this matter.

Now it is to be consider'd, that Mankind being fallen

into

into a way of commuting in this manner, to serve their occasions, some are more provident, others more profuse; some by their Industry and Judgment raise more Fruits from the Earth, than they consume in supplying their own occasions; and then the surplus remains with them, and is Property or Riches.

And Wealth thus contracted, is either commuted for other Mens Land (supposing all men to have had some) or massed up in heaps of Goods; be the same of Mettals, or any thing valuable. And those are the Rich, who transmit what they have to their Posterity; whereby particular Families become rich; and of such are compounded Cities, Countries, Nations, &c.

And it will be found, that as some particular men in a Town grow richer, and thrive better than others; so also do Nations, who by Trade serving the occasions of their Neighbours, supply themselves with what they have occasion for from abroad; which done, the rest is laid up, and is Silver, Gold, &c. for as I said, these being commutable for every thing, and of small bulk, are still preferr'd to be laid up, till occasion shall call them out to supply other Necessaries wanted.

Now Industry and Ingenuity having thus distinguisht Men into Rich and Poor; What is the consequence? One rich Man hath Lands, not only more than he can manage, but so much, that letting them out to others, he is supplied with a large over-plus, so needs no farther care.

Another rich Man hath Goods; that is, Mettals, Manufactures, &c. in great quantity, with these he serves his own occasions, and then commutes the rest in Trade; that is, supplies others with what they want, and takes in exchange what they had of, beyond their own occasions, whereby managing cunningly, he must always advance.

Now as there are more Men to Till the Ground than

3   have

have Land to Till, so also there will be many who want
Stock to manage; and also (when a Nation is grown
rich) there will be Stock for Trade in many hands, who
either have not the skill, or care not for the trouble of
managing it in Trade.

But as the Landed Man letts his Land, so these still
lett their Stock; this latter is call'd Interest, but is
only Rent for Stock, as the other is for Land. And in
several Languages, hiring of Money, and Lands, are
Terms of common use; and it is so also in some Counties in *England*.

Thus to be a Landlord, or a Stock-lord is the same
thing; the Landlord hath the advantage only in this :
That his Tenant cannot carry away the Land, as the
Tenant of the other may the Stock; and therefore Land
ought to yield less profit than Stock, which is let out at
the greater hazard.

These things consider'd, it will be found, that as
plenty makes cheapness in other things, as Corn, Wool,
&c. when they come to Market in greater Quantities
than there are Buyers to deal for, the Price will fall;
so if there be more Lenders than Borrowers, Interest
will also fall; wherefore it is not low Interest makes
Trade, but Trade increasing, the Stock of the Nation
makes Interest low.

It is said, that in *Holland* Interest is lower than in
England. I answer; It is, because their Stock is greater
than ours. I cannot hear that they ever made a Law
to restrain Interest, but am certainly informed, that at
this day, the Currant Interest between Merchant and
Merchant, when they disburse Money for each others
Account, is 6 *per Cent.* and the Law justifies it.

I allow Money is many times lent at 3, and 4 *per
Cent.* but it is upon Mortgages, out of which the State
hath a Duty, and by the course of Titles there, such
dealing is perfectly safe; and this is still by private

4   consent

consent and agreement, and not by co-ersion and order of Law.   The like often happens here, when poor Widows and Orphans purchase the Security of their Livelihoods, and punctual Payment, by lending at small Interest, to such as need not the Money.

It might not be amiss in this place, to say somewhat of the Publick Banks that are in Forreign Parts, as *Amsterdam, Venice*, &c. but that is a Subject I have not time to dilate upon : I shall only say, that it is a cunning way of supplying the Government once with a great Sum; and as long as the Government stands, it is no loss to them that have the Credit, nor no great Inconveniency; for all Bills of Exchange are made by Law payable in Bank, and not otherwise; for Dealers in Exchanges it is best that way, and such as want their Money, find no difficulty in selling their Credits, the price of which riseth and falleth according to Demanders, as of other things.

I do not understand that true, two Banks pay any Interest; it is true there are several Funds, *viz.* The Mint in *Venice*, and the Chamber in *Amsterdam*, with several others in those, and other Cities, where Money is put out at Interest for Lives, and several other ways, and at different Rates, more or less, according to the Credit these Funds have, which are the Security; and these may, by mistake, be called the Banks, which they are not, being only such as the Chamber of *London, East-India House*, &c. were.

I do not believe, but the Usurer, according to the saying, will take half a Loaf, rather than no Bread : But I averr, that high Interest will bring Money out from Hoards, Plate, &c. into Trade, when low Interest will keep it back.

Many Men of great Estates, keep by them for State and Honour, great Quantities of Plate, Jewels, &c.

which certainly they will be more inclin'd to do, when Interest is very low, than when it is high.

Such as have nothing to subsist by, but the Interest of Money, must either let it out, or Trade with it themselves, and be contented with what they can get; but that hinders not, but very many other Men, who are rich, and not so prest, may, if Interest be very low, choose to make use of their Stocks in Jewels, Plate, &c. rather than run the hazards, and be at the trouble of dealing with necessitous and knavish Men, such as many Borrowers are, for inconsiderable gains.

So that it cannot be denied, but the lowering of Interest may, and probably will keep some Money from coming abroad into Trade; whereas on the contrary. high Interest certainly brings it out.

Next is to be considered, that Dealings between Borrowers and Lenders are of two kinds : 1. Upon Mortgage, or Pawn. 2. Upon Personal Security, and that either by single Bond, or with Sureties; all which, as they differ in goodness, so ought in reason to bear different Prizes. Shall any Man be bound to lend a single Person, upon the same Terms, as others lend upon Mortgages, or Joynt Obligations ?

Then again it is to be considered, that the Moneys imployed at Interest in this Nation, are not near the Tenth part, disposed to Trading People, wherewith to manage their Trades; but are for the most part lent for the supplying of Luxury, and to support the Expence of Persons, who though great Owners of Lands, yet spend faster than their Lands bring in ; and being loath to sell, choose rather to mortgage their Estates.

So that in truth an Ease to Interest, will rather be a Support to Luxury, than to Trade ; the poor Trading Man, who hath but a narrow Stock, or none at all, supplies himself by buying Goods of rich Men at time,

and

and thereby pays Interest, not at the rate of 5, 6, or 8, but 10, 12, and more *per Cent*. And this is not in the Power of any Legislature to prevent, or remedy.

It may be said, let him take Money at Interest, and not buy at Time. But then Men must be found, that will lend; the Legislative must provide a Fund to borrow upon.

The Trade of setting out Ships, runs very much upon this course, wherein it is usual to Bum 'em (as they call it) at 36 *per Cent*. And this cannot be remedied; and if it were, it would be a stop, as well to the Building, as the setting out of many Ships; whereby, after all, not only the publick, but the private Persons concern'd are Gainers for the most part.

Thus when all things are considered, it will be found best for the Nation to leave the Borrowers and the Lender to make their own Bargains, according to the Circumstances they lie uuder; and in so doing you will follow the course of the wise *Hollanders*, so often quoted on this account: and the consequences will be, that when the Nation thrives, and grows rich, Money will be to be had upon good terms, but the clean contrary will fall out, when the Nation grows poorer and poorer.

Let any one Answer me, why do not the Legislators in those poor Countries, where Interest is at 10, & 12 *per Cent*. make such Laws to restrain Interest, and reduce it for the good of the People? If they should attempt it, it wou'd soon appear, that such Laws would not be effectual to do it. For when there are more Borrowers than Lenders, as in poor Countries, where if a rich Man hath 100*l*. to dispose, and there are four, five or more Men striving for it; the Law would be evaded by underhand Bargains, making Loans in Goods, drawing Bills, and a thousand ways beside; which cannot be prevented.

It is probable that when Laws restrain Interest of

7 Money

Money, below the Price, which the Reason of Trade settles, and Traders cannot (as we will suppose) evade the Law, or not without great difficulty, or hazard, and have not Credit to borow at Legal Interest, to make, or increase their Stock; so much of Trade is lopt off; and there cannot be well a greater obstruction to diminish Trade then that would be. The consideration of all these Matters, makes out an universal Maxime, That as more Buyers than Sellers raiseth the price of a Commodity, so more Borrowers than Lenders, will raise Interest.

And the State may with as much Justice make a Law that Lands which heretofore have been Lett for 10*s. per* Acre, shall not now be Lett for above 8*s. per* Acre, as that Money, or Stock, from 5 *per Cent.* shall be Lett for 4 *per Cent.* the Property being as good, and as much the Substance of the Kingdom in the one, as in the other.

I will not say any thing to the Theological Arguments against Interest of Moneys; by those 3 *per Cent*: is no more lawful, than 4, or 12. But this I shall maintain Politically, that if you take away Interest, you take away Borrowing, and Lending. And in consequence the Gentry, who are behind hand, be it for what cause soever, must sell, and cannot Mortgage; which will bring down the Price of Land. And the Trader whatever his skill is, if he hath no Stock, must either sit still, or buy at Time, which is Interest under another Name. And they who are poor, will always be so, and we should soon relapse into the state of One Thousand Years ago.

And whereas the Stock of the Nation is now reckon'd great, let it be fairly valued, and it will be found much less than it seems to be; for all the Monies that are owing upon Land Securities, must be struck off, and not estimated; or else you will have a wrong Account;

8   for

for if a Gentleman of 500*l. per Annum*, owes 8000*l.* and you value his Land, and the Lender's Stock both, you make an account of the same thing twice.

And whereas we make great Accounts of Money'd Men in the Nation, in truth there are but few; for suppose all that have lent upon Mortgage had Land for their Moneys, as indeed in strictness of Law they have, there wou'd be but few Money'd Men in the Nation left. The borrowing of Money of one, to pay another, call'd, Robbing of *Peter* to pay *Paul*, so much practis'd now a-days, makes us think the Nation far richer than it is.

A

A *Discourse of* Coyned Money.

IN the former Discourse, it hath been already made appear, that Gold and Silver for their scarcity, have obtained in small quantities, to equal in value far greater quantities of other Metals, &c. And farther, from their easie Removal, and convenient Custody, have also obtained to be the common Measure in the World between Man and Man in their dealings, as well for Land, Houses, &c. as for Goods and other Necessaries.

For the greater Improvement of this Convenience, and to remove some Difficulties, which would be very troublesome, about knowing quantities and qualities in common and ordinary dealing: Princes and States have made it a matter of Publick concern, to ascertain the Allay, and to determine the Weights, *viz.* the quantities of certain Pieces, which we call Coyn, or Money : and such being distinguish'd by Stamps, and Inscriptions, it is made difficult, and highly Penal to Counterfeit them.

By this means the Trade of the World is made easie, and all the numerous species of several Commodities have a common Measure. Besides the Gold and Silver being thus coyned into Money, and so become more useful for Commerce than in the Log or Block, hath in all places, except in *England* since the free Coynage, reasonably obtained a greater value than it had before : And that not only above the real charge of making it so, but is become a State-Revenue (except as before) tho' not very great. Whereas if Silver coyned and uncoyned bore the same rate, as it doth with us in

England, where it is coyned at the Charge of the Publick; it will be lyable frequently to be melted down, as I shall shew anon.

Money being thus the Common Measure of Buying and Selling, every body who hath any thing to sell, and cannot procure Chapmen for it, is presently apt to think, that want of Money in the Kingdom, or Country is the cause why his Goods do not go off; and so, want of Money, is the common Cry; which is a great mistake, as shall be shewn. I grant all stop in Trade proceeds from some cause; but it is not from the want of specifick Money, there being other Reasons for it; as will appear by the following Discourse.

No Man is richer for having his Estate all in Money, Plate, &c. lying by him, but on the contrary, he is for that reason the poorer. That man is richest, whose Estate is in a growing condition, either in Land at Farm, Money at Interest, or Goods in Trade: If any man, out of an humour, should turn all his Estate into Money, and keep it dead, he would soon be sensible of Poverty growing upon him, whilst he is eating out of the quick stock.

But to examine the matter closer, what do these People want, who cry out for Money? I will begin with the Beggar; he wants, and importunes for Money: What would he do with it if he had it? buy Bread, &c. Then in truth it is not Money, but Bread, and other Necessaries for Life that he wants. Well then, the Farmer complains, for the want of Money; surely it is not for the Beggar's Reason, to sustain Life, or pay Debts; but he thinks that were more Money in the Country, he should have a Price for his Goods. Then it seems Money is not his want, but a Price for his Corn, and Cattel, which he would sell, but cannot. If it be askt, if the want of Money be not, what then is

11   the

the reason, why he cannot get a price? I answer, it must proceed from one of these three Causes.

1. Either there is too much Corn and Cattel in the Country, so that most who come to Market have need of selling, as he hath, and few of buying: Or, 2. There wants the usual vent abroad, by Transportation, as in time of War, when Trade is unsafe, or not permitted. Or, 3. The Consumption fails, as when men by reason of Poverty, do not spend so much in their Houses as formerly they did; wherefore it is not the increase of specifick Money, which would at all advance the Farmers Goods, but the removal of any of these three Causes, which do truly keep down the Market.

The Merchant and Shop-keeper want Money in the same manner, that is, they want a Vent for the Goods they deal in, by reason that the Markets fail, as they will always upon any cause, like what I have hinted. Now to consider what is the true source of Riches, or in the common Phrase, plenty of Money, we must look a little back, into the nature and steps of Trade.

Commerce and Trade, as hath been said, first springs from the Labour of Man, but as the Stock increases, it dilates more and more. If you suppose a Country to have nothing in it but the Land it self, and the Inhabitants; it is plain that at first, the People have only the Fruits of the Earth, and Metals raised from the Bowels of it, to Trade withal, either by carrying out into Foreign Parts, or by selling to such as will come to buy of them, whereby they may be supplyed with the Goods of other Countries wanted there.

In process of time, if the People apply themselves industriously, they will not only be supplied, but advance to a great overplus of Forreign Goods, which improv'd, will enlarge their Trade. Thus the *English* Nation will sell unto the *French, Spaniards, Turk,* &c.

12   not

not only the product of their own Country, as Cloath, Tin, Lead, &c. but also what they purchase of others, as Sugar, Pepper, Callicoes, &c. still buying where Goods are produc'd, and cheap, and transporting them to Places where they are wanted, making great advantage thereby.

In this course of Trade, Gold and Silver are in no sort different from other Commodities, but are taken from them who have Plenty, and carried to them who want, or desire them, with as good profit as other Merchandizes. So that an active prudent Nation groweth rich, and the sluggish Drones grow poor; and there cannot be any Policy other than this, which being introduc'd and practis'd, shall avail to increase Trade and Riches.

But this Proposition, as single and plain as it is, is seldom so well understood, as to pass with the generality of Mankind; but they think by force of Laws, to retain in their Country all the Gold and Silver which Trade brings in; and thereby expect to grow rich immediately: All which is a profound Fallacy, and hath been a Remora, whereby the growing Wealth of many Countries have been obstructed.

The Case will more plainly appear, if it be put of a single Merchant, or if you please to come nearer the point, of a City or County only.

Let a Law be made, and what is more, be observ'd, that no Man whatsoever shall carry any Money out of a particular Town, County, or Division, with liberty to carry Goods of any sort: so that all the Money which every one brings with him, must be left behind, and none be carried out.

The consequence of this would be, that such Town, or County were cut off from the rest of the Nation; and no Man would dare to come to Market with his Money there; because he must buy, whether he likes,

or

or not : and on the other side, the People of that place could not go to other Markets as Buyers, but only as Sellers, being not permitted to carry any Money out with them.

Now would not such a Constitution as this, soon bring a Town or County to a miserable Condition, with respect to their Neighbours, who have free Commerce, whereby the Industrious gain from the slothful and luxurious part of Mankind? The Case is the same, if you extend your thought from a particular Nation, and the several Divisions, and Cities, with the Inhabitants in them, to the whole World, and the several Nations, and Governments in it. And a Nation restrained in its Trade, of which Gold and Silver is a principal, if not an essential Branch, would suffer, and grow poor, as a particular place within a Country, as I have discoursed. A Nation in the World, as to Trade, is in all respects like a City in a Kingdom, or Family in a City.

Now since the Increase of Trade is to be esteem'd the only cause that Wealth and Money increase, I will add some farther Considerations upon that subject.

The main spur to Trade, or rather to Industry and Ingenuity, is the exorbitant Appetites of Men, which they will take pains to gratifie, and so be disposed to work, when nothing else will incline them to it; for did Men content themselves with bare Necessaries, we should have a poor World.

The Glutton works hard to purchase Delicacies, wherewith to gorge himself; the Gamester, for Money to venture at Play; the Miser, to hoard; and so others. Now in their pursuit of those Appetites, other Men less exorbitant, are benefitted; and tho' it may be thought few profit by the Miser, yet it will be found otherwise, if we consider, that besides the humour of every Generation, to dissipate what another had collected, there is benefit from the very Person of a covetous Man; for

if

if he labours with his own hands, his Labour is very beneficial to them who imploy him; if he doth not work, but profit by the Work of others, then those he sets on work have benefit by their being employed.

Countries which have sumptuary Laws, are generally poor; for when Men by those Laws are confin'd to narrower Expence than otherwise they would be, they are at the same time discouraged from the Industry and Ingenuity which they would have imployed in obtaining wherewithal to support them, in the full latitude of Expence they desire.

It is possible Families may be supported by such means, but then the growth of Wealth in the Nation is hindered; for that never thrives better, then when Riches are tost from hand to hand.

The meaner sort seeing their Fellows become rich, and great, are spurr'd up to imitate their Industry. A Tradesman sees his Neighbour keep a Coach, presently all his Endeavours is at work to do the like, and many times is beggered by it; however the extraordinary Application he made, to support his Vanity, was beneficial to the Publick, tho' not enough to answer his false Measures as to himself.

It will be objected, That the Home Trade signifies nothing to the enriching a Nation, and that the increase of Wealth comes out of Forreign Trade.

I answer, That what is commonly understood by Wealth, *viz.* Plenty, Bravery, Gallantry, &c. cannot be maintained without Forreign Trade. Nor in truth, can Forreign Trade subsist without the Home Trade, both being connected together.

I have toucht upon these matters concerning Trade, and Riches in general, because I conceive a true Notion of them will correct many common Errors, and more especially conduce to the Proposition I chiefly aim to prove; which is, that Gold and Silver, and, out of them,

15   Money

Money, are nothing but the Weights and Measures, by which Traffick is more conveniently carried on than could be done without them: and also a proper Fund for a surplusage of Stock to be deposited in.

In confirmation of this, we may take Notice, That Nations which are very poor, have scarce any Money, and in the beginnings of Trade have often made use of something else; as *Sueden* hath used Copper, and the *Plantations*, Sugar and Tobacco, but not without great Inconveniences; and still as Wealth hath increas'd, Gold and Silver hath been introduc'd, and drove out the others, as now almost in the Plantations it hath done.

It is not necessary absolutely to have a Mint for the making Money plenty, tho' it be very expedient; and a just benefit is lost by the want of it, where there is none; for it hath been observed, that where no Mints were Trade hath not wanted a full supply of Money; because if it be wanted, the Coyn of other Princes will become current, as in *Ireland*, and the *Plantations;* so also in *Turky*, where the Money of the Country is so minute, that it is inconvenient for great Payments; and therefore the Turkish Dominions are supplied by almost all the Coyns of Christendom, the same being current there.

But a Country which useth Forreign Coyns, hath great disadvantage from it; because they pay strangers for what, had they a Mint of their own, they might make themselves. For Coyned Money, as was said, is more worth than Uncoyned Silver of the same weight and allay; that is, you may buy more Uncoyned Silver, of the same fineness with the Money, than the Money weighs; which advantage the Stranger hath for the Coynage.

If it be said, That the contrary sometimes happens, and coyned Money shall be current for less than Bullion

shall

shall sell for. I answer, that whereever this happens, the Coyned Money being undervalued, shall be melted down into Bullion, for the immediate Gain that is had from it.

Thus it appears, that if you have no Mint whereby to increase your Money, yet if you are a rich People, and have Trade, you cannot want Specifick Coyn, to serve your occasions in dealing.

The next thing to be shewed is, That if your Trade pours in never so much Money upon you, you have no more advantage by the being of it Money, then you should have were it in Logs, or Blocks; save only that Money is much better for Transportation than Logs are.

For when Money grows up to a greater quantity than Commerce requires, it comes to be of no greater value than uncoyned Silver, and will occasionally be melted down again.

Then let not the care of Specifick Money torment us so much; for a People that are rich cannot want it, and if they make none, they will be supplied with the Coyn of other Nations; and if never so much be brought from abroad, or never so much coyned at home, all that is more than what the Commerce of the Nation requires, is but Bullion, and will be treated as such; and coyned Money, like wrought Plate at second hand, shall sell but for the Intrinsick.

I call to witness the vast Sums that have been coyned in *England*, since the free Coynage was set up; What is become of it all? no body believes it to be in the Nation, and it cannot well be all transported, the Penalties for so doing being so great. The case is plain, it not being exported, as I verily believe little of it is, the Melting-Pot devours all.

The rather, because that Practice is so easie, profitable, and safe from all possibility of being detected,

as

as every one knows it is. And I know no intelligent Man who doubts, but the New Money goes this way.

Silver and Gold, like other Commodities, have their ebbings and flowings: Upon the arrival of Quantities from *Spain,* the Mint commonly gives the best price; that is, coyned Silver, for uncoyned Silver, weight for weight. Wherefore is it carried into the *Tower,* and coyned? not long after there will come a demand for Bullion, to be Exported again: If there is none, but all happens to be in Coyn, What then? Melt it down again; there's no loss in it, for the Coyning cost the Owners nothing.

Thus the Nation hath been abused, and made to pay for the twisting of straw, for Asses to eat. If the Merchant were made to pay the price of the Coynage, he would not have sent his Silver to the *Tower* without Consideration; and coyned Money would always keep a value above uncoyned Silver: which is now so far from being the case, that many times it is considerably under, and generally the King of *Spain's* Coyn here is is worth One penny *per* Ounce more than our New Money.

This Nation, for many Years last past, hath groaned, and still groans under the abuse of clipt Money, which with respect to their Wisdom, is a great mistake; and the *Irish* whom we ridicule so much, when in Peace, would not be so gulled, but weighed their (Pieces of Eight) Cobbs, as they call them, Piece by Piece; this Errour springs from the same Source with the rest, and needs no other Cure then will soon result from Noncurrency. Whereof I shall set down my thoughts.

There is great fear, that if clipt Money be not taken, there will be no Money at all. I am certain, that so long as clipt Money is taken, there will be little other: And is it not strange, that scarce any Nation, or People

18   in

in the whole World, take diminisht Money by Tale, but the *English ?*

What is the reason that a New Half-crown-piece, if it hath the least snip taken from the edge, will not pass ; whereas an Old Half-crown clipt to the very quick, and not intrinsically worth Eighteen Pence, shall be currant ?

I know no reason, why a Man should take the one, more than the other; I am sure, that if New Money should pass clipt, there would soon be enough served so. And I do not in the least doubt, unless the currency of clipt Money be stopt, it will not be very long before every individual piece of the Old Coynes be clipt.

And if this be not remedied, for fear of the Evil now, how will it be born hereafter, when it will be worse? surely at length it will become insupportable, and remedy itself as Groats have done ; but let them look out, in whose time it shall happen ; we are all shoving the Evil-Day as far off as may be, but it will certainly come at last.

I do not think the great Evil is so hard to be remedied, nor so chargeable as some have judged ; but if rightly managed, it may be done with no intolerable loss, some there will be, and considerable; but when I reflect where it will fall, I cannot think it grievous.

The general Opinion is, That it cannot be done otherwise, then by calling in of all the Old Money, and changing of it, for doing which the whole Nation must contribute by a general Tax ; but I do not approve of this way, for several Reasons.

For it will be a matter of great trouble, and will require many hands to execute, who will expect, and deserve good pay ; which will add to the Evil, and increase the Charge of the Work ; and the Trust of it is also very great, and may be vastly abused.

        Now

Now before I give any Opinion for the doing this thing, let some estimate be made of the loss, wherein I will not undertake to compute the Total, but only how the same may fall out in One Hundred Pound : There may be found in it Ten Pound of good New Money, then rests Ninety Pound; and of that I will suppose half to be clipt Money, and half good; so there will be but Five and Forty, in One Hundred Pounds, whereupon there will be any loss; and that will not surely be above a Third part : so I allow 15*l. per Cent.* for the loss by clipt Money, which is with the most, and in such Computes, it is safest to err on that side.

Now in case it should be thought fit, that the King should in all the Receipts of the Publick Revenue, forbid the taking of clipt Coyn, unless the Subject were content to pay it by weight at 5*s.* 2*d. per* Ounce, every Piece being cut in Two, (which must be especially and effectually secured to be done) I grant it would be a great surprize, but no great cause of Complaint when nothing is required, but that the Publick Revenue may be paid in lawful *English* Money.

And those who are to make Payments, must either find good Money, or clip in two their clipt Money, and part with it on such terms; by this Example it would like wise be found, that in a short time, all Men would refuse clipt Money in common Payment.

Now let us consider, where the loss would light, which I have estimated to be about 15 *per Cent.*

We are apt to make Over estimates of the Quantities of current Money; for we see it often, and know it not again; and are not willing to consider how very a little time it stays in a place; and altho' every one desires to have it, yet none, or very few care for keeping it, but they are forthwith contriving to dispose it; knowing that from all the Money that lies dead, no benefit is to be expected, but it is a certain loss.

20   The

The Merchant and Gentleman keep their Money for the most part, with Goldsmiths, and Scriveners; and they, instead of having Ten Thousand Pounds in Cash by them, as their Accounts shew they should have, of other Mens ready Money, to be paid at sight, have seldom One Thousand in Specie; but depend upon a course of Trade, whereby Money comes in as fast as it is taken out: Wherefore I conclude, that the Specifick Money of this Nation is far less than the common Opinion makes.

Now suppose all the loss by clipt Money should happen and fall where the Cash is, it would be severe in very few Places. It could do no great harm to Hoards of Money; because those who intend to keep Money, will be sure to lay up that which is good. It would not signifie much to the poor Man, for he many times hath none; and for the most part, if he hath any, it is very little, seldome Five Shillings at a time. The Farmer is supposed to pay his Landlord, as fast as he gets Money; so it is not likely he should be catcht with much: Wherefore it will light chiefly upon Trading Men, who may sometimes be found with Hundreds by them; and frequently not with many Pounds. Those who happen to have such great Cashes at such time would sustain loss.

In short, clipt Money is an Evil, that the longer it is born with, the harder will the Cure be. And if the Loss therein be lain on the Publick, (as the Common Project is) the Inconveniences are (as hath been shewed) very great; but in the other way of Cure it is not such a terrible Grievance, as most Men have imagined it would be.

So to conclude, when these Reasons, which have been hastily and confusedly set down, are duly considered, I doubt not but we shall joyn in one uniform Sentiment:

21   That

That Laws to hamper Trade, whether Forreign, or Domestick, relating to Money, or other Merchandizes, are not Ingredients to make a People Rich, and abounding in Money, and Stock. But if Peace be procured, easie Justice maintained, the Navigation not clogg'd, the Industrious encouraged, by indulging them in the participation of Honours, and Imployments in the Government, according to their Wealth and Characters, the Stock of the Nation will increase, and consequently Gold and Silver abound, Interest be easie, and Money cannot be wanting.

POSTSCRIPT.

POSTSCRIPT.

*Upon farther Consideration of the Foregoing Matters, I
think fit to add the following Notes.*

WHEN a Nation is grown rich, Gold, Silver,
Jewels, and every thing useful, or desirable, (as
I have already said) will be plentiful; and the Fruits of
the Earth will purchase more of them, than before,
when People were poorer: As a fat Oxe in former Ages,
was not sold for more Shillings, than now Pounds.
The like takes places in Labourers' Wages, and every
thing whatever; which confirms the Universal Maxim
I have built upon, *viz*. That Plenty of any thing makes
it cheap.

Therefore Gold and Silver being now plentiful, a
Man hath much more of it for his labour, for his Corn,
for his Cattle, &c. then could be had Five Hundred
Years ago, when, as must be owned, there was not
near so much by many parts as now.

Notwithstanding this, I find many, who seem willing
to allow, that this Nation at present abounds with
Gold and Silver, in Plate and Bullion; but are yet of
Opinion, That coyned Money is wanted to carry on the
Trade, and that were there more Specifick Money,
Trade would increase, and we should have better
Markets for every thing.

That this is a great Error, I think the foregoing
Papers make out: but to clear it a little farther, let it
be considered, that Money is a Manufacture of Bullion
wrought in the Mint. Now if the Materials are ready,
and the Workmen also, 'tis absurd to say, the Manufacture is wanted.

For

For instance: Have you Corn, and do you want Meal? Carry the Corn to the Mill, and grind it. Yes; but I want Meal, because others will not carry their Corn; and I have none: say you so; then buy Corn of them, and carry it to the Mill your self. This is exactly the Case of Money. A very rich Man hath much Plate, for Honour and Show; whereupon a poorer Man thinks, if it were coyned into Money, the Publick, and his self among the rest, would be the better for it; but he is utterly mistaken; unless at the same time you oblige the rich Man to squander his new coyn'd Money away.

For if he lays it up, I am sure the matter is not mended: if he commutes it for Diamonds, Pearl, &c. the Case is still the same; it is but changed from one hand to another: and it may be the Money is dispatcht to the *Indies* to pay for those Jewels: then if he buys Land, it is no more than changing the hand; and regarding all Persons, except the Dealers only, the Case is still the same. Money will always have an Owner, and never goeth a Beggar for Entertainment, but must be purchast for valuable consideration *in solido*.

If the use of Plate were prohibited, then it were a sumptuary Law, and, as such, would be a vast hindrance to the Riches and Trade of the Nation: for now seeing every Man hath Plate in his House, the Nation is possest of a solid Fund, consisting in those Mettals, which all the World desire, and would willingly draw from us; and this in far greater measure than would be, if Men were not allowed that liberty. For the poor Tradesman, out of an ambition to have a Piece of Plate upon his Cupboard, works harder to purchase it, than he would do if that humour were restrain'd, as I have said elsewhere.

There is required for carrying on the Trade of the Nation, a determinate Sum of Specifick Money, which varies, and is sometimes more, sometimes less, as the

24   Circumstances

Circumstances we are in require. War time calls for more Money than time of Peace, because every one desires to keep some by him, to use upon Emergencies; not thinking it prudent to rely upon Moneys currant in dealing, as they do in times of Peace, when Payments are more certain.

This ebbing and flowing of Money, supplies and accommodates itself, without any aid of Politicians. For when Money grows scarce, and begins to be hoarded, then forthwith the Mint works, till the occasion be filled up again. And on the other side, when Peace brings out the Hoards, and Money abounds, the Mint not only ceaseth, but the overplus of Money will be presently melted down, either to supply the Home Trade, or for Transportation.

Thus the Buckets work alternately, when Money is scarce, Bullion is coyn'd; when Bullion is scarce, Money is melted. I do not allow that both should be scarce at one and the same time; for that is a state of Poverty, and will not be, till we are exhausted, which is besides my subject.

Some have fancied, that if by a Law the Ounce of Silver were restrained to 5s. value, in all dealings, and at the *Tower* the same were coyned into 5s. 4d. or 5s. 6d. *per* Ounce, all the Plate in *England* would soon be coyned. The answer to this, in short, is: That the Principle they build upon is impossible. How can any Law hinder me from giving another Man what I please for his Goods? The Law may be evaded a thousand ways. As be it so: I must not give, nor he receive above 5s. *per* Ounce for Silver; I may pay him 5s. and present him with 4d. or 6d. more; I may give him Goods in barter, at such, or greater profit; and so by other contrivances, *ad Infinitum*.

But put case it took effect, and by that means all the Silver in *England* were coyned into Money; What then? would any one spend more in Cloaths, Equipages, House-keeping, &c. than is done? I believe not; but rather the contrary: For the Gentry and Commonalty being nipt in their delight of seeing Plate, &c. in their Houses, would in all probability be dampt in all other Expences: Wherefore if this could be done, as I affirm it cannot, yet instead of procuring the desired effect, it would bring on all the Mischiefs of a sumptuary Law.

Whenever the Money is made lighter, or baser in allay, (which is the same thing) the effect is, that immediately the price of Bullion answers. So that in reality you change the Name, but not the thing: and whatever the difference is, the Tenant and Debtor hath it in his favour; for Rent and Debts will be paid less, by just so much as the intrinsick value is less, then what was to be paid before.

For example: One who before received for Rent or Debt, 3*l.* 2*s.* could with it buy twelve Ounces, or a Pound of Sterling Silver; but if the Crown-piece be worse in value than now it is, by 3*d.* I do aver, you shall not be able to buy a Pound of such Silver under 3*l.* 5*s.* but either directly or indirectly it shall cost so much.

But then it is said, we will buy an Ounce for 5*s.* because 'tis the Price set by the Parliament, and no body shall dare to sell for more. I answer, If they cannot sell it for more, they may coyn it; And then what Fool will sell an Ounce of Silver for 5*s.* when he may coyn it into 5*s.* 5*d.*?

Thus we may labour to hedge in the Cuckow, but in vain; for no People ever yet grew rich by Policies; but it is Peace, Industry, and Freedom that brings Trade and Wealth, and nothing else.

26

Considerations

ON THE

EAST-INDIA TRADE;

Wherein all the OBJECTIONS to that TRADE, with relation,

I. To the Exportation of BULLION, for Manufactures consumed in *England:*

II. To the Loss of Employment for our own Hands:

III. To the Abatement of Rents:

ARE FULLY ANSWER'D.

With a Comparison of the EAST-INDIA and FISHING TRADES.

LONDON:

Printed for J. ROBERTS, near the *Oxford Arms*, in *Warwick-Lane*. MDCCI.

To the Reader.

MOST of the things in these Papers are directly contrary to the receiv'd Opinions, and therefore ought not to be sent abroad without the clearest Evidence; For this, instead of using only comparative and superlative Words to amuse the Reader, the Author has endeavour'd after the manner of the *Political Arithmetick*, to express himself in Terms of Number, Weight, and Measure; and he hopes, he shall not be thought to speak with confidence, of any thing that is not as certain as the very Principles of *Geometry*. The *East-India* Trade, the Division of the Companies, the influence of that upon Publick Affairs, are become the general Subject of Conversation; every Man, with the greatest freedom, bestows his Censure upon these things. Some are for the Dissolution of one, others of both the Companies; some are for an Union, many are against the Trade itself, as that which carries away the Bullion, destroys the Manufactures, and abates the Rents of the Kingdom. The Author too, as well as others, has thought of these things, and is convinc'd himself, that the Bullion, the Manufactures, and the Rents of *England*, are increas'd by the *East-India* Trade; that the same is of all others, the most profitable to the Kingdom; that it is become still more so, by the competition of the two Companies; and that by the Dissolution of both, it wou'd be carried on to the very utmost Advantage. He has often said these

things

To the Reader.

things among his Friends; to these, his Reasons have
been so very convincing, that they have advis'd the
Author, that the present time were not unseasonable
to make 'em Publick. But then, that the Season for
doing this shou'd not be over, the Composition has
been very hasty; the same attended with frequent and
very melancholy Interruptions, and at last carried to
the Press without the Correction, and indeed without
so much as the Review of the Author. Wherefore,
he thinks himself oblig'd to beg the Reader's Pardon
for his unnecessary Repetitions, for his Negligences,
for his Affectations, and for every other Fault,
but only want of Demonstration: This he hopes is
never wanting, and if it is, he does not ask Forgive-
ness. The Author has compar'd the Trade to the *East-
Indies* with only that of Fishing; he had also design'd
to compare it with other Trades, but was forc'd to
break off by the loss of his dearest Friend. He has
too much Tenderness in his composition, to think at
such a time of any other Subject.

The

The Contents.

The Contents.

Imployment, and the Destruction of our Manufactures; is answered and prov'd:

1. That by means of this Trade, no Imployment of the People is lost that is worth our keeping; no manufacture is destroy'd which is profitable to the Kingdom, Chap. 10.

2. That this very Trade is the way to make more Imployment for the People:

(1.) By inlarging their Business in the former Manufactures, by reduction of their Price, Chap. 11. and this without abating Wages, and without any other inconvenience to the Labourer, Chap. 12.

(2.) By setting on foot new Imployments for the People, Chap. 13.

III. To the last Objection against the *East-India* Trade, *viz.* The Abatement of Rents is answer'd and deny'd:

1. That the value of the Produce of the Estate is lessen'd by exportation of Bullion, Chap. 14.

2. By diminution of Consumers, *ibid.*

3. By abatement of Wages, *ibid.*

4. By letting the Produce of *India* into all the *English* Markets, to destroy the Monopoly of the Landholder: To which is answered,

(1.) That the unwrought things of the *East-Indies* do not lessen the value of the Produce of *English* Estates, much less can the *Indian* Manufactures, *ibid.*

(2.) That the importation of Manufactures can only abate the price of Labour mix'd with the Produce of the Estate, and thereby must raise the value of the Produce of the Estate it self. Chap. 15.

(3.) That this is confirm'd by Examples, Chap. 16.

(4.) That consequently, Money and Buyers increase as Sellers, and like things for Sale; and thus the Landholder is not the worse for the loss of his Monopoly, Chap. 17.

Thirdly, A comparison of the *East-India* and Fishing-Trades: Wherein it is affirm'd,

I. That the Herring Fishing-Trade is not so profitable as the importation of *Irish* Cattel, or of *Indian* Manu-

factures

The Contents.

factures, and more likely than either to abate Rents, Chap. 18.

II. That in the present circumstances, the Herring Fishing-Trade is not practicable in *England*, Chap. 19.

III. That the Ways to enable *England* to carry on this Trade, are,

1. To enable us to afford our Herrings for as little profit as the *Dutch;* and the Ways for effecting this, Chap. 20.

2. To enable us to catch and cure our Herrings as cheap; which is to be effected,

(1.) By making all Materials for the Fishing-Trade as cheap in *England,* Chap. 21.

(2.) By making all our Labour and Preparation in that Trade as cheap, Chap. 22.

CHAP. I.

The Objections against the East-India *Trade; viz. The Exportation of Bullion for Manufactures to be consum'd in* England; *the loss of the Labourer's Employment; the Abatement of Rents are enforc'd.*

IT is generally objected against the *East-India* Trade, That it carries great quantities of Bullion into *India*, and returns chiefly Manufactures to be consum'd in *England;* there are also particular Complaints against this Trade by the Labourer, That he is driven from his Employment; by the Landholder, That his Rents must be abated. I shall endeavour to give as much Force to every one of these Objections, as if I believ'd 'em all my self.

To begin with the first, and most general Complaint *The general Complaint, that Bullion,* against this Trade, The Bullion must needs be exported into *India*, for Manufactures to be consum'd in *England.* The cheapest things are ever bought in *India;* as much Labour or Manufacture may be had there for two Pence, as in *England* for a Shilling. The Carriage thence is dear, the Customs are high, the Merchant has great Gains, and so has the Retailer; yet still with all this Charge, the *Indian* are a great deal cheaper than equal *English* Manufactures. Every Man will buy the best Penyworth; if this is to be had from *India*, the Bullion will be carried thither.

There is no reason to believe, that the *Indians* will *and not Manufactures,* take off any of our Manufactures, as long as there is such a difference in the Price of *English* and *Indian* Labour, as long as the Labour or Manufacture of the *East-Indies* shall be valued there at but one sixth Part of the

1   Price

Price of like Labour or Manufacture here in *England*; an *English* Manufacture worth a Shilling, after the Charge of so long a Voyage, will be seldom sold for more than two Pence, the Returns of this will be seldom sold for twelve Pence here; and of this a great deal must be paid to Freight and Customs. Such a Trade will soon undo the Merchant; and therefore, unless now and then for Curiosities, *English* Manufactures will seldom go to *India*.

must be chang'd for Manufactures Without the help of Laws, we shall have little reason to expect any other Returns for our Bullion, than only Manufactures, for these will be most profitable; for the Freight of unwrought things from *India* is equal to the Freight of so much Manufacture; the Freight of a Pound of Cotton is equal to the Freight of so much Callico, the Freight of raw Silk to that of wrought Silk; but the Labour by which this Cotton or raw Silk is to be wrought in *England*. is a great deal dearer than the Labour by which the same would be wrought in *India*. Therefore of all things which can be imported thence, Manufactures are bought cheapest; they will be most demanded here, the chief Returns will be of these, little then will be return'd from *India*, besides Manufactures.

to be consum'd in England. And when these shall be imported, here they will be likely to stay: in *France, Venice*, and other Countries, *Indian* Manufactures are prohibited, the great consumption must be in *England*. It has been prov'd by Arguments, that Bullion, and chiefly Bullion, is carried into *India*, that chiefly Manufactures must be return'd, and that these must be consum'd in *England*; But instead of all other Arguments, is Matter of Fact; Cargo's of Bullion are every Year carried into *India*, while almost every one at home is seen in *Indian* Manufactures. And this is thought sufficient to make good the first Charge against this Trade, That it carries great quan-

2   tities

tities of Bullion into *India,* and returns chiefly Manufactures to be consumed in *England.*

The Labourer's Complaint,

The next Complaint against this Trade, is of the Labourer, That he is driven from his Employment, to beg his Bread; by the Permission of *Indian* Manufactures to come to *England, English* Manufactures must be lost; *Indian* Manufactures are imported with less labour, they do not employ so many People, they must therefore starve for want of Business so many as wou'd be employ'd to make the *English* Manufactures more than are necessary, to procure the like things from the *East-Indies.*

That Indian *Manufactures are procur'd by Labour of less Price,*

And first, to shew how much more labour is necessary to make an *English* Manufacture, than to procure a like thing from the *East-Indies,* all that need be done, is to compare the Prices both of the one, and the other Labour. Of an *East-India* Manufacture, a small part of the Price is the Price of the Labour by which it is procur'd, of a piece of Muslin of the price of six Pounds, perhaps two thirds of this Price go either to the King for Customs, or to the Merchant's and Retailer's Gains; if this be so, then not above one third of this Price goes to pay the labour of fitting and providing a Ship and Cargo of Bullion out to *India,* of conducting and returning the Ship and Manufactures thence: Whether this be exactly true or no, a great part of the Price of an *Indian* Manufacture is to pay the Customs of the King, the Merchant's, and the Retailer's Gains; and consequently, so much less of the Price must pay the Labour by which it was procur'd. But now of a piece of Cloth of the price of six Pounds, almost all the six Pounds are divided to Carders, Spinners, Weavers, Dyers, Fullers, and other Labourers; of an equal *English* Manufacture the King has no Customs, the Merchant has no Gains, almost the whole price is the price of Labour by which the same was made; a less part of the price of an equal *Indian* Manufacture suffices to pay the Labour by which the same was procur'd. Wherefore *Indian* Manufactures are procur'd by Labour of less price than equal *English* Manufactures.

And therefore by less Labour than English *Manufacture* The Labour here in *England* bears proportion to the Wages that are given for it, it must be measur'd by the price, so that Labour of less price must be accounted less Labour; *Indian* Manufactures are procur'd by Labour of less price, and therefore by less Labour than equal *English* Manufactures.

And therefore must starve the People. The Manufactures of this Kingdom by so many hands perform'd, yet do not find imployment for all the People in it; many are already upon the Parishes, many for want of imployment, are forc'd every Year to sell themselves to the Plantations: The *East-India* Trades does not reduce the Manufactures into fewer hands, it procures them by less Labour, by the Labour of fewer People than are necessary to make the like in *England;* wherefore it must bring still more upon the Parishes, it must drive still more out of *England* to seek for imployment in other Countries.

The reason of the Thing is plain, and yet 'tis confirm'd by Matter of Fact. *Norwich* and *Canterbury* are imploy'd in the same kind of Manufactures that are imported from the *East-Indies*: As the *East-India* Trade has increas'd, so have the poor of those Cities; of late the Trade has been driven so very close, that both those Cities are almost reduc'd to Beggery. We need not for our instruction, resort to the Cries of the Weavers; the Rates to the Poor of every Parish, are sufficient Evidence how many Beggars are made by the *East-India* Trade. Wherefore we are very safely come to the conclusion which was propos'd before, The *East-India* Trade starves for want of imployment, so many as would be imploy'd to make the *English* Manu-

4   factures

factures more than are sufficient to procure the like from the *East-Indies*.

The last is the Complaint of the Landholder against this Trade, that his Rents must be abated by it. The value of the Produce of the Estate must be lessen'd, by the exportation of Bullion; by the diminution of Consumers; by the abatement of Wages; by letting the Produce of *India* into all the *English* Markets. *The Landholder's Complaint, That Rents must be abated by*

It cannot be imagin'd, that if there were but one Million Sterling to buy the same quantity of Meat, or Corn, or Cloaths, or other Produce of the Estate, that as much can be given for every Pound of Meat, or for every Bushel of Corn, or for every Yard of Cloth, as if the Sum were doubled. An hundred and fifty Years since, seldom more than Five Shillings were given for a Quarter of Wheat, in our Age seldom less than Forty Shillings; the proportion of Money to the conveniences of Life, is greater now than so many Years ago: Hence it is certain, the less the Proportion of Money to the Produce of the Estate, the less must needs be given for it: By the Exportation of Bullion into *India*, the Proportion of Silver to the Produce of the Estate must needs be lessen'd, consequently the Value of it must be abated. *Exportation of Bullion.*

And so it must, by the diminution of Consumers, the price of the Produce of the Estate cannot be so great when the number of Buyers shall be lessen'd: The *East-India* Trade, by doing the same Work with less labour; by imploying fewer hands; must needs remove great numbers of People from their Business; must force many out of *England*; must disable many of those that stay behind; the Buyers must be diminish'd, so consequently must the value of the Produce of the Estate. *Diminution of Consumers.*

Also the Wages of People will be abated by this Trade; by this they will be disabled to give the Land- *Abatement of Wages.*

holder

holder so much for the Produce of his Estate. The Wages of all Men will be abated by the free Allowance of *Indian* Manufactures; some *English* Manufactures will be intirely lost by the importation of the like, at less prices from *India;* some that were imploy'd in those, will betake themselves to other Manufactures, and (as it always happens in a great increase of Labourers,) they will be forc'd to work at less Wages, and by taking less Wages themselves, they will force down the Wages of other People; the abatement of Wages will be universal: And thus *English* Labourers, that is, the Body of the People, will have less to give the Landholder for the Produce of his Estate, and so the price of it must be abated.

Destruction of the Land-holder's Monopoly.

But if there is never the less Bullion in *England* for what is carried into *India,* if Buyers are still as many, Wages as high as ever; yet without an increase of Money and Buyers, the value of the Produce of *English* Estates must be lessen'd, by letting the Produce of *India* into all the *English* Markets, by the increase of Sellers, and of like things for Sale beyond the former Proportion of Money and Buyers.

The same Money and Buyers are not so much in proportion to the Corn of *Dantzick* and *England,* as to *English* Corn alone; nor to the *English* Cattel, *Irish* Beef, and *Dutch* Herrings, as to only *English* Cattel, nor to the Woollen and *Indian* Manufactures as to only Woollen Manufactures; consequently an increase of Sellers, and like things for Sale, without an increase of Money and Buyers, is an increase of them beyond the former Proportion of Money and Buyers: The *East-India* Trade exports the Bullion, lessens the number of Consumers, at least it increases neither Money nor Buyers; but for the increase of Sellers and like things for Sale, the *East-India* Merchant is become a Seller as well as the Landholder of *England,* the Produce of *India* is

6   brought

brought to the same Markets with the Produce of *English* Estates; wherefore the *East-India* Trade increases the Sellers, and like things for Sale against the *English* Landholders, and the Produce of their Estates beyond the former Proportion of Money and Buyers.

Lastly, If Money and Buyers shall not be increas'd, can the Landholder demand as high a price for his Corn in a Market stock'd with Corn from *Dantzick*, or for his Beef and Mutton in a Market full of *Dutch* Herrings and *Irish* Cattel, or for his Wooll in a Market, full of the Manufactures of *India* and other Countries, as if all these things were prohibited, and he might have all the Market to himself? Wherefore, by the increase of Sellers and of like things for Sale, beyond the former Proportion of Money and Buyers, the Landholder is disabled to demand as good a price for the Produce of his Estate: The *East-India* Trade is very guilty of this, of increasing Sellers and like things for Sale, against the Landholder and the Produce of his Estate, beyond the former Proportion of Money and Buyers; consequently by this Trade, by letting the Produce of *India* into all the *English* Markets, the value of the Produce of *English* Estates must be lessen'd.

Thus, by the Exportation of Bullion, by the Diminution of Consumers, by the Abatement of Wages, by letting the Produce of *India* into *English* Markets, the price of the Produce of *English* Estates, that is, Rents are abated.

And therefore all the Objections against this Trade are maintain'd, the Bullion is exported for Manufactures to be consum'd in *England*, the Labourer is driven from his Imployment, the Rents are abated.

7   CHAP.

CHAP. II.

The Exportation of Bullion for Indian *Manufactures, is an exchange of less for greater Value.*

BUT now 'tis time to think of Answers to these Objections. And to the First, *viz.* The Exportation of Bullion and the Consumption of *Indian* Manufactures, may be said, That the Exportation of Bullion for *Indian* Manufactures, is an exchange of less for greater value; that 'tis the most likely way to import more Bullion; that the Kingdom is not more impoverish'd by the Consumption of *Indian* than by that of *English* Manufactures.

To Export Bullion for *Indian* Manufactures, is to exchange less for greater value; it is to exchange Bullion for Manufactures more valuable, not only to the Merchant, but also to the Kingdom. Certainly the worth of every quantity of Silver is not infinite: There must be some way to state, determine, and compare the value of this with other things. No Man will say, that all the Manufactures in *England* are not worth a Shilling; or that the least quantity of Silver is more valuable to the Kingdom than the greatest of such things. The Manufactures, or other things, which are sufficient to procure from a Foreign Country any quantity of Bullion, are of so much value: Thus if an Hundred Yards of Cloth may be exchang'd with *Spain* for an Hundred Pounds in Money, they are of equal value; and therefore, more than an Hundred Yards being sufficient to procure a greater Sum, must needs be more valuable. So that this is certain, our Manufactures, or other things, or how much soever of them it is, that may be exchang'd with a Foreign Country for Bullion, are as valuable to the Kingdom as so much Bullion.

And so without doubt are the Manufactures, or other

The things that may be exchang'd abroad,

8   things,

things, which may be sold in *England* for Money; these *and much* are certainly as valuable to the Kingdom as so much *more those that may be* Money, that is, as so much Bullion. For these are *exchang'd at* better than the Manufactures which wou'd be exported *home for Bul-* abroad for so much Bullion. We cannot certainly *valuable.* know how many things must be carried out of *England* to purchase Bullion; but in general we may be assur'd, that more or better will not be sent abroad for any quantity of Bullion, than can be bought for the same in *England*. The Merchant wou'd soon be weary of such a Trade. The Cloth which he bought for an Hundred Pounds in *England*, he will expect to sell for more in Foreign Markets; or, if he shall expect no more abroad, he certainly bought his Cloth for less at home. So that of this we may be sure, better Manufactures will not be exported to procure Bullion than can be bought for the same in *England*. And therefore, if those that may be exchang'd with any Foreign Country for any quantity of Bullion, are of so much value; without doubt, the Manufactures that may be exchang'd in *England* for Bullion, are as valuable to the Kingdom as so much Bullion.

The Manufactures that may be exchang'd with Foreign *And therefore* Countries, and much more those that may be exchang'd *the Manufac-* in *England* for any quantity of Bullion, are of so much *tures return'd* value to the Kingdom. But certainly, better are return'd *for Bullion,* from the *East-Indies* for the Bullion sent thither, than *are more* wou'd be bought for the same in *England*. This is the *valuable.* very cause of Complaint against the Trade, and it is also Matter of Fact. Wherefore, better Manufactures are return'd from *India* for the Bullion sent thither, than those which are prov'd to be equivalent to the same. And thus the exchange is of less for greater value.

Again, That the Kingdom is a gainer by this Exchange; the Manufactures return'd from *India* for Bullion, are not only better than those that might be

exchang'd

exchang'd in *England*, or abroad, for so much Bullion; they may also themselves be exported and sold for more in Foreign Markets.

The Consumption of *Indian* Manufactures here in *England* will last but little longer, the Prohibition is drawing on apace, yet still the Bullion is running out as much as ever for Manufactures, which must not be consum'd at home, and which therefore must be carried out to Foreign Markets. Now the Merchants wou'd never venture their Money to *India* for Manufactures which must not be sold in *England* at all, and which cannot be sold in Foreign Markets for more Bullion. Wherefore, to Trade with Bullion into the *East-Indies*, is to Exchange the same for Manufactures which may be exchang'd for more abroad, that is, to exchange less for greater value.

The Manufactures return'd the Principal, and more valuable Riches. Lastly, The true and principal Riches, whether of private Persons, or of whole Nations, are Meat, and Bread, and Cloaths, and Houses, the Conveniences as well as Necessaries of Life; the several Refinements and Improvements of these, the secure Possession and Enjoyment of them. These for their own sakes, Money, because 'twill purchase these, are to be esteemed Riches; so that Bullion is only secondary and dependant, Cloaths and Manufactures are real and principal Riches. Are not these things esteem'd Riches over all the World? And that Country thought richest which abounds most with them? *Holland* is the Magazin of every Countries Manufactures; *English* Cloth, *French* Wines, *Italian* Silks, are treasur'd up there. If these things were not Riches, they wou'd not give their Bullion for 'em; or they would soon convert 'em into Bullion, without staying for the Market. The summ of this is, to shew, that Cloaths are part of the true and principal Riches, and therefore more valuable in their own nature; and that Bullion is only secondary

10 and

and dependent, and therefore by nature not so valuable; wherefore to exchange Bullion for Cloaths, is to exchange the Riches naturally not so valuable, and which are of no use but to be exchang'd, for the more valuable Riches, and which are of more immediate use; consequently, to exchange Bullion for more Cloaths, for more Manufactures than are to be had elsewhere for the same Bullion, is to exchange the less for the greater value: To export Bullion to the *East-Indies* for the Manufactures of those Countries, is to exchange the Bullion for more and better Manufactures, than are elsewhere to be procur'd for so much Bullion; it is consequently to exchange the less for the greater value.

To exchange Bullion for *Indian* Manufactures, is to exchange the same for Manufactures more valuable than the Manufactures which were exported to procure, and are equivalent to so much Bullion: is to exchange the same for Manufactures which may themselves be exchang'd for more Bullion; is to exchange the secondary, for more of the principal Riches than are elsewhere to be had upon the same Terms: And therefore it is sufficiently prov'd, that the Exchange of Bullion for *Indian* Manufactures, is an Exchange of less for greater value.

C H A P. III.

A more Open East-India-Trade, is more profitable to the Kingdom.

'TIS objected, and deny'd, That the *East-India-*Trade, as at present manag'd, is an Exchange of less for greater Value; for that the Emulation of two Companies contending one against another, has

11   utterly

utterly destroy'd the Profit of the Trade, has driven
the Trade so very close, has run the Prices of things so
high in *India*, so very low in *England*, that no more can
be imported from *India* for any sum of Money, than will
be made in *England* for the same Money. Bullion,
and so much Manufacture as can be purchas'd for it,
are equivalent. Wherefore for any quantity of Bullion,
if no more can be imported from *India*, than wou'd be
made in *England*, the Exchange is not of less for
greater value; the Kingdom is not the richer for this
Exchange.

The Bullion is exchang'd for more Manufactures, than will be made in England for it. First 'tis answer'd, That the Merchant still carries
on his Trade to the *East-Indies*; wherefore upon the
return of his Manufactures, he finds sufficient value to
pay the Freight and Cargo outwards, sufficient to pay
the Customs of the King, and some Profit to himself
besides; and still he is able to sell the *Indian*, cheaper
than he can buy an equal *English* Manufacture.
Therefore notwithstanding the Emulation of two Companies, notwithstanding the Prices rais'd in *India*, and
abated in *England*, still the Bullion is exchang'd with
India for more Manufactures than will be made in
England for it; still the Exchange is of less for greater
value.

But for a farther Answer to this Objection of two
Companies trading one against another, it must be
said, That the *East-India*-Trade, the more open, and
the closer driven, must needs import more Profit to the
Kingdom, and less disturb the *English* Manufactures.

'Tis very probable the profit of an open Trade is a
great deal less in proportion to the Stock imploy'd in
it, and therefore the Merchant that feels the difference,
will be very ready with his Complaints; 'tis without
doubt, more profitable for a Merchant to imploy his
Stock in Trade, so as at the end of the Year to receive
his Principal again, with Gain besides of twenty for

12   every

every Hundred, than to imploy as much Stock for half as much Profit. But 'tis better and more profitable for the Kingdom, that 300*l*. should be imployed in Trade for the profit of 10 *per Cent*. than but 100*l*. for the profit of 20 *per Cent*. wherefore, less in proportion and more in quantity, must be esteem'd as greater profit.

This then will be the consequence of the *East-India* Trade, laid more open and closer driven; the profit will be less in proportion but more in quantity. 'Tis reasonable to believe, that a Company cannot trade so much to the publick Benefit; a Company of Merchants trading with a Joint-stock, is but one only Buyer, one only Seller; they manage their Trade with the pride and charge that become the State of Kings; they expect to be follow'd by the Market, and therefore never stir beyond the Warehouse, whither if Customers come, they are forc'd to wait till the Auction is ready to begin; in an open Trade, every Merchant is upon his good Behaviour, always afraid of being undersold at home, always seeking out for new Markets in Foreign Countries; in the mean time, Trade is carried on with less Expence: This is the effect of Necessity and Emulation, things unknown to a single Company. A Trade so far extended, so much better husbanded, however less profitable in proportion to the Merchant's Stock, must needs import more absolute Profit to the Kingdom. *Companies trade at more charge than private Persons.*

Also, the Examples of parallel Cases make it very credible, that a more open *East-India* Trade and closer driven, tho' it may be less profitable in proportion to the Bulk of it, will yet be more profitable to the Kingdom. In the time of Sir *Thomas Gresham*, perhaps he was the only Merchant in *England :* Wonderful things are storyed of Trade and profit of Trade in that Age; for every Hundred Pounds at the end of the Year, besides the Principal return'd again, Two or Three Hun- *Other Examples.*

13   dred

dred Pounds are said to have been divided between the
Customs of the King and the Merchant's Gain. 'Tis
scarce credible, that at this time more than the profit
of 20 or 30 *per Cent.* can be divided between the Merchant and the King; but then from the difference of
Customs, and for other Reasons, we may very well
believe, that for every Hundred Pounds in the Age of
Sir *Thomas Gresham,* Ten Thousand Pounds are now
imploy'd in Trade; and consequently, for every Hun-
dred Pounds gain'd in that Age, at least a Thousand
Pounds are gain'd in this; indeed a great deal less in
proportion to the Stock, but more in quantity. The
African Trade was very lately like that of the *East-
Indies,* carried on by the Joint-stock of one single
Company: it is not laid quite open now, only private
Traders are admitted upon payment of a Mulct to the
Company; the consequence of this is, that Ten ships
are imploy'd in that Trade for one before, Ten hundred
Pounds for one before. It will hardly be pretended by
the Company, that when the Trade was all their own,
they divided more to the King and Company than 100
per Cent. And it will hardly be deny'd by the present
Traders, that 20 or 30 *per Cent.* is divided to the Customs and their own Profit: and this is likewise less in
proportion to the present Bulk of the Trade, yet more
in quantity. Now, if this has been the consequence of
other Trades enlarg'd and closer driven, why should it
not be the same of the *East-India* Trade enlarg'd and
closer driven.

Also of the East-India Trade, prove an open Trade most profit-able. But indeed, this is the consequence: The *East-India*
Trade enlarg'd by the Emulation of two Companies,
may be less profitable to the Merchant; certainly it
must import more profit to the Kingdom. While one
only Company enjoy'd that Trade, I will believe, that
every Hundred Pounds exported into *India,* return'd in
value besides the Principal, 50*l.* to the Customs, and

14   double

double that Sum to the Merchant's Gain; in all 150*l.* this was great Profit. But at this time, the Stock in that Trade is four times as great as 'twas before, that is, Four hundred Pounds for one; Four hundred Pounds must now return in value, besides the Principal, as much in proportion to the Customs, in all Two hundred Pounds, and something over to the Merchant's Gains, perhaps One hundred Pounds for all the four. And thus the Trade is four times as great as 'twas before; the Profit is only doubled; the Profit is less in proportion to the Bulk of the Trade, but more in quantity.

Less Profit in proportion but greater in quantity, is greater Profit; from Reason, from the Experience of other Trades, and even of this very Trade, it appears, the more open the same shall be, and closer driven, it may indeed import less Profit in proportion to the Bulk of the Trade, yet must import more in quantity, and consequently must needs be more profitable to the Kingdom: And thus again, notwithstanding the prices of things rais'd in *India*, abated here, the Bullion is still exchang'd for greater value.

'Tis true, if this Trade shall be carried on with the greatest freedom, if every one shall be permitted to imploy his Stock in it, by degrees it will be driven so very close, that nothing of Profit will be glean'd from it; the Merchant will be disabled to import the *Indian* Manufactures cheaper than as good things may be made in *England*. Then there will be truth in his Complaint, the Exchange will be unprofitable, and must be given over. But then 'tis fit the Merchant should be told, that the *East-India* Trade is not carried on for his sake, but for the Kingdom's; when Manufactures are not to be imported cheaper from *India* than they can be made in *England*, our End is gain'd; we have reap'd the utmost Profit that is to be obtain'd by that

Tho' driven so close as to be left off.

15   or

or any other Trade; our Manufactures will then be quiet; they will not be disturb'd by the cheaper *Indian* Manufactures; these will not rule the price of ours, neither in our own nor foreign Markets: And thus one of the great Objections against this Trade wou'd be answer'd; the *East-India* Trade the more open and closer driven, will less disturb the *English* Manufactures, and import the greatest Profit into *England*.

Objections that a more open East-India *Trade not good.* Yet against a more open *East-India* Trade will be objected, That the Trade is not to be carried on at all without Forts and Factories; that these are not to be maintain'd without the Joint-stock of a Company; and 'tis but reasonable the Company that bears the charge, shou'd reap the Profit of the Trade. Wherefore 'tis every day insinuated, That the late Act for erecting a new Company, was gain'd by Violence and Injustice; that it is continu'd only for the sake of the Loan to the Government, at excessive Interest; that to be restor'd to their former Right of the whole Trade, the Old Company is ready to pay the Loan, and will be content with half the Interest; and 'twill be unreasonable, if an *English* Parliament shall refuse to do a piece of Justice so very profitable to the Kingdom, where as it ought to be done tho' to our greatest Disadvantage. And besides, Political Reasons concur with this, that the Kingdom may be once more at quiet. What Heats and Animosities have been caus'd by this Division? What Distractions in the Publick Counsels? Our Elections are not free, neither our Debates of Parliament. The Publick Business is very often at a stand; every one is engag'd on the side of the one or the other Company. If either can be gain'd to the Publick Interest, this is sure, tho' for no other reason, to meet with Opposition. Indeed of late, the Resolutions have been brave; the King has been Address'd to enter into great Alliances, for the preservation of our

16   Selves,

Selves, our Neighbours, our Religion, and the Peace of
Europe. Nevertheless it cannot presently be forgotten,
that it was some struggle to resolve upon the Peace of
Europe, that Speeches were made in favour of the
Duke of *Anjou*'s Title to the Crown of *Spain*, and that
it has been thought almost crime enough for an Im-
peachment, to advise the King to disown it. All which
is imputed to the Quarrel of the two Companies; Men
are afraid, that this in time may clog the Wheels of
the Government; so that we may be forc'd to stand
still, and see a coalition of *France* and *Spain*, the Empire broken, *Holland* devour'd in one or two Cam-
pagnes, and *England* left alone to deal with all this
Power. Our *Mediterranean* Trade is already at the
mercy of this Conjunction; when *Holland's* gone, the
French are Masters of all the Coast upon the Continent; our *Baltic* Trade and all our Naval Stores are
gone. Our *East* and *West-India* Trades might languish yet a little longer, but must decay for want of
Places to take off our Returns, and may yet be sooner
broken by this united Power. But why shou'd we be
in any Disquiets for our Trade, as if that alone were in
danger? If this Conjunction holds, we must submit
our selves, and be contented with Laws and Vice-Roys,
such as *France* will please to send us. 'Tis said, that
this Division of the Companies must certainly disable
us to use our Naval Strength, to harass the Coasts of
France and *Spain*, to cut off their Communication with
their *Indian* Kingdoms, to intercept and confiscate their
Treasures there to the use of a War so necessary; leave
must be had of both the Companies to spirit the Discontents of *Spain*, to encourage the Friends of the
House of *Austria* to shew themselves, and call aloud
for change of Government: These and an hundred
other invidious things, are charg'd upon this Division;
if they are true, we pay too dear for this Enlargement

17   of

of our Trade; 'twere far better that both the Companies were broken, and all the Profit of the Trade were lost for ever.

Answer'd. But certainly, to break both Companies is not the way to lose the Profit of the Trade; the Trade is then laid open, the Profit thereof must needs encrease; the necessary Forts and Castles may be as well maintain'd at the Publick Charge; and this may be better paid by the greater Gain of an open Trade. The want of Factories can be no Complaint: A greater Trade must needs increase these; it has done so in every Country; the Reason is alike in all; our Factories must be as well secur'd by Forts and Castles, under the immediate care of the Government, as if the same were maintain'd by the Joint-stock of a Company.

If it has really enter'd into the Thoughts of any Gentleman of the Old Company, to offer to advance this Loan to the Parliament at half the interest for all the Trade; if this is intended to be propos'd to the Wisdom of a Nation as a beneficial Bargain, this of all things is most extravagant and amazing. The Kingdom, that is, the Body of the People, is neither richer nor poorer, whether an Hundred thousand Pounds *per Annum* be paid to a Company of *English* Merchants, or remain at the disposal of the Government. But the Nation possibly, is by half a Million yearly richer, as long as this Trade is so much enlarg'd by the Emulation of two Companies, than if 'twere reduc'd to the Joint-stock of one. If so great a yearly Profit is not to be given up to Peace and Justice, 'twill never be given away for nothing; the Wisdom of Parliament will never be so far over-reach'd by the cunning of Merchants.

I rather hope to hear of Ways and Means to pay this Loan of both the Companies, to buy their Forts and Castles, and whatsoever is their Right of Trade: These

18   might

might be valu'd by a Jury of Twelve indifferent and understanding Men; whatever by these shou'd be Awarded, wou'd soon be paid by the Customs of this Trade: And thus the Trade wou'd be laid quite open to all the good People of *England;* by this means no Injustice wou'd be done, and these Advantages wou'd be obtain'd.

First of all, an end wou'd be put to the Trade of Stock-jobbers; uuskilful and unwary Men are entic'd away, from certain Profit to pursue uncertain Hopes; after great Revolutions of the Game, their Hopes at last are disappointed, their Stocks are left among the Artists, their Industry is lost to the Kingdom, their Families are undone. 'Tis in vain to forbid the thing by Laws; Laws are eluded by the subtlety and cunning of Men; the thing is practis'd more than ever: To break both Companies, is not only to forbid the Corruption, but to tear it up by the very Roots. *The dissolution of the Companies, the way to destroy Stockjobbing,*

Stocks in the Warehouses of private Merchants rise and fall, and no Man knows it but themselves; however, they rise in value in spight of Wars. Companies are frighted by Wars and rumours of Wars; the Jointstocks fall, and every one must hear it: And this engages the private Interest of some, the Fear of others, to disturb the publick Resolutions; to be rid of this inconvenience were worth a great deal to the Nation; to break both Companies were half the way to do it. *To restore Freedom to the publick Debates,*

Of Companies, Committees have always separate interests of their own; Commands of Ships, Places, and Governments to sell; however it fares with the Jointstock, the Trade to these Men is always profitable. These do not care to part with their places; and this perhaps has chiefly held off the Union of both the Companies. The Corruptions which they have practis'd themselves, they have learn'd to practise upon greater Men than themselves Vast sums are gone, *To put an end to many Corruptions,*

19

which

38

which are not yet, nor ever will be brought to account. To break both Companies, is the surest way to break these Practices; to make Men honest, is to take from them all Temptations to be otherwise.

To restore Peace among the People. By this, our Heats and Animosities will be remov'd, our Breaches heal'd, the Kingdom once again in peace. If such Mischiefs have been created by the distracted Counsels of both Companies, what may be fear'd from the united Strength of both?

To purchase these Advantages, nothing is given away that's valuable; the Trade already enlarg'd by the Emulation of two Companies, by the dissolution of both, will yet be more enlarg'd. A Trade more open and closer driven, will be more profitable to the Kingdom. Prices of things may be rais'd in *India*, abated here; nevertheless, as long as this Trade shall be carried on, the same will be an exchange of less for greater value; and when it ceases to be such, 'twill then be time to give it over.

CHAP. IV.

The East-India *Trade does not so much diminish the Riches of some private Persons, as it increases the Riches of the Kingdom.*

An Objection, That as much Value of English Manufacture is destroy'd, as is imported of Indian Manufactures. AGAIN, it is objected against this Trade, If the same is an Exchange of less for greater value, yet the Kingdom, the Body of the People is not the richer for this Exchange. The *East-India* Trade procures Manufactures at less Price, and by less Labour than the like wou'd be made in *England*; perhaps as much value at the price of one Shilling, and consequently by one Man's Labour, as will be made here by three, and for the price of three Shillings. But then

two

two are depriv'd of their Employments; for every one brought from *India*, so much *English* Manufacture is destroy'd: the *East-India* Trade does the Work with fewer Hands, but then no more is done. Few do the Business of many, but then the rest are forc'd to stand still; few possess themselves of all the Riches, and leave nothing for the rest of the People. Thus the Riches of the Kingdom are not greater, they are only translated into fewer Hands; what is gain'd by the exchange of Bullion for a better thing, is lost again by the loss of so much *English* Manufacture. Wherefore, tho' indeed the Exchange is for greater Value, yet all the Benefit is to private Persons; many others are undone; the Body of the People is not the richer, the Kingdom is not enrich'd.

To this Objection may be answer'd, If the Riches *The same is* of the Kingdom by this Trade are only translated into *Answer'd.* fewer Hands, if they are not greater, yet they are not less for this Translation. Of an 100*l.* the Value is the same, whether collected into the Hands of few, or distributed into the Hands of many. The same quantity of Silk, or Cloth, or Callico, or other Manufacture, will cloath as many Backs, the Value of 'em will feed as many Bellies, whether procur'd by the Labour of one, or by the equal Labour of three. If the same Work is done by one, which was done before by three; if the other two are forc'd to sit still, the Kingdom got nothing before by the Labour of the two, and therefore loses nothing by their sitting still. And thus if the Riches of the Kingdom are not greater, they are not less for being procur'd by fewer Hands. Nevertheless, this is not an Answer to the Objection, That tho' the Exchange is profitable to private Persons, yet the Kingdom is not the richer for it.

Therefore certainly the publick Stock must be increast. If one Man procures as much Value by his

labour

Labour from *India*, as three produc'd before in *England* : if one Man does the Work of three, his Riches are increas'd, he possesses as much as all the three before. The Riches of the other two are not reduc'd to nothing; perhaps their Labour is less valuable, yet still it is worth something; and whatsoever it is worth is Gain to the Kingdom. The Riches of one are as great as of all the three before, those of the other two are not reduc'd to nothing : And thus the increase of the Stock of a Part exceeding the diminution of that of the rest of the People, must be esteem'd an increase of the Riches of the whole People. If any *English* Manufactures are destroy'd by the Importation of those of the *East-Indies*, yet still there is left Employment for the People; and thus the Exchange of Bullion for *Indian* Manufactures is not only profitable to those that make it, but also to the Kingdom.

Whence it may be concluded, that notwithstanding the Emulation of two Companies, and the Influence of that upon the prices of things both here and in the *East-Indies*; notwithstanding the loss of some *English* Manufactures by the Importation of like and cheaper things from *India*, yet still the Trade with that Country is an Exchange of Bullion for Manufactures more valuable than those equivalent of so much Bullion; of Bullion for Manufactures that may be exchang'd for more; of less of the secondary for more of the principal Riches than are otherwise to be had upon the same Terms, is consequently an exchange of less for greater Value. And this may serve for a first Answer to the Exportation of our Bullion.

CHAP

(571)

CHAP. V.

The East-India Trade is the way to Increase our Bullion.

BUT if without regard to quantity, Bullion shall be esteem'd more valuable than Manufactures, because these are to be consum'd, and that may be preserv'd; it must be affirm'd, That the exchange of Bullion for *Indian* Manufactures, is the most likely way to procure more, by enabling us to export more Manufactures than were exported for so much Bullion.

The East-India Trade the most likely way to import more Bullion.

For this does not grow in *England,* 'tis imported from abroad; it is receiv'd in exchange for the Manufactures which are exported; these are exported and Bullion is return'd. Thus, for an Hundred Yards of Cloth carried into *Spain,* an Hundred Pounds in Money are return'd: so, for Three Hundred Yards of Cloth or equivalent Silks and Callicoes, more Silver is return'd; therefore the more Manufactures shall be exported, more Bullion will be imported. By the exportation of this into *India* for Manufactures, we have more of these than were carried out to procure this Bullion; we are therefore enabled to export more Manufactures, and consequently to import more Bullion. And thus the exportation of Bullion into *India* for the Manufactures of that Country, is the most likely way to increase it.

And indeed, by whatsoever means the Bullion is increas'd, more Plate is seen in Churches, more in Private Houses, more Goldsmiths, and Men who deal in Bullion, than ever heretofore. Besides, the plenty of Money is greater, more Money is given for Lands, more for Merchandizes, more for all manner of Pur-

And has actually increas'd the Bullion.

23   chaces.

chaces. Before the noise of a War with *France*, the Joint-stocks and Funds were rising every day; the credit of the Government was very much increas'd. Money lyes at less interest, it Trades for less profit, it makes a greater shew than ever; all this is demonstration that Bullion is increas'd. And, what other thing is so likely to be the cause of this, as the *East-India* Trade? It exchanges the Bullion gain'd by one for more and better Manufactures; it increases our Plenty, it must needs increase our Exportations, it must consequently be the cause of importing more Bullion.

CHAP. VI.

The East-India *Trade must increase our Exportations.*

Notwithstanding the increase of our Luxury;

TO this is objected, That the *East-India* Trade can be no cause of increasing our Bullion, that it cannot increase our Exportations; that *Indian* Manufactures are forbid in Foreign Countries, and Foreign Markets are already stock'd with ours; so that neither can the former be again exported, nor by being consum'd in *England*, can they be the cause of exporting more of *English* Manufactures. Consequently our Luxury and Consumption may increase with our Abundance, our Exportations cannot be greater, our Bullion cannot be increas'd.

Nevertheless, the most likely way to increase our Exportations, is the *East-India* Trade, and that by increasing our Plenty too fast for our use, too fast for our Luxury and Consumption. This Trade is a continual exchange of the Bullion procur'd by less for more and better Manufactures; and therefore of less for more and better Manufactures; it is therefore of

24   all

all other Trades, the most likely to increase our Plenty of those too fast for our Luxury and Consumption.

Again, Nothing will be kept in *England* to perish without use, all that is too much to be spent at home will be exported. Of all Trades, the *East-India* Trade is most likely to increase our Manufactures too fast for our Luxury and Consumption; it is therefore most likely to increase our Exportations.

Wherefore, in spight of Prohibitions, our *Indian* Manufactures will find out Foreign Markets. In spight of Laws people will buy cheapest, Foreigners will find out ways to get such things into their own Countries, or they will come after 'em into ours. Nothing can be so cheap in *Europe* as *Indian* Manufactures: Therefore such of these as are too much for the use of *England*, will be exported, or Foreigners will come hither; as our Plenty shall increase our People will increase. *Notwithstanding the Foreign Prohibitions of Indian Manufactures;*

Or, if all that are imported shou'd be consum'd within *England*, so many of our Manufactures will be spar'd; for if we shall have too many either of our own, or of *Indian* Manufactures, either those will be consum'd at home, and then the *Indian* will be exported; or these will be consum'd in *England;* and then, tho' Foreign Markets are already stock'd with *English* Manufactures, yet these will be exported. Foreign Markets perhaps will not take off more at the present price; by the free Allowance of *Indian*, the price of *English* Manufactures must be abated, (and this without inconvenience to any one as shall be shown hereafter) and then more of these will be exported. *Notwithstanding Foreign Markets are stock'd with English Manufactures.*

Of all Trades, that of the *East-Indies* is most likely to increase our Plenty beyond the power of our Luxury and Consumption ; and therefore, notwithstanding the Foreign Prohibitions of *Indian* Manufactures, and tho'

Foreign

Foreign Markets are already full of ours, the *East-India* Trade is the likeliest way to increase our Exportations, and consequently our Bullion.

CHAP. VII.

Notwithstanding the idleness of the Mint, the Money and the Bullion are increas'd.

An Objection that neither Money nor Bullion is increas'd because the Mint stands still.

AGain, That the *East-India* Trade may not have the credit of having increas'd our Bullion, 'tis deny'd that this is increas'd. If our Bullion were increas'd (say some) there wou'd be a greater plenty of Money. The whole Increase of Bullion wou'd not be manufactur'd into Plate; some wou'd be carried to the Mint; this has had no business but to recoin the Old Money, otherwise it has stood still for many Years; wherefore the Money is not increas'd, nor by consequence the Bullion.

The same is answer'd.

Yet notwithstanding the idleness of the Mint, Money is increas'd; and tho' this were not, the Bullion is increas'd. Foreign Money becomes every day more and more current, *French* Pistoles at Par with so much *English* Gold, are as plenty every where as Guineas; *Spanish* Silver is easie to be had on payment of the Difference. A plenty of Foreign Money very easily supplies the want of *English* Coin; tho' our own Mint stands still, with a sufficient plenty of Foreign Money we can never be in want; and thus notwithstanding the idleness of the Mint, the Money is increas'd.

And yet, tho' it were not, it cou'd be no Argument against the Increase of Bullion. The Increase of which does not prove that any of it must be carry'd to the Mint. Bullion by being coin'd, is made current only here in *England*; 'tis restrain'd from going into

26   any

any other Country; before, when 'twas current over all the World, 'twas more valuable than now, when 'tis confin'd to only *England,* so that 'tis made less valuable by being coin'd. It is not likely therefore that any Man will coin his Bullion, that it may become less valuable than 'twas before; wherefore the increase of the same is no necessary Argument, that any of it must be coin'd, consequently, notwithstanding the idleness of the Mint, the Bullion may be increas'd.

Tho' the Mint has stood still for many Years, the Money is increas'd, and if it were not, yet the Bullion is; the former Arguments are not shaken by this Objection.

CHAP. VIII.

The increase of Paper Money is to be ascrib'd to the increase of real Money, rather than the apparent plenty of Money to the increase of current Paper.

BUT Men are more ready to assign any thing as a reason of the greater apparent plenty of Money, than the *East-India* Trade; and therefore they say, the increase is all imaginary, Paper is current every where; the great plenty of this it is that makes a shew; that makes so much Money for Purchaces, so much to lye at low Interest, so much to Trade at little Profit. The current Money is little else but Paper; the increase of this is great, but not of real Money. *The apparent Plenty of Money is by some ascrib'd to the increase of current Paper.*

Notwithstanding all which, the apparent plenty of Money is not to be ascrib'd to the increase of current Paper; the increase of this is rather to be ascrib'd to that of real Money.

And first, it is not Paper that lyes at low interest; *But untruly.* that trades at little profit. If I deposit Money with a

27   Banker,

Banker, and take his Bills to answer the Demand, tho'
these shou'd pass Ten thousand times in Payment, yet
as long as so much Money lyes in the Hands of the
Banker, his Bills are real Money, For while these are
current, that in the mean time lyes dead; if the Bills
were call'd in, the Money wou'd do the work as well,
wou'd pass as well in payment. So that such kind of
Notes as these are not a new created Species, are not
imaginary or Paper only, but so much real Money.
In like manner, if I take up Bills of a Banker, and
bring no Cash into his Bank, those are no longer
imaginary or Paper only, than till an equal Cash is
paid in; when that is done, these are also real Money.
So that meer Paper money are Bills without a Cash to
answer them. And these are always paying excessive
Interest to the Banker, above the common Interest
above the ordinary Profit of Trade. For a Banker will
not make himself liable to answer the Demands of
ready Money for nothing; he will therefore expect to
receive the Value whensoever he gives out Bills, or
Interest above the common Rate, if without Money he
undertakes himself to answer the Demand; wherefore
meer Paper is always paying excessive Interest. Such
Money will neither endure to be let out at low Interest,
nor to be employ'd in Trade for little Profit; not by
the Borrower, he will not take up Money of the
Banker at high Interest to let out the same again at
less, or to Trade with it for little Profit; he therefore
borrows to pay off Debts that will not stay, to satisfie
his impatient Creditor. Nor by his Creditor, he is not
so impatient for his Money, as to oblige his Debtor to
borrow the same at higher Interest, that he may let it
out again at less, he wou'd rather take high Interest of
his Debtor than oblige him to pay it to the Banker;
so that he also wants his Money for more pressing
Occasions. Therefore this new created Species, this

28   imaginary

imaginary or meer Paper Money, is never lett at little Interest, is never imploy'd in Trade for little Profit, is not the Money that makes this mighty shew; and thus the apparent plenty of Money is not to be ascrib'd to Paper.

Rather the increase of this must be ascrib'd to that of real Money. When there was but little Money, the Credit also was very little; we have had late and sad Experience of this; Bills were discounted every day; so that Credit is always most, when there is most Money to satisfie the same. Paper Money is nothing else but Credit; from the increase of which, we are sure that Credit is increas'd; this is the present State of *England,* and consequently there is a greater plenty of real Money.

Real as well as Paper Money may be increas'd; 'tis very possible for both to be increas'd together; then the abundance of current Paper is no Argument that real Money, much less that Bullion, is not increas'd.

The present plenty of Money is not apparent only, 'tis also real; the little Profit for which it is employ'd in Trade, is the best Argument of the plenty of real Money. The idleness of the Mint is no Argument that Money, much less that Bullion is not increas'd. Of all Trades, this of the *East-Indies* is most likely to make our Plenty too great for our Luxury and Consumption, 'tis most likely to increase our Exportations, and consequently to increase our Bullion. And thus a second answer is given to the Exportation of Bullion for Manufactures to be consum'd in *England.*

CHAP.

C H A P. IX.

The Kingdom is not more impoverish'd by the Consumption of Indian *than of* English *Manufactures.*

The Consumption of English Manufactures is a loss of more value.

Lastly, The Kingdom is not more impoverish'd by the Consumption of *Indian* than of *English* Manufactures. Indeed whatsoever is consum'd in *England,* is loss, it can be no profit to the Nation; but yet to permit the Consumption of the *Indian,* is not the way to lose so much as if we shall restrain our selves to only *English* Manufactures. Things may be imported from *India* by fewer hands than as good wou'd be made in *England;* so that to permit the Consumption of *Indian* Manufactures, is to permit the loss of few Men's labour; to restrain us to only *English,* is to oblige us to lose the labour of many; the loss of few Men's labour must needs be less than that of many: Wherefore, if we suffer our selves to consume the *Indian,* we are not so much impoverish'd as if we were restraind to the Consumption of only *English* Manufactures.

It must be confess'd, that of Manufactures, whether *English* or *Indian,* of equal value, and already in our possession, the Consumption of one can be no more loss than of the other. But a Law to restrain us to use only *English* Manufactures, is to oblige us to make them first, is to oblige us to provide for our Consumption by the labour of many, what might as well be done by that of few; is to oblige us to consume the labour of many when that of few might be sufficient. Certainly we lose by being restrain'd to the Consumption of our own, we cannot be so much impoverish'd by the free and indifferent use of any Manufactures.

It was the first and most general Objection against

the

the *East-India* Trade, That it carries great quantities of Bullion into *India*, and returns chiefly Manufactures to be consum'd in *England;* the Matter of Fact is not deny'd, but then it has been answer'd and made evident, That the exportation of Bullion for *Indian* Manufactures, is an exchange of less for greater value, is the way to import more Bullion into *England*, and that we are not more impoverish'd by the consumption of *Indian* than of *English* Manufactures; and these are sufficient Answers to the first Objection.

CHAP. X.

The East-India *Trade destroys no imployment of the People which is profitable to the Kingdom.*

AND thus I think, I have remov'd the first great Charge against the *East-India* Trade. The next is, That Manufactures are procur'd from thence by the labour of fewer hands than the like, or as good can be made in *England;* that therefore, many must stand still at home for want of imployment.

People imploy'd to make Manufactures that might be imported from India, are imploy'd to no profit of the Kingdom.

To which is answer'd, That the *East-India* Trade cannot destroy any profitable Manufacture, it deprives the People of no business which is advantagious to the Kingdom; contrary, it is the most likely means to make full employment for the People.

The *East-India* Trade destroys no profitable *English* Manufacture; it deprives the People of no imployment, which we shou'd wish to be preserv'd. The foundation of this Complaint is, That Manufactures are procur'd from the *East-Indies* by the labour of fewer People, than are necessary to make the like in *England;* and this shall be admitted. Hence it follows, that to reject the *Indian* Manufactures that like may be made by the

labour

labour of more Hands in *England*, is to imploy many to do the work that may be done as well by few; is to imploy all, more than necessary to procure such things from the *East-Indies*, to do the work that may be done as well without 'em.

A Saw-mill with a pair or two of Hands, will split as many Boards as thirty Men without this Mill; if the use of this Mill shall be rejected, that thirty may be imployed to do the work, eight and twenty are imploy'd more than are necessary, so many are imploy'd to do the work that may be done as well without 'em. Five Men in a Barge upon a Navigable River, will carry as much as an hundred times so many Horses upon the Land, and twenty times as many Men; if the Navigation of this River shall be neglected, that the same Carriage may be perform'd by Land, nineteen in twenty of these Men, and all these Horses, are more than are necessary to do the work, so many are imploy'd to do the work that may be done as well without them. So, if by any Art, or Trade, or Engine, the labour of one can produce as much for our consumption or other use, as can otherwise be procur'd by the labour of three; if this Art, or Trade, or Engine, shall be rejected, if three shall rather be imploy'd to do the work, two of these are more than are necessary, so many are imploy'd to do the work that may be done as well without 'em; so in all cases, all that are imploy'd more than are necessary to do any work, are imploy'd to do the work that may be done as well without 'em: Wherefore, the People imploy'd to make Manufactures here, more than are necessary to procure the like from *India*, are People imployed to do the work that may be done as well without 'em, so many are imploy'd to no profit of the Kingdom. For, if the Providence of God wou'd provide Corn for *England* as *Manna* heretofore for *Israel*, the People wou'd not be well imploy'd, to

Plough,

Plough, and Sow, and Reap for no more Corn than might be had without this labour. If the same Providence wou'd provide us Cloaths without our labour, our Folly wou'd be the same, to be Carding, Spinning, Weaving, Fulling and Dressing, to have neither better nor more Cloaths than might be had without this labour. Again, if *Dantzick* wou'd send us Corn for nothing, we shou'd not refuse the Gift, only that we might produce the same quantity of Corn by the sweat of our Brows. In like manner, if the *East-Indies* wou'd send us Cloaths for nothing, as good or equivalent of those which are made in *England* by prodigious labour of the People, we shou'd be very ill imploy'd to refuse the Gift, only that we might labour for the same value of Cloaths which might be as well obtain'd by sitting still. A People wou'd be thought extravagant and only fit for Bedlam, which with great stir and bustle shou'd imploy it self to remove Stones from place to place, at last to throw 'em down where at first they took 'em up. I think the Wisdom of a People wou'd be little greater, which having Cloaths and Victuals, and other necessaries of Life already provided sufficient for their use, shou'd nevertheless abstain from the use of these things, till after the Penance of having carry'd them seven Miles upon their Shoulders; so in no case are any number of People well imploy'd, or to any profit of the Kingdom, who only do the work which might be done as well without 'em, who with great pains and labour provide for their own, or for the use of other People, the same or no better things than might be had without this pains and labour. Wherefore, to imploy to make Manufactures here in *England*, more People than are necessary to procure the like from *India*, to imploy so many to do the work which might be done as well without them, is to imploy so many to no profit of the Kingdom.

Then Manufactures made in *England*, which, or the

like

like of which, might be procur'd by the labour of fewer Hands from the *East-Indies*, are not profitable to the Kingdom ; wherefore, to procure such things from *India* by the labour of fewer Hands, to spare a great many Hands which wou'd be imployed in *England* to do the same things, is not to deprive the People of any imployment which we shou'd wish to be preserv'd, is not to lose any profitable Manufacture ; still the same things are done, only the labour of doing them is a great deal less than it was before.

To imploy People to make Manufactures which might be imported from India, is a loss to the Kingdom. To imploy to make Manufactures here, more Hands than are necessary to procure the like things from the *East-Indies*, is not only to imploy so many to no profit, it is also to lose the labour of so many Hands which might be imploy'd to the profit of the Kingdom. Certainly, every individual Man in *England*, might be imploy'd to some profit, to do some work which cannot be done without him ; at least, the contrary is not evident, as long as *England* is not built, beautify'd, and improv'd to the utmost Perfection, as long as any Country possesses any thing which *England* wants, *Spain* the Gold and Silver of *America*, *Holland* the Fishing and other Trades, *France* the Wines, as long as *Campagne* and *Burgundy* are not drunk in every Parish ; some of these things might be appropriated to *England ;* *English* Labour might be exchang'd for others ; these things wou'd be imployment enough for all, and a great many more than all the People of the Kingdom, tho' every one were imploy'd to the best advantage, tho' not the labour of any Hand in *England* were thrown away ; whence it may very well be concluded, that every individual Man in *England*, might be imploy'd to some profit of the Kingdom.

Then to imploy to Manufacture things in *England*, more Hands than are necessary to procure the like from *India*, is to imploy so many to no profit, which

34   might

might otherwise be imploy'd to profit, is the loss of so
much profit. If nine cannot produce above three
Bushels of Wheat in *England*, if by equal Labour they
might procure nine Bushels from another Country, to
imploy these in agriculture at home, is to imploy nine
to do no more work than might be done as well by
three; is to imploy six to do no more work than might
be done as well without them; is to imploy six to no
profit, which might be imploy'd to procure as many
Bushels of Wheat to *England*; is the loss of six Bushels
of Wheat; is therefore the loss of so much value. So, if
nine by so much Labour, can make in *England* a Manufacture but of the value of 10*s*. if by equal Labour they
can procure from other Countries, thrice as much value
of Manufactures, to imploy these Men in the *English*
Manufacture, is to imploy to no profit six of the nine
which might be imploy'd to procure twice as much value
of Manufactures from abroad, is clearly the loss of so
much value to the Nation. Thus Idleness, vain Labour,
the unprofitable imployment of the People, which might
be imploy'd to profit, is the loss of so much profit.
Wherefore, to imploy in *English* Manufactures more
Hands than are necessary, to procure the like from the
East-Indies, and Hands which might be imploy'd to
profit, is the loss of so much profit to the Nation.

Manufactures made in *England*, the like of which
may be imported from the *East-Indies*, by the labour
of fewer Hands, are not profitable, they are a loss to
the Kingdom; the Publick therefore loses nothing by
the loss of such Manufactures.

We are very fond of being restrain'd to the con- *The conse-*
sumption of *English* Manufactures, and therefore con- *quences of*
prohibiting
trive Laws either directly or by high Customs, to pro- Indian *Manu-*
hibit all that come from *India;* By this time, 'tis easie *factures.*
to see some of the natural Consequences of this Prohibition.

It

It is to oblige the things to be provided by the
Labour of many, which might as well be done by few;
'tis to oblige many to labour to no purpose, to no profit
of the Kingdom, nay, to throw away their Labour,
which otherwise might be profitable. 'Tis to oblige us
to provide things for our own Consumption by the
labour of many, when that of few wou'd be sufficient.
To provide the conveniences of Life at the dearest and
most expensive Rates, to labour for things that might
be had without. 'Tis all one as to bid us refuse Bread
or Cloaths, tho' the Providence of God or Bounty of
our Neighbours wou'd bestow them on us; 'tis all one
as to destroy an Engine or a Navigable River, that the
work which is done by few may rather be done by
many. Or, all these things may be comprehended in
this, to prohibit the consumption of *Indian* Manufactures, is by Law to establish vain and unprofitable
Labour.

Again, instead of making work, 'tis the direct way
to lessen the business of the People; to imploy more
Hands than are necessary, is the way to make our
Manufactures too dear for Foreign Markets. By
having less to do in Foreign Markets, we shall have
so much the less imployment for our People here at
home. If to make work for the People, a Law is
made this Year to destroy the Trade of the *East-Indies*,
some other such Law will be wanted the very next.
We may well hope, that in time the Navigation of the
Thames, of every other River, will be destroy'd, that
many may be imploy'd in the Carriage, which is now
perform'd by few. By degrees, not an Art or Engine
to save the labour of Hands, will be left in *England*.
When we shall be reduc'd to plain Labour without any
manner of Art, we shall live at least as well as the Wild
Indians of *America*, the *Hottantots* of *Africa*, or the
Inhabitants of New *Holland*.

As

As often as I consider these things, I am ready to say with my self, that God has bestowed his Blessings upon Men that have neither hearts nor skill to use them. For, why are we surrounded with the Sea? Surely that our Wants at home might be supply'd by our Navigation into other Countries, the least and easiest Labour. By this we taste the Spices of *Arabia*, yet never feel the scorching Sun which brings them forth; we shine in Silks which our Hands have never wrought; we drink of Vinyards which we never planted; the Treasures of those Mines are ours, in which we have never digg'd; we only plough the Deep, and reap the Harvest of every Country in the World.

C H A P. XI.

The East-India *Trade is the most likely way to inlarge the business in the present Manufactures.*

MAnufactures are procur'd from the *East-Indies* by the labour of fewer Hands than the like can be made in *England;* if by this means any numbers of People are disabled to follow their former business, the *East-India* Trade has only disabled so many to work to no profit of the Kingdom; by the loss of such Manufactures, of such ways of imploying the People, the Publick loses nothing. Nevertheless, to the Labourer's Objection of being driven from his imployment, it must be also answer'd, That the *East-India* Trade is the most likely way to make work for all the People, by inlarging their business in the present, by being the cause of setting on foot new imployments for the People.

It is very true, that *English* Manufactures cannot be sold dear, as if as good shall be imported cheap from *India;* so that the importation of cheaper must needs abate the price of the same kind of *English* Manufac-

The East-India Trade,

by abating the price of English Manufactures

87

tures.

tures. Of equal Labour in one and the same Country, the price will not be very different; and therefore, if the *East-India* Trade shall oblige Men to work cheaper in some kind of Manufactures, this very thing will have an influence upon others. Or thus, the *East-India* Trade will put an end to many of our *English* Manufactures; the Men that were imploy'd in these, will betake themselves to others, the most plain and easie; or to the single Parts of other Manufactures of most variety, because the plainest work is soonest learn'd: By the increase of Labourers, the price of work will be abated; and thus the *East-India* Trade must needs abate the price of *English* Manufactures.

and conse-quently by increasing their Vent, If the price of *English* Manufactures shall be abated, more People will be enabled to buy in the former Markets, the abatement of the price will pay for the Carriage into new Markets. Thus of Cloth, perhaps a Yard may be sold abroad for Ten Shillings, it were as easie to sell two if a fifth part of that price might be abated. It is certain, that more Stockings are sold since the Framework has reduc'd the price. For the same reason that more of the cheaper labour of Engines can be sold than of the dearer labour of Hands, more of *Indian* than of the dearer *English* Manufactures; for the very same, the cheaper *English* Manufactures can be sold, the more will be sold: Wherefore the *East-India* Trade by abating the price, must increase the vent of *English* Manufactures.

and consequently by increasing the Manufactures, Again, The more *English* Manufactures can be sold, the more of them will be made; consequently, the *East-India* Trade by increasing the vent, will also increase the *English* Manufactures.

makes more work for the People. Lastly, More People will be imploy'd to make Two hundred Yards of Cloth to produce as many Bushels of Wheat, to procure from the *East-Indies* as many pieces of Callicoe, and so of other things, than to procure

38   but

but half the quantity of these things; more People are imploy'd to make a greater than a less quantity of Manufactures: Wherefore the *East-India* Trade, by causing an increase of our Manufactures, is the most likely way to increase the imployment of the People.

CHAP. XII.

By being the cause of the Invention of Arts and Engines, of order and regularity in our Manufactures, the East-India Trade, without abating the Wages of Labourers, abates the price of Manufactures.

BUT if the Labourer was afraid that the importation of *East-India* Manufactures wou'd lessen his imployment, he will not be better pleas'd that to increase the same, the price of *English* Manufactures shou'd be abated. For by this, the price of Labour, that is Wages, will be abated. *It is objected, that by abating the price of Manufactures, Wages must be abated,*

And consequently, the Labourer will be oblig'd to work more for Wages enough to buy the same conveniences of Life. For, tho' there is a mixture of Labour with these things, tho' the price of Labour is a part of the price of the conveniences of Life, tho' by the abatement of Wages the price of these things is also abated, yet the price of the conveniences of Life is not so much abated as the Wages which are to buy them. This might be prov'd by Reason; but an Example will serve instead of Demonstration. Suppose that a third part of the price of Labour, a third part of every Man's Wages is abated, then my Wages of Ten Shillings for Ten days Labour, are abated to Six Shillings and Eight Pence: Again, Of a yard of Cloth of the price of Ten Shillings, a part of the price is the price of Labour by which the same was wrought, per- *consequently the Labourer must work more for the same things.*

haps

haps One Shilling is the price of Wool, Nine Shillings the price of Labour bestow'd upon it; by abatement of a third part of the price of Labour, the price of Wool is not abated, the price of the Manufacture is abated to Six Shillings; and thus the price of the Cloth is reduc'd to Seven Shillings: With my Wages of Ten Shillings for Ten Days labour, I was able to buy a Yard of Cloth of the price of Ten Shillings; but with the Wages of Six Shillings and Eight Pence for Ten Days labour, I am not able to buy the Yard of Cloth of the price of Seven Shillings, I must be oblig'd to work more than Ten Days for Wages enough to buy the Yard of Cloth; and therefore, if the *East-India* Trade shall abate the Wages of the Labourer, he will be oblig'd to work more for Wages enough to buy the same things.

Also, his share of Things must be lessen'd.

Again, By abatement of the price of Labour, the Labourer's share of things is lessen'd; there is a mixture of Labour with all the conveniences of Life: As of a piece of Cloth, a great part of the price is the price of Labour by which the same is made, the Labourer's share of the Cloth is as much in proportion to the whole Cloth as the price of Labour is in proportion to the whole price; then, if the *East-India* Trade shall abate the price of Labour without abating the rest of the value of Things, it will render the price of Labour less in proportion to the whole price of Things, it will consequently abate the Labourer's share of Things. Then he will have no reason to be pleas'd with the *East-India* Trade, if to increase the imployment of the People, it must abate the price of Manufactures.

Wages are not abated.

I am very ready to believe, that the *East-India* Trade by the importation of cheaper, must needs reduce the price of *English* Manufactures; nevertheless it is Matter of Fact, that the Wages of Men are not abated.

40   As

(589)

As much Wages are given to the Plough-man, to the
Sea-man, to the Weaver, to all kinds of Labourers as
ever heretofore; so that the *East-India* Trade by reducing the price of Manufactures, has not yet abated
Wages.

That this thing may not seem a Paradox, the *East-*
India Trade may be the cause of doing things with less
Labour, and then tho' Wages shou'd not, the price of
Manufactures might be abated. If things shall be done
with less labour, the price of it must be less tho' the
Wages of Men shou'd be as high as ever. Thus a Ship
is navigated with a great number of Hands at very
great charge; if by being undermasted and spreading
less Canvass the same shou'd be navigated by two-thirds
of that number, so as the difference of Speed shall be
very inconsiderable, the Ship wou'd be navigated with
less charge, tho' the Wages of Sea-men shou'd be as
high as ever. In like manner of any *English* Manufacture perform'd by so many Hands, and in so long a
time, the price is proportionable, if by the invention of
an Engine, or by greater order and regularity of the
Work, the same shall be done by two-thirds of that
number of Hands, or in two-thirds of that time; the
labour will be less, the price of it will be also less, tho'
the Wages of Men shou'd be as high as ever. And
therefore, if the *East-India* Trade shall be the cause of
doing the same things with less labour, it may without
abating any Man's Wages abate the price of Manufactures.

Arts, and Mills, and Engines, which save the labour
of Hands, are ways of doing things with less labour,
and consequently with labour of less price, tho' the
Wages of Men imploy'd to do them shou'd not be
abated. The *East-India* Trade procures things with
less and cheaper labour than would be necessary to

41   make

The East-India Trade the cause of doing things with Arts, and Engines, and more Regularity.

Engines without abating Wages, abate the price of Manufactures;

make the like in *England*; it is therefore very likely to be the cause of the invention of Arts, and Mills, and Engines, to save the labour of Hands in other Manufactures. Such things are successively invented to do a great deal of work with little labour of Hands; they are the effects of Necessity and Emulation; every Man must be still inventing himself, or be still advancing to farther perfection upon the invention of other Men; if my Neighbour by doing much with little labour, can sell cheap, I must contrive to sell as cheap as he. So that every Art, Trade, or Engine, doing work with labour of fewer Hands, and consequently cheaper, begets in others a kind of Necessity and Emulation, either of using the same Art, Trade, or Engine, or of inventing something like it, that every Man may be upon the square, that no man may be able to undersel his Neighbour. And thus the *East-India* Trade by procuring things with less, and consequently cheaper labour, is a very likely way of forcing Men upon the invention of Arts and Engines, by which other things may be also done with less and cheaper labour, and therefore may abate the price of Manufactures, tho' the Wages of Men should not be abated.

And so does Order and Regularity

Again, The *East-India* Trade is no unlikely way to introduce more Artists, more Order and Regularity into our *English* Manufactures, it must put an end to such of them as are most useless and unprofitable; the People imploy'd in these will betake themselves to others, to others the most plain and easie, or to the single Parts of other Manufactures of most variety; for plain and easie work is soonest learn'd, and Men are more perfect and expeditious in it; And thus the *East-India* Trade may be the cause of applying proper Parts of Works of great variety to single and proper Artists, of not leaving too much to be perform'd by the skill of

42   single

single Persons; and this is what is meant by introducing greater Order and Regularity into our *English* Manufactures.

The more variety of Artists to every Manufacture, *Cloth*; the less is left to the skill of single Persons; the greater the Order and Regularity of every Work, the same must needs be done in less time, the Labour must be less, and consequently the price of Labour less, tho' Wages shou'd not be abated. Thus a piece of Cloth is made by many Artists; one Cards and Spins, another makes the Loom, another Weaves, another Dyes, another dresses the Cloth; and thus to proper Artists proper Parts of the Work are still assign'd; the Weaver must needs be more skilful and expeditious at weaving, if that shall be his constant and whole imployment, than if the same Weaver is also to Card and Spin, and make the Loom, and Weave, and Dress, and Dye the Cloth. So the Spinner, the Fuller, the Dyer or Clothworker, must needs be more skilful and expeditious at his proper business, which shall be his whole and constant imployment, than any Man can be at the same work, whose skill shall be pusled and confounded with variety of other business.

A Watch is a work of great variety, and 'tis possible *Watches;* for one Artist to make all the several Parts, and at last to join them altogether; but if the Demand of Watches shou'd become so very great as to find constant imployment for as many Persons as there are Parts in a Watch, if to every one shall be assign'd his proper and constant work, if one shall have nothing else to make but Cases, another Weels, another Pins, another Screws, and several others their proper Parts; and lastly, if it shall be the constant and only imployment of one to join these several Parts together, this Man must needs be more skilful and expeditious in the composition of these several Parts, than the same Man cou'd be if he were

also

also to be imploy'd in the Manufacture of all these Parts. And so the Maker of the Pins, or Wheels, or Screws, or other Parts, must needs be more perfect and expeditious at his proper work, if he shall have nothing else to pusle and confound his skill, than if he is also to be imploy'd in all the variety of a Watch.

Ships made with more Order and Regularity, are cheaper. But of all things to be perform'd by the labour of Man, perhaps there is not more variety in any thing than in a Ship: The Manufacture of the Keel, the Ribbs, the Planks, the Beams, the Shrouds, the Masts, the Sails, almost thousands of other Parts, together with the composition of these several Parts, require as much variety of skill. And still as the Sizes and Dimensions of Ships differ, the skill in the Manufacture of the several Parts, and again in the Composition of them, must needs be different; it is one kind of skill to make the Keel, or Ribbs, or Planks, or Beams, or Rudders, or other Parts of a Ship of One hundred Tons, and another to make the same Parts of a Ship of Five hundred; and in the same manner, the composition of Parts of different Scantlings and Dimensions must needs be different. Wherefore, if the Demand of Shipping shall be so very great, as to make constant imployment for as many several Artists as there are several different Parts of Ships of different dimensions, if to every one shall be assign'd his proper work, if one Man shall be always and only imploy'd in the Manufacture of Keels of one and the same dimensions, another of Ribbs, another of Beams, another Rudders, and several others of several other Parts, certainly the Keel, the Ribbs, the Beams, the Rudders, or other Parts, must needs be better done and with greater expedition, by any Artist whose whole and constant imployment shall be the Manufacture of that single Part, than if he is also to work upon different Parts or different Scantlings. Thus the greater the Order and Regularity of every Work,

the

the more any Manufacture of much variety shall be distributed and assign'd to different Artists, the same must needs be better done and with greater expedition, with less loss of time and labour; the Labour must be less, and consequently the price of Labour less, tho' Wages shou'd continue still as high as ever. And therefore the *East-India* Trade, if it is the cause that greater Order and Regularity is introduc'd into every Work, that Manufactures of much variety are distributed and assign'd to proper Artists, that things are done in less time and consequently with less labour, then without abating the Wages of the Labourer, it may well abate the price of Labour.

The *East-India* Trade, whether by setting forward the invention of Arts and Engines to save the labour of Hands, or by introducing greater Order and Regularity into our *English* Manufactures, or by whatsoever other means, lessens the price of Labour. However, Wages are not abated; wherefore, without reducing Wages, this Trade abates the price of Labour, and therefore of Manufactures.

The *East-India* Trade abates only the price of Manufactures, not the Wages of the Labourer; then he is able to buy more Manufactures, more conveniences of Life with the same Labour; he is not obliged to labour more for Wages enough to buy the same things.

Lastly, If Wages are not abated, if only the price of things is abated, the Labourer's share of the conveniences of Life may well be lessen'd without any inconvenience, without taking from the share of the Labourer, but by adding to the share of other People: And this is no hurt to any Man. Among the wild *Indians* of *America*, almost every thing is the Labourer's, ninety nine Parts of an hundred are to be put upon the account of Labour: In *England*, perhaps the Labourer has not two thirds of all the conveniences of Life, but

45   then

then the plenty of these things is so much greater here, that a King of *India* is not so well lodg'd, and fed, and cloath'd, as a Day-labourer of *England*.

Thus, without any Objection, without abating the Wages of any Man, without any inconvenience to the Labourer, the *East-India* Trade, by abating the price of Manufactures, increases their Vent; by increasing the Vent increases the Manufactures; by increasing the Manufactures makes more imployment for the People.

CHAP. XIII.

The East-India *Trade is the most likely way to set on foot new Manufactures for imployment of the People.*

THE *East-India* Trade is the most likely way not only to increase the business in the former Manufactures, it is also the way to introduce new Manufactures, new Imployments, into *England*, by creating a greater plenty of Money for this purpose; the greater the plenty shall be of Money, the same will be less likely to be hoarded, less likely to lye still; wanton Purses will be always open to build, beautifie, and improve the Kingdom; Shipping and Navigation will every day increase, new Trades will be discover'd.

Trade will be driven so very close, till as little is to be gain'd by it as is the present Interest of Money; and as Money shall every day be drawn out of Trade, to lye at Interest, to purchace Lands, the value of these will rise, the interest of Money will fall, till at last Land shall become too dear for Purchasers, till too little is to be gain'd at Interest; and thus the restless Treasure will be driven into Trade again.

When the plenty of Money shall become as great as among any of our Neighbours, some of their Manufactures may be attempted; perhaps this is the way to

46   carry

carry on the Fishing-Trade in *England*: For this, in vain, Corporations have been projected, Incouragements have been given; Money is not drug enough in *England*; more is to be gain'd at present, by letting it out to Interest, by imploying the same in every other Trade: Corporations will not be contented more than private Persons to trade to loss, or to manage a less profitable Trade, while more profit is to be made of any other. The price of Labour is not enough abated; there is not a sufficient plenty of Money in *England* to do the thing; as soon as we shall have enough of this, private Persons will be able to carry on the Trade; there can be no need of Incouragements, no need of Corporations.

Then the *East-India* Trade, by doing more work with fewer Hands, by increasing our Superfluities, by increasing our Exportations, by making more Returns of Bullion into *England*, by increasing our Money, is the most likely means to set on foot new Imployments for the People.

The *East-India* Trade, by inlarging the business of the old, by setting on foot new, Manufactures, is the most likely way to make most imployment for the People; however, it deprives the People of no Manufacture which can be thought profitable to the Kingdom; and it were altogether as well that the People shou'd stand still, as that they shou'd be imploy'd to no profit. And this is what may be answer'd to the Labourer's Objection against the *East-India* Trade, the destruction of *English* Manufactures, and the loss of his Imployment.

CHAP.

CHAP. XIV.

The East-India *Trade does not abate the Rents, by the exportation of Bullion, by the diminution of Consumers, by the abatement of Wages; the importation of* Indian *Manufactures is less likely to abate Rents than the importation of the unwrought Produce of* India.

THE last Complaint is of the Landholder, that his Rents must be abated by the *East-India* Trade; that the value of the Produce of the Estate must needs be lessen'd by the exportation of Bullion, by the diminution of Consumers, by the abatement of Wages, by letting the Produce of *India* into all the *English* Markets.

Rents not abated by the exportation of Bullion;

To the exportation of Bullion, it has been already answer'd, That there is never the less Bullion in the Kingdom; that the Carriage of it into *India* is the way to increase our Exportations, to make Returns of more Bullion. Then there will be still as much in *England* to be given for the Produce of the Estate; the price of this is not likely to be abated for want of Bullion.

nor by diminution of Consumers;

To the diminution of Consumers, may be answer'd, That the *East-India* Trade reduces the price of Labour, by which the Produce of the Estate is manufactur'd; then more will be enabled at home, more will be invited from abroad to buy it: This Trade does not lessen the number of Buyers, it does not abate the value of the produce of the Estate.

nor by abatement of Wages.

To the abatement of Wages, may be answer'd, That the Matter of Fact has been deny'd; the *East-India* Trade indeed may have abated the price of Labour, by shortning every Work, by introducing Arts and Engines,

48   Order

Order and Regularity into every Manufacture, by which
the same may be done with less labour and greater
expedition; yet no Man's Wages are abated; every
Labourer has still as much to give the Landholder for
the Produce of his Estate.

To the Argument, That the value of the Produce of
English Estates must be abated, by letting the Produce
of *India* into all the *English* Markets, by destroying
the Monopoly of the Gentleman, by increasing the
number of Sellers and of like Things, for Sale, beyond
the former proportion of Money and Buyers, may be
answer'd, That Landholders think the Produce of their
Estates is in no danger from the unwrought Things of
India, they have less reason to be afraid of *Indian*
Manufactures; the importation of these can reduce
only the price of Labour, and therefore the price of the
Produce of the Estate cannot be abated by it; indeed,
there is very good reason that the value of that shou'd
be advanc'd by it; and this is also confirm'd by the
experience of many Countries in like cases; upon all
which, it must be deny'd, That the *East-India* Trade
increases the Sellers and like Things for Sale, against
the Landholder and the Produce of his Estate, beyond
the former proportion of Money and Buyers: And thus
the Landholder is not at all the worse for the loss of
his Monopoly.

Indian Manufactures cannot hurt the Rents of *Eng-* *The un-*
land; for, 'tis the sense of People, that the unwrought *wrought*
Things of
Things of *India* cannot do it; Men are very careful to *India are*
preserve their Rents; for this reason they keep every *more likely to*
abate Rents
thing out of *England* from whence any danger may be *than the*
apprehended; *Irish* Cattel are prohibited, and so are *Manufactures.*
the Manufactures of many Countries; we must rather
want plenty at home, than import the same from abroad;
and all this is done, that the value of the Produce of
English Estates may be preserv'd. But above all,

49   Gentlemen

Gentlemen are in the greatest disquiets for their Wool; this is watch'd with as much care and jealousie as the Golden Apples of the *Hesperides* ; a poor Man must not have leave to carry an old Sheet to his Grave ; both the Living and the Dead must be wrapt in Woollen ; indeed, no other Law is wanted to complete the business, but only one, That our Perukes shou'd be made of Wool. This demonstrates the great care of the Gentleman, to suffer nothing that may be dangerous to his Rents. Nevertheless, the unwrought Things of *India* are let alone ; these are neither directly, nor by high customs prohibited ; these therefore, in the opinion of Gentlemen, are not dangerous to the Rents, are not likely to abate the price of the Produce of the Estate.

But certainly, the importation of *Indian* Manufactures is not so likely to abate the value of the meer Produce of *English* Estates, as the unwrought Things of *India:* To import *Irish* Cattel, does not take up so many Hands, does not draw so many Labourers from the Plough, from the Loom, from the Manufacture of the rest of the Produce of *English* Estates, as the Fishing-Trade, which requires as many Hands to import so much value of Fish, and many more to build Busses, make Netts, and to work in all the Appendages of this Trade. In like manner, to import Callicoes, Stuffs, wrought Silks, and other *Indian* Manufactures, does not require so many Hands, does not draw so many from the Manufacture of the meer Produce of the Estate, as to import Cotton, Wool, Raw-silk, and the other unwrought Produce of *India*, which requires as many Hands to import them, and many more to perfect them : So in all cases, Foreign Manufactures are not likely to spend so much of our Labour as the unwrought Things of Foreign Countries; they are less likely to make a scarcity of Labourers to work up the Produce of the Estate, less likely to obstruct the demand of this, by

50   raising

raising the price of Labour that must be bestow'd upon
it. And thus the importation of *Indian* Manufactures
is not so like to abate the value of the meer Produce
of the Estate, as the unwrought Things of *India;* these,
as is already shewn in the judgment of Gentlemen, are
not like to do it; wherefore, they ought not to apprehend any danger to the Produce of their Estates from
the importation of *Indian* Manufactures.

CHAP. XV.

The Importation of Indian *Manufactures abates only
the price of Labour, but raises the price of the Produce of the Estate.*

THE foregoing Argument is not demonstrative, it
is only credible, that Gentlemen do not mistake
their own interest: Wherefore, that *Indian* Manufactures cannot abate the price of the meer Produce of
the Estate, is now to be demonstrated from Principles
which are evident.

I believe it will be granted, That a Manufacture will
not be made in *England* by dearer, if as good an one
shall be procur'd from *India* by cheaper Labour; so
that the Labour that makes the *English*, must not be
dearer than the Labour that produces the *Indian* Manufacture; the price then of that which makes the
English must be abated, till the same is nothing higher
than the price of the Labour that procures the
Indian Manufacture; or so much of the difference of
the price between both manufactures as is caus'd by
dearer Labour, must be abated upon Labour.

And this is the whole difference; for Wool is not
dearer than so much Cotton, Raw-silk, or other the
unwrought Produce of *India;* wherefore, whatsoever

51   the

the *English* exceeds in price the *Indian* Manufacture; the difference is not from the dearness of the unwrought Produce of *England;* this is not dearer, the Labour only that makes the *English* is dearer than the Labour that procures the *Indian* Manufacture; the whole difference of the price betwixt both Manufactures, is caus'd by dearer Labour.

All the difference of the price caus'd by dearer Labour, is abated upon Labour, and that is the whole difference; wherefore the whole difference is abated upon Labour.

By the importation of *Indian* Manufactures, only so much of the price of the *English* as exceeds the price of an *Indian* Manufacture is abated : for, if more shou'd be abated, then the *English* Manufacture wou'd be cheapest, then the *Indian* cou'd not be sold, and consequently wou'd not be imported, contrary to the Fact, and also contrary to the Supposition; therefore, all that is abated of the *English* Manufacture is the difference of the price : All this is abated upon Labour ; so that all that is abated, is abated upon Labour.

Or only the price of Labour that makes the *English*, is abated by the importation of *Indian* Manufactures, therefore the price of the Produce of the Estate is not abated.

On the contrary, the value of the Produce of the Estate is very likely to be rais'd by the importation of *Indian* Manufactures; for by this, the price of Labour will be abated, the demand of the Produce of the Estate will be increas'd, more will be invited, more will be enabled to buy the same at higher prices.

More of our own People will be able to buy Wool at two Shillings *per* pound, with the Labour and Manufacture of the price of Six Shillings, than to buy so much Wool for One Shilling if the Manufacture must be Nine. Or, if at home Men might be compell'd to buy

52

buy at any price, yet Foreigners are not subject to *English* Laws, they will rather buy our Wool with the price of Manufacture abated. The abatement of the price of the Manufacture, will pay for the carriage of our Wool into distant Markets; so then, if the *East-India* Trade shall reduce the price of the Labour and Manufacture, it must needs invite and enable more People to buy the Produce of the Estate.

Again, If almost every one in *England* shall be able to buy the Gentleman's Wool, the Demand of it must be greater, and so must the price, than if Multitudes shall be disabled. Also, if People upon the Coasts of Foreign Countries shall be invited and enabled to buy the Wool, than if the same shall be restrain'd to only *English* Markets. Lastly, If People at greater distances from those Coasts shall buy our Wool, than if only *English* Men, or the Coasters of Foreign Countries, shall be our Customers. So in all cases, the more People shall be enabled to buy the Produce of the Estate, the Demand must be the greater, and so must the Price. Then the importation of *Indian* Manufactures, abates the price of Labour, invites and enables so many the more to buy the Produce of the Estate, increases the Demand, increases the value of the Produce of the Estate.

C H A P. XVI.

And this is confirm'd by Examples.

THIS is Reason, and this is also confirm'd by the experience of many Countries: The *Romans* conquer'd great Nations, they injoin'd the conquer'd People to send them Tributes of their Manufactures, the Manufactures of every Nation were to be seen at *Rome;* from *Sicily, Africa,* and other neighbouring Provinces,

The Roman *Lands not impair'd by the Tributes;*

Provinces, they receiv'd their Corn; this was not done for want of Land enough for Tillage in *Italy*; we are taught by their Historians, that *Italy* was always able to bear Corn sufficient for their Inhabitants. Yet in such quantities 'twas imported, that the *Romans* were forc'd from their antient Husbandry, they were disabled this way to make profit of their lands; yet their Lands did not lye idle, the Produce of their Estates preserv'd its value, their Rents were not abated.

Nor the Dutch *Lands by their vast Imports;* But, Men are afraid of comparisons with the *Romans*, therefore later instances must be given: The *Dutch* import things of Foreign Growth and Manufacture, not so cheap indeed as the antient *Romans*, and 'tis to be hop'd they never will, yet cheaper far than like things can be brought into any other Country, and this they do with the greatest Freedom. They import into *Holland*, Corn, Wine, and grown Cattel, so very cheap, that they quite deprive themselves of the Articles of Tillage and Breeding. Pasture, Dairy, and the production of Flax and Madder, are almost all the imployment they have for Lands in *Holland*; yet, as if they wou'd have no use of their Pasture, they import such quantities of Herrings and fatted Cattel, as are sufficient for many such Countries as *Holland*, and so very cheap that no Country can do the like. As if they intended to spoil their Dairies, they import from *Sweden* such quantities of Butter, that they are forc'd to look out Foreign Markets for their own. And, as if they intended to run down the price of every thing at home, they import with the greatest freedom and in the greatest quantities, Hemp and Flax from the *East* Country, Linens from *Germany*, and other Manufactures from the *East-Indies*. They labour as it were, to abate the value of the Produce of their own Lands; in vain, for in no other Country are the Rents of Lands so high as those of *Holland*.

54   Again,

Again, *England* imports neither so many things, nor *Nor indeed the* English.
so cheap as *Holland;* yet of late, the Importations have
been very great; the Customs are greater far than ever
heretofore. Prodigious quantities of Silks, Callicoes,
and other *Indian* things have been imported, equal as
is said, to all the Woollen Manufacture. *Norwich* and
Canterbury are almost beaten out of their Trades:
However, in general the Woollen Manufacture has
flourish'd, Wool has carried a better price, and generally Rents have been rais'd over all the Kingdom.

If the price of Wool is not abated by the importation
of *Indian* Manufactures, why shou'd the importation of
Corn, of Wine, of Cattel, of Herrings, abate the
Rents of *England?* Why shou'd the price of the
Produce of the Estate be abated by any Importations?

The Rents of Lands in *Holland,* are generally higher
than the Rents of the same kind of Lands in *England,*
and perhaps at a medium are as high again. If the
importation of Wine, of Corn, of Cattel, has not
abated the higher Rent of *Holland,* Why shou'd it
abate the lesser Rent of *England?* If the *Dutch* Pasture is not abated below the Rent of Forty Shillings,
by the importation of Butter, Fish, and Fatted Cattel,
why shou'd the Rent of as good Pasture here be less
than Twenty Shillings, tho' all these things shou'd be
imported into *England.*

It is in vain to say, There is but little Land in *Hol-* *A small quan- tity of Land does not there- fore yield a greater Rent.*
land, that therefore Rents are higher there than in any
other Country, but if they had Land as much as *Eng-*
land, their Rents wou'd be soon affected by such mighty
Importations. This can never be a reason that the
Rents are high in *Holland.* Indeed, where there is
little Land and many Purchasers, the Purchace must
be dearer; but the Tenant, the Yearly Renter, will
give no more Rent than can be made of the Produce
of the Estate; and besides the Rent for the Landlord,

he will expect a living Profit for himself. Wherefore Rents in *Holland* are not high, a great price is not given for the Produce of the Estate, because there is but little Land in *Holland.*

Besides, *Holland* is upon the Continent; the Lands adjoining are large enough in reason; Are any other Lands impair'd in Yearly value by their Neighbourhood to *Holland?* The Rents of *Holland* are higher far than those of any other Country; the Yearly value of other Lands is always greater, the less their distance is from thence; great Importations into *Holland* have neither abated the Rents of that nor any other place: And therefore, as great Importations wou'd not abate the Rents in *England,* neither upon the Coast, nor in the midland Country.

The most likely ways to raise the Rents. Wherefore, better Reasons may be given; that the importation of things of Foreign Growth and Manufacture, is not the way to impair the Yearly value of the Lands of any Country. It is certainly the way to create a plenty of the conveniences of Life; this will invite Purchasers and People thither, and these will preserve the Yearly value of the Lands. Again, if plenty shall invite People into any Country, the value of such a Country must needs be rais'd; the People will give more for the Produce of Lands at home, than for like things at a greater distance, to be at the charge of Carriage. Besides, the increase of our Superfluities must needs increase our Exportations, must return more Bullion into *England,* must multiply Money to be given for the Produce of the Estate. Lastly, The importation of things of Foreign Growth and Manufacture is the most likely way to abate the price of Labour, which is to be mix'd with the Produce of the Estate, it is consequently the way to raise the value of the Produce of the Estate.

Whatsoever shall become of these Reasons, Matter

56   of

of Fact is certain; great Importations have always rais'd the value of every other Country, there is no reason to believe they can impair the Rents of *England*. And thus the Experience of several Countries, especially of our own, might teach Gentlemen to apprehend but little danger from the *Indian* Manufactures.

C H A P. XVII.

The East-India *Trade does not abate the Rents of the Landholder by destroying his Monopoly.*

AND now the Answer will be very easie to the last part of the Objection, That the permission of *Indian* Manufactures to be sold in *English* Markets, destroys the Monopoly of the Gentleman. As good a price as ever is given for the Produce of the Estate; wherefore it is deny'd, That by the permission of *Indian* Manufacture, the Sellers and like things for sale, are increas'd beyond the former proportion of Money and Buyers, which before were ready for the Produce of the Estate.

It is very true, That an Hundred thousand Pounds in Money, and as many Buyers, are not in proportion so much to any quantity of Meat, or Corn, or Cloaths, as the same Money and Buyers wou'd be to half the quantity of any of those things: But, to the single Butcher of a Country-Village, add as much Meat and as many Butchers as are in *London*, if the People and Money shall increase in proportion, Meat will bear as good a price. To the *English* Corn, add all the Corn of *Europe*, yet if all must come to the *English* Markets, if Money and Buyers shall increase in proportion to the increase of Corn, the price of Corn will never fall. So to the Woollen Manufactures, add those of *India* and other Countries, yet if Money and Buyers shall increase in proportion, the price of Cloth may be as

The increase of things does not reduce the price of Money, and Buyers increase in proportion.

57   high

high as ever. The reason why the increase of Sellers and of like things for sale, abates the price of things, is because the increase is beyond the proportion of Money and Buyers; and therefore, if these shall increase as fast, if there shall be still as great a proportion of them to the Produce of the Estate, the price of it will not be abated.

Now the importation of *Indian* Manufactures, and the permission of them to be sold in *English* Markets, does indeed abate the price of *English* Manufactures; so that the proportion of Money and Buyers to English Manufactures must needs be lessen'd. But then the whole abatement is upon the price of Labour by which the same are made; and by the abatement of the price of Labour, more are invited and enabled both at home and abroad, to buy the Produce of the Estate. In Fact as much is given for this as ever, the proportion of Money and Buyers to the Produce of the Estate, is not abated; and therefore, Money and Buyers are increas'd to the Produce of the Estate, in proportion to the increase which is made of Sellers and of like things for Sale, by the importation of *Indian* Manufactures. And consequently, this does indeed destroy the Monopoly of the Landholder; nevertheless, the value of the Produce of his Estate is not abated by it.

What has been said of the permission of *Indian* Manufactures to be sold in *English* Markets, is, That *Indian* Manufactures are not so likely to abate the price of the meer Produce of *English* Estates as the unwrought Produce of *India;* they can only abate the price of Labour; by abating the price of this, they must raise the value of the Produce of the Estate; this is reason, and this is confirm'd by experience. And thus, by the destruction of his Monopoly, the Landholder loses nothing; Money and Buyers increase, as Foreign Things are added to the Produce of the Estate; the

58   value

value of this is not abated by the permission of *Indian* Manufactures to be sold in all the *English* Markets.

There is still, notwithstanding the exportation of Bullion, as much Money in the Kingdom, as much Money and as many Buyers for the meer Produce of the Estate; the Labourer is still able to give as good a price; and indeed, as the price of Labour shall be lessen'd, both he and others must be forc'd to give a better: So that Rents are not abated by the importation of *Indian* Manufactures.

And thus Answers are given to every Objection against this Trade: to the exportation of Bullion for Manufactures to be consum'd in *England*; that the exchange is of less for greater value, of less for more Bullion; and that nothing more is lost to the Kingdom by the consumption of *Indian*, than of *English* Manufactures. To the complaint of the Labourer, and the loss of his imployment; that the loss of this is no loss to the Publick; and on the contrary, that the *East-India* Trade is the most likely way to make imployment for the People. The last Objection is deny'd, the Rents are not abated.

CHAP. XVIII.

The Fishing-Trade is not so profitable as the importation of Irish *Cattel, or of* Indian *Manufactures; and is more likely than either to abate the Rents of* England.

TO illustrate a Reason or two of this Discourse, instances were taken from the Fishing-Trade, from the importation of *Irish* Cattel, and of *Indian* Manufactures. Men are all fond of a Fishery; certain Landholders are jealous of the *Irish* Cattel, but every one is afraid of *Indian* Manufactures. Wherefore, it

59   may

may not be altogether improper to make a comparison of these things, that it may be seen with how little reason Men take up Aversions and Inclinations, how easily they mistake their Country's Interest and their own. The comparison may farther recommend the *Indian* Manufactures.

First then, The Fishing-Trade is not so profitable to the Kingdom as the importation of *Irish* Cattel, or of *Indian* Manufactures. It procures no greater value of Herrings, but with greater Labour than is necessary to procure so much value of *Irish* Cattel, or of *Indian* Manufactures. Herrings are not catch'd and cur'd with so little labour as will procure the same value of *Irish* Cattel or of *Indian* Manufactures.

Let any quantity of Herrings be taken of any value whatsoever, of these the King has no Customs, the King is to pay a Reward upon their exportation, and he has no increase of Tonnage and Poundage upon the Returns: Yet with all this Encouragement, the Merchant does not fit out busses. Wherefore, no part of the price is the share of the Merchant; when he shall have paid for the Labour by which the Fish were taken, there will be nothing left for himself. The whole price of the Herrings will do no more than pay the Labour.

It is not so in the case of *Irish* Cattel of the same price or value; if the Merchant were to have no part of the price, he wou'd not import, there wou'd be no need of Prohibitions, but the contrary is evident; wherefore, the whole price of the *Irish* Cattel did not go to pay the Labour by which they were procur'd.

Of *Indian* Manufactures of the same value; the King has great Customs, the Merchant and Retailer have great Gains; a small part of the price is sufficient to pay the Labour by which they were procur'd. Wherefore, Herrings are purchac'd by Labour of

60   greater

greater price than the same value of *Irish* Cattel, or of *Indian* Manufactures.

And, because Labour is proportionable to the price, and Labour of greater price is greater Labour, they are also procur'd by greater Labour.

Lastly, Since to procure the same value of things with greater Labour than is necessary, does not leave so many Hands at liberty to purchase other Benefits to the Commonwealth, it is not therefore so profitable; it follows, that to procure any value of Herrings with greater Labour than were sufficient to procure the same value of *Irish* Cattel, or of *Indian* Manufactures, is by no means so profitable to the Kingdom.

Again, The Fishing-Trade is more likely to abate Rents than the importation of *Irish* Cattel, or of *Indian* Manufactures; it is natural to believe, That it must take up more of the People's Labour, and leave a great deal less to the Plough, to the Loom, to the Manufacture of the rest of the Produce of the Land-holder's Estate; whence it is also natural to believe, That it is more likely to raise the price of Labour, and consequently to abate the value of the Produce of the Estate than the importation of *Irish* Cattel, or of *Indian* Manufactures.

CHAP. XIX.

The Herring-Fishery not practicable in the present Cir-cumstances of England; *the* Dutch *can sell cheaper*.

MEN are very full of Panegyricks upon the Fish-ing Trade, as if by this we were to increase our Shipping and Navigation, to make imployment for every individual Creature in the Kingdom; as if by this we were to enrich the Shoar with all the Spoils of the Sea, to extend our Trade into Foreign Countries, to gain the Balance of Trade over all the rest of *Europe;* they see these Effects of the Fishing-Trade in *Holland;* they expect presently the same Effects in *England,* and without any more ado we are to apply our selves to Fishing. And indeed, I shou'd be of their opinion, when Herrings can be catch'd and cur'd at less charge than will be paid by all their value, when the Merchant can obtain such a price for his Herrings, as besides the hire of the Fisher-man, and all the rest of his Charges, shall leave sufficient profit to himself; then these Panegyricks may be allow'd, then the Labourer may wish for the Fishing-Trade; the Landholder will have no reason to be jealous of it, he will have no reason to be afraid that his Rents will be abated by it. Whenever this shall happen, Money will be very much increas'd; more People will be invited into *England;* there will be more Purchacers to buy the Produce of the Estate; the Fishing-Trade has not abated the Rents of *Holland;* all the Lands adjoining are the richer for it; the Fishing-Trade will not abate the Rents of *England.*

But in the present posture of Affairs, whether profitable or unprofitable, 'tis neither to be hop'd nor fear'd, that the Fishery can be ours; the *Dutch* can afford their Herrings cheaper, and are therefore sure of all the Markets.

England has few Advantages for Fishing which Holland wants. Some have fondly imagin'd, that we might do the business cheaper, that we might wrest the Fishing-Trade from *Holland;* They content themselves to give no better Reasons than these for their opinion, That we have Timber of our own growth, and that there is none of this in *Holland;* that the *Dutch* pay great Excises upon their Victuals, and therefore *English* Fisher-men may work at less Wages; that the Herrings are upon our own Coast, and therefore we are

not

not to pay for the loss of so much time in sailing to and from our Ports; that we are nearer to the Land for taking in of Fresh-water, for drying of our Netts, which are Privileges that might be deny'd to *Holland*. Yet possibly these Advantages are not very great; for if Timber for building Busses is bought in Foreign Countries and imported cheaper into *Holland*, than as good Timber can be bought in *England*, and brought to any place of Building; if the *Dutch-man* pays Excises upon his Victuals, yet if his Victuals are so much cheaper, or if he pays no Excises upon the Fish he eats at Sea; Lastly, If we are nearer to the Herrings, yet if we are so much farther off from almost all the Markets our Advantages are but little. And if we were upon the square in other things, whether by these Advantages we are able to fish cheaper than the *Dutch* by One Shilling in twenty, or not by One in an hundred, must be left to others to determin.

But indeed, we are not upon the square in other things; the *Dutch* have advantages for the Fishing-Trade greater far than we; they catch and cure their Herrings with less charge, they can also sell for less profit.

Tho' the ordinary charge of catching and curing Herrings were alike to both, yet the *Dutch* are able to sell cheaper; they do not manage their Trade with so much contingent charge and hazard as we in *England*. *Law is less expensive and dilatory in Holland.* They have no Law-suits upon controverted Titles of their Busses; indeed they can have none; their Busses are all registred; the Owners can borrow Money upon 'em every where, without the charge of Procuration. Their other Controversies in the Fishing and other Trades, are in a Summary way with little charge determin'd by Men of Skill in the business. In *England* all is contrary; no certain Titles of Busses, frequent Controversies, dilatory and expensive Suits, but the gain of the Fishery is to pay for all; the Herrings

63 must

must be sold for such a price, as besides the rest of the charges may be sufficient to pay for this contingent Charge and Hazard. The Dutch do not want any price upon this account; wherefore, they are able to sell their Herrings for less profit.

The Dutch *must be content with less profit, for want of more profitable Trades;*

The *Dutch* pursue their Fishing-Trade for little profit, because they can make no more by any other Trade: In *England*, more is to be made of Mony in trading to the *Plantations*, to the *Straights*, to *Africa*, to the *East-Indies*; also, in the Purchace of Tallies, of Annuities upon the Government, of Joint-Stocks. As long as this can be done, no single Person, no Corporation in *England*, will level it self to such Gains as must content the *Dutch* in Fishing.

And also by their greater plenty of Money.

Besides, there is a greater plenty of Money in *Holland*; there are so many lenders, that every one is forc'd to be contented with half the Interest that will be expected here in *England*: and for the same Reason, there are so many trading one against another, that every one must be well satisfy'd with half the *English* profit. Let it be suppos'd then, that for an Hundred Pounds imploy'd a Year in the Fishing-Trade, a like quantity of Herrings may be catch'd and cur'd by both; if the *English* Merchant will expect for his Herrings, all his Principal with a profit of Twenty *per Cent.* it follows, that the *Dutch* Merchant will sell a like quantity of Herrings for Ten *per Cent.* besides his Principal, that is, he will sell as many Herrings Ten Pounds cheaper. So that a greater plenty of Money obliges the *Dutch* Fisherman to be contented with less profit than will serve in *England*.

The *Dutch* are not subject to so much contingent Charge and Hazard in carrying on their Fishing-Trade; they are not invited from the little profit of Fishing to so many other more profitable ways of imploying their Money; they are oblig'd by the greater plenty

64   of

to confirm by the examples of *Cæsar*, *Alexander*, and others, who hating covetousness, atchieved many acts and victories by lavish gifts and liberal expences. Unto which they add also the *little fruit* which came by that *great summ of money* which King *David* laid up and left to his son *Solomon*, who notwithstanding this, and all his other rich Presents and wealthy Traffique in a quiet reign, consumed all with pomp and vain delights, excepting only that which was spent in building of the Temple. Whereupon (say they) if so much treasure gathered by so just a King, effect so little, what shall we hope for by the endeavours of this kind in other Princes? *Sardanapalus* left ten millions of pounds to them that slew him. *Darius* left twenty millions of pounds to *Alexander* that took him; *Nero* being left rich, and extorting much from his best Subjects, gave away above twelve millions of pounds to his base flatterers and such unworthy persons, which caused *Galba* after him to revoke those gifts. A Prince who hath store of mony hates peace, despiseth the friendship of his Neighbours and Allies, enters not only into unnecessary, but also into dangerous Wars, to the ruin and over-throw (sometimes) of his own estate: All which, with divers other weak arguments of this kind (which for brevity I omit), make nothing against the lawful gathering and massing up of Treasure by wise and provident Princes, if they be rightly understood.

For first, concerning those worthies who have obtained to the highest top of *honour* and *dignity*, by their great gifts and expences, who knows not that this hath been done rather upon the spoils of their Enemies than out of their own Cofers, which is indeed a Bounty that causeth neither loss nor peril? Whereas on the contrary, those Princes which do not providently lay up Treasure, or do imoderately consume the needs be less; and yet 'tis lessen'd still by artificial Cutts and Channels, that all may be perform'd by Water. In *England*, the Workmen are but few, and these dispers'd, and almost all the Carriage perform'd by Men and Horses upon the Land; and this must raise the price of Labour here.

The Buss is not constantly imploy'd, there must be intervals; in these, the *Dutch* Buss is lodg'd secure from Wind and Weather, in artificial Trenches before the Door of the Fisherman, without the charge of Anchor, Cable, or of Watchman. In *England*, at all this charge the Buss must ride in the River, must endure the unkindness of frequent Tides, must suffer more Damage, must be refitted with greater Cost and Labour. *The Busses are cheaper Harbour'd.*

In *Holland*, they abound with Mills and Engines; such things are there promoted and incourag'd, to save the labour of Hands: But, has more than one only Saw-mill been seen in *England?* By wonderful Policy, the People here must not be depriv'd of their Labour; rather every Work must be done by more Hands than are necessary. Certainly, such things must make the Labour less, must also make the price of Labour less. *They abound more with Arts and Engines.*

Lastly, the *Dutch* are already in possession of the Trade; they are therefore able to husband all their equal Advantages better, by saving time, making less waste, an hundred other things that cannot all be thought of on the suddain.

The Work is done in *Holland* with great order and regularity: the Carriage there is less, and all perform'd by Water; their Busses are better secur'd in the intervals of Fishing, are with less Expence and Labour refitted; they have more Mills and Engines, more Ways and Means to save the work of Hands. Upon all which, it may be concluded, That their whole Preparation for this Trade is cheaper far than ours.

67　　　　　　They

4¹

Herrings as cheap, and to sell them for as little profit as they do in *Holland*.

That we may sell for as little profit; our Fisher-men must not be at more contingent charge or hazard; they must not be invited from the Fishing Trade to other more profitable ways; our plenty of Money must be as great as it is in *Holland*.

Our Busses and all other Ships might be registred; *Registers and* by this many Controversies wou'd be prevented; for a *Law-Mer-* *chant.* more easie and speedy Determination of others, a Law-Merchant might be erected. The Forms of Tryals in other cases might continue still the same without any Alteration; but these are not thought altogether so convenient for this purpose. Perhaps if this were done, our Fishing-Trade wou'd not be carried on with any more contingent charge or hazard.

That no Man might reject the small gain that is *Corporations* made of Fishing, for the greater profit of any other *in Trade* *hurtful.* Trade; all our Trades both foreign and domestick, might be driven with the greatest freedom, Corporations and other Restraints might be destroy'd; consequently, so many wou'd be trading one against another; all kinds of Trade wou'd be driven so very close, till at last no Man in *England* wou'd be able to gain more by any other way, than every Man in *Holland* does by that of Fishing; then certainly, no Man wou'd reject the small profit that is made of Fishing, for the hopes of greater profit by any other Trade.

By such an universal Freedom of Trade, our Super- *Free-Trade* fluities wou'd be multiply'd, our exportations wou'd *the way to* *increase our* be enlarg'd, our Bullion wou'd be increas'd, and the *Money.* more Money wou'd be still imploy'd in Trade. The profit of this wou'd be run as low as the present Interest of Money; and still as Money shou'd be drawn out of Trade to purchace Lands or lye at

Interest,

Interest, the Value of those wou'd rise, Interest wou'd
fall, Men wou'd be forc'd to trade on for little gain.
When Interest shall be the same, when the profit of
Trade shall be no greater than it is in *Holland*, our
plenty of Money must be as great.

And thus, when our hazard in Trade shall be no
greater, when we shall be able to make no greater
profit by any other Trade, when our plenty of Money
shall be as great, we shall be content to afford our
Herrings for as little profit as does content the *Dutch*.

CHAP. XXI.

That the way to enable England *to catch and cure their*
Herrings as cheap as Holland, *is, first to have*
Materials for that Trade as cheap: and that this is
most likely to be done, by discharging the Customs
upon such things, by making the Trade for them free
and open, by making the Carriage of them as cheap
as it is in Holland; *and that the last is not to be*
done without reduction of the price of Shipping: And
the way for effecting this.

Our first
Costs of things
necessary for
the Fishing-
Trade, are or
may be as
little as in
Holland.

THAT we may also catch and cure Herrings as
cheap as those of *Holland*, our things necessary
for the Fishing-Trade, our Labour bestow'd upon them,
must be as cheap.

It is said, That Salt as good and sizable for curing
Herrings, may be made so very near the Coal-pits, so
near a Navigable River, that tho' it should be sold for
more profit by the Maker, it may nevertheless be deliver'd as cheap to *English* Fisher-men, as like Salt
can be sold in *Holland*.

Timber fit for building Busses, grows as cheap in
Ireland, and perhaps in *England*, as in any Countrey
from whence 'tis carried into *Holland*. Iron also might

be

be made as cheap. And by a Law, to oblige of the Lands of every Parish a small proportion to be sown with Hemp and Flax, the Tax wou'd be very small upon the Kingdom, and new Materials for imployment of the People would be cheaply distributed up and down the Country. Now by opening the Navigation of some of our Rivers, perhaps these things might be brought as cheap to any place convenient for the Fishing-Trade, as like things are brought to *Holland*.

However, we buy the Timber, Iron, Hemp, the Rozin, Pitch and Tar, of the East-Country, as cheap as *Holland*; from the East-Country we might Navigate our Ships with as few Hands, we might import these things as free of Customs: By the same Methods by which Fishermen wou'd be oblig'd to sell their Herrings for as little profit, the importers of Materials for the Fishing-Trade, must also afford such things for as little as will suffice in *Holland*. If the Merchant buys Materials for the Fishing-Trade as cheap, if he imports these things as free of Customs, if he must also sell for as little profit, if he imports with as few hands, why shou'd not our *English* Fisher-men buy them as cheap as they are bought in *Holland*? There can be no other reason why they shou'd not, unless that Sea-men's Wages are higher, and Ships are dearer Victuall'd here, or that our Voyage for these things is longer, and consequently more of the price of them must go to the Wages of the Sea-man, to the Provisions, to the Wear and Tear of the Ship; or, that our Shipping for the importation of these things, is dearer than it is in *Holland*. Certainly, neither are our Wages nor the price of Provisions so great as they are there. But, the length of our Voyage is something greater, our Shipping is a great deal dearer. Wherefore, if by any Method this last shall become so much cheaper as to be sold for sufficient profit into *Holland*, this will ballance our greater distance from

Our Ships might be Navigated with as few Hands; and things might be imported as free of Customs; and as free a Trade wou'd oblige us to sell for as little profit as they do in Holland.

71　　　　　　　the

the East-Country ; this will enable our People to buy their Timber, Iron, Hemp, their Rozin, Pitch and Tar, as cheap as they do in *Holland*.

That English *Shipping might be cheaper than that of* Hol-land, *they must build in the Plantations.*

Wherefore, that the *English* Shipping may be cheaper than that of *Holland*, Ships might be built in our Plantations, to be sold for sufficient profit to the *Dutch*, altho' the Freight from the Plantations were not enough to pay their Passage hither.

Materials are cheaper there

Ships are built in the Plantations of cheaper Materials, and might be also by cheaper Labour. Materials there for Building, are cheaper. 'Tis true indeed, that Iron, Sails and Rigging, are bought in *Europe*, and therefore must be dearer in the Plantations ; however, these things are carried thither in Ships that otherwise must carry empty Holds and Ballast, so that they are not dearer for the Carriage : Besides, the Customs upon these things to *England*, are drawn back upon their Exportation ; so that they are cheaper in our Plantations than here in *England*, and indeed but little dearer than in *Holland*. But, if these things are something dearer, Timber, Rozin, Pitch and Tar, are so much cheaper ; that at a medium, Materials are nothing near so dear in our Plantations.

How Negroes might build with as much Skill,

Materials for Building there are cheaper ; that these may be wrought by cheaper Labour, the Work might be perform'd by Negroes. To single Parts of Ships, single Negroes might be assign'd, the Manufacture of Keels to one, to another Rudders, to another Masts ; to several others, several other Parts of Ships. Of which, the variety wou'd still be less to puzle and confound the Artist's Skill, if he were not to vary from his Model, if the same Builders wou'd still confine themselves to the same Scantlings and Dimensions, never to diminish nor exceed their Patterns. And of Ships for the same kind of Trade, and for ordinary and common use ; when once a good Model can be found, why shou'd the same

72   be

be often chang'd. So that the same Negroes might be imploy'd in only single Parts of Ships of the same Scantlings and Dimensions, by which the Work of every one wou'd be render'd plain and easie. That it may not seem impossible for Negroes to be always imploy'd in the same Parts of Ships; either by Law, or by some small encouragement to begin the Work, our Ships for that Trade might all be built in the Plantations: Such Fleets are every Year us'd between *England* and the Plantations, as wou'd find full and constant work for Numbers of Builders equal to all the different Parts: And therefore, Negroes might always be imploy'd in only single, plain, and easie Parts of Ships. And, thus a way is shewn to build in our Plantations by the hands of Negroes, to render a Work of such variety plain and easie, to enable Negroes to build with as much skill as those in *Holland*.

The Strength of Negroes is as great; a way is shewn *and Expe-* to make their Skill as great; wherefore, they might be *dition,* taught to build as well, and with equal expedition.

The Wages of Negroes are not so great as of the *and for as Dutch* Builders; the annual Service of a Negroe might *little Wages as Dutch Buil-* be hir'd for half the Price that must be given to one of *ders.* these. Only high Wages, or slow and clumsy Workmanship, make Labour dear. Negroes may build as good Ships with equal Expedition, for half the Wages that must be given in *Holland*. And therefore, Ships of cheaper Materials built by cheaper Labour in our Plantations, must needs be cheaper than equal Ships in *Holland*.

If Ships of Materials a great deal cheaper, might be built in our Plantations by Labour of half the price that must be given in *Holland*, they must needs be cheaper, and possibly by 20 or 30 *per Cent*. or by Thirty or Forty Shillings in every Ton.

Such

Ships built in the Planta-tions, might be Navigated to England without charge. Such Ships indeed, wou'd be built at a very great distance from *England*, but yet 'twou'd cost us nothing to get them hither; their Passage hither might well be paid by the present usual Freight from thence, and perhaps by one quarter of the present usual Freight, tho' all the Mariners to Navigate these Ships were still to be hired out of *England*.

I have heard, that for Ships not Overmasted, five Mariners are enough to every Hundred Tons; and that so many might be hired for Forty Pounds from *England*; so much wou'd be sufficient to pay the Wages and Passage of Seamen from *England* to any of our Plantations. As much more wou'd be sufficient to pay their Provisions and Wages back again to *England*; and this is all discharg'd by Freight of Sixteen Shillings for every Ton. Less than this wou'd pay the Wear and Tear of a Ship for a Voyage of so few Weeks; so that Thirty Shillings *per* Ton wou'd then be thought enough to pay the Passage of Ships from our Plantations into *England*.

'Tis true, that Freight so low will pay no profit to the Owner; but if a Ship can be built of Materials as cheap again, by Labour of half the price, that is, Thirty or Forty Shillings *per* Ton cheaper than such another can be built in *Holland*; the same wou'd bring sufficient profit to the Owner, tho' it shou'd come for Freight so low, nay, tho' all the Freight to *England* were not enough to pay the Passage; 'tis gain sufficient to the Builder, to sell his Ship for the profit of Twenty Shillings for every Ton.

Consequences of reducing Freight from the Planta-tions by cheap Shipping. And thus a Method is propos'd for building Ships in *America*, that may be sold for sufficient gain to the *Dutch*, altho' the Freight from our Plantations hither, were brought down to Thirty, Twenty, or less than Twenty Shillings for every Ton. If Ships might be

built

built so cheap in our Plantations, 'tis very likely the Freight from thence to *England* wou'd be run so low by emulation of our Plantation Builders.

For Freight so low from the Plantations, no Ships from *England* wou'd carry empty Holds and Ballast thither; the greatest part of those that come from thence, wou'd be sold and left in *England*; the few that wou'd return, wou'd always carry Cargoes of Manufactures and Mariners; the former for the use of the People there, the latter to navigate their Ships from thence: 'Twou'd be some benefit to *England*, to save the Carriage of empty Holds and Ballast, so long a Voyage, to save so much vain and unprofitable Labour.

By Freight so low from our Plantations, Tobacco, Sugar, and all the Produce of those Places, wou'd be imported so much cheaper; more wou'd be sold from *England*, our Foreign Trade wou'd be enlarg'd; and this wou'd be a greater benefit.

Timber, Pitch and Tar, and other Naval Stores, are bought for half the price in the Plantations, for which they can be bought in *Europe*: but Freight has always been too high to import such things so long a Voyage for profit: For Freight so low from our Plantations, these things might be imported thence a great deal cheaper into *England*, than they can be bought in any place in *Europe*. Certainly, 'twou'd be beneficial to *England* to become the Magazine of Naval Stores for all the rest of *Europe*. Besides, this were the way for *England* to have many Materials for the Fishing-Trade, cheaper than the same can be had in *Holland*.

'Tis not to be thought, that Busses, Dogger-boats and Vessels, for the immediate use of Fishermen, nor many other kind of Ships, can come from our Plantations; but Rudders, Masts and Keels, and other Parts of Ships of any kind, already fitted to certain Sizes and Dimensions, by the cheaper Labour of those Places,

75   might

might be imported into *England*; nothing need be left
to *English* Labour, but only to lay these several Parts
together. If Freight from the Plantations cou'd be
reduc'd so low, *England* might either build Busses to
Fish her self, or cheap enough to sell to *Holland*. Then
for the present, we might allow the *Dutch* to catch the
Herrings, if they wou'd buy of us their Busses.

Ships of any kind brought to *England* so very cheap,
will reduce the price of others here; no Ships will be
dear as long as any kind is cheap. To build as cheap
in *England*, Men will be forc'd to keep more to the
same Models in Ships of ordinary and common use;
they will be forc'd upon the invention of Mills and
Engines, to save the charge of Hands: they will be
forc'd to work with more Order and Regularity, by
which their Labour may be afforded cheaper. To reduce the price of building Ships by Methods such as
these, wou'd be a benefit to *England*.

But far the greatest benefit of all, wou'd be, that our
Shipping shou'd be render'd cheaper than that of *Holland*. The *Dutch* wou'd then buy their Ships of us;
however, they must be contented to let us trade with
cheaper Shipping. This were the way for us to become
the Carriers of the World, to profit by all that others
eat, and drink, and wear: This were a surer way, and
less odious to our Neighbours, than any Act of Navigation for only *English* Bottoms to be imploy'd, in the
Carriage of Things to and from our own Country.
Tho' our distance is a little greater than that of *Holland*
from the East-Country, this wou'd balance that Disadvantage, our Carriage thence wou'd be as cheap.

We buy our Fishing-Stores as cheap as *Holland*;
these may be brought hither as free of Customs; by
reducing the price of Shipping by the Methods that
have been propos'd, the Carriage hither might be as
cheap; a way is shewn for the Importer to expect as

little

little profit: And this is all that is necessary to render Materials for the Fishing-Trade, as cheap in *England* as they are in *Holland*.

CHAP. XXII.

The way to make English *Labour in the Fishing-Trade as cheap as that of* Holland; *that the People here must cohabit as close together; and the most probable Methods for effecting this, are to erect a Free-port, to impower Parishes to send their Pensioners to it, to give Privileges to such a Place: Also, all other Arts of working cheap must be allow'd.*

L Astly, that the *Dutch* may have no Advantage over us for the Fishing-Trade by their cheaper Labour, The People might be brought to live as close together here for the better carrying on of this Trade, as they do in *Holland*. In *England*, they might for this purpose be brought as close together, without any publick Charge, and with exceeding Profit to the Kingdom.

First, By erecting any convenient Place in *England* into a Free-Port; this wou'd be a way of bringing great Numbers of People close together, very easie to the Publick; the thing wou'd be done at the voluntary charge of Merchants. The Merchant must be very much disabled to gain by his Trade, if either he shall be compell'd to carry out his imported Merchandises within the Year before the Foreign Markets call for them, or after the Year without drawing back the Customs. It is without doubt, the interest of Merchants to be oblig'd to neither of these things. Now the way to be compell'd to neither, is, that a Free-Port shou'd be erected in any convenient Place in *England*, that Houses and Ware-house shou'd be built for the reception of Goods, which at all times may be freely imported

A Free-Port might be erected without Publick Charge,

77   hither

hither, and may again be as freely exported. Such a Place wou'd soon be built and peopled; the Interest of Merchants wou'd do the thing; it wou'd be done without any publick Charge. This wou'd be a way very easie to the Kingdom, of drawing great Numbers of People close together.

and to the Publick Benefit. And it were also a very profitable way; from a Free-Port at all times, all things may be exported, they pay no Customs at their coming in, and therefore are not limited to Times for drawing back their Customs, in order to their being carried out again; so that to erect a Free-Port, is to enable the Merchant to wait his own time; not to oblige him to carry out his Goods before the Foreign Markets call for them: it is consequently to enable him to sell his Goods so much dearer, it is to increase the Riches of the Merchant. The Riches of every individual Man is part of the Riches of the whole Community. Wherefore, if to erect a Free-Port is to increase the Riches of the Merchant, it must increase the Riches of the Kingdom. A Free-Port then wou'd be a very easie, 'twou'd be likewise a very profitable way of drawing great Numbers of People close together. And indeed, if this were done, if it shou'd please God to press the *Dutch* with greater difficulties than they will be able to overcome, whither is it so likely that they wou'd run their great Estates for shelter as into *England;* but the want of a Free-Port, together with the Act of Navigation, (which in other respects, is the best that was ever made for the security and improvement of our Trade,) makes *England* more dangerous than Rocks and Sands to *Holland.*

Parishes might send the Pensioners to this Free-Port; this wou'd not be chargeable, For increasing the People of this Place, Parishes might be impower'd to send their Pensioners to it; this also wou'd be done at the voluntary charge of every Parish, like the present way of removing poor Persons from one Parish to another; the Publick

wou'd

wou'd not feel it, the Way must needs be easie to the Kingdom.

And also, it wou'd be very profitable ; the poor People *but very* collected thus together, wou'd find more variety of *profitable to the Publick.* Imployments, fit for Persons of all conditions, in a place exceeding Populous, abounding with variety of Business and full of Manufactures, than as now, dispers'd over all the Kingdom, confin'd to Parishes, in which they are of little use, disabled to go where proper Business calls for them. The Blind and Lame, Young and Old, Women and Children, by their united Labours, might be serviceable to one another, they are now dispers'd ; they are neither useful to the Publick nor Themselves. Collected altogether, the Poor wou'd be more likely to provide their own Maintenance, to ease the Publick of this Charge ; so that, to impower Parishes to send their Pensioners to this Free-Port, wou'd be a profitable way of bringing great Numbers to cohabit close together : At least, thus the Poor cou'd not be more chargeable to the Kingdom, than when dispers'd and confin'd to Parishes that have no Business for them, and which are therefore willing to part with them ; so that if to collect the Poor together shou'd import no profit, yet it cou'd never hurt the Publick. But for the Reasons before, we may venture to conclude, That to impower Parishes to send their Pensioners to this Place, wou'd be a very easie and a very profitable way of making great Numbers of People cohabit close together.

Lastly, To give present Privileges to such a Place, *Privileges of* to give it a Freedom from Taxes, Customs, and Ex- *a Place, the* cises, must needs increase the People. And what hurt *way to increase the* were this to the Publick, that people who chiefly live *People.* on Charity, shou'd be eas'd of Charges which they cannot bear ? That it shou'd be made more easie for them to earn their own Living, by abating the prices of things ? By this the Publick wou'd suffer no damage,

and

and without doubt great Numbers of People wou'd be added to the place. So that Ways are shewn for bringing People together without any Publick Charge, and with exceeding Profit to the Kingdom.

Now, after all other Preliminaries settled, the chief Application of this place, must be to Fishing, to building Busses, making Netts, and the several Appendages of this Trade; it must be suppos'd, that all things necessary might be imported hither as cheap, and might be sold here for as little profit as they are in *Holland*. Why then, in so close a cohabitation of People of the same Trade and Profession; besides that, Cheats and extravagant Prices wou'd be prevented; every one wou'd be a cheque upon his Neighbour's Price, every one wou'd be oblig'd to live frugally, and sell cheap, for fear of being undersold by his more frugal Neighbour. It wou'd follow also, that every Work of as great variety, might be done with as much Order and Regularity as any like is done in *Holland*. No such wou'd be left to the slow and clumsy performance of single Persons; every one wou'd have his proper Share of every Manufacture; 'twou'd be the emulation and care of every one, to work as well and as cheap as others; so that every one wou'd be still advancing to farther Perfection upon the Invention of others. And thus perhaps, our whole Business might be done with as much Perfection and Expedition, with as little and as cheap Labour as it is in *Holland*.

So close a cohabitation of the People, wou'd still abate the price of things, by abating the Labour bestow'd upon them; the Carriage of things from one Work-man to another, wou'd be so much less: And yet, still it might be lessen'd by Navigable Cutts and Channels, to save the charge of Carriage.

Trenches also might be made, where, in the intervals of Fishing, the Buss might lodge secure, and be refitted

with

with less Cost. Mills, and Engines, and all other Arts, shou'd be allow'd to save the Labour of Hands. And whatsoever other Obstructions there are, these also shou'd be remov'd. But, perhaps I have already nam'd enough to create a despair of the thing, to make it credible, That our Herrings are not likely to pay the Cost and Charge that must be bestow'd upon them. If I have done so, I have reinforc'd my former Argument; The Fishing-Trade is not so profitable as the Importation of *Irish* Cattel, or of *Indian* Manufactures.

F I N I S.

INDEX.

A

Absolute Government—See *Government*

Abyssinia, bullion brought from, 15; character of its inhabitants, *ib.*

Account of comparative cost of spices, indigo, and silk, at Aleppo and in the East Indies, 11, 12; of cost of spices, &c. in India, and of their sale in England, 20; account of our coinage of gold and silver, from Oct. 1599, to Nov. 1675, (76 years,) 386—390

Accounts, knowledge of, necessary to a merchant, 122; he ought to be a good accountant by the noble order of " Debtor and Creditor," in use only among merchants, *ib.*

Acres, extent of England in acres, 352, 452

Acts of Parliament—Act called " Trade Encouraged," quoted as favourable to inclosures, 267; evil operation of navigation laws on trade, 317, 318, 327, 624; evil effects of acts against the importation of Irish cattle, 318; the 12 Chas. II., cap. 22, against export of wool ineffectual, 323; acts as to navigation enumerated, 327

Adulteration of wine with molasses, arsenic, &c., 420

Africa, corn furnished from thence to ancient Rome, 601, 602

African Company, patent of, and its injurious effects on trade, 332, 333; great privileges of the Company, *ib.*; partial opening of the African trade, and benefits thereof, 562

Alehouses, their increase and evils thereof, 376, 379; selling ale, &c., and letting lodgings in London too commonly end in the gallows, 380

Aleppo, its former importance as a mart, 10; cost of spices, &c. there, 11; trade of, 13; decay of its trade, to England, 32

Alexander, wealth taken by him from Darius, 186

Alexandria, its former importance as a mart, 10, 13

Algiers, our loss by the pirates of, 451, 472; encouragement given to them by the French, 472

Aliens, arguments for and against the settlement of foreigners in England, 219, 224, 226, 263, 265, 358, 359; why foreigners desire to dwell here, 220; colonies of foreigners settled in different parts of England, 264, 398; list of laws against aliens, 358; naturalization of foreign Protestants recommended, 358, 359

Alliances—See *Leagues*

Alloy, quantity used for coinage in England and elsewhere, 243, 244

Alsatia, destruction of villages in, 263

Alva, Duke of, Flemish manufacturers driven by his tyranny into England, 398, 431

America, discovery of, 102, 103, 386; English and Spanish emigration thereto, 350; cheap ship-building in America, 622, 623

Ammunition—See *Munitions*

Amsterdam, her merchant companies a main cause of her great traffic, 86; while London has 100,000 shopkeepers, Amsterdam has but 5000, 445; bank of Amsterdam, 519

Answers to objections to the East India trade, 7-47, 556-607

Antiquity, we prize all the sapless papers and fragments of antiquity, while notions of trade are turned into ridicule, 357

Antwerp, trade of, temp. Henry VII., 103, 104; decay of its trade, and cause thereof, 105, 432; English staple there, 399

Apparel, expense in apparel to be countenanced under restrictions, 235; English preferable to French tailors, 234; influence of fashion, 234,

money, and the Dutch but three.
318, 345, 518; no interest allowed
in France, 318, 345; the East India
Company pay 5 per cent. on their
debt, 341; interest should not be
restrained by law, 510, 516-523;
usual arguments for the abatement
of, 515; answers thereto, 516;
interest only rent for stock, 518;
causes of the rise and fall thereof,
518; more lenders than borrowers,
ib.; effect of high interest in drawing money from hoards, &c., 519,
520; mortgage and personal security, 520; when the nation
thrives, money will be had on good
terms, but the clean contrary when
she is poor, 521; all laws to restrain
interest ineffectual, 521, 522; it
would be as just to restrain the
rent of land as the interest of
money, 522; "if you take away
interest, you take away borrowing
and lending." *ib.*
Inventions, operations of laws as to
patents, 367; advantage of inventions for economy of labour, 580,
581, 615; frame-work for stockings,
586; the East India trade a stimu-
lus to invention, 587; they are the
effects of necessity and emulation,
590.
Ireland, yearly store of timber and
other provisions imported thence
by the India Company, 24; evil
effects of the Acts prohibiting the
importation of Irish cattle, 318,
351, 403, 404, 405; wool openly
exported thence at the low price
of 6s. or 7s. the tod, 321, 406; the
peopling of Ireland after the Irish
massacre, 350; English emigration
to, 380, 442; Irish woollen manufacture, 402; successful competition
of Irish butter, cheese, beef, &c.,
404, 406, 407, 408; former cessation
of exports from England to Ireland,
404, 405; Irish exports to the plantations, 406; rise of rents in Ireland
while the English sink, 407; expiring of the Irish Acts and consequence thereof, *ib*, 408; Irish
shipping, 414; manufacture of
frieze, 418; a hard matter to reclaim the Irish from drawing with
their horses' tails, 502; our fishing
trade not so profitable as the importation of Irish cattle, 607-609.
Iron, our imports of, from Sweden,
Flanders, and Spain, 418; iron
works in Kent, Sussex, and Surrey, 418; number of families de-

pendent on our iron manufacture,
ib.
Israelites, their discontent and its
punishment, 271-273
Italy, encouragement of the arts by
some of the Italian states, 15; industry, trade, and manufactures of
the Italians, 133, 137, 307, 402;
banks in, 137; how the Italians
furnish Spain with money in Flanders, 175; woollen manufacture in
Italy, 402; our former export of
fish to, 409; Italian wines, 419;
she was always able to bear sufficient corn for her inhabitants, 602

J.

Jamaica, the English population nearly
trebled since Sir Thomas Muddiford was Governor, 415
James I, his care that English cloth
was dyed before being exported, 75;
Dutch fishing trade in his time, 432
Japan, the English East India Company
have no trade there, 339; trade
thither of the Dutch East India
Company, 339
Jesuits, collections of money carried out
of the country by them, 207, 429,
451
Jews, Riches and discontent of the
ancient Jews, 272, 273, 503; encouragement given to the Jews by
the French King, and the Duke of
Tuscany, 366; civil disabilities of
Jews in England, 366
Joint Stock Companies, joint companies
for foreign merchandize an encouragement to traffic, 85, 86;
answer to objection that Companies
are impediments to free trade, 244,
245; constitution of our foreign
trading companies, and their consequence in trade, 331-348; distinction between regulated and joint
stock companies, 332; injurious
effects of the patents of the East
India and African Companies, 333;
account of the original stocks of
the English and Dutch East India
Companies, 341, 342; companies
trade at more charge than private
persons, 561
Josephus referred to, 503
Justice, Courts of, tedious and chargeable proceedings complained of,
368; evils of the little courts about
London, 368; a disputable groat
forces the expenditure of £3 or £4,
368

CL Press

A Fraser Institute Project

https://clpress.net/

Professor Daniel Klein (George Mason University, Economics and Mercatus Center) and Dr. Erik Matson (Mercatus Center), directors of the Adam Smith Program at George Mason University, are the editors and directors of CL Press. CL stands at once for classical liberal and conservative liberal.

CL Press is a project of the Fraser Institute (Vancouver, Canada).

CL Press includes a series called CL Reprints. CL Reprints was undertaken to make selected older works—no longer under copyright, chiefly—more available.

People:

Dan Klein and Erik Matson are the co-editors and executives of the imprint.

Jane Shaw Stroup is Editorial Advisor, doing especially copy-editing and text preparation.

Zachary Yost is Production Manager for CL Reprints.

An Advisory Board:

Jordan Ballor, *Center for Religion, Culture, and Democracy*

Caroline Breashears, *St. Lawrence Univ.*

Donald Boudreaux, *George Mason Univ.*

Ross Emmett, *Arizona State Univ.*

Knud Haakonssen, *Univ. of St. Andrews*

Björn Hasselgren, *Timbro, Uppsala Univ.*

Karen Horn, *Univ. of Erfurt*

Jimena Hurtado, *Univ. de los Andes*

Nelson Lund, *George Mason Univ.*

Daniel Mahoney, *Assumption Univ.*

Deirdre N. McCloskey, *Univ. of Illinois–Chicago*

Thomas W. Merrill, *American Univ.*

James Otteson, *Univ. of Notre Dame*

Catherine R. Pakaluk, *Catholic Univ. of America*

Sandra Peart, *Univ. of Richmond*

Mario Rizzo, *New York Univ.*

Loren Rotner, *Univ. of Austin*

Marc Sidwell, *New Culture Forum*

Craig Smith, *Univ. of Glasgow*

Emily Skarbek, *Brown Univ.*

David Walsh, *Catholic Univ. of America*

Richard Whatmore, *Univ. of St. Andrews*

Barry Weingast, *Stanford Univ.*

Lawrence H. White, *George Mason Univ.*

Amy Willis, *Liberty Fund*

Bart Wilson, *Chapman Univ.*

Todd Zywicki, *George Mason Univ.*

Why start CL Press?

CL Press publishes good, low-priced work in intellectual history, political theory, political economy, and moral philosophy. More specifically, CL Press explores and advance discourse in the following areas:

- The intellectual history and meaning of liberalism.
- The relationship between liberalism and conservatism.
- The role of religion in disseminating liberal understandings and institutions including: humankind's ethical universalism, the moral equality of souls, the rule of law, religious liberty, the meaning and virtues of economic life.
- The relationship between religion and economic philosophy.
- The political, social, and economic philosophy of the Scottish Enlightenment, especially Adam Smith.

www.ingramcontent.com/pod-product-compliance
Lightning Source LLC
Chambersburg PA
CBHW011833020426
42335CB00024B/2837